Brain Injury Claims

Second Edition

Brain Injury Claims

Second Edition

Dr Martin D van den Broek

and

Dr Sundeep Sembi

SWEET & MAXWELL

First Edition   2017
Second Edition   2020

Published in 2020 by Thomson Reuters, trading as Sweet & Maxwell. Registered in England & Wales, Company No.1679046.
Registered Office and address for service: 5 Canada Square, Canary Wharf, London, E14 5AQ.

For further information on our products and services, visit *www.sweetandmaxwell.co.uk*

Typeset by Letterpart Limited, Caterham on the Hill, Surrey, CR3 5XL.

Printed and bound in Great Britain by Printed and bound by CPI Group (UK) Ltd, Croydon, CR0 4YY.

No natural forests were destroyed to make this product: only farmed timber was used and re-planted.

A CIP catalogue record of this book is available from the British Library.

ISBN: 978-0-414-07483-5

Thomson Reuters, the Thomson Reuters Logo and Sweet & Maxwell ® are trademarks of Thomson Reuters.

Crown copyright material is reproduced with the permission of the Controller of HMSO and the Queen's Printer for Scotland.

All rights reserved. No part of this publication may be reproduced, or transmitted in any form, or by any means, or stored in any retrieval system of any nature, without prior written permission, except for permitted fair dealing under the Copyright, Designs and Patents Act 1988, or in accordance with the terms of a licence issued by the Copyright Licensing Agency in respect of photocopying and/or reprographic reproduction. Application for permission for other use of copyright material, including permission to reproduce extracts in other published works should be made to the publishers. Full acknowledgement of the author, publisher and source must be given.

© 2020 Thomson Reuters

Contributors

Niruj Agrawal
Consultant Neuropsychiatrist, Regional Neurosciences Centre, St George's Hospital, London

Jebet Beverly Cheserem
Department of Neurosurgery, Regional Neuroscience Centre, St George's Hospital, London

Fay Greenway
Department of Neurosurgery, Regional Neurosciences Centre, St George's Hospital, London

Shawn Halpin
Medical Director, DMC Imaging Ltd, London

Martin Hillier
Placement Consultant, Working Out, Community Head Injury Service, Buckinghamshire Healthcare NHS Trust

Nigel S. King
Consultant Clinical Neuropsychologist, Community Head Injury Service, Buckinghamshire Healthcare NHS Trust, and Oxford Institute of Clinical Psychology Training, Oxford Health NHS Foundation Trust and University of Oxford

The Hon Mr Justice Brian Langstaff
Queen's Bench Division, London

Denzil Lush
Master of the Court of Protection (1996–2007) and Senior Judge of the Court of Protection (2007–2016), Court of Protection, London

Caz Lyall
Occupational Therapist, Medico-Legal Consultant, Somek & Associates, Chesham

CONTRIBUTORS

William Norris QC
39 Essex Chambers, London

Jonathan Watt-Pringle QC
Temple Garden Chambers, London

Sundeep Sembi
Consultant Clinical Neuropsychologist, Psychology Chambers Ltd, London

Wolfgang Schady
Consultant Neurologist, Calderbank Medical Chambers, Manchester

Simon Stapleton
Consultant Neurosurgeon, Department of Neurosurgery, Regional Neuroscience Centre, St George's Hospital, London

Nathan Tavares QC
Outer Temple Chambers, London

Andy Tyerman
Consultant Clinical Neuropsychologist, Community Head Injury Service, Buckinghamshire Healthcare NHS Trust

Martin van den Broek
Consultant Clinical Neuropsychologist, The Neuropsychology Clinic, Guildford

Ingram Wright
Consultant Neuropsychologist and Associate Professor of Clinical Neuropsychology, University Hospitals Bristol NHS Trust

Andrew Worthington
Clinical Director/Consultant in Neuropsychology and Rehabilitation, Headwise, Birmingham, and
Honorary Chair, College of Medicine and College of Human and Health Sciences, Swansea University

Sarah, Tom, Alex and George ≈ Martin van den Broek

and

Ravinder and Krishan ≈ Sundeep Sembi

Preface to Second Edition

In the last 30–40 years there have been substantial changes in brain injury litigation. Whereas initially the focus of claims was on the individual's physical injuries and resulting disability, it soon became apparent that in many cases people can survive even significant brain trauma with little in the way of physical disability. Individuals may have physical limitations, such as balance and motor impairments, headache and epilepsy, but they may not always be significantly limiting. On the other hand, cognitive, emotional and personality issues such as impulsiveness, depression and executive dysfunction, are common and, in the absence of external physical disability, have led to the widely cited description of head trauma as representing a hidden disability. Many individuals are ambulant and communicate normally and in many respects appear, superficially at least, to have little in the way of lasting impairment from their injuries but, to those who know them well, particularly their family, they may have changes in their abilities, judgment and personality that indicate that they have not survived unscathed. Not only are these changes common, but they have been found to be important determinants of whether the individual reintegrates into their previous roles, establishes and maintains relationships, and resumes former leisure activities. Most importantly for litigation, they have also been found to be important determinants of whether the individual returns to employment, either part- or full-time or in an alternative role, and therefore they require careful assessment and evaluation because of the impact of loss of earnings on the value of a claim. Similarly, changes in cognition and personality are invariably the primary determinants of care requirements and whereas many survivors do not require hands-on care or support, they may nevertheless need assistance to compensate for faulty judgment or planning, as well as prompting and supervision with daily routines. As support may be required throughout the week and for many years, or even lifelong, this can also be a significant issue not only in terms of cost, but also affecting the individual's autonomy and independence. Breakdown in relationships are also commonplace bringing further distress and impact upon mental health but also additional care requirements as well as consideration of factors such as additional support for childcare. Addressing these complaints has in turn led to a growth in services from case managers, support workers, occupational therapists, speech therapists, physiotherapists, and neuropsychologists, as well as other professionals such as neuropsychiatrists, which can represent a further significant cost.

While the mechanisms involved in brain trauma are relatively well understood, and in many cases there may be objective evidence of neurological trauma on imaging, it may nevertheless be difficult to ascertain the extent to

PREFACE TO SECOND EDITION

which an individual has changed, if at all, from their previous functioning. As many of the reported complaints and obstacles to resuming everyday functioning are subjective, such as fatigue, pain and loss of concentration, new complaints may be difficult to disentangle from pre-existing or concomitant life or personality issues. Further the psychosocial impact, particularly on mental state can emerge after years of apparent recovery and sound coping and adjustment and increased rates for dementia are also now recognised. In addition, recent research has shown that a significant proportion of claimants have invalid presentations when assessed in civil claims, so further complicating the picture. This combination of factors and high-value litigation make brain injury claims particularly challenging for both lawyers and clinicians.

Building on the first edition, *Brain Injury Claims* (2nd edition) updates several key chapters as well as addressing two further aspects of traumatic brain injury not covered in the first edition: detailed consideration of the impact of brain injury in children, as well as reviewing the evidence for and against subtle brain injury and relating this to current case law.

Brain Injury Claims describes the medical aspects of brain trauma and the mechanisms by which the brain is injured, which in litigation invariably involves a motor vehicle accident, industrial accident or fall, as well as the use of neuroradiological investigations and the neurological sequelae. The neuropsychological and neuropsychiatric aspects are also reviewed, including neurorehabilitation, and the complex issues of returning to work and education and assessing care requirements. The controversies surrounding subtle brain injury are considered in detail and the assessment of capacity and the Mental Capacity Act, together with case studies. It has been said that whatever the complexity of a claim, the lawyer's advocacy is ultimately directed to convince the court, rather than anyone else, and so the critical role of judicial reasoning in appraising the evidence is reviewed.

Dr Martin D van den Broek

Dr Sundeep Sembi

Acknowledgements

Chapter 3 Figure 1: Anatomy of the brain—lateral view, midline view, and ventricular system is reproduced with the kind permission of KenHub.

Chapter 3 Figure 3: Diagrammatic view of the process of herniation of the brain as an intracranial mass expands is reproduced with the kind permission of Radiopaedia (https://radiopaedia.org/articles/cerebral-herniation by Dr Matt Skalski, Radiopaedia.org, rID: 45683).

Chapter 5 Table 1: Injury severity ratings for traumatic brain injuries is reproduced with the kind permission of the American Psychiatric Association.

Chapter 5 Table 2: American Congress of Rehabilitation Medicine mTBI Committee definition of mild traumatic brain injury is reproduced with the kind permission of Wolters Kluwer Health, Inc.

Chapter 5 Table 3: Definition of mTBI developed by National Centre for Injury Prevention and Control is reproduced with the kind permission of the Centers for Disease Control and Prevention.

Chapter 5 Table 4: World Health Organization collaborating Centre task force definition of mTBI is reproduced with the kind permission of Journal of Rehabilitation Medicine (originally published by Taylor & Francis).

Chapter 5 Table 5: Neuropsychological complaint base rates in a family practice control group and non-TBI claimants is reproduced with the kind permission of Oxford University Press.

Chapter 5 Table 6: Symptom endorsement percentages reported by individuals without a brain injury in various studies is reproduced with the kind permission of Oxford University Press.

Chapter 7 Figure 1: Number of publications annually with the keyword "malingering" from 1980 to 2009 is reproduced with the kind permission of Springer Science + Business Media, LLC.

Chapter 7 Figure 2: Number of US federal and state cases in five-year epochs between 1978 and 2008 used as a basis for polynomial regression for the subsequent 15 years is reproduced with the kind permission of Taylor & Francis.

Chapter 7 Table 1: Base rate of probable malingering or symptom exaggeration in litigating/compensation seeking cases by diagnosis is reproduced with the kind permission of Taylor & Francis.

Chapter 7 Table 2: Faking bad response styles is reproduced with the kind permission of *The Forensic Examiner* (American College of Forensic Examiners Institute).

Chapter 7 Figure 3: Schematic model outlining the overlap between exaggeration, poor effort, and malingering is reproduced with the kind permission of Taylor & Francis.

ACKNOWLEDGEMENTS

Chapter 7 Panel: Diagnostic categories and criteria for malingering of neurocognitive dysfunction is reproduced with the kind permission of Taylor & Francis.

Chapter 7 Figure 4: Brain MRI at one year of age showing bilateral volume loss is reproduced with the kind permission of Taylor & Francis.

Chapter 11 Table 1: 10 differences between therapeutic and forensic relationships is reproduced with the kind permission of American Psychological Association.

The publishers have made every effort to trace the copyright holders and to obtain their permission for the use of copyright material. If any have been inadvertently overlooked, the publisher would be happy to make any necessary arrangement at the first opportunity.

TABLE OF CONTENTS

	PAGE
Contributors	v
Preface to Second Edition	ix
Acknowledgements	xi
Table of Cases	xxvii
Table of Legislation	xxxiii

	PARA
1. Acquired Brain Injury and Civil Litigation *William Norris QC and Nathan Tavares QC*	
Chapter Layout	1–001
1. Litigation Issues	
Why the medicine matters	1–002
Relevance to damages	1–003
Identifying the nature of the brain injury	1–004
The importance of the medico-legal expert to litigation	1–005
Diagnosis: what the lawyer must look out for	1–006
Categories of head injury	1–007
The role of the expert	1–008
How to choose an expert	1–010
Changing experts	1–011
Treating doctors as experts	1–012
Expert's consultation with the client	1–013
Funding and bias	1–014
What the expert must see	1–015
What must be disclosed apart from final expert reports	1–016
Preparation for and attendance at trial	1–017
Handling litigation for brain injured individuals	1–019
The seriously unwell claimant	1–021
Duties owed to clients	1–022
Evidence from the incapacitated claimant	1–025
The claimant who retains capacity with the aid of support	1–026
2. Case Studies	1–029
Case Study 1—Subtle brain injury	
Clarke v Maltby [2010] EWHC 1201 (QB)	
Background	1–030
Comment	1–031

CONTENTS

Case Study 2—Difficulty in assessment of cognitive ability
Ali v Caton [2013] EWHC 1730 (QB)
    Background 1–032
    Comment 1–033
Case Study 3—Damages assessment for moderate brain injury
Edwards v Martin [2010] EWHC 570 (QB)
    Background 1–035
    Comment 1–036
Case Study 4—Illegality following brain injury
Wilson v Coulson [2002] P.I.Q.R. P22
    Background 1–040
    Comment 1–041
Case Study 5—Somatisation disorder
Giblett v P & NE Murray Ltd (1999) 96(22) L.S.G. 34; Times, 25 May 1999
    Background 1–043
    Comment 1–044

2. Assessing Capacity: The Law *Denzil Lush*

Introduction 2–001
1. Common Law Tests of Capacity
Common law tests of capacity 2–002
Capacity to litigate
    Summary 2–003
    Masterman-Lister 2–004
    Cases after Masterman-Lister 2–006
Where medical evidence cannot be obtained 2–008
Capacity to manage one's property and financial affairs 2–009
Capacity to manage property and affairs: a checklist 2–010
    The extent of the person's property and affairs 2–011
    Personal information 2–012
    The person's vulnerability 2–013
Capacity to enter into a contract
    Contractual capacity 2–014
    Contracts made by persons lacking capacity are voidable 2–015
    Necessary goods or services 2–016
Capacity to make a lasting power of attorney 2–017
    The two types of lasting power of attorney 2–018
    The packs provided by the Office of the Public Guardian 2–019
    The digital lasting power of attorney service 2–020
    The prescribed form 2–021
    The certificate provider 2–022
    The test for capacity to create a lasting power of attorney 2–023
    Capacity to revoke a lasting power of attorney 2–024
Capacity to make a will—testamentary capacity
    The time at which testamentary capacity is required 2–025
    The test in Banks v Goodfellow 2–026
    Capacity to make a will—"the golden rule" 2–027

CONTENTS

    Capacity to revoke a will 2–028
Capacity to make a gift 2–029
Capacity to marry or enter into a civil partnership 2–030
Capacity to consent to medical treatment 2–031
Capacity to consent to sexual relationships 2–032
Capacity to make decisions regarding residence, contact, and
care 2–033
    Residence 2–034
    Contact 2–035
    Care 2–036
Capacity to use the internet and social media 2–037
Claimants' knowledge of the amount of their damages award 2–038
2. Mental Capacity Act 2005 sections 1–3 2–041
Section 1: The principles 2–042
Commentary on section 1
    The presumption of capacity and the burden of proof 2–043
    All practicable steps 2–044
    Supported decision-making 2–045
    Unwise decisions 2–046
    Best interests 2–047
    Less restrictive alternative 2–048
Section 2: People who lack capacity 2–049
Commentary on section 2
    The diagnostic threshold 2–050
    Matter specific and time specific 2–051
    The causative nexus 2–052
    Temporary impairment 2–053
    Age 2–054
    Standard of proof 2–055
Section 3: Inability to make decisions 2–056
Commentary on section 3
    All four elements in section 3(1) must be applied in full 2–057
    The relevant information 2–058
    Understanding relevant information 2–059
    Retaining relevant information 2–060
    Using or weighing relevant information 2–061
    Communicating the decision 2–062
    The Mental Capacity Act 2005 Code of Practice 2–063
    What the court expects 2–064
3. Mental Capacity Act Case Studies 2–065
Case Study 1
    LBL v RYJ [2010] EWHC 2665 (COP); [2010] C.O.P.L.R.
    Con. Vol. 795 2–066
Case Study 2
    Re S; D v R [2010] EWHC 2405 (Fam); [2010] C.O.P.L.R.
    Con. Vol. 1112 2–067

King v Wright Roofing Co Ltd 2020 EWHC 2129 (QB)

CONTENTS

Case Study 3
  PH v A Local Authority [2011] EWHC 1704 (Fam); [2012]
  C.O.P.L.R. 128 2–068
Case Study 4
  CC v KK [2012] EWHC 2136 (COP); [2012] C.O.P.L.R. 627 2–069
Case Study 5
  PC v City of York Council [2013] EWCA Civ 478; [2013]
  C.O.P.L.R. 409 2–070
Case Study 6
  IM v LM [2014] EWCA Civ 37; [2014] C.O.P.L.R. 246 2–071
Case Study 7
  Heart of England NHS Foundation Trust v JB [2014] EWHC
  342 (COP) 2–072
Case Study 8
  London Borough of Redbridge v G; C and F [2014] EWHC
  485 (COP); [2014] C.O.P.L.R. 292...2–073
Case Study 9
  Norfolk CC v PB [2014] EWCOP 14; [2015] C.O.P.L.R. 118.........2–074
Case Study 10
  A Local Authority v TZ (No.2) [2014] EWHC 973 (COP);
  [2014] C.O.P.L.R. 159 2–075
Case Study 11
  King's College Hospital NHS Foundation Trust v C [2015]
  EWCOP 80; [2016] C.O.P.L.R. 50...2–076
4. Judicial Observations on Capacity 2–077
  1. The court must make the ultimate decision 2–078
  2. The court must survey all the available evidence.............................2–079
  3. The forward looking focus of the Court of Protection 2–080
  4. The presumption of capacity 2–081
  5. All practicable steps must be taken...2–082
  6. Unwise decisions 2–083
  7. Unwise decisions: the fact that a decision is unwise is a
  relevant consideration for the court to take into account when
  considering whether a person lacks capacity 2–084
  8. Unwise decisions: the distinction between an unwise decision,
  which a person has the right to make, and a decision based on a
  lack of understanding of the risks...2–085
  9. Unwise decisions: the space between an unwise decision and
  one which an individual does not have the mental capacity to
  take 2–086
  10. The danger of applying an "outcome approach" whereby the
  patient is regarded as capable of making a decision that follows
  medical advice but incapable of making one that does not 2–087
  11. Qualifications and qualities of the assessor.....................................2–088
  12. Qualifications and qualities of the assessor 2–089
  13. Qualifications and qualities of the assessor 2–090
  14. A suggestion that a surgeon lacked the expertise to assess
  capacity..2–091

CONTENTS

15. Psychological tests and psychiatric tests 2–092
16. Stock responses 2–093
17. The burden of proof 2–094
18. The burden of proof 2–095
19. Standard of proof: the balance of probabilities 2–096
20. The standard of proof: the seriousness of the underlying issue 2–097
21. A single visit 2–098
22. The judge seeing the patient in private 2–099
23. Danger of imposing too high a test of capacity 2–100
24. A combination of clinical judgment and cognitive testing 2–101
25. Avoid impractical and unnecessary distinctions that could diminish the scope of a person's capacity 2–102
26. The causative nexus ("because of") 2–103
27. The causative nexus: it does not matter in what order the expert addresses the issues 2–104
28. Impairment of, or disturbance in the functioning of, the mind or brain 2–105
29. Existence of factors other than an impairment or disturbance in the functioning of the mind or brain 2–106
30. Every single issue of capacity must be evaluated by applying section 3(1) of the Act in full 2–107
31. Understanding: what is required is a broad, general understanding of the kind that is expected from the population at large 2–108
32. Relevant information: salient details 2–109
33. Relevant information: salient details 2–110
34. There has to be a practical limit on what needs to be envisaged as "reasonably foreseeable consequences" 2–111
35. Use or weigh: in some cases the ability to use information will be critical; in others, it will be necessary to weigh competing considerations 2–112
36. Use or weigh: different individuals may give different weight to different factors 2–113
37. Use or weigh: setting the bar too high 2–114
38. Use or weigh: where the person being assessed chooses to withhold information 2–115
39. Use or weigh: the inability to factor into her thought processes the realities of the harm that she will suffer 2–116
40. Use or weigh as part of the decision-making process 2–117
41. Where "the ability to use and weigh information is unlikely to loom large in the evaluation of capacity" 2–118
42. When a refined analysis is necessary because for a particular individual an otherwise simple decision is not a simple one 2–119
43. Inconsistency, confusion and incapacity 2–120
44. Inconsistency, confusion and incapacity 2–121
45. Indecision, avoidance and vacillation should not be confused with incapacity 2–122

CONTENTS

    46. Conflating a capacity assessment with a best interests analysis 2–123
    47. Vulnerability 2–124
    48. The vulnerable person's protective imperative 2–125
    49. The vulnerable person's protective imperative 2–126
    50. Judicial criticism of an expert's report 2–127
    5. Conclusion 2–128

3. Acquired Brain Injuries: Primary and Secondary Mechanisms
Fay Greenway, Jebet Beverly Cheserem, Simon Stapleton

Introduction 3–001
1. Economic Impact of Head Injury 3–002
2. Public Health Measures to Reduce Head Injury 3–003
    Speed limits 3–004
    Helmets 3–005
    Seat belts 3–006
    Infant and child seats 3–007
3. Basic Clinical Anatomy and Physiology of Head Injury
    Anatomy of the brain 3–008
    Neurophysiology 3–009
    Intracranial pressure 3–010
    Cerebral blood flow 3–011
    Brain herniation 3–013
    Glasgow Coma Scale 3–015
4. Types of Injury and Pathophysiology 3–016
    Diffuse brain injury 3–017
    Intracranial haematomas 3–018
    Severe diffuse injuries 3–019
    Chronic subdural haematoma 3–020
5. Head Injury at the Extremes of Age 3–021
6. Management of Head Injury 3–023
7. Long Term Surgical Complications
    Infection following head injury 3–026
    Hydrocephalus 3–027
    Cranioplasty 3–028
8. Conclusions 3–029
References 3–030

4. Neurological and Neuroradiological Evaluation of Traumatic Brain Injuries *Wolfgang Schady and Shawn Halpin*

Introduction 4–001
1. Assessment of Head Injury Severity 4–002
2. Physical Consequences of Traumatic Brain Injury
    The post-traumatic syndrome 4–004
    Impairments of mobility 4–007
    Special senses 4–008
    Bulbar functions 4–010
    Sphincter functions 4–011

CONTENTS

3. Imaging after Traumatic Brain Injury 4–012
   Computed tomography 4–013
   Magnetic resonance imaging 4–016
   Functional magnetic resonance imaging... 4–017
   Radionuclide studies 4–018
4. Delayed Complications of Traumatic Brain Injury
   Hydrocephalus... 4–019
   Post-traumatic epilepsy 4–020
   Alzheimer's disease... 4–022
   Hypopituitarism... 4–023
   Other delayed complications... 4–024
5. Extremes in the Spectrum of Severity of Traumatic Brain Injury
   Problems in the assessment of minor head injuries 4–025
   The persistent vegetative state 4–027
6. Life Expectancy 4–028
7. Conclusions 4–032
References 4–033

5. Neuropsychological Perspectives of Traumatic Brain Injury
Martin van den Broek and Sundeep Sembi

Introduction 5–001
   Difficulties in determining injury severity 5–003
   Neuropsychological examination.. 5–005
   Intellectual assessment.. 5–007
   Attention and memory 5–009
   Executive skills 5–011
   Secondary influences on neuropsychological impairment.................. 5–013
      Depression.. 5–014
      Anxiety... 5–015
      Fatigue.. 5–016
      Pain... 5–017
      Alcohol and substance use... 5–018
   Psychological and emotional functioning... 5–019
   Moderate and severe injuries 5–023
   Test disclosure 5–025
   Third party observers 5–026
   Conclusions 5–027
References 5–028

6. Neuropsychiatric Aspects of Brain Injury *Niruj Agrawal*

Introduction 6–001
1. Extent of Problem 6–002
2. Causation of Neuropsychiatric Problems following Traumatic
   Brain Injury 6–004
3. Mild Traumatic Brain Injury and Post-Concussion Syndrome............. 6–006
4. Acute Post-Traumatic Amnesia/Post-Traumatic Agitation................... 6–011
5. Mood Disorders
   Depression.. 6–013

Suicide 6–015
Affective dysregulation 6–016
Anxiety disorders 6–017
6. Apathy—Amotivation... 6–020
7. Psychosis 6–022
8. Organic Personality and Behavioural Change.. 6–023
9. Alcohol and Drugs 6–025
10. Functional Neurological Disorders and Factitious Disorder................... 6–028
11. Risk for Dementia 6–030
12. Management 6–033
References 6–034

7. Malingering and Exaggeration *Martin van den Broek and Sundeep Sembi*
1. Validity Issues in Litigation.. 7–001
2. Base-Rate of Non-Credible Presentations 7–003
3. Definitions of Malingering 7–005
4. Panel: Diagnostic Categories and Criteria for Malingering of Neurocognitive Dysfunction (MND; Slick et al., 1999) 7–008
5. Litigation and its Effects... 7–009
6. Assessment of Non-Credible Presentations... 7–010
7. Performance Validity Assessment... 7–011
   State full effort was applied... 7–012
   Over-state good effort 7–013
   Ignore the performance validity test.. 7–014
   Ignore other performance validity test results 7–015
   Performance validity test failure coexisting with genuine deficits 7–016
   Performance validity test and malingering... 7–017
8. Symptom Validity Assessment.. 7–018
9. Faking Good and Faking Bad... 7–020
10. Malingering, Exaggeration and the Courts... 7–021
11. Practical Significance of Validity Measures 7–022
12. Conclusions 7–024
References 7–025

8. Neurorehabilitation After Acquired Brain Injury
Andrew Worthington
Introduction 8–001
1. Brain Injury and Brain Recovery
   Acute treatment: preventing nerve cell death... 8–002
   Does (lesion) size matter?.. 8–004
   Neuroplasticity and rehabilitation... 8–005
   Use it or lose it.. 8–006
   Use it and improve it 8–007
   Specificity.. 8–008
   Repetition matters 8–009
   Intensity matters 8–010

CONTENTS

Time matters 8–011
Salience matters 8–012
Age matters 8–013
Transference 8–014
Interference 8–015
2. Understanding Disability 8–016
3. Models of Rehabilitation and Service Provision 8–017
Rehabilitation pathways 8–019
4. Stages of Rehabilitation
Very early rehabilitation 8–020
Rehabilitation in hospital 8–022
Residential rehabilitation 8–025
Slow stream rehabilitation 8–026
Neurobehavioural rehabilitation 8–027
Rehabilitation in the community 8–028
Case management 8–030
Neurorehabilitation in practice 8–032
    Identifying impairments and constraints on learning 8–033
    Neuropsychological constraints on rehabilitation 8–034
    Attention, processing speed and learning 8–035
    Executive functions 8–036
    Fatigue 8–037
Constraints on psychological therapy 8–038
    Motivation for change 8–039
    Inertia and avoidance 8–040
Cognitive and behavioural rehabilitation 8–041
    Environmental modification 8–042
    Compensatory strategies 8–043
    Task specific training 8–044
    Metacognitive training 8–045
    Therapy versus scaffolding 8–046
    Relapse prevention 8–047
    Crisis intervention 8–048
5. Service Organisation
Teamwork 8–049
Goal setting 8–052
Outcome evaluation 8–054
6. Quality and Evidence in Brain Injury Rehabilitation
Quality standards 8–055
Efficacy and cost-effectiveness of neurorehabilitation 8–056
    Mild traumatic brain injury 8–057
    Severe brain injury 8–058
7. Conclusions and Future Trends 8–060
References 8–061

CONTENTS

9. Paediatric Acquired Brain Injury *Ingram Wright*
Chapter Layout 9–001
1. Neurodevelopmental Aspects of Childhood Brain Injury
   Why a developmental perspective matters 9–002
   Healthy central nervous system maturation 9–003
   Post-injury central nervous system and cognitive development ... 9–004
      Plasticity (biological) 9–005
      Plasticity (cognitive/behavioural) 9–006
      Vulnerability (biological/behavioural/cognitive) 9–007
   Critical periods in development 9–008
   Impact of age at injury on outcome following brain injury 9–009
2. Issues in Childhood Brain Injury Litigation
   Age at which reliable prognosis can be determined 9–010
   Estimating pre-injury functioning in childhood 9–014
   Impact of intervention and rehabilitation in childhood 9–015
3. Specific Challenges in Paediatric Acquired Brain Injury
   Mild traumatic brain injury and normal brain imaging 9–017
   Special case of frontal lobe functioning and emergence of
   dysexecutive symptoms 9–018
   Capacity to litigate and manage finances and broader issues on
   reaching majority 9–020
   Intellectual ability and adaptive function/care needs,
   employment 9–022
Summary 9–024
References 9–025

10. Subtle Brain Injury Claims *Jonathan Watt-Pringle QC and Martin van den Broek*
Introduction 10–001
1. Post-Traumatic Amnesia 10–002
2. Post-Injury Complaints 10–006
3. Explanations for Subtle Brain Injury Complaints 10–010
   Emotional and mood disorders 10–013
   Acute and chronic pain 10–014
   Iatrogenesis 10–015
   Validity issues 10–017
   Critogenic influences 10–018
4. Conclusions 10–020
   Case Study 1
      Van Wees v Karkour [2007] EWHC 165 (QB) 10–021
   Case Study 2
      Clarke v Maltby [2010] EWHC 1201 (QB); [2010] EWHC
      1856 (QB) 10–024
   Case Study 3
      Siegel v Pummell [2014] EWHC 4309 (QB); [2015] EWHC
      195 (QB) 10–026
   Case Summary 4
      Hibberd-Little v Carlton [2018] EWHC 1787 (QB) 10–030

CONTENTS

References 10–034

11. Return to Work and Vocational Rehabilitation *Andy Tyerman, Nigel King and Martin Hillier*
Introduction..11–001
1. Vocational Outcomes/Needs
   Return to work after traumatic brain injury........................11–003
   Factors influencing return to work......................................11–005
   Vocational needs after brain injury 11–009
2. Disability Discrimination 11–011
   The Equality Act 2010 11–012
      Direct discrimination 11–013
      Indirect discrimination..11–014
      Discrimination arising from disability 11–015
      Failure to make reasonable adjustments 11–016
      Harassment 11–018
      Victimisation..11–019
   Public Sector Equality Duty and positive action.................11–020
   Obligations of employers 11–021
      Selection 11–022
      Ongoing employment and adjustments........................11–023
   Obligations in higher and further education 11–024
      Selection 11–026
      Current students...11–027
   Disability discrimination in vocational rehabilitation practice..........11–028
      In employment..11–029
      Further and higher education 11–031
3. Vocational Assessment
   What is vocational assessment? 11–032
   Illustrative acquired brain injury vocational assessment
   programme..11–034
   Expert neuropsychological assessment and opinion...........11–037
4. Vocational Rehabilitation 11–039
   Supported return to previous work 11–040
   Preparation for new or alternative employment 11–042
   Return to alternative occupation 11–045
   Effectiveness of vocational rehabilitation after brain injury 11–047
5. Vocational Rehabilitation Service Provision in the UK 11–049
6. Conclusions 11–052
References...11–053

12. Assessing Care Needs After Acquired Brain Injury *Caz Lyall*
Introduction 12–001
1. Introduction to Acquired Brain Injury................................12–002
   Impact of acquired brain injury on family members and
   spouses..12–004
2. Skill Base of the Care Expert..12–006
3. Assessment of a Claimant with Brain Injury 12–007

xxiii

CONTENTS

   4. Assessment Process
      Introduction 12–008
      Assessment techniques 12–010
      Pre-existing disabilities 12–013
      Timing of care assessments 12–014
      Use of standardised assessments and the potential for
      exaggeration 12–015
      Assessment of past care 12–016
      Conclusion 12–017
   5. Future Recommendations in Terms of Rehabilitation 12–018
      Introduction 12–019
      Recommendations for rehabilitation 12–020
      Support workers and their role in rehabilitation 12–021
      Trials of independent living 12–023
      Care packages where active rehabilitation approach is not
      required 12–024
      Predicting future care needs and differing view of care experts 12–025
      What are the main areas of disagreement between care
      experts? 12–027
      Management of neuropsychiatric conditions 12–028
   6. "Care" Packages and Working Time Directives 12–029
      Monitoring the care package 12–032
      Agency and direct employment 12–033
      Live-in care and working time directives 12–034
      Double-up care 12–036
   7. Recommendations for Case Management Input 12–037
      Case manager role and standards of practice 12–038
      Effectiveness of a dynamic and well managed rehabilitation
      programme and care package 12–041
      Effectiveness of case management after brain injury 12–044
   8. Longer-Term Recommendations 12–045
      References 12–046

13. **Whose Evidence Should We Accept? How Judges Reach Their Decisions** *The Hon Mr Justice Langstaff, William Norris QC, Nathan Tavares QC and Martin van den Broek*
    1. The Issue 13–001
    2. Evaluating Brain Injury Claims (MB) 13–002
       Coarse bias 13–003
       Subtle biases 13–005
          Base rates 13–006
          Hindsight bias 13–007
          Confirmatory bias 13–008
    3. Judicial Decision-Making 13–009
       Expert evidence 13–012
       Lay witnesses: how do we decide between them? 13–013
       Guthrie Featherstone and the "judicial nose" 13–015
       Science versus art 13–016

CONTENTS

4. Judicial Perspectives 13–019
References 13–023

                                                                             PAGE
Index 507

TABLE OF CASES

Paragraph numbers in **bold** represent case studies

A (Capacity: Social Media and Internet Use: Best Interests) Re, [2019] EWCOP 2; [2019] Fam. 586; [2019] 3 W.L.R. 59; [2019] 2 WLUK 284; [2019] C.O.P.L.R. 137; [2019] Med. L.R. 135; (2019) 168 B.M.L.R. 58 2–037
A Local Authority v AK [2012] EWHC B29 (COP); [2013] C.O.P.L.R. 163 .... 2–097, 2–119
A Local Authority v TZ (No.2) [2014] EWHC 973 (COP); [2014] C.O.P.L.R. 159 .. **2–075**, 2–085, 2–0126
A v Powys Local Health Board [2007] EWHC 2996 (QB) 1–027
A v X [2012] EWHC 2400 (COP); [2013] W.T.L.R. 187; [2013] C.O.P.L.R. 1 2–009
AB v John Wyeth & Brother Ltd (No.1) [1992] 1 W.L.R. 168; [1992] 1 All E.R. 443; [1992] P.I.Q.R. P437; [1992] 3 Med. L.R. 190 1–016
AB v Royal Devon and Exeter NHS Foundation Trust [2016] EWHC 1024 (QB) ... 1–026, 1–027, 1–042
ABC v St. George's Healthcare NHS Trust [2020] EWHC 455 (QB) 1–023
Air Canada v Secretary of State for Trade (No. 2) [1983] 2 A.C. 394; [1983] 2 W.L.R. 494; [1983] 1 All E.R. 910 13–014
Ali v Caton [2013] EWHC 1730 (QB) **1–032**
Allen v British Rail Engineering Ltd (BREL) [2001] EWCA Civ 242; [2001] I.C.R. 942; [2001] P.I.Q.R. Q10 1–004
Allen Tod Architecture Ltd (In Liquidation) v Capita Property and Infrastructure Ltd (previously Capita Symons Ltd) [2016] EWHC 2171 (TCC); [2016] B.L.R. 592; 168 Con. L.R. 201; [2016] C.I.L.L. 3881 1–011
Armagas Ltd v Mundogas SA (The Ocean Frost) [1986] A.C. 717; [1986] 2 W.L.R. 1063; [1986] 2 All E.R. 385; [1986] 2 Lloyd's Rep. 109; (1986) 2 B.C.C. 99197; (1986) 83 L.S.G. 2002; (1986) 130 S.J. 430 13–011
Attorney General v Parnther (1792) 3 Bro. C.C. 441, 2 Dick 748; 29 E.R. 962 2–043
AWG Group Ltd (formerly Anglian Water Plc) v Morrison [2006] EWCA Civ 6; [2006] 1 W.L.R. 1163; [2006] 1 All E.R. 967 13–019
B v A Local Authority [2019] EWCA Civ 913; [2019] 3 W.L.R. 685; [2019] 6 WLUK 122; [2019] 2 F.L.R. 1001; [2019] C.O.P.L.R. 347; (2019) 22 C.C.L. Rep. 336; [2019] Med. L.R. 371 CA 2–036, 2–037
B (A Child) (Care Proceedings: Threshold Criteria) Re, [2013] UKSC 33; [2013] 1 W.L.R. 1911; [2013] 3 All E.R. 929; [2013] 6 WLUK 280; [2013] 2 F.L.R. 1075; [2013] 2 F.C.R. 525; [2013] H.R.L.R. 29; [2013] Fam. Law 946; (2013) 157(24) S.J.L.B. 37 13–009
B (Capacity: Social Media: Care and Contact) Re, [2019] EWCOP 3; [2019] 2 WLUK 298; [2019] C.O.P.L.R. 163; [2019] Med. L.R. 143; (2019) 168 B.M.L.R. 72 2–037
Bailey v Warren [2006] EWCA Civ 51; [2006] C.P. Rep. 26; [2006] M.H.L.R. 211; [2006] W.T.L.R. 753 .... 2–003, 2–006, 2–007
Baker Tilly (A Firm) v Makar [2013] EWHC 759 (QB); [2013] 3 Costs L.R. 444; [2013] C.O.P.L.R. 245 2–008
Banks v Goodfellow (1869–70) L.R. 5 Q.B. 549 2–026
Barker v Corus UK Ltd [2006] UKHL 20; [2006] 2 A.C. 572; [2006] 2 W.L.R. 1027; [2006] 3 All E.R. 785; [2006] I.C.R. 809; [2006] P.I.Q.R. P26; (2006) 89 B.M.L.R. 1; (2006) 103(20) L.S.G. 27; (2006) 156 N.L.J. 796; (2006) 150 S.J.L.B. 606; [2006] N.P.C. 50 13–001
Beacon Insurance Co Ltd v Maharaj Bookstore Ltd [2014] UKPC 21; [2014] 4 All E.R. 418; [2014] 2 All E.R. (Comm) 558 .... 13–001, 13–011
Beaney (Deceased), Re [1978] 1 W.L.R. 770; [1978] 2 All E.R. 595; (1977) 121 S.J. 832 2–029
Beck v Ministry of Defence [2003] EWCA Civ 1043; [2005] 1 W.L.R. 2206; [2003] C.P. Rep. 62; [2004] P.I.Q.R. P1; (2003) 100(31) L.S.G. 31 1–011
Bennett v Compass Group UK & Ireland Limited [2002] EWCA Civ 642; [2002] C.P. Rep. 58; [2002] C.P.L.R. 452; [2002] I.C.R. 1177 1–011
Biogen Inc v Medeva plc [1996] 10 WLUK 486; [1997] R.P.C. 1; (1997) 38 B.M.L.R. 149; (1997) 20(1) I.P.D. 20001 13–009
Bird v Luckie 68 E.R. 375; (1850) 8 Hare 301 2–046
Blamire v Cumbria Health Authority [1992] 10 WLUK 104; [1993] PIQR Q1 .... **10–023**

TABLE OF CASES

BMG (Mansfield) Ltd v Galliford Try Construction Ltd [2013] EWHC 3183 (TCC); [2014] C.P.
  Rep. 3; [2017] T.C.L.R. 4; [2014] C.I.L.L. 3437 1–011
Booth v Warrington Health Authority [1992] P.I.Q.R. P137 1–016
Boughton v Knight (1872–75) L.R. 3 P. & D. 64 2–014
Brown v Mujibal [2017] 4 WLUK 42 1–025
Buckenham v Dickinson [2000] W.T.L.R. 1083 2–027
C v Kemp [2011] CSOH 43; 2011 G.W.D. 18–432 1–028
C.A.F, Re 1961 No. 2367 Unreported 25 March 1962 .... 2–009, 2–010
Cattermole v Prisk [2006] 1 F.L.R. 693; [2006] Fam. Law 98 2–027
CC v KK and STCC [2012] EWHC 2136 (COP); [2012] C.O.P.L.R. 627 ... 2–042, 2–044, 2–058,
  2–069, 2–078,
  2–083, 2–095, 2–110, 2–123
Clark v Greater Glasgow Health Board [2016] CSOH 126; 2016 Rep. L.R. 126; 2016
  G.W.D.. 1–027
Clarke v Maltby [2010] EWHC 1201 (QB) 1–004, **1–030**, 10–001, **10–024**, 10–029,
  13–017
Clarke v Maltby (Costs) [2010] EWHC 1856 (QB) 1–031, **10–024**
Cloutt, Re Unreported 7 November 2008 COP 2–024
Clunis v Camden and Islington Health Authority [1998] Q.B. 978; [1998] 2 W.L.R. 902; [1998] 3
  All E.R. 180; (1997–98) 1 C.C.L. Rep. 215; (1998) 40 B.M.L.R. 181; [1998] P.N.L.R. 262;
  (1998) 95(2) L.S.G. 23; (1998) 142 S.J.L.B. 38 .... 1–040, 1–042
Coombs v Dorset NHS Primary Care Trust [2013] EWCA Civ 471; [2014] 1 W.L.R. 111; [2013] 4
  All E.R. 429; (2013) 16 C.C.L. Rep. 376; [2013] P.I.Q.R. P16; [2013] M.H.L.R. 194 1–021
Corr v IBC Vehicles Ltd [2008] UKHL 13; [2008] 1 A.C. 884; [2008] 2 W.L.R. 499; [2008] 2 All
  E.R. 943; [2008] I.C.R. 372; [2008] P.I.Q.R. P11; (2008) 105(10) L.S.G. 28; (2008) 152(9)
  S.J.L.B. 30 1–042
Crookdake v Drury. *See* Sowden v Lodge
Derby & Co Ltd v Weldon (No.9) [1990] 11 WLUK 50 1–009
DN v Greenwich London Borough Council [2004] EWCA Civ 1659; [2005] 1 F.C.R. 112; [2005]
  B.L.G.R. 597; [2005] E.L.R. 133; (2005) 149 S.J.L.B. 25 1–012
Dunhill v Burgin (Nos 1 and 2) [2014] UKSC 18; [2014] 1 W.L.R. 933; [2014] 2 All E.R. 364;
  [2014] R.T.R. 16; [2014] C.O.P.L.R. 199; (2014) 17 C.C.L. Rep. 203; [2014] P.I.Q.R. P13;
  (2014) 137 B.M.L.R. 1; [2014] M.H.L.R. 387; (2014) 164(7599) N.L.J. 20; (2014) 158(12)
  S.J.L.B. 41 .... 2–007, 2–015
Eagle v Chambers (No.2) [2004] EWCA Civ 1033; [2004] 1 W.L.R. 3081; [2005] 1 All E.R. 136;
  [2005] P.I.Q.R. Q2; [2004] Lloyd's Rep. Med. 413; (2005) 82 B.M.L.R. 22; (2004) 154 N.L.J.
  1451; (2004) 148 S.J.L.B. 972................................ 1–027
Edwards v Martin [2010] EWHC 570 (QB)......................... **1–035**
Edwards-Tubb v JD Wetherspoon Plc [2011] EWCA Civ 136; [2011] 1 W.L.R. 1373; [2011] C.P.
  Rep. 27; [2011] P.I.Q.R. P16; (2011) 121 B.M.L.R. 70; (2011) 155(9) S.J.L.B. 31 1–011
Excelsior Commercial & Industrial Holdings Ltd v Salisbury Hamer Aspden & Johnson (Costs)
  [2002] EWCA Civ 879; [2002] C.P. Rep. 67; [2002] C.P.L.R. 693 .... 1–030, 13–017
EXB (A Protected Party) v FDZ [2018] EWHC 3456 (QB); [2018] 12 WLUK 233; [2019] P.I.Q.R.
  P7 .... 2–038, 2–039
EXP v Barker [2017] EWCA Civ 63; [2017] Med. L.R. 121; (2017) 155 B.M.L.R. 18 1–014
Farrugia v Burtenshaw Unreported 22 January 2014 QBD 12–036
Folks v Faizey [2006] EWCA Civ 381; [2006] C.P. Rep. 30; [2006] M.H.L.R. 239 2–006
Gartside v Outram [1857] 26 L.J. Ch. 113 1–023
Gestmin SGPS SA v Credit Suisse (UK) Ltd [2013] EWHC 3560 (Comm) 10–005, 13–009,
  13–011
Giblett v P & NE Murray Ltd (1999) 96(22) L.S.G. 34 .... **1–043**
Gray v Thames Trains Ltd [2009] UKHL 33; [2009] 1 A.C. 1339; [2009] 3 W.L.R. 167; [2009] 4
  All E.R. 81; [2009] P.I.Q.R. P22; [2009] LS Law Medical 409; (2009) 108 B.M.L.R. 205;
  [2009] M.H.L.R. 73; [2009] Po. L.R. 229; (2009) 159 N.L.J. 925; (2009) 153(24) S.J.L.B.
  33 1–042
Hajigeorgiou v Vasiliou [2005] EWCA Civ 236; [2005] 1 W.L.R. 2195; [2005] 3 All E.R. 17;
  [2005] C.P. Rep. 27; (2005) 102(18) L.S.G. 22; [2005] N.P.C. 39 1–011
Harman (A Child) v East Kent Hospitals NHS Foundation Trust Queen's Bench Division, 11 June
  2015 [2015] EWHC 1662 (QB); [2015] P.I.Q.R. Q4; [2016] Med. L.R. 305 12–017
Hart v O'Connor [1985] A.C. 1000; [1985] 3 W.L.R. 214; [1985] 2 All E.R. 880; [1985] 1 N.Z.L.R.
  159; (1985) 82 L.S.G. 2658; (1985) 129 S.J. 484 2–015
Hayden v Maidstone and Tunbridge Wells NHS Trust [2016] EWHC 3276 (QB) 1–004

TABLE OF CASES

Heart of England NHS Foundation Trust v JB [2014] EWHC 342 (COP); (2014) 137 B.M.L.R. 232 .... 2–031, **2–072**, 2–087, 2–091, 2–102, 2–108, 2–122
Heil v Rankin [2001] Q.B. 272; [2000] 2 W.L.R. 1173; [2000] 3 All E.R. 138; [2000] I.R.L.R. 334; [2000] P.I.Q.R. Q187; [2000] Lloyd's Rep. Med. 203; (2000) 97(14) L.S.G. 41; (2000) 150 N.L.J. 464; (2000) 144 S.J.L.B. 157 1–037
Hibberd-Little v Carlton [2018] EWHC 1787 (QB); [2018] 7 WLUK 133 . 1–032, 10–009, 10–012, 10–030
HM (A Child), Re [2012] Med. L.R. 449; [2014] Med. L.R. 40; [2012] W.T.L.R. 281 1–026
Hoff v Atherton [2004] EWCA Civ 1554; [2005] W.T.L.R. 99 2–027
Housecroft v Burnett [1986] 1 All E.R. 332; (1985) 135 N.L.J. 728 1–035
Housen v Nikolaisen [2002] 2 S.C.R. 235; 2002 SCC 33 13–001
Howell-Smith v Official Solicitor [2006] P.N.L.R. 21 1–024
Hoyle v Rogers [2014] EWCA Civ 257; [2015] Q.B. 265; [2014] 3 W.L.R. 148; [2014] 3 All E.R. 550; [2014] C.P. Rep. 30; [2014] 1 C.L.C. 316; [2014] Inquest L.R. 135 1–012
Ikarian Reefer (No.1), The. *See* National Justice Compania Naviera SA v Prudential Assurance Co Ltd (The Ikarian Reefer) (No.1)
IM v LM (Capacity to Consent to Sexual Relations) [2014] EWCA Civ 37; [2015] Fam. 61; [2014] 3 W.L.R. 409; [2014] 3 All E.R. 491; [2014] 2 F.C.R. 13; [2014] C.O.P.L.R. 246; (2014) 17 C.C.L. Rep. 39; [2014] Med. L.R. 345; (2014) 158(5) S.J.L.B. 37 . 2–032, 2–057, 2–058, 2–061, **2–071**, 2–080, 2–107, 2–111, 2–112, 2–118
Imperial Loan Co Ltd v Stone [1892] 1 QB 599 2–015
J (A Minor) (Child Abuse: Expert Evidence), Re [1990] 7 WLUK 344 [1991] F.C.R. 193 1–009
Jackson v Barry Railway Co [1893] 1 Ch. 238 13–019
Jackson v Marley Davenport Ltd [2004] EWCA Civ 1225; [2004] 1 W.L.R. 2926; [2005] C.P. Rep. 8; [2005] B.L.R. 13; [2005] P.I.Q.R. P10; [2005] 1 E.G.L.R. 103; (2004) 101(38) L.S.G. 29; (2004) 148 S.J.L.B. 1121 1–016
K (Enduring Powers of Attorney), Re; Re F [1988] Ch. 310; [1988] 2 W.L.R. 781; [1988] 1 All E.R. 358; [1988] 2 F.L.R. 15; [1988] Fam. Law 203; (1987) 137 N.L.J. 1039; (1987) 131 S.J. 1488 2–023
Kenward v Adams, Times, 29 November 1975 2–027
Key v Key [2010] EWHC 408 (Ch); [2010] 1 W.L.R. 2020; [2010] M.H.L.R. 308; [2010] W.T.L.R. 623 2–027
King's College Hospital NHS Foundation Trust v C [2015] EWCOP 80; [2016] C.O.P.L.R. 50 .... 2–052, 2–061, 2–076, 2–079, 2–083, 2–105, 2–114, 2–117
Kirkman v Euro Exide Corp (CMP Batteries Ltd) [2007] EWCA Civ 66; [2007] C.P. Rep. 19; (2007) 104(6) L.S.G. 31; (2007) 151 S.J.L.B. 164 1–012
KJP, Re [2016] EWCOP 6; [2016] W.T.L.R. 687 2–024
Lawrence v Kent County Council [2012] EWCA Civ 493 1–012
LBL v RYJ [2010] EWHC 2665 (Fam); [2011] 1 F.L.R. 1279; [2011] Fam. Law 242; [2010] C.O.P.L.R. Con. Vol. 795 .... 2–058, 2–061, **2–066**, 2–109, 2–113, 2–120, 2–121, 2–124
LBX v K, L, M. *See* X v K
Lindsay v Wood [2006] EWHC 2895 (QB); [2006] M.H.L.R. 341 .... 1–026, 2–006
Livingstone v Rawyards Coal Co (1880) 5 App. Cas. 25; (1880) 7 R. (H.L.) 1 12–006
London Borough of Redbridge v G; C and F [2014] EWHC 485 (COP); [2014] C.O.P.L.R. 292 .... **2–073**, 2–081, 2–088, 2–089, 2–096
Loughlin v Singh [2013] EWHC 1641 (QB); [2013] Med. L.R. 513 .... 12–042, 12–043
M (a child) v Lambeth London Borough Council [2014] EWHC 57 (QB) 1–019
Mann v Bahri unreported 12 March 2012, Central London County Court 10–001, 10–029
Masterman-Lister v Jewell; Masterman-Lister v Brutton & Co [2002] EWCA Civ 1889; [2003] 1 W.L.R. 1511; [2003] 3 All E.R. 162; [2003] C.P. Rep. 29; (2004) 7 C.C.L. Rep. 5; [2003] P.I.Q.R. P20; [2003] Lloyd's Rep. Med. 244; (2003) 73 B.M.L.R. 1; [2003] M.H.L.R. 166; [2003] W.T.L.R. 259; (2003) 147 S.J.L.B. 60
Miller v Minister of Pensions [1947] 2 All E.R. 372; 63 T.L.R. 474; [1947] W.N. 241; [1948] L.J.R. 203; 177 L.T. 536; (1947) 91 S.J. 484 .... 2–004—2–006, 2–009, 2–010, 2–043
Miller v Minister of Pensions [1947] 2 All E.R. 372 2–055
Mitchell v Alasia [2005] EWHC 11 (QB) 2–006

TABLE OF CASES

Montgomery v Lanarkshire Health Board [2015] UKSC 11; [2015] A.C. 1430; [2015] 2 W.L.R. 768; [2015] 2 All E.R. 1031; 2015 S.C. (U.K.S.C.) 63; 2015 S.L.T. 189; 2015 S.C.L.R. 315; [2015] P.I.Q.R. P13; [2015] Med. L.R. 149; (2015) 143 B.M.L.R. 47; 2015 G.W.D. 10–179 2–031
Morrow v Shrewsbury Rugby Football Club Ltd [2020] EWHC 379 (QB) 1–025
Mugweni v NHS London (formerly South East London SHA) [2011] EWHC 334 (QB) . . . 13–014
Murray v Martin Devenish [2017] EWCA Civ 1016 1–011
Mustard v Flower [2019] EWHC 2623 (QB); [2019] 10 WLUK 167 10–019
NHS Trust v Dr A [2013] EWHC 2442 (COP); [2014] Fam. 161; [2014] 2 W.L.R. 607; [2013] Med. L.R. 561; (2014) 136 B.M.L.R. 115 2–046
National Justice Compania Naviera SA v Prudential Assurance Co Ltd (The Ikarian Reefer) (No.1) [1995] 1 Lloyd's Rep. 455, [1994] 12 WLUK 105 . . . . 1–009, 13–012
Newman v Laver [2006] EWCA Civ 1135 10–011
Norfolk CC v PB [2014] EWCOP 14; [2015] C.O.P.L.R. 118 . 2–052, **2–074**, 2–099, 2–104, 2–106, 2–115, 2–116
Ocean Frost, The. *See* Armagas Ltd v Mundogas SA (The Ocean Frost)
Onassis v Vergottis [1968] 2 Lloyd's Rep. 403; (1968) 118 N.L.J. 1052 . . . . 13–010, 13–014
Owen v Brown [2002] All E.R. (D) 534 1–027
Page v Plymouth Hospitals NHS Trust [2004] EWHC 1154 (QB); [2004] 3 All E.R. 367; [2004] P.I.Q.R. Q6; [2004] Lloyd's Rep. Med. 337; (2005) 82 B.M.L.R. 1; (2004) 101(26) L.S.G. 27; (2004) 154 N.L.J. 853 1–027
Page v Smith [1996] A.C. 155; [1995] 2 W.L.R. 644; [1995] 2 All E.R. 736; [1995] 2 Lloyd's Rep. 95; [1995] R.T.R. 210; [1995] P.I.Q.R. P329; (1995) 92(23) L.S.G. 33; (1995) 145 N.L.J. 723; (1995) 139 S.J.L.B. 173 1–043
Park, In the Estate of [1954] P. 112; [1953] 3 W.L.R. 1012; [1953] 2 All E.R. 1411; (1953) 97 S.J. 830 2–030
Parker v Felgate (1883) 8 P.D. 171; (1883) 52 L.J.P. 95 PDAD 2–025, 2–029
PBM v TGT [2019] EWCOP 6; [2019] 3 WLUK 728; [2019] C.O.P.L.R. 427; [2019] W.T.L.R. 995 2–039
PC v City of York Council [2013] EWCA Civ 478; [2014] Fam. 10; [2014] 2 W.L.R. 1; (2013) 16 C.C.L. Rep. 298; [2013] Med. L.R. 213; [2013] C.O.P.L.R. 409 . . 2–047, 2–052, **2–070**, 2–086, 2–103
Perrins v Holland [2010] EWCA Civ 840; [2011] Ch. 270; [2011] 2 W.L.R. 1086; [2011] 2 All E.R. 174; [2010] W.T.L.R. 1415; 13 I.T.E.L.R. 405; (2010) 160 N.L.J. 1076; (2010) 154(29) S.J.L.B. 34 . . . . 2–025, 2–026
Peters v East Midlands SHA [2009] EWCA Civ 145; [2010] Q.B. 48; [2009] 3 W.L.R. 737; (2009) 12 C.C.L. Rep. 299; [2009] P.I.Q.R. Q1; [2009] LS Law Medical 229; (2009) 153(9) S.J.L.B. 30; Times, March 16, 2009 1–021
PH v A Local Authority [2011] EWHC 1704 (Fam); [2012] C.O.P.L.R. 128 . . **2–068**, 2–090, 2–094, 2–098, 2–100, 2–125
Pickford v Imperial Chemical Industries Plc [1998] 1 W.L.R. 1189 10–011
Polivitte Ltd v Commercial Union Assurance Co Plc [1987] 1 Lloyd's Rep. 379; [1986] 10 WLUK 128 1–009
R. v C [2009] UKHL 42; [2009] 1 W.L.R. 1786; [2009] 4 All E.R. 1033; [2010] 1 Cr. App. R. 7; [2009] M.H.L.R. 189; [2010] Crim. L.R. 75; (2009) 153(31) S.J.L.B. 30 2–032
R. v Lucas (Lyabode Ruth) [1981] Q.B. 720; [1981] 3 W.L.R. 120; [1981] 2 All E.R. 1008; (1981) 73 Cr. App. R. 159; [1981] Crim. L.R. 624 13–010
Reaney v University Hospital of North Staffordshire NHS Trust [2015] EWCA Civ 1119; [2016] P.I.Q.R. Q3; [2016] Med. L.R. 23 12–013
Rhesa Shipping Co SA v Edmunds (The Popi M) [1985] 1 W.L.R. 948 10–010
Rialis v Mitchell, Times, 17 July 1984 1–037
S, Re Unreported 1 March 1997 2–024
S, Re; D v R [2010] EWHC 2405 (Fam); [2011] W.T.L.R. 449; [2010] C.O.P.L.R. Con. Vol. 1112 . . . . 2–047, **2–067**, 2–084, 2–092, 2–093, 2–101, 2–127
Sabatini, Re (1969) 114 S.J. 35. 2–028
Sarwar v Ali [2007] EWHC 1255 (QB); [2007] LS Law Medical 375 1–028
Saulle v Nouvet [2007] EWHC 2902 (QB); [2008] LS Law Medical 201; [2008] M.H.L.R. 59; [2008] W.T.L.R. 729 . . . . 1–028, 2–006
Scammell v Farmer [2008] EWHC 1100 (Ch); [2008] W.T.L.R. 1261; (2008) 152(23) S.J.L.B. 31 2–027

TABLE OF CASES

Sharp v Adam [2006] EWCA Civ 449; [2006] W.T.L.R. 1059; (2007–08) 10 I.T.E.L.R. 419 2–027
Sheffield City Council v E [2004] EWHC 2808 (Fam); [2005] Fam. 326; [2005] 2 W.L.R. 953; [2005] 1 F.L.R. 965; [2005] Lloyd's Rep. Med. 223; [2005] Fam. Law 279; (2005) 102(9) L.S.G. 30 2–030
Siegel v Pummell [2014] EWHC 4309 (QB) 1–010, 1–032, 10–001, 10–006, **10–026**
Siegel v Pummell [2015] EWHC 195 (QB); [2015] 3 Costs L.O. 357, [2015] 2 WLUK 77 . **10–026**
Simpson (Deceased), Re; Schaniel v Simpson (1977) 121 S.J. 224 2–027
Singellos v Singellos [2010] EWHC 2353 (Ch); [2011] Ch. 324; [2011] 2 W.L.R. 1111; [2011] W.T.L.R. 327 2–029
Sowden v Lodge; sub nom. Crookdake v Drury [2004] EWCA Civ 1370; [2005] 1 W.L.R. 2129; [2005] 1 All E.R. 581; [2005] Lloyd's Rep. Med. 86; (2004) 148 S.J.L.B. 1282 . . 1–035, 1–037
Stephens v Cannon [2005] EWCA Civ 222; [2005] C.P. Rep. 31; [2006] R.V.R. 126 13–014
Summers v Fairclough Homes Ltd [2012] UKSC 26; [2012] 1 W.L.R. 2004; [2012] 4 All E.R. 317; [2012] 4 Costs L.R. 760; [2013] Lloyd's Rep. I.R. 159; (2012) 162 N.L.J. 910; (2012) 156(26) S.J.L.B. 31 13–017
Synclair v East Lancashire Hospital NHS Trust [2015] EWCA Civ 1283; [2016] Med. L.R. 1 1–006
TB v KB (Capacity to Conduct Proceedings) [2019] EWCOP 14; [2019] 4 WLUK 486 2–007
Three Rivers DC v Bank of England (No.3) (Summary Judgment) [2001] UKHL 16; [2003] 2 A.C. 1; [2001] 2 All E.R. 513; [2001] Lloyd's Rep. Bank. 125; (2001) 3 L.G.L.R. 36 1–031
Toth v Jarman [2006] EWCA Civ 1028; [2006] 4 All E.R. 1276 (Note); [2006] C.P. Rep. 44; [2006] Lloyd's Rep. Med. 397; (2006) 91 B.M.L.R. 121 1–014
Ure v Ure Unreported 13 July 2007 QBD 1–028
Van Wees v Karkour [2007] EWHC 165 (QB) 10–001, 10–002, 10–021
Vernon v Bosley (No.1) [1997] 1 All E.R. 577; [1997] R.T.R. 1; [1998] 1 F.L.R. 297; [1997] P.I.Q.R. P255; (1997) 35 B.M.L.R. 135; [1997] Fam. Law 476; (1996) 146 N.L.J. 589 1–009
W v Edgell [1989] EWCA Civ 13 1–023
Watt v ABC [2016] EWCOP 2532; [2016] 11 WLUK 66; [2016] C.O.P.L.R. 605; [2017] W.T.L.R. 159; [2017] W.T.L.R. 739; [2017] 1 P. & C.R. DG9 1–026
White v Fell Unreported 12 November 1987 .... 2–009, 2–010
White v Kuzych [1951] A.C. 585; [1951] 2 All E.R. 435; [1951] 2 T.L.R. 277; (1951) 95 S.J. 527 13–019
Whitehouse v Jordan [1981] 1 W.L.R. 246; [1981] 1 All E.R. 267; (1981) 125 S.J. 167 .... 1–009, 13–011
Whiten v St George's Healthcare NHS Trust [2011] EWHC 2066 (QB); [2012] Med. L.R. 1; (2011) 108(33) L.S.G. 28 1–037
Williams v Jervis [2008] EWHC 2346 (QB); [2008] 10 WLUK 165 .... 5–026, 10–029
Wilson v Coulson [2002] P.I.Q.R. P22 .... **1–040**
Wiszniewski v Central Manchester Health Authority [1998] P.I.Q.R. P324; [1998] Lloyd's Rep. Med. 223 1–025
X v K [2013] EWHC 3230 (Fam); [2013] 6 WLUK 532 2–033
Young v AIG Europe Ltd [2015] EWHC 2160 (QB) 1–004

TABLE OF LEGISLATION

1832	Reform Act (c.45)...........2–128		(1) ..2–050, 2–051, 2–052, 2–053,
1837	Wills Act (c.26) 2–027			2–066,
	s.18 2–027			2–073
	s.18B 2–027		(a)................2–059
	s.20 2–027		(2) 2–053
1948	Law Reform (Personal Injuries) Act		(4) 2–055, 2–058
	(c.41)................1–021		(5) 2–054
1976	Fatal Accidents Act (c.30)......1–042		s.3 ....2–002, 2–056, 2–057, 2–066,
1979	Sale of Goods Act (c.54)			2–073
	s.3...................2–016		(1) ..2–057, 2–061, 2–067, 2–071,
1980	Limitation Act (c.58)..........2–004			2–077,
1983	Mental Health Act (c.20). .1–021, 2–050			2–107
	Pt VII.................2–004		(a)................2–070
1985	Enduring Powers of Attorney Act		(a)–(d) 2–071
	(c.29)................2–023		(b) 2–060
1989	Children Act (c.41)...........2–054		(c)................2–071
1990	National Health Service and Community		(d) 2–062
	Care Act (c.19)...........8–025		(2) 2–059, 2–128
1998	Working Time Regulations (SI		(3) 2–060
	1998/1833) 12–034		(4) 1–019
	Civil Procedure Rules (SI		s.4..................2–047
	1998/3132) 1–025, 13–014		(2) 2–047
	Pt 18 10–010		(3) 2–053
	Pt 21 ..1–025, 2–004, 2–007, 2–008		(4) 1–019, 2–045, 2–128
	PD to Pt 35 ....1–016, 13–012		(6) 2–076
	Pt 35 .1–008, 1–012, 1–016, 10–010,		(11) 2–047
	12–006,		s.5.............2–048, 2–053
	13–012		s.6..................2–048
	r.35.1 1–008		s.7..................2–016
	r.35.3 12–026		s.8..................2–048
	(2) 13–012		s.13(2) 2–024
	r.35.4 1–008		s.15 2–075
	r.35.10 1–016		s.18(3) 2–054
2000	Adults with Incapacity (Scotland) Act		s.21 2–054
	(asp 4) 8–051		s.48 2–053
2003	Sexual Offences Act (c.42)		Sch.A1 2–068
	s.30 2–032	2006	Compensation Act (c.29)
2004	Civil Partnership Act (c.33).....2–027		s.3 13–001
2005	Mental Capacity Act (c.9). 1–024, 1–026,		National Health Service Act
	2–001, 2–021, 2–023,		(c.41)................1–021
	2–024, 2–006, 2–032,	2007	Lasting Powers of Attorney, Enduring
	2–040, 2–041, 2–044,		Powers of Attorney and Public
	2–047, 2–050, 2–063,		Guardian Regulations (SI 2007/1253)
	2–065, 2–066, 2–070,		reg.8(3) 2–022
	2–071, 2–073, 2–076,	2010	Equality Act (c.15) 1–038, 11–011,
	2–128, 8–027, 8–051,		11–012, 11–019,
	9–020, 12–031		11–020,
	Pt 1 2–070		11–027, 11–028,
	s.1 ....2–042, 2–043		11–030, 11–031
	(2) 2–042, 2–043	2015	Lasting Power of Attorney, Enduring
	(3) ..1–026, 2–042, 2–044, 2–128		Powers of Attorney and Public
	(4) 2–042, 2–046		Guardian (Amendment) Regulations
	(5) 2–042, 2–047		(SI 2015/899)............2–021
	(6) 2–048	2017	Public Guardian (Fees, etc.)
	ss.1—3 ....2–041, 2–070		(Amendment) Regulations (SI
	s.2 ....2–049, 2–050, 2–074		2017/503)
			reg.3 2–021

TABLE OF LEGISLATION

Court of Protection Rules (SI 2017/1035)
    Pt 15 2–064

PD 15A 2–064

CHAPTER 1

Acquired Brain Injury and Civil Litigation

William Norris QC and Nathan Tavares QC

CHAPTER LAYOUT

This chapter is split into two parts. Part 1 addresses aspects of medico-legal practice and procedure relevant to all involved in brain injury litigation. Part 2 consists of case studies from claims which have actually been adjudicated upon by courts in England. The cases serve as a guide as to how some of the common issues in this type of litigation have been addressed in practice.

1–001

1. LITIGATION ISSUES

Why the medicine matters

Whether one is a lawyer litigating a personal injury or clinical negligence claim or an expert involved in such litigation, a good understanding of the medicine is key to doing the job properly. The authors write this introductory chapter with both kinds of reader in mind. For that same reason, we refer to "patient" and "claimant" interchangeably[1] and shall endeavour to focus on the practical aspects of medico-legal practice without undue concentration on any discussion of legal principle. For all questions of principle, the reader should to refer to standard textbooks such as *Kemp & Kemp, The Quantum of Damage* (Kemp Quantum) and *Kemp, Personal Injury Law, Practice and Procedure* (Kemp Practice).

1–002

The medicine matters at every stage of the analysis for those engaged in personal injury and clinical negligence litigation. In the case of catastrophic injury, a claimant's brain damage may result in physical disability which is in reality very similar to a major spinal injury in the sense that there is a similar dependence on nursing care and support but with the added complication of impaired intelligence, understanding or awareness. In such cases, there may be no significant dispute between the experts on either side as to the mechanism of injury, diagnosis or extent of disability. Rather, the areas of controversy are more

---

[1] Likewise, gender: "he" is used for convenience when we really mean "he or she".

likely to be confined to the prognosis (including life expectancy[2]) and to arguments about the extent to which the claimant reasonably requires (say) care, specialised accommodation, aids and equipment, therapies and so forth.

Relevance to damages

1–003 The relevance of medical opinion to assessing the appropriate level of compensation is obvious. Whether the claim is dealt with as a lump sum award or by way of periodical payments, it is impossible to carry out any sort of calculation without knowing the answer to the "what is needed and what will it cost?" question.[3] That will be informed by the experts' views on issues such as "what care?" or "which piece of equipment will actually be useful?". This requires input both from the doctor who knows the claimant's clinical needs and the specialist in, say, care or occupational therapy. Without that evidence, it will be impossible accurately and fairly to assess either the multiplicand for the capitalised value or the annual award for the periodical payments (and any elements of future loss which are in fact capitalised).

Further, in all serious head injury cases, there will also need to be a consideration of whether the patient's life expectancy is impaired. If it is, an issue of considerable importance to every aspect of the claim will be deciding the extent of such impairment. Of course, the power to award periodical payments mitigates the artificiality of the exercise as regards the provision of lifetime care and case management which will, typically be the largest component of any big claim as well as the issue of most concern to the injured claimant and his family.

But that is not to say the issue is not important in all cases since every significant claim will have at least some elements of future loss which are likely to be capitalised on the basis of a multiplier and multiplicand. To those, an assessment of life expectancy is a necessary ingredient of the calculation. Of course, such assessments are based on statistical material but they are also informed by clinical judgment and other, possibly equally artificial, assessments are often required in head injury claims, such as deciding the claimant's lifetime risk of developing epilepsy.[4] Again, the doctors' opinions are likely to be crucial, and the expert most likely to be able to address issues both in relation to life expectancy and epilepsy risk (often overlapping issues), will be a neurologist—albeit a neurorehabilitation or a neuropsychiatrist could deal with such issues in an appropriate case. Traumatic brain injury may also give rise to depressive illness and an associated suicide risk which may make an expert psychiatric view particularly important to life expectancy.

---

[2] Most practitioners will be familiar with the issues surrounding assessment of life expectancy both by statisticians and clinicians. For further analysis, see Kemp Quantum, para.4-033.
[3] Here, the starting point of the assessment is what is known as the "100% principle" and how far, if at all, it is qualified by considerations such as reasonableness, proportionality, and/or cost versus benefit, see the discussion in Chapter 1 of Kemp Quantum.
[4] Albeit the artificiality of the assessment is also mitigated by the court's power to award provisional damages—see Kemp Quantum, Chapter 25.

Identifying the nature of the brain injury

What are, perhaps, the more difficult cases will include those where the brain injury is less obvious, which some practitioners like to characterise as involving "subtle brain injury".[5] Here, the issue between the parties may be more binary: did the claimant suffer a significant organic injury or did he not?

1–004

The questions that need to be answered in such cases are usually along the following lines: Is the injury alleged consistent with what is known of the index accident? Is there evidence (and, preferably, corroboration) of the head injury from material surrounding the index accident or from other sources? What do the scans show? What is the independent evidence of any enduring effects? Is the claimant genuine or may he be exaggerating his symptoms (and, if so, is that deliberate or not)? Are there other possible causes of the symptoms which the claimant attributes to the accident? Has the litigation any part to play in the continuation of those symptoms? What does the future hold? And so forth.

In some instances, the argument may be more about cause than effect. Let us take the example of a different type of injury. All personal injury (PI) lawyers will have done cases in which the claimant says he is suffering from a bad back as a result of an accident. An issue of causation often arises is in such claims. Typically, the question the court must answer tends to be posed in what, to doctors, may appear simplistic terms as "but for the accident, for how many years would the claimant be likely to have remained symptom free?".[6] Whilst doctors may be instinctively reluctant to speculate along those lines, this is a practical requirement (or, if you prefer, a necessary evil) of medico-legal work as otherwise there can be no sensible basis for assessing compensation.

Similar problems can arise in relation to head injury claims. Sometimes, the issue of causation is, in effect, an absolute one and can be put very simply: Has the claimant demonstrated, on a balance of probabilities, that his condition was caused by the tort? As a matter of principle, what is true of spinal injury is equally true of brain injury. *Young v AIG Europe Ltd*,[7] for example, is a case where the issue was whether the claimant had suffered not only a myocardial infarction as a result of the accident (such causative link being admitted) but whether it also had caused a spinal haematoma rendering him paraplegic. To resolve such an issue, it is necessary for the court to understand the possible mechanisms and, in the end, to make a judgment as to the most probable cause.

In other instances, the issue will not be absolute but the court's judgment on causation will again be substantially informed by the medical experts. There will be many cases in which the court will need to answer the question as to whether the tort has made a "material contribution" to the claimant's disability or has caused a "material increase in risk".[8]

---

[5] An example is *Clarke v Maltby* [2010] EWHC 1201 (QB) which we discuss in more detail in the case studies at the end of this chapter.

[6] These are known as "acceleration" cases and the typical answer, at least in many back injury examples, is "five to ten years". The decision of Jay J in *Hayden v Maidstone and Tunbridge Wells NHS Trust* [2016] EWHC 3276 (QB) contains a valuable review and application of principle and authority.

[7] [2015] EWHC 2160 (QB).

[8] For further discussion which is beyond the scope of the present work, see Kemp Quantum, Chapter 2. In such cases, the medical experts may also need to do their best to try and disentangle tortious and

The importance of the medico-legal expert to litigation

1–005 To summarise, then, we as lawyers need to know what we are talking about if we are to do our job properly. We have to assess the strength or weakness of a case in consultation with those experts. We may be advocates who will have to explain the medicine to the judge or to cross-examine witnesses who take a contrary view from our own. If we do not have a reasonable understanding of the science behind any analytical process about which we ask questions, then the chances of embarrassment are high and the prospects of a favourable outcome will be unnecessarily diminished. This is probably true of all areas of evidential expertise but medical science in general and head injuries in particular are subjects which certainly require some background education over and above analysis of the specific issues arising in the context of the particular claim. Likewise, others from whatever discipline who have any involvement in this area of personal injury and medical litigation will, we hope, find value in what this work provides.

Diagnosis: what the lawyer must look out for

1–006 The heading of this section suggests that our focus here is on the lawyer-as-reader but, for reasons we have given already, what we say will apply equally to clinicians. The simple message is that the process of assessment of any condition—diagnosis certainly, prognosis usually—depends not just on examination and study of the presenting condition but on the patient's history.

In the case of a head injury, therefore, it is crucial to establish:

- Is there any record[9] of a head injury or of altered consciousness in the records created following the accident? If the accident was a road traffic accident (RTA), this will involve looking at the police report. Always look at the ambulance records and be prepared to investigate further by interviewing the individuals referred to in such records.
- Check carefully to see if there is any record of a Glasgow Coma Scale (GCS)[10] which is abnormal (or, indeed, normal).
- Do witnesses to the accident giving rise to the claim say anything to confirm or refute the contention that there was a head injury or altered consciousness?
- Consider the patient's memory (usually what matters is continuous memory rather than islands of recollection) before and after the event. Note that the length of time before the return of continuous memory (post-traumatic amnesia) after the event will be an important factor for the clinicians to consider and the better the record of that element the more reliable will be this indicator.
- What do the triage and hospital/nursing notes record?

---

non-tortious causes unless the case is truly one of "indivisible injury"—see *Allen v British Rail Engineering Ltd (BREL)* [2001] EWCA Civ 242; [2001] I.C.R. 942—and/or to help with identifying any "material increase in risk" if the case is one where that is the basis on which causation is determined.

[9] A useful discussion of the importance of contemporary documentary records can be found in *Synclair v East Lancashire Hospital NHS Trust* [2015] EWCA Civ 1283; [2016] Med. L.R. 1.

[10] This is a 3 to 15 point scale where 15 indicates full consciousness.

LITIGATION ISSUES

- If there is little or no record of any head injury (or loss of consciousness however transient), may that be explained by the fact that the emergency services and (say) those providing intensive care were primarily concerned with other more immediately serious, possibly life-threatening injuries?[11] Lawyers often experience cases where there has been no reference in the hospital records to any head injury, but where the claimant's mental functioning and/or behaviour can be seen after a while, and given the accident circumstances, to be suggestive of a brain injury.
- Do family and friends or work colleagues report any alterations in the person's character and behaviour at home or following a return to work? Their account of any such change—which the doctors may see as evidence of neurobehavioural deficit—will be valuable. Bear in mind that there are many head injury cases in which a claimant asserts that he has suffered a significant loss of earnings as a result of a reduction in intellectual function following the accident or even because of a loss of confidence, stamina or powers of concentration. In such cases, the inquiring mind, be it medical or legal, will look to see if that is supported by any written record or by the observation of those who knew and know the person in question. Needless to say, one must be careful to resist the understandable wish to see everyone as promising[12] and looking forward to what would, absent the index accident, have been a successful career.
- What do the claimant's previous work and medical records reveal? In some areas of medico-legal practice, this line of inquiry will be as routine as it is useful. For example, it is grossly careless (at least in the medico-legal context) to accept without checking a patient's word that he or she had "no previous trouble with his back" whilst asserting that, absent the accident, he might have been expected to have remained symptom-free for X number of years into the future. Similarly, if one is looking at a head injury claim where the patient complains of headaches since the accident or of some other behavioural change, it is equally important to see what the independent material—created outside the context of any claim—says about the person in question.
- Clearly, the medical records will usually show what treatment the patient has had. This may seem obvious, but it is not just a question of looking back and seeing how such-and-such a course of treatment may have helped. Sometimes what has or what has not been tried in the past may help with diagnosis. In the case of head injury patients, there may often be a fine line between identifying the symptoms of organic brain damage and the effects of a mild but untreated psychiatric illness such as depression. Here it may be necessary to see whether attempts have or have not been made to treat such a condition before deciding that his problems have an organic cause.
- The other side of the coin is that what has or has not been tried in the past may be relevant to the assessment of future loss. Take a claimant with a recognised head injury and a record of depressive illness. What medication

---

[11] Even then, there is usually some record (Ambulance or Police Report or Admission Note) which will show, often by diagram, where a patient's injuries were observed to be.

[12] Just as there is a moment in everyone's life when we last beat our children at tennis, so each of us will have a moment when we were last regarded as "promising".

has been tried hitherto? May a course of treatment so far untried give grounds for optimism? Would some therapeutic intervention—cognitive behavioural therapy (CBT), for example—be worth trying? And so forth.
- Lawyers will also need to be alert to the signs of a head injury even in a claimant who denies that he has suffered one, if the accident circumstances may have given rise to such an injury and his post-accident behaviour is of concern. Careful and sometimes skilful questioning is required to elucidate subtle post-accident changes, and the extent and quality of evidence will often be better as time goes by, meaning too early a settlement of the case may not be in the claimant's best interests.

Categories of head injury

1–007 Those who seek guidance on the level of award appropriate in respect of pain, suffering and loss of amenity ("general damages") will see that the Judicial College (formerly Judicial Studies Board) divides head injuries into those causing "very severe brain damage", those which are "moderately severe" or "moderate", and those which are "minor". Practitioners will also refer to the guidelines for cases of psychiatric injury—which may often be the product of or associated with head injury—and the separate section which deals with epilepsy.

From the clinician's perspective, the class of injury known as traumatic (or "acquired") brain injury is often sub-divided into primary and secondary injuries. A primary injury is typically caused by a direct blow to the head or by sudden acceleration or deceleration. This may result in direct damage (as in the case of a penetrative injury) or may cause the brain to strike the inside of the skull with similar consequences (sometimes called a "contrecoup" injury). A secondary injury is one which is not caused by any mechanical process at the moment of impact but occurs thereafter and/or is super-imposed on an already damaged brain.

There is also a distinction to be drawn between focal and diffuse injuries. A typical focal injury would be a fractured skull—such as when the head strikes the ground or windscreen. Diffuse injuries typically arise as a result of acceleration/ deceleration and will include diffuse axonal injury, hypoxic/ischaemic damage, meningitis and vascular injury.

For our purposes it should suffice to identify the differences between acquired brain injury (traumatic and non-traumatic; diffuse or focal) and to grade those conditions, as the JC Guidelines do, into those which are mild, moderate and severe or even very severe. But categorisation and grading are only the starting point for the assessment of damages. One might have a claimant with a major head injury but who is still able to lead a life which is largely independent without the need for external support and only a small claim for loss of earnings. The award in monetary terms in such a case could easily be very much less than that which would be made to a high-flying businessman who has suffered only a mild concussive injury but the result of which is a "loss of edge" with major consequences for the earnings claim.

The role of the expert

What follows applies to expert medical evidence and, indeed, to all expert evidence given in the context of litigation. We shall concentrate on some of the more obvious issues which we encounter.

1–008

To the legal profession in general and the judiciary in particular, expert witnesses tend to be regarded as a necessary evil. They are necessary to explain matters to us laymen that we are not able to understand without their help. The evil is not so much that the expert may trespass on matters which are the true province of the judge. Rather, it is that long and bitter experience leads us to doubt whether many experts are really giving their own, independent, view irrespective of the party on whose behalf they are instructed. Instead, many seem to see their role as putting matters in the best possible light from the perspective of their instructing party and, in extreme cases, will even go so far as to enter the field of argument on that side. That, of course, is the job of the advocate and should be none of the expert's business.

Practitioners have long and frequently tried to address the problem of the expert who takes sides. Lord Woolf's reforms[13] had the control of expert evidence at their heart and he identified this issue as one that required particularly careful case management and control. Civil Procedure Rules (CPR) Part 35, for example, at CPR rule 35.1, mandates that expert evidence should be confined to that which is reasonably required and, where possible, a single joint expert is used especially in lower-value cases. Indeed, CPR rule 35.4 states that no party may call any expert evidence without the court's permission.[14]

The problem—which no amount of well-intentioned guidance by rules committees or judges can ever overcome—is that our approach, in which the claimant's and defendant's teams are on opposing sides, literally and metaphorically, is an almost inevitable consequence of an adversarial system. Experience suggests that an expert will often, perhaps instinctively, join the "side" by whom they are instructed. Nor are single, joint, experts a perfect solution to this. We are naturally cautious about entrusting too much power to a single joint expert in whom we may not have absolute confidence. Similarly, if we are to investigate and value cases properly and, by doing so, reach a consensual settlement without a court trial, we need to be able to have frank discussions with our experts and to do so without our opponents listening. But, that apart, there remains that unavoidable—if subtle—element of team instinct which develops as soon as the expert is engaged on one side rather than the other. A similar thing often happens when someone comes to court with us just to see how the job is done. It is absolutely commonplace that such a person tends to see things from "our" point of view. To an extent, it is probably even a product of the fact that one sits on different sides of the court—taking sides in a very real sense.[15]

Having said all that, the best expert is one that maintains an independent detachment. One who can be seen to be taking an over-enthusiastic part in the

1–009

---

[13] See Lord Woolf's *Access to Justice* Report.
[14] Chapter 23 of *Kemp Practice* has an invaluable discussion of the key provisions in the rules and in practice.
[15] A point made about "taking sides" by Thorpe LJ in *Vernon v Bosley (No.1)* [1997] 1 All E.R. 577 at 612.

trial process—gown-tugging, eye rolling, note passing—will very soon be shown up as having entered the arena of argument and his evidence is likely to be treated with appropriate scepticism.

It goes without saying that every expert should not only sign but should adhere both to the letter and to the spirit of the declaration at the end of his report. Hired guns are not welcome in any judicial saloons in this country and there is no more useful summary of the duties and responsibilities of an expert than Mr Justice Cresswell's well-known exposition in *The Ikarian Reefer (No.1)*[16]:

> "The duties and responsibilities of expert witnesses in civil cases include the following:
> 1. Expert evidence presented to the court should be, and should be seen to be, the independent product of the expert uninfluenced as to form or content by the exigencies of litigation: *Whitehouse v. Jordan* [1981] 1 W.L.R. 246 at 256, per Lord Wilberforce.
> 2. An expert witness should provide independent assistance to the court by way of objective, unbiased opinion in relation to matters within his expertise: *Polivitte Ltd. v. Commercial Union Assurance Co. plc* [1987] 1 Lloyd's Rep. 379 at 386, Garland J. and *Re J* [1990] F.C.R. 193, Cazalet J. An expert witness in the High Court should never assume the role of an advocate.
> 3. An expert witness should state the facts or assumptions upon which his opinion is based. He should not omit to consider material facts which could detract from his concluded opinion (Re J, supra).
> 4. An expert witness should make it clear when a particular question or issue falls outside his expertise.
> 5. If an expert's opinion is not properly researched because he considers that insufficient data is available, then this must be stated with an indication that the opinion is no more than a provisional one (*Re J*, supra). In cases where an expert witness, who has prepared a report, could not assert that the report contained the truth, the whole truth and nothing but the truth without some qualification, that qualification should be stated in the report: *Derby & Co. Ltd. and others v. Weldon and others*, The Times, 9 November 1990, per Staughton L.J.
> 6. If, after exchange of reports, an expert witness changes his view on a material matter having read the other side's expert's report or for any other reason, such change of view should be communicated (through legal representatives) to the other side without delay and when appropriate to the court.
> 7. Where expert evidence refers to photographs, plans, calculations, analyses, measurements, survey reports or other similar documents, these must be provided to the opposite party at the same time as the exchange of reports (see 15.5 of the Guide to Commercial Court Practice)."

How to choose an expert

1–010 We are assuming here that the choice is being made in the context of litigation. The best expert to choose is someone that you would feel confident about recommending to someone else. Ask around. Look for someone with a current clinical practice, preferably holding a consultant's position. Avoid those who do only defendant or only claimant work unless you are confident that their reputation transcends the inevitable suspicion that such a person sees things only from one perspective. Establish whether the expert has been the subject of

---

[16] [1993] 2 Lloyd's Rep. 68.

judicial criticism in other cases but simply because one judge on a different day in a different case did not accept the opinion of the expert may not matter as much as one might initially expect. However, if the judge's criticism was that the expert in question had behaved unprofessionally, was unduly partisan or was simply useless, you would be well advised not to have instructed him in the first place. These matters are, after all, easy to establish these days.[17]

There are plenty of experts who have prepared many medico-legal reports, but who have little if any experience giving oral evidence in court. It goes without saying that performance in court can be crucial to a case and hence prior experience can be a real asset. In all cases, however, giving the expert a detailed indication of what sort of questions they might be expected to address in cross examination is invaluable preparation. But coaching the expert in his answer, even in a subtle way, is wholly wrong.

In brain injury cases a particular problem may be knowing what type of experts you need. A neurologist may be a good starting point, but do you need a neurorehabilitation expert, a neurologist, a neuropsychiatrist, and/or a neuroradiologist? Each case will raise its own different issues, and hopefully the contents of this book will help inform the reader as to which particular areas of expertise he might need. In our experience the problem is not so often knowing who to instruct to enable diagnosis of the brain injury, but who to instruct to give an expert prognosis in relation to care and support needs. It is often the case that a small team of experts comprising a neurorehabilitation expert and a neuropsychologist and/or neuropsychiatrist is required. And like experts in any type of litigation, those who are the best are highly sought after and often unavailable (or even unaffordable) when you need them.

In some cases the claimant and defendant will have instructed experts of different disciplines to opine on the same issue. An example of this is *Siegel v Pummell*[18] where the defendant's neuropsychiatrist had refused to meet with the claimant's neuropsychologist due to lack of overlapping expertise even though they were considering similar issues.

Changing experts

A word of warning about expert-shopping: be careful about getting reports from experts you decide not to use. If at some stage you want to change from the expert for which the court has given permission and whose report you have disclosed, you will be expected to reveal if you have solicited other opinions. You may then be required to disclose such reports as a condition of being allowed to instruct a new one in place of that which you to discard.[19]

1–011

---

[17] The internet has, of course, transformed our lives in this kind of line of inquiry and in many other respects. Who would imagine that it was only 15 years ago that an opponent made a comment to the Court of Appeal about a Commonwealth case that "Mr Norris had apparently found on his internet machine"? We smiled even then.
[18] [2014] EWHC 4309 (QB).
[19] See *Edwards-Tubb v JD Wetherspoon Plc* [2011] EWCA Civ 136; [2011] 1 W.L.R. 1373 and, more recently, *Murray v Martin Devenish* [2017] EWCA Civ 1016.

There may be any number of good reasons why you might wish to change your expert. But, as the *Edwards-Tubb* case[20] makes clear, the court will exercise tight control over whether (and on what terms) you are allowed to do so. Expert shopping—going from one expert to another and so forth until you find a favourable report is rightly deplored and will not be permitted. Hence an application to change can only be made when there is a good reason to make that change and is likely to be conditional on disclosure of earlier opinions even if not now relied upon. It is very unlikely to be allowed if the other side will suffer any significant prejudice or a trial date is threatened and, if the court has evidence of actual or apparent expert shopping, it may go beyond simply requiring undisclosed reports and may consider ordering disclosure of all communications in which the substance of the "unserved" expert's opinions are contained, including attendance notes of conferences, side letters, emails and the like.[21]

Claimants can potentially prevent expert shopping by a defendant by only permitting disclosure of his confidential medical records to a named expert.[22] It would then be a serious matter if the defendant disclosed the records to another expert in an unauthorised manner bearing in mind the claimant's article 8 rights under the European Convention of Human Rights (ECHR).

Treating doctors as experts

1-012 This is not the place to offer any detailed commentary on the constraints upon expert evidence under CPR Part 35 or the admissibility of expert and/or opinion evidence outside its confines. Those who seek further guidance on those matters should consult the rules themselves, *Phipson on Evidence*, Kemp Practice (Chapter 23), the White Book and cases such as *Hoyle v Rogers*[23]; *Kirkman v Euro Oxide*[24]; *DN v Greenwich London Borough Council*[25] and *Lawrence v Kent County Council*.[26]

Here we are simply concerned with the question of whether a party—save in very exceptional circumstances, this is assumed to be the claimant—should call the treating expert. His evidence would, in any case, be admissible as evidence of fact[27] but there is certainly no bar and there may be good reasons for him also

---

[20] [2011] EWCA Civ 136. See also *Beck v Ministry of Defence* [2003] EWCA Civ 1043; [2005] 1 W.L.R. 2206; *Hajigeorgiou v Vasiliou* [2005] EWCA Civ 236; [2005] 1 W.L.R. 2195.

[21] See the judgment of Edwards-Stuart J in *BMG (Mansfield) Ltd v Galliford Try Construction Ltd* [2013] EWHC 3183 (TCC); [2014] C.P. Rep. 3 where such an extensive order was contemplated in circumstances where there was actual or apparent "expert shopping". And see *Allen Tod Architecture Ltd (In Liquidation) v Capita Property and Infrastructure Ltd (previously Capita Symons Ltd)* [2016] EWHC 2171 (TCC); [2016] B.L.R. 592—which applied *BMG*—for a more recent statement of the relevant principles.

[22] In *Bennett v Compass Group UK and Ireland Ltd* [2002] EWCA Civ 642; [2002] C.P. Rep. 58, Clarke LJ noted (at 40) that a defendant should only be allowed to see a claimant's medical records in carefully defined circumstances.

[23] [2014] EWCA Civ 257; [2015] Q.B. 265.

[24] [2007] EWCA Civ 66; [2007] C.P. Rep. 19.

[25] [2004] EWCA Civ 1659; [2005] 1 F.C.R. 112.

[26] [2012] EWCA Civ 493. A case in which the claimant's daughter and a surveyor from the local authority offered opinions about the dangerous state of the highway. This evidence was ruled admissible and relevant but had to be treated with particular caution given the lack of independence in their positions.

[27] See *Kirkman* [2007] C.P. Rep. 19.

giving that side's—or joint—expert opinion evidence. The practical key must be to satisfy oneself that the expert's independence and objectivity are not affected by the doctor/patient relationship. And the doctor in question must be crystal clear that he can only provide opinion evidence as a court expert if he recognises that this duty overrides the ordinary duty owed by a doctor to his patient. Clearly the defendant must not instruct one of the claimant's former or current treating doctors without express permission from the claimant.

Expert's consultation with the client

It may be that the brain injured client is unable to give a reliable account of themselves due to cognitive or emotional deficits. With such individuals it is important to ensure that an appropriate individual accompanies them to expert consultations. This is to try and ensure that reliable information is provided to the expert, but also to help prevent exploitation by the unscrupulous of a suggestible claimant. It has not been unheard of for psychiatrists or other opposing experts to discuss inappropriate topics with claimants such as what size of award they are expecting to get, or what their evidence is on matters of liability. It is always advisable to have the claimant's litigation friend attend appointments with them and, if not, the case manager or another responsible individual. Another sensible precaution is to make sure that consultations with the opposing party's experts only take place after relevant witness statements have been served by the claimant. This will help prevent needless questioning on topics covered by the statements, questioning which could otherwise lead potentially to inconsistent answers.

1–013

Funding and bias

If the expert is to maintain any independence, he cannot have any commercial interest in the outcome of the litigation or have a close personal relationship with the parties.[28] Accordingly, the Protocol for the Instruction of Experts,[29] approved by the Civil Justice Council, makes it clear that a contingency fee arrangement is not permitted though the expert can agree to defer payment until after the case is won (or lost).

1–014

What the expert must see

We have looked at this above but it is worth repeating that the easiest way to undermine any expert witness, however confidently he may have given a written opinion or oral evidence, is by demonstrating that they have not seen or read everything relevant. So the expert must be sure he has studied:

1–015

- All written records that exist in relation to the event on which the cause of action is founded (accident book entries, police/ambulance reports, medical records, etc).

---

[28] See *EXP v Barker* [2015] EWHC 1289 (QB). Any possible conflict of interest should be disclosed—see *Toth v Jarman* [2006] EWCA Civ 1028; [2006] 4 All E.R. 1276 (Note).
[29] For further discussion, see paras 23-024 and following of Kemp Practice.

- All witness evidence—such as friends or work colleagues who paint the "before and after" picture.
- All relevant expert reports from all parties.
- All relevant medical/nursing/case management notes.

A sensible step for the instructing solicitor to take is to prepare a schedule listing all the documentation the experts are required to take account of. This schedule can then be sent to each expert and annexed to their report. It will aid consistency and prevent the experts listing different documents in different reports.

It may also be desirable, if the case does come to court and it is not disproportionately expensive, that the expert spends enough time in court to see relevant witnesses give evidence. Even if that is not possible, he must, as a bare minimum, ask about (or read a note of) the evidence that was given. An increasingly common and welcome development in High Court trials is to have live transcription of evidence and daily transcripts. The cost for such services is not high compared to the overall trial costs, and the transcripts produced can be invaluable for updating or reminding witnesses as to what has been said in court.

What must be disclosed apart from final expert reports

1–016 CPR rule 35.10 requires experts to comply with the Practice Direction to Part 35 and the key requirement is that the disclosed report must contain the complete professional opinion of the expert. If there are side letters or supplementary reports which qualify the opinion as disclosed, then they too should be disclosed.

That does not, however, mean that earlier drafts need to be disclosed: these remain privileged and so are outside the scope of CPR Part 35—*Jackson v Marley Davenport Ltd*.[30] Documents referred to in expert reports must be disclosed if they have been relied upon or deployed in some way by the expert.[31]

Preparation for and attendance at trial

1–017 We shall assume that the case has not settled and that the medical expert witness will have had at least one conference with the legal team in advance of the trial. As we said at the beginning, it is important that the lawyers are able to explain any medical issue themselves without simply deferring to their expert: hence providing the lawyers with a crash course in sometimes complex medical science often forms a key part of the expert's job.

It is also entirely legitimate for the expert to help with the preparation of cross-examination of his opposite number. But here the blurring of the divide between dispassionate independence and a partisan role can very easily occur. If the line is crossed—as it is when the expert is obviously entering the fray in court by his words or conduct—then the expert will have done more harm than good.

When giving evidence, the expert should be clear that any literature on which he wishes to rely has been identified in his report and has been made available to

---

[30] [2004] EWCA Civ 1225; [2004] 1 W.L.R. 2926.
[31] See *AB v John Wyeth & Bros Ltd (No.1)* [1992] 1 W.L.R. 168; [1992] 1 All E.R. 443 and *Booth v Warrington Health Authority* [1992] P.I.Q.R. P137. *Kemp & Kemp: Personal Injury Practice and Procedure* has a more detailed discussion of this topic in Chapter 23.

LITIGATION ISSUES

his opposite number. Remember also that he will have had a joint meeting with his opposite number in order to establish and, if possible, reduce the areas of disagreement. There will have been a joint statement produced. The easiest way for an expert to make sure it properly records what he wanted to say is to take charge of the drafting. But, if that is not possible, it is crucial that he ensures that any reservations of frank disagreements are set out in the final draft. Courts are meticulous in their insistence that it is not legitimate to inquire into the background to and process of discussion. Accordingly, what matters is the final draft and it is about that that the expert witness can expect to be closely questioned. In passing, however, we comment that our experience is that experts sometimes need to be cautioned not to make concessions purely in a misguided attempt to try and settle issues, if not the whole case. Any agreement reached in the joint statement must be on a principled basis which can be defended in the witness box. The task of settling the case, if appropriate, is the lawyer's job and not the expert's.

When the expert does actually go into the witness box, his report (or reports) will almost always be taken as read. The court may permit some—or no—examination in chief. Sometimes, the evidence in chief does not extend beyond the expert identifying his name, his signature on the report and a statement that it contains his full opinion and remains unchanged. Some judges will allow a little more to be led but there are few examinations in chief which, in a typical four-day trial, are allowed to go on for more than 20 or 30 minutes. If one is allowed even that much leeway, the advocate's strategy must be to bed his witness in and, by the choice of a few important points, establish him as authoritative and reliable.

1–018

The good witness is one who not only knows his subject but is fair, careful and balanced and answers the question rather than one who cannot give any response without embarking on a lecture or getting into an argument. He who keeps his answers (and his report) short and properly structured and ensures that they are not overstated will prosper.

Handling litigation for brain injured individuals

For lawyers instructed by brain injured claimants there are often challenges not faced by other litigators. Whether the injury is profound or very subtle, sensitivity and understanding is required during interactions with the client. The issue of capacity will need to be kept under review at all stages and there will be cases where the client's inability to manage their affairs will only become apparent over time, possibly after their ability to manage an interim payment is seen, or when decisions on significant matters in the litigation are required. Even if capacity to litigate has been lost and the claimant has a litigation friend, it is still necessary to involve the claimant so far as possible in the decision making. This is not just good practice, it is required by the law.[32] Capacity often raises a number of complications for the lawyers, such as where the claimant himself does not agree he lacks capacity, or where there is no obvious litigation friend so that the Official

1–019

---

[32] Mental Capacity Act 2005 s.4(4).

Solicitor needs to act, or where the person acting as litigation friend is uncooperative or may have ulterior motives.[33]

In terms of actually handling the client, unlike most health professionals, lawyers are not routinely trained in how to interact with brain injured individuals. Consideration needs to be given to many issues not faced by other litigators. For example, is the client going to be unduly stressed coming to your offices? What time of day is the client going to be most alert? How can the language and legal issues be simplified? Would an informal or mental health advocate for the client improve communication in the current situation? How should expert examinations be organised so as to cause the minimum of distress and disruption? Should expert visits all be domiciliary and/or with someone who knows the client well?

One of the big challenges for brain injury lawyers is implementing the steps necessary to assess the quantum of the claim. Going back only a couple of decades, claimants' lawyers tended merely to put a schedule of loss together based on the initial reports of the medical experts. These days, the quantification process is much more involved and the lawyers are much more pro-active. The legal team may, for example, organise multi-disciplinary conferences or get involved in discharge planning from hospital or rehabilitation. They may actively enable the rehabilitation process, liaise with statutory services whilst trying to keep the claimant's family on board and cooperating with the care regime.

1–020   This enlargement of the lawyers' role coincides with the development of case management as a discipline which has only really been going since the 1980s. Very often the client will have been discharged from hospital post injury with little or no support or follow-up from any healthcare body or from social services, so getting a competent brain injury case manager engaged at the outset is often vital. However, in cases where there is no or no substantial interim funding, this will not be possible, and the lawyer may find he has to take on a role akin to that of case manager. He will also need to make sure that the medico-legal experts will have the information necessary to form opinions in relation to long-term need. In all these circumstances, therefore, the lawyer should get the medico-legal team together (including the care expert) early so that he can be guided by them.

The legal timetable may need to be skilfully managed to ensure that there is appropriate time for proper assessment of the claimant including trials of independent living if necessary. This can be a huge challenge in an age of costs budgeting, and the involvement of experts will need to be carefully controlled whilst ensuring that the evidence is not stale by the time the case comes on for trial. The work needed in properly preparing a complicated brain injury case often means a considerable amount of front-loading, and this can cause problems with the costs budgeting judge who is encouraged to take a dim view of front-loaded costs. We would suggest, therefore, that the key is to keep the other party abreast of expert involvement and the treatment/care being given to the claimant, and to use staged budgets whenever possible; it is not always necessary or sensible to budget the case through to trial at the first costs and case management conference.

---

[33] For a case in which there was an obstructive litigation friend, see *M (a child) v Lambeth London Borough Council* [2014] EWHC 57 (QB).

The seriously unwell claimant

If the client is acutely unwell, making them suicidal or dangerously unstable and aggressive, they could be the subject of compulsory detention in a mental health facility against their will if they present with a mental disorder of a nature or degree that makes it appropriate for them to receive assessment or treatment, and that detention is necessary in the interests of their health, safety or for the protection of others. If the client is detained in a mental health unit under the Mental Health Act and the mental disorder giving rise to the detention is causally related to the index injury, compensation from the tortfeasor could still be claimed to enable the claimant to fund inpatient treatment under detention in a private mental health facility. We know from *Peters v East Midlands SHA*[34] that a claimant can opt for self-funding and damages for accommodation and care rather than relying on statutory services, and that the same applies to medical treatment pursuant to the Law Reform (Personal Injuries) Act 1948. In *Coombs v Dorset NHS Primary Care Trust*[35] the court also held that there was nothing inherent in the Mental Health Act 1983 (MHA), the National Health Service Act 2006, or by way of public policy to exclude absolutely the possibility of detained patients or their families paying for, or contributing to, the cost of their treatment or care as long as such treatment was not in conflict with the recommendations of the responsible clinician. In that case the claimant who had long-standing psychiatric history sustained traumatic brain injuries as a result of the defendant's negligence. He required detention under the MHA and his family wanted a wider range of psychiatric inpatient units available to him than was available through the NHS. Private provision of this nature was held to be permissible.

1–021

Duties owed to clients

What should the lawyer or clinician do if they believe the claimant needs to be sectioned? What if they are told that the claimant is making preparations to take his own life? What if the claimant is putting others at risk, say by mentioning harming his children at the same time as himself? Is there any duty to act to prevent the harm occurring?

1–022

Clearly there is a duty to act in the interests of one's client, but one should not breach confidences and must respect their autonomy, so if they do not want their lawyer to do anything, the lawyer may be left with a problem. Protection of confidential information is a fundamental feature of our relationship with clients (in so far as we are concerned with confidential information rather than legal professional privilege—which is absolute). In addition, English law strongly favours the individual's autonomy unless there is evidence that the person is lacking mental capacity or is being coerced. If a solicitor or barrister breached confidentiality against the clients' wishes it could lead to disciplinary proceedings and/or to being sued.

Where a client has indicated their intention to commit suicide or serious self-harm, the Ethics Guidance from the Solicitors Regulation Authority (dated 25 November 2019) is as follows:

---

[34] [2009] EWCA Civ 145.
[35] [2013] EWCA Civ 471.

> "Where you believe the client is genuine in their intention to commit suicide or serious self-harm and there is no other way of dealing with the issue, you should consider seeking consent from the client, if appropriate, to disclose the information to a third party so that help might be given. e.g. to a ward nurse where the client is in hospital. Where it is not possible or appropriate to get consent you may decide, to protect the client or another, to disclose that information without consent."

1–023 Obviously "consent" here means "informed consent". If confidence is going to be breached, who should be contacted with the relevant information? It is vital to keep the disclosure of confidences to the bare minimum, as once the information is passed to others, control of it may be lost. If the claimant is not already in hospital, then contact may be to the GP to invoke the involvement of the Community Mental Health Team, the case manager, the treating psychiatrist if they have one, a close relative, a social worker, or even the police if circumstances warrant it.

If serious harm to others is threatened the situation is more straightforward: there is no confidence in an iniquity, and communications that further a criminal purpose are simply not privileged (*Gartside v Outram*,[36] *W v Edgell*,[37] and *ABC v St George's Healthcare NHS Trust et al*[38]).

In either case the best course of action is to:

- limit the amount of information being disclosed to that which is strictly necessary, and
- keep a careful attendance note detailing the cause for concern and the factors considered prior to making the disclosure. This should include the reasons why it was not considered appropriate or practicable to obtain the client's consent to the disclosure.

1–024 Should the client be told that confidentiality has been breached? The SRA suggests:

> "having made the disclosure to the appropriate party, you should assess whether it is appropriate to disclose to the client the fact that you have passed confidential information to a third party. Your fiduciary duty to clients makes your position very difficult if you have disclosed their confidential information to others without their consent. Where you believe that disclosure would result in risk of harm to your client or a third party, or would prejudice an investigation, you may feel it would not be appropriate to inform the client."

If, after taking reasonable steps to assess the client's mental capacity to consent to disclosure of confidential information, the client appears to lack capacity, one can act in the client's best interests under the Mental Capacity Act 2005. It is important to note that the capacity issue in question will not be the same as the issue of capacity to litigate or capacity manage property. In *Howell-Smith v Official Solicitor*,[39] the Court of Appeal held that a solicitor had a duty to protect the interests of a client who was under a disability, and in certain circumstances

---

[36] [1857] 26 L.J. Ch. 113.
[37] [1989] EWCA Civ 13.
[38] [2020] EWHC 455 (QB).
[39] [2006] P.N.L.R. 21.

that would require breaching the client's confidence. In that case, the solicitor had acted properly in requiring the client's psychiatrist to return monies she had invested with him and reporting his professional conduct, although they had no instructions from the client to do so.

Evidence from the incapacitated claimant

A common issue when dealing with claimants who lack capacity is whether or not to call them to give evidence at trial. In some cases it will be wholly impractical to call the claimant due to the degree of mental disability, but in other cases, particularly where there is a dispute about capacity between the parties, the court may be invited to draw adverse inferences against the claimant if he is not called.[40] Of course, no such inference could be drawn if it is not reasonable to expect the witness to be called to give evidence. It must always be remembered that as regards the litigation and the requirements of CPR Part 21, the assessment of capacity is a matter of mixed law and fact to be decided by the court: it is not a matter for the experts alone to determine. At the same time, however, the court will have to guard against forming snap judgments about an individual's capacity based purely on his presentation for a relatively short period of time in the witness box. In some cases something of a half-way house might be reached in which a statement is served from the claimant dealing only with basic details of any physical injuries and his pre-accident employment and living circumstances. The court might then be willing to limit questioning (particularly cross-examination) to such matters rather than the issues pertinent to extent of brain injury. Even if no witness statement is served on behalf of the claimant on the basis that there is no intention of them giving evidence at trial, however, the court has the power to allow the defendant to call the claimant to be cross-examined if hearsay evidence from him has been served.[41] Typically expert reports will contain hearsay statements from the claimant so in theory he can be cross-examined on those statements. It should be noted that under its general case management powers the court can make special provisions regarding the giving of oral evidence by vulnerable witnesses. In the context of civil proceedings, there are no specific provisions dealing with vulnerable parties either in legislation or in the Civil Procedure Rules, but in August 2019, the Civil Justice Council issued a consultation paper on this issue. The paper recognises that vulnerability may be caused by a person's mental condition which may "hamper" access to justice. A useful example of a personal injury trial in which a claimant was treated as a vulnerable witness is *Morrow v Shrewsbury Rugby Union Football Club Ltd*.[42]

1–025

---

[40] *Wiszniewski v Central Manchester Health Authority* [1998] P.I.Q.R. P324.
[41] See *Brown v Mujibal* [2017] 4 WLUK 42, per HHJ Mark Gargan sitting as a Deputy Judge of the High Court.
[42] [2020] EWHC 379 (QB), Farby J at [20]–[49].

The claimant who retains capacity with the aid of support

1–026 It is common in brain injury litigation to have claimants who are competent to manage the litigation or their property and affairs as long as they are given appropriate support.[43] The Mental Capacity Act 2005 expressly states: "a person is not to be treated as unable to make a decision unless all practicable steps to help him to do so have been taken without success".[44] The form of support required can often pose a problem; for example, a claimant may well have capacity to conduct proceedings so long as he has some help with reading, correspondence and appointments. Typically a spouse or close relative will provide such support, but what is to be done if the spouse or relative does not wish to act? In that case, some alternative form of support would need to be arranged but this can often be problematic in practice and the lack of available support may lead to a conclusion that capacity is lost.

A vexed issue frequently relates to how the claimant should be supported in managing his property and affairs. When he lacks capacity to manage his finances there is no real issue: a Court of Protection deputy will be appointed on his behalf, usually a professional deputy, and any costs for both the past and the future deputyship will be recoverable as a matter of course for as long as the incapacity is likely to last.[45] In appropriate cases a trust can be set up in place of deputyship.[46] However, when the claimant does not lack mental capacity but needs support with his finances because of vulnerabilities (such as to exploitation, or to impulsive behaviour) the nature of appropriate support may not be straightforward, and claiming compensation for such support may be legally controversial. Setting up a trust is one obvious means of protecting a vulnerable but capacitous claimant as this enables the trustees to have oversight of expenditure, and they can challenge the claimant over any inappropriate expenditure requests. The problem with a trust set up for an individual who retains capacity is that he, as beneficiary, will generally have the absolute power to wind up the trust thereby overcoming the protection it can afford.[47] This is something that many medico-legal experts who advocate the setting up of a trust as a means of protection for the claimant may not fully appreciate. Clearly there is little protection if the claimant can be put under pressure by others, or by his own impetuousness, to dissolve the trust vehicle and seize its assets. Such trusts will only work if there is a very good reason to suppose that the claimant will respect the advice of the trustees and continue to permit their input.

The experience of the authors is that not infrequently apparently reliable and advice-taking claimants succumb to all sorts of pressures following settlement such that significant parts of their awards are misused. Hence the seemingly neat

---

[43] Sometimes informally referred to as "dependent capacity" or "supported capacity".
[44] Mental Capacity Act 2005 s.1(3), discussed more in Chapter 2 along with all other aspects of mental capacity.
[45] In *AB v Royal Devon and Exeter NHS Foundation Trust* [2016] EWHC 1024 (QB), for example, the court awarded the costs of a professional trustee for one year following trial after which capacity was expected to return, failing which it would be self-induced through drug taking.
[46] See *Re HM* [2012] Med. L.R. 449 and *Watt v ABC* [2017 4 W.L.R. 24.
[47] Trusts law is beyond the scope of this book, but the authors understand there to be no basis for preventing the competent beneficiary of a discretionary personal injury trust from having the power to wind it up.

solution of recommending that a claimant retains the capacity to manage his property and affairs with the implementation of a trust really does call in to question whether they should not in fact be deemed to lack capacity in the first place.[48]

Another feature of such trusts is that, where a professional trustee is involved for a claimant with capacity, there is no means for the court to oversee or involve itself over the costs the trustee is incurring and charging the claimant—unlike the situation applicable to a professional deputy who will have to account to the Court of Protection. Indeed, the very costs of a professional trustee may be a powerful incentive for a claimant to wind-up the trust sooner rather than later. And given the discretionary nature of a trust, it may fall prey to the argument that it is merely a means by which the claimant voluntarily chooses to manage his money, and therefore is not a cost the defendant should be required to bear.[49] In the case of *Owen v Brown*,[50] for example, the claimant's neuropsychologist had recommended that some form of trust fund be arranged to protect his financial interests for the future because the expert was not confident he would be able to use the necessary judgment and discretion to manage a large amount of money. Silber J made the following comments and rejected any claim for the costs of the trust:

1–027

> "The claimant is not a patient and therefore he will not be subject to the jurisdiction of the Court of Protection. He is also over the age of 18. In those circumstances, the defendant says correctly in my view that as the claimant would be the sole beneficiary to the trust, he would be entitled at any time as of right to determine the trust at will and to call for the trust property to be transferred to him by invoking the rule in *Saunders v. Vautier* (1841) Beav 115. No contrary submission was adduced.
>
> 162. A second difficulty confronting the claimant is that the trust is unlikely to achieve its aim, which would be to lead to, in the words of the claimant's skeleton, 'a vital cooling off period to reflect on his proposed course of action'. The trust could at any time be determined by the claimant if he was dissatisfied with a decision of the trustees.
>
> 163. In other words, the trust would only last for as long as the claimant wanted it to and so its existence would afford no protection for him] and thus this claim (Item F.8.8) cannot succeed."

The above reasoning was followed by Irwin J in *AB v Royal Devon and Exeter NHS Foundation Trust*[51] where the costs of a trust were not allowed. In *A v*

---

[48] See *Lindsay v Wood* [2006] EWHC 2895 (QB) where this issue was considered by Stanley Burnton J, who determined that vulnerability to exploitation did not of itself lead to the conclusion that there was lack of capacity. The issue was whether the person concerned had the mental capacity to make a rational decision.

[49] It is clear that there can be no claim in respect of investment advice or for the costs of managing investments. This is so whether or not the claimant is a patient: *Page v Plymouth Hospitals NHS Trust* [2004] EWHC 1154 (QB); [2004] 3 All E.R. 367 and *Eagle v Chambers (No.2)* [2004] EWCA Civ 1033; [2004] 1 W.L.R. 3081. Accountancy costs in relation to managing an award were not allowed in *A v Powys Local Health Board* [2007] EWHC 2996 (QB) as Lloyd Jones J considered that they fell into the same category as investment advice.

[50] [2002] All E.R. (D) 534. Note that an element of the first instance award, namely nursing care, was appealed to the Court of Appeal. Unfortunately, the question of trust costs was not considered on the appeal.

[51] [2016] EWHC 1024 (QB).

Powys Local Health Board[52] arguments were made for the provision of a trust for a claimant who had severe physical disability but who was not lacking capacity. Lloyd Jones J did not consider there to be need for such a trust. He noted that the claimant had a supportive and protective family, and that many of the tasks it was suggested should be managed by a professional trustee were matters which were really the responsibility of the case manager. He did, however, permit the costs of a premier banking service as the claimant was unable to handle cash, or bank cards.

In the recent Scottish case of *Clark v Greater Glasgow Health Board*,[53] Lord Stewart sitting in the Outer House did allow trust costs for a neurologically impaired claimant, stating[54]:

> "My decision is that provision should be made for the cost of putting any damages awarded to the pursuer into trust for the benefit of the pursuer during her lifetime. Because of the neurological injuries which have devastated the pursuer's motor functions, the pursuer is completely dependent on others. While the pursuer's intellect has been spared, she cannot communicate at all with non-family members except by using assistive technology, a painstaking business for her. The pursuer would be unable to administer her damages personally and would be vulnerable to exploitation. She offers evidence on affidavit, bearing to be executed by a solicitor on her behalf before a notary, to the effect that she does not have the experience to manage a huge sum of money. It is her intention to have any damages awarded placed in trust. This could protect her eligibility for certain state benefits and could offer tax advantages. The care model favoured by the defenders' care-cost expert (see below) envisages trustees as the employers of the pursuer's support workers. Parties agree that the cost of setting up a trust would be £3,000 plus VAT; and that the annual cost of trust administration and accounting including making tax returns would be £23,750 plus VAT. This is irrespective of the care model."

1–028 It is understood that the defender did not dispute the claim for trust costs. One could also cite the comments of Mr Andrew Edis QC, sitting as a judge of the High Court in *Saulle v Nouvet*[55] where he said:

> "I also draw attention to the proposition discussed in argument that where a person is held to have capacity because he is able to understand and seek suitable professional advice, as here, it may be necessary to include in the award a sum which is designed to enable him to retain such advisers."

It is also of note that in a number of English cases the parties have agreed that trust costs are to be provided for in the compensation, even where the claimants have retained capacity.[56]

It is our view that, if the court determines that the claimant retains capacity to manage his property and financial affairs but only on condition that he has protective steps in place via a trust vehicle to help support his decision-making and control access to his award, it would be reasonable to allow the costs

---

[52] [2007] EWHC 2996 (QB).
[53] [2016] CSOH 126.
[54] At 7.
[55] [2007] EWHC 2902 (QB) at [58].
[56] An example is *Sarwar v Ali* [2007] EWHC 1255 (QB). See also *Ure v Ure* unreported 13 July 2007 QBD, and the Scottish case of *C v Kemp* [2011] CSOH 43 at 9.

associated with the operation of that vehicle on normal compensatory principles. A necessary condition precedent would be a high degree of confidence that the claimant will accept the involvement and advice of trustees in the long term. If on the other hand there is a reasonable expectation that the trust would not survive the claimant's wilfulness or vulnerability, the court will need to question whether the claimant truly has the capacity to manage his affairs. Support of a claimant may take many forms, however, and it would be sensible to consider solutions beyond provision of a discretionary trust, but if a trust is to be recommended, it is important that the medico-legal experts advocating it understand its limitations.

2. CASE STUDIES

The object of this section of the chapter is to look at some reported cases in which claimants have suffered traumatic head injuries of varying severity. In each case we include in full the Lawtel headnote and offer some commentary on lessons to be learned (as, we acknowledge, lessons can be learned by every person engaged in every case in whatever capacity). 　1–029

Case Study 1—Subtle brain injury

Clarke v Maltby [2010] EWHC 1201 (QB)

Background

The claimant (C) sought an order that the defendant (M) pay her costs of personal injury proceedings on the indemnity basis. 　1–030

M had admitted liability for personal injuries sustained by C in a road traffic accident. At the trial for quantum, M contested the general effect of the injuries on C and the effect of the injuries on her ability to pursue her career as a solicitor. C was awarded general damages and damages for loss of earnings.

Held: Judgment for claimant. M's counter-schedule had called into question the genuineness of the symptoms described by C, and the clear implication was that she was deliberately exaggerating her symptoms. That was also the basis on which the prolonged cross-examination of C and that of other witnesses was conducted. Although it was appropriate for M to test the degree of C's injuries, the manner in which the case was conducted went far beyond that. Critically, there was simply no support for the allegation of deliberate exaggeration in any of the medical evidence on which M relied. On the contrary, each expert specifically disavowed any suggestion of deliberate exaggeration by C. It was also relevant that the allegation of deliberate exaggeration to substantiate a fraudulent claim was being made in relation to a solicitor. That was plainly distressing to C, and would have had the most serious consequences if well-founded. Furthermore, the counter-schedule had implied serious professional impropriety by the solicitors representing C, an implication that was unreservedly withdrawn at trial. All of those factors plainly took the case out of the norm, and M would be ordered to pay C's costs on the indemnity basis, *Excelsior Commercial & Industrial Holdings Ltd v Salisbury Hamer Aspden & Johnson (Costs)*[57] followed.

Judge: Owen J

Comment

1–031　This case, involving what we call a "subtle brain injury", which had serious consequences for the claimant, has multiple lessons for lawyers and clinicians alike.

As the headnote records, the claimant, a 45-year-old solicitor, was a front seat passenger in a car involved in a very serious road accident (a combined collision speed of 80–110 mph: the driver of the other car was killed) in September 2004. Although a careful study of the contemporaneous records would have disclosed that she did indeed hit her head and that there was some evidence of unconsciousness, most of those records understandably focused on her life-threatening orthopaedic injuries including spinal fractures, other broken bones and a pneumothorax of the left lung.

The claimant went on to make a good physical recovery and returned to work (as a solicitor in private practice). On the face of things, her career progressed onwards and upwards. Nevertheless, the medical records showed that she continued to seek help for persisting psychiatric problems and noted that she was finding work a strain and she had sessions of CBT in 2007 although she moved to a new job as a fixed equity partner in May 2008.

The claimant's first year's appraisal (in 2009) was good but coincided with her request to move to a three-day week. She told her supervising partner that this was for "personal reasons" but the judge accepted that it was really because she was finding it increasingly difficult to cope and had been advised to cut down her work by a clinical psychologist she consulted. In fact, that did not help much and by mid-December 2009 she went off work completely and was still off sick at the date of the trial in March 2010.

The defendant's advisers evidently felt that none of this added up. They served a counter-schedule/opening which asserted that there was very little wrong with her and included the very clear implication that she had given up work for no good reason and, worse still, had probably done so to maximise her claim and on the advice of her lawyers. As the later judgment on costs makes clear,[58] that was an assertion that was unfounded even in the defendant's own medical evidence and should never have been made.

Once the judge accepted—as he did, without reservation—that the claimant's symptoms were genuine and not exaggerated, the debate turned to whether they had an organic cause (that is, were the result of injury to the brain) or were the symptoms of psychiatric illness. In one sense, this may not matter much so long as one can decide whether they are genuine or not and can assess the personal and financial consequences. On the other hand, it may be thought that cognitive

---

[57] [2002] EWCA Civ 879; [2002] C.P. Rep. 67.
[58] *Clarke v Maltby (Costs)* [2010] EWHC 1856 (QB).

CASE STUDIES

dysfunction which is not the product of physical injury will be more susceptible of treatment and have a better prognosis.

In the event, the judge preferred all the claimant's medical evidence and found that her symptoms were indeed the consequence of a traumatic brain injury. He went on to assess the loss of earnings claim (and other lesser claims) on that basis.

There are (at least) the following lessons to be learned from the case:

(1) It is an elementary error to overstate one's case either in a medical report or in a schedule, counter-schedule or opening. It is also wrong[59] to make any assertion of dishonesty (= deliberate exaggeration) without clear evidential support and a properly pleaded case.

(2) Just because one or other doctor expresses doubts about a claimant, the legal team needs to consider closely whether such doubts are well-founded and, specifically, how and in what terms they can properly be expressed. To take the approach that this was "only a minor head injury" and "she has evidently done well since" may be a legitimate starting point for a sceptical line of inquiry but it is utterly unscientific to reach a concluded view that there is nothing much wrong with a claimant without studying the entirety of the evidence.

(3) That evidence should include all records of the accident and the likely forces involved and all records of the claimant's physical or psychological state before and after it.

(4) The evidence of those who knew the claimant well before and after the accident, whether at work or at home, is always enormously valuable. Of course, one should take account of records that a GP may have or which may be found in an employment appraisal suggesting that someone is doing well. But one should bear in mind that someone may be putting a brave or optimistic face on matters for perfectly good reason.

(5) No doctor should be allowed within a million miles of the witness box unless he has first carefully studied all the relevant material and taken account of facts and matters that contradict as well as those that support whatever thesis is being advanced in the report.

(6) Lawyers need to have a reasonable understanding of different kinds of organic brain damage and of the interrelation of organic and non-organic injuries as well as what may—or may not—be revealed on scans.[60]

---

[59] And contrary to para.704(c) of the Bar's Code of Conduct: see also *Three Rivers District Council v Bank of England* [2003] 2 A.C. 1.
[60] Other "subtle brain injury" cases in which one finds further helpful analysis are *Siegel v Pummell* [2014] EWHC 4309 (QB) and *Hibberd-Little v Carlton* [2018] EWHC 1787 (QB). Saggerson J's decision in the latter case provides a valuable analysis of the medical issues and of the quality of the expert evidence arising in such cases.

Case Study 2—Difficulty in assessment of cognitive ability

Ali v Caton [2013] EWHC 1730 (QB)

Background

1–032 A car being driven by C at about 50 mph struck J causing him a very severe brain injury and significant orthopaedic injuries. C was uninsured and the defence was conducted by the second defendant Motor Insurers' Bureau (MIB). A trial on liability was compromised before judgment on the basis that C was negligent and 80% responsible for the accident. On the assessment of damages, the MIB's case was that J was malingering, that any ongoing cognitive defects were mild and that, once the litigation was over, he would be motivated to function and would function at a far higher level than he had so far exhibited.

The MIB contended that (1) J showed a level of cognitive performance and motivation which was inconsistent with his case that his injuries had serious consequences for his ability to lead an independent life; (2) psychometric tests consistently returned results strongly indicating that J was deliberately exaggerating his difficulties; (3) J's daily performance was inconsistent with and worse than his assessment while in residential rehabilitation; (4) on his own initiative, J had taken and passed the UK Citizenship Test, a task that was wholly inconsistent with his level of cognitive disability.

Held: Judgment for claimant. (1) J had consistently presented with significant memory problems from a time when he had been in no fit state to contemplate feigning (see [243] of judgment). (2) On the evidence J's cognitive deficit attributable to the accident was not accurately reflected in the various test results that had been recorded ([250]). (3) On a daily level, J had been performing less than optimally, despite having engaged constructively with rehabilitation but the root causes were the accident and its sequelae, not his deliberate or fraudulent under-performance ([251]). (4) The evidence showed that J had suffered lasting cognitive deficit as a result of the accident, the scope and extent of which could not be quantified with precision. It was not as severe as a number of the test results had indicated; otherwise he would not have been able to pass the citizenship test. However, the effects were significant and profoundly damaging in their impact on J's everyday life ([252]). J was awarded damages and interest totalling £988,902, after allowing for interim payments and benefits and the 20% deduction. The award included general damages of £147,500, past losses of £376,850 and future losses of £1,134,660, excluding future care and case management ([319]).

On appeal: The judge had not erred in finding that a personal injury claimant suffered from a significant cognitive disability despite the fact that he had passed the UK Citizenship Test, a task which was inconsistent with his apparent level of cognitive disability. The judge had been entitled to take all of the evidence into account and there were no grounds for altering the award of damages.

Judge: Stuart-Smith J

CASE STUDIES

Court of Appeal: Tomlinson LJ, McCombe LJ, Beatson LJ

Comment

Most brain injury claims are resolved by compromise after varying degrees of negotiation. Not many go to trial. Those which do frequently involve allegations of malingering. Typically, the claimant will be claiming for the financial consequences of serious ongoing disability whereas the defendant will be alleging that the symptoms have been deliberately exaggerated for financial gain. If the parties are wedded to their respective positions, the disparity of approach makes settlement impossible. This was just one such case.

There was no dispute that the claimant had suffered a very severe brain injury in the index accident. His GCS had been recorded as 3/15 at the scene of the accident and was 7/15 on arrival at hospital. There were skull fractures, a right extra-axial haematoma with displacement of the extra-dural surface, a left parietal "contrecoup" contusion, and diffuse swelling of the brain as well as a number of orthopaedic and chest injuries. He required bilateral frontal decompressive craniotomy following which a bone flap was left out.

The claimant developed epilepsy, and the brain injury resulted in physical problems in the form of residual ataxia, dysarthria, and communicative problems from pronunciation and articulatory imprecision. There were also cognitive problems the extent of which were in dispute. It was the claimant's case that the brain injury had serious consequences for his ability to lead an independent life, whereas the defendant contended that he had been consistently malingering, that the residual cognitive defects were mild and that once the trial was over he would be motivated and function at a far higher level than he had exhibited thus far. A point made by the defendant's neurologist, however, was that the severity of initial injury does not correlate well with long-term outcome. The defendant relied on four major points to support its argument: first, that following the accident the claimant attended a further education college thereby showing a level of cognitive performance and motivation inconsistent with that being advanced on his behalf. Secondly, that in the psychometric tests administered by both side's neuropsychologists, the claimant consistently failed the symptom validity tests (SVTs). Thirdly, his day to day performance was inconsistent with the findings during his rehabilitation. He had received extensive residential rehabilitation at Queen Elizabeth's Foundation for Disabled People at Banstead, a recognised centre of excellence, during which he was able to access the local community independently, demonstrate road safety awareness, and shop independently, though there was also some suggestion that he appeared more independent before going to Banstead than after. Fourthly, he had since the accident taken his UK Citizenship Test and passed it. A number of experts called on both the defendant and claimant side considered that passing the Test, whether fairly or by cheating, was inconsistent with the level of cognitive disability reportedly displayed on a day to day basis since the accident. The passing of the Test was therefore central to the defendant's allegation that the claimant was malingering and would perform much better when the exigencies of the litigation were over.

1–033

1-034 The neuropsychology evidence The parties' neuropsychologists agreed that the nature of the brain injury was such as likely to give rise to deficits disadvantaging the claimant in employment and social function. They agreed that he had not cooperated in the assessment process and had failed symptom validity testing in a profound manner when seen by each of them. They were unable to determine the motivation underlying that failure, but agreed that the failures rendered all of the neuropsychometric results unreliable and that they probably underestimated his true level of ability, albeit there would be a degree of genuine deficit. They found the claimant a complex person to assess. The claimant's expert concluded that he lacked capacity to manage his affairs or the litigation and was significantly handicapped. The claimant was not, the expert thought, capable of consistently exaggerating his presentation and leading, in effect, a double life, particularly given the time he had spent at Banstead where he was considered to have significant cognitive deficits. By contrast the defendant's neuropsychologist took the view that a reliable conclusion could not be reached without objective scientific evidence, and that such evidence was lacking given the comprehensive failure of the SVTs. Instead he preferred to emphasise the evidence that was inconsistent with significant ongoing cognitive deficit, and considered that this was proof of the claimant malingering.

The trial judge considered the neuropsychological evidence to be particularly important in this case—as did the neurologists. He found that on at least some occasions the claimant had not merely failed to do his best in the psychometric testing, but had deliberately under-performed. In consequence he found that quantitative estimates of cognitive deficit recorded outside the medico-legal sphere (where SVTs were not performed) could not be relied upon. He considered that no neuropsychologist could properly reach an opinion purely on the test results. He concluded that:

> "when the neurological and rehabilitative evidence is taken into account, it shows that the consequences of very severe traumatic brain injuries are poorly understood and incapable of either prediction or accurate definition. Specifically, in a case such as the present, the determinants of behaviour and effective functional ability are multifactorial, depending upon injuries to parts of the body other than the brain, physical abilities and disabilities, perception, mood, and the ability of rehabilitation to enable the patient to function independently on a day to day basis. The presence of reliable test results is useful but not determinative; their absence does not absolve clinicians or the court from reviewing all of the available evidence in order to form an opinion".[61]

Overall the judge preferred the "measured and cautious" approach taken by the claimant's neuropsychologist to the evidence as opposed to the "dogmatic and frequently unjustifiable" approach of the defendant's expert whom he considered to have formed a hardened view of the claimant, making disparaging remarks which the expert felt compelled to withdraw in the course of cross-examination. The judge found that after proper scrutiny, the claimant could be shown to have consistently presented with significant memory problems from a time when he was in no fit state to contemplate feigning. As regards the defendant's trump card, the Citizenship Test, the judge considered that the claimant had learned the

---

[61] At [230].

CASE STUDIES

answers by rote and struck lucky with the questions, but that the fact of passing compelled a conclusion that the claimant retained cognitive function which should have allowed him to operate at a better level than he had done on a day to day basis. The explanation for the general under-performance was multifactorial, complex and subtle. The judge had no hesitation in finding that whilst the effect of the severe brain injury was uncertain, the claimant was one of the majority of individuals who fail to flourish after suffering such an injury, and the scope and extent of the deficit could not be quantified with precision. Though the effects were not as significant as various tests suggested, they were nevertheless profoundly damaging in their impact being imposed as they were on a person of low average IQ. It is interesting to note that the judge also found that after the claimant eventually realised his return to normal life would not be complete he adopted a sick role which was not motivated by a desire for financial compensation "but by a deep seated realisation that he was not going to be able to function as a normal young man again. Once he slipped into the role it became intractable and pervasive".[62]

On the issue of the claimant's capacity to manage his property and affairs, the judge found it to be finely balanced, but concluded that the cognitive impairments in memory, attention and executive skills were sufficient to justify the finding (supported by the claimant's medical experts) that he lacked capacity. It was noted that he was suggestible, and needed support with all personal finances and benefits. His problems would be compounded when in receipt of a large award of damages.

There were a number of other issues addressed in the judgment of the trial judge including his care needs, his prospects of marrying, and his earning capacity. On appeal the appellant argued, amongst other things, that the trial judge had wrongly equated inability to manage large sums of money with lack of capacity, and that he was wrong to have made the assumption that the claimant "struck lucky" in passing the Citizenship Test, and that if the judge had attributed the correct weight to the Test he would have found that the claimant had either been malingering or consciously exaggerating. After careful review of the evidence the Court of Appeal upheld the judge's decision on all counts. It is worth noting that the judgment at first instance was extremely thorough, running to 345 paragraphs, which meant there was little reason to suggest that the trial judge had not properly considered all relevant issues.

The following lessons can be learned from this case:

(1) The long-term consequences of brain injury are idiosyncratic and can take a considerable amount of time and evidence to tease out. Evidence from lay witnesses can be very important in this regard. It must be remembered that experts only get a snapshot of the claimant—and may only have met him once or twice before trial. Moreover, any psychometric testing will have its limitations, particularly where SVTs are failed.
(2) Brain injured individuals can also present in an inconsistent fashion which makes assessment difficult. Their performance, as in the present case, can vary significantly depending upon the environment they are in, their mood, and physical state. Memory function might appear tolerable in a controlled

---

[62] At [254].

test, but may be poor in an environment with multiple distractions or sources of anxiety, i.e. a "real world" situation, though in the present case it was also poor in tests.

(3) Exaggeration may be a feature of the presentation, but it is not necessarily conscious and may be a reaction to the change in personality and life circumstances the claimant finds himself in. The litigation process can also wear down the claimant with seemingly endless medico-legal appointments and assessments which have a demoralising effect. If an allegation of malingering is going to succeed, there has to be very clear evidence, and this may be particularly hard to come by when someone has suffered a severe brain injury.

(4) Any expert who personally takes against a claimant is going to come unstuck in front of a judge. It is important that an expert is balanced and measured in their approach at all times and does not give a hint of personal animosity or bias.

Case Study 3—Damages assessment for moderate brain injury

Edwards v Martin [2010] EWHC 570 (QB)

Background

1–035 E had sustained a severe and life-threatening head injury resulting in a permanent loss of cognitive functioning with permanent emotional and behavioural problems, diagnosed as an organic personality disorder. E moved into a home with his partner and their child, but their relationship later deteriorated and he moved out and purchased another home. However, court proceedings later commenced in relation to his contact with his child. Liability in the instant case was admitted, subject to a deduction of 15% for the risk of finding contributory negligence for a failure to wear a seat belt.

M submitted that when considering recoverability of the cost of accommodation, the case should be distinguished from those in which the need for new accommodation arose from a claimant's physical disabilities as E's separation from his partner and his consequent need to obtain alternative accommodation were not reasonably foreseeable consequences of M's actions.

Held: Damages assessed.

(1) This was a case that fell within the "moderate brain damage" category of the Judicial Studies Board Guidelines. There was no more than modest intellectual deficit, but the personality change was sufficiently severe and multi-faceted that an award towards the upper range of the second level was appropriate. Moreover, there remained a residual small risk of epilepsy and an appropriate figure for pain, suffering and loss of amenity was £90,000.

(2) The court assessed E's past loss of earnings against the background of annual increases having been awarded to his employee comparators throughout the years since the accident.

(3) E was also entitled to his past miscellaneous expenses, past care and case management costs and costs of the Court of Protection and appointment of a financial deputy.
(4) The psychiatric effects of E's head injury made it impractical for him to continue to live with his family. Such a situation was reasonably foreseeable as a consequence of the injury that he suffered, *Crookdake v Drury*[63] and *Housecroft v Burnett*[64] considered. Consequently, E was entitled to the expenses incurred in the purchase and furnishing of his new property.
(5) The disputed family court proceedings also arose as a foreseeable consequence of the breakdown of E's relationship with his former partner. E had sought to pursue a claim for staying in contact with his child which was a manifestation of his rigid thinking and lack of insight into his condition, both arising from the condition itself. His partner had resisted that contact on reasonable grounds. A sum for the proceedings was therefore also recoverable.
(6) E would not be unfit for all remunerative employment for the rest of his normal working lifetime. The defects in his cognitive abilities, executive functioning and memory were considered mild. His behavioural and personality problems were more severe but not such as to rule out future part-time routine work. To reflect the inevitable setbacks, substantial employment breaks and difficulties in finding new jobs, the agreed multiplier for future loss of earnings was 3.68.
(7) E was also entitled to future accommodation, DIY costs, therapy and holiday costs, assessed by the court.

Judge: David Clarke J

Comment

Although the claimant's head injury was only classified as "moderate" and the cognitive, executive and memory deficits were mild, the actual consequences of the injury as regards his day to day life were significant and all too familiar: he had difficulty managing his money, his relationship with his partner broke down, and he lost his job after 16 months. There was radiological evidence of organic brain damage with multiple foci of signal loss throughout the cerebral hemispheres. Fortunately there was no residual physical neurological impairment, but there was an organic personality disorder and the claimant was left with lack of motivation, irritability and temper, rigid and at times obsessive thinking, total loss of libido, depression and phobic anxiety. The prospects for his future looked bleak.

The relevance of this case is that it included consideration of many if not most of the issues that can arise in brain injury litigation including (the now seemingly ubiquitous) video surveillance, care needs, accommodation requirements, employment prospects, and capacity issues.

1–036

---

[63] [2003] EWHC 1938 (QB); (2004) 76 B.M.L.R. 99.
[64] [1986] 1 All E.R. 332.

ACQUIRED BRAIN INJURY AND CIVIL LITIGATION

Video surveillance It is not worth dwelling on the video surveillance as its use has been mentioned in other case studies, but it is as well to note that it showed the claimant performing perfectly normally and without any hint of disability in certain situations. An example was him playing golf with friends without needing any obvious support—including attending a golfing break in Ireland. The witness evidence before the judge, including from the case manager, was that golf was an important pre-accident activity for the claimant and much emphasis was put on him continuing with it and maintaining his group of golfing friends. As for the tour to Ireland, he had little involvement in its organisation. The witness evidence was important to qualify and put into context what was seen on the video. Suffice it to say that the judge did not find the video surveillance to support a contention that the claimant was exaggerating.

1–037
The defendant had argued that inconsistent effort in the psychometric tests administered by the parties' psychologists also indicated exaggeration. However, the judge found that the claimant passed some tests which he would have expected to fail had he been consciously exaggerating, and that far from trying to exaggerate his disability for financial gain he had consistently shown no interest in the litigation.

Care needs Like so many brain-injured individuals, the claimant was reluctant to accept care or support. In the early stages the only way to implement support was for his sister to take on the role of paid support worker as that was all he would accept. Latterly he did permit the engagement of a professional support worker, and that resulted in significant improvement in his rehabilitation. As for the future, there was a fundamental difference in approach between the parties' neuropsychiatrists. The opinion of the claimant's expert was that care and support was required to prevent deterioration and to maintain quality of life. The defendant's expert took a more minimal approach and considered that care should be increased if and when problems arise and decreased when independence improves. The trial judge applied what is termed the "100%" or "full compensation" principle, namely that the claimant must so far as reasonably possible be put in the position he would have been in had the injuries not been sustained. This meant the care necessary for the maintenance of a reasonable quality of life, not just crisis provision on top of a minimal baseline provision of care. In many cases the judge will be well able to determine what constitutes "reasonable" provision without too much difficulty, but there remain legal issues regarding the extent to which concepts of proportionality and fairness to the paying party bear upon what is considered to be reasonable need.[65] The judge awarded long-term future care in the form of 10 hour per week paid support worker time on an agency basis plus 80 hours per year of case management. The

---

[65] There is a long established line of cases which support the proposition that where there is a range of "reasonable options" to meet the claimant's needs, the question is not in the first instance whether some other provision is reasonable, but whether the provision claimed for on behalf of the claimant is reasonable—see *Sowden v Lodge* [2004] EWCA Civ 1370 and *Rialis v Mitchell, Times*, 17 July 1984. However it has also been held that what is "reasonable" must not result in injustice to the defendant and includes consideration of proportionality as between the cost to the defendant and the extent of benefit which would be derived by the claimant—see per Swift J in *Whiten v St George's Healthcare NHS Trust* [2011] EWHC 2066 (QB) relying on Lord Woolf MR in *Heil v Rankin* [2001] 2 Q.B. 272 at [22]. There is tension between these two approaches, but this is not the place for a jurisprudential discussion about them.

support worker was to be an "enabler" without whose help he said the claimant would have an impoverished quality of life. The judge observed that it was also the quality of the care that was crucial to the claimant's functioning and quality of life, not the quantity.

Another of the judge's findings was that the claimant's relationship with his partner had broken down due to the effects of the head injury. The defendant argued that the future care should be reduced because of the prospect the claimant would find another partner who would look after him. This argument was rejected. The claimant had no libido, was no longer interested in women, was selfish, moody and lacking drive or initiative. The judge held it most improbable that he would find another partner.

The breakdown in the claimant's pre-existing relationship was, the judge found, a direct result of his injuries. The cost of the claimant moving to alternate accommodation was therefore one he could recover, but a discount was made for the small chance the relationship would have broken down in any event. The separation led to the claimant being denied contact with his daughter from the relationship largely due to unreasonableness on his part. The defendant argued that it should not be responsible for the costs associated with the claimant's unreasonableness, but the judge held that it he could recover the costs he incurred in bringing proceedings in the Family Court to secure access to his child. Brain injuries often result in family breakdown, and the costs associated with restoring the family relationships will generally be recoverable as part of the compensation. In some cases this involves housing the claimant separately from his or her spouse and children if the injury prevents them from living together amicably. An alternative may be to house the claimant in a separate annex to the main family home where care can be provided unobtrusively.

Loss of earnings The claimant went back to work as an HGV driver within six months of the accident. He was able to manage mainly part time work with some HGV driving for 16 months before his driving licence was revoked. The judge said that the return to work was premature and ill-advised and probably did more harm than good. Again, this is a commonly encountered problem, and an early return to work may not be a reliable prognosticator for long-term employability or function. The only reason he (and so many other claimants) managed to last as long as he did in his employment was due to the significant allowances the employer made for his recovery—a recovery that never fully materialised.

The case also highlights the often-contentious issue of driving. A brain-injured claimant who has avoided visual field defects will often return to driving as soon as possible and before medical advice is sought or the injury reported to the DVLA or any driving assessment undertaken. When the claimant in the present case eventually did undergo a driving assessment five years after the accident it was found that he was road-aware and physically capable of the task of driving under direct supervision, but his personality disorder, rigid thinking and susceptibility to stress in difficult situations were serious impediments. In practice it is probably rare that someone who lacks the capacity to manage their property and affairs will be considered fit to drive and to manage the complex interactions experienced on today's roads.

The judge was not prepared to find that the claimant, who was 41 at trial, would never gain any form of remunerative employment, but he thought the

1–038

ACQUIRED BRAIN INJURY AND CIVIL LITIGATION

prospects of early re-employment to be remote and applied an earnings multiplier which assumed disability within the definition of the disability discrimination legislation.[66] A residual earnings multiplicand of £9,000 pa was applied to this multiplier.

1–039
Capacity This was a borderline case in so far as capacity to manage property and affairs was concerned. The judge reminded himself of the strong presumption of capacity, but found that the claimant was unfit to make more than the most simple and low-level decisions about his financial affairs. An important point noted by the judge was the relief from stress which the appointment of a deputy brought to the claimant's life. He also noted that the claimant had waived any financial interest he had in the property he had lived in with his former partner without first taking any professional advice or even discussing it with his family. This showed a lack of awareness of the importance of what he did and supported the judge's conclusion that he lacked capacity.

The following lessons can be learned from this case:

(1) Detailed witness evidence from those who know the claimant well, such as family, is often the best evidence of function. It is particularly helpful if such evidence is measured and acknowledges where improvements have been made as well as the negatives.
(2) Return to pre-accident activities following brain injury should not be rushed and should involve medical advice following proper rehabilitation wherever possible, advice and rehabilitation which may be hard to come by under the NHS. The imperative to return to work promptly because of financial need should be tempered by interim funding if such is available.
(3) As support workers for the walking wounded such as this claimant are more buddies than carers, it is necessary to find suitably experienced individuals with whom the injured person can get on well. This may mean someone of a similar age, sex, or with similar interests. Although there is a reluctance to employ family members or friends in the role, sometimes this will be the only solution in the early stages of rehabilitation.
(4) Special care needs to be taken not to seek to settle the claim too soon before the likely longer-term prognosis can be reliably predicted. It is of note that the present case only came to trial nine years after the accident. Whilst every case need not take that long to quantify, it is by no means unusual.

Case Study 4—Illegality following brain injury

Wilson v Coulson [2002] P.I.Q.R. P22

Background

1–040
Mr Wilson claimed damages for personal injury following a road accident in September 1995 in which he had suffered brain damage as a passenger in a car driven negligently by Mr Coulson. As a result of the brain damage some of his personality and cognitive functions were impaired. Mr Wilson had a history of drug taking. Whilst depressed and suffering from headaches, he took some heroin

---

[66] Now the Equality Act 2010 definition of disability.

in about November 1995. He became addicted and took an overdose in February 1996. As a result he suffered further brain damage causing weakness in his left leg. Thereafter, he continued to be addicted to heroin until April 1998 when he was detoxified. Since that date he had remained drug free. Mr Wilson argued that the defendant was liable for the consequences of the overdose because it would not have occurred but for the accident. The defendant argued that the chain of causation had been broken by the fact that the claimant's use of heroin was unreasonable and that as a matter of public policy the claimant should not be permitted to rely on his own criminal behaviour.

Held: giving judgment for the defendant, that

(1) the claimant's track record relating to the use of drugs was such that there was a substantial risk that he would have used heroin at some time in the future even if the accident had not occurred, and
(2) the taking of heroin after the accident could not be excused by his condition at the time. His action in doing so was both unreasonable and illegal and he should not be allowed to profit from his actions. He was the author of his own misfortune and what followed was caused by his own conduct. It did not matter whether it was put on the basis of unreasonable conduct breaking the chain of causation or of public policy relating to criminal conduct. Both were applicable and, in either event, the result was the same, *Clunis v Camden and Islington Health Authority*[67] followed.

Judge: Harrison J

Comment

The issues for the court to determine broadly included the following: first, whether the heroin use was caused by the original traumatic brain injury sustained in the accident; secondly, what injury was caused by the heroin overdose; and thirdly, whether the defendant should be liable for any loss suffered as a result of the heroin use or overdose.

The brain injury sustained in the original RTA was severe. The claimant suffered post-traumatic amnesia (PTA) of two to three weeks duration, he had a depressed right fronto-temporal skull fracture and a fracture of the right zygoma and roof of the right orbit which left him blind in the right eye. The judge found there to be damage affecting the right temporal and frontal lobes. The claimant had mild right sided weakness and incoordination of the limbs with unsteadiness of gait and poor balance. His memory and organisational ability were impaired, and he suffered significant personality change becoming apathetic, irritable and lacking in personal hygiene. He had troubling headaches, and he suffered epilepsy. All this for a previously fit and healthy 27-year-old man in regular employment (he worked in a brewery) was quite devastating. A couple of months or so after the accident the claimant started to use heroin to relieve his headaches and before he knew it he was addicted to the drug. Less than three months later he was found unconscious from a heroin overdose. He was taken to hospital but had

1–041

---
[67] [1998] Q.B. 978.

multi-organ failure including renal failure requiring dialysis, pancreatitis, and rhabdomyolosis (a blood disorder). One of the expert psychiatrists called to give evidence said that it was the most severe overdose he had heard of where the patient survived. The claimant was, however, left with left hemi-paresis causing weakness of the left leg, and damage to the left sciatic nerve. There was an issue as to what if any additional cognitive damage was caused by the overdose: the claimant denied there was any such damage whilst the defendant suggested there was significant additional damage. The judge heard evidence from one expert that it was very unusual for a patient who survives a large opiate overdose to suffer brain damage, whilst another said he had not seen brain damage from a heroin overdose, but that it was common from anoxia following other abuse of other substances such as ecstasy. The judge concluded that the claimant did sustain further brain damage of a diffuse nature from the overdose. He noted that the claimant had suffered respiratory failure, had low oxygenation of the blood, and low blood pressure. In these circumstances an anoxic injury was likely, and damage was exacerbated by the vulnerable state of the brain following the RTA.

The judge was required to apportion the claimant's overall neurobehavioural disability between the two brain injuries, though the experts had declined to do so. The parties' neuropsychologists were only prepared to go so far as to say that:

> "Although it is not possible to put a precise figure on the additional neurobehavioural consequences of that overdose, it is possible to state that his condition would have been less severe and his recovery would have been more rapid and complete had he not suffered additional brain damage following the overdose, and if he had not continued to take heroin".

Doing the best that he could, the judge determined that 25% of the claimant's non-physical or neurobehavioural disability was due to the heroin overdose.

1–042
As regards the question of whether or not the defendant should be liable for the heroin addiction, the judge was constrained by case law to determine that he should not be. This was on the grounds of public policy.[68] The evidence was that albeit the heroin use potentially arose as a result of the headaches and mood disorder following the accident, it was a voluntary choice for the claimant to start taking it. There had been no suggestion that he lacked the mental capacity to make the choice of whether to take heroin, and it was noteworthy that subsequently he had been able to give up the drug with the help of a detox programme. Heroin is a Class A drug and taking it was a criminal act. It was therefore contrary to public policy to allow the claimant to recover damages consequent upon its use.[69] The judge held that the claimant's actions in taking heroin were both unreasonable and illegal and he should not be allowed to profit from his actions. It should be noted that there was in any event significant doubt as to whether the heroin use was caused by the initial brain injury given that even before the RTA the claimant had been a habitual cannabis user, and had taken

---

[68] Following the legal principle defined by the Latin phrase *ex turpi causa non oritur action*.
[69] See *Clunis v Camden and Islington Health Authority* [1998] 2 W.L.R. 902, or more recently, *Gray v Thames Trains Ltd* [2009] UKHL 33. For a recent case in which even a long-term drug addict was not permitted to recover damages associated with his addiction following a spinal cord injury, see *AB v Royal Devon and Exeter NHS Foundation Trust* [2016] EWHC 1024 (QB).

ecstasy twice and cocaine once. His younger brother was also a heroin addict, though this fact may have been protective against the claimant following the same devastating course.

The case is interesting in that it illustrates the problems faced by claimants trying to attribute certain aberrant acts to brain injury. On the current state of the law a party liable to compensate a victim for an acquired brain injury will not be liable for illegal, immoral or unreasonable acts carried out in consequence. Such acts will be considered to have broken the chain of causation. A similar example is the case of *Gray v Thames Trains Ltd*.[70] Mr Gray was a victim of the Ladbroke Grove rail crash and suffered severe PTSD as a consequence. Whilst suffering the disorder he killed a man and he then claimed losses arising from his eventual imprisonment against the train operator responsible for the crash (he had pleaded guilty to manslaughter on ground of diminished responsibility). The House of Lords rejected his claim on grounds of public policy. And in the recent case of *AB v Royal Devon and Exeter NHS Foundation Trust*,[71] the claimant, who had a longstanding polysubstance misuse disorder was not permitted, on grounds of public policy, to recover Court of Protection and deputyship costs which arose because his addiction deprived him of his capacity. By contrast, suicide may not invoke the public policy prohibition: in *Corr v IBC Vehicles Ltd*[72] Mr Corr had suffered severe head injuries from malfunctioning machinery for which the defendant was liable. He went on to develop PTSD and depression, and subsequently committed suicide. Mrs Corr brought a Fatal Accidents Act 1976 for loss of dependence on her husband which the House of Lords permitted.

Case Study 5—Somatisation disorder

Giblett v P & NE Murray Ltd (1999) 96(22) L.S.G. 34; Times, 25 May 1999

Background

Mrs Giblett appealed against an award of general damages of £12,500 for pain, suffering and loss of amenity arising from personal injuries sustained when the vehicle in which she was travelling as a front seat passenger was struck from behind by Murray Ltd's (the defendant's) vehicle. The defendant conceded liability, but a dispute arose as to the cause of Mrs Giblett's injuries and quantum of damages. Medical evidence showed that Mrs Giblett had sustained mild to moderate whiplash injuries, but Mrs Giblett sought damages for the exacerbation of pre-existing neurosis and for temporary cessation of her sexual relationship with her partner.

Held: dismissing the appeal, that the increase in general damages above the accepted band of £3,500 to £6,000 for mild to moderate whiplash reflected the psychiatric aspect of Mrs Giblett's injuries. However, the judge below had erred in holding that the cessation of sexual relations was too remote and not

1–043

---

[70] [2009] UKHL 33.
[71] [2016] EWHC 1024 (QB).
[72] [2008] UKHL 13.

foreseeable. The correct test was to determine whether, on the balance of probabilities, the accident either caused or materially contributed to the development or increased the duration of a pre-existing psychiatric illness, *Page v Smith*[73] applied. To succeed, therefore, Mrs Giblett had only to show that her physical or psychiatric injury was reasonably foreseeable by the defendant and that the negligence caused her injury. She did not have to prove that either the injury, in the form it took, or its manifestation as a disease or condition arising from a pre-existing condition, would have been reasonably foreseeable by the defendant. On the facts, however, the judge's error on foreseeability did not assist Mrs Giblett as to causation, as there was sufficient evidence of difficulties in the relationship to enable the judge to reject the causative link between the accident and the temporary cessation of sexual relations.

Judges: Roch LJ; Otton LJ; Pill LJ

Comment

1-044 This case highlights the problem the courts have in assessing claimants who present with somatisation or conversion disorders. Whilst the case did not involve traumatic brain injury, there would appear to be no reason why mildly head-injured claimants could not suffer similar disorders.

The motor collision in which the claimant was involved was relatively minor in nature. The damage to her car cost just £346 to repair. The immediate injury was a neck whiplash of mild to moderate severity, and any continuing organic disability (if any) was minimal by the time of trial. However, over the nine years between the accident and trial, the claimant complained of grossly disabling symptoms, including "total body pain" which could not be accounted for on an organic basis. It was claimed that the disability prevented the claimant in engaging in normal domestic or work activities, and that it ruined her sex life and her marriage.

It was accepted by all of the medical experts that the claimant's presentation had to be explained psychiatrically save to the extent that there was conscious exaggeration, and the diagnosis of somatisation disorder (under the old DSM-III) was generally accepted. The main issue at the trial was the extent and severity of the psychiatric condition. Determination of this depended to a great extent upon the claimant's truth or accuracy of her alleged disabilities. This of course presented a dilemma for the judge because exaggeration of symptoms is one of the manifestations of somatisation disorder, thereby making the claimant a patently unreliable witness. Teasing out the extent and genuineness of disability is a common problem, and the court therefore needs to look for objective evidence as far as possible. In this case the defendant mounted a full frontal attack on the claimant's credibility and suggested that she deliberately mislead the court about the severity of her symptoms. Their expert psychiatrist considered that most of her symptomology was not in any way due to the accident. The defendant subjected her to covert video surveillance which appeared to demonstrate her

---

[73] [1996] A.C. 155.

functioning relatively normally. In addition there was no evidence of the muscle wasting which would have been expected had she been disabled to the extent she claimed.

The trial judge failed to clearly address the extent to which the symptoms the claimant complained of were genuine as opposed to consciously exaggerated, but the award he made implied that he had accepted some of the ongoing complaints as being genuine. The Court of Appeal held that the judge should have included in his judgment more analysis into his reasoning, and should have set out how the claimant would have been had she not suffered the road traffic accident.

1–045

The defendant's expert psychiatrist suggested that the litigation itself was a major psychological issue hanging over the claimant and that her chances of improvement would be considerably enhanced when the litigation was over. This is a common suggestion in cases where an injury has given rise to an adverse psychological reaction—probably with a good deal of validity. It is, of course, impossible to test the theory for the benefit of the trial judge. There has been some academic study into the follow-up of mental disorder following resolution of litigation,[74] but it might be a fruitful area for further study.

The inherent unreliability of evidence from a claimant suffering a somatisation disorder poses a problem not just for the judge, but also for the claimant's own legal team. How are they to assess the claimant's veracity and the proper value of the case? Ultimately their role is not to judge the claimant but to make an assessment of what the judge is likely to conclude at trial, but the present case indicates the problems with leaving it until trial for the judge to determine the outcome. The claimant had sought damages of more than £500,000 but only recovered a tiny fraction of that. Such a disappointing outcome can have a significant financial effect on the claimant's lawyers (who are typically funded under no-win no-fee agreements) as the claimant may not recover most of the costs incurred by her in the litigation. One solution may be for the claimant's lawyers themselves to undertake some covert video surveillance. As long as it is done with the claimant's prior consent albeit without giving away the precise time and location of the surveillance, any ethical issues ought to be overcome.

In conclusion, somatisation disorders[75] are problematic for all concerned in personal injury litigation. It does not help that they are not well understood by many in the medical profession, some of whom insist that the absence of a readily understood organic cause of disability implies malingering. Even with a good understanding of the somatisation disorders the courts are faced with the prospect of claimants who may not engage well with treatment, and whose potential for improvement may not be known until the conclusion of the litigation. If the claimant's alleged somatisation disorder is not accepted by the court, the judge has to deliver a judgment which might itself be a crushing blow to an already psychologically fragile claimant. The judge in this case had tried to spare the claimant detailed analysis of what he thought of her and was criticised for doing so. As Lord Justice Otton eloquently put it he "tempered the wind to the shorn lamb and spared the plaintiff a good deal of pain and humiliation".

---

[74] Renee L. Binder, MD; Michael R. Trimble, FRCP, FRCPsych; and Dale E. McNiel, PhD, "Is Money a Cure? Follow-up of Litigants in England", *Bull Am Acad Psychiatry Law*, Vol.19, No.2, 1991. See also Chapter 7 for discussion regarding the effects of litigation on claimants.

[75] Currently included in DSM-5 under the title "Somatic Symptom and Related Disorders".

CHAPTER 2

Assessing Capacity: The Law

Denzil Lush

INTRODUCTION

This chapter contains five parts: 2–001

(1) Part 1 considers several of the more important common law tests of capacity.
(2) Part 2 looks at the provisions of the first three sections of the Mental Capacity Act 2005 (MCA 2005) and includes a brief commentary on each of them.
(3) Part 3 describes 11 cases in which judges have determined whether an individual has capacity or lacks it under the MCA 2005.
(4) Part 4 contains a selection of 50 judicial observations from the 11 cases summarised in Part 3 on how to assess capacity and what the court expects from an expert witness.
(5) Part 5 is a brief conclusion which summarises the anticipated changes in the law, practice and procedure over the next decade.

1. COMMON LAW TESTS OF CAPACITY

Common law tests of capacity

In a legal context, "capacity" refers to a person's ability to do something, 2–002 including making a decision, which may have legal consequences for that person, or for other people. Having a mental disability alone does not render someone incapable of doing various things or making certain decisions. The law tends to focus less on the disability itself than the extent of the impairment it causes. If the impairment crosses a particular threshold, then that person will be regarded as lacking capacity. Over several centuries, judges have developed different tests of capacity, each of which is designed to assess a person's ability to enter into a specific type of transaction or relationship. These are known as the common law tests of capacity and they operate in some of the most important areas of the law. They tend to be decision-specific, though the capacity to manage one's property and affairs generally covers a broader range of actions and decision-making. These common law tests of capacity are not incompatible with the test in section

ASSESSING CAPACITY: THE LAW

3 of the MCA 2005 because they focus primarily on the relevant information that the person making the decision needs to be able to understand, retain and use or weigh. Here are some examples.

Capacity to litigate

Summary

2–003 In the Court of Appeal's judgment in the case of *Bailey v Warren* Lady Justice Arden gave the following summary of matters that need to be considered when assessing whether a person has litigation capacity[1]:

(1) The assessment of capacity to conduct proceedings depends to some extent on the nature of the proceedings in contemplation.
(2) The person being assessed would need to understand how the proceedings were to be funded.
(3) He would need to know about the chances of not succeeding and about the risk of an adverse order as to costs.
(4) He would need to have capacity to make the sort of decisions that are likely to arise in litigation.
(5) Capacity to conduct such proceedings would include the capacity to give proper instructions for and to approve the particulars of a claim, and to approve a compromise.
(6) To have capacity to approve a compromise, he would need insight into the compromise, an ability to instruct his solicitors to advise him on it, and an understanding of their advice and an ability to weigh their advice.
(7) He would need to know what he was giving up and what would happen if he refused to accept the offer of compromise.

Masterman-Lister

2–004 The capacity to litigate was hived off from the capacity to manage one's property and affairs generally by the Court of Appeal in the case of *Masterman-Lister v Brutton & Co*.[2] Part 21 of the Civil Procedure Rules 1998 (CPR), which relates to children and protected parties, requires a "protected party" (in other words, someone who lacks capacity to conduct the proceedings) to have a litigation friend to conduct the proceedings on their behalf.

Martin Masterman-Lister was born in 1963. After leaving school, he became an apprentice technician with British Aerospace and on 9 September 1980, while he was on his way to work on a motorbike, he overtook a vehicle on a bend and collided with a milk float owned by Home Counties Dairies and driven by Mr Jewell. Martin sustained various orthopaedic injuries and a head injury.

Brutton & Co, Solicitors, acted for him in the subsequent personal injury proceedings, and in September 1987, on counsel's advice, the claim settled for £76,000—half its value on full liability on account of Martin's contributory

---

[1] [2006] EWCA Civ 51; [2006] C.P. Rep. 26 per Arden LJ at [125].
[2] [2002] EWCA Civ 1889; [2003] 1 W.L.R. 1511.

negligence. Several years later, Martin came around to thinking that his claim may have been settled at an under-value and he sought to re-open it.

His new solicitors—Stewarts—obtained a medical report from an expert in acquired brain injury, Dr Martyn Rose of St Andrew's Hospital, Northampton, who was of the opinion that Martin was a patient for the purposes of Part VII of the Mental Health Act 1983, and that he had been a patient ever since his accident in 1980. This view was shared by Dr Graham Powell, a leading clinical neuropsychologist. The defendants, however, obtained reports from equally distinguished medical practitioners and clinical psychologists to support their contention that Martin was not a patient. Essentially, if he were a patient, time would not have run against him under the Limitation Act 1980 and he could re-open the case, because the original settlement would have been a nullity, as it had not been approved by the court.

The trial began before Mr Justice Wright on 28 January 2002 and lasted 15 days. The judge upheld some earlier unreported English authorities on the capacity to manage one's property and affairs and whether a person is or is not a patient or protected party. He concluded that Martin may very well have been a patient for the first three years after his accident in 1980, but that he had not been a patient since 1983; that he had survived for the last 20 years without any major or even minor catastrophe; and that his affairs had, in fact, been perfectly adequately managed. Accordingly, the claim was statute-barred.

2–005

Martin appealed and the Court of Appeal heard matter over five days in November 2002 and handed down its judgment on 19 December 2002. It upheld Mr Justice Wright's decision and in the process hived off the capacity to litigate from the capacity to manage one's property and affairs generally. In particular, Lord Justice Chadwick held that[3]:

> "For the purposes of [Part 21 of the CPR] the test to be applied, as it seems to me, is whether the party to legal proceedings is capable of understanding, with the assistance of such proper explanation from legal advisers and experts in other disciplines as the case may require, the issues on which his consent or decision is likely to be necessary in the course of those proceedings. If he has capacity to understand that which he needs to understand in order to pursue or defend a claim, I can see no reason why the law—whether substantive or procedural—should require the interposition of a [litigation friend]."

And he added[4]:

> "More pertinently, I reject the submission that a person who would be incapable of taking investment decisions in relation to a large sum received as compensation is to be held, for that reason, to be incapable of pursuing a claim for that compensation."

Cases after Masterman-Lister

The Queen's Bench Division (QBD) of the High Court is the usual forum for adjudicating on major personal injury claims and, following the Court of Appeal's decision in *Masterman-Lister*, there was a series of cases in the QBD

2–006

---

[3] *Masterman-Lister v Jewell* [2002] EWCA Civ 1889 at [75].
[4] *Masterman-Lister v Jewell* [2002] EWCA Civ 1889 at [83].

which sought to dissect the capacity to litigate into discrete decisions relating to the various decisions that a claimant may have to make during the course of personal injury proceedings.[5] This process came to a climax in *Bailey v Warren*,[6] the facts of which were as follows.

Late at night on 3 May 1998, Ronald Bailey was crossing a four-lane dual-carriageway in Stockport, on his way home from the pub, when he was knocked down by a car driven by Matthew Warren. He suffered a severe head injury. He got in touch with some solicitors and in November 2000, after consulting his family, he agreed to accept an offer made by Mr Warren's insurers to compromise liability on a 50:50 basis. Proceedings were commenced in April 2001, though it was not until 4 December 2001 that the court formally entered judgment in his favour for 50% of the full liability of damages to be assessed. In July 2003 Professor Neary, a neurologist, expressed the view that Mr Bailey was a protected party (or "patient", to use the expression that appeared in the legislation at that time). The district judge ordered that a litigation friend be appointed and referred the question of when and for what periods Mr Bailey had been a patient to a judge of the QBD to decide.

The judge, Mr Justice Holland, found that Mr Bailey had been a patient on 4 December 2001, when judgment on liability was entered, but not in November 2000, when he agreed to compromise his claim on a 50:50 basis, and directed that the 50:50 apportionment should stand. In reaching this decision, the judge considered that a distinction could be drawn between the claimant's understanding of the issues relating to liability and his understanding of the issues relating to quantum, and that Mr Bailey had had sufficient understanding in respect of the extent of his liability.

Mr Bailey appealed to the Court of Appeal, which is a three-judge tribunal. One of the principal issues was whether litigation capacity should be assessed in the context of discrete decisions or the conduct of the proceedings as a whole. There was a 2:1 majority decision. The dissenting judge was Lady Justice Hallett, who said[7]:

> "It is becoming increasingly common for the issues of liability and quantum to be split and separate trials ordered. Thus, within the ambit of the Civil Procedure Rules the word 'issue' will often encompass the issue of liability alone and the ethos of the CPR is to encourage issues to be dealt with separately if they can be done fairly and cost effectively. In my judgment the construction [leading counsel] seeks to put on the words 'issue' and 'transaction' would be to give ordinary English words an extraordinary meaning. Transaction is usually defined as 'a piece of business done'. In my view, in the present case, the issue was the issue of liability and the piece of business done was the compromise of the issue of liability not the conduct of the whole of the litigation."

2–007   By contrast, Lady Justice Arden (with whom Lord Justice Ward agreed) said that[8]:

---

[5] For example: *Mitchell v Alasia* [2005] EWHC 11 (QB); *Lindsay v Wood* [2006] EWHC 2895 (QB); *Folks v Faizey* [2006] EWCA Civ 381; *Saulle v Nouvet* [2007] EWHC 2902 (QB).
[6] [2006] EWCA Civ 51.
[7] *Bailey v Warren* [2006] EWCA Civ 51 at [73] and [74].
[8] *Bailey v Warren* [2006] EWCA Civ 51 at [122] and [123]. Lord Justice Ward's approval is at [176].

"I do not think that a distinction can be drawn in this way. Obviously, where the transaction is self-contained and clearly separate from other matters, it is easy to determine the issue to which capacity should be related. Examples would include the making of a gift or the making of a will. It may not be so easy, however, to determine the issue to which capacity should be related where the transaction is multi-faceted, and a choice exists as to whether to break the transaction down into its component parts, to which capacity is related seriatim, or to treat the transaction as a single indivisible whole. A will may consist of a series of gifts but on the authorities the question of capacity is assessed in relation to the will as a whole. A person making a will is not making a series of separate decisions as to gifts but is making a decision as to the nature and effect of the claims of all the persons who might have claims upon him. Thus the gifts are interdependent and connected. Likewise this court in the *Masterman-Lister* case considered that litigation down to the administration of any award of damages was to be treated as a single transaction and not as a series of individual steps. Kennedy LJ regarded this conclusion as one of common sense (para.27).

It seems to me that the right approach must be to ask as a matter of common sense whether the individual steps formed part of a larger sequence of events which should be seen as one, or whether they were in fact self-contained steps which were not connected with each other."

Lady Justice Arden added that[9]:

"One of [leading counsel's] submissions was that, if the judge were right, the solicitors would have to assess their client's capacity on a number of occasions in the course of litigation. A separate assessment might thus have to be made as to capacity to decide whether to issue a pre-action letter, whether to accept an offer on liability, whether to accept an offer on quantum and whether to issue proceedings and so on. The conclusion that I prefer avoids that result. I accept that, if an assessment of the client's capacity in relation to transactions occurring before the start of the litigation but closely connected with it, has to be in relation to each individual transaction, the law would impractical. That is one of the reasons why I prefer the conclusion that the appropriate test in this case is whether the client had capacity to start proceedings. That would include the question whether he would have capacity for the purposes of an offer of compromise. I would add that, in my judgment, where a client seeks damages for personal injury because he has suffered a brain injury, capacity is a question that ought in general routinely to be considered by those representing him. In cases of doubt, this will usually mean that the solicitor has to arrange for a medical opinion to be obtained."

Lady Justice Arden then summarised the following matters that should be taken into account when assessing someone's capacity to conduct proceedings[10]:

"The assessment of capacity to conduct proceedings depends to some extent on the nature of the proceedings in contemplation. I can only indicate some of the matters to be considered in assessing a client's capacity. The client would need to understand how the proceedings were to be funded. He would need to know about the chances of not succeeding and about the risk of an adverse order as to costs. He would need to have capacity to make the sort of decisions that are likely to arise in litigation. Capacity to conduct such proceedings would include the capacity to give proper instructions for and to approve the particulars of claim, and to approve a compromise. For a client to have capacity to approve a compromise, he would need

---

[9] *Bailey v Warren* [2006] EWCA Civ 51 at [125].
[10] *Bailey v Warren* [2006] EWCA Civ 51 at [125].

insight into the compromise, an ability to instruct his solicitors to advise him on it, and an understanding of their advice and an ability to weigh their advice. So far as Mr Bailey was concerned, the receipt of damages could have a substantial impact upon him. He would need to know what he was giving up and what would happen if he refused to accept the offer of compromise."

In *Dunhill v Burgin*,[11] the Supreme Court held that the test of capacity to conduct proceedings for the purpose of CPR Part 21 is the capacity to conduct the claim or cause of action which the claimant in fact has, rather than to conduct the claim as formulated by her lawyers.

In *TB v KB*,[12] Mr Justice Macdonald observed that:

"In addition, the nature of the *dispute* is not the only component of the relevant subject matter required to be considered in the context of determining whether a litigant has capacity to conduct proceedings. More fundamentally, the nature of legal proceedings themselves, and in particular the specific demands they make on litigants, also fall to be considered. I accept Dr Barker's characterisation of legal proceedings as not being simply a question of providing instruction to a lawyer and then sitting back and observing the litigation, but rather a dynamic transactional process, both prior to and in court, with information to be recalled, instructions to be given, advice to be received and decisions to be taken, potentially on a number of occasions over the span of the proceedings as they develop. ... [L]egal proceedings are not a 'one off' decision but rather a process of decision making that requires the ongoing ability to recall information in the context of an evolving situation and the ability to use and weigh that information in the context in which it is needed in the proceedings."

Where medical evidence cannot be obtained

2–008   Although there is no requirement in CPR Part 21 for a judge to consider medical evidence, or to be satisfied as to incapacity before a party to civil proceedings is to be treated as a protected party, the court should always, as a matter of practice, at the earliest opportunity, investigate the question of capacity whenever there is reason to suspect that a party to the proceedings may lack capacity. This means that, even where the issue is not contentious, a judge who is responsible for case management will almost certainly require the assistance of a medical report before being able to be satisfied that the party lacks capacity.

In the case of *Baker Tilly v Makar*[13] Mira Makar was a litigant in person in proceedings relating to the assessment of the costs she was required to pay to Baker Tilly, a firm of accountants. The sum claimed by Baker Tilly was £520,340. During the hearing before the Costs Master, Ms Makar became distressed, left the room, and lay rolling on the floor outside screaming. The Costs Master was concerned that she may lack capacity to conduct the litigation, but she absolutely refused to let anyone assess her capacity or access her medical records. The Costs Master eventually decided that she lacked capacity and Ms Makar appealed his decision. The judge allowed the appeal and said that medical evidence would ordinarily be required before a court would make a finding of lack of capacity on the ground of an impairment of the mind or brain, but its

---

[11] [2014] UKSC 18; [2014] C.O.P.L.R. 199 at [18].
[12] *TB v KB (Capacity to Conduct Proceedings)* [2019] EWCOP 14 at [29] and [36].
[13] [2013] EWHC 759 (QB); [2013] C.O.P.L.R. 245.

absence could not be a bar to making such a finding. Where circumstances arise in which medical evidence cannot be obtained, the court should be most cautious before making such a finding. The Master had given too much weight to one incident and had not taken into account Ms Makar's appearances before other judges, and his finding of fact of incapacity should be set aside.

Capacity to manage one's property and financial affairs

> "The general concept of managing affairs is an ongoing act and, therefore, quite unlike the specific act of making a will or making a [lasting] power of attorney. The management of affairs relates to a continuous state of affairs whose demands may be unpredictable and may occasionally be urgent."[14]

2–009

The leading case on the capacity to manage one's property and affairs is the decision in *Masterman-Lister v Brutton & Co, Masterman-Lister v Jewell*,[15] in which the Court of Appeal upheld the decision of the first instance judge, Mr Justice Wright.[16] He had approved and applied two previously unreported decisions, one in the Court of Protection, and the other in the QBD. They were:

(1) Mr Justice Wilberforce's decision on 23 March 1962 in *Re C.A.F.*[17] Although there is no surviving transcript of his decision, the judgment of the then Master of the Court of Protection, which Mr Justice Wilberforce upheld on appeal, had survived and the case was cited in a footnote in Heywood & Massey, *Court of Protection Practice* as authority for the proposition that

> "the question of the degree of incapacity of managing and administering a patient's property and affairs must be related to the circumstances, including the state in which the alleged patient lives and the complexity and importance of the property and affairs he has to manage or administer."

C.A.F. was the granddaughter of an earl and the widow of an ambassador and lived in a Grade II* Georgian house set in a thousand acres of parkland. She suffered several strokes in 1957, when she was 66, and started giving away some rather valuable heirlooms. Her son applied to be appointed as her receiver and C.A.F. opposed the application, but was unsuccessful, both at first instance and on appeal.

(2) Mr Justice Boreham's decision in a personal injury claim, *White v Fell*, on 12 November 1987. He held that the meaning of the expression "incapable of managing his property and affairs" should be construed in a common sense way as a whole. Few people have the capacity to manage all their affairs unaided, and whether they are capable of managing their property and affairs depends on whether they are capable of taking, considering, and acting upon appropriate advice.

---

[14] *A v X* [2012] EWHC 2400 (COP); [2013] C.O.P.L.R. 1 per Hedley J at [41].
[15] [2002] EWCA Civ 1889; [2003] 1 W.L.R. 1511.
[16] *Masterman-Lister v Jewell* [2002] EWHC 417 (QB).
[17] SI 1961/2367.

Capacity to manage property and affairs: a checklist

2–010 Mr Justice Wright, the first instance judge in *Masterman-Lister*, also approved the following checklist, which appeared in the first edition of *Assessment of Mental Capacity: Guidance for Doctors and Lawyers*, published jointly by the British Medical Association and the Law Society in 1995, which to a large extent incorporated the principles identified in *Re C.A.F*, and *White v Fell*.[18]

The extent of the person's property and affairs

2–011 This would include an examination of:

- the value of the person's income and capital (including savings and the value of the home);
- financial needs and responsibilities;
- whether there are likely to be any changes in the person's financial circumstances in the foreseeable future;
- the skill, specialised knowledge, and time it takes to manage the affairs properly, and whether a mental disorder is affecting the management of the assets; and
- whether the person would be likely to seek, understand and act upon appropriate advice where needed in view of the complexity of the affairs.

Personal information

2–012 Personal information about the patient might include:

- age;
- life expectancy;
- psychiatric history;
- prospects of recovery or deterioration;
- the extent to which the incapacity could fluctuate;
- the condition in which the person lives;
- family background;
- family and social responsibilities; and
- the degree of back-up and support the person receives or could expect to receive from others.

The person's vulnerability

2–013 Other issues which should be considered might be:

- could inability to manage the property and affairs lead to the person making rash or irresponsible decisions?
- could inability to manage lead to exploitation by others—perhaps even members of the person's family?

---

[18] *Masterman-Lister v Jewell* [2002] EWHC 417 (QB) at [25].

- could inability to manage lead to the position of other people being compromised or jeopardised?

Capacity to enter into a contract

Contractual capacity

The test for contractual capacity is whether a person is capable of understanding the nature and effect of the particular contract he is entering into.[19] So the degree of capacity required will vary according to the complexity of the transaction. A low degree of understanding might be required for a simple contract, such as renewing a Senior Railcard, whereas a more complicated transaction, such as entering into an equity release scheme, would require a higher degree of understanding.

2–014

Contracts made by persons lacking capacity are voidable

With the exception of a contract for "necessaries", a contract made by someone who lacked capacity to make it at the material time is voidable, but not void. This means that the contract is binding upon him (even if it is unfair),[20] unless he can show that the other party knew of his incapacity at the material time or ought to have been aware of it.[21]

2–015

Necessary goods or services

A different rule applies in respect of "necessaries". Section 3 of the Sale of Goods Act 1979 (as amended), which is headed "Capacity to buy and sell", provides that:

2–016

"(1) Capacity to buy and sell is regulated by the general law concerning capacity to contract and to transfer and acquire property.
(2) Where necessaries are sold and delivered to a minor or to a person who by reason of mental incapacity or drunkenness is incompetent to contract, he must pay a reasonable price for them.
(3) In subsection (2) above 'necessaries' means goods suitable to the condition in life of the minor or other person concerned and to his actual requirements at the time of the sale and delivery."

Section 7 of the MCA 2005, which is headed "Payment for necessary goods and services", says broadly the same thing:

"(1) If necessary goods or services are supplied to a person who lacks capacity to contract for the supply, he must pay a reasonable price for them.
(2) 'Necessary' means suitable to a person's condition in life and to his actual requirements at the time when the goods or services are supplied."

---

[19] *Boughton v Knight* (1872-75) L.R. 3 P. & D. 64 at 72.
[20] *Hart v O'Connor* [1985] A.C. 1000.
[21] *Imperial Loan Co Ltd v Stone* [1892] 1 QB 599. See also *Dunhill v Burgin* [2014] UKSC 18; [2014] 1 W.L.R. 933 at [25].

ASSESSING CAPACITY: THE LAW

The Mental Capacity Act Code of Practice gives the following commentary on these provisions[22]:

> "The aim is to make sure that people can enjoy a similar standard of living and way of life to those they had before lacking capacity. For example, if a person who now lacks capacity previously chose to buy expensive designer clothes, these are still necessary goods—as long as they can still afford them. But they would not be necessary for a person who always wore cheap clothes, no matter how wealthy they were. Goods are not necessary if the person already has a sufficient supply of them. For example, buying one or two pairs of shoes for a person who lacks capacity could be necessary. But a dozen pairs would probably not be necessary."

Capacity to make a lasting power of attorney

2–017 A lasting power of attorney (LPA) is a deed in which one person ("the donor") confers upon one or more other persons ("the attorney(s)") the authority to act on the donor's behalf. An LPA cannot be used until it has been registered with the Office of the Public Guardian (OPG), and the power of attorney lasts, or remains in force, after the donor has lost capacity.

The two types of lasting power of attorney

2–018 There are two types of LPA:

(1) An LPA for financial decisions (LP1F), which, subject to any restrictions or conditions contained in the LPA itself, enables the attorney to make decisions about the donor's property and financial affairs, including:
   (a) selling the donor's house;
   (b) running the donor's bank or savings account;
   (c) managing or selling the donor's investments;
   (d) receiving the donor's income; and
   (e) paying the donor's bills.
(2) An LPA for health and care decisions (LP1H), which enables the attorney to make decisions about the type of health care and medical treatment the donor receives, including life-sustaining treatment, where the donor lives, and day-to-day matters such as the donor's diet and daily routine. These decisions can only be made by the attorney(s) if the donor is incapable at the material time of making the decision personally.

The packs provided by the Office of the Public Guardian

2–019 A pack of forms may be obtained from the OPG or downloaded from GOV.UK. The complete pack consists of:

- LP1F or LP1H—the prescribed form of LPA and the application for registration.

---

[22] Mental Capacity Act Code of Practice, paras 6.58 and 6.59.

COMMON LAW TESTS OF CAPACITY

- LP3—"Form to notify people". This form only needs to be completed if there are "people to notify" (also called "people to be told" or "named people") listed in the LPA.
- LP12—"Make and register your lasting power of attorney: a guide". The guide is 47 pages long.
- LPA120—"LPA and EPA fees". This sets out the fees payable with effect from April 2017. The application for registration fee is £82. The application for repeat registration is £41. The form also explains the circumstances in which an exemption or remission is available.
- LPC—"Continuation sheets". There are four different continuation sheets:
  (1) Continuation sheet 1—Additional people;
  (2) Continuation sheet 2—Additional information;
  (3) Continuation sheet 3—If the donor cannot sign or make a mark;
  (4) Continuation sheet 4—Trust corporation appointed as an attorney in an LPA for property and financial affairs.

The digital lasting power of attorney service

Alternatively, the digital LPA service helps a donor make an LPA online. The donor is asked some questions and for each question will need to give some information or make choices. There are links to detailed guidance. The donor can stop at any time and save the information that has already been entered. Donors may want to do this if they need longer to think about a decision or to discuss the LPA with someone. They can sign back in when they are ready to continue. 2–020

With the digital LPA service the donor cannot complete the whole process online—they need to print and sign their LPA and send it to the OPG to be registered. They also need to print the completed LPA document so that they and the other people involved can sign it. The law currently requires an LPA to be a paper document with handwritten signatures or marks. Accordingly, there are three stages:

(1) creating the LPA online and paying the registration fee online;
(2) printing and signing the LPA: making sure that all the required people sign the LPA in the correct order; and
(3) posting the LPA to the OPG, including all documentary evidence required (for example, to pay a reduced fee), as well as a cheque if the applicant is not paying online.

The prescribed form

An LPA must be in the form prescribed by the current Lasting Powers of Attorney, Enduring Powers of Attorney and Public Guardian Regulations at the time when it is signed by the donor. 2–021

There have been three prescribed forms for each type of LPA since the MCA 2005 came into force on 1 October 2007. The current forms are those prescribed by the Lasting Power of Attorney, Enduring Powers of Attorney and Public Guardian (Amendment) Regulations 2015 (SI 2015/899), which came into force on 1 July 2015. They can be downloaded from the OPG's website.

ASSESSING CAPACITY: THE LAW

In the prescribed form of LPA for financial decisions, form LP1F:

(1) Section 1 contains the donor's name, address, date of birth and email address (optional).

(2) Section 2 contains the attorneys' names, addresses, dates of birth and email addresses.

(3) Section 3 asks "How should your attorneys make decisions?" If only one attorney is to be appointed, tick the relevant box. If more than one attorney is to be appointed, there are three options: (a) jointly and severally, where the attorneys can make decisions on their own or together; (b) jointly, where the attorneys have to act unanimously; and (c) jointly for some decisions and jointly and severally for other decisions, which the donor has to specify.

(4) Section 4, on replacement attorneys, is optional.

(5) Section 5, "When can your attorneys make decisions?" requires the donor to tick one of two boxes: (a) as soon as my LPA has been registered, or (b) only when I do not have mental capacity.

(6) Section 6, listing the people to notify when the LPA is registered, is optional. A maximum of five people can be notified.

(7) Section 7 contains the donor's "preferences" and "instructions". The attorneys do not have to follow the donor's preferences, but should bear them in mind. They do have to follow the donor's instructions.

(8) Section 8 sets out "Your legal rights and responsibilities". Everyone signing the LPA (i.e. the donor, the certificate provider, and the attorneys) must read this information.

(9) Section 9 is where the donor signs the LPA in the presence of a witness who is aged 18 or over. An attorney or replacement attorney cannot witness the donor's signature.

(10) Section 10 is for the certificate provider. The certificate provider signs to confirm they have discussed the lasting power of attorney (LPA) with the donor, that the donor understands what they are doing and that nobody is forcing them to do it. The certificate provider should be either:
    (a) someone who has known the donor personally for at least two years, such as a friend, neighbour, colleague or former colleague;
    (b) someone with relevant professional skills, such as the donor's GP, a healthcare professional or a solicitor.
A certificate provider cannot be one of the attorneys.

(11) Section 11 is where the attorney or replacement attorney signs the LPA in the presence of a witness aged 18 or over. The donor cannot witness an attorney's or replacement attorney's signature. Section 11 must not be signed until after the certificate provider has signed section 10.

After section 11, the form states "Now register your LPA", and the remainder of the form contains the application for registration.

(12) Section 12 must be completed by the applicant, who can be either the donor or an attorney (all the attorneys if they were appointed to act jointly). The donor and attorneys should not apply together.
(13) Section 13 asks "Who do you want to receive the LPA?" There are three choices:
(a) the donor,
(b) the attorney(s), or
(c) someone else, such as a solicitor.
(14) Section 14 is about the application fee of £82.[23] It asks whether the applicant would like to pay by card or by cheque or whether they wish to pay a reduced fee (either completely exempted or with a 50% remission). Section 14 also covers the repeat application fee of £55 if a previous application was made no more than three months ago and it was not possible at that time for the OPG to register the LPA.
(15) Section 15 is where the applicant signs.

The completed form should then be sent to the Office of the Public Guardian, PO Box 16185, Birmingham B2 2WH.

The prescribed form of LPA for health and care decisions (LP1H) is essentially the same as LP1F, except for section 5, in which the donor must choose whether the attorneys can give or refuse consent to life-sustaining treatment on the donor's behalf. Life-sustaining treatment means care, surgery, medicine or other medical assistance to keep the donor alive, for example:

(1) a serious operation, such as a heart bypass or organ transplant;
(2) cancer treatment; and
(3) artificial nutrition or hydration (food or water given other than by mouth).

The certificate provider

The certificate provider must read LPA sections 8 and 10 before they sign the LPA. They can then fill in their name and address, and sign and date section 10. The "certificate provider" signs to confirm that:

(1) they have discussed the LPA with the donor,
(2) the donor understands what they are doing and that nobody is forcing them to do it.

The "certificate provider" should be either:

(1) someone who has known the donor personally for at least two years, such as a friend, neighbour, colleague or former colleague; or
(2) someone with relevant professional skills, such as the donor's GP, a healthcare professional or a solicitor.

---

[23] Public Guardian (Fees, etc.) (Amendment) Regulations 2017 (SI 2017/503) reg.3.

ASSESSING CAPACITY: THE LAW

The certificate provider cannot be[24]:

(1) an attorney or replacement attorney named in this LPA or any other LPA or enduring power of attorney for the donor;
(2) a member of the donor's family or of any of the attorneys' families, including husbands, wives, civil partners, in-laws and step-relatives;
(3) an unmarried partner, boyfriend or girlfriend of either the donor or one of the attorneys (whether or not they live at the same address);
(4) the donor's or an attorney's business partner;
(5) the donor's or an attorney's employee; and
(6) an owner, manager, director or employee of a care home where the donor lives.

The test for capacity to create a lasting power of attorney

2–023 It has been possible for a donor to create an LPA since the MCA 2005 came into force on 1 October 2007. Prior to that, it was possible to create an Enduring Power of Attorney (EPA). The Enduring Powers of Attorney Act 1985 came into force on 10 March 1986 and was repealed by MCA 2005. Since 1 October 2007 it has no longer been possible to create an EPA, but applications can still be made to the OPG to register EPAs made before that date.

The capacity required to create an EPA was described by Mr Justice Hoffmann (later Lord Hoffmann), in *Re K; Re F*,[25] in the following terms:

> "First (if such be the terms of the power), that the attorney will be able to assume complete authority over the donor's affairs). Secondly (if such be the terms of the power), that the attorney will in general be able to do anything with the donor's property which he could have done. Thirdly, that the authority will continue if the donor should be or become mentally incapable. Fourthly, that if he should be or become mentally incapable, the power will be irrevocable without confirmation by the court."

There are several differences between an EPA and an LPA, and it is suggested that the donor of an LPA would need to know:

(1) Who the attorneys are.
(2) What authority they have: in other words, what decisions they can lawfully make.
(3) That the LPA cannot be used until it has been registered by the OPG.
(4) That the LPA will remain in force if the donor becomes mentally incapable.
(5) There is a change of emphasis between an LPA for financial decisions and an LPA for health and care decisions. In particular, the attorney under an LPA for health and care can only make decisions that the donor is incapable of making himself at the time the decision needs to be made.

---

[24] The list of persons who are disqualified from giving an LPA certificate can be found in the Lasting Powers of Attorney, Enduring Powers of Attorney and Public Guardian Regulations 2007 (SI 2007/1253) reg.8(3).
[25] [1988] 1 All E.R. 358.

COMMON LAW TESTS OF CAPACITY

(6) Unlike an EPA, the donor can revoke an LPA at any time, provided that he has the capacity to do so, without the need for the Court of Protection to confirm the revocation.
(7) The authority created by an LPA, unlike an EPA, is subject to the provisions of the MCA 2005, and in particular section 1 (the principles) and section 4 (best interests).
(8) The statutory definition of incapacity in the MCA 2005 requires the donor to be aware of the foreseeable consequences of making or not making an LPA.

Capacity to revoke a lasting power of attorney

The donor may revoke an LPA at any time when he has capacity to do so.[26] The MCA 2005 does not set out what is required to revoke an LPA. There is no presumption that a later LPA automatically revokes an earlier LPA, though an act that is inconsistent with the continued operation of an LPA might amount to implied revocation. The completion of the certificate provider's certificate in a subsequent LPA is not proof by implication that the donor had capacity to revoke an LPA; only capacity to grant one.[27] The most satisfactory way of revoking an LPA is to execute a deed of revocation and immediately to serve notice of the revocation on the attorneys under the existing LPA. There is no prescribed form of deed of revocation in the LPA regulations.

2–024

As far as the donor's capacity is concerned, it was suggested, that the donor should understand[28]:

(1) who the attorney is, or who the attorneys are; and, if more than one, whether they were appointed to act jointly or jointly and severally;
(2) what authority they have;
(3) why it is necessary or expedient to revoke the LPA; and
(4) the foreseeable consequences of revoking the LPA.

The foreseeable consequences might be:

(1) that the donor personally makes decisions about his property and affairs or health and welfare;
(2) that it may be necessary or expedient to create a new LPA; or
(3) that the Court of Protection will have to appoint a deputy to make property and financial decisions or health and welfare decisions on behalf of the donor, if the donor is incapable of making such decisions himself.

Capacity to make a will—testamentary capacity

The time at which testamentary capacity is required

A person should have testamentary capacity at two stages:

2–025

---

[26] MCA 2005 s.13(2).
[27] *Re Cloutt* unreported 7 November 2008.
[28] *Re S* unreported 1 March 1997 and confirmed in *Re KJP* [2016] EWCOP 6 at [48]–[50].

ASSESSING CAPACITY: THE LAW

(1) when giving instructions to a solicitor for the preparation of a will or, if the will is written or typed by the testator personally, at the time of writing or typing it; and
(2) when the will is executed.

However, where the testator becomes ill, or their condition deteriorates, between giving instructions and executing the will, the rule in *Parker v Felgate*[29] may apply. This rule was approved and applied by the Court of Appeal in *Perrins v Holland*[30] to declare a will valid where the testator had given instructions in April 2000 but did not execute the will until September 2001, at which point it was accepted that he lacked testamentary capacity. The Court of Appeal summarised the rule as follows:

> "Where the testator loses some of his faculties between giving instructions and executing the will ... one must then ask
> (i) whether at the time he gave the instructions he had the ability to understand and give proper consideration to the various matters which are called for, that is, whether he had testamentary capacity,
> (ii) whether the document gives effect to his instructions,
> (iii) whether those instructions continued to reflect his intentions, and
> (iv) whether at the time he executed the will he knew what he was doing and thus had sufficient mental capacity to carry out the juristic act which that involves.
> If all those questions can be answered in the affirmative, one can be satisfied that the will accurately reflects the deceased's intentions formed at a time when he was capable of making fully informed decisions."

The test in Banks v Goodfellow

2–026 The capacity to make a will is often referred to as "testamentary capacity" and the person who makes a will is known as the "testator" if he is a man, and "testatrix" if she is a woman. The requirements for testamentary capacity were described by the Chief Justice in *Banks v Goodfellow* as follows, though the original text did not contain bullet points[31]:

> "It is essential that a testator shall:
> • understand the nature of the act and its effects;
> • shall understand the extent of the property of which he is disposing;
> • shall be able to comprehend and appreciate the claims to which he ought to give effect;
> • and with a view to the latter object, that no disorder of mind shall poison his affections, pervert his sense of right, or prevent the exercise of his natural faculties—that no insane delusion shall influence his will in disposing of his property and bring about a disposal of it which, if the mind had been sound, would not have been made."

The test in *Banks v Goodfellow* was considered in *Perrins v Holland* by Mr Justice Lewison, who said that:

---

[29] (1883) 8 P.D. 171; (1883) 52 L.J.P. 95 PDAD.
[30] [2010] EWCA Civ 840; [2011] Ch. 270.
[31] (1869-70) L.R. 5 Q.B. 549 at 565.

COMMON LAW TESTS OF CAPACITY

"There are six points that I should make. First, since the test is a common law test it is capable of being influenced by contemporary attitudes. Second, our general understanding of impaired mental capacity of adults has increased enormously since 1870. Third, we now recognise that an adult with impaired mental capacity is capable of making some decisions for himself, given help. Thus, fourth, we recognise that the test of mental capacity is not monolithic, but is tailored to the task in hand. Fifth, contemporary attitudes towards adults with impaired capacity are more respectful of adult autonomy. Sixth, even the traditional test must be applied to the context of the particular testator and the particular estate. A testator with a complex estate and many potential beneficiaries may need a greater degree of cognitive capability than one with a simple estate and few claimants ...

> 'The criteria in *Banks v Goodfellow* are not matters that are directly medical questions, in the way that a question whether a person is suffering from cancer is a medical question. They are matters for common sense judicial judgment on the basis of the whole of the evidence. Medical evidence as to the medical condition of a deceased may of course be highly relevant, and may sometimes directly support or deny a capacity in the deceased to have understanding of the matters in the *Banks v Goodfellow* criteria. However, evidence of such understanding may come from non-expert witnesses. Indeed, perhaps the most compelling evidence of understanding would be reliable evidence (for example, a tape recording) of a detailed conversation with the deceased at the time of the will displaying understanding of the deceased's assets, the deceased's family and the effects of the will. It is extremely unlikely that medical evidence that the deceased did not understand these things would overcome the effect of evidence of such a conversation'."[32]

In a consultation paper on *Making a will*, published on 13 July 2017, the Law Commission discussed various differences between the test in *Banks v Goodfellow* and the test for mental capacity set out in the MCA 2005, and observed that:

> "There is one obvious criticism about the law here: it is uncertain. The uncertainty matters because potential differences between the two tests have been identified. It also matters because the fact of the existence of two tests, and any differences between them, may cause confusion to those responsible for undertaking capacity assessments and make it that much more difficult for them to develop knowledge and expertise in relation to assessing testamentary capacity."[33]

For these reasons, the Law Commission provisionally proposed that "the test for mental capacity set out in the MCA 2005 should be adopted for testamentary capacity and that the specific elements of capacity necessary to make a will should be outlined in the MCA Code of Practice".[34]

---

[32] *Perrins v Holland* [2009] EWHC 1945 (Ch) at [40].
[33] Law Commission Consultation Paper 231, *Making a Will* (2017), p.29, para.2.45.
[34] Law Commission Consultation Paper 231, *Making a Will* (2017), p.35, consultation question 3.

ASSESSING CAPACITY: THE LAW

Capacity to make a will—"the golden rule"

2–027   Although its origins are historical, "the golden rule" was first described as such the case of *Kenward v Adams*[35]:

> "When a solicitor is drawing up a will for an aged testator or one who has been seriously ill, it should be witnessed or approved by a medical practitioner, who ought to record his examination of the testator and his findings. That was the golden if tactless rule, Mr Justice Templeman said when finding that the testatrix, Mrs Martha Price, retired hospital almoner of Mitcham, did not have testamentary capacity when she signed a second will in 1972 or the capacity to revoke a will of 1951 by destroying it, if in fact she did destroy it. Other precautions were that, if there was an earlier will, it should be examined and any proposed alterations should be discussed with the testator."

The same judge, Mr Justice Templeman, repeated the golden rule two years later in *Re Simpson (Deceased)*,[36] and added that, wherever possible, in cases of borderline capacity it is preferable that the testator be seen by a solicitor who knows him.

More recently the following comments have been made on the golden rule by various judges:

(1) "Miss Hall not only fully complied with this, but did everything conceivably possible, short of submitting Mr Adam to a wholly impracticable full scale series of neurophysiological tests and examinations, to satisfy herself that Mr Adam had testamentary capacity. Mr Cooper, on behalf of the appellants, came quite close to submitting that such meticulous compliance with the golden rule should in principle be determinative. In our view, this would go too far. The opinion of a general practitioner, unimpeachable in itself and supported by that of one or more solicitors, may nevertheless very occasionally be shown by other evidence to be wrong. The golden rule is a rule of solicitors' good practice, not a rule of law giving conclusive status to evidence obtained in compliance with the rule. Nevertheless, where a testator's apparent mental state is observed and recorded at the time when he actually executes the will in complete compliance with the rule and with the care with which it was in the present case; and where professional people concerned reached a properly informed and recorded conclusion that the testator does have testamentary capacity, it will require very persuasive evidence to enable the court to dislodge that conclusion." *Sharp v Adam*.[37]

(2) "Compliance with the Golden Rule does not, of course, operate as a touchstone of the validity of a will, nor does non-compliance demonstrate its invalidity. Its purpose, as has repeatedly been emphasised, is to assist in the avoidance of disputes, or at least in the minimisation of their scope. As the expert evidence in the present case confirms, persons with failing or

---

[35] Times, 29 November 1975; subsequently approved in *Buckenham v Dickinson* [2000] W.T.L.R. 1083; *Hoff v Atherton* [2005] W.T.L.R. 99; *Cattermole v Prisk* [2006] 1 F.L.R. 693; and in *Scammell v Farmer* [2008] EWHC 1100 (Ch) at [117]–[123].
[36] *Re Simpson (Deceased); Schaniel v Simpson* (1977) 121 S.J. 224.
[37] [2006] EWCA Civ 449 per May LJ at [27].

impaired mental faculties may, for perfectly understandable reasons, seek to conceal what they regard as their embarrassing shortcomings from persons with whom they deal, so that a friend or professional person such as a solicitor may fail to detect defects in mental capacity which would be or become apparent to a trained and experienced medical examiner, to whom a proper description of the legal test for testamentary capacity had first been provided." *Key v Key*.[38]

Capacity to revoke a will

A will can be revoked in one of three ways: 2–028

(1) by validly executing a new will, in which former wills and codicils are expressly revoked[39];
(2) by the testator subsequently entering into a marriage or civil partnership. An existing will is automatically revoked by operation of law, unless it was expressed to be made in contemplation of the marriage or civil partnership[40]; and
(3) by the testator personally burning, tearing or otherwise destroying the will with the intention of revoking it, or by the testator authorising someone else to burn, tear or destroy it in his presence and by his direction.[41]

The capacity to revoke a will by destruction was considered in *Re Sabatini*.[42] Ruth Sabatini was the divorced wife of the novelist Rafael Sabatini (1875–1950). In 1940 she made a will leaving her residuary estate to her nephew, Anthony. On 16 September 1965, when she was suffering from advanced dementia, she tore up the will. She died on 14 May 1966, aged 92. A total of seven nieces and nephews were equally entitled to her estate equally on her intestacy. Anthony contended that his aunt had lacked capacity to revoke the will. Counsel for the other nephews and nieces contended that a lower standard of capacity was acceptable when a will is revoked by destruction. The judge rejected this argument and said that, as a general rule, a testator must have the same degree of understanding, when destroying his will, as when he made it. It would be illogical if different methods of revocation were to be judged by different standards. In view of the evidence, the only possible conclusion was that the destruction of Mrs Sabatini's will was not a rational act, and that she was not of sound disposing mind, memory and understanding when she destroyed it.

Capacity to make a gift

The common law on capacity to make a gift has not developed an entirely 2–029 independent test of capacity, but instead has applied elements of two tests applicable to other transactions, namely the capacity to enter into a contract

---

[38] [2010] EWHC 408 (Ch); [2010] W.T.L.R. 623 per Briggs J at [8].
[39] Wills Act 1837 s.20.
[40] Wills Act 1837 ss.18 and 18B. Section 18B was inserted into the Wills Act 1837 by the Civil Partnership Act 2004 with effect from 5 December 2005.
[41] Wills Act 1837 s.20.
[42] (1969) 114 S.J. 35.

(essentially, being able to understand the nature and effect of the transaction) in respect of smaller gifts, and the capacity to make a will in respect of larger gifts.

The leading case on capacity to make a large gift is *Re Beaney (Deceased)*.[43] Mrs Beaney was a 64-year-old widow with three grown-up children. She lived with her elder daughter Valerie in a semi-detached house in Middlesex. In 1973, when she was suffering from advanced dementia, she signed a deed purporting to transfer her house to Valerie. She died intestate a year later and her estate was worth £1,150, whereas the house was worth £14,000. Her younger son and daughter applied to the court for a declaration that the transfer was void because their mother had lacked capacity when she signed it. The judge held that, in this case, the degree of understanding required was as high as that required to make a will. In the circumstances, Mrs Beaney had not been capable of making a valid transfer of the house, and the transfer was void and of no effect. In the course of his judgment, the judge said[44]:

> "The degree or extent of understanding required in respect of any instrument is relative to the particular transaction which it is to effect. In the case of a will, the degree required is always high. In the case of a contract, a deed made for consideration or a gift *inter vivos*, whether by deed or otherwise, the degree required varies with the circumstances of the transaction. Thus, at one extreme, if the subject-matter and value of a gift are trivial in relation to the donor's other assets, a low degree of understanding will suffice. But, at the other, if its effect is to dispose of the donor's only asset of value and thus for practical purposes to pre-empt the devolution of his estate under his will or on his intestacy, then the degree of understanding required is as high as that required for a will, and the donor must understand the claims of all potential donees and the extent of the property to be disposed of."

Although in most cases the relevant time to determine the donor's capacity is the time when the gift is made, the rule in *Parker v Felgate*[45] has also been applied in respect of inter vivos transactions. In *Singellos v Singellos*[46] Mrs Singellos had the necessary capacity when she gave instructions to her accountant, but when she signed the multiple documents involved she only understood that she was giving effect to her previous instructions. Declaring that the documents had been validly executed, the judge said[47]:

> "... if the *Parker v Felgate* approach is not applied to *inter vivos* dispositions, that will mean that the test of capacity applicable to *inter vivos* gifts may be more onerous than that applicable to testamentary dispositions. In the *Re Beaney* type of case, the full *Banks v Goodfellow* capacity test would be applicable but could only be applied at the date of execution of the deed even if it could have been satisfied when instructions for the deed were given. This seems counter-intuitive and illogical."

---

[43] [1978] 2 All E.R. 595.
[44] *Re Beaney (Deceased)* [1978] 2 All E.R. 595 per Martin Nourse QC at 601f–h.
[45] (1883) 8 P.D. 171; (1883) 52 L.J.P. 95 PDAD.
[46] [2010] EWHC 2353 (Ch); [2011] Ch. 324.
[47] *Singellos v Singellos* [2010] EWHC 2353 (Ch) per Andrew Simmonds QC at [167].

Capacity to marry or enter into a civil partnership

The leading case on capacity to marry is *Sheffield City Council v E*,[48] the facts of which were very briefly as follows. E was a 21-year-old woman with physical and intellectual disabilities. S, aged 37, was a Schedule 1 offender with a substantial history of sexually violent crimes, for which he had received a total sentence of eight years' imprisonment. They met in January 2004. She moved in with him in June 2004 and Sheffield City Council discovered that they planned to marry on 18 September 2004. The Council began proceedings to stop them marrying or associating and asserted that it was in E's best interests neither to marry nor to associate with S.

At [141] of the judgment Mr Justice Munby summarised his principal conclusions as follows:

> "(i) The question is *not* whether E has capacity to marry X rather than Y. The question is *not* (being specific) whether E has capacity to marry S. The relevant question is whether E has capacity to marry. If she does, it is not necessary to show that she also has capacity to take care of her own person and property.
> (ii) The question of whether E has capacity to marry is quite distinct from the question of whether E is wise to marry: either wise to marry at all, or wise to marry X rather than Y, or wise to marry S.
> (iii) In relation to her marriage the only question for the court is whether E has capacity to marry. The court has no jurisdiction to consider whether it is in E's best interests to marry or to marry S. The court is concerned with E's capacity to marry. It is not concerned with the wisdom of her marriage in general or her marriage to S in particular.
> (iv) In relation to the question of whether E has capacity to marry the law remains today as it was set out by Singleton LJ in *In the Estate of Park deceased, Park v Park* [1954] P. 112 at 127:Was the deceased ... capable of understanding the nature of the contract into which he was entering, or was his mental condition such that he was incapable of understanding it? To ascertain the nature of the contract of marriage a man must be mentally capable of appreciating that it involves the responsibilities normally attaching to marriage. Without that degree of mentality, it cannot be said that he understands the nature of the contract.
> (v) More specifically, it is not enough that someone appreciates that he or she is taking part in a marriage ceremony or understand its words.
> (vi) He or she must understand the nature of the marriage contract.
> (vii) This means that he or she must be mentally capable of understanding the duties and responsibilities that normally attach to marriage.
> (viii) That said, the contract of marriage is in essence a simple one, which does not require a high degree of intelligence to comprehend. The contract of marriage can readily be understood by anyone of normal intelligence.
> (ix) There are thus, in essence, two aspects to the inquiry whether someone has capacity to marry. (1) Does he or she understand the nature of the marriage contract? (2) Does he or she understand the duties and responsibilities that normally attach to marriage?
> (x) The duties and responsibilities that normally attach to marriage can be summarised as follows: Marriage, whether civil or religious, is a contract, formally entered into. It confers on the parties the status of husband and wife, the essence of the contract being an agreement between a man and a woman

---

[48] [2004] EWHC 2808 (Fam); [2005] Fam. 326.

to live together, and to love one another as husband and wife, to the exclusion of all others. It creates a relationship of mutual and reciprocal obligations, typically involving the sharing of a common home and a common domestic life and the right to enjoy each other's society, comfort and assistance."

Capacity to consent to medical treatment

2–031   In *Heart of England NHS Foundation Trust v JB*[49] Mr Justice Peter Jackson summarised capacity to consent to treatment (in this case, a partial amputation of the patient's right leg) as follows:

> "The question is whether JB can understand, retain and use and weigh the relevant information in coming to a decision. As in C's case, what is in my view required is that she should understand the nature, purpose and effects of the proposed treatment, the last of these entailing an understanding of the benefits and risks of deciding to have or not to have one or other of the various kinds of amputation, or of not making a decision at all.
>
> What is required here is a broad, general understanding of the kind that is expected from the population at large. JB is not required to understand every last piece of information about her situation and her options: even her doctors would not make that claim. It must also be remembered that common strategies for dealing with unpalatable dilemmas—for example indecision, avoidance or vacillation—are not to be confused with incapacity. We should not ask more of people whose capacity is questioned than of those whose capacity is undoubted."

In *Montgomery v Lanarkshire Health Board*[50] the UK Supreme Court held that[51]:

> "An adult person of sound mind is entitled to decide which, if any, of the available forms of treatment to undergo, and her consent must be obtained before treatment interfering with her bodily integrity is undertaken. The doctor is therefore under a duty to take reasonable care to ensure that the patient is aware of any material risks involved in any recommended treatment, and of any reasonable alternative or variant treatments. The test of materiality is whether, in the circumstances of the particular case, a reasonable person in the patient's position would be likely to attach significance to the risk, or the doctor is or should reasonably be aware that the particular patient would be likely to attach significance to it."

Capacity to consent to sexual relationships

2–032   On a number of occasions, both before and after the implementation of the MCA 2005, judges had formed the view that the test for capacity to consent to sexual relationships is general and issue specific, rather than person or event specific.

The information relevant to the decision that a person needs to understand is:

(1)   the mechanics of sexual intercourse in basic terms;
(2)   the reasonably foreseeable consequences of sexual intercourse; for example, the risks of pregnancy and of acquiring or transmitting a sexually transmissible disease; and

---

[49] [2014] EWHC 342 (COP); (2014) 137 B.M.L.R. 232.
[50] [2015] UKSC 11; [2015] A.C. 1430.
[51] *Montgomery v Lanarkshire Health Board* [2015] UKSC 11 at [87].

COMMON LAW TESTS OF CAPACITY

(3) that they have a choice whether to agree to, or to refuse, intercourse.

However, in *R. v C*,[52] when considering a criminal appeal under section 30 of the Sexual Offences Act 2003 (Sexual activity with a person with a mental disorder impeding choice), Baroness Hale remarked that[53]:

> "[I]t is difficult to think of an activity which is more person-and-situation specific than sexual relations. One does not consent to sex in general. One consents to this act of sex with this person at this time and in this place. Autonomy entails the freedom and the capacity to make a choice of whether or not to do so. This is entirely consistent with the respect for autonomy in matters of private life which is guaranteed by article 8 of the European Convention for the Protection of Human Rights and Fundamental freedoms."

In the case of *IM v LM*[54] the Court of Appeal attempted to reconcile these two different approaches and held that the approach taken by the judges of the Court of Protection in regarding the test for capacity to consent to sexual relationships as being general and issue specific, rather than person or event specific, was the correct approach within the terms of the MCA 2005 and that it is not at odds with the observations of Baroness Hale, which were made in a different legal context. Her comments had been made in the context of a criminal prosecution for acts that had already taken place, whereas the decisions the judges of the Court of Protection are required to make relate to decisions that need to be made now or at some time in the future.[55]

Capacity to make decisions regarding residence, contact, and care

The case of *LBX v K, L, M*[56] was an application made to the Court of Protection by the London Borough of Waltham Forest for orders relating to residence and contact in respect of a man referred to as L, who was 29 at the time of the court's judgment in 2013. He had a diagnosis of mild mental retardation and his IQ had been assessed at 59. He was the elder of the two sons of his father, K, and his mother had disappeared from the scene when he was a baby. He was initially looked after by a paternal aunt in Trinidad, and since 2001 he had lived with his father and younger brother in London. Although K acknowledged that it would be in L's best interests eventually to move into supported living accommodation with a view to attaining greater independence, he was of the view that the local authority was striving to achieve this too soon. In her judgment, Mrs Justice Theis approved the following lists, which had been drawn up by the Official Solicitor, setting out the "relevant information" that L would need to be able to understand, retain, and use and weigh in order that it could be said that he had capacity to make decisions regarding his residence, contact and care.

2–033

---

[52] [2009] UKHL 42; [2009] 1 W.L.R. 1786.
[53] *R. v C* [2009] UKHL 42 at [27].
[54] [2014] EWCA Civ 37.
[55] *IM v LM* [2014] EWCA Civ 37 at [79].
[56] [2013] EWHC 3230 (Fam) at [43] to [48].

ASSESSING CAPACITY: THE LAW

Residence

2–034
(1) what the options are, including information about what they are, what sort of property they are and what sort of facilities they have;
(2) in broad terms, what sort of area the properties are in (and any specific known risks beyond the usual risks faced by people living in an area if any such specific risks exist);
(3) the difference between living somewhere and visiting it;
(4) what activities L would be able to do if he lived in each place;
(5) whether and how he would be able to see his family and friends if he lived in each place;
(6) in relation to the proposed placement, that he would need to pay money to live there, which would be dealt with by his appointee, that he would need to pay bills, which would be dealt with by his appointee, and that there is an agreement that he has to comply with the relevant lists of dos and don'ts, otherwise he will not be able to remain living at the placement;
(7) who he would be living with at each placement;
(8) what sort of care he would receive in each placement in broad terms, in other words, that he would receive similar support in the proposed placement to the support he currently receives, and any differences if he were to live at home; and
(9) the risk that his father might not want to see him if L chooses to live in the new placement.

The judge considered that the following matters should not be included in the list because they would set the bar too high:

(1) the cost of the placements and the value of money;
(2) the legal nature of the tenancy agreement or licence; and
(3) what his relationship with his father might be in 10 or 20 years' time if L chooses to live independently now.

Contact

2–035
(1) who his contacts are, and in broad terms the nature of his relationship with them;
(2) what sort of contact he could have with each of them, including different locations, differing durations and differing arrangements regarding the presence of a support worker;
(3) the positive and negative aspects of having contact with each person. This will necessarily and inevitably be influenced by L's evaluations. His evaluations will only be irrelevant if they are based on demonstrably false beliefs. For example, if he believed that a person had assaulted him when they had not. But L's present evaluation of the positive and negative aspects of contact will not be the only relevant information. His past pleasant experience of contact with his father will also be relevant and he may need to be reminded of them as part of the assessment of capacity;

(4) what might be the impact of deciding to have or not to have contact of a particular sort with a particular person; and
(5) family are in a different category.

Care

(1) what areas he needs support with;
(2) what sort of support he needs;
(3) who will be providing him with support;
(4) what would happen if he did not have any support or he refused it; and
(5) that carers might not always treat him properly and that he can complain if he is not happy about his care.

2–036

The judge expressed the view that the following matters were not to be regarded as "relevant information" for the purposes of having capacity to make a decision on care:

(1) how the care would be funded; and
(2) how the overarching arrangements for monitoring and appointing care staff work.

In *B v A Local Authority*, the Court of Appeal stated that it saw no principled problem with these lists, provided that they are "treated and applied as no more than guidance to be expanded or contracted or otherwise adapted to the facts of the particular case".[57]

Capacity to use the internet and social media

On 21 February 2019 Mr Justice Cobb delivered judgments in two cases in which similar issues arose relating to the use of the internet and social media: namely, *Re A (Capacity: Social Media and Internet Use: Best Interests)*[58] and *Re B (Capacity: Social Media: Care and Contact)*.[59] A was a 21-year-old gay man with a learning disability, whose use of the internet included compulsive searching for pornographic and paedophilic sites. The local authority applied to the Court of Protection for decisions relating to his residence, care, contact with others, and his use of the internet. At [28] and [29] of his judgment in *Re A*, the judge set out the following list of "relevant information" that an individual needs to be able to understand, retain, and use and weigh in order to demonstrate that he has capacity to use the internet and social media:

2–037

"Information and images (including videos) which you share on the internet or through social media could be shared more widely, including with people you don't know, without you knowing or being able to stop it.
1. It is possible to limit the sharing of personal information or images (and videos) by using 'privacy and location settings' on some internet and social media sites; [see paragraph below].

---

[57] [2019] EWCA Civ 913; [2019] 3 W.L.R. 685 at [62].
[58] [2019] EWCOP 2.
[59] [2019] EWCOP 3.

2. If you place material or images (including videos) on social media sites which are rude or offensive, or share those images, other people might be upset or offended; [see paragraph below].
3. Some people you meet or communicate with ('talk to') online, who you don't otherwise know, may not be who they say they are ('they may disguise, or lie about, themselves'); someone who calls themselves a 'friend' on social media may not be friendly.
4. Some people you meet or communicate with ('talk to') on the internet or through social media, who you don't otherwise know, may pose a risk to you; they may lie to you, or exploit or take advantage of you sexually, financially, emotionally and/or physically; they may want to cause you harm.
5. If you look at or share extremely rude or offensive images, messages or videos online you may get into trouble with the police, because you may have committed a crime [see paragraph below].
29. With regard to the test above, I would like to add the following points to assist in its interpretation and application:
  a. In relation to 2 above, I do not envisage that the precise details or mechanisms of the privacy settings need to be understood but P should be capable of understanding that they exist, and be able to decide (with support) whether to apply them;
  b. In relation to 3 and 6 above, I use the term 'share' in this context as it is used in the 2018 Government Guidance: 'Indecent Images of Children: Guidance for Young people': that is to say, 'sending on an email, offering on a file sharing platform, uploading to a site that other people have access to, and possessing with a view to distribute';
  c. In relation to 3 and 6 above, I have chosen the words 'rude or offensive' – as these words may be easily understood by those with learning disabilities as including not only the insulting and abusive, but also the sexually explicit, indecent or pornographic;
  d. In relation to 6 above, this is not intended to represent a statement of the criminal law, but is designed to reflect the importance, which a capacitous person would understand, of not searching for such material, as it may have criminal content, and/or steering away from such material if accidentally encountered, rather than investigating further and/or disseminating such material. Counsel in this case cited from the Government Guidance on 'Indecent Images of Children' (see 2 above). Whilst the Guidance does not refer to 'looking at' illegal images as such, a person should know that entering into this territory is extremely risky and may easily lead a person into a form of offending. This piece of information (in 6) is obviously more directly relevant to general internet use rather than communications by social media, but it is relevant to social media use as well."

Mr Justice Cobb applied the same list in *Re B*, in respect of which an appeal on other aspects of the case was lodged, and the Court of Appeal commented: "We see no principled problem with the list provided that it is treated and applied as no more than guidance to be expanded or contracted or otherwise adapted to the facts of the particular case".[60]

---

[60] *B v A Local Authority* [2019] EWCA Civ 913 at [62].

Claimants' knowledge of the amount of their damages award

In accordance with international human rights law, ordinarily, a claimant should be given full details of their personal injury award and to deny them knowledge of the overall amount would constitute an interference with their rights. However, in some circumstances, it may be in their best interests not to be told how large the award is, because greater harm could be caused by imparting that information than from withholding it. This has been an issue for many years, but has only recently received judicial attention and was considered in two judgments in 2018 and 2019.

2–038

The first case was *EXB v FDZ*,[61] the facts of which were as follows. In October 2013, when he was 26, EXB was a back-seat passenger in a car driven by FDZ, which collided with a vehicle and then collided with a tree. As a result of these collisions, he suffered orthopaedic injuries and a brain injury. In 2015 the Court of Protection appointed Ivan Barry of Prince Evans, Solicitors, Uxbridge, to be his deputy for property and affairs, and in June 2018 they discussed whether he should be told the amount of his award. EXB's view was that he did not want to know how much it was, his reason being that he would "probably end up spending it", and liken it to having just "won the lottery or something".

Mr Barry felt that his role as deputy would be made easier if he were able to say to EXB, if he should ask the value of the award, "I can't tell you because the court has said so". This would also remove the burden of being perceived as a gatekeeper of such information from the litigation friend, litigation solicitor, or member of the support team. Accordingly, he applied to the court for an order that "the deputy shall not disclose information to EXB about the total value of his settlement award and shall direct others who have knowledge of this information not to inform him".

The case was heard by Mr Justice Foskett, who not only approved the settlement in the Queen's Bench Division but also, as a High Court judge, was a nominated judge of the Court of Protection. Having heard evidence from, among others, Dr Gemma Wall, a clinical neuropsychologist who "gave an impressive analysis that is worth recording", the judge considered that EXB lacked capacity in relation to the matter in question and that it was unlikely that he would have capacity to make this decision in future. He also found that the evidence that it would not be in EXB's best interests to know the amount of the award was overwhelming. Accordingly, he made the order sought, but stipulated that EXB's condition should be kept under periodic review.

2–039

The second case was *PBM v TGT*.[62] PBM is in his mid-twenties and lives in Wales. He has an acquired brain injury as a result of a deliberate injection of insulin by his father when he was 12 months old. He received a substantial award of compensation from the Criminal Injuries Compensation Authority, which is managed by a solicitor, TGT, who was appointed as his deputy for property and affairs in 2013. It was PBM's wish that he should be told about the extent of his assets, but the deputy disagreed.

---

[61] [2018] EWHC 3456 (QB).
[62] [2019] EWCOP 6.

ASSESSING CAPACITY: THE LAW

Since 2016 PBM had been in a relationship with his fiancée, MVA. They had planned to get married in June 2018, and in anticipation of that event, in May 2018 the deputy applied to the court for the following orders:

(1) whether PBM has capacity to marry his fiancée;
(2) whether PBM has capacity to enter into a prenuptial agreement; and
(3) whether PBM should be informed of the extent of his assets.

2–040 By the time that the matter came to final determination by Mr Justice Francis in January 2019, it was agreed by all parties that PBM did have the capacity to marry, to make a will, and to enter into a prenuptial agreement, but that he lacked capacity to manage his property and financial affairs, in respect of which the deputy should take steps to assist him to develop the requisite skills. The only contentious issue remaining was whether PBM had capacity to decide whether he should be informed about the extent of his assets. In spite of the properly articulated argument on behalf of the deputy, the judge formed the clear conclusion that PBM did have the capacity to be informed about the extent of his assets, and, in any event, it was important for him to be provided with that information because:

(1) The prenuptial agreement which he needed to make would be less effective without the information. There was a risk, therefore, that failure to provide the information would deprive him of an opportunity to protect his assets in the event of marital breakdown.
(2) PBM had expressed the clearest desire to enter into a prenuptial agreement and to make a will. His ability to effect these would be greatly enhanced by knowing about the extent of his assets.
(3) PBM was already aware that he is worth a substantial amount. "Substantial" is a word that means different things to different people, but it is possible that PBM thinks that he is worth more, rather than less, than the sum that he is actually worth.
(4) The existence of the deputyship has been an effective safeguard against financial abuse.
(5) Disclosure accords with the principles of the MCA 2005 and with the principles laid down in the UN Convention of the Rights of Persons with Disabilities which include:
    (a) respect for inherent dignity, individual autonomy including the freedom to make one's own choices, and independence of persons;
    (b) non-discrimination;
    (c) full and effective participation and inclusion in society.

The judge concluded by saying that "when PBM is informed of the extent of his assets it is important that he is supported emotionally, as well as assisted to build and develop life skills".

2. MENTAL CAPACITY ACT 2005 SECTIONS 1–3

Part 2 of this chapter considers the first three sections of the Mental Capacity Act 2005 (MCA 2005) and provides a brief commentary on them. The sections are: 2–041

(1) The principles;
(2) People who lack capacity; and
(3) Inability to make decisions.

Section 1: The principles

Section 1 of the MCA 2005 provides that: 2–042

"(1) The following principles apply for the purposes of this Act.
(2) A person must be assumed to have capacity unless it is established that he lacks capacity.
(3) A person is not to be treated as unable to make a decision unless all practicable steps to help him to do so have been taken without success.
(4) A person is not to be treated as unable to make a decision merely because he makes an unwise decision.
(5) An act done, or decision made, under this Act for or on behalf of a person who lacks capacity must be done, or made, in his best interests.
(6) Before the act is done, or the decision is made, regard must be had to whether the purpose for which it is needed can be as effectively achieved in a way that is less restrictive of the person's rights and freedom of action."

An imaginary line needs to be drawn between subsections (4) and (5) of section 1 of the Act to emphasise the fact that subsections (2), (3) and (4) fall within the domain of assessing capacity. Anything on the other side of the threshold is within the domain of doing things and making decisions in the best interests of a person who lacks capacity. In practice, there is a danger that professionals may objectively conflate a capacity assessment with a best interests analysis.[63]

Commentary on section 1

The presumption of capacity and the burden of proof

The presumption of capacity in section 1(2) has been part of English common law for centuries.[64] It is what is known as a "rebuttable presumption". In other words, the court must assume that something is true until someone successfully rebuts it and proves to the contrary. A similar rebuttable presumption is the "presumption of innocence" in criminal law. The burden of proof is on the person asserting the contrary. So, in criminal law, the burden of proof is on the prosecutor to prove that the accused is guilty, and in mental capacity law, the burden of proof is on anyone who claims that the person concerned lacks capacity. 2–043

---

[63] *CC v KK and STCC* [2012] EWHC 2136 (COP) at [65] per Baker J.
[64] See, for example, *Attorney General v Parnther* (1792) 3 Bro. C.C. 441, 2 Dick 748.

There used also to be a "presumption of continuance". Once it had been established that a person concerned lacked capacity, his incapacity was presumed to continue until the contrary was proved. It is unlikely that this presumption of continuance still exists in English law because in the case of *Masterman-Lister v Brutton & Co*, the Court of Appeal held that:

> "It is common ground that all adults must be presumed to be competent to manage their property and affairs until the contrary is proved, and that the burden of proof rests on those asserting incapacity. (Counsel) submitted that where, as in the present case, there is evidence that as a result of a head injury sustained in an accident the doctors who have been consulted agree that for a time the claimant was incapable of managing his property and affairs he can rely on the presumption of continuance. That I would not accept. Of course, if there is clear evidence of incapacity for a considerable period then the burden of proof may be more easily discharged, but it remains on whoever asserts incapacity."[65]

All practicable steps

2–044   Section 1(3) of the MCA 2005 provides that "a person is not to be treated as unable to make a decision unless all practicable steps to help him do so have been taken without success".

The Explanatory Notes that accompanied the MCA 2005 suggested that:

> "This could include, for example, making sure that the person is in an environment in which he is comfortable or involving an expert in helping him express his views."

The Mental Capacity Act Code of Practice, which goes into greater detail than the Explanatory Notes, suggests, at paragraph 4.49, that the following practical steps should be taken when assessing capacity:

> "Anyone assessing someone's capacity will need to decide which of these steps are relevant to their situation:
> - They should make sure that they understand the nature and effect of the decision to be made themselves. They may need access to relevant documents and background information (for example, details of the person's finances if assessing capacity to manage affairs).
> - They may need other relevant information to support the assessment (for example, healthcare records or the views of staff involved in the person's care).
> - Family members and close friends may be able to provide valuable background information (for example, the person's past behaviour and abilities and the types of decisions they can currently make). But their personal views and wishes about what *they* would want for the person must not influence the assessment.
> - They should again explain to the person all the information relevant to the decision. The explanation must be in the most appropriate and effective form of communication for that person.
> - Check the person's understanding after a few minutes. The person should be able to give a rough explanation of the information that was explained. There

---

[65] *Masterman-Lister v Jewell* [2002] EWCA Civ 1889; [2003] 1 W.L.R. 1511 per Kennedy LJ at [17].

are different methods for people who use non-verbal means of communication (for example, observing behaviour or their ability to recognise objects or pictures).
- Avoid questions that need only a 'yes' or 'no' answer (for example, did you understand what I just said?). They are not enough to assess the person's capacity to make a decision. But there may be no alternative in cases where there are major communication difficulties. In these cases, check the response by asking questions again in a different way.
- Skills and behaviour do not necessarily reflect the person's capacity to make specific decisions. The fact that someone has good social or language skills, polite behaviour or good manners doesn't necessarily mean they understand the information or are able to weigh it up.
- Repeating these steps can help confirm the result."

In *CC v KK and STCC*[66] Mr Justice Baker stated that:

"It is inappropriate to start with a 'blank canvas'. The person under evaluation must be presented with detailed options so that their capacity to weigh up those options may be fairly assessed ... The statute requires that, before a person can be treated as lacking capacity to make a decision, it must be shown that all practicable steps have been taken to help her do so. As the Code of Practice makes clear, each person whose capacity is under scrutiny must be given 'relevant information' including 'what the likely consequences of a decision would be (the possible effects of deciding one way or another).' That requires a detailed analysis of the effects of the decision either way, which in turn necessitates identifying the best ways in which each option would be supported."[67]

The requirement that all practicable steps be taken to help a person make a decision is sometimes referred to as "assisted decision-making" or "supported decision-making", which is discussed in further detail in the following section.

Supported decision-making

Supported decision-making is a relatively new concept that has attracted attention internationally as a result of its endorsement by the United Nations Convention on the Rights of Persons with Disabilities, which was adopted by the UN General Assembly in 2006. It originally developed in Canada as a means of overcoming some of the barriers for people with intellectual disabilities in exercising their capacity and it emphasises the interdependent nature of most of our lives. The important decisions that everyone makes are often made with support (such as advice from family, friends, carers, counsellors or professional advisers). People with mental disabilities may simply need additional support to make decisions themselves.

2–045

The concept of supported decision-making includes a range of support mechanisms, both informal and formal, such as:

- providing and explaining information to someone in a way they understand;
- spending time with a person to help them consider the options available and the risks and consequences of those options;

---

[66] [2012] EWHC 2136 (COP); [2012] C.O.P.L.R. 627.
[67] *CC v KK* [2012] EWHC 2136 (COP) at [68].

- spending time with the person to ascertain their wishes and preferences;
- helping the person to communicate their decision to others; and
- taking action to ensure that the person's decisions are respected and implemented.

Once it is established that a person lacks capacity, someone else may have the authority to step in and make a decision in that person's best interests, but the principle of supported decision-making still applies. Section 4(4) of the MCA 2005 requires that the person making the determination as to what is in a person's best interests, "must, so far as reasonably practicable, permit and encourage the person to participate, or to improve his ability to participate, as fully as possible in any act done for him and any decision affecting him".

Unwise decisions

2–046 This principle confirms the common law right of a person to make decisions that others may regard as unwise.[68] To a large extent, it is related to risk, and there have been several decisions in the Court of Protection which have cautioned that there is a danger that all professionals involved with treating and helping a person—including a judge—may feel drawn towards an outcome that is more protective of the adult and thus, in certain circumstances, fail to carry out an assessment of capacity that is both detached and objective.[69]

The Mental Capacity Act Code of Practice states at paragraph 2.11 that:

> "There may be cause for concern if somebody:
> - repeatedly makes unwise decisions that put them at significant risk of harm or exploitation or
> - makes a particular unwise decision that is obviously irrational or out of character.
>
> These things do not necessarily mean that somebody lacks capacity. But there might be a need for further investigation, taking into account the person's past decisions and choices. For example, have they developed a medical condition or disorder that is affecting their capacity to make particular decisions? Are they easily influenced by undue pressure? Or do they need more information to help them understand the consequences of the decision they are making?".

The principle in section 1(4) of the MCA 2005 that a person is not to be treated as unable to make a decision merely because he makes an unwise decision has been the subject of judicial comment in a number of cases. For example:

---

[68] In *Bird v Luckie* (1850) 8 Hare 301, the Vice-Chancellor Knight-Bruce remarked that, although the law insists that individuals should be capable of understanding the nature and effects of their actions, it does not require them to behave "in such a manner as to deserve approbation from the prudent, the wise, or the good". He went on to state that "a testator is permitted to be capricious and improvident, and is, moreover, at liberty to conceal the circumstances and motives by which he was actuated in his dispositions".

[69] *An NHS Trust v Dr A* (2013) EWHC 2442 (COP) per Baker J at [34].

"There is a space between an unwise decision and one which an individual does not have the mental capacity to take. ... It is important to respect that space, and to ensure that it is preserved, for it is within that space that an individual's autonomy operates."[70]

"The significance of section 1(4) must not be exaggerated. The fact that a decision is unwise or foolish may not, without more, be treated as conclusive, but it remains a relevant consideration for the court to take into account in considering whether the criteria of inability to make a decision for oneself in section 3(1) are satisfied. This will particularly be the case where there is a marked contrast between the unwise nature of the impugned decision and the person's former attitude to the conduct of his affairs at a time when his capacity was not in question."[71]

Best interests

It is a key principle of the MCA 2005 that all steps and decisions taken for someone who lacks capacity must be taken in the person's best interests: section 1(5). The best interests principle is an essential aspect of the Act and builds on the common law while offering further guidance. Given the wide range of acts, decisions and circumstances that the Act covers, the notion of "best interests" is not defined in the Act. Rather, section 4(2) makes it clear that determining what is in a person's best interests requires a consideration of "all the relevant circumstances". "Relevant circumstances" are defined in section 4(11) as those of which the person making the determination is aware, and which it would be reasonable to regard as relevant.

2–047

Section 4 contains a list of particular steps that *must* be taken when determining whether a particular act or decision is in the best interests of the person who lacks capacity. Best interests is not a test of "substituted judgment" (what the person would have wanted), but rather it requires a determination to be made by applying an objective test as to what would be in the person's best interests. All the relevant circumstances, including the factors mentioned in section 4 must be considered, but none carries any more weight or priority than another. They must all be balanced in order to determine what would be in the best interests of the person concerned. The factors in section 4 do not provide a definition of best interests and are not exhaustive.

In 2009, four years after the enactment of the MCA 2005, the United Kingdom ratified the United Nations Convention on the Rights of Persons with Disabilities (CRPD). On 11 April 2014 the UN committee that monitors the CRPD published a General Comment on Article 12 of the Convention, following which the Ministry of Justice launched an investigation into whether the MCA 2005 is compliant with the CRPD. It commissioned the Essex Autonomy Project, based at the University of Essex, to provide technical advice and assistance, which culminated in a report, "Achieving CRPD Compliance", published on 22 September 2014.

The report found that the best-interests decision-making framework of section 4 of the MCA 2005 fails to satisfy the requirements of CRPD article 12(4), which requires safeguards to ensure respect for the rights, will and preference of

---

[70] *PC v City of York Council* [2013] EWCA Civ 478; [2013] C.O.P.L.R. 409 at [54].
[71] *Re S; D v R* [2010] EWHC 2405 (COP); [2010] C.O.P.L.R. Con. Vol. 1112.

disabled persons in matters pertaining to the exercise of legal capacity, and recommended that the best-interests decision-making framework on which the MCA 2005 relies should be amended to establish a rebuttable presumption that, when a decision must be made on behalf of a person lacking in mental capacity, and the wishes of that person can be reasonably ascertained, the best-interests decision-maker shall make the decision that accords with those wishes. This recommendation was endorsed by the Law Commission, which in 2015 proposed that:

> "Section 4 of the Mental Capacity Act should be amended to establish that decision-makers should begin with the assumption that the person's present wishes and feelings should be determinative of the best interests decision."[72]

Less restrictive alternative

2–048 Section 1(6) of the MCA 2005 requires that, before anybody acts or makes a decision in the best interests of a person who lacks capacity, they must consider whether they can achieve the desired objective in a way that would interfere less with the person's rights and freedom of action. This "less restrictive" alternative will not necessarily be the "least restrictive" option because the person's best interests should always have priority.

Although it is not expressly stated in the Act, it is generally accepted that the appointment of a deputy to make decisions on behalf of a person who lacks capacity to make such decisions should be a last resort and that less formal arrangements should be preserved wherever possible. In the context of personal welfare decision-making, particularly in relation to care and treatment, sections 5, 6 and 8 of the MCA 2005 provide a framework for decision-making that does not require the intervention of the Court of Protection.

Section 2: People who lack capacity

2–049 Section 2 of the MCA 2005 states that:

> "(1) For the purposes of this Act, a person lacks capacity in relation to a matter if at the material time he is unable to make a decision for himself in relation to the matter because of an impairment of, or a disturbance in the functioning of, the mind or brain.
> (2) It does not matter whether the impairment or disturbance is permanent or temporary.
> (3) A lack of capacity cannot be established merely by reference to:
>   (a) a person's age or appearance, or
>   (b) a condition of his, or an aspect of his behaviour, which might lead others to make unjustified assumptions about his capacity.
> (4) In proceedings under this Act or any other enactment, any question whether a person lacks capacity within the meaning of this Act must be decided on the balance of probabilities.
> (5) No power which a person ('D') may exercise under this Act:
>   (a) in relation to a person who lacks capacity, or

---

[72] Law Commission, Consultation Paper No.222, *Mental Capacity and Deprivation of Liberty* (7 July 2015), p.166.

(b) where D reasonably thinks that a person lacks capacity, is exercisable in relation to a person under 16.

(6) Subsection (5) is subject to section 18(3).""

Commentary on section 2

The diagnostic threshold

Section 2(1) provides that: 2–050

> "For the purposes of this Act, a person lacks capacity in relation to a matter if at the material time he is unable to make a decision for himself in relation to the matter because of an impairment of, or a disturbance in the functioning of, the mind or brain."

This is often referred to as "the diagnostic threshold" and in its report on *Mental Incapacity*, which is the legislative source of the MCA 2005, the Law Commission stated that:

> "The arguments for and against such a diagnostic hurdle are very finely balanced ... In the event, most respondents agreed with our preliminary view that a diagnostic hurdle did have a role to play in any definition of incapacity, in particular in ensuring that the test is stringent enough not to catch large numbers of people who make unusual or unwise decisions."[73]

However, the Law Commission was eager to move away from the term "mental disorder", which applied in Court of Protection proceedings under the Mental Health Act 1983, and said that[74]:

> "Many respondents to our medical treatment consultation paper were concerned to ensure that all the conditions which can result in incapacity to take medical decisions should be included in the new definition. Some of these will have very little in common with psychiatric illnesses or congenital impairments of the kind addressed by the 1983 Act. It was argued that some relevant conditions might not qualify as disorders or disabilities 'of mind' at all. Temporary toxic confusional states (whether resulting from prescription or illicit drugs, alcohol or other toxins) and neurological disorders were given as examples. Some doctors would argue that these are properly labelled disorders of *brain* rather than mind. One respondent pointed out that women can lack capacity to take obstetric decisions after prolonged labour, and queried whether the effects of pain and exhaustion were a disability 'of mind'. We are persuaded that there are many good reasons from departing from the 1983 Act definition."

Matter specific and time specific

The definition of incapacity in section 2(1) is both "matter specific" and "time 2–051 specific". A person lacks capacity in relation to a matter if at the material time he is unable to make a decision for himself in relation to the matter because of an impairment of, or a disturbance in the functioning of, the mind or brain.

---

[73] Law Commission Report No.231, *Mental Incapacity* (HMSO, 1995), para.3.8.
[74] Law Commission Report No.231, *Mental Incapacity* (HMSO, 1995), para.3.11.

ASSESSING CAPACITY: THE LAW

The Mental Capacity Act Code of Practice consists of 16 chapters. The first page of each chapter from the second chapter onwards contains a caption (almost like the government health warning on a packet of cigarettes) that "in this chapter, as throughout the Code, a person's capacity (or lack of capacity) refers specifically to their capacity to make a particular decision at the time it needs to be made".

The causative nexus

2–052 Section 2(1) provides that "a person lacks capacity in relation to a matter if at the material time he is unable to make a decision for himself in relation to the matter *because of* an impairment of, or a disturbance in the functioning of, the mind or brain". The words "because of" have been described as "the causative nexus between mental impairment and inability to decide".[75]

The Mental Capacity Act Code of Practice states that there is a "two stage test of capacity" (Stage 1: Does the person have an impairment of, or a disturbance in the functioning of, their mind or brain? Stage 2: Does the impairment or disturbance mean that the person is unable to make a specific decision when they need to?).[76]

However, in order not to water down the causative nexus, judges have suggested that capacity should be assessed in the order set out in section 2(1): namely, first the person's inability to decide and secondly the existence of an impairment of or disturbance in the functioning of the mind or brain.[77] So, for example, in one case, having found that C was not unable to make a decision for herself, the judge announced that there was no need for him to go on to consider the diagnostic test.[78]

Temporary impairment

2–053 Referring to the diagnostic threshold in section 2(1), whereby a person's inability to make a decision must be "because of an impairment of, or a disturbance in the functioning of, the mind or brain", section 2(2) provides that "it does not matter whether the impairment or disturbance is permanent or temporary". The Code of Practice states that[79]:

> "Some people have fluctuating capacity—they have a problem or condition that gets worse occasionally and affects their ability to make decisions. For example, someone who has manic depression may have a temporary manic phase which causes them to lack capacity to make financial decisions, leading them to get into debt even though at other times they are perfectly able to manage their money. A person with a psychotic illness may have delusions that affect their capacity to make decisions at certain times but disappear at others. Temporary factors may also affect someone's ability to make decisions. Examples include acute illness, severe pain,

---

[75] *PC v City of York Council* [2013] EWCA Civ 478; [2013] C.O.P.L.R. 409 per McFarlane LJ at [58].
[76] Mental Capacity Act Code of Practice, paras 4.10–4.13.
[77] *PC v City of York Council* [2013] EWCA Civ 478; [2013] C.O.P.L.R. 409 per McFarlane LJ at [58]. But see *Norfolk CC v PB* [2014] EWCOP 14; [2015] C.O.P.L.R. 118 per Parker J at [90].
[78] *King's College Hospital NHS Foundation Trust v C* [2015] EWCOP 80 per Macdonald J at [93].
[79] Mental Capacity Act Code of Practice, para.4.26.

the effect of medication, or distress after a death or shock. More guidance on how to support someone with fluctuating or temporary capacity to make a decision can be found in chapter 3, particularly paragraphs 3.12–3.16. More information about factors that may indicate that a person may regain or develop capacity in the future can be found at paragraph 5.28."

As in any other situation, an assessment must only examine a person's capacity to make a particular decision at the time when it needs to be made. If an urgent decision is needed, then someone else or the court may be able to intervene and make the decision on the person's behalf if it is in their best interests to make the decision without delay.[80] However, when considering what is in the person's best interests, the best interests decision-maker must consider whether it is likely that the person will at some time have capacity in relation to the matter in question and, "if it appears that he will, when that is likely to be".[81] In effect, this means that, in a situation where there is no real urgency, it may be more appropriate to wait until the person has capacity to make the decision himself.

Age

Section 2(5) of the MCA 2005 states that powers under the Act generally only apply where the person lacking capacity is 16 or over. However, powers in relation to property and financial affairs might be exercised in relation to a younger person who has disabilities, which will cause the incapacity to last into adulthood: see section 18(3). This usually arises in the context of children who have suffered brain damage as a result of personal injury or clinical negligence and have received a damages award by way of compensation. Any overlap with the jurisdiction under the Children Act 1989 can be dealt with by orders under section 21 relating to the transfer of proceedings to the more appropriate court.

2–054

Standard of proof

Section 2(4) of the MCA 2005 provides that: "In proceedings under this Act or any other enactment, any question whether a person lacks capacity within the meaning of this Act must be decided on the balance of probabilities". This is known as "the standard of proof".

2–055

At common law there has always been a distinction between the standard of proof in criminal cases and that the standard of proof in civil cases. In criminal law a judge or jury has to be satisfied that the person on whom the burden of proof falls has proved his case "beyond reasonable doubt", whereas in civil proceedings a lower standard of proof is required, namely "the balance of probabilities".

If the evidence is such that the judge can say "I think that it is more probable than not", the burden is discharged, but if the probabilities are equal the burden is not discharged to the required standard.[82] Expressing this in percentage terms, if a

---

[80] For example, a carer could make a decision under s.5 of the MCA 2005, and the court could make an interim order or directions under section 48 if it is in P's best interests to make the order, or give the directions without delay.
[81] MCA 2005 s.4(3).
[82] *Miller v Minister of Pensions* [1947] 2 All E.R. 372 per Denning J.

judge concludes that it is 50% likely that the person on whom the burden of proof falls (the applicant) is right, then the applicant will lose, but if the judge decides that there is a 51% likelihood that the applicant is right, then the applicant will win.

When the Law Commission was reviewing the mental capacity legislation in England and Wales in the early 1990s, it received submissions that the criminal standard of proof should be applied in any enquiry into an individual's mental capacity because of "the drastic consequences" of an adverse finding. The Law Commission, however, considered that these representations took a purely negative view of intervention, which can have a positive side and can benefit and protect the individual concerned. It also noted that: "... although the normal civil standard is the 'balance of probabilities', this is qualified by the requirement that the graver the consequences the greater the standard of proof required. We consider that this is entirely appropriate".[83]

Section 3: Inability to make decisions

2–056 Section 3 of the MCA 2005 provides that:

> "(1) For the purposes of section 2, a person is unable to make a decision for himself if he is unable —
> (a) to understand the information relevant to the decision,
> (b) to retain that information,
> (c) to use or weigh that information as part of the process of making the decision, or
> (d) to communicate his decision (whether by talking, using sign language or any other means).
> (2) A person is not to be regarded as unable to understand the information relevant to a decision if he is able to understand an explanation of it given to him in a way that is appropriate to his circumstances (using simple language, visual aids or any other means).
> (3) The fact that a person is able to retain the information relevant to a decision for a short period only does not prevent him from being regarded as able to make the decision.
> (4) The information relevant to a decision includes information about the reasonably foreseeable consequences of—
> (a) deciding one way or another, or
> (b) failing to make the decision."

Commentary on section 3

All four elements in section 3(1) must be applied in full

2–057 Section 3(1) contains four elements. The first three should be applied together. If a person cannot do these three things, they will be treated as unable to make the

---

[83] The Law Commission, Consultation Paper No.128 (1993), *Mentally Incapacitated Adults and Decision-Making: A New Jurisdiction*, page 35, para.3.42.

decision. The fourth only applies in situations where people cannot communicate their decision in any way.[84] In its judgment in *IM v LM*[85] the Court of Appeal held that:

> "For the avoidance of doubt, every single issue of capacity which falls to be determined under Part 1 of the Act must be evaluated by applying section 3(1) in full and considering each of the four elements of the decision-making process that are set out at (a)–(d) in that subsection ... The extent to which on the facts of any individual case there is a need for a sophisticated, or for a more straightforward, evaluation of any of these four elements will naturally vary from case to case and from topic to topic."[86]

The relevant information

The information relevant to a decision will depend on the nature and effect of the particular decision. Section 2(4) of the Act states that it also includes the reasonably foreseeable consequences of deciding one way or another or of making no decision at all.[87]

2–058

As will be seen from Part 1 of this chapter, common law tests of capacity usually identify the relevant information that a person needs to understand, retain and use or weigh before taking action or making a decision.

Judicial observations in some of the cases considered in Parts 3 and 4 of this chapter have indicated that:

(1) it is not necessary for a person to demonstrate a capacity to understand and weigh up every detail of the respective options, but merely the salient features[88]; and
(2) there has to be a reasonably practical limit on what needs to be envisaged as the "reasonably foreseeable consequences".[89]

Understanding relevant information

The origin of section 2(1)(a) of the MCA 2005—"a person is unable to make a decision for himself if he is unable to understand the information relevant to the decision"—can be found in the Law Commission's report on *Mental Incapacity*, published in 1995.[90]

2–059

> "Respondents favoured our suggestion that it was more realistic to test whether a person can understand information, than to test whether he or she can understand 'the nature of' an act or decision. It was, however, suggested that an ability to 'appreciate' information about the likely consequences of a decision might be conceptually different from such information. We prefer to approach this in a

---

[84] Mental Capacity Act Code of Practice, para.4.15.
[85] [2014] EWCA Civ 37 [2014] C.O.P.L.R. 246.
[86] *IM v LM* [2014] EWCA Civ 37; [2014] C.O.P.L.R. 248 per Sir Brian Leveson, President of the Queen's Bench Division at [73].
[87] See also Mental Capacity Act Code of Practice, para.4.16.
[88] See *LBL v RYJ* [2010] EWHC 2665 (Fam) and *CC v KK* [2012] EWHC 2136 (COP).
[89] *IM v LM* [2014] EWCA Civ 37.
[90] Law Commission Report No.231, *Mental Incapacity* (HMSO, 1995), para.3.16.

slightly different way, on the basis that information about consequences is one of the sorts of information which a person with capacity understands. Respondents supported the express mention of foreseeable consequences in our draft test, and we still see advantage in drawing attention to the special nature of information about likely consequences, as information which will in every case be relevant to the decision."

Section 3(2) of the MCA 2005 provides that:

"A person is not to be regarded as unable to understand the information relevant to the decision if he is able to understand an explanation of it given to him in a way that is appropriate to his circumstances (using simple language, visual aids or any other means."

The legislative intention of this subsection was as follows[91]:

"In the draft test of incapacity which appeared in the consultation papers we suggested that a person should be found to lack capacity if he or she was unable to understand an explanation of the relevant information in broad terms and simple language. Many respondents supported this attempt to ensure that persons should not be found to lack capacity unless and until someone has gone to the trouble to put forward a suitable explanation of the relevant information. This focus requires an assessor to approach any apparent inability as something which may be dynamic and changeable. As one commentator on our original draft test has written, we chose 'to import the patient's right to information by implication into the test of capacity.' Further guidance on the way the new statutory language may impinge on the methods of assessing capacity in day to day practice should be given in a code of practice accompanying the legislation."

The Code of Practice contains extensive further guidance in Chapter 3, and also at paragraph 4.18, where it gives the following three examples specifically in the context of the requirements of section 3(2):

"A person with a learning disability may need somebody to read information to them. They might also need illustrations to help them to understand what is happening. Or they might stop the reader to ask what things mean. It might be helpful for them to discuss information with an advocate.

A person with anxiety or depression may find it difficult to reach a decision about treatment in a group meeting with professionals. They may prefer to read the relevant documents in private. This way they can come to a conclusion alone, and ask for help if necessary.

Someone who has a brain injury might need to be given information several times. It will be necessary to check that the person understands the information. If they have difficulty understanding, it might be useful to present information in a different way (for example, different forms of words, pictures or diagrams). Written information, audiotapes, videos and posters can help people remember important facts."

---

[91] Law Commission Report No.231, *Mental Incapacity* (HMSO, 1995), para.3.18.

Retaining relevant information

2–060 Section 3(1)(b) of the MCA 2005 provides that a person is unable to make a decision for himself if he is unable to retain information relevant to the decision. Section 3(3) amplifies this by confirming that "the fact that a person is able to retain the information relevant to a decision for a short period only does not prevent him from being regarded as able to make the decision". The Code of Practice further amplifies this point by stating that "the person must be able to hold the information in their mind for long enough to use it to make an effective decision", and that the length of time involved "depends on what is necessary for the decision in question. Items such as notebooks, photographs, posters, videos and voice recorders can help people record and retain information".[92]

Using or weighing relevant information

2–061 In its report on *Mental Incapacity*, published in 1995, the Law Commission noted that:

> "There are cases where the person concerned can understand information but where the effects of a mental disability prevent him or her from using that information in the decision-making process ... Certain compulsive conditions cause people who are quite able to absorb information to arrive, inevitably, at decisions which are unconnected to the information or their understanding of it. An example is the anorexic who always decides not to eat. There are also some people who, because of a mental disability, are unable to exert their will against some stronger person who wishes to influence their decisions or against some force majeure of circumstances ... Common to all these cases is the fact that the person's eventual decision is divorced from his or her ability to understand the relevant information. Emphasising that the person must be able to use the information which he or she has successfully understood in the decision-making process deflects the complications of asking whether a person needs to 'appreciate' information as well as understand it. A decision based on compulsion, the overpowering will of a third party or any other inability to act on relevant information as a result of mental disability is not a decision made by a person with decision-making capacity."[93]

The need to be able to use or weigh information has attracted more judicial comment than any of the other three elements in section 3(1) of the MCA 2005. For example:

(1) In some cases, the ability to use information will be critical; in others, it will be necessary to weigh competing considerations.[94]
(2) Different individuals may give different weight to different factors.[95]
(3) The ability to use and weigh information is unlikely to loom large in the evaluation of capacity to consent to sexual relations.[96]

---

[92] Mental Capacity Act Code of Practice, para.4.20.
[93] Law Commission Report No.231, *Mental Incapacity* (HMSO, 1995), para.3.17.
[94] *IM v LM* [2014] EWCA Civ 37; [2014] C.O.P.L.R. 246 at [52].
[95] *LBL v RYJ* [2010] EWHC 2665 (COP); [2010] C.O.P.L.R. Con. Vol. 795.
[96] *IM v LM* [2014] EWCA Civ 37; [2014] C.O.P.L.R. 246 at [81].

(4) It may be setting the test for capacity too high if one expects the person being assessed to be able to demonstrate significant using and weighing of information with a balanced, nuanced, used and weighted position.[97]

Communicating the decision

2–062 Section 3(1)(d) of the MCA 2005 provides that "a person is unable to make a decision for himself if he is unable to communicate his decision (whether by talking, using sign language, or any other means". The intention of the legislators was that[98]:

> "[T]hose who cannot communicate decisions should be included within the scope of the new jurisdiction. We had in mind particularly those who are unconscious. In some rare conditions a conscious patient may be known to retain a level of cognitive functioning but the brain may be completely unable to communicate with the body or with the outside world (Guillain-Barre or "locked-in" syndrome). In other cases, particularly after a stroke. It may not be possible to say whether or not there is cognitive dysfunction. It can, however, be said that the patient cannot communicate any decision he or she may make. In either case, decisions may have to be made on behalf of such people, and only two respondents expressed the purist view that they should be excluded from our new jurisdiction because they do not suffer from true 'mental incapacity'. It appears to us appropriate that they should be brought within the scope of our new legislation rather than being left to fend for themselves within the uncertain and inadequate principles of the common law."

The Mental Capacity Act 2005 Code of Practice

2–063 The Mental Capacity Act 2005 Code of Practice is paperback, A4 size, 296 pages long, and contains 16 chapters, most of which begin with a "quick summary". Each chapter is also prefaced with the following reminder, which stands out like a health warning on a packet of cigarettes, emphasising the fact that capacity is both issue-specific and time-specific: "In this chapter, as throughout the Code, a person's capacity (or lack of capacity) refers specifically to their capacity to make a particular decision at the time it needs to be made".

At the end, instead of an index, there is a glossary of "key words and phrases used in the Code", and an annex containing contact details for various organisations with an interest in this area. Each chapter includes a number of "scenarios". These are vignettes or case studies designed to illustrate the meaning of the legislation described in the main text of the code. However, page six of the introduction to the code contains a rather unhelpful disclaimer, which says that "the scenarios should not in any way be taken as templates for decisions that need to be made in similar situations".

The first five chapters of the Code of Practice are as follows:

Chapter 1 *What is the Mental Capacity Act 2005?* This introduces the Act; describes what decisions are covered by it, and what decisions are excluded, and briefly summarises what the Act says about the Code of Practice itself.

---
[97] *King's College Hospital NHS Foundation Trust v C* [2015] EWCOP 80.
[98] Law Commission Report No.231, *Mental Incapacity* (HMSO, 1995), para.3.13.

Chapter 2 *What are the statutory principles and how should they be applied?* This discusses the five principles set out in section 1 of the MCA 2005, and how they should be applied in practice.

Chapter 3 *How should people be helped to make their own decisions?* This describes how the Act requires people to be given the right amount of help and support to make their own decisions. It considers providing relevant information, communicating in an appropriate way, and making the person feel at ease.

Chapter 4 *How does the Act define a person's capacity to make a decision and how should capacity be assessed?* The contents of this chapter are as follows:
- Quick summary
- What is mental capacity?
- What does the Act mean by "lack of capacity"?
- What safeguards does the Act provide around assessing someone's capacity?
- What proof of lack of capacity does the Act require?
- What is the test of capacity?
- What does the Act mean by "inability to make a decision"?
- What other issues might affect capacity?
- When should capacity be assessed?
- Who should assess capacity?
- What is "reasonable belief" of lack of capacity?
- What other factors might affect an assessment of capacity?
- What practicable steps should be taken when assessing capacity?
- When should professionals be involved?
- Are assessment processes confidential?
- What if someone refuses to be assessed?
- Who should keep a record of assessments?
- How can someone challenge a finding of lack of capacity?

Chapter 5 *What does the Act mean when it talks about "best interests"?* This considers what acting in someone's best interests means, and discusses the checklist set out in section 4 of the MCA 2005.

What the court expects

A practice direction on expert evidence, numbered 15A, supplements Part 15 of the Court of Protection Rules 2017.[99] It sets out the court's general requirements on expert evidence and its specific requirements with regard to the form and content of an expert's report and questions asked for the purpose of clarifying the expert's report.

In 2019 the *International Journal of Law and Psychiatry* published an article by a multidisciplinary team of authors—Alex Ruck-Keene, Nuala B. Kane, Scott Y.H. Kim and Gareth S. Owen—called "Taking capacity seriously? Ten years of

2–064

---

[99] Court of Protection Rules 2017 (SI 2017/1035 (L.16)) came into force on 1 December 2017. Practice Direction 15A can be accessed online free of charge. A search "Court of Protection Practice Direction 15A" should direct you to the Courts and Tribunals Judiciary website: *https://www.judiciary.uk/publications/15a-expert-evidence* [Accessed 16 January 2020].

mental capacity disputes before the Court of Protection".[100] For psychiatrists, and others whose function is to assess capacity, the authors suggested that the implications of their findings were as follows:

> "(1) Given the extent to which the principle of decision-specificity is (rightly) upheld in the Court of Protection, psychiatrists preparing evidence for the court should be mindful that working to understand and delineate the relevant decision(s) forms an important pre-condition to assessing the person's capacity.
> (2) Because of the statutory requirement that the decision-making inability be 'caused by' the person's impairment of mind or brain, and not merely co-exist with it, psychiatrists should expect to give evidence on this 'causative nexus'.
> (3) Given that most contested cases hinge on the 'use or weigh' ability, psychiatrists should be aware that good quality evidence is particularly pertinent in court.
> (4) Our findings show that Court of Protection judgments on mental capacity have grown up on particular types of clinical soil—covering some impairments (learning disability, dementia, and, to a lesser extent, psychosis) but not others (notably mood and substance disorders). This needs to be held in mind when extending the concept of mental capacity, as evolved in the court, to impairments and contexts for which the Court of Protection has less experience.
> (5) We wish to draw attention to the importance of asking whether those charged with making determinations of capacity have explained the basis upon which they have reached their conclusion. Only if they have done so in a fashion which transparently and robustly addresses the relevant statutory criteria can it be said that the determination is a satisfactory one."

3. MENTAL CAPACITY ACT CASE STUDIES

2–065 Part 3 consists of summaries of 11 cases that have been reported on the British and Irish Legal Information Institute (BAILII) website,[101] and, in most cases, also in the Court of Protection Law Reports (C.O.P.L.R.). Although only a few of these cases relate to claims for personal injury or clinical negligence, they do illustrate a variety of issues relating to the interpretation of the Mental Capacity Act 2005 (MCA 2005) and what the court expects from expert witnesses who report on an individual's capacity. Part 4 contains a number of verbatim judicial observations that appear in these cases.

---

[100] *International Journal of Law and Psychiatry* 62 (2019) 56–76.
[101] The BAILII website can be accessed free of charge. For Court of Protection judgments, take the following steps. (1) go to the BAILII homepage at *https://www.bailii.org*; (2) on the left-hand side of the homepage under BAILII Databases, click England and Wales; (3) under England and Wales Case Law, Courts, click England and Wales Court of Protection; (4) access judgments by browsing the title from A to Z or by browsing the year. There is a continuous set of Court of Protection judgments since 2009.

Case Study 1

LBL v RYJ [2010] EWHC 2665 (COP); [2010] C.O.P.L.R. Con. Vol. 795

Judge: Macur J
22 September 2010

RYJ was an 18-year-old woman who, as a result of brain injury at birth, had epilepsy, significant learning difficulties and significant language and communication difficulties. She lacked the capacity to litigate. She had a difficult relationship with her mother, VJ, who came from Zambia, and preferred to spend most of the year at the National Centre for Young People with Epilepsy at Lingfield, Surrey, where her care was funded by the local authority, and during the holidays she lived with her maternal aunt, J. However, there was some inconsistency in her approach towards contact with her mother. Her mother objected to both RYJ's current educational placement and her apparent preference for living with the aunt, and argued that she did not have capacity to make these decisions. The mother had applied to the Special Educational Needs and Disability Tribunal, requesting that RYJ be educated elsewhere.

2–066

The local authority (LBL) sought a declaration as to RYJ's capacity to make decisions concerning daily life and, if she did have such capacity, asked the court to make a "best interests" declaration under the inherent jurisdiction, essentially in order to give the local authority the power to direct where the young woman should reside and be educated and with whom she should have contact. The Official Solicitor argued that the use of the inherent jurisdiction for such a purpose would subvert the statutory scheme of the MCA 2005.

Held: declaring that the presumption of capacity had not been displaced, and dismissing the application for a declaration as to best interests:

(1) The phrase "a person lacks capacity in relation to a matter if at the material time he is unable to make a decision for himself in relation to the matter" in section 2(1) of the MCA 2005, was to be read as meaning that capacity was to be assessed in relation to the particular type of decision at the time the decision needed to be made, not the person's ability to make decisions generally or in abstract (see [25]).

(2) The fact of inconsistency was not necessarily a sign of confusion. Equally, confusion was not necessarily an indication of incapacity. A change of mind might reflect the circumstances, wishes, desires of the moment, a reluctance to engage, or genuine indecision. In this case inadequate regard had been paid to the young woman's potential to teenage ennui, manipulation and fickleness, which were not traits confined to those lacking capacity. Further, if an initial expression of views was effectively challenged by continual repetitive questioning, as had happened in this case, any person, even one without impairment, might begin to doubt his or her initial response (see [33], [49] and [50]).

(3) When considering the test of capacity in section 3 of the MCA 2005, the correct interpretation was that the person under review must comprehend and weigh the salient details relevant to the decision to be made. It was not

necessary that the person should be able to give weight to every consideration that would otherwise be utilised in forming a decision objectively in her "best interests". In this case the young woman did not need to understand all the details within her statement of special educational needs (see [58]).

(4) The inherent jurisdiction was available to supplement the protection afforded by the MCA 2005 for those who had capacity for the purposes of the Act but who were "incapacitated" by external forces outside their control from reaching a decision. However, the inherent jurisdiction could not be used to impose a decision as to welfare or finance in the case of an adult with capacity. It had not been established that the young adult in this case was unable to recognise and withstand external pressure to an appropriate degree, or that she was likely to be subjected to physical constraint or behaviour impacting on her free will and capacity to reach decisions concerning residence and contact (see [62]–[64] and [66]).

Case Study 2

Re S; D v R [2010] EWHC 2405 (Fam); [2010] C.O.P.L.R. Con. Vol. 1112

Judge: Henderson J
4 October 2010

2–067   S was born in 1933. In April 2005 he suffered a stroke and requested help with various chores. He was befriended and assisted by Mrs D, who was his solicitor's secretary. In February 2006 he signed an Enduring Power of Attorney appointing Mrs D and two partners in another firm of solicitors to be his attorneys, and between January 2006 and April 2007 he made gifts to Mrs D totalling £549,141. On 9 October 2007 S's daughter, R, was appointed by the Court of Protection as his deputy for property and affairs and she commenced proceedings on his behalf in the Chancery Division to set aside the gifts on the ground that they had been procured by undue influence. It was S's clearly expressed wish that the Chancery proceedings should never have been commenced in the first place and that they should be discontinued immediately. S wished Mrs D to keep the money he had given her. Mrs D applied to the court for a determination as to whether S had capacity to decide whether the Chancery proceedings should be discontinued.

Held:
(1) A decision to discontinue, or to continue to prosecute or to settle proceedings could only be validly taken if the person concerned was capable of having, and had, a basic understanding of the nature of the claim, of the legal issues involved, and of the circumstances which gave rise to the claim (see [43]).
(2) Where the claim is founded on a rebuttable presumption of undue influence, for the donor to be able to decide whether or not to pursue such a claim, he must be able to understand:
  (a) the nature and extent of the relationship of trust and confidence arguably reposed by him in the donee;

- (b) the extent to which it may be said that the gifts cannot readily be accounted for by the ordinary motives or ordinary people in such a relationship; and
- (c) the nature of the evidential burden resting on the donee to rebut any resumption of undue influence (see [44]).

(3) Although S was able to communicate his views, he was unable to make the decision whether or not to continue the Chancery proceedings because in terms of section 3(1) of the MCA 2005 he was unable:
- (a) to understand the information relevant to the decision;
- (b) to retain that information; and
- (c) to use or weigh that information as part of the decision-making process (see [153]).

Case Study 3

PH v A Local Authority [2011] EWHC 1704 (Fam); [2012] C.O.P.L.R. 128

Judge: Baker J
30 June 2011

PH was a 49-year-old-man who suffered from Huntington's disease. He had lived with his partner in the community, but became difficult to care for in this setting as his condition deteriorated. He was admitted to a residential placement (Y Court) having been told it was a temporary arrangement, when in fact it was permanent. He wanted to return home, and issued proceedings challenging the standard authorisation put in place by the local authority under Schedule A1 to the MCA 2005 authorising his deprivation of liberty at Y Court. The first matter that fell to be determined was whether PH lacked capacity to make decisions about his residence for the purposes of Schedule A1. An independently instructed psychiatrist concluded on the basis of a single assessment that PH had capacity to decide where to live. PH's treating psychiatrist, social worker and two general practitioners, who had assessed PH, considered that he lacked capacity in this regard.

2–068

Held: PH lacked capacity to decide where to reside; his capacity to be reviewed after a period of six months:

(1) PH lacked capacity to decide the narrow question under MCA 2005 Schedule A1 whether or not he should be accommodated at Y Court for the purpose of being given care and treatment (see [64]). PH also lacked capacity to decide the broader question of where he should reside (see [65]). He was unable to understand, retain and weigh salient information about each decision.

(2) Specifically, PH was not aware of the full extent of his personal care needs and behavioural problems. He did not understand what care he would require if he returned home, what it would be like to receive 24-hour care at home, and that his care arrangements would be different from previously.

He was unable to consider the realities of what life would be like if he were to go home, and did not understand why his care at home had broken down in the past (see [59]–[61]).

(3) There was no reason to require that a finding of a lack of capacity should only be made where the quality of the evidence in support of such a finding was "compelling". Nor should the statutory test be construed narrowly (see [16(xii)]).

(4) In assessing the evidence of capacity, the opinion of independently-instructed experts and treating clinicians and other experts working with P should be considered. The court must be aware of the risk that all professionals involved with treating and helping that person may feel drawn towards an outcome that is more protective of the adult and thus, in certain circumstances, fail to carry out an assessment of capacity that is detailed and objective (see [16(xiii)]).

Case Study 4

CC v KK [2012] EWHC 2136 (COP); [2012] C.O.P.L.R. 627

Judge: Baker J
26 July 2012

2–069 KK was an 82-year-old woman with partial paralysis, Parkinson's disease and vascular dementia. She was being looked after very well in a nursing home (STCC), but wanted to go home to the bungalow where she had lived before her admission to STCC. After assessment by Dr T a standard authorisation was granted by CC, the supervisory body under the Deprivation of Liberty Safeguards. KK commenced proceedings challenging the authorisation. Interim orders were made directing trial home visits for KK during the day and further independent assessment by Dr TH. A further capacity assessment by Dr T concluded that KK did not have capacity and a further standard authorisation was granted. Dr TH also concluded that KK lacked capacity to make decisions regarding her care needs and residence. In the light of the interim orders, CC declined to give STCC any further standard authorisation on the basis that KK was not now being deprived of her liberty. This hearing was held to decide whether: (1) KK lacked capacity to make decisions regarding her care and residence; and (2) she had been, or was being, deprived of her liberty.

Held: finding that the burden of proving that KK lacked capacity was not discharged and KK's circumstances did not amount to a deprivation of liberty:

(1) Although there was a consensus amongst the professionals that KK had lost the capacity to make decisions concerning her residence, it was the court alone that was in the position to weigh up all the evidence and analyse the professional evidence in the context of all the other evidence and, in particular, KK's own evidence (see [62]).

(2) Whilst KK may have underestimated or minimised some of her needs, she did not do so to an extent that suggests that she lacks capacity to weigh up information. In evaluating capacity the court must recognise that different

individuals may give different weight to different factors. There was a danger that professionals, including judges, may objectively conflate a capacity assessment with a best interests analysis and conclude that the person under review should attach greater weight to the physical security and comfort of a residential home and less importance to the emotional security and comfort that the person derives from being in their own home (see [65]–[67]).

(3) In order to understand the likely consequences of deciding to return home, KK should have been given full details of the care package that would or might be available. The choice which KK should have been asked to weigh up was not between the nursing home and a return home with no or limited support, but rather between staying in the nursing home and a return home with all practicable support (see [68]).

Case Study 5

PC v City of York Council [2013] EWCA Civ 478; [2013] C.O.P.L.R. 409

Court of Appeal: Richards, McFarlane and Lewison LJJ
1 May 2013

PC was a 48-year-old woman diagnosed with a mild learning disability. Her husband, NC, was shortly to be released from prison where he had been serving a sentence for serious sexual offences. PC did not accept that NC was guilty of the offences and, therefore, did not consider that he posed a risk to her. NC and PC wanted to live together on his release from prison. At first instance, the court held that PC lacked capacity to decide to resume married life with NC, but that it was in her best interests to do so, notwithstanding the risks posed to her.

The Official Solicitor, on behalf of PC, appealed on three grounds. The first ground was that the judge had wrongly identified the issue for determination as being whether PC had capacity to "resume married life", rather than by reference to the established domains of care, contact and residence. As a result, the Official Solicitor contended, the judge had conflated the relevant issues. The second ground was that the judge had failed to give proper weight to the fact that PC and NC had contracted a valid marriage in 2006 and there had been no relevant change in circumstances since that time to bring the validity of the marriage into question. The third ground was that, in any event, the judge wrongly applied a person-specific, rather than an act-specific, test in determining capacity.

2–070

Held: allowing the appeal and setting aside the judge's finding that PC lacked capacity to decide whether or not to go and live with her husband, NC:

(1) The determination of capacity under Part 1 of the MCA 2005 is decision-specific. Some decisions, for example, agreeing to marry or consenting to divorce, are status or act-specific. Some other decisions, for example, whether P should have contact with a particular individual, may be person-specific. But all decisions, whatever their nature, fall to be evaluated within the straightforward and clear structure of the MCA 2005

sections 1 to 3, which require the court to have regard to "a matter" requiring "a decision". The judge was correct to focus on the decision in hand, and the requirement in MCA 2005 section 3(1)(a) to "understand the information relevant to the decision" in this particular case must include reference to information specifically relevant to NC in the light of his conviction and its potential impact on the decision before the court (see [35], [39] and [40]).

(2) In a case where an apparently vulnerable person wishes to make an unwise decision, the structure and provisions of the MCA 2005 are to be applied with clarity and care in order to ensure that the autonomy of the individual is not eroded by the court in a case which, in reality, does not come within the statutory provisions. The causative nexus between mental impairment and the inability to make a decision must be established. Where a person has capacity to make other, related, decisions, there is a need to delineate why and how her mental impairment is sufficient to be the cause of her asserted inability to make the decision at issue (see [51] and [61]).

(3) On the facts, there was no sufficiently cogent evidence on which the court could have concluded that, despite PC having capacity to marry, she lacked capacity to decide to resume married life with her husband (see [59]).

Case Study 6

IM v LM [2014] EWCA Civ 37; [2014] C.O.P.L.R. 246

Court of Appeal: Sir Brian Leveson, President of the Queen's Bench Division, and Tomlinson and McFarlane LJJ

24 January 2014

2–071   LM was born in October 1972 and at the time of this appeal was 41. Her adult life had been chaotic. She had an extensive history of alcohol and drug abuse and convictions for offences related to prostitution. She had three children by a former abusive partner, all of whom had to be looked after by others at various stages during their childhood. On 16 July 2010, during gastro-intestinal surgery for liver disease, LM suffered a cardiac arrest leading to hypoxic brain injury, causing significant amnesia with moments of lucid thought that resulted in her displaying frustration, agitation and physical and verbal aggression.

AB, who had a significant criminal record and had been IM's sexual partner for a number of years, had been barred from the hospital in which she was being treated for what was described as inappropriate behaviour. He commenced proceedings in the Court of Protection to challenge the legality of the restrictions. Declarations had been made that LM lacked capacity to make decisions about her residence, care and contact with others, and that it was in her best interests to live in a residential placement before moving to independent supported living in around 12 months' time, and to continue to have her contact with AB restricted, but with an expectation that a reduction in restrictions should at least be trialled.

The issue of LM's capacity to consent to sexual relations was raised following the report of an independent psychiatrist, Dr G, who noted that LM wished to re-establish a sexual relationship with AB. Dr P, LM's clinical neuropsychologist, considered that LM understood the nature and character of the act of sexual intercourse but was concerned about her ability to withstand pressure or manipulation. Dr G confirmed that LM understood the mechanics of the sexual act, was able to say that heterosexual intercourse could give rise to pregnancy, and was aware of the risks of sexually transmitted infections. However, she was not able to weigh up the risks to herself of pregnancy or the potential risks to any children, and nor was she able to take appropriate action to avoid sexually transmitted infections, partly due to apathy and a lack of initiation arising from her brain injury, and partly due to a lack of general awareness of her own state of health. Dr G concluded that LM lacked capacity to consent to a sexual relationship on the basis that she could not weigh up information about the risks of pregnancy and sexually transmitted disease.

On 22 January 2013 the judge at first instance, Peter Jackson J, concluded that LM had capacity to consent to sexual relations. LM's mother, IM, appealed, arguing that the judge had:

(1) modified the correct standard of proof (which was simply on the balance of probabilities);
(2) erroneously took various irrelevant factors into account (such as her demonstrated sexualised behaviour prior to and following her brain injury);
(3) failed to appreciate that far from the opportunities for AB to have sex with LM being limited, the local authority will be under an obligation to facilitate such activity;
(4) failed to recognise that an inability to understand the implications of pregnancy demonstrated a lack of capacity to consent; and
(5) failed to have regard to the account of the clinicians that LM was unable to understand the nature of her relationship with others so as to be vulnerable to abuse and, in so doing, failed to explain why he disagreed with their views.

Held: dismissing the appeal:

(1) For the avoidance of doubt, every single issue of capacity which falls to be determined under the MCA 2005 must be evaluated by applying section 3(1) in full and considering each of the four elements of the decision-making process that are set out at (a)–(d) in that subsection. The extent to which on the facts of any individual case there is a need either for a sophisticated, or for a more straightforward, evaluation of any of these four elements will naturally vary from case to case and from topic to topic (see [73]). In the context of capacity to consent to sexual relations, the ability to use and weigh information was unlikely to loom large; the notional process of using and weighing information attributed to the protected person should not involve a refined analysis of the sort which did not typically inform the decision to consent to sexual relations made by a person of full capacity (see [81]). Similarly, the information regarded by persons of full capacity as relevant to the decision whether to consent to sexual relations was relatively limited (see [82]).
(2) Decisions about capacity within the Court of Protection have a necessary forward looking focus, in contrast to the criminal law which focus on the

specific occasion when capacity is actually deployed and consent is either given or withheld (see [75]). The test for capacity to consent to sexual relations under the MCA 2005 was general and issue specific, rather than person or event specific (see [79]).

Per curiam: The terminology that has developed in this field ("person-specific", "act-specific", "situation-specific" and "issue-specific") although superficially attractive, tends to disguise the broad base of the statutory test which, when applied to the question of capacity in the wide range of areas that is covered by the MCA 2005, will inevitably give rise to different considerations. It is important to emphasise that section 3(1)(c) of the MCA 2005 refers to the ability to use or weigh information as part of the process of making the decision. In some circumstances, having understood and retained relevant information, and ability to use it will be what is critical; in others, it will be necessary to be able to weigh competing considerations (see [52]).

Case Study 7

Heart of England NHS Foundation Trust v JB [2014] EWHC 342 (COP)

Judge: Peter Jackson J
17 February 2014

2–072   JB was a 62-year-old woman, who had been suffering from paranoid schizophrenia since her 20s. In addition, she had several chronic physical disabilities including hypertension, poorly-controlled insulin-dependent diabetes, retinopathy and anaemia. She developed ulcers on her feet and by August 2013 her right foot had become gangrenous. She refused to have an amputation of part of her right leg to prevent the spread of gangrene. There were differing views on whether she had capacity to refuse treatment and on 6 February 2014 the NHS Trust applied to the Court of Protection for a declaration that JB lacked capacity to make a decision about serious medical treatment.

Held: dismissing the Trust's application—that JB undoubtedly had a disturbance in the functioning of her mind in the form of paranoid schizophrenia (as to which she lacked insight) but that it had not been established that she thereby lacked the capacity to make a decision about surgery for herself. On the contrary, the evidence established that she did have capacity to decide whether to undergo an amputation of whatever kind (see [43]).

Case Study 8

London Borough of Redbridge v G; C and F [2014] EWHC 485 (COP); [2014] C.O.P.L.R. 292

Judge: Russell J
26 February 2014

2–073   The London Borough of Redbridge received complaints regarding C and F and their influence over a frail 94-year-old woman, G, who was British African

Caribbean and had no relative living in the UK. Having investigated the complaints, Redbridge brought proceedings under the MCA 2005.

Held: (a) declaring that G was incapable of making decisions in relation to the people who lived with her; contact with others; financial matters; and litigation capacity in respect of these three areas; (b) appointing an independent panel deputy to manage G's property and affairs:

(1) The evidence of the independent psychiatric expert in this regard was to be preferred to that of the independent social worker. The social worker was not qualified, as was the psychiatrist, to reach decisions as to mental impairment or disturbance (see [61]).
(2) On the evidence before the court, whilst it appeared that certain information was being deliberately withheld from her, it was also clear that the impairment gave rise to difficulties in retaining information and formulating decisions. The influence of C and F further compromised her ability to make decisions and understand what was happening to her. G therefore lacked capacity within the meaning of sections 2 and 3 of the MCA 2005 and her case fell under the jurisdiction of the Court of Protection, rather than the inherent jurisdiction (see [78]–[82]).

Case Study 9

Norfolk CC v PB [2014] EWCOP 14; [2015] C.O.P.L.R. 118

Judge: Parker J
21 March 2014

PB was a 79-year-old woman with a schizoid disorder and cognitive problems. TB was her husband, who suffered from schizophrenia. Both suffered from incontinence and required assistance with personal care. There was a history of PB being left without assistance by TB and being found in insanitary conditions. The local authority sought declarations that PB lacked capacity to make decisions about her care and residence and contact with TB, and that it was in her best interests to live at a residential home, where TB could visit and have overnight stays. The court heard evidence from PB's treating psychiatrist and an independent psychiatrist. The Official Solicitor for PB and the Official Solicitor for TB submitted that the presumption of capacity had not been rebutted, because it had not been shown that the reason for PB's alleged incapacity was her mental impairment rather than her beliefs about the importance of her marriage to TB.

2–074

Held: making final declarations as to PB's capacity and interim declarations as to PB's best interests:

(1) In determining whether the causative nexus between an individual's mental impairment and an inability to make a decision was satisfied for the purposes of section 2 of the MCA 2005, the question was whether the impairment or disturbance of mind was an effective, material or operative cause of the incapacity, even if other factors came into play (see [86]). PB's

compromised executive functioning and her anxiety were the cause of her inability to use and weigh information about the relevant matters (see [92] and [107]). The influence of TB on PB was also a relevant consideration of PB's capacity, and was not limited to the causal nexus between impairment or disturbance of functioning of mind and brain and inability to make a decision (see [103]).

(2) If PB had capacity, the court could have exercised its inherent jurisdiction to require PB's placement in the care home in any event, even if that entailed a deprivation of her liberty (see [113] and [121]).

Case Study 10

A Local Authority v TZ (No.2) [2014] EWHC 973 (COP); [2014] C.O.P.L.R. 159

Judge: Baker J
1 April 2014

2–075 TZ, who was born in 1989, had mild learning disabilities, atypical autism and Attention Deficit Hyperactivity Disorder. Despite the concerns of professionals and his adoptive parents, he formed a relationship with another man, A. The responsible local authority filed an application in the Court of Protection seeking declarations as to his capacity and orders as to his welfare. The principal focus of the attention of the parties and the court was the issues that might arise as TZ endeavoured to meet, and form intimate relations with, other men. TZ was clear that he wished to have the opportunity to have these experiences, and all professionals involved in supporting him agreed that he should be given that opportunity. The question was whether he had the capacity in respect of decisions that may have to be made when that opportunity arises. It was agreed that the issues that arise could be summarised as:

(1) What was the relevant decision in respect of which the question of capacity arose?
(2) Did TZ lack capacity in respect of that decision?
(3) If yes, what orders could be made in TZ's best interests?
(4) And should the court appoint the local authority to act as TZ's welfare deputy?

Held: declaring that TZ lacked the relevant decision-making capacities, and making observations as to the content of the care plan that should be put in place for TZ in his best interests:

(1) On a proper analysis, the questions as to capacity were: (a) whether TZ had the capacity to make a decision whether or not an individual with whom he might wish to have sexual relations was safe; and, if not, (b) whether he had the capacity to make a decision as to the support he required when having contact with an individual with whom he might wish to have sexual relations. On a balance of probabilities, he did not have the requisite capacity in respect of either of these decisions (see [18] and [37]–[40]).

(2) In determining what care plan would be in TZ's best interests, the court would have regard to a number of principles, including the obligation under section 4(6) of the MCA 2005 to have regard to his wishes and feelings; the obligation under article 8 of the European Convention for the Protection of Human Rights and Fundamental Freedoms 1950 to respect his right to private and family life; the provisions of article 23 of the CRPD and the state's obligation to protect him from harm. The court proposed a care plan focused upon education and empowerment. The court would deliberately not set out a draft plan in detail, that being a matter for the local authority support team to prepare in collaboration with TZ himself and his litigation friend, the Official Solicitor (see [45]–[54] and [87]).

(3) This was not an appropriate case for the appointment of a personal welfare deputy (see [82]–[86]).

Case Study 11

King's College Hospital NHS Foundation Trust v C [2015] EWCOP 80; [2016] C.O.P.L.R. 50

Judge: Macdonald J
30 November 2015

C was a 50-year-old woman who was described as "living a life characterised by impulsive and self-centred decision making without guilt or regret". She had been married four times and was "an entirely reluctant and at times completely indifferent mother" to her three daughters. She was diagnosed with breast cancer in December 2014 and underwent a lumpectomy and radiotherapy. Thereafter her life rapidly disintegrated and she lost "her sparkle". On 7 September 2015 she attempted suicide by swallowing 60 paracetamol tablets with champagne. She was subsequently taken to King's College Hospital, where she was treated for severe damage to her liver and kidneys. She refused haemodialysis treatment to her kidneys, knowing that without such treatment she would die. In November 2016 two psychiatrists, Dr R and Professor P, both concluded that C lacked capacity to make decisions about her medical treatment.

2–076

Kings College Hospital applied to the Court of Protection for a declaration under section 15 of the MCA 2005 that C lacked capacity to make decisions about her medical care and treatment and a further declaration that the Trust and its staff be authorised to provide such medical care and treatment as they judged to be clinically indicated, to prevent C from leaving the hospital without agreement and to use necessary and reasonable restraint for the purpose of providing the medical care and treatment.

Held: dismissing the application by the Trust:

(1) The court was not satisfied that the Trust had established on the balance of probabilities that C lacked capacity at the material time to decide whether or not to accept treatment by way of dialysis (see [95]). In the circumstances, the court had no jurisdiction to interfere with the decision making process (see [98]).

ASSESSING CAPACITY: THE LAW

(2) A capacitous individual is entitled to decide whether or not to accept treatment from his or her doctor. The right to refuse treatment extends to declining treatment that would, if administered, save the life of the patient and, accordingly, a capacitous patient may refuse treatment even in circumstances where that refusal will lead to his or her death (see [96]).

(3) The ongoing discomfort of treatment, the fear of chronic illness and the fear of lifelong treatment and lifelong disability were factors that weighed heavily in the balance for C in reaching a decision to refuse dialysis (see [97]).

(4) Although C's decision could be characterised as an unwise one that did not accord with the expectations of many in society, this was not evidence of lack of capacity (see [97]).

(5) The court being satisfied that, in accordance with the provisions of the MCA 2005, C had capacity to decide whether or not to accept the treatment, C was entitled to make her own decision on that question based on the things that are important to her, in keeping with her own personality and system of values and without conforming to society's expectation of what constitutes the "normal" decision in this situation. As a capacitous individual C is, in respect of her own body and mind, sovereign (see [97]).

4. JUDICIAL OBSERVATIONS ON CAPACITY

2–077 Part 4 contains some judicial observations on capacity and its assessment taken from the eleven decisions summarised in Part 3. The judicial observations are set out in detail after the following index.

1. The court must make the ultimate decision
2. The court must survey all the available evidence
3. The forward looking focus of the Court of Protection
4. The presumption of capacity
5. All practicable steps must be taken
6. Unwise decisions
7. Unwise decisions: the fact that a decision is unwise is a relevant consideration for the court to take into account when considering whether a person lacks capacity
8. Unwise decisions: the distinction between an unwise decision, which a person has the right to make, and a decision based on a lack of understanding of the risks
9. Unwise decisions: the space between an unwise decision and one which an individual does not have the mental capacity to take
10. The danger of applying an "outcome approach" whereby the patient is regarded as capable of making a decision that follows medical advice but incapable of making one that does not
11. Qualifications and qualities of the assessor
12. Qualifications and qualities of the assessor
13. Qualifications and qualities of the assessor
14. A suggestion that a surgeon lacked the expertise to assess capacity

JUDICIAL OBSERVATIONS ON CAPACITY

15. Psychological tests and psychiatric tests
16. Stock responses
17. The burden of proof
18. The burden of proof
19. Standard of proof: the balance of probabilities
20. The standard of proof: the seriousness of the underlying issue
21. A single visit
22. The judge seeing the patient in private
23. Danger of imposing too high a test of capacity
24. A combination of clinical judgment and cognitive testing
25. Avoid impractical and unnecessary distinctions that could diminish the scope of a person's capacity
26. The causative nexus ("because of")
27. The causative nexus: it does not matter in what order the expert addresses the issues
28. Impairment of, or disturbance in the functioning of, the mind or brain
29. Existence of factors other than an impairment or disturbance in the functioning of the mind or brain
30. Every single issue of capacity must be evaluated by applying section 3(1) of the MCA 2005 in full
31. Understanding: what is required is a broad, general understanding of the kind that is expected from the population at large
32. Relevant information: salient details
33. Relevant information: salient details
34. There has to be a practical limit on what needs to be envisaged as "reasonably foreseeable consequences"
35. Use or weigh: in some cases the ability to use information will be critical; in others, it will be necessary to weigh competing considerations
36. Use or weigh: different individuals may give different weight to different factors
37. Use or weigh: where the person being assessed chooses to withhold information
38. Use or weigh: setting the bar too high
39. Use or weigh: the inability to factor into her thought processes the realities of the harm that she will suffer
40. Use or weigh as part of the decision-making process
41. Where "the ability to use and weigh information is unlikely to loom large in the evaluation of capacity"
42. When a refined analysis is necessary because for a particular individual an otherwise simple decision is not a simple one
43. Inconsistency, confusion and incapacity
44. Inconsistency, confusion and incapacity
45. Indecision, avoidance and vacillation should not be confused with incapacity
46. Conflating a capacity assessment with a best interests analysis
47. Vulnerability
48. The vulnerable person's protective imperative
49. The vulnerable person's protective imperative

ASSESSING CAPACITY: THE LAW

50. Judicial criticism of an expert's report

1. The court must make the ultimate decision

2–078 "I acknowledge that there is consensus amongst the professionals who gave evidence that KK has lost the capacity to make decisions concerning her residence. These opinions are of course important evidence, but as stated above it is the court alone that is in the position to weigh up all the evidence as to the functional test and thus it is the court that must make the ultimate decision". *CC v KK* [2012] EWHC 2136 (COP); [2012] C.O.P.L.R. 627 per Baker J at [62].

2. The court must survey all the available evidence

2–079 "Finally, I of course bear in mind that my decision does not accord with the considered opinions of two very experienced psychiatrists. Whilst I have some concern that Dr R in particular set the test for capacity too high in this case in looking for C to demonstrate significant using and weighing of information demonstratively ending with a balanced, nuanced, used and weighed position, the fact that I have differed from Dr R and Professor P is in large part a product of this being a finely balanced case in which a number of reasonable interpretations of the information available are possible. In reaching my decision I must survey all the available evidence (see *PH v A Local Authority* [2011] EWHC 1704 (COP) at [16]). In the final analysis, having had the benefit of surveying the entirety of the information available to the court, I have come to a different interpretation of the finely balanced evidence to that favoured by the two psychiatrists, to both of whom I am grateful for their considered and extremely helpful evidence". *King's College Hospital NHS Foundation Trust v C* [2015] EWCOP 80 per Macdonald J at [94].

3. The forward looking focus of the Court of Protection

2–080 "[There is] a distinction between the general *capacity* to give or withhold consent to sexual relations, which is the necessary forward looking focus of the Court of Protection, and the person-specific, time and space specific, *occasion* when that capacity is actually deployed and the consent is either given or withheld, which is the focus of the criminal law". *IM v LM* [2014] EWCA Civ 37; [2014] C.O.P.L.R. 246 per Sir Brian Leveson, President of the Queen's Bench Division at [75].

4. The presumption of capacity

2–081 "Taking as my starting point the assumption that G has capacity I ignore the wisdom or otherwise of allowing strangers to live in her house and control her finances. I turn to the evidence regarding G's capacity or lack of it". *London Borough of Redbridge v G; C and F* [2014] EWHC 485 (COP); [2014] C.O.P.L.R. 292 per Russell J at [76].

5. All practicable steps must be taken

2–082 "This danger is linked, in my view, to a further problem with the local authority's approach in this case. I agree with Miss Hurst that, in assessing capacity it is inappropriate to start with a 'blank canvas'. The person under evaluation must be presented with detailed options so that their capacity to weigh up those options may be fairly assessed. I find that the local authority has not identified a complete package of support that would or might be available should KK return home. The statute requires that, before a person can be treated as lacking capacity to make a decision, it must be shown that all practicable steps have been taken to help her do so. As the Code of Practice makes clear, each person whose capacity is under scrutiny must be given 'relevant information' including 'what the likely consequences of a decision would be (the possible effects of deciding one way or another).' That requires a detailed analysis of the effects of the decision either way, which in turn necessitates identifying the best ways in which each option would be supported. In order to understand the likely consequences of deciding to return home, KK should be given full details of the care package that would or might be available. The choice which KK should be asked to weigh up is not between the nursing home and a return to the bungalow with no or limited support, but rather between staying in the nursing home and a return home with all practicable support. I am not satisfied that KK was given full details of all practicable support that would or might be available should she return home to her bungalow". *CC v KK* [2012] EWHC 2136 (COP); [2012] C.O.P.L.R. 627 per Baker J at [68].

6. Unwise decisions

"The decision C has reached to refuse dialysis can be characterised as an unwise one. That C considers that the prospect of growing old, the fear of living with fewer material possessions and the fear that she has lost, and will not regain, 'her sparkle' outweighs a prognosis that signals continued life will alarm and possibly horrify many, although I am satisfied that the ongoing discomfort of treatment, the fear of chronic illness and the fear of lifelong treatment and lifelong disability are factors that also weigh heavily in the balance for C. C's decision is certainly one that does not accord with the expectations of many in society. Indeed, others in society may consider C's decision to be unreasonable, illogical or even immoral within the context of the sanctity afforded to life by society in general. None of this however is evidence of lack of capacity. The court being satisfied that, in accordance with the provisions of the MCA 2005, C has capacity to decide whether or not to accept treatment C is entitled to make her own decision on that question based on things that are important to her, in keeping with her own personality and system of values and without conforming to society's expectation of what constitutes the 'normal' decision in this situation (if such a thing exists). As a capacitous individual C is, in respect of her own body and mind, sovereign". *King's College Hospital NHS Foundation Trust v C* [2015] EWCOP 80 per Macdonald J at [97]. 2–083

7. Unwise decisions: the fact that a decision is unwise is a relevant consideration for the court to take into account when considering whether a person lacks capacity

"The significance of section 1(4) must not, however, be exaggerated. The fact that a decision is unwise or foolish may not, without more, be treated as conclusive, but it remains, in my judgment, a relevant consideration for the court to take into account in considering whether the criteria of inability to make a decision for oneself in section 3(1) are satisfied. This will particularly be the case where there is a marked contrast between the unwise nature of the impugned decision and the person's former attitude to the conduct of his affairs at a time when his capacity was not in question". *Re S; D v R* [2010] EWHC 2405 (COP); [2010] C.O.P.L.R. Con. Vol. 1112 per Henderson J at [43]. 2–084

8. Unwise decisions: the distinction between an unwise decision, which a person has the right to make, and a decision based on a lack of understanding of the risks

2–085 "I find on a balance of probabilities that TZ does not have the capacity to decide whether a person with whom he may wish to have sexual relations is safe. I base that finding on the assessments, which include extensive conversations with TZ in which he himself has acknowledged that he lacks capacity. In particular, while he has the ability to understand and retain information, he lacks the ability to use or weigh up the information, including the ability to assess risk and, in the language of section 3(4), to understand the reasonably foreseeable consequences of the decision. This is, in my judgment, a good example of the distinction identified in paragraph 4.30 of the Code of Practice between, on the one hand, unwise decisions, which a person has the right to make, and, on the other hand, decisions based on a lack of understanding of risks and the inability to weigh up the information concerning a decision". *A Local Authority v TZ (No.2)* [2014] EWHC 973 (COP); [2014] C.O.P.L.R. 159 per Baker J at [37].

9. Unwise decisions: the space between an unwise decision and one which an individual does not have the mental capacity to take

2–086 "Mr Butler's reference to Baroness Hale's description of the approach that underpins the MCA 2005 is timely; the court's jurisdiction is not founded upon professional concern as to the 'outcome' of an individual's decision. There may plainly be women who are seen to be in relationships with men regarded by professionals as predatory sexual offenders. The Court of Protection does not have jurisdiction to act to 'protect' these women if they do not lack the mental capacity to decide whether or not to be, or continue to be, in such a relationship. The individual's decision may be said to be 'against the better judgment' of the woman concerned, but the point is that, unless they lack mental capacity to make that judgment, it is against *their* better judgment. It is a judgment that they are entitled to make. The statute respects their autonomy so to decide and the Court of Protection has no jurisdiction to intervene.

Mr Bowen correctly submits that there is a space between an unwise decision and one which an individual does not have the mental capacity to take and he powerfully argues that it is important to respect that space, and to ensure that it is preserved, for it is within that space that an individual's autonomy operates". *PC v City of York Council* [2013] EWCA Civ 478; [2013] C.O.P.L.R. 409 per McFarlane LJ at [53] and [54].

10. The danger of applying an "outcome approach" whereby the patient is regarded as capable of making a decision that follows medical advice but incapable of making one that does not

2–087 "At all events, it is for the Trust to displace the presumption that JB has capacity on a balance of probabilities. It is important that the right question is asked ... There is a danger in a difficult case like this that the patient is regarded as capable of making a decision that follows medical advice but incapable of making one that does not". *Heart of England NHS Foundation Trust v JB* [2014] EWCOP 342 per Peter Jackson J at [27] and [28].

JUDICIAL OBSERVATIONS ON CAPACITY

11. Qualifications and qualities of the assessor

"Mr Gillman-Smith is not qualified, as Dr Barker is, to reach decisions as to mental impairment or disturbance. As a social worker, albeit a highly experienced and well-qualified one, he does not have the knowledge and training that a psychiatrist possesses in that respect. Rather his field is in welfare and as such he is well placed to give an opinion on relationships and inter-personal functioning within G's household; he is well qualified to advise on what steps could or should be taken to assist G to regain capacity and what should be put in place to reduce her dependency on C. He did not apply the tests in sections 2 and 3 of the MCA in his report nor was he instructed to do so in the letter of instruction which directed him instead to section 4". *London Borough of Redbridge v G; C and F* [2014] EWHC 485 (COP); [2014] C.O.P.L.R. 292 per Russell J at [61].

2–088

12. Qualifications and qualities of the assessor

"For the purposes of section 2 I must decide whether it is more likely than not that there is an impairment of, or a disturbance in the functioning of, the mind or brain of G. When it comes to this question I prefer the evidence of Dr Barker, for reasons I have alluded to previously. He is an expert in Old Age Psychiatry and eminently qualified to reach the conclusion that he did; finding evidence of significant cognitive impairment on the basis of his examination of G which included carrying out tests recognised and approved by the National Institute for Health and Care Excellence (NICE). There is no evidence from an equally well qualified expert to gainsay his evidence and on the balance of probabilities I find that G has an impairment of her mind or brain". *London Borough of Redbridge v G; C and F* [2014] EWHC 485 (COP); [2014] C.O.P.L.R. 292 per Russell J at [77].

2–089

13. Qualifications and qualities of the assessor

"Although neither Dr A nor Dr B nor Dr C has a curriculum vitae as academically distinguished as Dr Rickards, in my view they each have obvious and valuable expertise in Huntington's disease. Interestingly, each of them brings a slightly different type of expertise to the case—Dr A as a consultant psychiatrist specialising in old age and dementia. Dr B is a GP but with a unique depth of expertise in Huntington's disease through his years working at Y Court, and Dr C, with his expertise in mental capacity assessment and interest in medico-legal matters. With respect to Dr Rickards, I consider that the overall expertise of Doctors A, B and C, coupled with their much greater experience of PH as a patient, justifies the court attaching greater weight to their combined views in this case. In addition, D, although not as experienced as the clinicians, was to my mind a manifestly fair and perceptive witness whose opinion demands very great respect". *PH v A Local Authority* [2011] EWHC 1704 (Fam); [2012] C.O.P.L.R. 128 per Baker J at [58].

2–090

14. A suggestion that a surgeon lacked the expertise to assess capacity

"It was, perhaps surprisingly, suggested to Mr Collin that he lacked the expertise to assess capacity. He accepted that the assessment of mental illness was outside his remit but said that he was well qualified to assess the capacity of patients to consent to operations. I agree. All doctors and many non-medical professionals (for example, social workers and solicitors) have to assess capacity at one time or another. Bearing in mind JB's longstanding mental illness it is entirely appropriate

2–091

that the core assessment of her capacity comes from psychiatrists, but other disciplines also have an important contribution to make". *Heart of England NHS Foundation Trust v JB* [2014] EWCOP 342 per Peter Jackson J at [38].

15. Psychological tests and psychiatric tests

2–092

"I now turn to the question whether Mr S is able to use or weigh the relevant information. In view of the conclusion which I have already reached about his inability to understand the information, I can deal with this question comparatively briefly. All of the matters which I have already mentioned on the issue of understanding apply, with equal or greater force, to the question whether he is able to use or weigh the relevant information as part of the decision-making process. In addition, I have the clear and firm evidence of both Professor Beaumont and Dr Barker that Mr S cannot satisfy this requirement, even on the assumption that he does understand the relevant information. Their evidence on this part of the case was not significantly shaken in cross-examination, and I have the added comfort of knowing that they agree in their conclusion although they approach it from the perspective of their different disciplines as a psychologist and a psychiatrist. I do not wish to express any view on the question whether the avowedly scientific tests administered by a psychologist have intrinsically greater value than the bedside tests and clinical insights of a psychiatrist. Both professions have much to contribute when the subject matter is something as profound and mysterious as the workings of the human brain. For present purposes, the important point is that both Professor Beaumont and Dr Barker are in agreement." *Re S; D v R* [2010] EWHC 2405 (COP); [2010] C.O.P.L.R. Con. Vol. 1112 per Henderson J at [148].

16. Stock responses

2–093

"At this point, Professor Beaumont returned to the theme that Mr S has a number of set phrases which he tends to use habitually, such as 'I did what I did and that's an end of it', which Mr S had said to him a number of times. When asked what he concluded from this, Professor Beaumont replied:

'What I conclude is that, as with many patients who have these kinds of executive disorders and problems with reasoning, is that they fall back on relatively stereotyped social speech and interaction. In fact my view may be partly coloured by the fact that in my hospital job I work with clients who have extremely severe and profound brain injury ... Now, I am not suggesting that this is the case for [Mr S], but he is on the road to that which is what one commonly sees in dementias of the kind that [he] has. Because he has difficulties with his cognition, he falls back on a relatively restricted range of comments and remarks and responses which he makes, which are acceptable in the situation but are not ... freely reasoned in the way that a normal intact individual would do.'

Professor Beaumont gave us another example of a repeated phrase used by Mr S, his expression that '[Mrs D] touched me very deeply'. He added that the point of such responses was that they were socially quite helpful to Mr S in that they prevented further discussion of his reasons for having acted as he did.

...

I think there is force in Professor Beaumont's observation that Mr S tends to have recourse to stock responses, that he often fails to offer an explanation for his stated position, and that his reactions are not those of a person of ordinary prudence. None of these points is more than an indicator, and I am, of course, well aware of the

JUDICIAL OBSERVATIONS ON CAPACITY

statutory principle that a decision is not necessarily made without capacity merely because it is an unwise one. Nevertheless, in the context of all the other evidence in the case I think that the probable explanation for these features of Mr S's current behaviour is that the deterioration in his mental faculties has left him unable to reason his way to a conclusion in a novel situation". *Re S; D v R* [2010] EWHC 2405 (COP); [2010] C.O.P.L.R. Con. Vol. 1112 per Henderson J at [125] and [152].

17. The burden of proof

"Just as there is no justification for imposing any threshold conditions before a best interests assessment under the DOLS [Deprivation of Liberty Safeguards] can be carried out, so in my judgment there is no reason for adopting the approach, also advanced by Miss Morris on behalf of the Official Solicitor, that the statutory test should be construed 'narrowly'. The statutory scheme is, as I have already observed, carefully crafted. I agree with the submission made on behalf of Z Ltd (in written submissions by Mr Vikram Sachdeva who did not appear at the hearing) that the question of incapacity must be construed in accordance with the statutory test—'no more and no less'". *PH v A Local Authority* [2011] EWHC 1704 (Fam); [2012] C.O.P.L.R. 128 per Baker J at [16 (xii)]. 2–094

18. The burden of proof

"This case illustrates the importance of the fundamental principle enshrined in section 1(2) of the 2005 Act—that a person must be assumed to have capacity unless it is demonstrated that she lacks it. The burden lies on the local authority to prove that KK lacks capacity to make decisions as to where she lives. A disabled person, and a person with a degenerative condition, is as entitled as anyone else to the protection of this presumption of capacity. The assessment is issue-specific and time-specific. In due course, her capacity may deteriorate. Indeed that is likely to happen given her diagnosis. At this hearing, however, the local authority has failed to prove that KK lacks capacity to make decisions as to where she should live". *CC v KK* [2012] EWHC 2136 (COP); [2012] C.O.P.L.R. 627 per Baker J at [74]. 2–095

19. Standard of proof: the balance of probabilities

"For the purposes of section 2, I must decide whether it is more likely than not that there is an impairment of, or a disturbance in the functioning of, the mind or brain of G. When it comes to this question I prefer the evidence of Dr Barker, for reasons I have alluded to previously. ... There is no evidence from an equally well qualified expert to gainsay his evidence and on the balance of probabilities I find that G has an impairment of her mind or brain". *London Borough of Redbridge v G; C and F* [2014] EWHC 485 (COP); [2014] C.O.P.L.R. 292 per Russell J at [77]. 2–096

20. The standard of proof: the seriousness of the underlying issue

"Mr Bagchi submits that, since the underlying subject matter here consists of a duly celebrated marriage, the court should not take any decision which might lead to the subsequent annulment of the marriage unless the evidence is compelling. It is not easy go correlate this with section 2(4) of the MCA 2005, which expressly imposes 'the balance of probabilities' as the standard of proof. Whilst that therefore has to be the standard, I will keep in mind the seriousness of the underlying issue when reaching my decision and will not decide lightly that the prescribed standard has 2–097 been met by the local authority". *A Local Authority v AK* [2012] EWHC B29 (COP); [2013] C.O.P.L.R. 163 per Bodey J at [15].

21. A single visit

2–098

"I acknowledge the expertise of Dr Rickards and find his approach to his assessment to have been appropriately objective and professional but I was struck by the fact that his report, and the answers to the supplementary questions posed by the other parties, seemed somewhat superficial. This may have been a reflection of the fact that he was basing his opinion on a single interview of 90 minutes. It would be an over-simplification to describe it as a snapshot but it is, to my mind, a disadvantage that the assessment was based on a single visit". *PH v A Local Authority* [2011] EWHC 1704 (Fam); [2012] C.O.P.L.R. 128 per Baker J at [56].

22. The judge seeing the patient in private

2–099

"I was asked prior to the hearing, and when I had no opportunity to assess the background, whether I would see PB at the hearing. I reserved that decision for the trial. At court I was also asked to see TB. I was happy to do so, but stressed that care has to be taken as to how a meeting shall be treated. The protected party does not give a sworn/affirmed account, and in particular if the meeting takes place only in the presence of the judge, with no opportunity to test the evidence, then in my view no factual conclusions save those that relate to the meeting itself should be drawn, in particular with regard to capacity (see *YLA v PM* [2013] EWHC 4020 (COP); [2014] C.O.P.L.R. 114 at [35]". *Norfolk CC v PB* [2014] EWCOP 14; [2015] C.O.P.L.R. 118 per Parker J at [42].

23. Danger of imposing too high a test of capacity

2–100

"In *Re E (An Alleged Patient): Sheffield City Council v E and S* [2004] EWHC 2808 (Fam) (a case concerning capacity to marry before the implementation of the MCA 2005) Munby J (as he then was) said (at [144]): 'We must be careful not to set the test of capacity to marry too high, lest it operate as an unfair, unnecessary and indeed discriminatory bar against the mentally disabled.' Although that observation concerned the capacity to marry, I agree with the submission made by Miss Morris on behalf of the Official Solicitor in this case that it should be applied to other questions of capacity. In other words, courts must guard against imposing too high a test of capacity to decide issue such as residence because to do so would run the risk of discriminating against persons suffering from a mental disability. In my judgment, the carefully-drafted detailed provisions of the MCA 2005 and the Code of Practice are consistent with this approach". *PH v A Local Authority* [2011] EWHC 1704 (Fam); [2012] C.O.P.L.R. 128 per Baker J at [16(xi)].

24. A combination of clinical judgment and cognitive testing

2–101

"In answer to questions from Mr Marshall, Dr Barker said that he had been unusually impressed by Professor Beaumont's report, and he was reassured by the fact that Professor Beaumont had adopted a dual approach, relying on his clinical judgment as well as the cognitive testing in which he had special expertise". *Re S; D v R* [2010] EWHC 2405 (COP); [2010] C.O.P.L.R. Con. Vol. 1112 per Henderson J at [139].

25. Avoid impractical and unnecessary distinctions that could diminish the scope of a person's capacity

"Nor do I accept the Official Solicitor's submission that the issue is whether JB has the capacity to consent to a below-knee amputation as opposed to operations no longer proposed by the Trust, i.e. through-knee or above-knee amputations. As explained above, what is required is an understanding of the nature, purpose and effects of the proposed treatment. In this sense 'the proposed treatment' is surgical treatment for a potentially gangrenous limb, and is not limited to one of the possible operations. Treating each type of amputation as different is an impractical and unnecessary distinction that would diminish the scope of JB's capacity and potentially lead to unprofitable reassessments with every change in treatment programme". *Heart of England NHS Foundation Trust v JB* [2014] EWHC 342 (COP) per Peter Jackson J at [43].

2–102

26. The causative nexus ("because of")

"It would be going too far to hold that in approaching matters in this way Hedley J plainly erred in applying the law. His judgment refers to the key provisions and twice refers to the nexus between the elements of an inability to make decisions, set out in section 3(1), and mental impairment or disturbance required by section 2(1). There is, however, a danger in structuring the decision by looking to section 2(1) primarily as requiring a finding of mental capacity and nothing more, and in considering section 2(1) first before then going on to look at section 3(1) as requiring a finding of inability to make a decision. The danger is that the strength of the causative nexus between mental impairment and inability to decide is watered down. That sequence—'mental impairment' and then 'inability to make a decision'—is the reverse of that in section 2(1)—'unable to make a decision … *because of* an impairment of, or a disturbance in the functioning of, the mind or brain' [emphasis added]. The danger of using section 2(1) simply to collect the mental health element is that the key words 'because of' in section 2(1) may lose their prominence and be replaced by words such as those deployed by Hedley J: 'referable to' or 'significantly relates to". *PC v City of York Council* [2013] EWCA Civ 478; [2013] C.O.P.L.R. 409 per McFarlane LJ at [58].

2–103

27. The causative nexus: it does not matter in what order the expert addresses the issues

"Ms Street and Mr Reeder also submit that Dr Khalifa approached the test the wrong way round. They submit that the Code of Practice stipulates that the first step is to decide whether there is a disturbance of mind, and the second to decide on capacity, whereas McFarlane LJ in *PC v City of York* [2013] EWCA Civ 478; [2013] C.O.P.L.R. 409 stated that this should be considered in reverse order. In my view McFarlane LJ did not purport to lay down a different test: nor did he take the questions in the reverse order, but simply stressed that there must be a causative nexus between the impairment and the incapacity.

I do not consider that it matters what order the expert addressed the issues so long as he or she observes the causative nexus. Dr Khalifa identified the impairment or disturbance, which she described compellingly and in detail, and then clearly advised that this caused the inability to use and weigh". *Norfolk CC v PB* [2014] EWCOP 14; [2015] C.O.P.L.R. 118 per Parker J at [89] and [90].

2–104

28. Impairment of, or disturbance in the functioning of, the mind or brain

2–105 "Having found that C is not a person unable to make a decision for herself for the purposes of section 3(1) it is not necessary for me to go on to consider the so called 'diagnostic test'. It is right to record that, as I observed at the conclusion of the hearing, had I been satisfied that C was unable to use and weigh information in the manner contended for by the Trust, I believe that I would have had difficulty in deciding that this inability was, on the balance of probabilities, because of an impairment of, or a disturbance in the functioning of the mind or brain. Whilst it is accepted by all parties that C has an impairment of, or a disturbance in the functioning of, the mind or brain, the evidence as to the precise nature of that impairment or disturbance was far from conclusive. Further, and more importantly, with regard to the question of causation, and in particular whether what was being seen might be the operation of a personality disorder or simply the thought processes of a strong willed, stubborn individual with unpalatable and highly egocentric views the evidence was likewise somewhat equivocal. However, as I say, I need say no more about this in light of my conclusions as set out above". *King's College Hospital NHS Foundation Trust v C* [2015] EWCOP 80 per Macdonald J at [93].

29. Existence of factors other than an impairment or disturbance in the functioning of the mind or brain

2–106 "I agree with Ms Burnham that where there are several causes it is logically impossible for one of them to be 'the effective cause'. I agree that to hold otherwise would lead to an absurd conclusion because even if impairment or disturbance were the most important factor, wherever there were other factors (however little part they might play) the s.2 MCA test would not apply.

There is nothing Convention incompatible in the concept that multiple factor may affect a decision. Otherwise a person with impaired capacity whose disturbance/impairment of mind operates to disable her from weighing and using information would not fall within the protection of the Act.

It seems to me that the true question is whether the impairment/disturbance is an effective, material or operative cause. Does it cause the incapacity, even if other factors come into play? This is a purposive construction". *Norfolk CC v PB* [2014] EWCOP 14; [2015] C.O.P.L.R. 118 per Parker J at [84]–[86].

30. Every single issue of capacity must be evaluated by applying section 3(1) of the Act in full

2–107 "For the avoidance of doubt, every single issue of capacity which falls to be determined under Part 1 of the [Mental Capacity] Act must be evaluated by applying section 3(1) in full and considering each of the four elements of the decision-making process that are set out at (a)–(d) in that subsection ... The extent to which on the facts of any individual case there is a need either for a sophisticated, or for a more straightforward, evaluation of any of these four elements will naturally vary from case to case and from topic to topic". *IM v LM* [2014] EWCA Civ 37; [2014] C.O.P.L.R. 246 per Sir Brian Leveson, President of the Queen's Bench Division at [73].

31. Understanding: what is required is a broad, general understanding of the kind that is expected from the population at large

"The question is whether JB can understand, retain and use and weigh the relevant information in coming to a decision. What is in my view required is that she should understand the nature, purpose and effects of the proposed treatment, the last of these entailing an understanding of the benefits and risks of deciding to have or not to have one or other of the various kinds of amputation, or of not making a decision at all. What is required here is a broad, general understanding of the kind that is expected from the population at large. JB is not required to understand every last piece of information about her situation and her options: even her doctors would not make that claim. It must also be remembered that common strategies for dealing with unpalatable dilemmas—for example, indecision, avoidance or vacillation—are not to be confused with incapacity. We should not ask more of people whose capacity is questioned than of those whose capacity is undoubted". *Heart of England NHS Foundation Trust v JB* [2014] EWHC 342 (COP) per Peter Jackson J at [25] and [26].

2–108

32. Relevant information: salient details

"In Dr Rickard's view it is unnecessary for his determination of RYJ's capacity that she should understand all the details within the Statement of Special Educational Needs. It is unnecessary that she should be able to give weight to every consideration that would otherwise be utilised in formulating a decision objectively in her 'best interests'. I agree with his interpretation of the test in section 3 which is to the effect that the person under review must comprehend and review the salient details relevant to the decision to be made. To hold otherwise would place greater demands on RYJ than others of her chronological age/commensurate maturity and unchallenged capacity". *LBL v RYJ* [2010] EWHC 2665 (COP); [2010] C.O.P.L.R. Con. Vol. 795 per Macur J at [58].

2–109

33. Relevant information: salient details

"When considering KK's capacity to weigh up the options for her future residence, I adopt the approach of Macur J in *LBJ v RYJ*, namely that it is not necessary for a person to demonstrate a capacity to understand and weigh up every detail of the respective options, but merely the salient factors. In this case, KK may lack the capacity to understand and weigh up every nuance or detail. In my judgment, however, she does understand the salient features, and I do not agree that her understanding is 'superficial'". *CC v KK* [2012] EWHC 2136 (COP); [2012] C.O.P.L.R. 627 per Baker J at [69].

2–110

34. There has to be a practical limit on what needs to be envisaged as "reasonably foreseeable consequences"

"The requirement for a practical limit on what needs to be envisaged as 'reasonably foreseeable consequences' derives not just from pragmatism but from the imperative that the notional decision-making process attributed to the protected person with regard to consent to sexual relations should not become divorced from the actual decision-making process carried out in that regard on a daily basis by persons of full capacity. That process ... is largely visceral rather than cerebral,

2–111

owing more to instinct and emotion than to analysis". *IM v LM* [2014] EWCA Civ 37; [2014] C.O.P.L.R. 246 per Sir Brian Leveson, President of the Queen's Bench Division at [80].

35. Use or weigh: in some cases the ability to use information will be critical; in others, it will be necessary to weigh competing considerations

2–112 "We endorse the language of Macfarlane J and express concern that the terminology that has developed in this field ('person-specific', 'act-specific', 'situation-specific' and 'issue-specific'), although superficially attractive, tends to disguise the broad base of the statutory test, which, when applied to the question of capacity in the wide range of areas that is covered by the act, will inevitably give rise to different considerations. It is important to emphasise that section 3(1)(c) of the act refers to the ability to use or weigh information as part of the process of making the decision. In some circumstances, having understood and retained relevant information, an ability to use it will be what is critical; in others, it will be necessary to weigh competing considerations". *IM v LM* [2014] EWCA Civ 37; [2014] C.O.P.L.R. 246 per Sir Brian Leveson, President of the Queen's Bench Division at [52].

36. Use or weigh: different individuals may give different weight to different factors

2–113 "I read section 3 to convey, amongst other detail, that it is envisaged that it may be necessary to use a variety of means to communicate relevant information, that it is not always necessary for a person to comprehend all peripheral details and that it is recognised that different individuals may give different weight to different factors". *LBL v RYJ* [2010] EWHC 2665 (COP); [2010] C.O.P.L.R. Con. Vol. 795 per Macur J at [24].

37. Use or weigh: setting the bar too high

2–114 "Whilst I have some concern that Dr R in particular set the test for capacity too high in this case in looking for C to demonstrate significant using and weighing of information demonstratively ending with a balanced, nuanced, used and weighed position, the fact that I have differed from Dr R and Professor P is in large part a product of this being a finely balanced case in which a number of reasonable interpretations of the information available are possible". *King's College Hospital NHS Foundation Trust v C* [2015] EWCOP 80 per Macdonald J at [94].

38. Use or weigh: where the person being assessed chooses to withhold information

2–115 "[Dr Barker] said that assessment of whether she was unable to use and weigh might be skewed if PB had chosen to withhold information. She might have different thought processes but was choosing not to disclose that to him. There is evidence that she understands the issue but she may not want to give evidence which may 'damage her cause', this may be a natural denial". *Norfolk CC v PB* [2014] EWCOP 14; [2015] C.O.P.L.R. 118 per Parker J at [66].

JUDICIAL OBSERVATIONS ON CAPACITY

39. Use or weigh: the inability to factor into her thought processes the realities of the harm that she will suffer

"I have had the advantage, which the experts have not, of surveying all the material in this case and in particular the oral evidence of Ms Thompson. PB, notwithstanding her high intellectual capacity and verbal dexterity, and in spite of her superficial and partial acknowledgment of the risks, is simply unable to factor into her thought processes (i.e. use and weigh) the realities of the harm that she will suffer if she resumes living with TB or has uncontrolled contact with him. And perhaps, even more importantly, she is unable to weigh up the risks to her of being in an unsupported environment, with or without him, without a package of care. This is not paternalistic, or to fail to allow her to experience an acceptable degree of risk. It is not a question of allowing her 'to make the same mistakes as all other human beings are at liberty to make and not infrequently do'". *Norfolk CC v PB* [2014] EWCOP 14; [2015] C.O.P.L.R. 118 per Parker J at [108].

2–116

40. Use or weigh as part of the decision-making process

"It is important to note that section 3(1)(c) is engaged where a person is unable to use and weigh the relevant information as part of the process of making the decision. What is required is that the person is able to employ the relevant information in the decision making process and determine what weight to give it relative to other information required to make the decision. Where a court is satisfied that a person is able to use and weigh the relevant information, the weight to be attached to that information in the decision making process is a matter for the decision maker. Thus, where a person is able to use and weigh the relevant information but chooses to give that information no weight when reaching the decision in question, the element of the functional test comprised by section 3(1)(c) will not be satisfied, Within this context, a person cannot be considered to be unable to use and weigh information simply on the basis that he or she has applied his or her own values or outlook to that information in making the decision in question and chosen to attach no weight to that information in the decision making process". *King's College Hospital NHS Foundation Trust v C* [2015] EWCOP 80 per Macdonald J at [38].

2–117

41. Where "the ability to use and weigh information is unlikely to loom large in the evaluation of capacity"

"It is for that reason also that the ability to use and weigh information is unlikely to loom large in the evaluation of capacity to consent to sexual relations. It is not an irrelevant consideration; indeed (as we have emphasised) the statute mandates that it be taken into account, but the notional process of using and weighing information attributed to the protected person should not involve a refined analysis of the sort which does not typically inform the decision to consent to sexual relations made by a person of full capacity ... Perhaps yet another way of expressing the same point is to suggest that the information typically, and we stress typically, regarded by persons of full capacity as relevant to the decision whether to consent to sexual relations is relatively limited. The temptation to expand that field of information in an attempt to simulate more widely-informed decision-making is likely to lead to what Bodey J rightly identified as both paternalism and a derogation from personal autonomy". *IM v LM* [2014] EWCA Civ 37; [2014] C.O.P.L.R. 246 per Sir Brian Leveson, President of the Queen's Bench Division at [81] and [82].

2–118

42. When a refined analysis is necessary because for a particular individual an otherwise simple decision is not a simple one

2–119 "[In *Re MM* [2007] EWHC 2003 (Fam) at [134] Munby J] explained that the test of being able to 'understand, retain and weigh up' under section 3 is just as applicable where the question is whether an individual has the capacity to marry as it is where the question is whether he or she has the capacity to take any other decision: '... it is simply that such a refined analysis is probably not necessary where the issue is as simple as the question whether someone has the capacity to marry, or to consent to sexual relations.' In other words, because for most people, marriage is regarded as a fairly straightforward concept (compared for example with litigating, or with many medical procedures) one would not normally need to spend too much time on an individual's ability to 'understand, retain, use and weigh' the information about marriage which is referred to in *Sheffield*. Nevertheless, there will occasionally be cases where the degree and/or nature of the individual's impairments does make it necessary to do so, because for him or her a decision about marrying is not actually a simple one. This is one such case. I shall need to revert to the point below on the issue of how Dr S struggled with the test in law and came to the original conclusion that AK had capacity". *A Local Authority v AK* [2012] EWHC B29 (COP); [2013] C.O.P.L.R. 163 per Bodey J at [15].

43. Inconsistency, confusion and incapacity

2–120 "I consider that there has been inadequate regard paid by LBL and VJ to RYJ's potential tendency to teenage ennui, manipulation and fickleness which are traits not confined to those lacking capacity. For example, I was struck by the fact that Ms. Stevenson approached RYJ's 'inconsistency' as to contact with VJ in a particular and somewhat blinkered way. It is clear that RYJ's answer 'maybe' in response to a question whether she wished to see VJ was interpreted to mean that, at worse—in terms of capacity—she was unable to reach a decision on the matter or else, at best, frightened that her decision would not be given effect, not that she was at that stage undecided. I accept the evidence of Mr Sinclair that it is necessary for those who deal with RYJ not to underestimate her ability to attempt to manipulate a situation as with many other teenagers in similar stage of maturity and chronology age. At the time of this response RYJ was 'away' from her family living in somewhat isolated conditions". *LBL v RYJ* [2010] EWHC 2665 (COP); [2010] C.O.P.L.R. Con. Vol. 795 per Macur J at [33].

44. Inconsistency, confusion and incapacity

2–121 "Immediately thereafter Ms Stevenson refers to guidance in Chapter 3 of the Code of Practice relating to the assistance to be proffered in facilitating the decision making process of an individual in accordance with their particular limitations. It seems to me that in RYJ's case in August 2010 on occasions it was more honoured in the breach than in its observance. Quite clearly the fact of inconsistency is not necessarily a sign of confusion. Equally, confusion is not necessarily an indication of incapacity.

In this case RYJ had made known her particular views which, even if adjudged objectively to vary according to date, time and interviewer are not diagnostic of lack of capacity. Ms Stevenson did not appear to consider that RYJ's change of mind may reflect the circumstances/wishes/desires of the moment; a reluctance to engage or genuine indecision. What is more, it seems that those particular views were effectively challenged by continual repetitive questioning to 'confirm' the same. In those circumstances it is unsurprising that any person without impairment may begin to doubt that which they said initially.

In the circumstances I am not satisfied on the balance of probabilities that this inconsistency was anything other than a wish to bring to an end the repeated questioning which she was being subject to. Nor am I satisfied that it is anything other than the facility employed by R to effectively move on during the day without interruption to her plans". *LBL v RYJ* [2010] EWHC 2665 (COP); [2010] C.O.P.L.R. Con. Vol. 795 per Macur J at [49], [50] and [51].

45. Indecision, avoidance and vacillation should not be confused with incapacity

"It must also be remembered that common strategies for dealing with unpalatable dilemmas—for example, indecision, avoidance or vacillation—are not to be confused with incapacity. We should not ask more of people whose capacity is questioned than of those whose capacity is undoubted". *Heart of England NHS Foundation Trust v JB* [2014] EWCOP 342 per Peter Jackson J at [26].

2–122

46. Conflating a capacity assessment with a best interests analysis

"A fundamental point in this case is the principle articulated by Macur J in *LBJ v RYJ* that in evaluating capacity the court must recognise that different individuals may give different weight to different factors. There is, I perceive, a danger that professionals, including judges, may objectively conflate a capacity assessment with a best interests analysis and conclude that the person under review should attach greater weight to the physical security and comfort of a residential home and less importance to the emotional security and comfort that the person derives from being in their own home. I remind myself again of the danger of the 'protection imperative' identified by Ryder J in *Oldham MBC v GW and PW*. These considerations underpin the cardinal rule, enshrined in statute, that a person is not to be treated as unable to make a decision merely because she makes what is perceived as being an unwise one". *CC v KK* [2012] EWHC 2136 (COP); [2012] C.O.P.L.R. 627 per Baker J at [65].

2–123

47. Vulnerability

"RYJ's vulnerability is assessed by Mr Sinclair as that which is associated with her age and limited intellectual functioning. I am not satisfied that it has been established before me that she is unable to recognise and withstand external pressure to appropriate degree nor that she is or is likely to be subject to physical constraint to reach decisions concerning residence, care and contact. All the evidence in the papers before me suggests that even during her minority she was able to withstand the external desires of others by physical resistance to the same; that she has been able to withstand decisions enforced upon her and that she has been able to verbalise her wishes. The difficulty, as I apprehend it to be, arises from the approach of others to the expression of those wishes". *LBL v RYJ* [2010] EWHC 2665 (COP); [2010] C.O.P.L.R. Con. Vol. 795 per Macur J at [63].

2–124

48. The vulnerable person's protective imperative

"In assessing the question of capacity, the court must consider all the relevant evidence. Clearly, the opinion of an independently-instructed expert will be likely to be of very considerable importance, but in many cases the evidence of other

2–125

clinicians and professionals who have experience of treating and working with P will be just as important and in some cases more important. In assessing that evidence, the court must be aware of the difficulties which may arise as a result of the close professional relationship between the clinicians treating, and the key professionals working with P. In *Oldham Metropolitan Borough Council v GW and PW* [2007] EWHC 136 (Fam); 2 FLR 597, a case brought under Part IV of the Children Act 1989, Ryder J referred to a 'child protection imperative', meaning 'the need to protect a vulnerable child' that for perfectly understandable reasons may lead to a lack of objectivity on the part if a treating clinician or other professional involved in caring for a child. Equally, in cases of vulnerable adults, there is a risk that all professionals involved with treating that person—including, of course, a judge in the Court of Protection—may feel drawn towards an outcome that is more protective of the adult and thus, in certain circumstances, fail to carry out an assessment of capacity that is detached and objective. Having identified that hypothetical risk, however, I add that I have seen no evidence of any lack of objectivity on the part of the treating clinicians and social worker who gave evidence in this case". *PH v A Local Authority* [2011] EWHC 1704 (Fam); [2012] C.O.P.L.R. 128 per Baker J at [16(xiii)].

49. The vulnerable person's protective imperative

2–126

"In reaching these conclusions as to capacity, I have reminded myself, again, of the need to avoid what could be called the vulnerable person's protective imperative—that is to say, the dangers of being drawn towards an outcome that is more protective of the adult and thus fail to carry out an assessment that is detached and objective. I do not consider that I have fallen into that trap in this case". *A Local Authority v TZ (No.2)* [2014] EWHC 973 (COP); [2014] COPLR 159 per Baker J at [41].

50. Judicial criticism of an expert's report

2–127

"Before I leave the question of Mr S's understanding of the relevant information, I need to say a little more about Professor Howard's reports. In his second report, he addressed the question whether the Chancery proceedings should have been issued. As a preliminary comment, it should be noted that this is not quite the same as the question whether they should now be continued, although rather surprisingly Professor Howard seemed unable to appreciate the distinction between the two questions when it was put to him in cross-examination. In that report, he expressed the opinion that, although Mr S's memory was extremely poor, if prompted 'he quickly recognises the facts and issues involved.' Professor Howard then went on to say that, with prompting, Mr S could recall the gifts and his reasons for making them, the fact that R was trying to recover the money, and the existence of the chancery proceedings. However, it emerged from Mr Marshall's skilful cross-examination that this opinion was based on only a superficial acquaintance with the case on the part of Professor Howard, which he readily acknowledged. I have already referred to the relevant passages in his cross-examination, and I will not repeat them. It is, in my judgment, a fair criticism to say that Professor Howard should not have expressed a clear opinion in these terms without also making clear the limited nature of his own understanding of the facts and issues, and the precise steps which he had taken to remind or inform Mr S about them. A related, and equally valid, criticism is that he failed to comply with the mandatory requirements in the Practice Direction to Part 15 of the Court of Protection Rules 2007 to include in his report 'a statement setting out the substance of all facts and instructions given to [him] which are material to the opinions expressed in the report or upon which those opinions are based.' An acceptable alternative, as the Practice Direction makes clear, would have been to annex his instructions insofar as they were in writing. None of these elementary steps was taken, and the result (unintended, I am sure, but nevertheless potentially very worrying) is that the report rests on a much flimsier foundation than a reading of it would naturally suggest. The rules are there for a good reason, and if they are not complied with, a report, even from the most eminent of experts, is likely to lack the transparency and objectivity which the court rightly insists upon in expert evidence. I do not wish to be too critical, because the report appears to have been produced under some time pressure (although I must say it is not clear to me what the urgency was), and because Professor Howard and Hunters may have thought of it essentially as a supplement to the first report which he had produced in April 2008. Nevertheless, I have to say that there is substance in at least some of the severe criticisms of this report which Mr Marshall advanced in his closing submissions". *Re S; D v R* [2010] EWHC 2405 (COP); [2010] C.O.P.L.R. Con. Vol. 1112 per Henderson J at [146].

5. CONCLUSION

Since the Reform Act of 1832, which is often regarded as the seminal moment at which the United Kingdom became a modern parliamentary democracy, we have revised our mental capacity legislation about once in a generation: every 25 to 30 years on average.

The date of the current legislation, the Mental Capacity Act 2005 (MCA 2005), is misleading. The MCA 2005 was originally drafted by the Law Commission as the Mental Incapacity Bill in 1995 and it was then shelved by the government for several years for political reasons. It summarises the thinking on mental capacity and human rights during the first half of the 1990s, and does so very well, but we have moved on since then.

In 2009, four years after it enacted the MCA 2005, the United Kingdom Parliament ratified the United Nations Convention on the Rights of Persons with Disabilities (CRPD), which requires states to revise their mental capacity legislation in order to give persons with disabilities access to the support necessary for them to make, communicate and participate in decisions affecting their lives. All three territorial jurisdictions in the United Kingdom need new legislation in order to comply with the CRPD and it is likely that there will be at least four significant changes in practice and procedure. They are as follows:

(1) Although the MCA contains provisions that actively promote supported decision-making—for example, sections 1(3), 3(2) and 4(4)—the CRPD envisages something much more robust. Currently, expert witnesses in personal injury and clinical negligence proceedings merely assess whether someone is a protected party and whether they will require a deputy to manage their damages award when the claim finally settles. Very few of these experts have regard to section 1(3) of the MCA 2005 and take all practicable steps to help a disabled person make a decision before concluding whether they lack capacity. This practice needs to change and inevitably it will change.

(2) The word "mental" in the MCA 2005 violates the equality and non-discrimination provisions in article 5 of the CRPD, and new legislation

2–128

will almost certainly omit any reference to the diagnostic threshold—"an impairment of, or a disturbance on the functioning of, the mind or brain".

(3) In future, any decisions made on behalf of someone who lacks capacity will have to respect their "rights, will and preferences" in accordance with article 12.4 of the CRPD, rather than apply the current best interests criteria. This is likely to present a significant challenge to those who handle cases where individuals have suffered traumatic brain injury and have a lack of insight and awareness, and emotional and behavioural problems such as impulsivity and disinhibition.

(4) Finally, the new legislation will need to ensure that there are "appropriate and effective safeguards to prevent abuse in accordance with international human rights law" and that any measures taken are "free of conflict of interest and undue influence".[102] The MCA 2005 deals with a single issue—mental capacity. It does not consider undue influence or the vast grey area between incapacity and undue influence, which is inhabited by people who have a mild or moderate cognitive impairment that does not amount to actual incapacity, but nevertheless leaves them vulnerable to predators. The main problem in this regard is that hitherto incapacity has been fairly easy to define, assess and prove, whereas vulnerability is much more elusive.

---

[102] United Nations Convention on the Rights of Persons with Disabilities, art.12.4.

CHAPTER 3

Acquired Brain Injuries: Primary and Secondary Mechanisms

Fay Greenway, Jebet Beverly Cheserem, Simon Stapleton

INTRODUCTION

"Acquired brain injury" is a term applicable to any insult to the brain sustained as a result of factors in the environment. This covers a multitude of possible mechanisms, including stroke, traumatic brain injury, brain tumours, and infection. Traumatic brain injury is not only the most common mechanism but is also the most studied. Head injury is the commonest cause of death and disability in people aged 1–40 years in the UK. Each year, 1.4 million people attend emergency departments in England and Wales with a recent head injury (NICE, 2014). This chapter looks at the public health measures to prevent head injury, basic neuroanatomy and physiology, types of traumatic brain injury, and initial neurosurgical management of head injury. The UK and Eire have 34 neurosurgical units all of which receive emergency referrals of head injured patients every day. This may be in the context of multiple injuries or more minor blows to the head, and involves the initial management and early rehabilitation of patients. The essential role of clinicians in the acute phase of management is to prevent secondary insults to the brain through mechanisms such as expanding blood clots in the head, hypoxia (inadequate oxygenation of neurons), hypotension (inadequate blood pressure) and infection. 3–001

The long-term management of head injured patients requires a multidisciplinary team with active involvement from neurologists, neuro-rehabilitation physicians, physiotherapists, occupational therapists, speech and language therapists, psychologists, psychiatrists, and social workers, and is discussed in more detail later in this book. The absence of mass lesions requiring neurosurgical intervention does not equate to normal neuronal function; indeed, some patients may have devastating neurological defects or personality change despite an apparently moderate injury on imaging. According to Headway, the largest brain injury charity in the UK, acquired brain injury continues to represent a growing proportion of hospital attendances and admissions. Of the 1.4 million attending emergency departments each year, between 33% and 50% are children under the age of 15 years (NICE, 2014). In the UK in 2016–17 there were 348,453 admissions to hospital with acquired brain injury (including stroke and traumatic brain injury). That is 531 admissions per 100,000 of the population, with men being 1.5 times more likely than women to be admitted with a head injury. Of these, 155,919 admissions were for head injury (Tennant, 2015). The worldwide pattern of head injury varies with middle to low income countries being over-represented by work-related or road traffic accidents. The most common causes of TBI are falls, road traffic accidents, assault and blast injuries in war zones (Langlois et al., 2006). Sports and recreation are also major causes of TBI and are increasingly recognised. Falls are the most common cause of TBI in young children and the elderly; road traffic accidents, sports related injuries, assault and occupational injuries are most common in young adults (Bruns and Hauser, 2003).

Traumatic brain injury represents a very broad group of patients from those with minor head injury (the vast majority of cases) who recover without specific or specialist intervention, to catastrophic head injuries that result in death or significant long-term disability—some of which can be due to the effects of complications that could potentially be minimised or avoided with early detection and appropriate treatment.

1. ECONOMIC IMPACT OF HEAD INJURY

3-002   Head injuries contribute a significant proportion of disability on a temporary and permanent basis. In the immediate phase there is the loss of earnings from days off work and the need for carer leave, especially when children are involved. Significant injury can result in both a long-term loss of earnings due to a physical or cognitive inability to return to work, as well as significant financial costs associated with the provision of hospital and community healthcare. Studies also suggest a link between moderate and severe head injury and an increased risk of developing Alzheimer's disease (Lye and Shores, 2000; Tripodis et al., 2017); the long-term impact this has on healthcare resources is not insignificant. The financial costs of traumatic brain injury are difficult to calculate and not as well understood as its immediate consequences, in part due to difficulties in quantifying human emotional cost, and because of how brain injuries affect some victims more severely than others. There have been several studies worldwide looking at the economic costs of brain injury in the US (Finkelstein et al., 2006), Australia (Collie, 2009), and Europe (Olesen et al., 2012), but they all have their own limitations and cannot easily be extrapolated to other countries due to multiple differences in the types of data collected, different population statistics, and different healthcare systems. The review by the European Brain Council, published in 2012, (Olesen et al., 2012) gave some insight into the annual costs of providing health and social care, plus economic output losses as a result of long-term disability (but not premature mortality) of victims. The data showed a total cost of €798 billion per annum for all disorders of the brain, €33 billion of which were costs due to traumatic brain injury. The figures covered direct healthcare, direct non-medical, and indirect costs of all resources used or lost owing to illness, and were thought to be conservative due to the lack of accurate data for some conditions. Data suggests that the annual cost of traumatic brain injury in the UK is in the region of £15 billion (Parsonage, 2016), but this figure is again likely to be an underestimate due to the lack of good quality data enabling more accurate analysis.

2. PUBLIC HEALTH MEASURES TO REDUCE HEAD INJURY

Given the economic burden resulting from head injuries, various attempts have been made to reduce the risk of them occurring. These include motor vehicle safety measures, health and safety initiatives at work, and road safety education.

3–003

Speed limits

As engineering has refined various vehicles (including bicycles, scooters, trucks, cars), there have been significant advances in the rate of acceleration, maximum speed achievable and effectiveness of braking systems. However, speed limits are needed to limit damage, particularly in vehicle versus pedestrian collisions, with the most vulnerable groups being children and the elderly. It is estimated that a 5% increase in speed can result in a 10% increase in accidents and a 20% increase in fatalities—depending on the type of road (Box and Bayliss, 2012). Increasing the speed from 30mph to 50mph results in the increased risk of fatal pedestrian injuries from approximately 10% to 70% (Box and Bayliss, 2012).

3–004

Helmets

Modern helmets are made in a wide variety of materials with the principle aim being absorption of energy to reduce acceleration/deceleration injury to the brain, reduce shearing forces and reduce direct trauma to the skull by sharp or blunt objects. Helmets are designed to match the expected direction of force and expected energy at impact for a particular activity. This accounts for the simple cycle helmet with minimal padding to more extensive head coverage in motorcycle or motorsports where a higher energy at impact and multidirectional forces are expected.

3–005

The most robust data on the use of helmets for cyclists is from the Cochrane review published in 1999. It analysed data from five case-controlled studies, concluding that:

> "Helmet use reduces the risk of head injury by 85%, brain injury by 88% and severe brain injury by at least 75%. The protective effect of helmets for facial injury is 65% for the upper and mid facial regions. No protection is provided for the lower face and jaw" (Thompson et al., 1999).

In a subsequent analysis of the American National Trauma Data Bank of 2012, 6,267 patients in bicycle related accidents were included and the use of helmets was noted to result in a 51% reduced odds of severe traumatic brain injury and 44% reduced odds of mortality (Joseph et al., 2017).

With regard to motorcycle helmets, a systematic review by Cochrane published in 2008 found that helmets reduced the risk of death by 42% and the risk of head injury by 62% (Liu et al., 2008). The review included 61 observational studies. There is currently limited evidence to support one style of helmet over another. In 2007, the British Government's Department for Transport, as part of their consumer information programme, established SHARP

(Safety Helmet Assessment and Rating Programme), a scheme designed to guide motorcycle users in helmet purchasing. It provides online advice on the fitting of helmets and their safety ratings based on scientific and technical impact studies. It was introduced with the objective to improve motorcycle road safety, and draws on data and conclusions primarily from the European COST 327 study published in 2001 (Chinn et al., 2001).

Seat belts

3–006 The evolution of seat belts dates back to the early 1900s when doctors in the US starting fitting their own vehicles with lap belts. In the 1950s the Sports Car Club of America required competing drivers to wear lap belts, and Volvo began designing vehicles with two-point cross-chest belts. In 1958 a Volvo design engineer patented the three-point safety belt. The early 1960s saw the introduction of seat belts in America, and in 1965 it became compulsory for all new vehicles built in Europe to be fitted with front seat belts. In 1967 it became law that all new cars in the UK should be fitted with front seat belts. During the 1970s there were several government bills proposed to make the wearing of seat belts compulsory but it was not until 1981 that it actually became law.

The initial lap belts increased the risk of internal and vertebral injuries as they acted as a fulcrum. Subsequently the shoulder belt was introduced to provide a three-point fixation. Seatbelts are designed to restrain the passenger from colliding with parts of the motor vehicle on impact, thereby reducing the risk of injury. They prevent the head from hitting the windscreen, the chest from hitting the steering wheel, and the pelvis from overriding the femur. Seatbelts prevent head injuries particularly when there is more than 30% impact of the car body in the collision (Lindquist et al., 2006). Wearing a seat belt reduces the risk of death among drivers and front seat occupants by 45–50%, and the risk of death and serious injuries among rear seat occupants by 25% (World Health Organization, 2018).

Airbags are designed to further reduce the risk of injury by helping to diffuse the energy on impact. They inflate rapidly, and then immediately deflate, cushioning the occupant and preventing or reducing the level of contact with the steering wheel or dashboard. They are an effective secondary safety measure that reduce the risk of injury for vehicle occupants in more severe collisions. However, a number of problems with airbags have been identified and there is no legal requirement in the UK for cars to be fitted with them. The Royal Society for the Prevention of Accidents does support their use, but only to be in conjunction with, and not in place of, seatbelts.

Infant and child seats

3–007 Infants are at high risk of injury during road traffic accidents. They have relatively large heads compared to older children and have several structural features of their neck and spine that place them at particularly high risk of head and spine injuries. Car seats are mandatory within the UK for infants and children up to 12 years or 135cm, whichever comes first. Seats are either height or weight-based, and must be rear facing until the child is over 15 months old. In some countries it is now recommended that children remain rear-facing until the age of 4 years (or around 18 kilograms weight). Infant seats are secured facing the rear usually on the back seat, or rear-facing in the front seat with the airbag disengaged. It is thought that in the event of a collision, they work by transmitting energy primarily through the back of the safety seat to the infant's back, which is the strongest point anatomically.

The American Pediatric Association guidelines highlight that current evidence indicates child safety seats reduce the risk of injury by 71% to 82% (Arbogast et al., 2004; Zaloshjna et al., 2007; Elliott et al., 2006) and reduce the risk of death by 28% when compared with those for children of similar ages in seat belts. Booster seats are also noted to reduce the risk of nonfatal injury among 4-to 8 year olds by 45% (Arbogast et al., 2009).

The failure to wear a helmet or to use a seat belt or safety seat for children could contribute significantly to the severity of any subsequent head injury.

3. BASIC CLINICAL ANATOMY AND PHYSIOLOGY OF HEAD INJURY

Anatomy of the brain

Figure 1 shows the anatomy of the surface of the brain with the various lobes of the cerebral cortex labelled and the structures of a midline section through the brain with the anatomical structures mentioned in the text. This includes the brainstem, made up of the midbrain, pons and medulla. It is the extension of the spinal cord within the brain which contains the neural centres essential for maintenance of respiration, blood pressure and heart rate, as well as the origin of the cranial nerves and centres for coordinating eye movements. It also contains neural structures essential for the maintenance of consciousness (the reticular activating system) and all the motor and sensory pathways contained in the spinal cord pass through the brainstem. The thalamus acts as the main relay station in the motor and sensory pathways passing to and from the cerebral cortex. The corpus callosum is the large bundle of white matter fibres connecting the two cerebral hemispheres. The cerebellum is a structure attached to the back of the brainstem and is important in ensuring smooth, coordinated movements.

3–008

Neurophysiology

Other than preventative measures to reduce the likelihood of head injury or to protect the head on impact, little can be done to mitigate the effects of the primary injury to the brain. The aim in the early clinical management of the head injured patient is to reduce the effects of the secondary insult triggered by the initial traumatic insult. Secondary brain injury can occur either at adjacent or remote intracranial sites, for example, at the point of impact of a direct blow or distant to that site. It begins immediately and then evolves over days. Common

3–009

patterns of secondary brain injury include oedema (swelling), hypoxia (insufficient oxygen delivered to the brain tissue), impaired autoregulation and cerebral blood flow (see para.3–011), and the production of free radicals and destruction of cell membranes.

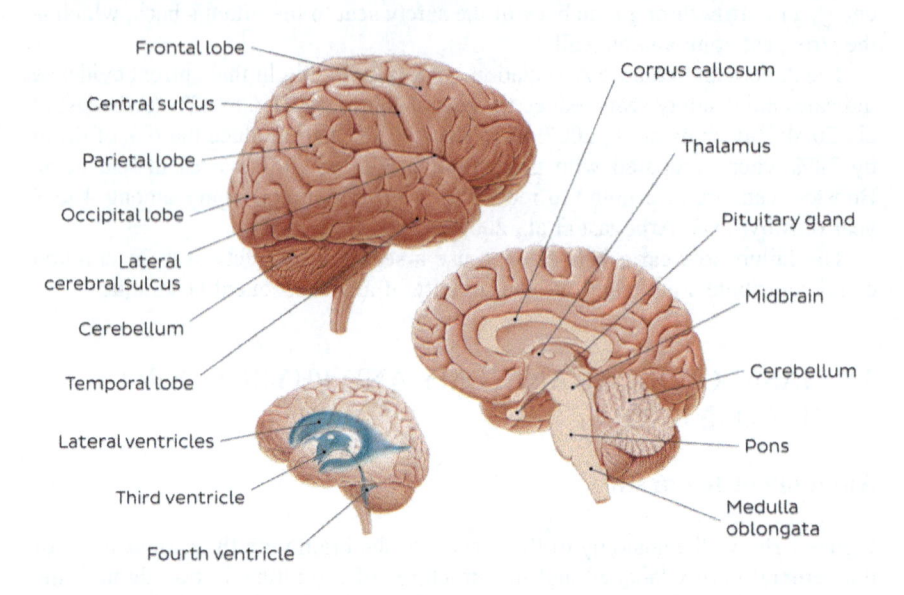

Figure 1: Anatomy of the brain—lateral view, midline view, and ventricular system

Intracranial pressure

3–010   Any insult to the brain causes cerebral oedema (brain swelling) as part of the inflammatory response to that injury. Since the skull provides a rigid container for the brain, any increase in volume of the contents (brain, cerebrospinal fluid and blood), such as brain swelling or bleeding (haematoma), will cause a rise in the pressure within the skull. Rises in pressure within the head have two main deleterious effects: (i) effects on blood flow to the brain and (ii) brain herniation (shifts).

Cerebral blood flow

3–011   At rest about 15% of the output of blood from the heart goes to the brain. This is in order to maintain the high metabolic rate of the cerebral cortex and other highly active areas of the brain. Neurones require a continuous supply of oxygen and glucose from the blood to function. If neurones are completely deprived of oxygen or glucose, even for short periods (minutes), they will start to die. They may tolerate a moderate reduction in the supply of these essential nutrients but, if sustained, this will begin to cause cell death. This has led to the concept of an ischaemic insult to the brain causing an area where neurones will die within minutes and cannot be salvaged (the *ischaemic core*), surrounded by an area where neurones can survive if the blood flow is restored in a timely fashion (the *ischaemic penumbra*). If cells in the ischaemic penumbra do not have their

BASIC CLINICAL ANATOMY AND PHYSIOLOGY OF HEAD INJURY

oxygen supply restored within minutes they will contribute to an enlarging ischaemic core. Hence, the principle of management is to restore oxygen supply to that tissue to prevent further damage.

Blood flow to the brain depends upon the arterial blood pressure (the pressure of blood entering the head through vessels in the neck) and the intracranial pressure (the "back pressure" in the head against the arterial pressure). The perfusion of the brain tissue itself with oxygen and nutrients is thus dependent on both these components:

Cerebral perfusion pressure = Mean arterial pressure − Intracranial pressure

The arterial blood pressure provides the brain with a continuous flow of blood and the healthy brain is able to maintain a constant flow in the face of variations in blood pressure by altering the calibre of its blood vessels (autoregulation). It is not until blood pressure falls considerably that blood flow, and hence cell survival, will be affected adversely. The injured brain loses the ability to autoregulate its blood flow and this means that blood flow to the brain may be reduced with even moderate falls in blood pressure as the flow varies passively with pressure.

If intracranial pressure rises, as with an expanding intracranial haematoma or cerebral oedema, cerebral perfusion pressure will fall causing a fall in cerebral blood flow if autoregulation is not intact.

The management of the head injured patient is therefore directed at maintaining cerebral blood flow by correcting both falls in blood pressure and rises in intracranial pressure to restore cerebral perfusion pressure to normal.

3–012

Blood pressure may need to be maintained with fluids, including blood, if necessary, or with the use of inotropic drugs such as noradrenaline, which have effects on the heart and blood vessels to increase the blood pressure.

Intracranial pressure may be controlled by:

(1) Measures directed at the cause, for example, by removing an intracranial haematoma.
(2) Diuretic drugs to "dehydrate" the brain, e.g. mannitol.
(3) Removing cerebrospinal fluid (CSF).
(4) Altering the calibre of cerebral blood vessels by controlling the carbon dioxide level in the blood.
(5) Increasing the volume of the head; in practice, this means removing part of the skull vault to allow the brain to swell (decompressive craniectomy).
(6) Removal of contused and irretrievably damaged brain.

Brain herniation

Herniation is a term used to describe the shift of one organ, or part of, from its normal anatomical location into another, abnormal, location. An expanding mass such as an intracranial haematoma or swelling of the brain will cause shift of the brain contents within the skull, resulting in parts of the brain herniating from their usual site to another with associated stretching and damage of the connecting fibres. The intracranial contents are divided into three compartments by folds of

3–013

dura, the thick membrane which covers the brain: two supratentorial compartments (right and left) separated by the vertical *falx cerebri* in the midline, and one infratentorial compartment, beneath the horizontal *tentorium cerebelli*.

Brain herniation can occur between these compartments (see Figure 2):

(1) Subfalcine herniation when a part of the cingulate lobe of the cerebral cortex slips beneath the falx from one supratentorial compartment to the other.
(2) Tentorial (uncal) herniation when the uncus of the temporal lobe is forced through the tentorial hiatus from one supratentorial compartment to the infratentorial compartment.
(3) Foraminal (tonsillar) herniation, also called *coning*, when the cerebellar tonsils and brainstem are forced out of the skull through the foramen magnum.

Each of these herniations can have significant effects on brain function and are manifest clinically as a neurological decline in the patient's consciousness level with rising intracranial pressure.

3–014 Subfalcine herniation may be seen on CT scans as an intracranial haematoma develops and may be associated with contralateral hydrocephalus as the Foramen of Monro (the opening between the lateral and third ventricles) is obstructed by the shift of the midline structures. Clinically there may be a deterioration in the level of consciousness.

Tentorial herniation (see Figure 3) may cause an ipsilateral third nerve palsy due to direct pressure on the nerve by the uncus of the temporal lobe as it passes through the tentorial hiatus. This will be seen as a fixed and dilated pupil. The opposite cerebral peduncle may be compressed against the free edge of the tentorium. This will cause an ipsilateral hemiparesis (explaining why some head injured patients may have a weakness on the same side as the haematoma). With further downward pressure the other pupil will also become fixed and dilated.

Foraminal herniation results in compression of the medulla (part of the brainstem), the site of centres essential for maintenance of breathing, blood pressure and heart rate. Continued pressure on the medulla results in respiratory arrest, cardiac arrest and ultimately death. Clinical signs of medullary compression will include a further deterioration in conscious level and a "Cushing reflex" when the blood pressure rises and the heart rate falls (hypertension and bradycardia) prior to respiratory and cardiac arrest.

The signs of deteriorating conscious level, pupillary abnormalities and altered pattern of breathing and heart rate are therefore indicative of shifts of the brain within the cranial cavity and will rapidly result in death if left untreated. These parameters are therefore those most closely monitored in the early management of the head injured patient.

Glasgow Coma Scale

3–015 The central role played by alterations in conscious level as the most important sign of rising intracranial pressure and hence as a means of assessing the severity of a brain injury led to the development of the Glasgow Coma Score (GCS) as a

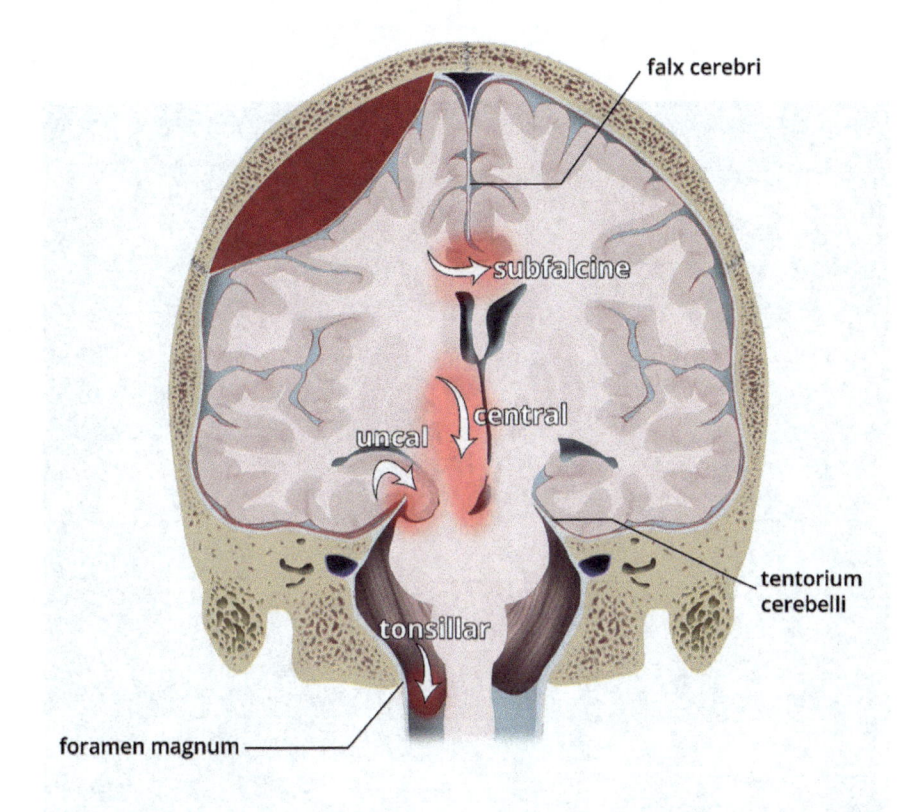

Figure 2: Diagrammatic view of the process of herniation of the brain as an intracranial mass expands

reliable, reproducible and simple method for establishing and recording the conscious state of a patient following a head injury (Teasdale and Jennett, 1974). Changes in the conscious level as assessed by the GCS reflect changes in the severity of the condition of the patient. It is clear that the conscious level following an injury provides a simple measure of the severity of a head injury and is highly predictive of the subsequent outcome. The score, as an assessment of the conscious level, is based on best performance of three parameters easily assessed at the bedside as a response to external stimuli (conversation, asking the patient to perform a task, assessing their response to a painful stimulus): eye opening, verbal and motor responses.

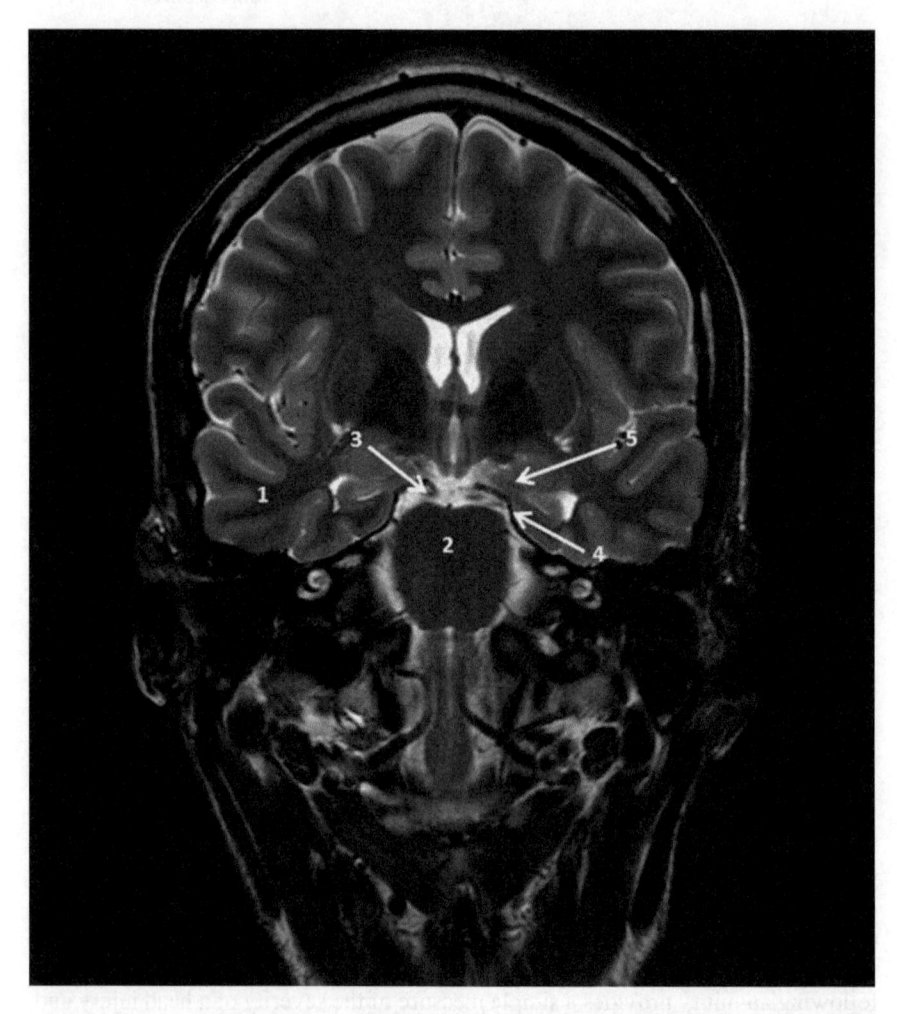

Figure 3: Coronal MRI of brain—showing temporal lobe (1) and brainstem—pons (2). The third (oculomotor) cranial nerve (3) runs from the brainstem alongside the tentorium (4) and is susceptible to compression by the uncus (5) of the temporal lobe when downward pressure is exerted by an expanding mass. Clinically, this is manifest as a deteriorating level of consciousness and a fixed dilated pupil on the side of the lesion.

TYPES OF INJURY AND PATHOPHYSIOLOGY

Table 1: Glasgow Coma Scale

Criteria	Score
Eye opening	
Spontaneous	4
To sound	3
To pain	2
None	1
Verbal response	
Orientated	5
Confused	4
Words	3
Sounds	2
None	1
Motor response	
Obey commands	6
Localising	5
Normal flexion	4
Abnormal flexion	3
Extension	2
None	1

GCS Score = (E[4] + V[5] + M[6]) = Best possible score 15; worst possible score 3
*If an area cannot be assessed, no numerical score is given for that region, and it is considered "non-testable, NT".

It is important to remember that it is the best response possible, so that, for example, a weakness on one side would not prejudice the scoring. Similarly, the verbal response cannot be scored in a patient who is intubated or has an injury directly affecting the speech areas of the brain or an injury to the jaw or mouth itself, for example. The motor response is thus the single best measure of the severity of an injury to the head. After several weeks in coma, sleep-waking cycles return with eye opening occurring spontaneously. At this stage an apparent improvement in the eye-opening score is not necessarily indicative of an improved conscious level.

4. TYPES OF INJURY AND PATHOPHYSIOLOGY

The circumstances in which the head is injured are numerous, ranging from minor scalp injuries and concussion to major injuries as a result of high-speed road accidents or high velocity missile injuries. In general, a distinction should be drawn between focal injuries where the energy of the blow to the head is

3–016

delivered in a single discrete area and those injuries where the energy is distributed throughout the head and brain. Furthermore, the effect of an injury may be primary, as a result of the initial impact, or secondary, due to the evolution of subsequent events.

Focal injuries to the head include scalp lacerations and haematomas and depressed fractures of the skull vault. The impact on the head is localised and the energy imparted is generally low. This means that the effects on the brain, if at all, are limited to the brain underlying the injury and are not transmitted throughout the brain itself. Low velocity penetrating injuries will cause localised injury to the scalp, skull, dura (the tough membrane lining the inside of the skull and covering the brain) and underlying brain. There exists an important distinction between closed injuries where the scalp remains intact and open or compound injuries where the scalp has been breached allowing contamination of the wound and subsequent infection. Given sufficient force, foreign material, as well as tissue including hair, skin and bone may be driven into the brain.

High velocity injuries, such as gunshot wounds, impart a far higher energy to the brain causing far more extensive injury. As the projectile travels through the head it is preceded by a shock wave producing a wide area of disruption and cavitation of brain tissue, as well as driving fragments of scalp and bone into the wound. The exit wound also leads to considerable tissue damage. The energy imparted is proportional to the square of the velocity, therefore with modern weapons this type of injury is usually fatal.

Diffuse brain injury

3–017 Diffuse injury to the head occurs when the impact of the blow is distributed throughout the brain. This is usually associated with a decelerating force such as in a fall or collision. The energy imparted to the brain determines the severity of the injury. In a mild or low velocity injury there will be only transient effects on the function of the brain (concussion) without evidence of structural damage. In more energetic events there may be disruption of brain tissue (contusions, cerebral haemorrhage) causing permanent alterations in brain structure and function. This latter is termed a *diffuse axonal injury*.

Contusions of the brain (in effect bruising which may coalesce to form a haematoma in the brain substance) usually occur underlying the site of trauma and as result of the movement of the brain within the skull on impact. Common sites for these contusions to occur are the frontal lobes and anterior temporal lobes due to the rough bony contour of the base of the skull in these regions. Injuries at the site of impact can be described as "*coup*" and opposite the site of impact, due to inertia of the brain within the skull, as "*contrecoup*". Contusions represent a primary insult to the brain parenchyma and when seen on brain imaging may correlate with injury severity. They are also of significance as a secondary insult due to the associated cerebral oedema (brain swelling) which develops in the days following an injury, with the subsequent effects of increased intracranial pressure.

Aside from deceleration forces, most significant closed injuries to the head also involve rotational and shearing forces in the brain. This type of injury produces widespread damage to the white matter tracts of the brain (diffuse

TYPES OF INJURY AND PATHOPHYSIOLOGY

axonal injury) and characteristically affects the corpus callosum and the brainstem. The secondary effects of brain swelling due to the tissue disruption can also lead to severe rises in intracranial pressure.

Intracranial haematomas

Once at the neurosurgical unit an expanding intracranial haematoma with deteriorating conscious level will require urgent surgery. Haematomas may occur in the extradural space (between the skull and its lining, the dura; see Figure 4), in the subdural space (beneath the dura but external to the arachnoid membrane; see Figure 5), or within the brain itself, intracerebral haematoma (see Figure 6). 3–018

Extradural haematomas usually occur at the site of a skull fracture and are often seen in children and young adults, not necessarily with major force applied. Since much of the impact has been absorbed by the skull, if the clot is evacuated in a timely fashion, there may be very little injury to the underlying brain. The prognosis for a full recovery is therefore generally good if the clot is removed in sufficient time to prevent secondary insults, as described above under blood flow and herniations (paras 3–011, 3–013 and 3–014).

In contrast, acute subdural haematomas are often associated with a significant impact coupled with shear and rotatory forces and are often associated with major underlying brain contusion and swelling and generally have a much worse outlook due to the primary direct effect on the brain.

For extradural and most subdural haematomas, surgery involves a craniotomy (opening the scalp and a trap-door of bone to gain access to the intracranial contents) and evacuation of the clot. Although a burr hole alone may relieve raised pressure briefly in a dire emergency, it is not sufficient to remove an intracranial haematoma, which consists of clotted blood and will not drain through such a small opening.

Severe diffuse injuries

Severe diffuse injuries without significant intracranial haematomas will in general require monitoring on the neurological intensive care unit. These patients require assisted ventilation to protect the airway and to ensure adequate oxygenation. Cardiovascular support may also be required to ensure adequate perfusion of the injured brain. Observation of the pupillary responses and of any limb deficits is also carried out. Drug induced neuromuscular paralysis is often necessary to aid ventilation and prevent rises in intracranial pressure. As a result, the Glasgow Coma Score cannot be used to assess conscious level and monitoring of intracranial pressure directly is usually required. The intracranial pressure can be measured by a transducer placed on the surface of the brain via a twist-drill hole in the skull or through a drain placed in the ventricular system of CSF. Intracranial pressure monitoring can be used to help establish the adequacy of cerebral perfusion and to direct treatment, as well as to determine the effectiveness of measures used to reduce the intracranial pressure. The peaks in intracranial pressure usually occur in the first 72 hours following a severe diffuse injury to the brain and thereafter with suitable measures to control it, the intracranial pressure may start to decline. 3–019

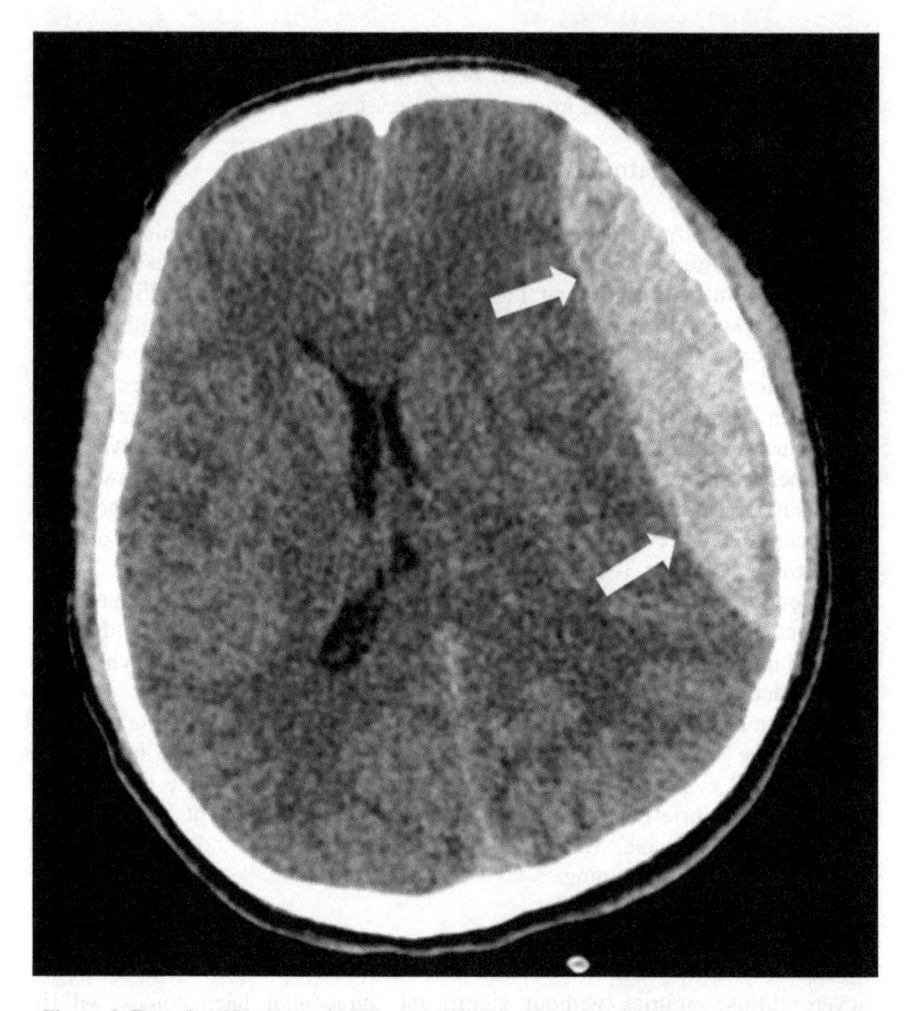

Figure 4: Extradural haematoma. CT scan of the head showing the high density "lentiform" shape of an extradural haematoma—between the skull and the dura (lining of the brain) (solid arrows)—following a blow to the head.

Numerous studies have looked at the effectiveness of various other methods to attempt to control intracranial pressure, cerebral blood flow and metabolism. Steroids may be effective in controlling brain oedema due to tumours, but has been shown not to be effective in the management of head injuries (CRASH Study) (Roberts et al., 2004). Similarly, barbiturates reduce the cerebral metabolic rate, but have not been shown conclusively to improve outcome in these circumstances (Roberts et al., 2012) and indeed may cause detrimental effects due to hypotension and infection. Hypothermia (body temperature down to 32°C) again reduces metabolic rate and ICP, but no clinical trials have shown a definite improvement in outcome (Andrews et al., 2015).

However, despite intensive monitoring and management of rising intracranial pressure some injuries cause progressive rises in pressure which are not amenable to further medical treatment. Decompressive craniectomy (removal of a portion

TYPES OF INJURY AND PATHOPHYSIOLOGY

of the skull to allow the brain to swell) and removal of severely contused areas of brain (one temporal or frontal lobe, but not bilaterally) may sometimes be considered in these circumstances. Nevertheless, all too often the injury will have had devastating consequences for the function of the brain without the prospect of meaningful recovery or of an independent existence. Evidence shows that such surgery does improve survival rates, but results in an increase in the number of people surviving with a poor neurological outcome (Cooper et al., 2011; Hutchinson et al., 2016). This poor prognosis will need to be discussed with the family and carers in a sensitive, but realistic manner. Continued uncontrolled rises in intracranial pressure will lead to ischaemic changes in the brainstem and brain herniations ultimately leading to brainstem death.

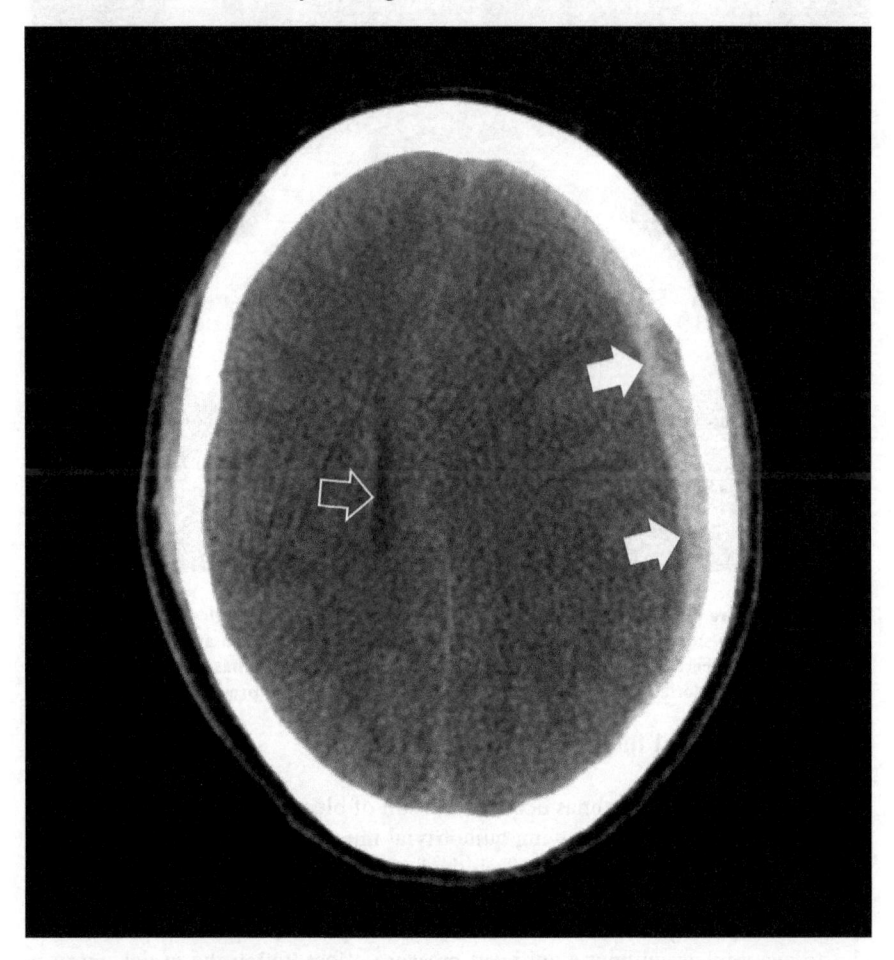

Figure 5: Acute subdural haematoma. CT scan of the head showing the high density "crescentic" shape of an acute subdural (between the dura and the brain) haematoma (solid arrows). There is effacement of the lateral ventricle and shift of the midline structures away from the blood clot (the ventricle of the opposite side is visible (open arrow) whereas the lateral ventricle on the side of the clot has been compressed and is therefore not visible).

ACQUIRED BRAIN INJURIES

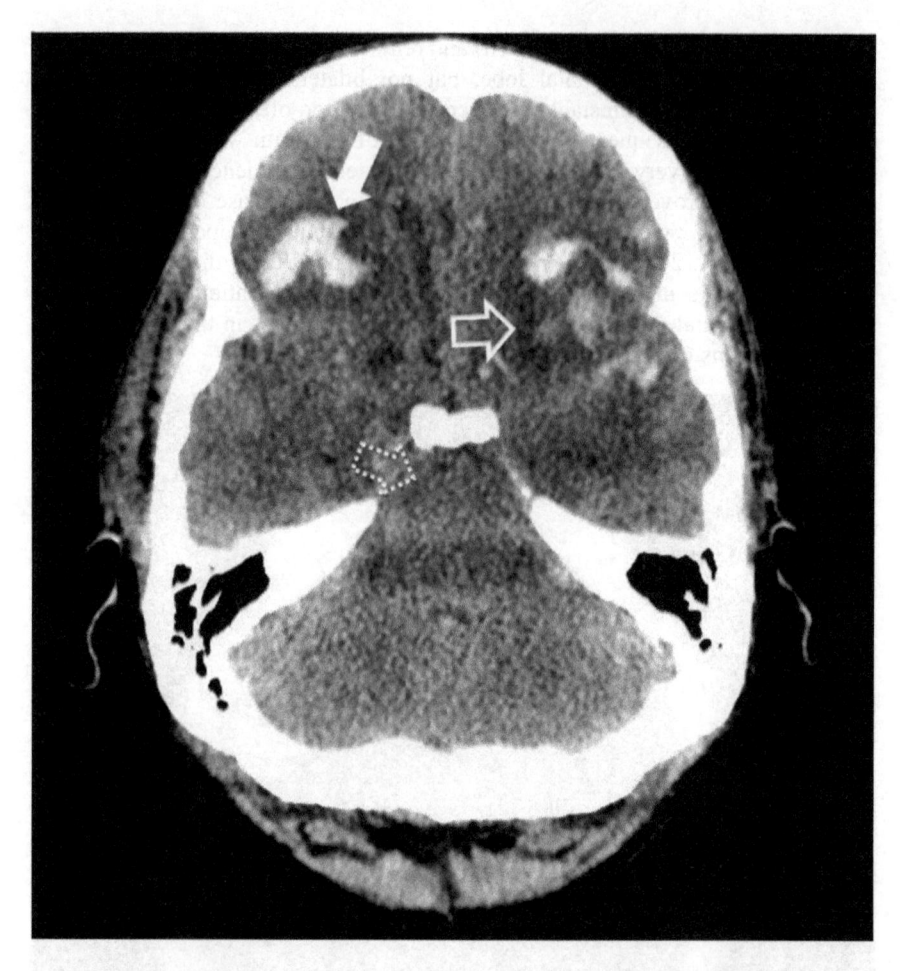

Figure 6: Severe diffuse axonal injury. CT scan of the head showing high density blood clot within the brain substance (solid arrow) with areas of low density (open arrow), indicative of brain swelling (cerebral oedema). The CSF filled spaces around the base of the brain have been obliterated (dotted arrow) due to the swelling suggesting high pressure within the head.

Chronic subdural haematoma

3–020 Chronic subdural haematomas occur as a result of bleeding in the subdural space, often in elderly patients following quite trivial injuries to the head. Low pressure bleeding from bridging veins between the brain and the skull may initially cause a blood clot to develop without significant mass effect on the brain. This occurs due to the shrinkage of the brain with age (atrophy) allowing more space for the clot to accumulate without significant pressure effect. Often the initial injury is not sufficient to seek medical attention, but over the course of the next few weeks the clot may expand (due to breakdown of the blood products) and begin to cause pressure on the underlying brain. Once symptomatic, chronic subdural haematomas can be drained through one or two burr holes, since the clot has liquefied, allowing the fluid to drain under its own pressure through a small opening. Since there is usually very little underlying damage to the brain the prognosis for recovery is generally good.

5. HEAD INJURY AT THE EXTREMES OF AGE

The pattern of head injury is affected by age. This is due to two factors, the anatomical and structural differences between children and adults, and different mechanisms of injury.

The infant skull is comprised of several bony plates which are yet to fuse together. They are thus able to over-ride each other or expand to some extent. This compliance serves an important role during the birth process, affording the infant brain some protection against injuries which may occur during descent through the birth canal. The bone plates subsequently fuse along suture lines, with the process typically being almost complete by the age of 2 years.

Different injuries occur depending on the physical forces involved in the injury and the anatomical structures which are involved.

Between the bony skull and the surface of the brain is the dura—a reasonably thick membrane between the surface of the brain and the inner aspect of the skull. Trauma to the head can result in blood clots on or within the brain. In children and young adults, the dura can be easily stripped off the inner surface of the skull, resulting in blood clots forming in the extradural space (extradural haematoma). These typically occur with direct impact to the skull.

Shearing forces induced by severe translational and rotational forces applied to the head will cause diffuse axonal injuries with severe consequences, some of which may only be apparent as the child develops. Brain insults suffered early in life can manifest in a delayed fashion when a child may fail to meet various developmental milestones such as fine or gross motor skills, social behaviours or cognitive abilities.

With advancing age, the brain atrophies (shrinkage of the brain with loss of brain cells resulting in overall loss of brain volume). At the same time, the dura becomes increasingly adherent to the skull making extradural haemorrhage less likely. In the elderly, since the brain has shrunk away from the skull vault, the bridging veins between the brain and the skull are susceptible to tearing even with relatively minor injuries, which results in bleeding in the subdural space. These patients may often be on anticoagulants for the treatment of other medical conditions such as previous stroke or heart attack. This inevitably makes bleeding into the subdural space more common, causing acute or chronic subdural haematomas.

The brain atrophy associated with aging means there is physically more space available in the head for a blood clot before it might cause a physical mass effect on the rest of the brain, and become clinically symptomatic. As a result, many elderly patients may not present immediately with an acute haemorrhage and it is only with slow expansion of a blood clot, sometimes over weeks, that symptoms become evident. This is frequently the course of events in chronic subdural haematomas. Nevertheless, severe injuries to the brain in the elderly are not well tolerated and recovery, if it occurs, is often poor.

ACQUIRED BRAIN INJURIES

6. MANAGEMENT OF HEAD INJURY

3–023   The chief aim of the medical team involvement in the early management of head injury is to prevent secondary insults to the brain. Major head injuries often occur in association with other injuries to the chest, neck, abdomen or limbs. Standard protocols for the receiving medical team should be established to prioritise effective and timely treatment of all injuries. The Advanced Trauma Life Support, ATLS, protocol was developed in 1976 following a plane crash in which an orthopaedic surgeon's wife died and three of his children were critically injured. They received injury care, but the resources and expertise they needed were not available. That surgeon went on to develop the programme to ensure appropriate training in advanced life support. ATLS is now almost universally accepted and practised. To match local need, the algorithm is often adapted to the demographics and resources of the area in question.

The initial assessment comprises a clinical assessment typically characterised by ABCDE:

A	Airway and cervical spine protection
B	Breathing
C	Circulation
D	Disability (GCS + pupillary reaction)
E	Exposure (examination of the whole patient including the back)

Ensuring adequate oxygenation and blood pressure (perfusion of the brain) immediately following a head injury is the priority. An assessment of the conscious level is also required. Thereafter, imaging of the brain is necessary to establish the extent of any injuries and to look for evolving intracranial haematomas. Computed tomography (CT scanning) is the preferred study in this context, since with modern scanners it is quick and easy to perform and generally provides the information required in the acute setting (unlike MRI which is more time consuming, difficult to interpret and subject to contraindications such as patients with metal implants and cardiac pacemakers). Bony injury and blood clots are well seen on CT and an assessment of the degree of brain swelling can be made.

3–024   There is a wide range of severity in head injury and not all injuries require CT scanning. In order to decide which group of patients require imaging, and in what sequence, the UK National Institute for Health and Care Excellence have developed head injury guidelines for both paediatric and adult patients. They were last reviewed in 2019, and guide clinicians on when a CT scan is required and in what time interval (NICE 2014; see Table 2).

Table 2

NICE Guidelines for CT Scanning—within 1 hour
GCS < 13 on initial assessment in Emergency Department
GCS < 15 at 2 hours after injury on assessment in Emergency Department
Suspected open or depressed skull fracture
Any sign of basal skull fracture (haemotympanum, 'panda' eyes, cerebrospinal fluid leakage from the ear or nose, Battle's sign)
Post-traumatic seizure
Focal neurological deficit
More than 1 episode of vomiting

NICE Guidelines for CT Scanning—within 8 hours
Age 65 years or older
Any history of bleeding or clotting disorders (including patient on anticoagulant medication)
Dangerous mechanism of injury (a pedestrian or cyclist struck by a motor vehicle, an occupant ejected from a motor vehicle or a fall from a height of greater than 1 metre or 5 stairs)
> 30 minutes' retrograde amnesia of events immediately before the head injury

Since CT scanners are now widely available there is no longer a place for skull x-rays, except as part of a skeletal survey in children with suspected non-accidental injury.

Once initial resuscitation and CT scanning have been carried out the subsequent management can be established based on the conscious level and CT appearances.

Patients who are not fully conscious or who have a significant abnormality on their CT scan require admission to hospital for observation. This should entail observation with assessment of their Glasgow Coma Score on an acute medical or surgical ward or dedicated observation unit. The timing of observations depends upon the injury and local unit policies. Consideration may need to be given to repeating the CT within 24 hours on the advice of the neurosurgical unit if there is concern about the possibility of an evolving intracranial haematoma.

Minor head injuries without loss of consciousness do not require admission to hospital and can safely be discharged with advice to return if their condition changes.

Patients with persistently poor or deteriorating levels of consciousness, a focal neurological deficit or a mass lesion seen on CT should be discussed with the local neurosurgical unit and urgent transfer arranged accordingly (see Table 3).

ACQUIRED BRAIN INJURIES

Table 3: Circumstances in which to Refer to Neurosurgical Unit

Persisting coma (GCS ≤ 8)
Unexplained confusion for > 4 hours
Deterioration in conscious level
Progressive neurological signs
Seizure without full neurological recovery
Compound or depressed skull fracture
Definite or suspected penetrating injury
Cerebrospinal fluid leak

7. LONG TERM SURGICAL COMPLICATIONS

Infection following head injury

3–026   Open injuries to the head, associated with a depressed skull fracture and potential laceration of the dura, carry a risk of contamination of the wound and ensuing infection. Debris, including dirt, hair and bone, may be driven into the brain and act as a focus for infection causing brain abscess. For this reason, contaminated open injuries should be cleaned and "debrided" (removal of dead and devitalised tissue) in the operating theatre. Prophylactic antibiotics should be considered for contaminated wounds. An established brain abscess requires surgical drainage and a prolonged course of antibiotics. The risk of post-traumatic seizures increases significantly if a brain abscess occurs.

Closed head injuries do not generally pose a risk of intracranial infection. However, if there has been a skull fracture with an associated tear of the dura through the skull base including one of the air sinuses or the middle ear, CSF may leak out of the nose, called CSF rhinorrhoea; or, if the ear drum has been perforated, through the ear, called CSF otorrhoea. There is therefore a risk of infection gaining entry through these routes causing meningitis. CSF leak itself is thought to occur in 11–45% of skull base fractures (Yilmazlar et al., 2006; Ziu et al., 2012). The overall risk of meningitis is thought to be 10–30% and is greatest within the first year after injury (Daudia et al., 2007). A Cochrane review in 2015, analysing the available literature, found no evidence to recommend the use of antibiotics to reduce the frequency of meningitis (Ratilal et al., 2015). If a leak persists and a source can be identified, surgical repair of the defect is required.

Hydrocephalus

3–027   Occasionally in the months after a severe head injury the CSF containing spaces within the brain (the ventricles) may enlarge causing hydrocephalus (clinical signs and symptoms secondary to rising intracranial pressure due to CSF accumulation). This may be recognised clinically as a reduction in alertness and attention causing a deterioration in the patient's ability to take part in rehabilitation. This may be due to a blockage of the normal absorption pathways for cerebrospinal fluid as a result of blood in the ventricles or CSF spaces around the base of the brain at the time of the injury. Treatment generally requires the insertion of a ventriculoperitoneal shunt. This diverts the CSF from the ventricles via narrow tubing passed under the skin into the abdominal cavity where it can be absorbed into the circulation of the blood by a different route. The enlargement of the ventricles under pressure seen in these circumstances must be differentiated from so-called *ex vacuo* dilatation due to shrinkage (atrophy) of the brain caused by loss of brain substance as a result of a severe injury. This condition will not respond to shunting.

Cranioplasty

Decompressive craniectomy has a limited place in the management of severely raised intracranial pressure. Once the brain swelling has subsided the bony defect can be repaired. This is usually carried out several months after a severe head injury and often only once a patient is in rehabilitation. Repair may be with the original piece of skull bone if this has been preserved in the patient's own abdominal wall or, more frequently, with a custom made cranioplasty made of titanium or other inert material. Surgery is not without its complications of post-operative haemorrhage and infection, but has the advantage of restoring the not insignificant cosmetic defect of a decompressive craniectomy and hence improving a patient's well-being and self-esteem, as well as assuaging any concerns over further injury whilst a portion of the skull is missing.

3–028

8. CONCLUSIONS

Head injuries are common and the vast majority are mild with no long-term sequelae but, more substantial injuries have lasting and often devastating long term effects, as described in later chapters. The early management of head injuries is prevention with strategies designed to prevent significant impact to the head and the resultant primary injury. Pre- and in-hospital treatment is aimed at minimising the consequences of secondary injury to the brain. Over many years much effort has gone into understanding the mechanisms of brain swelling following head injury and mitigating its effects to try to improve outcomes. Nevertheless, serious head injury remains a major cause of mortality and significant long-term disability in a relatively young group of people.

3–029

REFERENCES

Andrews, P.J., Sinclair, H.L., Rodriguez, A., Harris, B.A., Battison, C.G., Rhodes, J.K., Murray, G.D., Eurotherm 3235 Trial Collaborators (2015). "Hypothermia for intracranial hypertension after traumatic brain injury". *New England Journal of Medicine* 373(25): 2403–2412.

3–030

Arbogast, K.B., Durbin, D.R., Cornejo, R.A., Kallan, M.J., Winston F.K., "An evaluation of the effectiveness of forward facing child restraint systems" (2004) *Accident; Analysis and Prevention* 36(4): 585–589.

Arbogast, K.B., Jermakian, J.S., Kallan, M.J., Durbin, D.R., "Effectiveness of belt positioning booster seats: an updated assessment" (2009) *Pediatrics* 124(5): 1281–1286.

Box, E. and Bayliss, D., "Speed limits; A review of evidence. RAC Foundation" (2012). Available at: *https://www.racfoundation.org/assets/rac_foundation/content/downloadables/speed_limits-box_bayliss-aug2012.pdf.*

Bruns, J. and Hauser, W. (2003). "The epidemiology of traumatic brain injury: a review". *Epilepsia* 44(s10): 2–10.

Chinn, B., Canaple, B., Derler, S., Doyle, D., Otte, D., Schuller, E., Willinger R., (2001). "European Cooperation in the field of Scientific and Technical Research (COST). COST 327: Motorcycle safety helmets". Available at: *https://sharp.dft.gov.uk/wp-content/themes/sharp2017/pdfs/COST-327-Motorcycle-Safety-Helmets-Final-report.pdf.*

Collie A., "The economic cost of spinal cord injury and traumatic brain injury in Australia. Victorian Neurotrauma Initiative" (2009) Available at: *http://www.spinalcure.org.au/pdf/Economic-cost-of-SCI-and-TBI-in-Au-2009.pdf.*

Cooper, D.J., Rosenfeld, J., Murray, L., Arabi, Y., Davies, A., D'Urso, P., Kossmann, T., Ponsford, J., Seppelt, I., Reilly, P., Wolfe, R., "Decompressive craniectomy in diffuse traumatic brain injury" (2011) *New England Journal of Medicine* 364(16): 1493–502.

Daudia, A., Biswas, D., Jones, N.S., "Risk of meningitis with cerebrospinal fluid rhinorrhea" (2007) *Annals of Otology, Rhinology and Laryngology* 116(12): 902–5.

Elliott, M.R., Kallan, M.J., Durbin, D.R., Winston, F.K., "Effectiveness of child safety seats vs seat belts in reducing risk for death in children in passenger vehicle crashes" (2006) *Archives of Pediatric and Adolescent Medicine* 160(6): 617–621.

Finkelstein, E., Corso, P., Miller, T., *The Incidence and Economic Burden of Injuries in the United States* (New York: Oxford University Press, 2006)

Headway *https://www.headway.org.uk/media/2883/acquired-brain-injury-the-numbers-behind-the-hidden-disability.pdf.*

Hutchinson, P.J., Kolias, A.G., Timofeev, I.S., Corteen, E., Czosnyka, M., Timothy, J., Anderson, I., Bulters, D., Belli, A., Eynon, C., Wadley, J., Mendelow, A., Mitchell, P., Wilson, M., Critchley, G., Sahuquillo, J., Unterberg, A., Servadei, F., Teasdale, G., Pickard, J., Menon, D., Murray, G., Kirkpatrick, P., "Trial of decompressive craniectomy for traumatic intracranial hypertension" (2016) *New England Journal of Medicine* 375(12): 1119–30.

Joseph, B., Azim, A., Haider, A., Kulvatunyou, N., O'Keeffe, T., Hassan, A., Gries, L., Tran, E., Latifi, R., Rhee, P., "Bicycle helmets work when it matters the most" (2017) *American Journal of Surgery* 213(2): 413–7.

Langlois, J., Rutland-Brown, W., Wald, M., "The epidemiology and impact of traumatic brain injury: a brief overview" (2006) *Journal of Head Trauma Rehabilitation* 21(5): 375–8.

Lindquist, M.O., Hall, A.R., Björnstig, U.L. "Kinematics of belted fatalities in frontal collisions: A new approach in deep studies of injury mechanisms" (2006) *Journal of Trauma* 61: 1506–16.

Liu, B.C., Ivers, R., Norton, R., Boufous, S., Blows, S., Lo, S.K., "Helmets for preventing injury in motorcycle riders" (2008) *Cochrane Database of Systematic Reviews*, Issue 1. Art. No.: CD004333.

Lye, T.C. and Shores, E.A., "Traumatic brain injury as a risk factor for Alzheimer's disease: a review." (2000) *Neuropsychology Review* 10(2): 115–129.

REFERENCES

National Institute for Health and Care Excellence (NICE) (2014). "Head injury: assessment and early management, clinical guideline 176". Updated September 2019. Available at: *https://www.nice.org.uk/guidance/cg176*.

Olesen, J., Gustavsson, A., Svensson, M., Wittchen, H.U., Jonsson, B., "The economic cost of brain disorders in Europe" (2012) *European Journal of Neurology* 19(1): 155–62.

Parsonage, M., "Traumatic brain injury and offending—an economic analysis" (2016) Available at: *https://www.barrowcadbury.org.uk/wp-content/uploads/2016/07/Traumatic-brain-injury-and-offending-an-economic-analysis.pdf*.

Ratilal, B.O., Costa, J., Pappamikail, L., Sampaio, C., "Antibiotic prophylaxis for preventing meningitis in patients with basilar skull fractures" (2015) *Cochrane Database of Systematic Reviews*, Issue 4. Art. No.: CD004884.

Roberts, I., Yates, D., Sandercock, P., Farrell, B., Wasserberg, J., Lomas, G., Cottingham, R., Svoboda, P., Brayley, N., Mazairac, G., Laloë, V., Muñoz-Sánchez, A., Arango, M., Hartzenberg, B., Khamis ,H., Yutthakasemsunt, S., Komolafe, E., Olldashi, F., Yadav, Y., Murillo-Cabezas, F., Shakur, H., Edwards, P., "Effect of intravenous corticosteroids on death within 14 days in 10,008 adults with clinically significant head injury (MRC CRASH Trial): randomised placebo controlled trial" (2004) *Lancet* 364 (9442): 1321–8.

Roberts, I. and Sydenham, E., "Barbiturates for acute traumatic brain injury. Cochrane Database of Systematic Reviews" (2012) Issue 12. Art. No.:CD000033.

Teasdale, G. and Jennett, B., "Assessment of coma and impaired consciousness. A practical scale" (1974) *The Lancet* 304(7872): 81–84.

Tennant A., "Acquired brain injury: the numbers behind the hidden disability" (2015). Available at: *https://www.headway.org.uk/media/2883/acquired-brain-injury-the-numbers-behind-the-hidden-disability.pdf*.

Thompson, D.C., Rivara, F., Thompson, R., "Helmets for preventing head and facial injuries in bicyclists" (1999) *Cochrane Database of Systematic Reviews*, Issue 4. Art. No.: CD001855.

Tripodis, Y., Alosco, M.L., Zirogiannis, N., Gavett, B.E., Chaisson, C., Martin ,B., McClean, M.D., Mez, J., Kowall, N., Stern, R.A., "The Effect of Traumatic Brain Injury History with Loss of Consciousness on Rate of Cognitive Decline Among Older Adults with Normal Cognition and Alzheimer's Disease Dementia" (2017) *Journal of Alzheimer's Disease* 59(1): 251–263.

World Health Organization, "Global status report on road safety: summary" (2018) *Geneva: World Health Organization*; (WHO/NMH/NVI/18.20). Available at: *https://www.who.int/violence_injury_prevention/road_safety_status/2018/English-Summary-GSRRS2018.pdf*.

Yilmazlar, S., Arslan, E., Kocaeli, H., Dogan, S., Aksoy, K., Korfali, E., Doygun, M., "Cerebrospinal fluid leakage complicating skull base fractures: analysis of 81 cases" (2006) *Neurosurgical Review* 29(1):64–71.

Zaloshnja, E., Miller, T.R., Hendrie, D., "Effectiveness of child safety seats vs safety belts for children aged 2 to 3 years" (2007) *Archives of Pediatric and Adolescent Medicine* 161(1): 65–68.

Ziu, M., Savage, J.G., Jimenez, D.F., "Diagnosis and treatment of cerebrospinal fluid rhinorrhea following accidental traumatic anterior skull base fractures" (2012) *Neurosurgical Focus* 32(6): E3.

CHAPTER 4

Neurological and Neuroradiological Evaluation of Traumatic Brain Injuries

Wolfgang Schady and Shawn Halpin

INTRODUCTION

In a medico-legal context, as well as in clinical practice, there is some overlap between the roles of a neurologist and a neurosurgeon. In both cases proper evaluation of the patient requires careful clinical and radiological examination. In the acute setting of a hospital emergency department neurosurgical input is essential, whereas a neurologist tends to become involved later in the patient's evolution, particularly if delayed complications arise. In both situations a history of complaints has to be obtained and the cranial nerves and limbs have to be examined for signs of brain damage. A disturbance of eye movements, a visual field defect, reduced manipulative skills or altered tendon reflexes may be picked up even when the patient has noticed little impact on function. 4–001

Different long-term consequences can be expected depending on whether the head injury has been focal or diffuse. In the former case, for example a penetrating skull vault fracture, the residual deficit may be confined to the function of the insulted brain region. In diffuse brain injuries damage is caused by shearing or rotating forces giving rise to serious physical and/or cognitive impairments even when the head looks outwardly intact.

The purpose of this Chapter is to consider the physical sequelae of acquired brain injury and the imaging that is available to correlate them with structural changes in the brain. Recognition of deficits is aimed at (a) identifying and managing those complications that are treatable, (b) providing information about mechanisms of injury and prognosis to patients and the treating team, and (c) in the medico-legal context, quantifying impediments that have a bearing on the assessment of damages. The first step is to ascertain the severity of the head injury. When it is mild, the commonest symptoms are those that are encompassed under the rubric of a post-traumatic syndrome. In more serious cases there will be identifiable impairments involving the limbs, special senses and bulbar or sphincter functions. Delayed complications may arise later, such as hydrocephalus or epilepsy. Imaging may help to clarify the underlying pathology at these various stages.

1. ASSESSMENT OF HEAD INJURY SEVERITY

4-002   Head injuries can be classified by pathology type, location, severity, outcome or prognosis. An assessment of the severity of the head injury is important in defining management in the early stages. The level of consciousness is the most commonly-used parameter. By assigning a numerical value to it on the Glasgow Coma Scale (GCS) it is easier to monitor fluctuations and thereby identify and correct downturns in the patient's condition. The GCS provides a score for eye opening, verbal response and motor function. A GCS score of 13–15 defines the head injury as mild, 9–12 as moderate and 3–8 as severe. From the clinical point of view it is important to provide the individual scores in addition to the total score. The later the GCS measurement is made (provided the patient is not sedated), the better its prognostic value. In other words, the most reliable score is that which is obtained after initial resuscitation within six hours post-injury. The disadvantage of the GCS is that it is not linear and there may be considerable differences in the condition of patients assigned the same score.

The duration of post-traumatic amnesia (PTA or post-acute brain injury confusional state) is also used as an index of the severity of a head injury. It is defined as the time between the event and the return of uninterrupted memory. During this period continuous memory fails because patients are unable to store and retrieve new information. Islands of memory may surface before the end of PTA. Using this criterion, a head injury is regarded as mild if the duration of PTA is less than an hour, moderate if the PTA is between one and 24 hours and severe if it exceeds a day.

By these definitions, 80–90% of head-injured patients attending A&E departments have a mild head injury, 5–10% have a moderate head injury and 5–10% have a severe head injury (Kraus and McArthur, 1996). These figures have to be viewed with some caution because of difficulties in ascertainment and in the allocation of patients into the three categories. Problems arise when the GCS score and the duration of PTA do not match, i.e. they put the head injury in different categories. The radiological findings must also be taken into account.

4-003   A degree of circumspection is thus necessary. The authors of an oft-quoted study (Annegers et al., 1998) divided traumatic brain injuries into three categories of severity. Severe traumatic brain injuries were characterised by one or more of the following features: brain contusion, intracranial haematoma or loss of consciousness or post-traumatic amnesia for more than 24 hours. Moderate traumatic brain injuries were characterised by one or more of the following: loss of consciousness or post-traumatic amnesia lasting between 30 minutes and 24 hours or a skull fracture. Mild traumatic brain injuries were characterised by an absence of fracture, and loss of consciousness or post-traumatic amnesia for less than 30 minutes.

These criteria have the advantage of being established and in widespread use. However, no single indicator can be regarded as the gold standard for determining traumatic brain injury (TBI) severity. A patient may have a brief period of PTA yet have abnormalities on the computed tomography (CT) brain scan. The Mayo classification system was introduced to overcome these difficulties (Malec et al., 2007). This system classifies TBI severity into three categories: moderate–severe (definite), mild (probable) and symptomatic (possible) according to the following criteria:

1. Moderate–severe (definite): death due to TBI, loss of consciousness of 30 minutes or more, PTA of 24 hours or more, worst GCS score in the first 24 hours of less than 13, or evidence of cerebral haematoma, contusion, penetrating TBI, haemorrhage or brainstem injury.
2. Mild (probable): loss of consciousness for less than 30 minutes, PTA shorter than 24 hours and/or radiological evidence of a skull fracture with intact dura.
3. Symptomatic (possible): blurred vision, confusion, dazed or dizzy state, focal neurological symptoms, headaches or nausea in the absence of the above criteria.

The Mayo system classifies patients with head injury more accurately than other systems, which is particularly important in research. It is also valuable to plan post-acute clinical care. The fact that it does not differentiate between moderate and severe TBI is a potential limitation. On the other hand, the introduction of the category of possible TBI highlights the potential overlap between minimal brain injury, post-concussional syndrome and psychological/psychiatric symptoms.

2. PHYSICAL CONSEQUENCES OF TRAUMATIC BRAIN INJURY

The post-traumatic syndrome

The terms post-traumatic syndrome (PTS) and post-concussional syndrome (PCS) are often used interchangeably, though strictly speaking the latter term is inappropriate if the head injury is not associated with signs of concussion, i.e. loss of consciousness or significant post-traumatic amnesia. The condition is characterised by a range of symptoms experienced by people in the aftermath of a head injury, including headaches, dizziness, visual disturbance, nausea, fatigue, disordered sleep, irritability, forgetfulness, noise sensitivity, inability to concentrate and intolerance of alcohol. About 50% of people have post-traumatic headaches after mild or moderate head injuries at work or in road traffic accidents (Long and Webb, 1983). There has been much debate about the cause of PTS. Some experts believe it to be due to a physical disturbance of brain function, while others regard it as primarily a psychological problem.

4–004

A number of interesting points have emerged from studies of the syndrome (Bruyn and Lanser, 1990; Evans, 1996). A PTS occurs infrequently in children or people who have suffered a sporting injury or a domestic accident. The symptoms are generally more prominent in those who have had a mild head injury than those with severe cranial trauma (Yamaguchi, 1992). Arguably, the effects of a head injury should be proportional to its severity, which is one of the reasons that emotional factors are sometimes regarded as paramount. The truth is that the

NEUROLOGICAL AND NEURORADIOLOGICAL EVALUATION OF TBI

condition is inadequately understood. In all probability a number of factors, both physical and psychological, are responsible for these complaints.

The prognosis of the PTS is usually good. Symptoms are often quite troublesome during the first few weeks but thereafter they gradually improve. Full recovery may take anything between three months and two years. One of the features that characterises a non-organic PTS (previously known as compensation or accident neurosis) is that symptoms do not improve as expected. Indeed, they fail to respond to standard symptomatic treatment and often worsen with the passage of time. In the absence of functional overlay most people are able to go back to work within weeks, although in severe cases some months may elapse before a return to full-time work and leisure pursuits is possible.

4–005   The commonest PTS is headache. Potential causes of headache following a mild head injury include muscle contraction, sensory nerve damage, tenderness of the scalp and injury to the soft tissues of the neck. A serious cause such as a chronic subdural haematoma can usually be identified from symptoms and signs of raised intracranial pressure, which should prompt a CT head scan. The type of headache varies to some extent depending on its cause. Scarring of the scalp may result in a steady sensation of pressure at the site of impact. Most commonly the headache takes the form of aching in a circumscribed area or a band around the head. Such muscle contraction headaches account for around 85% of all post-traumatic headaches (Evans, 1996). Muscle tension in anxiety states has the same effect. If there has been an associated whiplash injury or there is antecedent cervical spondylosis the two syndromes may merge, prolonging the headache syndrome. The best way of dealing with headaches originating in the muscles of the face, neck and scalp is to take simple painkillers such as paracetamol. Codeine-containing compounds should be avoided beyond the first few weeks because they have the potential to cause paradoxical persistence of the syndrome (so-called analgesic misuse headaches).

Migraine headaches are typically unilateral and throbbing. Post-traumatic migraine is not as common as muscle tension-type headaches following a head injury. There is sometimes a family history of migraine or a history of previous headaches, perhaps forgotten, in the sufferer's youth. Nausea, flashing lights and sensitivity to noise often accompany the headache and force the sufferer to retire to bed in a darkened room. The same type of medication can be used effectively in post-traumatic as in standard migraine. In the writers' view migraine triggered by a blow to the head cannot be attributed to the head injury on an indefinite basis. It would be counter-intuitive to suggest that headaches persisting, say, 10 years after a mild head injury should still be held to have been caused by it. Since migraine is normally a constitutional condition, it would be more reasonable to regard the aetiological impact of the accident as limited to 18–24 months.

Many people have more than one type of headache after a head injury. There may be a combination of pain from local tissue damage and scalp or neck muscle contraction. A lesion of the greater occipital, supra-orbital or infra-orbital nerve can cause neuralgia characterised by local tingling and shooting pain at the site of trauma. Scalp dysaesthesiae post-head injury may persist for weeks or months but rarely for more than one year (Evans, 1996). Emotional states such as fear of permanent damage and worry over employment may contribute to the headache. Depression can have the same effect, giving rise to insomnia, loss of appetite and despondency in addition to headaches.

Dizziness is the second commonest complaint in patients with a PTS. It is usually a temporary phenomenon that is rarely disabling. Some people complain of lightheadedness and darkening of vision on sitting up or getting out of bed. This is due to slow adjustment of their blood pressure to changes in posture. The dizziness is short-lived and does not require any action other than advice to get up more slowly. Other patients notice a feeling of faintness when they look up due to interference with the blood supply from the vertebral arteries.

4–006

Vertigo is a more troublesome form of dizziness. It is a feeling of giddiness or swaying brought on by movement, associated with nausea and loss of balance when standing. It points to an injury to the labyrinth that may be detected by vestibular function tests. If it is caused by direct trauma to the inner ear in the context of a petrous temporal fracture, there is always some associated loss of hearing. In the absence of a fracture, labyrinthine concussion can have a similar, though usually reversible, effect.

A mild or moderate head injury can cause benign paroxysmal positional vertigo (BPPV), a condition in which small crystals called otoconia become dislodged in the inner ear, migrating into the posterior semicircular canal. The fluid in the inner ear (the endolymph) is displaced, resulting in a sensation of vertigo on head movement. The diagnosis can be made by performing a Dix-Hallpike manoeuvre (rapid sitting up from a lying position with the head turned to one side). BPPV can usually be corrected with an Epley manoeuvre, normally carried out by a specialist physiotherapist.

Impairments of mobility

Limb movements may be disturbed for one of two reasons: either the limb is weak or it lacks coordination. Damage to the posterior frontal lobe can give rise to weakness down the opposite side of the body. This is called a hemiparesis if the weakness is partial and hemiplegia if it is complete. The affected limbs tend to be spastic or stiff as well because the healthy brain exerts inhibitory drive on the motor tracts. The arm or leg may be more severely affected, depending on where precisely the damage is located. When major bilateral damage has occurred, the patient presents with a tetraparesis or tetraplegia (four-limb weakness or paralysis, respectively). In extreme cases the patient adopts decorticate or decerebrate rigidity, which refers to abnormal positioning of the limbs. In both cases the lower extremities are extended and the ankles are plantar flexed (i.e. pointing down). The elbows are flexed in decorticate rigidity but extended in decerebrate rigidity.

4–007

In less severe cases patients walk stiffly and have difficulty using their hands for day-to-day tasks. In the most serious cases they may be virtually helpless, unable to stand or walk and dependent on others for all aspects of their personal care. Drugs like Baclofen or Dantrolene and local injections of Botulinum toxin are used, together with regular stretching exercises, to avoid secondary complications such as contractures.

An abnormality of gait is sometimes due to imbalance rather than weakness. Ataxia is a consequence of damage to the cerebellum or its connections in the brainstem. A different form of ataxia can occur when there is loss of feedback from insensate limbs. Such patients are particularly liable to fall if they close their eyes, whereas in cerebellar ataxia unsteadiness occurs as much when the eyes are open as when visual feedback is removed. A cerebellar syndrome also manifests with tremor, loss of dexterity of the hands, difficulty judging distances, slurring of speech (dysarthria) and wobbly eyes (nystagmus). All voluntary actions are affected because it is no longer possible to synchronise movement smoothly even though muscle strength is normal. Gait dyspraxia is an uncommon disorder characterised by difficulty walking in the absence of weakness or ataxia. It is due to damage to the frontal lobes and is often associated with urinary incontinence and executive dysfunction.

Special senses

4–008   Loss of the sense of smell is called anosmia or hyposmia if it is partial. In the setting of a head injury anosmia occurs when the olfactory nerves have been damaged. They enter the base of the anterior cranial fossa in the form of fine rootlets that are vulnerable to injury in blows to the front or, more commonly, the back of the head. About one in 20 head-injured people attending hospital develop anosmia, though the figure increases to about one in four following severe injuries when the base of the skull has been fractured (Zusho, 1982). In some people partial damage to the olfactory nerves causes not loss but distortion of smell (parosmia) or a perceived malodorous smell, as if caused by a fetid substance (cacosmia).

Anosmia is invariably accompanied by an alteration in the sense of taste. The perception of salty, bitter, sour or sweet tastes is conveyed by nerve branches supplying the tongue and is therefore preserved, but detection of other flavours depends on an intact sense of smell. It is common knowledge that when our nose is blocked the sense of taste is largely lost. Anosmia detected early on after a head injury may recover to some extent but if it is still present after a year it is very likely to be permanent. This evidently reduces the enjoyment of food and drink, which some patients find distressing.

Fractures of the petrous temporal bone may involve the inner and middle ear, causing loss of hearing either due to disruption of the cochlea or the ossicular chain or damage to the cochlear nerve. Audiometry reveals unilateral sensorineural deafness (failure of perception rather than conduction of sound) that is not normally amenable to correction with a hearing aid. There may be associated vertigo if the balance mechanisms in the inner ear have been disrupted.

Hearing loss may also occur in the absence of a skull base fracture. Whereas deafness from a skull fracture can be quite profound, that from inner ear concussion tends to be mild. Sufferers complain of difficulty hearing conversation above the background noise. The deafness is worse for high-frequency sounds. In most cases post-traumatic deafness due to inner ear concussion improves in a matter of weeks without the need for treatment, especially in young people.

Tinnitus is an unpleasant symptom that troubles some patients who have suffered a closed head injury with inner ear damage. A whistling, ringing or roaring sound is reported by the patient when consciousness is regained, invariably associated with some degree of hearing loss in the same ear. Tinnitus may be present all the time but many patients are only aware of it in a quiet environment, for instance, in bed at night. Attempts to mask it with white noise are frequently unsuccessful. Tinnitus is often more distressing and persistent than the associated hearing impairment.

4–009

Turning to vision, it may be affected by a blow to the head in one of two ways. Visual acuity diminishes if the eyeball itself has been injured, there is retinal detachment or the optic nerve has sustained damage. The assessment of such injuries belongs in the field of ophthalmology. When visual impairment is subtle it may go unnoticed until the patient realises he has a weak eye, in which case fundoscopy will reveal optic nerve atrophy (a pale optic disc as assessed with an ophthalmoscope).

If the patient complains of difficulty visualising objects on one side, examination may reveal a visual field defect. When both eyes are affected on the same side this is known as a homonymous hemianopia. For example, loss of the nasal half of the visual field in the left eye and of the temporal half of the visual field in the right eye would be described as a right homonymous hemianopia. It is due to damage to the contralateral optic radiation or occipital lobe. It causes patients to knock into obstacles on their blind side. They are classed as partially sighted and their driving licence is permanently revoked.

Double vision (diplopia) points to disturbance of the external ocular muscles. They are supplied by three cranial nerves, namely the oculomotor or third, trochlear or fourth and abducens or sixth. Sixth cranial nerve lesions cause double vision with horizontal separation of images when looking to the side of the lesion. Fourth cranial nerve lesions are most commonly responsible for diplopia after head injuries, giving rise to double vision with crossed images. Third cranial nerve lesions are associated with an enlargement of the pupil causing intolerance of bright lights. All such lesions are more likely to improve than traumatic optic neuropathy. No double vision will occur if a third, fourth or sixth nerve lesion is associated with an optic neuropathy, as in this case one of the images will be suppressed. By the same token, diplopia can be suppressed by wearing a patch over one eye.

Bulbar functions

The tongue and throat muscles are necessary for speech and swallowing. Dysarthria means slurring of speech, which can be due to motor disturbance or a cerebellar lesion. Widespread brain damage may lead to spasticity of the tongue that interferes with speech. In extreme cases the patient is anarthric (mute). Alternatively, a cerebellar syndrome can give rise to incoordination of tongue movements. The resulting dysarthria may be misinterpreted as drunkenness, with understandable annoyance on the part of the sufferer. The involvement of a speech and language therapist is essential to improve intelligibility and, in more severe cases, advise on electronic means of communication.

4–010

Dysphagia (difficulty swallowing) can be overcome by nasogastric feeding in the early stages after an acquired brain injury. Spontaneous improvement is the rule but if swallowing remains unsafe, food has to be delivered via a tube inserted into the stomach through the abdominal wall (a gastrostomy). The procedure can be carried out under X-ray control but more commonly it is performed endoscopically, hence the acronym PEG (percutaneous endoscopic gastrostomy). Dysphagia is a cause for concern because of its association with aspiration and pneumonia, thereby reducing life expectancy.

Sphincter functions

4-011   In the early stages after a severe head injury the unconscious patient is unaware of bodily functions, so the nursing staff must be alert to the possibility of either incontinence or retention of urine, since both can result from a so-called neurogenic bladder. A urethral catheter is used to drain the urine and is kept in the bladder until consciousness is regained. It carries a risk of urinary tract infection. In the long-term urinary incontinence is much more common than loss of bowel control. When it is due to a small, spastic bladder it often responds to anticholinergic medication.

The great majority of people who are incontinent in the early stages after a head injury regain control over their bladder. In those who have suffered severe brain damage this is not always the case. The sufferer may be left with diminished perception of bladder fullness and incomplete emptying. Nevertheless, as sensation and sphincter control are usually reduced rather than lost, bladder retraining can often be achieved. Undetected urinary retention can result in hydronephrosis (enlargement of the kidneys), hypertension and chronic renal failure. Assessments of bladder and kidney function are thus an integral part of rehabilitation after traumatic brain injury.

3. IMAGING AFTER TRAUMATIC BRAIN INJURY

4-012   There are many medical imaging modalities available for use after head injury. In the acute context, CT is the mainstay of imaging the brain, and is likely to remain so.

Computed tomography

4-013   In the UK, the National Institute for Health and Clinical Excellence (NICE) has produced guidelines for the use of CT in acute head injury. The guidance differs slightly for adults and children. CT scanning is recommended within one hour in acute trauma when the GCS is less than 13 for adults or 14 for children (less than 15 for babies) at first assessment, or when less than 15 at two hours after the injury. Further indications for CT scanning within one hour include a suspected skull fracture, a seizure, any focal neurological deficit or vomiting (once for adults, three times for children). A provisional written radiology report should be available within one hour of the scan. In less acutely sick patients, CT scans after head injury are recommended within eight hours in elderly patients, those taking

IMAGING AFTER TRAUMATIC BRAIN INJURY

anticoagulants, where there has been 30 minutes or more of retrograde amnesia or when there is a dangerous mechanism of injury.

NICE guidance therefore mandates CT scanning in moderate head injury. Most patients with mild head injury, such as those sustained on the sports field where the player may be momentarily shaken-up or disorientated, will not have scans. The use of CT is restricted to cases where it is likely to have an impact on immediate medical management, mainly because it involves a relatively high radiation dose to the patient. Even small doses of radiation are considered to raise the lifetime risk of fatal cancer, and CT is the largest cause of non-background radiation to the population in the Western world.

CT scans will reliably demonstrate fractures of the skull vault or skull base and macroscopic haemorrhage. This includes haematomas in the extradural, subdural, or subarachnoid compartments, and haemorrhagic contusions inside the brain itself (see Figures 1, 2, 3). In addition, CT allows the detection of mass effect from haemorrhage and other secondary effects of bleeding inside the skull, such as infarction from arterial compression and generalised brain swelling.

4-014
Neurosurgeons use CT scanning both to triage the treatment of patients with TBI and to monitor for and treat subsequent deterioration. Substantial haematomas may require craniotomy and evacuation. Generalised brain swelling usually responds to medical treatment, but some patients may need a craniectomy (removing a flap of bone) to reduce intracranial pressure.

The administration of intravenous iodinated contrast medium allows the depiction of brain arteries or veins, depending on the timing of the bolus of contrast and the scan's acquisition. It helps to demonstrate areas of the brain that have abnormal perfusion. This technique is not part of routine care but it can be used in selected patients when vascular injury is suspected, or to help make balanced judgments regarding the viability of brain tissue and the need for intervention.

As well as its value in acute head injury, CT can be useful in the follow-up of brain-injured patients. Later scans may demonstrate long-term loss of cerebral substance or brain atrophy after trauma. They also show focal areas of atrophy or evidence of scarring, known as gliosis. In combination with medical and neuropsychological assessments, CT can help refine the prognosis for long-term outcome.

4-015
The diagnosis of cerebral atrophy can be difficult if based on a single scan. The range of variation in the normal population is very wide (Figure 4), and the diagnosis of atrophy is often subjective. This point is frequently misunderstood in medico-legal practice. There are no definitive CT or magnetic resonance imaging (MRI) signs of mild or even moderate brain atrophy. Radiologists assess the size of the cerebral sulci and ventricles and make a judgment according to their experience and speciality. Some patients are born with relatively large ventricles, while others are born with small fluid spaces. In the absence of a previous scan for comparison, it is entirely possible to misdiagnose a normal scan as showing brain atrophy, or an abnormal scan as normal.

It is often helpful to compare radiological studies taken at or around the time of trauma with any subsequent scans obtained in the chronic phase. In this way patients act as their own control subjects. This comparison should confirm or refute the existence of brain atrophy as a consequence of TBI.

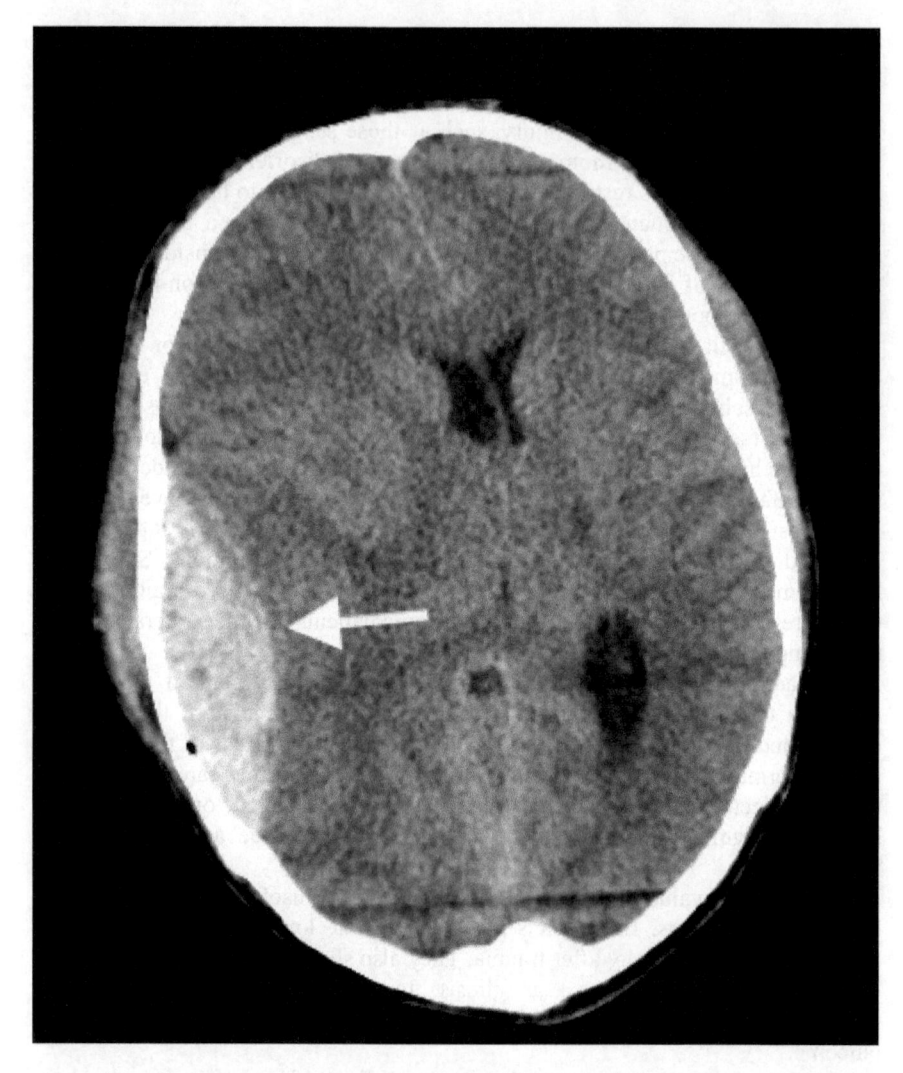

Figure 1: CT image of a patient with an acute extradural haematoma (arrow) over the right hemisphere (on the left of the image as we see it), displacing structures across the midline of the skull. Extradural haematomas present a convex surface to the brain

Magnetic resonance imaging

4–016   Whereas CT scanners generate images by the shadows cast by X-rays passing through tissue of different density, MRI scanners produce images gained by small signals generated from the tissue itself when it is strongly magnetised. MRI (magnetic resonance imaging) has much better contrast resolution than CT, but usually a worse spatial resolution. Soft tissues can be reliably distinguished, and there is a much clearer depiction of normal and diseased brain.

MRI is seldom used in acute head injury. This is mostly because CT provides all the information necessary to manage an acutely brain-injured patient in the short term, but also because the environment in an MRI scanner is difficult for

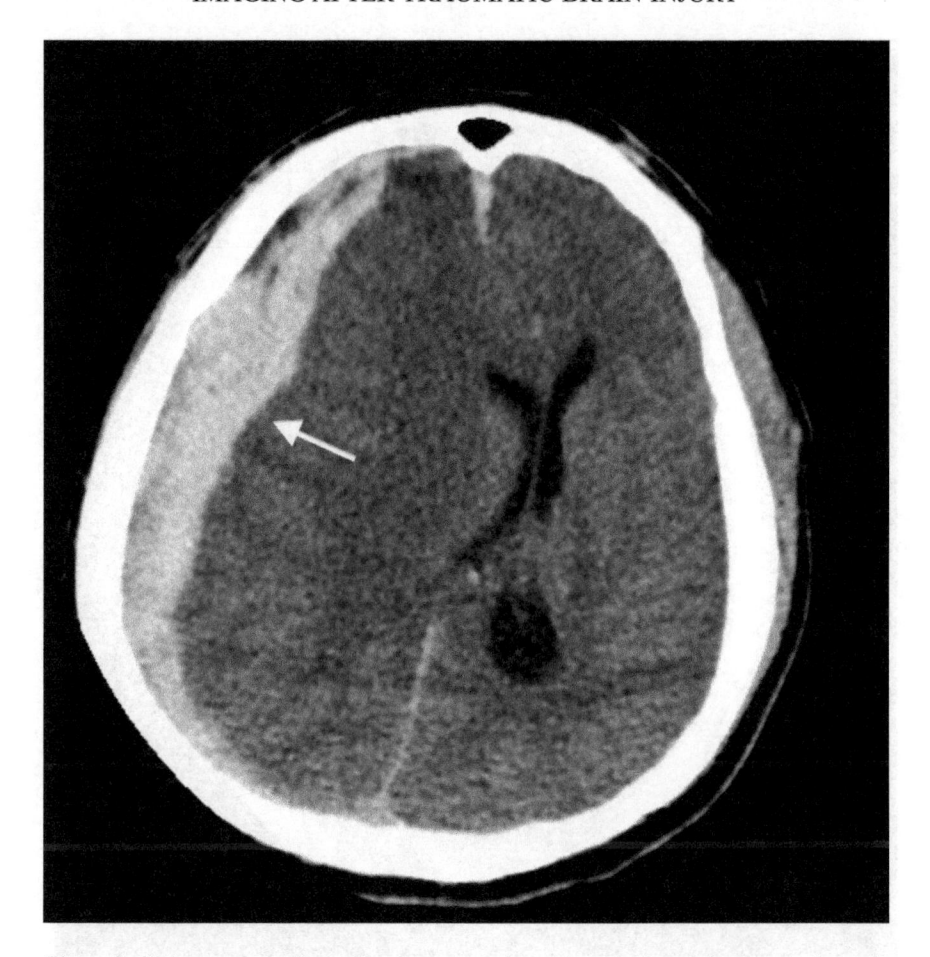

Figure 2: CT image of a patient with a large acute haematoma in the subdural space (arrow). Subdural collections present a concave surface to the brain. There is severe shift of midline structures to the left (the right side of the image as we see it)

acutely sick patients and for the medical staff looking after them. Any magnetic object in the scanner room is potentially a flying projectile, and the strong magnetic field brings dangers to patients with metallic implants or cardiac pacemakers. In addition, motion artefact is a major problem in MRI.

However, MRI does have several key advantages over CT. As mentioned, it is much more sensitive to subtle changes in brain structure. Whereas CT will detect only a small percentage of microscopic haemorrhages in the acute or chronic phases, gradient echo scans (GRE) and particularly susceptibility weighted images (SWI) are highly successful in demonstrating microhaemorrhages deposited by a shearing injury (Figure 5) (Mittal et al., 2009).

A similar MRI protocol can be useful in the later stages after TBI. In the medico-legal context, MRI may provide objective evidence of focal, multifocal or diffuse brain injury. The addition of SWI to scanning protocols is particularly helpful. Even so, it must be borne in mind that MRI, whilst very sensitive to brain injury, cannot detect 100% of lesions. No current imaging system will benignly

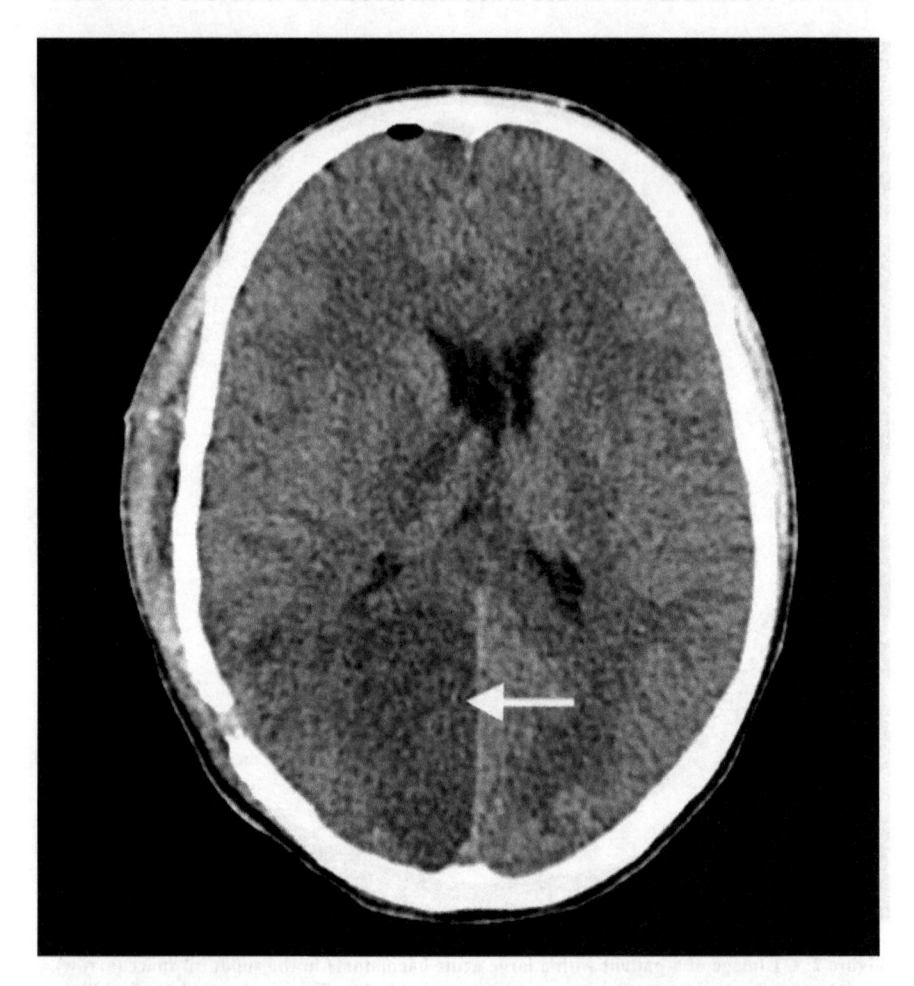

Figure 3: Same patient as Figure 1, taken after surgery to remove the extradural haematoma. The mass effect is relieved. There is extensive damage (infarction) of the right occipital lobe (arrow). This is one of the secondary effects of TBI. Severe midline shift has caused compression of the right posterior cerebral artery causing infarction of its dependant territory

pick up all abnormalities. Furthermore, MRI scan changes may not be specific to trauma. Cerebral microhaemorrhages have been described in the antiphospholipid syndrome, amyloid angiopathy and small vessel cerebrovascular disease, although the distribution and pattern of the changes will often aid in the distinction between these conditions and TBI.

Functional magnetic resonance imaging

4–017 This describes MRI techniques that examine which areas of the brain are activated during specific physical or cognitive tasks. Functional MRI (fMRI) relies on the fact that when an area of the brain is activated, it extracts oxygen from haemoglobin, forming deoxyhaemoglobin, which alters the MRI signal.

IMAGING AFTER TRAUMATIC BRAIN INJURY

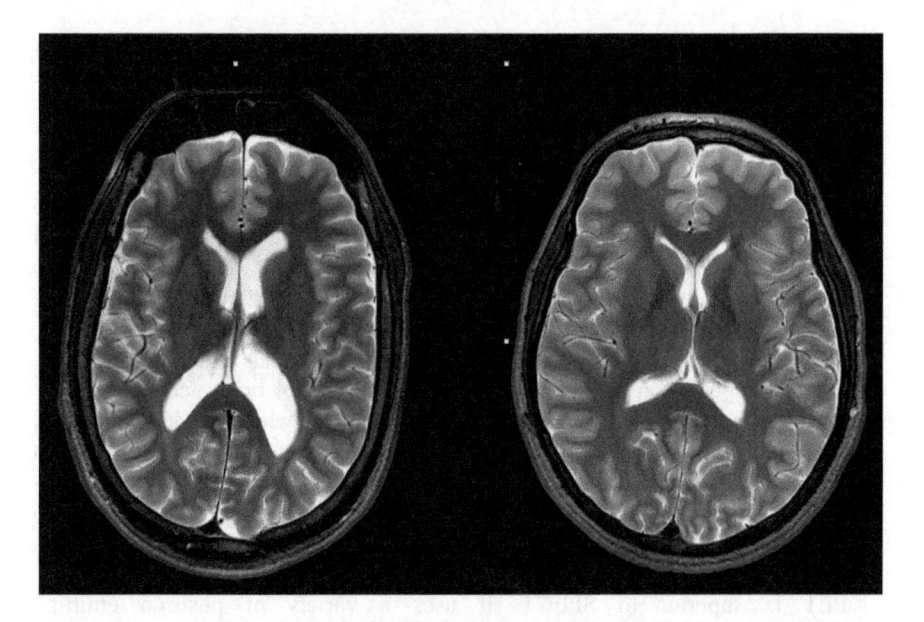

Figure 4: MRI scans of two asymptomatic individuals, illustrating the range of normal variation in the appearance of the brain in the population

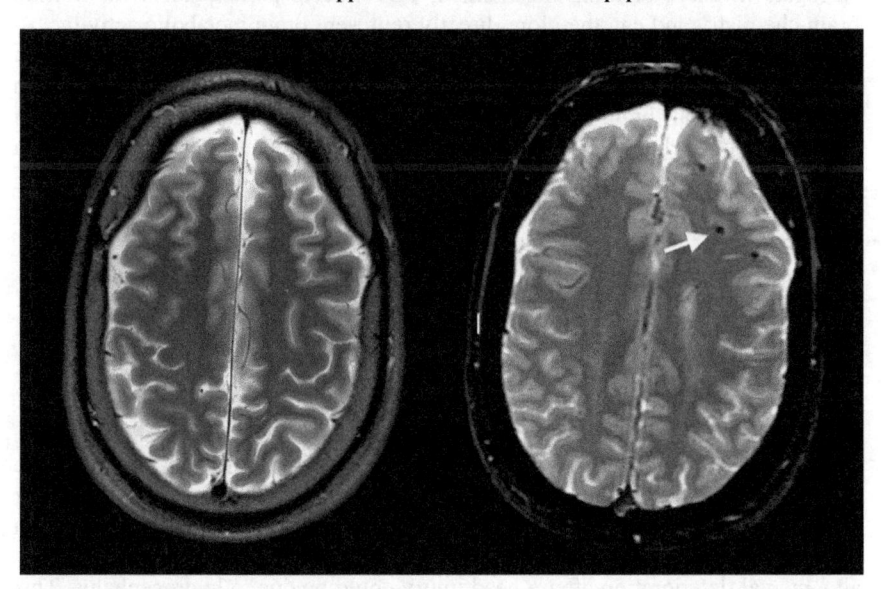

Figure 5: MRI of the same slice of the brain taken using T2 weighting (left) and T2* weighting by gradient echo (right). The gradient echo image shows foci of dark signal (middle lesion arrowed) at the junction of grey and white matter representing haemosiderin deposition from axonal shearing injury, yet the T2 image appears normal

Most fMRI studies have focused on changes in regional brain activation during a task. There are areas of the brain that are active even when the individual is not engaged in a specific task. It is possible to examine activation of such resting state networks using fMRI in patients complaining of difficulties in attention and concentration (Bonnelle et al., 2011). For the moment, fMRI of resting state networks remains a research tool.

Radionuclide studies

4–018 These comprise single photon emission computed tomography (SPECT) and positron emission tomography (PET). PET is undoubtedly superior in terms of spatial resolution and sensitivity. SPECT is widely available, and relatively cheap compared to PET. Both modalities investigate the regional metabolism of the brain, and are not strictly anatomical or structural.

SPECT studies normally use radiolabelled compounds such as HMPAO, which act as perfusion agents and surrogate markers for brain activity. SPECT images can be fused with CT, so-called SPECT/CT, which renders improved anatomical localisation. It has been shown that in some instances SPECT can demonstrate an abnormality in brain perfusion where CT and standard MRI scans have been normal. It has a particular place when MRI is contra-indicated due to implants or metallic foreign bodies. In practice, SPECT scanning is rarely used in TBI.

PET is superior to SPECT. It uses a variety of positron emitting radiopharmaceuticals linked to brain metabolism. Rather than providing a surrogate measure of brain metabolism, PET tracers participate in the normal brain chemistry and can therefore directly represent brain metabolic activity.

In chronic TBI cases PET has been shown to demonstrate abnormalities in glucose metabolism and neuronal activity. Some studies have shown a correlation between regional brain activity and cognitive impairment in brain-injured patients. Such techniques show promise for the future but are not currently in clinical use (Franck, 2015).

4. DELAYED COMPLICATIONS OF TRAUMATIC BRAIN INJURY

Hydrocephalus

4–019 Most of the consequences of a head injury improve with the passage of time. When there is worsening of the patient's condition in the months following the accident, this could be due either to the unmasking of a pre-existing disorder or the development of a delayed complication. Increasing headaches and confusion may signal a slowly expanding chronic subdural haematoma. Equally, progressive mental deterioration after a head injury could be due to hydrocephalus. This consists of an enlargement of the cavities deep in the brain (the ventricles) which contain the cerebrospinal fluid (CSF) that flows onto the surface of the brain and protects it. When there has been traumatic subarachnoid haemorrhage the mechanism of CSF absorption may be disrupted, causing it to accumulate steadily in the ventricles.

This can manifest clinically as a reduction in alertness and attention causing a deterioration in the patient's ability to take part in rehabilitation. Headaches worsen, sometimes with vomiting, and the patient becomes apathetic and confused. As intracranial pressure rises the brain and optic nerves become compressed. It is important to identify this complication because chronic pressure on the optic nerves would otherwise result in secondary optic atrophy causing concentric reduction in the visual fields and eventually blindness. This is a tragic outcome, fortunately rare, of a complication of head injury that is readily treatable.

The usual treatment is insertion of a ventriculo-peritoneal (VP) shunt. This diverts the CSF from the ventricles via narrow tubing under the skin to the abdominal cavity. The enlargement of the ventricles under pressure (true hydrocephalus) must be differentiated from so-called ex vacuo dilatation due to shrinkage of the brain (atrophy) caused by loss of cerebral substance from a severe injury. This will not respond to shunting.

Post-traumatic epilepsy

Epilepsy is a tendency to recurrent attacks of altered consciousness due to disturbed electrical activity in the brain. This definition encompasses two essential elements, namely that there must be more than one attack and that the disturbance is electrical. A single fit does not constitute epilepsy, nor do recurrent faints. The diagnosis hinges on a detailed history of the attacks, preferably corroborated by a witness.

4–020

People who suffer from epilepsy have fits or seizures with periods of normal health in-between. Seizures may be minor or major, depending on whether consciousness is completely lost. A minor attack can take the form of an absence, focal twitching or a so-called complex partial seizure. An "absence" consists of staring into space for a few seconds. A focal fit is one where there is twitching of a foot or a hand which then spreads up the limb. A complex partial seizure, as its name implies, is a combination of various bodily sensations (an odd smell, butterflies in the stomach), psychological features (such as out of body experiences) and motor automatisms (twitching or fidgeting). Major seizures are readily recognisable, for they cause sudden loss of consciousness, stiffening of the body and jerking of the limbs. They are known as tonic/clonic seizures. Such a convulsion usually lasts a few minutes and leaves the person feeling drained for several hours.

The timing of seizures is important. An isolated fit occurring at the scene of the accident is not necessarily an ominous development. Such first-week seizures are classed as early epilepsy. Many of them are focal motor fits or tonic/clonic seizures with a focal onset. Seizures in the first week increase the risk of the later development of post-traumatic epilepsy but an isolated fit at the scene, without recurrence, does not. Fitting that continues for half an hour or more is labelled status epilepticus. It should be treated as an emergency, as it carries a high morbidity and mortality. Patients who have had an episode of status have a higher risk of future status than patients with uncomplicated seizures.

The incidence of post-traumatic epilepsy has been the subject of many studies. The overall risk of seizures is greater than 50% in missile injuries but is much lower in the civilian population. It is known that the highest risk is in patients with a depressed skull fracture, dural tear and penetrating brain injury (Jennett, 1975).

4-021 Annegers and co-workers have shown that the risk of seizures after traumatic brain injury varies greatly depending on its severity and the time since injury (Annegers et al., 1998). Their work, which is widely quoted in the medico-legal setting, indicates that after a severe head injury the cumulative 30-year probability of epilepsy is 17%. In their study, patients were classed as having mild, moderate or severe head injuries using the criteria described in Part 1 of this Chapter. The risk of epilepsy was given as a percentage risk compared to that in the general population, which is 0.5–0.7%. According to this work a mild head injury carries a risk of epilepsy of 1.5–2% during year one, and 1% between years one and four post-injury. Thereafter the risk is equivalent to that in the population as a whole. Moderate head injuries carry a risk of 3.5–5% during year one, 1.5–2% between years one and nine and 0.9% by year 10. Lastly, following severe head injuries the risk is 47–66% during year one, 8–11.5% between years one and four, 6–8.5% between years five and nine, and 2% by year 10 and beyond.

A more recent study (Christensen et al., 2009) indicates that, relative to no brain injury, the risk of epilepsy is two times higher after mild brain injury and after skull fracture, and seven times higher after severe brain injury. Not surprisingly, the risk is highest during year one.

Whilst the diagnosis of epilepsy is alarming, there are many drugs available to treat it. With appropriate anticonvulsant medication control can be achieved in between two thirds and three quarters of patients (Chadwick, 1994). Someone with epilepsy will not be allowed to drive for a year from the date of the last seizure. Working with heavy machinery or at heights should be avoided at least during the same period. HGV and PSV drivers will lose their licences. Adverse effects are less common with newer anti-epileptic drugs but indigestion, rashes, weight gain and metabolic disturbance may occur. Adjustments in the medication can be made but ultimately the benefit of being seizure-free far outweighs, in the experience of most patients, the inconvenience of side-effects. Women on anticonvulsant medication should consult their doctors before considering becoming pregnant. One should also note that employers are often biased against people with epilepsy even when the condition is controlled.

Alzheimer's disease

4-022 It is intuitive to suppose that if someone has lost a proportion of their cerebral neurones as a result of TBI they will be at a higher risk of developing degenerative cerebral disorders associated with old age, in particular Alzheimer's disease (AD). Earlier studies yielded conflicting results (Schofield et al., 1997; Nemetz et al., 1999). A community-based study of the incidence of head injury in AD sufferers revealed an association between the two, either because of shortening of the pre-clinical period of AD or by a direct role in initiating the disease. On the other hand, a detailed study of all documented cases of TBI that occurred in Rochester between 1935 and 1984 found that the number of patients contracting AD was no greater than expected (Chandra et al., 1989). Careful ascertainment allowed the authors to minimise problems of insufficient power, selection bias, recall bias and referral bias.

However, meta-analyses of case-controlled studies support the view that there is an excess history of head injury in patients with AD (Mortimer et al., 1991; Fleminger et al., 2003). A recent population-based study found that after five years the risk of dementia in patients with TBI is 1.68 times greater than in the general population, after adjusting for socio-demographic characteristics and selected comorbidities (Wang et al., 2012).

In the MIRAGE study the odds ratio (risk relative to the general population) for dementia was 4.0 for head injury with loss of consciousness and 2.0 for head injury without loss of consciousness. Gardner et al. (2014) found an increased risk of dementia in patients with moderate-to-severe TBI at 55+ years or mild TBI at 65+ years. A very recent publication provided evidence that mild traumatic brain injury is associated with greater neurodegeneration and reduced memory performance in individuals at genetic risk for AD (Hayes et al., 2017).

On balance, it may be concluded that the risk of AD is increased by at least a factor of two and possibly four-fold in patients with severe TBI. The association is more notable in males and is strongest in patients who have a genetic variant of the apolipoportein gene, ApoE4, which results in a genetic predisposition to AD.

Hypopituitarism

Fatigue is a common complaint after TBI, usually proportional to the degree of residual physical and mental disability. This is understandable, since such patients have to put additional effort into everyday activities. There is a sub-group of patients who report intrusive fatigue after modest cranial trauma, sometimes as a delayed phenomenon. Examination often reveals no residual physical impediment and on psychometric testing there are mild or variable abnormalities in cognitive functioning. In the absence of firm signs of brain injury, fatigue is unlikely to arise from structural damage. In such cases it can be viewed as an extension of the PTS, especially if depression or other psychological factors are in evidence.

4–023

One must, however, consider the possibility of hypopituitarism. A number of publications in the medical literature have demonstrated endocrinological abnormalities after TBI (Benvenga et al., 2000; Agha et al., 2004). Diabetes insipidus accounts for about a third of the cases of post-traumatic hypopituitarism (PTHP). It causes excessive urine output due to loss of vasopressin production by the posterior lobe of the pituitary gland. In many cases it remits spontaneously. In the great majority of cases PTHP manifests within a year of injury but the diagnosis may be delayed if the syndrome is not recognised. Deficiencies in growth hormone and gonadal, adrenal or thyroid-stimulating hormones have been described, usually after severe head injuries with loss of consciousness. They can be confirmed or excluded by blood and urine tests. In addition to fatigue, loss of growth hormone impacts on mental well-being and cognitive function. These symptoms are readily reversed with hormone replacement treatment.

Other delayed complications

4-024 Movement disorders may be caused or aggravated by TBI, especially if it affects the basal ganglia. Trauma caused by motor vehicle accidents can transiently exacerbate pre-existing Parkinsonism, although without causing persistent increase in disability or an alteration in the course of the disease (Goetz and Stebbins, 1991). Kinetic tremors and dystonia have been noted in a small group of patients (Krauss et al., 1996). Parkinson's syndrome occurring de novo has been described in isolated cases of TBI affecting the deep nuclei of the brain (Doder et al., 1999).

Head trauma has sometimes been linked to chronic neurological disorders such as multiple sclerosis (MS) and motor neurone disease (amyotrophic lateral sclerosis). Studies applying strict methodological principles do not support the view that trauma plays a role in the aetiology of these conditions or in exacerbating the disease (Goodin et al., 1999). Having said that, patients with chronic motor impediments from disorders such as MS or muscular dystrophy may find it difficult to mobilise after a head injury and fail to regain their pre-accident baseline. In such cases it is a matter for the clinician to consider whether the natural evolution of the disease would have led to a loss of faculty equivalent to the step-down caused by the traumatic event.

5. EXTREMES IN THE SPECTRUM OF SEVERITY OF TRAUMATIC BRAIN INJURY

Problems in the assessment of minor head injuries

4-025 At the better end of the spectrum of severity are patients with a minor/mild head injury according to traditional criteria. Retained consciousness and absence of significant post-traumatic amnesia argue against concussion. There is therefore no pathological substrate for brain damage in these cases. Aside from the effects of a PTS, no enduring ill-health would be expected.

Having said that, there are patients who continue to report self-perceived cognitive problems several years post-injury. This raises the question of whether subtle brain damage, undetected by neurological examination or imaging, may have occurred. It is tempting to argue backwards along the lines that if cognitive difficulties persist they must be due to brain injury. This runs the risk of turning into a circular argument rather than adhering to first principles. It can lead to the suggestion that patients with whiplash injuries or indeed with chronic pain must have sustained cerebral damage if neuropsychological testing reveals impairments, however mild.

A meta-analysis of 17 studies found that financial compensation was a strong risk factor for long-term disability after mild TBI (Binder and Rohling, 1996). The insurance compensation system (tort versus no-fault) is one of the strongest factors associated with slower recovery (Carroll et al., 2004). Psychosocial factors, the process of litigation and other sources of anxiety all play a role in prolonging the syndrome.

Advanced techniques in MRI technology have been used to address the problem of patients with ongoing neuropsychological symptoms but apparently normal brain scans. Diffusion tension imaging (DTI) is a sensitive index of acute brain damage by measuring the diffusion of protons in the extracellular space. This space becomes distorted after cellular injury and water can no longer diffuse freely, resulting in a change in signal on DWI. It is a useful technique to investigate the integrity of the white matter bundles that connect the various lobes of the brain (see Figures 6a and 6b). A damaged white matter bundle will have fewer axons running in it, leading to an enlarged extra-axial space, and this subtle change can be demonstrated by DTI. There is literature indicating that abnormalities on DTI can point to past brain damage (Hulkower et al., 2013).

4–026

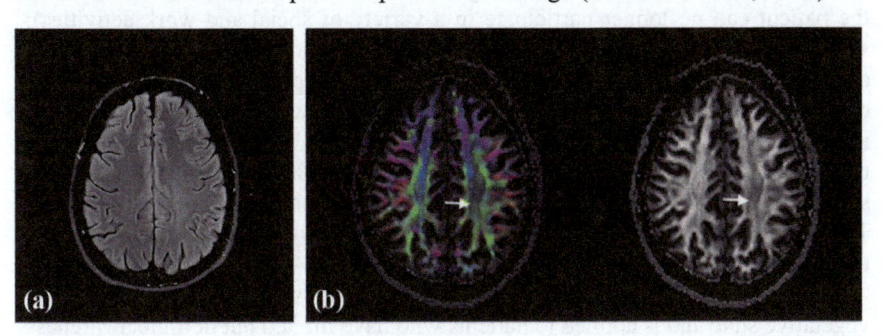

Figures 6a and 6b: MRI scans from a DTI study. Figure 6a shows normal appearing white matter. Figure 6b demonstrates two images from a DTI series at the same location as 6a. The monochrome image on the right is a representation of fractional anisotropy. A reduction in the brightness of FA signal indicates an abnormality of extracellular fluid, and by itself could represent oedema: correlation with the coloured image is necessary to confirm fibre tract disruption. Abnormal colour indicates abnormal fibre tract structure. The coloured DTI study shows fibres passing transversely as red; fibres crossing front to back as green; and fibres passing up and down as blue

There are caveats to the use of such techniques in clinical rather than research work. Interpretation of the detail should ideally be part of a quantitative analysis rather than the use of the naked eye, as in most radiological assessments. This requires dedicated computer software and the knowledge and experience to use it. The most accurate interpretation of clinical and radiological findings in mild TBI requires a joint assessment of the evidence by the radiologist, neuropsychologist and neurologist.

The persistent vegetative state

At the other end of the clinical spectrum is the patient in a vegetative or minimally conscious state. A vegetative state (VS) is characterised by (a) sleep/wake cycles with spontaneous eye opening, (b) preserved brainstem function so that circulation and respiration are spontaneously maintained, (c) no awareness of self or the environment, including absence of response (of a kind suggesting volition or conscious purpose) to a range of sensory stimuli, and (d) absence of language comprehension or meaningful expression.

4–027

A wakeful unconscious state that lasts longer than eight weeks is referred to as a persistent vegetative state (PVS). It does not necessarily imply irreversibility. If a patient remains vegetative six months after a head injury, in the absence of other factors that might suppress consciousness, the term permanent vegetative state is used. Its permanence is based on probabilities, like all diagnoses in medicine, not absolutes. Cases of misdiagnosis of the vegetative state have been described (Andrews et al., 1996), leading to the introduction of validated test protocols, the most detailed of which is the SMART (sensory modality assessment and rehabilitation technique). It can be repeated if there is evidence of recovery of consciousness later in the patient's evolution. In accordance with the Glasgow Outcome Scale (GOS), patients may attain one of the following prognostic categories: good recovery (resumption of normal occupational and social activities); moderate disability (resumption of almost all daily living activities but the patient can no longer participate in a variety of social and work activities); severe disability (loss of the capacity to engage in most previous personal, social and work activities); PVS; and death. Age is an important factor determining outcome: patients over the age of 40 years have a smaller chance of improvement. A meta-analysis of studies of patients in a vegetative state revealed the following outcomes at one year: 33% had died, 15% were in a PVS, 28% had severe disability, 17% had moderate disability and 7% had made a good recovery. The incidence of good recovery beginning at 6–12 months post-injury was less than 0.5% (American Academy of Neurology, 1994).

The minimally conscious state (MCS) refers to a level slightly above that of a vegetative state and is applied to patients who have limited but definite awareness of their environment despite profound cognitive impairment. Such awareness may be demonstrated by reproducible, albeit inconsistent, responses that are either localising or discriminating. This cohort has been further sub-divided into MCS-minus (patients who show non-reflexive movements such as pursuit or orientation to noxious stimuli) and MCS-plus (patients with more complex behaviours such as following commands).

Studies on the long-term outcome from an MCS have shown variable levels of recovery. In a majority of patients there is some improvement but virtually all continue to have life-long support requirements (Lamm et al., 2005).

6. LIFE EXPECTANCY

4–028 The life expectancy of people with TBI is a matter of considerable medico-legal interest. A number of papers on this subject have been published in the medical literature and there is general consensus that mortality in this group of patients is increased relative to their healthy peers. There are certain difficulties in quantifying this excess mortality and in translating the results of epidemiological studies into estimates of life expectancy for individual patients. It is important to point out that, although the courts are concerned with making an assessment of the survival of a particular claimant, this can never be quantified accurately. Life expectancy is the average survival time in a large group of similar persons. Provided the study cohorts and the claimant's relative characteristics are similar, statistically derived information can provide a guide about the claimant's likely survival time. In principle this is no different from predicting a person's life expectancy from standard Ogden tables.

LIFE EXPECTANCY

Older publications in the medical literature on life expectancy in TBI have a number of drawbacks. Often the samples are small, which means that life expectancy tables cannot be produced. Some studies deal with penetrating head injuries, the prognosis of which is quite different from that of head injuries incurred in civilian life. Older studies do not take into account subsequent advances in medical care and technology.

Mortality is highest during the first year after brain injury. Various studies have concentrated on the causes of death beyond that. Most patients succumb to aspiration, pneumonia, seizures, choking/suffocation, accidental injury and urinary and kidney complications. The incidence of respiratory and cardiovascular disease is increased, as is the risk of suicide. Reviewers have sometimes used cerebral palsy, mental retardation and spinal cord injury as proxies for TBI because there is an overlap between the functional disabilities caused by these conditions. There is a considerable literature on life expectancy in patients with cerebral palsy and spinal cord injury, in particular.

Strauss and co-workers (1998) studied the long-term survival of children and adolescents after TBI and found that the chief predictors of mortality were basic functional skills such as mobility and self-feeding. For high-functioning persons, life expectancy was only 3–5 years shorter than for the general population. By contrast, the remaining life expectancy for those without mobility six months after injury was only around 15 years. An Australian study obtained a mortality rate of 5.7% after an average of five years post-head injury (Baguley et al., 2000).

4–029

Harrison-Felix and co-workers (2004) looked at a cohort of over 2,000 individuals with severe TBI who had completed in-patient rehabilitation at one of 15 disability and rehabilitation institutes in the United States. They found that, relative to the general population, TBI increases mortality and decreases life expectancy. People with TBI were twice as likely to die compared to individuals of similar characteristics in the general population. The estimated average life expectancy reduction was seven years.

Pentland et al. (2005) published a paper on the mortality trends in a cohort of people admitted to a regional head injury unit in Scotland in 1981. They found that the commonest causes of death were related to alcohol, suicide or accidents. However, it should be noted that the great majority of the patients they studied had minor head injuries and only 93 had severe TBI, so their results would not be representative for the population of patients with severe TBI as a whole.

After the first year following TBI mortality drops sharply. It is generally accepted that thereafter there is a gradation in survival dependent on functional abilities; in other words, there is a correlation between mobility and mortality. Patients who are male, older and have the greatest functional restrictions fare worst. It is therefore important to study a sufficiently large cohort to enable it to be broken down into sub-groups by functional ability.

4–030

Shavelle and colleagues (2007) provided statistical data from the California Disabilities Database, incorporating data on over 1,700 people in a PVS and 3,600 persons over the age of 10 with TBI. The data set for TBI included 285,400 person-months. They were broken down by gender, age and severity of disability (walking and feeding ability), thereby generating life tables for each sub-group (PVS; cannot walk and is fed by others; cannot walk but self-feeds; some walking ability; and walks well alone). Different figures were provided for males and females, as women live on average 4–5 years longer than men. Data were provided by decade between the ages of 10 and 50.

Life expectancy is longer in the UK than the US. The reduction caused by acquired brain damage should be expressed in percentage terms and translated to the British population. For example, a 40-year-old American man with TBI who can walk 10 feet but does not balance well has a life expectancy of 28 years compared to 36.2 years in the general population. This represents a 22.6% reduction. According to 2012-based population projections produced by the Office for National Statistics, a 40-year-old British male has an expectation of life of 46.6 years. The 40-year-old British male used in this example would thus, on average, lose 10.5 years of life.

4-031 The accuracy of these figures relies on the use of projected mortality rates in the British population. This depends on the assumption that trends in mortality rates of long-term survivors of TBI have kept up with improving life expectancy in the general population. A recent study (Brooks et al., 2015) has shown that, contrary to what might be anticipated, the expectation of life of people with moderate-to-severe TBI who have survived beyond the acute post-injury period has not increased over the past 20 years. Similar findings have been reported for persons with disabilities arising from spinal cord injury. If this is correct, life expectancy figures for patients with TBI should be derived from comparisons with current rather than projected mortality rates in the population as a whole. The same study showed that the effect of quality of care on life expectancy is outweighed by the effects of patient-specific factors, namely age, sex and severity of disability.

Figures such as these are the baseline from which calculations of life expectancy in TBI patients can be derived. They take into account the most important factors, namely the person's age, gender, mobility and feeding ability, but not the presence of additional adverse or favourable factors that put the individual concerned into a worse or better than average category. For example, the life expectancy of people with poorly controlled epilepsy who have frequent tonic/clonic seizures and/or status epilepticus is reduced by up to 10 years (Gaitatzis et al., 2004). By the same token, a slim non-smoker who is well motivated to engage in rehabilitation can be expected to survive longer than average.

Smoking is known to be associated with serious risks to health. It has been argued that, since the Ogden tables incorporate both smokers and non-smokers, smoking should not be regarded as an adverse factor when calculating life expectancy. This is fallacious. If the population of TBI sufferers is divided into smokers and non-smokers, the former group will fare worse than the latter. Smoking, like obesity or diabetes, is an independent risk factor. It could only be discounted from calculations of life expectancy in smokers with TBI if the comparison were with the subpopulation of smokers as opposed to the population as a whole.

7. CONCLUSIONS

It is important to emphasise that the outcome of head injuries varies a good deal irrespective of the classification of severity that is used. Head injury should not be equated with brain injury since the first can exist without the second. Whereas any blow to the head is correctly labelled as a head injury, the term brain injury should be confined to cases where there is demonstrable cerebral dysfunction. Early classification allows predictions to be made about the likelihood of long-term sequelae. This, in turn, together with the evolution of the syndrome, helps to distinguish organic from functional syndromes.

There is an overlap between the cognitive and behavioural manifestations of diffuse axonal injury, a PTS and depression. Even when abnormalities are detected on brain imaging, the correlation with clinical features is often imprecise. The MRI finding of old microhaemorrhages does not rule out the possibility that the clinical picture is dominated by psychological factors. Conversely, CT and MRI scans may be normal in patients who have convincing signs of sequelae from a head injury. The organic versus non-organic dichotomy must be addressed in order to plan management and assess prognosis. In cases where a multi-disciplinary team is involved, the chances of successful rehabilitation will be enhanced if there is good understanding of the aetiology of any residual symptoms and agreement by all involved on the best management strategy.

4–032

REFERENCES

Agha, A., Rogers, B., Sherlock, M., et al., "Anterior pituitary dysfunction in survivors of traumatic brain injury" (2004) *J Clin Endocrinol Metab* 89: 4929–4936.

4–033

American Academy of Neurology, "Multi-society Task Force on PVS. Medical Aspects of the persistent vegetative state" (1994) *N Engl J Med* 330: 1499–1508.

Andrews, K., Murphy, L., Munday, R., Littlewood, C., "Misdiagnosis of the vegetative state: retrospective study in a rehabilitation unit" (1996) *B.M.J.* 313: 13–16.

Annegers, J.F., Hauser, W.A., Coan, S.P., Rocca, W.A., "A population-based study of seizures after traumatic brain injuries" (1998) *N Engl J Med* 338: 20–24.

Baguley, I., Slewa-Ounan, S., Lazarus, R., et al., "Long-term mortality trends in patients with traumatic brain injuries" (2000) *Br Ing* 14: 505–512.

Benvenga, S., Campenni, A., Ruggeri, R.M., Trimarchi, F., "Hypopituitarism secondary to head trauma" (2000) *J Clin Endocrinol Metab* 85: 1353–1361.

Binder, L.M., Rohling, M.L., "Money matters: a meta-analytic review of the effects of financial incentives on recovery after closed head injuries" (1996) *Am J Psychiatry* 153: 7–10.

Bonnelle, V., Kirsi, R.L., Kinnunen, M., et al., "Default mode network connectivity predicts sustained attention deficits after traumatic brain injury" (2011) *J Neurosci* 31: 1344–1351.

Brooks, J.C., et al., "Long-term survival after traumatic brain injury Part II: life expectancy" (2015) *Arch Phys Med Rehabil* 97: 1000–1005.

Bruyn, G.W., Lanser, J.B.K., "The post-concussional syndrome" in Vinken, P.J., Bruyn, G.W., Klawans, H.L. (eds), *Handbook of Clinical Neurology*, Vol.57 (Elsevier Science Publishers, 1990), pp.421–427.

Carroll, L.J., Cassidy, J.D., Peloso, P.M., et al., "Prognosis for mild traumatic brain injury: results of the WHO collaborating centre task force on mild traumatic brain injury" (2004) *J Rehabil Med* Suppl; 43: 84–105.

Chadwick, D., "Epilepsy" (1994) *J Neurol Neurosurg Psychiat* 57: 264–277.

Chandra, V., Kokmen, E., Schoenberg, S., Beard, C.M., "Head trauma with loss of consciousness as a risk factor for Alzheimer's disease" (1989) *Neurology* 39: 1576–1578.

Christensen, J., et al., "Long-term risk of epilepsy after traumatic brain injury in children and young adults: a population-based cohort study" (2009) *Lancet* 373: 1105–1110.

Doder, M., Jahanshahi, M., Torjanski, N., et al., "Parkinson's syndrome after closed head injury: a single case report" (1999) *J Neurol Neurosurg Psychiat* 66: 380–385.

Evans, R.W., "The post-concussion syndrome and the sequelae of mild head injury" in Evans (ed.), *Neurology and Trauma* (1996) pp.91–116.

Fleminger, S., Oliver, D.L., Lovestone, S., et al., "Head injury as a risk factor for Alzheimer's disease: the evidence ten years on; a partial replication" (2003) *J Neurol Neurosurg Psychiat* 74: 857–862.

Franck, C.K., Arciniegas, M.P., Brazaikis, K.C., et al., "Review of the effectiveness of neuroimaging modalities for the detection of traumatic brain injury" (2015) *J Neurotrauma* 32:1693–1721.

Gaitatzis, A., Johnson, A.L., Chadwick, D.W., et al., "Life expectancy in people with newly diagnosed epilepsy" (2004) *Brain* 127: 2427–2432.

Gardner, R.C., Burke, J.F., Nettiksimmons, J., et al., "Dementia risk after traumatic brain injury vs non-brain trauma: the role of age and severity" (2014) *JAMA Neurol* 71: 1490–1497.

Goetz, C.G., Stebbins, G.T., "Effects of head trauma from motor vehicle accidents on Parkinson's disease" (1991) *Ann Neurol* 29: 191–193.

Goodin, D.S., Ebers, G.C., Johnson, K.P., et al., "The relationship of MS to physical trauma and psychological stress" (1999) *Neurology* 52: 1737–1745.

Harrison-Felix, C., Whiteneck, G., De Vivo, M., et al., "Mortality following rehabilitation in the traumatic brain injury model systems of care" (2004) *NeuroRehabilitation* 19: 45–54.

Hayes, J.P., Logue, M.W., Sadeh, N., et al., "Mild traumatic brain injury is associated with reduced cortical thickness in those at risk for Alzheimer's disease" (2017) *Brain* 140: 813–825.

Hulkower, M.B., Poliak, D.B., Rosenbaum, S.B., et al., "A decade of DTI in traumatic brain injury: 10 years and 100 articles later" (2013) *Am J Neuroradiol* 34: 2064–2074.

Jennett, B., *Epilepsy after non-missile head injuries* (London: William Heinemann Medical Books, 1975).

Kraus, J.F., McArthur, D.L., "Epidemiology of brain injury" in R.W. Evans (ed.), *Neurology and Trauma* (Philadelphia: WB Saunders, 1996) pp.9–10.

Krauss, J.K., Tränkle, R., Kopp, K.-H., "Post-traumatic movement disorders in survivors of severe head injury" (1996) *Neurology* 47: 1488–1492.

Lamm, M.H., Smith, V.H., Tate, R.L., Taylor, C.M., "The minimally conscious state and recovery potential: a follow-up study 2–5 years after traumatic brain injury" (2005) *Arch Phys Med Rehabil* 86: 746–754.

REFERENCES

Long, C.J., Webb, W.L., "Psychological sequelae of head trauma" (1983) *Psychiatr Med* 1: 35–77.

Malec, J.F., Brown, A.W., Leibson, C.L., et al., "The Mayo Classification System for Traumatic Brain Injury Severity" (2007) *J Neurotrauma* 9: 1417–1424.

Mittal, S., Wu, Z., Neelavalli, J., Haacke, E.M., "Susceptibility-weighted imaging: technical aspects and clinical applications, Part 2" (2009) *Am J Neuroradiol* 30: 232–252.

Mortimer, J.A., van Dujn, C.M., Chandra, V., et al., "Head trauma as a risk factor for Alzheimer's disease: a collaborative re-analysis of case controlled studies" (1991) *Int J Epidemiol* 20 (Suppl 2): S28–35;

Nemetz, P.N., Leibson, C., Naessens, J.M., et al., "Traumatic brain injury and time to onset of Alzheimer's disease: a population-based study" (1999) *Am J Epidemiol* 149: 32–40.

Pentland, B., Hutton, L.S., Jones, P.A., "Late mortality after head injury" (2005) *J Neurol Neurosurg Psychiatry* 76: 395–400.

Schofield, P.W., Tang, M., Marder, K., et al., "Alzheimer's disease after remote head injury: an incidence study" (1997) *J Neurol Neurosurg Psychiat* 62: 119–124;

Shavelle, R.M., Strauss, D.J., Day, S.M., Ojdan, K.A., "Life Expectancy" in N.D. Zasler, D. Katz, R. Zafonte (eds), *Brain Injury Medicine: Principles and Practice* (New York: Demos Medical Publishing, 2007).

Strauss, D.J., Shavelle, R.M., Anderson, T.W., "Long-term survival of adolescents after traumatic brain injury" (1998) *Arch Phys Med Rehabil* 79: 1095–1100.

Wang, H.K., Lin, S.H., Sung, P.S., Tsai, K.J., "Population-based study on patients with traumatic brain injury suggests increased risk of dementia" (2012) *J Neurol Neurosurg Psychiat* 83: 1080–1085.

Yamaguchi, M., "Incidence of headache and severity of head injury" (1992) *Headache* 32: 427–431.

Zusho, H., "Post-traumatic anosmia" (1982) *Arch Otolaryngol* 108:90.

CHAPTER 5

Neuropsychological Perspectives of Traumatic Brain Injury

Martin van den Broek and Sundeep Sembi

INTRODUCTION

Cognitive assessment can be considered to have started in the latter part of the nineteenth and early twentieth century with the quantification of intellect in children in the school system, the determination of "mental retardation" in asylums and later by the military to determine whether individuals selected for service were capable of the rigours of military life. The advent of neuroscience refined these techniques such that initial attempts to quantify ability by a unitary construct broadened to an understanding of the functioning and biological underpinnings of the cognitive systems that allow independence in daily life. It was appreciated that damage to different parts of the brain affected a broad range of cognitive functions, albeit differentially, with those abilities most directly served by the damaged tissue being eliminated or significantly impaired, and associated abilities being less affected and those unrelated to the areas of damage remaining intact. The unevenness of impairment was also recognised temporally. Some functions were disrupted permanently, some impaired in the early stages and then improved, and some initially being intact, but deteriorating years later.

5–001

Historically the primary role of neuropsychologists in healthcare has been to contribute to neurological diagnosis using cognitive and personality measures, although over time their function has expanded to encompass a range of roles involving rehabilitation and therapeutic treatment and organising and evaluating services. Diagnostic work has remained important in determining patterns and profiles of abilities and impairment to identify disorders of brain functioning and aid diagnosis. This has included assessing abilities to assist in the localisation of lesion sites and identify pathological conditions of the brain and differentiating between psychological, psychiatric and neurological symptoms.

Over time the development of treatment interventions and the evaluation of rehabilitation effectiveness has become progressively more important and led to the development of neuropsychological rehabilitation programmes. A more recent development in North America and Europe has been the emergence of the neuropsychologist in criminal settings and, more commonly, in the field of civil litigation. In this arena the court is interested to know not only whether a brain injury has occurred, but the practical significance of the injury and how it affects the individual day-to-day and the implications for their capacity to look after themselves, work, and resume social and leisure activities, as well as what interventions or rehabilitation might be beneficial. The effects of brain trauma are heterogeneous and there are a wide range of potential long-term outcomes from those who make a good recovery and resume work and social relationships, through to those who are profoundly disabled and require constant care and supervision and those who are in a persistent vegetative state. The majority of injuries lie towards the mild end of the spectrum and mild traumatic brain injuries (mTBIs), such as from falls or sporting accidents, are estimated to account for around 80%, and for whom medical attention may not even be sought (Kraus and Chu, 2005). More significant trauma, however, can precipitate lasting disability and it has been consistently found that the most disabling effects tend to be psychological, rather than physical, and relate to the cognitive, emotional and personality changes an individual undergoes which, in turn, affects their ability to resume previous activities and roles. Moderate-to-severe injuries can be associated with motor impairments, vestibular problems, visual dysfunction, fatigue and sexual difficulties. Potentially any combination of complaints can be observed, which together with personality and cognitive issues, result in significant psychosocial limitations. These limitations may compromise the individual's independent living skills and a proportion will need supervision with activities such as shopping and financial management, have difficulty finding or holding down employment, studying, or maintaining marital or other relationships and emotional problems, particularly depression and anxiety, social anxiety, agoraphobia and obsessional states are also common (Dikmen et al., 2003; Olver et al., 1996; Ponsford, 2014; Hoofien et al., 2001; Whelan-Goodinson et al., 2009).

5–002   Although potentially any part of the brain can be injured, in practice the frontal and temporal lobes are the most commonly affected sites either because of direct insults to those areas (coup injuries) or because of rebound injury as the brain moves inside the skull (so-called contrecoup injuries) following a blow or blows to the head. Damage can be due to the effects of rotation of the head and brain resulting in a diffuse axonal injury, or from haemorrhage in or around the brain, and contusions (bruising). Alternatively, there may be later secondary injury, for example, due to inadequate oxygen (hypoxia). As the frontal and temporal lobes are intimately involved in key psychological processes, particularly personality functioning, executive skills and memory, in the event that the injury is sufficiently severe, then later neuropsychological sequelae may be found.

An important starting point in a legal assessment is ascertaining the nature of the injury and, indeed, whether a brain injury occurred at all and, if it did, the severity. Injuries are usually divided into one of three categories, mild, moderate or severe, on the basis of the duration of any loss of consciousness, the Glasgow Coma Scale (GCS), and the duration of post-traumatic amnesia (PTA) (see Table 1). Some classification systems also have an additional category of very severe injury (Russell and Smith, 1961). Typically, GCS readings between 13–15 denote a mild injury, 9–12 as moderate, and 3–8 as severe. A brief loss of consciousness, typically under 30 minutes, is viewed as indicating a mild event, up to 24 hours denotes moderate brain trauma, and longer durations are viewed as indicative of severe trauma. PTA typically refers to the period between the trauma to the head

INTRODUCTION

and resuming continuous memory and includes any interval of unconsciousness, disorientation and confusion. Patients may be asked to recall their memories after the injury in sequential order with the emphasis on what they actually remember, rather than what they have been told, until the examiner concludes that continuous recall is being described (King et al., 1997). Amnesia after the trauma is viewed as particularly important due to its association with subsequent outcomes with increasing PTA duration denoting greater injury severity (Ellenberg et al., 1996; Katz and Alexander, 1994; Asikainen et al., 1988, Walker et al., 2010). Typically patients also report an interval of amnesia preceding the injury (retrograde amnesia), which is usually shorter than the PTA, although not always. Retrograde amnesia may be momentary or last up to weeks, and sometimes longer, and although long durations tend to be associated with more severe injuries, it is not viewed as having the same prognostic significance as PTA. A particular difficulty is that there is no consensus as to how severity should be graded. For example, Russell and Smith (1961) suggested that PTA of less than an hour denoted a mild injury, 1–24 hours as moderate, 1–7 days indicated a severe injury, and more than seven days was classed as very severe. This contrasts with the system outlined in DSM-5 (American Psychiatric Association, 2013) which grades PTA quite differently (see Table 1) and which does not include a very severe category. An alternative is the Mayo classification system which also differs and differentiates between moderate-severe (definite) brain injury, mild (probable), and symptomatic (possible) brain trauma (Malec et al., 2007). Earlier classifications, such as Russell and Smith's, have tended to fall into abeyance and been superseded by more modern accounts, such as DSM-5 or the Mayo systems.

Mild brain injuries, in particular, have attracted several classification systems. The Mild Traumatic Brain Injury Committee of the Head Injury Interdisciplinary Special Interest Group of the American Congress of Rehabilitation Medicine (ACRM mTBI Committee, 1993) provided a definition which has a range of severity from unconsciousness to momentary confusion (see Table 2).

Table 1: Injury severity ratings for traumatic brain injuries (American Psychiatric Association, 2013)

Injury characteristic	Mild	Moderate	Severe
Loss of Consciousness	<30 Min	30 Min–24 Hours	>24 Hours
Post-Traumatic Amnesia	<24 Hours	24 Hours–7 Days	>7 Days
Glasgow Coma Scale	13–15	9–12	3–8

Table 2: American Congress of Rehabilitation Medicine mTBI Committee (1993) definition of mild traumatic brain injury

Traumatically induced physiological disruption of brain function, as manifested by *at least* one of the following:
1. Any loss of consciousness, 2. Any loss of memory for events immediately before or after the accident, 3. Any alteration in mental state at the time of the accident (e.g. feeling dazed, disoriented, or confused), and 4. Focal neurological deficit(s) that may or may not be transient. But where the severity of the injury does not exceed the following: 1. Loss of consciousness of approximately 30 minutes or less, 2. After 30 minutes, an initial Glasgow Coma Scale (GCS) of 13–15, and 3. Post-traumatic amnesia (PTA) not greater than 24 hours.

Alternative criteria were developed by the Centre for Disease Control working group on mTBI (National Center for Injury Prevention and Control, 2003) and are shown in Table 3, and by the World Health Organization (WHO, 2003) outlined in Table 4. A further potentially important distinction can be made between complicated and uncomplicated mTBIs, in which the criteria for a mild injury is met (i.e. GCS 13–15), but the injury is designated as complicated because of the presence of trauma on imaging, such as haemorrhage, contusion or oedema, whereas uncomplicated injuries have normal imaging. Some also include the presence of skull fractures as indicating a complicated injury, although increasingly the term is used primarily to refer to those with abnormal imaging. As might be expected, some investigations have found that complicated injuries are associated with more significant neuropsychological consequences and that they follow a course similar to those with moderate injuries, but such differences have not been consistently reported (Iverson, 2006a; McCrea, 2008; Iverson et al., 2012a; Veeramuthu et al., 2017).

Table 3: Definition of mTBI developed by National Center for Injury Prevention and Control (2003)

A case of MTBI is an occurrence of injury to the head resulting from blunt trauma or acceleration or deceleration forces with one or more of the following conditions attributable to the head injury during the surveillance period:

Any period of observed or self-reported transient confusion, disorientation, or impaired consciousness;
• Any period of observed or self-reported dysfunction of memory (amnesia) around the time of injury;
• Observed signs of other neurological or neuropsychological dysfunction, such as:
  — Seizures acutely following head injury;
  — Among infants and very young children: irritability, lethargy, or vomiting following head injury;
  — Symptoms among older children and adults such as headache, dizziness, irritability, fatigue, or poor concentration, when identified soon after injury, can be used to support the diagnosis of mild TBI, but cannot be

> used to make the diagnosis in the absence of loss of consciousness or altered consciousness. Further research may provide additional guidance in this area.
> - Any period of observed or self-reported loss of consciousness lasting 30 minutes or less.
>
> More severe brain injuries were excluded from the definition of MTBI and include one or more of the following conditions attributable to the injury:
> - Loss of consciousness lasting longer than 30 minutes;
> - Post-traumatic amnesia lasting longer than 24 hours;
> - Penetrating craniocerebral injury.

Table 4: World Health Organization Collaborating Centre Task Force definition of mTBI (Carroll, Cassidy, Holm, Krause and Coronado, 2004).

> mTBI is an acute brain injury from mechanical injury to the head from external physical forces and operational criteria for identification include:
>
> 1. One or more of the following: confusion or disorientation, loss of consciousness for 30 minutes or less, post-traumatic amnesia for less than 24 hours, and/or other transient neurological abnormalities such as focal signs, seizure, and intracranial lesion not requiring surgery.
> 2. Glasgow Coma Scale score of 13–15 after 30 minutes post-injury or later upon presentation for healthcare.
> 3. These manifestations of mTBI must not be due to drugs, alcohol, medications, caused by other injuries or treatment for other injuries (e.g. systemic injuries, facial injuries or intubation), caused by other problems (e.g. psychological trauma, language barrier or coexisting medical conditions) or caused by penetrating craniocerebral injury.

Difficulties in determining injury severity

As GCS readings are recorded by ambulance or hospital medical staff, they are usually available in the medical record and potentially provide a contemporaneous and independent indication of injury severity. However, Malec et al. (2007) observed that GCS scores may be affected by roadside sedation, for example, by the ambulance service, or prior intoxication, which can depress readings. In addition, although the GCS is used internationally, concerns have nevertheless been expressed about the inter-rater reliability of the measure, that is, the degree to which different raters arrive at the same score and the level of agreement between clinicians has not always been found to be optimal (Gill et al., 2004; Zuercher et al., 2009). Ascertaining the duration of any loss of consciousness and the PTA duration can also pose problems for an assessor. In the event that the ambulance service was on the scene when the claimant was unconscious, it will be clear that a loss of consciousness occurred and its likely duration may be relatively well-defined. However, when the individual regains consciousness before their arrival it may be erroneously recorded as uncertain or that no loss occurred. In these situations, the clinician may rely on the patient's account, although that may also be problematical. Sherer et al. (2015) examined the relationship between self-reported coma duration and the duration recorded in the medical records and found that patients overestimated by 8.2(±21) days the time

5–003

that they were unconscious, indicating that reliance on self-report may be inadvisable. Similarly, Mayou et al. (2000) found that patients' retrospective account was inaccurate and only 15% of those who thought they had been unconscious were established to have definitely lost consciousness.

On the other hand, they found that it was uncommon for patients to think that they had never lost consciousness when, in fact, they had. Lees-Haley et al. (2001) compared the complaints of mTBI claimants and a group of claimants with other injuries. The non-neurological group comprised those who had never had a brain injury and they were claiming for injuries following distressing motor accidents, sexual harassment, wrongful termination and various forms of discrimination, exposure to horrifying incidents, as well as orthopaedic injuries, lacerations, bruises and strains and various pain complaints. They found that 50% of the mTBI participants reported having had a partial loss of consciousness associated with their index injury, but 24% of the other injury group also reported a partial loss, despite never having had brain trauma. These findings suggest that reliance on self-report alone to ascertain whether unconsciousness occurred is potentially highly unreliable and can lead to inaccurate conclusions being drawn. Similar reservations have been expressed about patients' accounts of their post-traumatic amnesia. PTA is invariably seen as a key indicator in brain injury claims because its occurrence establishes that brain trauma has occurred and potentially its severity and it has a known association with subsequent neuropsychological impairment and restrictions (Walker et al., 2010).

However, while PTA is an important measure, this does not mean that its assessment is necessarily reliable. It is rarely, if ever, recorded in the Emergency Department where the primary behavioural measure of interest is the GCS. As a result, in legal claims PTA is necessarily assessed retrospectively and the assessor relies entirely on the individual's self-report and their recollection of events. However, the reliability and hence the accuracy of such assessments is often unknown, although potentially questionable, as they are usually undertaken years after the injury and rest on the individual's recollection. However, memories are not cinematic and remembered or recorded in a linear manner and so discontinuity of recall is to be expected, particularly months or years after the event and when the claimant may also complain of having memory difficulties. Friedland and Swash (2016) pointed out that the length of PTA is necessarily unverifiable and determining when it ends involves a subjective judgment on the part of the clinician, although the courts nevertheless rarely challenge such assessments. While some have suggested that retrospective PTA assessment can be reliable (McMillan et al., 1996), other investigations indicate that this is not always the case. Sherer et al. (2015) examined a group of patients with traumatic brain injuries and found that they retrospectively estimated their PTA as being 106($\pm$194) days, but this overestimated the actual recorded duration by 64($\pm$176) days. Similarly, Roberts et al. (2016) found that in 58% of patients, retrospective PTA was longer than that prospectively recorded and in 37% it was shorter, again indicating that what patients thought was not consistent with what had occurred. Gronwall and Wrightson (1980) examined mTBI patients and found that their account of their PTA tended to change over time, indicating a propensity to unreliability. Lees-Haley et al. (2001) found that 38% of an mTBI group reported having had PTA, but 21% of non-neurological claimants also reported a PTA

INTRODUCTION

experience despite never having had a brain injury. Amnesia for aspects of a traumatic event is a diagnostic feature of post-traumatic stress disorder (PTSD) which can co-occur with TBI, particularly following mild injuries (Hayes and Gilbertson, 2012). Typically it is attributed to dissociation and in practice indistinguishable retrospectively from PTA. McCarter et al. (2007) examined orthopaedic patients who had not had a brain injury and found that opiate analgesia induced PTA-type amnesia. Kemp et al. (2010) also examined orthopaedic patients, none of whom had a brain injury, and found that 38% described experiencing PTA-like phenomenon. They found that clinically significant anxiety after the injury and surgical procedures necessitating the administration of anaesthetic drugs were associated with PTA experiences. There was a range of reported PTA durations from 4 to 96 hours and 30% of the group described amnesia lasting 24 hours or more. They pointed out that this would usually be interpreted as indicating that they had experienced significant brain trauma and observed that their findings had significant medico-legal implications.

The significance of these studies is that assessors who rely on an individual's retrospective account of having been unconscious or amnesic potentially run the risk of coming to erroneous conclusions and inferring that the individual has suffered brain trauma and even significant injury, when a more minor event or, in fact, no brain injury has occurred. Sherer et al. (2015) observed that their findings raised substantial concerns about the accuracy of self-reported coma and PTA durations and in most cases the inaccuracy arose from patients overestimating both, and the overestimation was so large as to change injury severity classification. They noted that regression modelling showed that people with no coma might report 10 days of coma and, similarly, those with brief or no medically documented PTA reported several weeks of PTA, which would place them in a severe injury classification. These issues are particularly relevant in subtle brain injury claims when typically a brain injury is diagnosed some time, often years, after the event, and there may be an absence of objective evidence of neurological trauma, such as neuroimaging or contemporaneous medical records in the event that the claimant did not attend an Emergency Department. Subsequently cognitive complaints, such as memory and concentration difficulties or other behavioural changes, may attract the attention of a clinician or lawyer which then leads to an exploration of the possibility of a brain injury in lieu of a previously less significant diagnosis, such as whiplash. In these circumstances, the evidence that a brain injury took place may rest entirely on the claimant's retrospective account of having been unconscious or amnesic, which then leads to the possible erroneous conclusion that they have suffered brain damage. Given the potential uncertainties about retrospective assessment, arguably the most prudent approach when diagnosing is to rely primarily on contemporaneous emergency and medical evidence and objective observations, such as neuroimaging and neuropsychological data, with self-report being treated judiciously.

Neuropsychological examination

5-005 A clinical interview is the starting point of a neuropsychological examination and apart from providing the opportunity of obtaining the claimant's perspective of their difficulties it also offers the opportunity to form a judgment about their behaviour and insight. Claimants may be poor historians, lack awareness into the extent of their limitations, show denial or inadvertently report difficulties inaccurately. For example, they may be unable to differentiate between memory impairment and word finding difficulties, slowed processing speed, or sequencing difficulties, and so report all as being "memory problems". Wood (2009) pointed out that an interview provides the opportunity to note impulsive or careless replies, inappropriate conduct such as disinhibition, poor concentration and fatigue, or mood issues, such as indifference, elation, irritability and impatience. Concrete replies and denial of complaints, or alternatively symptom amplification, may be observed. Keesler et al. (2016) found that patients' inconsistent reporting of the date of injury and/or any loss of consciousness was associated with failure on performance validity testing. Observations during the interview potentially provide important information about the claimant's mental state and the potential impact of the injury and much of the assessment of an individual's capacity to understand language and communicate may be undertaken informally while exploring these issues. It is usually desirable to interview claimants on their own, so having the opportunity of observing these issues without interruption or editing from a relative or other interested individual, although a later interview with a family member, spouse or friend, should be mandatory, so providing the opportunity of contrasting the claimant's perception with another. As well as clarifying the individual's understanding of their situation, Wood (2009) observed that the opportunity can be taken to assess the emotional impact of the injury and how that might affect a cognitive assessment and observations of a depressed mood, excessive fatigue or impatience, may be especially pertinent when interpreting neuropsychological data. Having gathered such information, it is necessary to consider its consistency, for example, with the clinical records, family members' reports and the outcome of the cognitive assessment. Significant impairment in independence and mental state might be expected to be reflected in the medical and other records to a comparative degree and only passing mention of mild difficulties, or treatment with sub-therapeutic medication, may indicate inconsistency and discrepancy.

Following significant injury claimants may have difficulty reporting their limitations and disclose relatively few difficulties. Impaired self-awareness has been reported in up to 45% and sometimes more of those with moderate-to-severe injuries, although this is not a universal finding and some investigations have found good concordance between patient and other ratings (Flashman and McAllister, 2002; Pagulayan et al., 2007; Ownsworth and Fleming, 2014). Lack of awareness of deficits or partial awareness is usually assessed by contrasting the claimant's account with that of a relative or another individual who knows them well, or alternatively comparing their ratings on a checklist or questionnaire with a relative's ratings. Awareness deficits may vary with the nature of the individual's difficulties and there can be better awareness for physical limitations than for cognitive and emotional changes and patients may be more likely to

INTRODUCTION

report having difficulties in response to specific questions, rather than general open-ended questions (Sherer et al., 1998). Diminished awareness and insight has been viewed as being important in shaping willingness to engage in rehabilitation with patients refusing to undergo treatment or partially engaging for difficulties that they do not recognise. Alternatively, they may pursue inappropriate goals and unrealistically endeavour to return to a previous job, whereas accurate self-awareness has been found to be associated with good work outcomes (Sherer et al., 1998).

Although following moderate-to-severe injuries diminished awareness may have a neurological basis, it can represent a psychological defence (denial) or alternatively result from social factors, such as family protectiveness and excessive support which protects the individual from failure and being able to learn about their difficulties (Ownsworth and Fleming, 2014) or a combination of these factors. Addressing issues of self-awareness and insight is often viewed as being particularly important and a pre-requisite to successful rehabilitation, although early intervention when the individual is adjusting may be distressing, particularly when the issue is more psychologically based than neurological. Onsworth and Clare (2006) suggested that the balance of evidence supports the view that greater self-awareness is associated with better treatment outcomes and intervention is warranted when awareness deficits are an obstacle to the individual achieving their goals or there are safety concerns because of poor insight. They also suggested that intervention may be indicated when the emotional effect of enhancing insight is less detrimental than the persisting awareness deficit and there is support to manage the impact of raised self-awareness.

When injuries fall towards the less severe end of the spectrum a particular difficulty when considering claimants' complaints, is that many are non-specific and not pathognomonic of brain injury. Following severe injuries, individuals may have marked behavioural changes and become physically aggressive and threatening and assault others, or they may show disinhibited and sexually inappropriate behaviour, and in these circumstances there may be little doubt that they have changed due to brain trauma. However, most people do not show extreme changes and, indeed, their difficulties may be relatively subtle, with an emphasis placed on the disabling nature of fluctuating somatic complaints, such as headaches and dizziness, or diffuse problems such as feeling disorganised or experiencing diminished drive and fatigue which are reported to impair an effective return to activities such as work. Lees-Haley and Brown (1993) pointed out that claimants who report a high incidence of such symptoms are typically viewed as having had brain trauma. However, they gave a checklist of neuropsychological complaints to claimants undergoing a psychological assessment and compared them with a control group of outpatients attending a routine family practice. The claimants were assessed for psychological injuries following a range of stressful experiences and none of them had suffered a brain injury, whereas the family practice group were seen for common ailments such as flu, hypertension, and sore throats. Table 5 shows the percentage in each group that endorsed having each symptom and in most cases more of the claimants endorsed having the symptom than did the family practice controls. They suggested that clinicians need to examine closely whether such symptoms are indeed evidence

5–006

of brain-related impairment given that neither group had a neurological injury. Evidently there can be a high incidence of such complaints in litigation irrespective of whether the individual has suffered brain trauma, and they are not uncommon even in those receiving routine healthcare. Similarly, Iverson and McCracken (1997) found that 39% of a group of chronic pain patients had cognitive problems and met the full criteria for a post-concussive syndrome. A number of studies have found that symptoms that mimic and masquerade as brain trauma are not uncommon even among healthy normal individuals. Garden and Sullivan (2010) administered a post-concussion checklist to 96 predominantly young male healthy individuals (students and non-students). The list included complaints such as headache, dizziness, nausea and fatigue, as well as sleep disturbance and concentration difficulties. They found that high proportions, ranging from 37% to 81%, endorsed having symptoms. While mild symptoms were reported more often, they nevertheless found that approximately 60% of the sample met the ICD-10 diagnostic criteria for having a post-concussional syndrome and 29% endorsed symptoms at a moderate-to-severe level. Depressed mood was positively correlated with symptomatology and those who reported mild to severe depression reported having more complaints. McCrea (2008) noted that complaints such as headache, dizziness, irritability and cognitive problems affecting memory and concentration, have high base rates not only among those with mild head injuries, but also among other non-neurological groups including college students, pain, depression, and other litigating injuries. Zakzanis and Yeung (2011) looked at the incidence of neurological symptoms endorsed by healthy individuals from different ethnic groups including Africans, Chinese, Arab, Filipino and Caucasian subjects, and found a high incidence of symptom endorsement in the absence of a brain injury. There were no particular cultural differences, but complaints of depression and anxiety were commonly reported (see Table 6). Although clinicians may view such complaints as "neurogenic" and cite them as evidence that brain trauma has occurred sometimes in the absence of objective evidence (i.e. neuroimaging), this may not be justified. Such fallacious clinical reasoning can represent an instance of affirming the consequent in which the clinician erroneously associates a symptom with a specific cause. For example, while a brain injury can be associated with memory problems, having memory problems does not necessarily indicate that the individual has had a brain injury.

Intellectual assessment

5–007   There is no agreed structure as to what comprises a neuropsychological assessment and this leads to quite different approaches being taken and measures used by different clinicians, some of which are guided by custom and practice. For example, many clinicians ascribe to the practice that assessments should be separated by a six-month period to avoid practice effects and this view has permeated into the legal arena to the extent that some lawyers insist on it, although as Greiffenstein (2009) pointed out, the notion is based on a myth which has no known basis. The length of the assessment is determined by the problem but, as a rule, neuropsychological assessments tend to be lengthy; involving an interview with the claimant, cognitive testing, and an interview with a relative or

INTRODUCTION

another significant person in the head injured person's life, and it is not unusual for them to take the best part of a day. Some claimants are not able to tolerate a long assessment and in these circumstances it may be spread over more than one appointment or shortened because of the specific circumstances, although, as a rule, the length of the assessment is a reasonable indication of its comprehensiveness and depth. Although cognitive examinations vary, more often than not an assessment of intellectual ability is included. A number of ability tests exist, although the principle measure used in the UK is the Wechsler Adult Intelligence Scale (WAIS) which is currently in its fourth iteration (WAIS-IV). Since its inception in the 1930s successive generations of the WAIS have reflected the increasing use of intelligence testing in clinical, academic, vocational and legal settings by incorporating the growing number of clinical studies addressing theoretical advances, clinical research and practical need. The literature confirms that intelligence is composed of several broad domains of ability, each of which are further composed of more specific skills (Carroll, 1993; Horn and Noll, 1997).

The WAIS-IV is not a single test but, in fact, it consists of 15 different subtests (or 12 in adults over 69 years of age) which are organised into four index scales and from which an overall measure of ability is derived, the Full-Scale IQ. Of those 15 subtests, 10 are compulsory if an accurate determination of intelligence and the indexes is to be achieved. The additional five subtests provide extra clinical information that the assessor may choose to use as they see fit, although as assessments are invariably time-consuming, they are not always, or even often, administered. When the Wechsler measures were first developed the focus of clinical attention was on the IQ measure, but that approach has since waned and largely fallen into abeyance and instead attention is primarily paid to the various index measures and the individual subtests. This is because brain trauma, and most other neurological conditions, tend to have differential effects, that is, some abilities are affected, but not others, and so the profile of abilities is of more interest, whereas focusing on a single measure can obscure areas of ability or difficulty. The four indexes are:

- Verbal Comprehension Index (VCI): this index consists of measures assessing abstract concept formation, verbal reasoning and categorical thinking, acquired knowledge, and word knowledge.
- Perceptual Reasoning Index (PRI): measures fluid, non-verbal reasoning, and visual perception.
- Working Memory Index (WMI): measures attention, auditory processing, and mental manipulation and sequential processing and numerical reasoning.
- Processing Speed Index (PSI): measures the speed of mental processing using visual stimuli and graphomotor skills that are related to the efficient use of other cognitive abilities.

Table 5: Neuropsychological complaint base rates in a family practice control group and non-TBI claimants

Family practice group	Non-TBI claimants	Symptom
54%	93%	Anxiety or nervousness
52%	92%	Sleeping problems
32%	89%	Depression
62%	88%	Headaches
48%	80%	Back pain
58%	79%	Fatigue (mental or physical)
26%	78%	Concentration problems
36%	77%	Worried about health
38%	77%	Irritability
30%	74%	Neck pain
36%	65%	Impatience
18%	62%	Restlessness
24%	61%	Feeling disorganised
30%	60%	Loss of interest
16%	59%	Confusion
16%	56%	Loss of efficiency in carrying out everyday tasks
14%	55%	Shoulder pain
20%	53%	Memory problems
26%	44%	Dizziness
6%	41%	Sexual problems
12%	39%	Numbness
34%	38%	Nausea*
20%	34%	"Word finding problems, not finding the word you want, using the wrong word"*
28%	2%	Diarrhoea*
22%	32%	"Visual problems, blurring, or seeing double"*
8%	30%	Trembling or tremors

INTRODUCTION

Family practice group	Non-TBI claimants	Symptom
18%	29%	Hearing problems*
16%	29%	Constipation*
22%	24%	Foot pain*
12%	24%	Trouble reading*
20%	21%	Bumping into things*
12%	21%	Elbow pain*
16%	18%	Speech problems*
4%	15%	Impotence
12%	11%	Bleeding*
2%	4%	Seizures*
8%	2%	Broken bone or bones*

* Denotes symptoms where the percentages did not differ significantly between the groups; all other symptoms were endorsed more frequently by the claimant group (Lees-Haley and Brown, 1993).

An important issue is determining whether an individual has suffered some form of intellectual impairment, perhaps affecting their concentration or involving a degree of slowing, with reduced processing speed being one of the most common issues following brain trauma. This requires an assessment of ability, but also determining their likely level of functioning before being injured. This is important because a result that falls in the average range may be normal for one person, but represent an area of downgraded functioning or impairment for another. Determining the individual's prior, or premorbid, level can either be done with reference to past test results, which are rarely available, or by some form of estimation. Clinicians may estimate the claimant's premorbid ability on the basis of their clinical judgment taking into account factors such as their qualifications and past occupations, but this may not necessarily be reliable. Crawford et al. (2001) examined the accuracy of clinicians, all of whom were described as regularly conducting neuropsychological assessments for medico-legal purposes, to predict prior ability on the basis of a range of information including the individual's age, sex, occupation, years of education and social class and compared their accuracy with predictions derived from a statistical regression equation. They found that the statistical procedure was more accurate than the clinicians, perhaps because there are known limits to the ability of people to handle complex, multifaceted data.

5–008

Table 6: Symptom endorsement percentages reported by individuals without a brain injury in various studies (frequency, %); adapted from Zakzanis and Yeung, 2011

Symptoms	Caucasian	Chinese, Filipino, and South East Asia	Arab and West and South Asian	African	Chan (2001)	Iverson and Lange (2003)	Wang et al. (2006)
Headache	34.4	44.9	51.2	88.5	40	52.4	35.5
Forgetfulness	39.4	55.1	55.8	53.8	58.9	50.5	45.5
Dizziness	21.2	42.9	30.2	38.5	31.8	41.7	32.2
Noise sensitivity	15.1	16.3	25.6	23	2.4	39.8	33.9
Light sensitivity	12.1	20.4	14	23	35.3	—	20.7
Poor concentration	57.6	63.3	67.4	76.9	58.9	61.2	58.7
Blurred vision	15.1	22.4	27.9	15.3	41.2	—	28.1
Fatigue	84.8	81.6	74.4	76.9	53.5	75.7	76.9
Frustration	56.3	51	62.8	53.8	42.3	53.4	46.3
Irritable	51.5	55.1	62.8	26.9	43.6	71.8	42.1
Longer time to think	54.5	67.3	55.8	61.5	65.9	—	60.3
Sleep disturbance	72.7	51	55.8	53.8	50.6	62.1	50.4
Depressed or tearful	36.4	44.9	44.2	53.8	31.8	61.2	37.2
Nausea or vomiting	15.1	16.3	25.6	23	13	37.9	14.9

INTRODUCTION

The limitations of clinical judgment have been widely accepted and in most cases premorbid estimates are determined with statistical methods using information such as the person's reading proficiency or word recognition, combined with other demographic details such as their age, gender and educational background, rather than on the basis of the clinician's judgment alone. This may not always be possible, for example, when the claimant was injured in childhood and before they reach their asymptotic level and in these circumstances, the best estimates of their likely trajectory may be derived from a combination of previous education records and comparison with parental and sibling attainments.

When examining an individual's profile it is important to be mindful that it is commonplace for there to be variation in their abilities and that variability can sometimes be considerable, but nevertheless normal. Two erroneous assumptions are that when a person is "normal" then all of their scores on tests should be in the normal range and that an abnormal or particularly low result is synonymous with a deficit, such as from a brain injury. However, when several tests are considered simultaneously it is not uncommon for there to be scatter in the results with some being within normal limits and others relatively low and the incidence, or base rate, of this scatter can be considerable. For example, Iverson et al. (2012) pointed out that it is commonplace for a person of average ability to have up to 10% of their test scores on intelligence and memory testing to be at or below the fifth percentile, that is, falling in the bottom 5% of the population. While it may seem intuitively plausible to conclude that such low performance indicates impairment, particularly when an individual has evidence of brain trauma, nevertheless it may simply represent normal variation. Even someone of high average intelligence may have 5% of their results in that low range. Such results may be quite normal, but nevertheless interpreted as indicating areas of deficit or impairment, so resulting in misdiagnosis. In these circumstances, particularly when the claimant has subjective cognitive complaints, which themselves may not be uncommon, there is the potential for harmful iatrogenic effects by apparently confirming their complaints and concluding that they have lasting impairment due to brain damage. The risks of misdiagnosis increases substantially as ability decreases and, for instance, in the event that a person is of low average ability, it is commonplace to have up to 25% of their memory and intelligence results in the bottom 5% range and with those of unusually low intelligence, half of their results may be at that level. Slowed mentation is a common complaint after brain trauma with many people saying that they feel slowed up or sluggish and this may then be assessed using measures of processing speed. When an individual shows slowed functioning on these measures this may then be interpreted as consistent with their complaints and concluded that a deficit is present. However, in the order of 8% of those of average ability may have at least one or more measures in the bottom 5% and so such a finding may not necessarily indicate impairment, but instead normal variation. Likewise, among those of unusually low ability, 50% may have one or more processing speed measures at that level. Despite base rate data being available to help differentiate between what is normal and abnormal these issues can be overlooked in preference to a more subjective opinion about a person's profile with the attendant risks of concluding that impairment is present when it is not. Knowing the base rates of low scores in the general population and considering an individual's profile in the context of the many tests that have been administered, reduces the likelihood of misdiagnosis. In addition, it also avoids the opposite, namely concluding that there is no deficit when there is. Brooks et al. (2010) observed that if a clinician applies the same cut off scores for abnormality for low functioning individuals to those who are high functioning, there is a risk of concluding that they have no impairment (false-negative diagnosis) when impairment is present. They found that when using base rate data, a group of moderate-to-severe TBIs were 13.2 times more likely to be identified as having a low cognitive profile compared with healthy controls.

Attention and memory

5–009   Problems with attention and memory are among the more common complaints following brain trauma and important determinants of whether an individual returns to work or regains their independence with daily activities (Draper and Ponsford, 2008). Significant forgetfulness or distractibility raises important issues about the individual's safety at home and their ability to drive, use appliances, and reliably manage medication, so potentially necessitating care and support. As with other abilities, the evaluation of these issues is typically three-pronged and involves an assessment of the individual's self-report, the account of significant others, such as a relative or friend (significant other), and employing cognitive tests. A number of checklists are available for patients and relatives to report difficulties, although in practice they are infrequently used and usually reliance is primarily placed on the individual's account at interview, together with an interview with a relative or close friend. A consistent finding has been that the brain injured person's report about their concentration and memory may not correlate, or correlate well, with a significant other's perspective and they either overestimate or underestimate their abilities. The assessor therefore attempts to integrate the information from the patient, significant other and tests, and understand the reasons for any discrepancies between them taking into account the injury severity and other details, such as the individual's prior functioning. Having concentration and memory complaints can be a poor guide as to whether they are due to brain trauma or even pathological and they may correlate poorly with objective cognitive tests. For example, in the order of three quarters of claimants in the Lees-Haley and Brown (1993) study reported having problems with their concentration and around half endorsed having memory difficulties, although none had suffered brain trauma (see Table 5), and substantial proportions of normal individuals also have these complaints (see Table 6).

Gervais et al. (2009) examined the relationship between self-reported memory and cognitive complaints in non-head injury disability claimants and objective cognitive functioning on neuropsychological tests, and the relationship between subjective complaints and mood. They found no relationship between self-report and objective cognitive and memory measures and complaints were not a good predictor of an individual's neuropsychological status. However, having complaints was associated with ratings of emotional distress, suggesting that the primary driver for reporting difficulties was the person's emotional state, rather than their objective performance. Bay and Kalpakjian (2012) found that

INTRODUCTION

subjective memory complaints in a mild-to-moderate injury group were associated with increased age, time since the injury, chronic stress, somatic symptoms and communication difficulties and they suggested that some of these factors could be addressed with treatment. Jamora et al. (2012) compared a group of brain injured claimants with mild injuries and claimants with moderate-to-severe injuries. The moderate-to-severe groups' self-reported memory difficulties predicted their memory on testing, but not in the mTBI group. The mTBI group reported having significantly more problems with their attention and executive functioning compared with the moderate-to-severe group, and their self-ratings of PTSD were associated with attention and memory complaints, but not objective performance on testing. Jamora et al. (2012) noted that studies have shown that those with mild injuries tend to over-report complaints, particularly in the context of compensation seeking, whereas fewer complaints are reported by those with moderate-to-severe TBI, perhaps due to reduced self-awareness.

A significant other may describe the claimant as having substantial difficulties and problems may also be found on testing, but this may not be reflected in the individual's account, and the lack of congruence potentially provides useful pointers as to their insight and self-awareness which, in turn, may have implications for other issues, such as their ability to benefit from rehabilitation. On the other hand, when an individual has complaints or a relative reports that they have difficulties, this may be interpreted by experts as due to brain trauma despite the high base rate of complaints irrespective of neurological injury. When this is not confirmed by testing, a potential challenge may be that the tests are inaccurate or do not properly capture the individual's day-to-day functioning. The utility of tests will necessarily vary from one measure to the other and in some cases alternative measures may be preferable. However, this is but one of a number of potential reasons for a lack of convergence between reported and objective data. In the event that a claimant or relative describe disabling memory complaints following an mTBI, the clinician may be more likely to accept normal results as valid, and might interpret the reported complaints as indicating exaggeration and over-reporting. Other potential explanations include the misattribution of normal cognitive inefficiencies to the injury, personality and adjustment issues, mood disturbance, and symptom focusing. The account of a relative, such as a spouse or parent, is often seen as especially important in litigation because they have the advantage of living with the claimant and therefore they are in a position to observe them day-to-day. However, while potentially valuable, there are nevertheless important limitations to such accounts. Relatives or close friends may not necessarily be impartial or objective observers and nor are they professional observers and their observations may be coloured by the stresses they experience in their relationship with the claimant or other issues in their lives, their personality characteristics, and understandable sympathy and a wish to help the claim. In addition, while accurately reporting concentration and memory or other issues, they may not be in a position to identify the underlying reasons for those difficulties and attribute them to the index injury unaware of the significance of other potentially relevant factors.

5–010

Fuster (1995) defined memory as the capacity to retain information and utilise it for adaptive purposes. Many claimants and clinicians report a host of cognitive dysfunction under the term memory impairment, when the difficulties they have relate more to other disabilities, such as executive functions, speed of information processing, problem-solving or language disorders. Clinicians are usually interested in differentiating between difficulties that arise due to problems with assimilating information into memory, holding information in store and then later recovering it, and a range of measures are available to assess encoding, retention and retrieval difficulties. In addition, as memory is not unitary, typically clinicians differentiate between learning and remembering verbal material (such as conversations and written information) and visual material (such as routes and faces) as memory breakdown can be selective with deficits in one area coexisting with normal or better functioning in another. Differentiating between memory difficulties and other limitations that impact on learning can be difficult. Howieson and Lezak (1995) observed that problems with registering or assimilating information can be secondary to issues with attention, potentially due to difficulty focusing, directing or sustaining attention adequately, or due to a depleted capacity to hold information with the result that the individual feels overwhelmed and overloaded. In addition, a reduction in processing speed may be a contributory factor, such that an individual is incapable of processing conversations or instructions at a normal tempo and so information is lost to them. Subtle language difficulties that effect understanding may undermine learning and perceptual difficulties may compromise the ability to interpret visual information appropriately with the effect that daily functioning is impaired. Some executive limitations also impact on memory day-to-day, because of impulsivity or employing inefficient learning strategies, again resulting in disorganised or inconsistent learning and remembering. Such difficulties may be reported as being memory impairments, although the inefficiency may more accurately be viewed as secondary to other deficits.

Executive skills

5–011 Traumatic brain injuries invariably have diffuse effects throughout the brain, although the frontal structures are particularly vulnerable to injury. This is especially important as they are closely involved in executive, personality and emotional regulation and damage can be associated with impairments in appropriately planning and organising behaviour and effectively sustaining and completing activities. These difficulties are sometimes described as representing a frontal lobe syndrome, although increasingly the term dysexecutive syndrome is employed, reflecting the fact that such difficulties can occur in the absence of damage to the frontal structures. Describing these difficulties as a syndrome, however, implies that there is a recognised combination of signs and symptoms, whereas this is not the case and in practice there are a diverse and heterogeneous range of potential deficits and no diagnostic criteria. As a result the term can be misused and employed to describe disparate difficulties ranging from minor non-significant inefficiencies on a small number of cognitive tests through to grossly disturbed and disordered behaviour. Nevertheless, executive dysfunction is recognised as being among the most disabling impairments that can follow brain trauma and they are particularly implicated in difficulty managing daily activities and independent living. Despite otherwise relatively normal cognitive functioning, individuals may be impulsive, have difficulty controlling their

INTRODUCTION

behaviour or be inconsistent and have difficulty sustaining their motivation and drive, and so require supervision with planning activities or guidance to maintain appropriate behaviour. Similarly, being disorganised or unreliable may have implications for an individual's ability to work, despite retaining other abilities and competencies and appropriate social skills. In recent years increasing interest has turned to the effects of brain trauma on subsequent emotional and social behaviour. Problems of emotional regulation and inhibition may occur post-injury involving disinhibition, particularly following severe TBI, characterised by inappropriate comments or sexualised behaviour. Alternatively instead of behavioural excesses, there may be impairments in drive, indifference, aspontaneity and reduced engagement in activities. Rigidity of thought ("black-and-white" thinking) may potentially impair social interactions and the ability to empathise with others. Impaired social cognition can feature a loss of social sensitivity and ability to interpret other people's behaviour, comments or humour appropriately and respond flexibly to social cues. The individual may have residual competencies, but also have difficulty engaging with others in an appropriate and sensitive manner and show reduced empathy, interest and tolerance.

A particular difficulty when assessing executive impairments is that there can be a discrepancy between an individual's behaviour day-to-day and their performance on assessment, known as Mesulam's paradox or the frontal lobe paradox. Mesulam (1986) observed that some individuals with significant lesions of the frontal structures nevertheless have normal neurological and neuropsychological examinations and he suggested that assessing patients in the office provides structure and organisation that inadvertently suppresses their disabling behavioural tendencies and consequently difficulties can be overlooked. He noted that some individuals with a history of behavioural problems may nevertheless behave appropriately when interviewed in a clinical setting and respond normally to questioning. Manchester et al. (2004) suggested that a number of tests of executive function do not discriminate between those with and without brain damage and consequently they are insensitive and risk yielding a false negative diagnosis. They suggested that in medico-legal assessments the views of the claimant should be compared with those of a relative, partner or carer, and life-like cognitive tasks used and a greater emphasis placed on lay evidence and observation.

There are, however, difficulties with this approach, which are perhaps specific to the medico-legal setting. In particular, it is impossible to predict a priori when Mesulam's paradox will apply in any particular case and consequently not possible to distinguish between an instance of the paradox and the claimant not having incurred executive difficulties or having made a good recovery. As a result, referring to the paradox may be misused to refute or reject findings that do not substantiate the claimant's or relative's account, this being particularly problematical bearing in mind that assessments are undertaken to confirm, or otherwise, the alleged injuries and complaints. In these circumstances the risk is that clinical reasoning becomes inconsistent and abnormal results are accepted, whereas normal findings are not. A further difficulty is that the value of a measure is not whether it differentiates between those with or without brain damage, but whether it is sensitive to the presence of executive dysfunction. Not all individuals with brain damage have executive difficulties and not all of those with executive difficulties have brain damage. If a measure is completed satisfactorily, necessarily the individual retains the ability assessed by the test and they are not impaired in that area. Manchester et al. (2004) recommended that observation is employed and placed a strong emphasis on utilising lay evidence, particularly in claims when executive testing is normal, but everyday functioning reportedly is not. The account of others, such as a spouse or other family member, can undoubtedly be informative, but should not be accepted uncritically. Measures have been developed to assess the validity of a claimant's self-report, but no comparable instruments exist for assessing significant others' accounts. This is an important consideration, bearing in mind that in the order of 30–50% of claimant's show invalid presentations (see Chapter 7). In addition, while the utility of neuropsychological measures is usually known, the reliability and accuracy of relatives and friends is not. Lay evidence may be influenced by the vagaries of personal recall, idiosyncratic observations and the passage of time that can affect any individual and their accuracy may be further influenced by sympathy for the claimant and, in some cases, being potential beneficiaries of the claim. When their account is provided via witness statements an additional consideration is that they are collated by lawyers who are involved in the adversarial proceedings and have an interest in the outcome. In these circumstances, it is counterintuitive to subordinate objective data in preference to lay evidence with an unknown, but potentially significant, error rate.

5–012 While the absence of deficits on assessment have attracted understandable concern because of the risk of overlooking difficulties, the opposite can also be true and clinicians may be liable to over diagnose executive impairment. Karr et al. (2017) looked at the degree to which executive skills vary in the normal, healthy population and examined the normative data for three executive tests that assess verbal fluency, inhibition, and the ability to flexibly alternate responses. They found that 36% of normal individuals had one or more of their scores equal to or less than the bottom 5% of the population. Performance varied with intelligence and 67% of those of low average ability fell in that range, whereas the proportion was lower among those of high average intelligence, although nevertheless 16% had similar scores. Performance also varied according to the individual's educational level with lower scores being associated with lower educational involvement. For example, 54% of those with 9–11 years of education had at least one score at that level, whereas the proportion was substantially lower among those with 16 or more years of education, although nevertheless 22% showed a similar low level of performance. If such base rates are not taken into account, the risk of over-, rather than under-, diagnosing executive impairment is potentially considerable.

The complexities involved in assessing executive problems can potentially be compounded by the presence of pre-existing personality disorders or comorbid conditions, such as depression, anxiety, and trauma disorders such as PTSD, or psychiatric disorders such as schizophrenia and bipolar disorder (Basso et al., 2013; Clarke and MacLeod, 2013; Suchy, 2016) that may also be associated with executive weaknesses and which, along with normal variation, must be differentiated from the effects of brain trauma. In practice, few clinicians rely on cognitive measures alone when assessing executive skills or when conducting

INTRODUCTION

neuropsychological examinations more generally. Suchy (2016) recommended that collating information about the individual's premorbid executive ability is important when determining whether there has been a change. She recommended that a record review is undertaken, for instance, examining the individual's school records where there may be previous standardised tests, attendance or incident reports, and term and annual reports. Contact with educational psychology services may also provide additional information regarding the presence or absence of pre-existing learning or behavioural disorders. Review of the individual's work/personnel file and examining their application form, resume or letter of interest, and any test results that may have been required by the employer may be informative, together with annual performance evaluations, incident reports, disciplinary actions or remediation plans and an exit interview summary. In addition, Suchy (2016) recommended a review of past medical and psychiatric records, as well as any forensic records relating to previous convictions. This information provides a baseline of behaviour from which inferences can be drawn about the individual's previous executive functioning and personality for comparison with their current behaviour taking into account other issues, such as problems with sleep, pain or the individual's emotional state, and integrated with neuropsychological test data, to determine whether, and to what degree, there has been a change.

Secondary influences on neuropsychological impairment

A profile of impairment is not necessarily indicative of having had a brain injury and even following severe injury, other factors may influence an individual's performance. Secondary influences may be directly or indirectly associated with the index injury and it is important to consider whether they are causative or consequent upon the index event (Arnett, 2013). An individual with depression following a stroke may have a poor memory and concentration difficulties secondary to the effects of depression which is not attributable to the lesion caused by the stroke. Furthermore, although a stroke may directly precipitate depression, low mood may then have a reciprocal exacerbating impact on cognitive functioning. The significance of secondary factors, whether a direct consequence of brain trauma or the psychosocial sequelae or other life issues, is that they potentially impact functioning and exacerbate the effect of the injury or provide an alternative explanation for the claimant's difficulties. In subtle brain injury claims the role of secondary factors may be overlooked in preference to attributing impairment to brain trauma, despite their importance in shaping everyday complaints.

5–013

Although there are a range of secondary factors that can influence subjective complaints and functioning there may be a temptation to assume that the claimant's difficulties relate to the neurological insult alone. The situation can be further complicated because as well as myriad secondary influences, the litigation process itself might contribute to the claimant's distress and critogenic factors may compound matters (Gutheil et al., 2000; Grant et al., 2014). There may also be unrelated, concomitant conditions that have a bearing on the individual's presentation, such as long-standing learning difficulties, dyslexia, chronic obstructive pulmonary disorder, and cardiovascular disease and other coexisting neurological disorders, such as multiple sclerosis and Parkinson's disease, to name but a few. Pre-existing psychological issues may also colour post-injury progress, such as previous depression or other psychiatric conditions. Van Veldhoven et al. (2011) examined the relationship between past life events and recovery following mTBI. They found that 25% or more of an mTBI group had experienced stressful life events before their injuries, including having a life-threatening accident, being robbed using physical force or with a weapon, death of an immediate family member/romantic partner/very close friend as a result of an accident/homicide/suicide, and witnessing a murder or physical or sexual assault. They concluded that the presence of previous life events was a significant predictor of outcome following mild injuries. The significance of these and other secondary factors is that they may exacerbate or amplify brain injury-related complaints or explain their presentation. More importantly for the patient, as well as undergoing neurorehabilitation for their neurological injuries, clarifying and then addressing secondary factors may ameliorate their impact, so further improving their quality of life.

Depression

5–014   Depression is one of the most common psychological conditions following brain trauma. Whelan-Goodinson et al. (2009) found that 17% of a TBI group had depression before their injury, and 45% were depressed post-injury. A diagnostic feature of major depressive disorder is a diminished ability to think or concentrate and indecisiveness, as well as psychomotor slowing, fatigue and reduced interest (American Psychiatric Association, 2013). Iverson (2006b) studied a group of patients with depression and found between 31% and 85% endorsed having post-concussion symptoms, such as headaches, fatigue, concentration and memory difficulties, and between 10% and 57% rated having symptoms to a moderate-to-severe degree. However, depression has not always been found to be associated with impairment. Rohling et al. (2002) examined a group of medico-legal referrals of predominantly head injuries and other neurological disorders, as well as cases of depression and conditions such as chronic fatigue and orthopaedic injuries. The claimants who failed effort testing (42%) were excluded from the study and the remainder divided into those with high or low depression and the results indicated that they did not differ in their cognitive performance. Ferguson et al. (2012) proposed that cognitive complaints are common, but the influence of depression on performance can be variable. They noted that depression has been found to affect information processing, attention, memory and executive skills, but there is no particular pattern of deficit and considerable heterogeneity, and when limitations are found, they may vary significantly from mild to frank impairment. Others have also concluded that depression may be associated with cognitive limitations, but not uniformly or affecting all domains of functioning, and the severity has also been found to vary, although comorbid anxiety disorders tend to exacerbate deficits (Basso et al., 2013).

INTRODUCTION

Anxiety

The impact of anxiety on test performance has long been established (Eysenck, 1992). While a modest degree of anxiety may enhance performance by establishing a tonic level of alertness (Eysenck, 1982), more severe anxiety progressively causes impairment through over-arousal and a disrupting and narrowing of attentiveness. Acute anxiety or panic may indicate that an assessment should be postponed or drawn to a close until there has been some improvement. Whelan-Goodinson et al. (2009) reported that compared with before TBI, post-injury there was an increase in generalised anxiety disorder (5% vs 17%), PTSD (4% vs 14%), specific phobias (0% vs 7%), panic disorder (1% vs 6%) and social phobia (2% vs 6%). The effects of a TBI and anxiety-related conditions overlap and it can be difficult to differentiate between them. Cognitive complaints including difficulty concentrating are among the diagnostic criteria for generalised anxiety disorder and acute stress disorder and problems concentrating and memory difficulties are listed in the criteria for PTSD (American Psychiatric Association, 2013). Disassociation at the time of a traumatic event can also make it difficult to assess the duration of any post-traumatic amnesia and complicate determining whether a brain injury occurred. Lees-Haley et al. (2001) examined the rate of post-concussional complaints immediately following injury in mTBI claimants and claimants for other distressing events such as witnessing horrifying incidents, sexual harassment, vehicle accidents and various discriminations. A third of the non-TBI group had some loss of memory for what had happened and the two groups endorsed an equal number of complaints indicating considerable overlap between the effects of mTBI and other stressful experiences. Assessment can be further complicated by the fact that conditions, such as PTSD, may also coexist with other conditions, such as depression and phobic states, substance abuse, and pain.

5–015

Fatigue

Fatigue is commonly reported following head injury and sufferers often describe feeling tired, lacking in energy, and feeling depleted and disinterested. Olver et al. (1996) found that 68% of a group with moderate-to-severe TBIs reported suffering from fatigue two years post-injury. When they were followed up five years after their injuries, 73% reported continuing issues. Problems with insomnia, that is, going to sleep or maintaining sleep, excessive sleepiness and daytime napping, or a disturbed sleep-wake cycle, are the more common disturbances. However, fatigue and sleep disturbance are non-specific issues and occur in those with other neurological, medical, and psychiatric conditions. Self-reported fatigue also shows an inconsistent association with cognitive performance and Strober and DeLuca (2013) suggested that the notion that self-reported fatigue leads to performance detriment is potentially simplistic. Sanders et al. (2013) observed that sleep disturbance after brain injury affects mood, mental capacity and social functioning, as well as employment, although it may not always be a primary problem, but rather due to other factors such as depression or anxiety. Lifestyle issues, such as alcohol or substance misuse, may also impact on its incidence.

5–016

Pain

5-017 Headaches, and other pain complaints, are common following traumatic neurological injury, particularly when patients have extremity fractures, spine, head and facial trauma, and other bodily injuries. Uomoto and Esselman (1993) compared the incidence of pain complaints in a group with mTBIs and a combined group of patients with moderate and severe brain trauma. The most common complaint was headaches (mTBI 89% vs moderate/severe 18%), followed by a neck/shoulder pain (51% vs 4%), back pain (45% vs 2%), and other pains including knee, chest, hip, leg and arm pain (20% vs 2%). Only 5% of the mTBI had no pain-related complaints, whereas 78% of the moderate/severe group was without pain, a counterintuitive finding given the likelihood of other bodily injuries being more common in the moderate/severe group. The mTBI group also frequently reported having pain in more than one bodily site, whereas the moderate/severe group tended to have only one affected site. Uomoto and Esselman (1993) suggested that chronic pain, particularly headaches, is primarily a feature of mTBIs and associated with depression, anxiety and irritability, and that there is an overlap between TBI and pain patients' complaints, with a resulting risk of labelling such symptoms as due to brain injury. McCracken and Iverson (2001) examined 275 patients with chronic pain (excluding those with head injuries and stroke) and found that cognitive complaints were commonplace. The most frequent were forgetfulness (24%), having minor accidents (23%), difficulty finishing tasks (20%), and problems with attention (18%), and 54% reported having at least one problem with cognitive functioning. Munoz and Esteve (2005) found that cognitive complaints were common in chronic pain patients and anxiety and depression played an important role in their causation. Other investigations have also shown that those experiencing pain commonly report neuropsychological impairment with up to 60% of mixed chronic pain patients routinely describing difficulties in at least one cognitive domain with short-term memory, attention and concentration deficits being the most common (McCracken and Iverson, 2001; Epker and Ogden, 2013). Iverson and McCracken (1997) found that chronic pain patients (with no history of brain trauma) reported having difficulty maintaining their attention (18%), as well as having problems with their concentration and thinking (16%) and forgetfulness (29%), and proposed that pain should be considered when interpreting complaints following a head injury. Perceived cognitive problems are not always associated with objective impairment in daily life and some with chronic pain may describe cognitive impairments in excess of objective neuropsychological findings with litigation and financial gain also being found to be significant factors in reporting pain-related cognitive impairment (Epker and Ogden, 2013). Pain rarely occurs in isolation, but with comorbid conditions that may also affect performance. They include mood disturbance, somatisation, poor sleep and medication use causing diminished performance on measures of attention and psychomotor speed.

Alcohol and substance use

5-018 Alcohol and substance use can have a significant influence on problems following brain trauma and claimants may have a prior or post-injury history of

INTRODUCTION

substance use or heavy drinking which complicates their presentation and assessment. Lezak et al. (2012) suggested that following frontotemporolimbic injuries there can be a diminution in impulse control and reduced judgment, so increasing the risk of substance and alcohol use. The acute effects of alcohol are well known and it has been proposed that 33–50% of those with long-standing alcohol misuse have cognitive or motor impairments involving memory, executive functioning, visuospatial and motor skills, although they may be mild (Fama and Sullivan, 2014). Recreational substances, such as cannabis, cocaine and methamphetamine, potentially also have deleterious effects, with cannabis being the most commonly used illicit drug. Cattie and Grant (2014) noted that cannabis has acute effects on attention, executive functions, processing speed and memory, and is also associated with comorbid conditions including developmental and behavioural problems (such as attention-deficit hyperactivity disorder), other substance misuse and additional psychopathology. Silver et al. (2001) found alcohol abuse and dependency was more common in those with a head injury compared with those with no head injury (25% vs 10%), as was drug abuse and dependency (11% vs 5%). Bombardier et al. (2003) found that alcohol consumption decreased substantially from before the injury to a year afterwards, although approximately a quarter of their sample nevertheless reported heavy drinking and they found that pre-injury alcohol problems were predictive of post-injury alcohol difficulties, although it was uncommon for those who had previously been abstinent or normal drinkers to then drink excessively. Horner et al. (2005) found that 70% of their TBI sample were light or infrequent drinkers, but 15% were heavy drinkers, which was associated with being male, younger in age, a history of drug or alcohol use treatment before the brain injury, and a diagnosis of depression after injury, fair/moderate mental health and better physical function. They noted that heavy drinking was strongly associated with post-TBI depression, and it was unclear whether depression was due to drinking or drinking was a form of self-medication.

Psychological and emotional functioning

Following severe injury there may be marked changes in an individual's behaviour and emotional regulation featuring puerile, erratic or immature behaviour that is out of keeping with the individual's pre-accident personality and, in some cases, necessitates close and regular supervision. However, as the majority of injuries are relatively mild, then inevitably the problems that arise are less pronounced and they may represent exacerbations of pre-existing characteristics or be difficult to distinguish from the individual's previous behaviour, and cognitive changes may be intermingled with emotional and somatic complaints. Although increasing injury severity is usually associated with increasing disability, this is not invariant and there can be considerable individual variability with some making relatively good recoveries despite significant trauma, and others having enduring complaints following more minor events. Greater injury severity may establish a tendency to confirmatory bias whereby an assessor attributes the individual's emotional or behavioural issues to the injury, rather than pre-existing or other concomitant relevant factors, and having been labelled

5–019

as severely brain injured, a claimant's psychological and life problems may be perceived and interpreted in that context.

The role of neurological damage in precipitating and maintaining symptoms following mTBI is debated in the literature with a continuing dispute about the extent to which complaints are neurologically, as opposed to psychologically, determined. While symptoms may at least initially be precipitated by the direct effects of the head injury, the role of neurological factors in their subsequent maintenance is questionable. Fox (2017) observed that by definition an uncomplicated mTBI indicates that routine neurological and neuroradiological investigations, such as CT and MRI imaging, are normal. He noted that there are methodological problems with more advanced imaging techniques, such as diffusion tensor imaging, in determining whether findings are specific to head injury and whether they have a causal relationship to complaints, and observed that in the main neuropsychological investigations tend not to show persisting deficits following such injuries. In a review Sweet et al. (2013) noted that multiple investigations have shown that typically cognitive deficits resolve within three months of mTBI and in some cases within days and, as a result, rehabilitation, medication or prolonged rest are not required, although education and exercise may be beneficial. However, investigations have shown a consistent tendency for those with more minor injuries to nevertheless have more subjective cognitive and emotional complaints than those whose injuries have been more serious. Youngjohn et al. (1997) reported a paradoxical head injury severity effect when they examined self-reported complaints on a questionnaire (MMPI-2). They found that a claimant mTBI group had the highest elevations on the various clinical scales (i.e. more complaints), followed by a litigating severe TBI group, and the lowest elevations were among the most severely injured non-litigant group. Similarly, Youngjohn et al. (2011) found a paradoxical inverse relationship between reported head pain complaints and injury severity, with less severely injured individuals reporting greater complaints. They pointed out that previous research has also found more complaints among mTBIs than those with severe injuries, particularly in those pursuing litigation. Greiffenstein and Baker (2001) commented that premorbid records relating to an individual's personality are rarely available and consequently clinicians necessarily have to rely on the judgment of the claimant or a family member, which requires assumptions about their accuracy. They examined 23 claimants with predominantly mild injuries for whom there were pre-existing personality assessments (on the Minnesota Multiphasic Personality Inventory (MMPI)) and found that all had abnormal profiles predating their injury characterised by somatoform symptoms. They suggested that this was consistent with the notion of an "eggshell" claimant that is often referred to in the legal literature, although contrary to expectation, post-injury there was a trend towards them reporting decreased psychopathology.

5–020 McCrea (2008) has drawn attention to the variability in the estimates of those complaining following mild head injuries. Although it has been suggested that 15–20% of those with mTBI may have persistent problems after a year, he noted that there are methodological difficulties in assessing the base rate, such as the criteria used to define the syndrome. He concluded that the 15–20% estimate is severely inflated and represents clinical lore and the true incidence is far less than 5% of all mTBI cases. Part of the difficulty arises because of the non-specific

INTRODUCTION

nature of post-concussional complaints, which occur in other conditions, such as depression, pain, whiplash, and even among normal individuals, so leading to over-diagnosis. A further complication is the lack of concordance between diagnostic criteria. Boake et al. (2005) found that a post-concussional syndrome was diagnosed more frequently when ICD-10 criteria were employed (64%) than with the DSM-IV criteria (11%). This has the potential to create inconsistency between clinicians and affect treatment and confuse patients (Sweet et al., 2013). In other words, different criteria result in different opinions. Iverson et al. (2010) also found differences in the rate of symptom reporting depending on the assessment method that was used. They examined symptom reporting during an interview and later asked the same individuals to complete a symptom checklist. During the interview fewer symptoms were reported and symptoms endorsed on the checklist were endorsed as moderate or severe. Iverson and Lange (2011) suggested that clinicians often assume that because symptoms are reported long after an mTBI they must be causally related to the injury, but such symptoms can be caused and maintained or exacerbated by many unrelated factors and they are non-specific.

In litigation the importance of an individual's motivation and engagement during legal assessments has attracted widespread interest because of the evident potential role of effort and financial compensation in shaping claimants' presentation. Cognitive measures necessarily rely on the individual participating appropriately and applying satisfactory effort during the evaluative process and its absence may substantially influence the results, either deliberately or unintentionally, leading clinicians to erroneous conclusions. Green et al. (2001) found that poor effort suppressed performance on cognitive testing over four times more than having had a moderate-to-severe brain injury, highlighting the importance of measuring effort during evaluations. A World Health Organization investigation by Carroll et al. (2004) reviewed the literature on mild injuries and found that the majority of adults recover within 3–12 months and in the case of persistent complaints, there was minimal evidence for other factors being predictive apart from involvement in compensation claims, although some studies suggested that prior health, age and life stresses also shaped poor outcomes. The role of symptom and performance validity assessment in litigation and the issues of exaggeration and malingering are reviewed in Chapter 7 and consequently not discussed further here.

Complaints post-head injury may potentially be influenced by the nocebo effect (Hahn, 1997). Whereas in the case of the placebo effect, a benign treatment or innocuous intervention has beneficial effects and leads to improved well-being and health, the nocebo effect is the opposite and occurs when beliefs or expectations of harm become self-fulfilling and precipitate ill-health and deterioration. An illustration of this is a study conducted by Schweiger and Parducci (1981) who told college students to expect having headaches after being administered an electric current. Although no current was actually administered, nevertheless 71% reported developing headaches. While mild brain trauma may not have significant long-lasting effects, nocebo effects are thought to occur when the individual's expectations of illness or distress become self-fulfilling. Arguably many people view having a brain injury in negative, and sometimes dire, terms and their perception of what has occurred and their injuries may be

5–021

detrimental and become self-fulfilling. Nocebo effects are linked to the issue of an individual's expectations of illness and their beliefs about the likelihood of becoming disabled. Suhr and Wei (2013) suggested that when individuals are aware that they have suffered a head injury, they may then report more symptoms consistent with the expected effects of the head injury, together with a tendency to recall fewer symptoms in the past. Mittenberg et al. (1992) compared a group of 223 healthy control volunteers with 100 patients with head injuries and they were asked to complete a checklist of 30 symptoms. The control group was asked to indicate the symptoms that they currently experienced and then complete the checklist again and report the symptoms that they would have following a motor vehicle accident in which they had a head injury. The head injury group completed the same checklist, but were asked to rate their current symptoms and those they had before they were injured. They found that the controls expected symptoms at a frequency that did not differ from those actually reported by the patients and there was a good degree of concordance between their expectations and the actual experience of symptoms. The investigators also compared the incidence of symptoms reported by the patients pre-injury, with those currently reported by the control group, and found that the patients endorsed having fewer previous complaints. Mittenberg et al. (1992) suggested that expectations shape post-head injury complaints and symptoms such as depression, headache, anxiety, vertigo and confusion, may arise due to the anticipation of complaints. The role of cultural factors in shaping symptom expectations was explored by Ferrari et al. (2001) when they compared the expectations of post-concussive symptoms in participants in Edmonton, Canada, with participants in Kaunas, Lithuania. Healthy individuals in both countries completed a symptom checklist to indicate the complaints they expected to occur following a motor vehicle accident in which they had a head injury and lost consciousness. They also indicated how long they thought the expected symptoms would last after the injury. Both Canadian and Lithuanian groups endorsed similar symptoms as being likely, but the Canadians anticipated that they would last for months or years, in contrast to the Lithuanians who did not endorse chronicity, indicating cultural differences in symptom expectation. Ferrari et al. (2001) suggested that expectations may not themselves be causative, but interact with other factors, such as anxiety, iatrogenic influences and litigation and generate symptom focusing and amplification, and so establish long-standing complaints.

Litigation inevitably leads to medical investigation with claimants undergoing assessments for the provision of reports which are later followed by re-examinations by defence experts, and further examinations over time. Claimants find themselves in the position of repeating their symptoms, invariably over the course of years to clinicians who are sometimes sympathetic and at other times questioning. It has long been recognised that there are considerable risks of iatrogenic influences impacting on a claimant when told that they are brain injured and their difficulties will be permanent and have implications for their ability to work, manage and look after themselves, with these opinions then being repeated and challenged in reports. Lishman (1987) observed that the injured person is invited to complain and then finds that they must continue to complain repeatedly over the years to a number of specialists and repeated questioning from lawyers and doctors serves to focus their attention on early symptoms,

INTRODUCTION

which may have been due to recede, but which reinforces the prospect of them continuing and even raises the possibility of worse to come. Rehabilitation professionals may also spend much of their time raising the individual's insight, which involves endeavouring to help them acknowledge problems that they do not believe they have, but the clinician does, and accepting their impact on their life and the need to adopt various rehabilitation strategies. Investigations, such as CT and MRI scans and neuropsychological evaluations, instead of being reassuring, may indicate to the individual that their symptoms are significant and sufficiently concerning for them to be undertaken (Wood, 2004). As symptoms can be ambiguous and their causation not always clear or necessarily due to brain injury, investigations, reports and treatment can have counter-productive effects and recent studies have suggested that iatrogenic effects can be readily induced. Merckelbach et al. (2012) reported the case of a middle-aged woman with memory complaints and low mood, whose mother had Alzheimer's disease, and who was diagnosed by a neurologist as having the same condition. She was given a SPECT scan which was interpreted as showing frontal hypoperfusion, she had blood samples taken and she was enrolled in a research trial. However, a subsequent assessment, which included neuropsychological testing and another SPECT, was normal and it was concluded that she did not have the condition. Despite that, it was difficult to convince her that she did not have Alzheimer's disease and even when she eventually accepted it, she remained concerned about the condition and had intrusive thoughts about the misdiagnosis and catastrophised in response to non-significant memory lapses. Merckelbach et al. (2012) noted there had initially been an overreliance on brain imaging together with an absence of neuropsychological testing and a failure to rule out depression. They proposed that the case highlighted that misinformation (misleading information) is particularly likely to be influential when provided by a trusted person, repeated over time, and it is plausible (the patient had memory complaints and a family history of Alzheimer's disease). These conditions invariably apply in litigation where an injury has occurred and prestigious experts, treaters and lawyers make recommendations, and opinions are repeated and treatment may be provided over years. The effects of misinformation have been found to be relatively subtle and even influence normal individuals following briefly presented misleading information. Merckelbach (2011) asked normal volunteers to complete a checklist of symptoms after which they changed the volunteers' responses to indicate that they had greater cognitive difficulties than they had actually reported. The participants were then asked about their reasons for indicating that they had cognitive complaints when that had not previously been the case, that is, they were given false feedback and misinformed. For instance, when the participants had indicated that they did not have concentration difficulties they were asked why they had indicated such difficulties were present and asked to elaborate. The majority of participants accepted the misleading misinformation and when they were assessed again a week later, they increased their symptom ratings. Merckelbach et al. (2011) concluded that most individuals failed to detect when they were being misinformed and tended to adopt the erroneous information they were given. They suggested that expressions of concern about a condition and over-investigation, as well as other developments such as attending support groups, may all lead to symptom escalation.

5-022   A contributory factor to symptom reporting may be the claimant's response bias. A number of investigations have shown that litigants tend to see the past in more favourable terms than non-litigants, a tendency that has been termed the "good old days" bias. For example, in the Mittenberg et al. (1992) study it was found that when head injured patients were asked to rate their pre-injury functioning they reported having fewer difficulties than the normal control group reported currently experiencing, in other words, they saw the past as having been more favourable. Subsequent investigations have also found that claimants undergoing neuropsychological evaluations rate the past as having been less problematical than non-claimants (Lees-Haley et al., 1996; Lees-Haley et al., 1997). This can also be accompanied by a corresponding tendency to view the present as being more problematical, with the effect that the impact of an injury is magnified.

Suhr and Gunstad (2002) examined the issue of what they termed "diagnostic threat" in shaping expectations and an individual's performance. They suggested that drawing attention to a history of head injury and its possible effects might cause worse cognitive performance compared with those who do not have their attention drawn to a history of head injury. They studied a group of undergraduates who had reported a history of mild head injury, but who did not present with depression, and divided them into two groups. The first was asked to complete a number of cognitive tests and apply their best effort, whereas the second was told that they had been included in the study because they had a history of head injury/concussion and they were told that previous studies had shown that concussions were associated with having cognitive deficits on testing. The groups then underwent cognitive testing and it was found that they did not differ on measures of attention or psychomotor speed, but differed on selective measures of intellect and memory with the second group performing worse. Suhr and Gunstad (2002) found that those in the diagnostic threat group rated themselves as putting forth less effort on the tasks than those given neutral instructions and they also rated the tasks as being more difficult and felt that they had performed less well. They suggested that the diagnostic threat effect might be more significant in those who feel vulnerable or inferior in their abilities and who are undergoing medical or legal procedures. A further study also found evidence for the threat effect, but did not find that effort, anxiety or depression were explanations (Suhr and Gunstad, 2005). Not all investigations have confirmed that diagnostic threat undermines performance and Trontel et al. (2013) found that drawing attention to a previous head injury primarily affected the self perception of being effective, rather than causing a genuine practical difference.

Iverson and Lange (2011) drew attention to the literature on individual personality characteristics, which may also influence the production and maintenance of symptoms, with differences in coping style being relevant and some becoming overwhelmed by complaints, whereas others are minimally affected and view them as only an annoyance. An injurious event may have a particular emotional significance that for some evokes feelings of vulnerability, wanting retribution for being wronged or not being responded to when hurt and sick. For others, vulnerable personality characteristics, such as dependency traits, may shape their response. They suggested that the role of individual characteristics remains poorly understood, but they undoubtedly influence

INTRODUCTION

symptom reporting. The role of personality characteristics has long been noted in the literature with some investigators suggesting that those who pity themselves or have a tendency to "neurotic" tendencies may be particularly prone to developing somatic complaints, such as fatigue, insomnia and dizziness (Lishman, 1987). The emotional shock of being injured, together with the circumstances of the accident, may also precipitate obsessive ruminations, particularly when there is no post-traumatic amnesia to eradicate memory of the accident (Lishman, 1987).

Moderate and severe injuries

While psychological factors may shape the progress of those who have an mTBI, there is no a priori reason why they do not also influence, at least to some degree, those with moderate-to-severe injuries, particularly as there is a heterogeneous level of disability and brain trauma does not occur in a psychological or social vacuum and so individuals may also be subject to influences such as iatrogenic and expectation effects. However, in general the more severe the injury, the greater the likelihood that the direct neurological effects of the brain trauma are determinative, that the long-term neuropsychological effects will be greater and employment rates and functional abilities will be affected, and the claimant's difficulties will be enduring. In their review Sweet et al. (2013) noted that impairments affecting memory, processing speed and executive functioning, are common following moderate-to-severe injuries and as a rule the majority of recovery takes place in the initial five months post-injury, with fewer improvements in the next seven months, and few and potentially no improvement one–two years post-injury. Olver et al. (1996) reviewed a group of predominantly moderate-to-severe TBI patients at two and five years post-injury. At two years cognitive complaints were common, such as forgetfulness (69%), slower thinking (64%), and issues with concentration (63%) and planning (43%). Problems with fatigue (68%), irritability (68%) and impulsiveness (43%) were also found. At five years there were continuing issues with forgetfulness (71%), slower thinking (69%), concentration difficulties (60%) and planning issues (48%). In addition, fatigue (73%), irritability (66%), and impulsiveness (44%) remained. In a review of investigations, Ponsford (2014) noted that TBI tends to be associated with lower socio-economic and educational status, unstable employment, drug and alcohol use and psychiatric disorders, as well as past head injury and learning difficulties, and the long-term outcome for those with moderate or severe TBI can involve a complex interaction between the injury and these variables.

5–023

The practical implications of significant brain trauma have attracted considerable interest, particularly the implications for work, everyday independence, and the ability to resume or participate in leisure and interpersonal relationships. Most investigations have found that moderate-to-severe injuries invariably have a deleterious effect on employment. Dikmen et al. (2003) found that 30% of their sample of TBI patients were unable to work or go to school, and 10% reported significant changes in their job responsibilities, such as demotion or a pay cut, and 20% had difficulty fulfilling their responsibilities, such as having difficulty getting on with co-workers, taking longer at work or having more sick leave. On the other hand, 40% reported that their main activity (work or school) was not affected two–five years post-injury. Olver et al. (1996) reviewed a group with predominantly moderate-to-severe injuries between two and five years post-injury and found that of those who were employed at the time of their injury, 50% were working at two years and 40% at five years, and of those who were not working at two years only 12% had found work by five years. Most investigations have shown that long-term work prospects are deleteriously affected (see Chapter 9).

Everyday independence was examined by Olver et al. (1996) and they found that five years post-injury 81% were independent with light domestic chores (e.g. meal preparation, washing-up and dusting) and 72% with heavy chores (e.g. cleaning, laundry and gardening), 70% were independent with shopping and banking and 48% were driving. Dikmen et al. (2003) found that around 12% of their group was dependent/needed some help with personal care and ambulation and about 25% needed help with home management and approximately 35% with financial issues. Hoofien et al. (2001) examined a group on average just over 14 years post-injury and found that locomotion and independence and daily living skills were less prominent aspects of disability.

5–024 An important area for most individuals, particularly in the event that the TBI survivor does not return to work, is their ability to participate in social and recreational activities and maintain personal relationships. Olver et al. (1996) found that over half of their sample reported that they had lost friends and become more isolated, which they thought was unsurprising given their emotional and behavioural difficulties. Hoofien et al. (2001) found that TBI and family members evaluated their social activities as particularly problematical with 31% reporting having no friends at all outside of their family, and 8% reported complete social isolation. Dikmen et al. (2003) found that 10% had more difficulty relating to people and 25% reported a reduction in the number of friends, being unable to make new friends, or having less contact with family and friends. In addition, 10% were isolated and reliant on parents, family or staff for social contacts. On the other hand, 55% reported having no problems with social integration due to their injury. Ponsford (2014) concluded that significant brain trauma can have significant effects on family life and potentially create stresses that increase over time, primarily due to the individual's psychological disability, rather than any physical restrictions. On the other hand, this has not always been found and some families adjust and cope remarkably well.

The factors that shape long-term outcome are complex and multifaceted and include the duration of the post-traumatic amnesia, GCS severity, increasing age and premorbid functioning (psychiatric, education and employment status and intelligence) and the person's social support and cultural background and coping style (Ellenberg et al., 1996; Katz and Alexander, 1994; Walker et al., 2010; Ponsford, 2014; Iverson and Lange, 2011). While moderate-to-severe trauma can have widespread and deleterious effects there are, however, a range of outcomes and significant problems have not always been reported. Wood and Rutterford (2006) reviewed a cohort of 80 patients all of whom had severe brain trauma, and they were assessed on average 17 years after injury (range 10–32 years). They found that 72% were living independently and 29% were in full-time work and 60% were married or cohabiting. When asked to rate their life satisfaction, the mean rating was that they were "slightly dissatisfied", but serious emotional

INTRODUCTION

problems were not reported in their self-ratings of mood. Wood and Rutterford (2006) found that their competency and integration with community activities was just below that of non-disabled individuals and they concluded that overall the results suggested that long-term adjustment was better than might be expected from previous studies.

Test disclosure

With the growth in the role of neuropsychological assessment in litigation, attention has turned to the validity of experts' conclusions, particularly when they rely on psychometric measures and occasionally a request is made by claimant or defendant solicitors for copies of test data. Morel (2009) maintained that the dissemination of neuropsychological data and tests is an important area because breaches in test security can have a significant impact on the outcome of litigation and, more widely, affect the practitioner, test publishers, and even the legal system. As a rule, psychologists and neuropsychologists are discouraged by their professional bodies from disclosing test materials to unqualified individuals because of the importance of maintaining test confidentiality and the utility of cognitive measures both for the claimant, but also other claimants and the wider public as their dissemination would undermine their utility. The British Psychological Society (BPS) published a Statement (2007) advising that psychologists who use tests should respect the confidentiality of test materials and avoid releasing them into the public domain. The BPS pointed out that the leaking of confidential information into the public arena would damage the integrity of subsequent testing using the disclosed materials and when presenting evidence in open court a practitioner should refer to tests in a general way so as not to affect their later usefulness and they should not engage in a detailed presentational discussion of the materials. The BPS cited the American Psychological Association (1996) as describing the reasons for maintaining the security of test materials:

5–025

> "Availability of test items to an unqualified person can not only render the test invalid for any future use with that individual, but also jeopardises the security and integrity of the test for other persons who may be exposed to test items and responses. Such release imposes very concrete harm to the general public—loss of effective assessment tools. Because there are a limited number of standardised psychological tests considered appropriate for a given purpose (in some instances only a single instrument), they cannot easily be replaced or substituted if an individual obtains prior knowledge of item content or the security of the test is otherwise compromised.
>
> Development and refinement of items and norms for individual intelligence tests, personality assessment techniques, and achievement tests often require many years of research and considerable effort and expense. Improper disclosure of test items or other test materials also may result in damage to those parties which have developed or have ownership in the test and possibly result in breach of contract claims against psychologists who violate the terms of their test purchase or lease agreements." (American Psychological Association, 1996.)

Similarly, the National Academy of Neuropsychology provided a Position Statement (2000) saying that maintaining test security is critical because of the harm that can result from public dissemination of test procedures and the risks of coaching and manipulating results. They pointed out there is risk of public harm and tests becoming invalidated and the risk of violations of copyright and intellectual property. While neuropsychologists may not therefore disclose test materials or test data to non-psychologists there is, however, no reason why they should not disclose such information to another neuropsychology expert, provided there are assurances that the material will be properly protected. Another neuropsychologist may want to examine the original materials to check responses made by the claimant, compare results between assessments or understand the basis for any conclusions, and there is no reason why a request for disclosure should be denied, although it may best take place directly between the expert practitioners.

Third party observers

5–026 Occasionally lawyers ask for a claimant to be accompanied during a neuropsychological assessment, for example, by a case manager and, since the case of *Williams v Jervis*,[1] occasionally requests are also made to record an assessment. These requests are much more common in North America where accompanying witnesses have even accrued the title third person observer (TPO). TPOs, or third-party observation, refers to the direct or indirect observation of the client and psychologist or neuropsychologist during the assessment process when an involved individual attends and observes the examination. The observer is described as "involved" when they include a member of the family, legal team or a representative of a party involved in the proceedings, such as a case manager, but also includes observation via a one-way mirror and the use of audio or video recording (American Academy of Clinical Neuropsychology, 2001). Requests to include a TPO are invariably declined as there is a substantial body of research indicating that their presence adversely affects an individual's performance during assessment and negative effects have been found on measures of attention, learning, and memory (Lewandowski et al., 2016). These findings are perhaps unsurprising as direct or indirect observation can be expected to have a distracting effect on a claimant so that they no longer engage appropriately with the examination and instead turn their attention to the TPO, perhaps anticipating their reactions or later appraisal of their comments and performance, and so altering their responses and behaviour and affecting the validity of the examination. In addition, tests have not been standardised for use in such circumstances and consequently a TPO represents a deviation from consistent and standard practice and there is no basis for concluding that the results are valid or that they can be interpreted using the relevant normative data (Lewandowski et al., 2016). As the clinician has no control over the subsequent recording, particularly if it is covert, concerns about test security and the utility of tests for other individuals, both in and outside of the litigation, again comes into play, as well as concerns about copyright and intellectual property infringement.

In the circumstances it is not surprising that a number of bodies have advised clinicians not to agree to the presence of TPOs, including the National Academy

---

[1] [2008] EWHC 2346 (QB).

INTRODUCTION

of Neuropsychology, American Academy of Clinical Neuropsychology and the American Board of Professional Neuropsychology (Lewandowski et al., 2016).

Conclusions

While brain trauma is a common condition, it is not always easy or straightforward to diagnose in the absence of contemporaneous clinical evidence (i.e. ambulance and medical records) or objective evidence of brain trauma (i.e. neuroimaging). When there is evidence of brain damage, such as from CT or MRI imaging, then the clinician will be on firm ground, but such information is not always available and relying primarily on the patient's retrospective account may be an insecure foundation for diagnosis. Injuries towards the milder end of the spectrum are particularly likely to be multifactorial in nature with a range of influences potentially being relevant as well as the index injury. Physical and somatic issues (i.e. pain, sleep disturbance and fatigue, vestibular symptoms, and other bodily injuries) may exacerbate and maintain complaints, together with psychological factors (i.e. nocebo effects, expectations, the "good old days" bias, personality characteristics, and psychological/psychiatric issues such as depression, anxiety, and PTSD). Similarly, the individual's social and environmental context can have an influence (i.e. iatrogenic factors, critogenic factors, family responses and caring). The significance of these issues will vary from one person to another and in some cases be relevant, but not in others. Their importance may also vary over time while recovery, adjustment and rehabilitation take place, together with fluctuations in the individual's mood, pain, fatigue and other factors, such as substance or alcohol use. Assessment in the course of litigation may be further complicated by vagaries in the information available to the assessor (see Chapter 11) and the influence of litigation itself (see Chapter 7). While after moderate-to-severe injuries cognitive, emotional or physical changes can be expected, particularly with increasing injury severity, nevertheless, indices of severity may provide an imperfect guide to an individual's prognosis and long-term condition as there is considerable variability in outcome. While problems with maintaining relationships, social isolation and unemployment are common, nonetheless, investigations show that significant proportions do not have social difficulties and others return to work (Dikmen et al., 2003; Olver et al., 1996; Wood and Rutterford, 2006) underscoring the need to view injury severity as increasing the likelihood, but not the inevitability, of long-term disability. This variability may be due to injury-related factors, such as the force and nature of blows to the head and brain, the sites of injury and the occurrence of complications (i.e. haemorrhage, contusions or oedema), and the later opportunity for rehabilitation, as well as a range of other psychological and social factors. The individual's condition may also affect those around them, particularly a spouse, partner and family, and their response may in turn become another influence, such as through family distress or over-protectiveness. While the complexity of such issues may complicate determining the nature of an individual's difficulties, nevertheless, a clear understanding also provides important pointers for intervention and rehabilitation to address them. Ameliorating the effects of factors, such as depression, with rehabilitation, psychological therapies or medication, as well as addressing other issues such as self-fulfilling

5–027

negative expectations, misattribution and iatrogenic influences, may allow for a better understanding of the impact of the injury and, in due course, improve the individual's future quality of life.

REFERENCES

5–028   American Academy of Clinical Neuropsychology "Policy Statement on the Presence of Third-Party Observers in Neuropsychological Assessments" (2001) *Clinical Neuropsychologist (Neuropsychology, Development and Cognition: Section D)* 15, 433–439.

American Psychiatric Association (2013) *Diagnostic and Statistical Manual of Mental Disorders, 5th edition: DSM-5* (Arlington, VA: American Psychiatric Association).

American Psychological Association (1996) "Statement on the Disclosure of Test Data" *American Psychologist* 51 (6), 6, 644–648.

Arnett, P.A. (2013) "Introduction to secondary influences on neuropsychological test performance" in Arnett, P.A. (ed.), *Secondary Influences on Neuropsychological Test Performance: Research Findings and Practical Applications* (New York: Oxford University Press, 2013).

Asikainen I., Kaste M. and Sarna S., "Predicting late outcome for patients with traumatic brain injury referred to a rehabilitation programme: a study of 508 Finnish patients 5 years or more after injury" (1998) *Brain Injury* 12, 95–107.

Basso, M.R., Miller, A., Estevis E., and Combs, D., "Neuropsychological deficits in major depressive disorder: correlates and conundrums" in Arnett, P.A. (ed.), *Secondary Influences on Neuropsychological Test Performance: Research Findings and Practical Applications* (New York: Oxford University Press, 2013).

Bay, E.H. and Kalpakjian, C.Z., "Determinants of subjective memory complaints in community-dwelling adults with mild to moderate traumatic brain injury" (2012) *Brain Injury* 26, 941–949.

Boake, C., McCauley, S.R., Levin, H.S., Pedroza, C., Constant, C.F., Song, J.X., Brown, S.A., Goodman, H., Brundage, S.I. and Diaz-Marchan, P.J., Diagnostic criteria for postconcussional syndrome after mild-to-moderate traumatic brain injury (2005) *Journal of Neuropsychiatry and Clinical Neuroscience* 17 (3), 350–356.

Bombardier, C.H., Temkin, N.R., Machamer, J. and Dikmen, S.S., "The natural history of drinking and alcohol-related problems after traumatic brain injury" (2003) *Archives of Physical Medicine and Rehabilitation* 84 (2), 185–191.

British Psychological Society, *Statement on the Conduct of Psychologists Providing Expert Psychometric Evidence to Courts and Lawyers* (Leicester: BPS, 2007).

Brooks, B.L., Holdnack, J.A. and Iverson, G.L., "Advanced clinical interpretation of the WAIS-IV and WMS-IV: prevalence of low scores varies by level of intelligence and years of education" (2010) *Assessment* 18 (2), 156–167.

Carroll, J.B., *Human Cognitive Abilities: A Survey of Factor analytic studies* (New York: Cambridge University Press, 1993).

Carroll, L.J., Cassidy, J.D., Holm, L., Krause J. and Coronado, V.G., "Methodological Issues and Research Recommendations for Mild Traumatic Brain: The WHO Collaborating Centre Task Force on Mild Traumatic Brain" (2004a) *Journal of Rehabilitation Medicine* 43, 113–125.

Carroll, L.J., Cassidy, J.D., Peloso, P.M., Borg, J., van Holst, H., Holm, L., Paniak C. and Pepin, M., "Prognosis for mild traumatic brain injury: results of the WHO collaborating Centre task force on mild traumatic brain injury" (2004b) *Journal of Rehabilitation Medicine* 43, 84–105.

REFERENCES

Cattie, J.E. and Grant, I., "Cannabis" in Allen, D.N., and Woods, S.P. (eds), *Neuropsychological Aspects of Substance Use Disorders* (Oxford: Oxford University Press, 2014).

Chan, R.C.K. "Base rate of post-concussion symptoms among normal people and its neuropsychological correlates" (2001) *Clinical Rehabilitation* 15, 266–273.

Clarke, P. and MacLeod, C., "The impact of anxiety on cognitive task performance" in Arnett, P.A. (ed.), *Secondary Influences on Neuropsychological Test Performance: Research Findings and Practical Applications* (New York: Oxford University Press, 2013).

Crawford, J.R., Millar, J. and Milne, A.B., "Estimating premorbid IQ from demographic variables: a comparison of a regression equation vs clinical judgement" (2001) *British Journal of Clinical Psychology*, 40, 97–105.

Dikmen, S.S., Machamer, J.E., Powell J.M. and Temkin, N.R., "Outcome 3 to 5 years after moderate to severe traumatic brain injury" (2003) *Archives of Physical Medicine and Rehabilitation* 84 (10), 1449–1457.

Draper, K. and Ponsford, J., "Cognitive functioning 10 years following traumatic brain injury and rehabilitation" (2008) *Neuropsychology* 22, 618–625.

Ellenberg J.H., Levin H.S. and Saydjari, C., "Posttraumatic amnesia as a predictor of outcome after severe closed head injury" (1996) *Archives of Neurology* 53 (8), 782–91.

Epker, J. and Ogden, M., "The impact of pain and pain-related factors on cognitive functioning" in Arnett, P.A. (ed.), *Secondary Influences on Neuropsychological Test Performance: Research Findings and Practical Applications* (New York: Oxford University Press, 2013).

Eysenck, M.W., *Attention and arousal: cognition and performance* (Berlin: Springer, 1982).

Eysenck, MW., *Anxiety: the cognitive perspective* (Hove: Erlbaum, 1992).

Fama, R. and Sullivan, E.V., "Alcohol" in Allen, D.N. and Woods, S.P. (eds), *Neuropsychological Aspects of Substance Use Disorders: Evidence-Based Perspectives* (New York: Oxford University Press, 2014).

Ferguson, K.E., Iverson, G.L., Langenecker, S.A. and Young, A.H., "Depression in the Context of Workplace Injury" in Bush, S.S. and Iverson, G.L. (eds), *Neuropsychological Assessment of Work-Related Injuries* (New York: Guilford Press, 2012).

Ferrari, R., Obelieniene, D., Russell, A.S., Darlington, P., Gervais, R. and Green, P., "Symptom expectation after minor head injury. A comparative study between Canada and Lithuania" (2001) *Clinical Neurology and Neurosurgery* 103, 184–190.

Flashman, L.A. and McAllister, T.W., "Lack of awareness and its impact on traumatic brain" (2002) *Neurorehabilitation* 17, 285–296.

Fox, D.D., "Persistent Postconcussion Syndrome" in Boone, K.B. (ed.), *Neuropsychological Evaluation of Somatoform and Other Functional Somatic Conditions: Assessment Primer* (New York: Routledge, 2017).

Friedland, D. and Swash, M., "Post-traumatic amnesia and confusional state: hazards of retrospective assessment" (2016) *Journal of Neurology, Neurosurgery and Psychiatry* 87 (10), 1068–1074.

Fuster, J. M. *Memory in the Cerebral Cortex: An Empirical Approach to Neural Networks in the Human and Nonhuman Primate* (Cambridge, MA: MIT Press, 1995).

Garden, N. and Sullivan, K.A., "An examination of the base rates of post-concussion symptoms: the influence of demographics and depression" (2010) *Applied Neuropsychology* 17, 1–7.

Gervais, R.O., Ben-Porath, Y.S. and Wygant, D.B., "Empirical correlates and interpretation of the MMPI-2-RF cognitive complaints (COG) scale" (2009) *Clinical Neuropsychologist* 23, 996–1015.

Gill, M.R., Rieley, D.G. and Green, S.M., "Interrater reliability of Glasgow Coma Scale scores in the Emergency Department" (2004) *Annals of Emergency Medicine* 43 (2), 215–223.

Grant, GM., O'Donnell, ML., Spittal, MJ, Creamer, M., and Studdert, DM., "Relationship between Stressfulness of Claiming for Injury Compensation and Long-Term Recovery: A Prospective Cohort Study" (2014) *JAMA Psychiatry*, 1:71(4), 446–453.

Green, P., Rohling, M.L., Lees-Haley, P.R. and Allen, L.M., "Effort has a greater effect on test scores than severe brain injury in compensation claimants" (2001) *Brain Injury* 15 (12), 1045–1060.

Greiffenstein, M.F., "Clinical Myths in Forensic Neuropsychology" (2009) *Clinical Neuropsychologist* 23, 286–296.

Greiffenstein, M.F. and Baker, W.J., "Comparison of premorbid and post injury MMPI-2 profiles in late postconcussion claimants" (2001) *Clinical Neuropsychologist* 15 (2), 162–170.

Gronwall, D. and Wrightson, P., "Duration of post-traumatic amnesia after mild head injury" (1980) *Journal of Clinical Neuropsychology* 2(1), 51–60.

Gutheil, T.G., Bursztajn, H., Brodksy, A. and Strasburger, L.H., "Preventing 'Critogenic' Harms: Minimizing Emotional Injury from Civil Litigation" (2000) *Journal of Psychiatry and Law* 28(1), 1 5–18

Hahn, R.A., "The nocebo phenomenon: concepts, evidence, and implications for public health" (1997) *Preventative Medicine* 26 (5), 607–611.

Hayes, J.P. and Gilbertson, M.W., "Understanding Post-Traumatic Stress Disorder: Implications for Comorbid Post-Traumatic Stress Disorder and Mild Traumatic Brain Injury" in Vasterling, J.J., Bryant, R.A. and Keane, R.M. (eds), *PTSD and Mild Traumatic Brain* (New York: Guilford Press, 2012).

Hoofien D., Gilboa, A., Vakil, E. and Donovick, P.J., "Traumatic brain injury (TBI) 10–20 years later: a comprehensive outcome study of psychiatric symptomatology, cognitive abilities and psychosocial functioning" (2001) *Brain Injury* 15 (3), 189–209.

Horn, J.L. and Noll, J., "Human cognitive capabilities: Gf-Gc theory" in Flannagan, D.P., Genshaft, J.L. and Harrison, P.L. (eds), *Contemporary Intellectual Assessment: Theories, Tests and Issues* (New York: Guilford Press, 1977).

Horner, M.D., Ferguson, P.L., Selassie, A.W., Labbate, L.A., Kniele, K. and Corrigan, J.D., "Patterns of alcohol use one year after traumatic brain injury: a population-based, epidemiological study" (2005) *Journal of the International Neuropsychological Society* 11, 322–330.

Howieson D.B. and Lezak, M.D., "Separating Memory from other cognitive problems" in Baddeley, A.D., Wilson, B.A. and Watts, F. (eds), *Handbook of Memory Disorders* (New York: Wiley, 1995).

Iverson, G.L., "Complicated vs uncomplicated mild traumatic brain: acute neuropsychological outcome" (2006a) *Brain Injury* 13–14, 1335–1344.

Iverson, G.L., "Misdiagnosis of the persistent postconcussion syndrome in patients with depression" (2006b) *Archives of Clinical Neuropsychology* 21, 303–310.

Iverson, G.L. and Lange, R.T., "Examination of 'postconcussion-like' symptoms in a healthy sample" (2003) *Applied Neuropsychology* 10, 137–144.

Iverson, G.L., Brooks, B.L., Ashton V.L. and Lange, R.T., "Interview versus questionnaire symptom reporting in people with post-concussion syndrome" (2010) *Journal of Head Trauma Rehabilitation* 25 (1), 23–30.

REFERENCES

Iverson, G.L. and Lange, R.T., "Post-concussion syndrome" in Schoenberg, M.R., and Scott, J.G. (eds), *The Little Black Book of Neuropsychology: a syndrome-based approach* (Berlin: Springer, 2011).

Iverson, G.L., Lange, R.T., Waljas, M., Liimatainen, S., Dastidar, P., Hartikainen, K.M., Soimakallio, S., and Ohman, J., "Outcome from complicated versus uncomplicated mild traumatic brain" (2012a) *Rehabilitation Research and Practice* 2012, 1–7.

Iverson, G.L., Brooks, B.L. and Holdnack, J.A., "Evidence-based neuropsychological assessment following work-related injury" in Bush, S.S. and Iverson, G.L. (eds), *Neuropsychological Assessment of Work-Related Injuries* (New York: Guilford Press, 2012b).

Jamora, C.W., Young, A. and Ruff, R.M., "Comparison of subjective cognitive complaints with neuropsychological tests in individuals with mild vs more severe traumatic brain injuries" (2012) *Brain Injury* 26(1), 36–47.

Johns, P., *Clinical Neuroscience: An Illustrated Colour Text* (London: Elsevier Health Sciences, 2014)

Karr, J.E., Garcia-Barrera, M.A., Holdnack, J.A. and Iverson, G.L., "Using multivariate base rates to interpret low scores on an abbreviated battery of the Delis-Kaplan executive function system" (2017) *Archives of Clinical Neuropsychology* 32(3), 297–305.

Katz, D.I., Alexander, M.P., "Traumatic brain injury. Predicting course of recovery and outcome for patients admitted to rehabilitation" (1994) *Archives of Neurology* 51 (7), 661–670.

Keesler, M.E., McClung, K., Meredith-Duluba, T., Williams, K. and Swirsky-Sacchetti, T., "Red flags in the clinical interview may forecast invalid neuropsychological testing" (2016) *The Clinical Neuropsychologist*, 31 (3), 619–631.

Kemp, S., Agostinis, House, A. and Coughlan, A.K., "Analgesia and other causes of amnesia that mimic post-traumatic amnesia (PTA): a cohort study" (2010) *Journal of Neuropsychology* 4, 231–236.

King, N.S., Crawford, S., Wenden, F.J., Moss, N.E.G., Wade, D.T. and Caldwell, F.E.V., "Measurement of post traumatic amnesia: how reliable is it?" (1997) *Journal of Neurology, Neurosurgery, and Psychiatry* 62, 38–42.

Kraus, J.F. and Chu, L.D., "Epidemiology" in Silver, J.M., McAllister, T.W. and Yudofsky, S.C. (eds), *Textbook of Traumatic Brain* (Harlington: American Psychiatric Publishing Inc, 2005).

Lees-Haley, P.R. and Brown, R.S., "Neuropsychological complaint base rates of 170 personal injury claimants" (1993) *Archives of Clinical Neuropsychology* 8, 203–209.

Lees-Haley, P.R., Fox, D.D. and Courtney, J.C., "A comparison of complaints by mild brain injury claimants and other claimants describing subjective experiences immediately following their injury" (2001) *Archives of Clinical Neuropsychology* 16, 689–695.

Lees-Haley, P.R., Williams, C.W. and English, L.T., "Response bias in self-reported history of plaintiffs compared with non-litigating patients" (1996) *Psychological Reports*, 79, 811–818.

Lees-Haley, P.R., Williams, C.W., Zasler, M.D., Marguilies, S., English, L.T. and Stevens, K.B., "Response bias in plaintiffs' histories" (1997) *Brain Injury*, 11 (11), 791–799.

Lewandowski, A., Baker, W.J., Sewick, B., Knippa, J., Axelrod, B. and McCaffrey, R.J., "Policy statement of the American Board of Professional Neuropsychology regarding Third Party Observation and the Recording of Psychological Test Administration in Neuropsychological Evaluations" (2016) *Applied Neuropsychology: Adult* 23 (6), 391–398.

Lezak, M.D., Howieson, D.B., Bigler, E.D. and Tranel, D., *Neuropsychological Assessment* (New York: Oxford University Press, 2012).

Lishman, W.A., *Organic Psychiatry: the Psychological Consequences of Cerebral Disorder* (New Jersey: Blackwell Scientific Publications, 1987).

Malec, J.F., Brown, A.W., Leibson, C.L., Flaada, J.T., Mandrekar, J.N., Diehl, N.N. and Perkins, P.K., "The Mayo Classification System for Traumatic Brain Injury Severity" (2007) *Journal of Neurotrauma* 24, 1417–1424.

Manchester, D., Priestley, N. and Jackson, H., "The assessment of executive functions: coming out of the office" (2004) *Brain Injury* 18 (11), 1067–1081.

Mayou, R.A., Black, J. and Bryant, B., "Unconsciousness, amnesia and psychiatric symptoms following road traffic accident injury" (2000) *British Journal of Psychiatry* 177, 540–545.

McCarter, R.J., Walton, N.H., Moore, C., Ward, A. and Nelson, I., "PTA testing, the Westmead post-traumatic amnesia scale and opiate analgesia: a cautionary note" (2007) *Brain Injury* 21, 1393–1397.

McCracken, L.M. and Iverson, G.L., "Predicting complaints of impaired cognitive functioning in patients with chronic pain" (2001) *Journal of Pain and Symptom Management*, 21 (5), 392–396.

McCrea, M.A., *Mild Traumatic Brain and Postconcussion Syndrome: the New Evidence Base for Diagnosis and Treatment* (New York: Oxford University Press, 2008).

McMillan, T.M., Jongen, E.L.M.M. and Greenwood, R.J., "Assessment of post-traumatic amnesia after severe closed head injury: retrospective or prospective?" (1996) *Journal of Neurology, Neurosurgery, and Psychiatry*, 60, 422–427.

Merckelbach, H., Jelicic, M. and Jonker, C., "Planting a misdiagnosis of Alzheimer's disease and the persons mind" (2012) *Acta Neuropsychiatrica* 24, 60–62.

Merckelbach, H., Jelicic, M. and Pieters, M., "Misinformation increases symptom reporting—a test-retest experiment" (2011) *Journal of the Royal Society of Medicine Short Reports* 2(10), 1–6.

Mesulam, M.M., "Frontal cortex and behaviour" (1986) *Annals of Neurology* 19 (4), 320–325.

Mild Traumatic Brain Committee of the Head Injury Interdisciplinary Special Interest Group of the American Congress of Rehabilitation Medicine, "Definition of mild traumatic brain injury" (1993) *Journal of Head Trauma Rehabilitation* 8 (3), 86–87.

Mittenberg, W., DiGiulio, D., Perrin S. and Bass, A.E., "Symptoms following mild head injury: expectation as aetiology" (1992) *Journal of Neurology, Neurosurgery, and Psychiatry* 55, 200–204.

Morel, K.R., "Test Security in Medicolegal Cases: Proposed Guidelines for Attorneys Utilising Neuropsychological Practice" (2009) *Archives of Clinical Neuropsychology* 24 (7), 635–646.

Munoz, M. and Esteve, R., "Reports of memory functioning by patients with chronic pain" (2005) *Clinical Journal of Pain* 21 (4), 287–291.

National Academy of Neuropsychology, "Test security: Official Position Statement of the National Academy of Neuropsychology" (2000) *Archives of Clinical Neuropsychology* 15 (5), 383–386.

National Center for Injury Prevention and Control, *Report to Congress on Mild Traumatic Brain Injury in the United States: Steps to Prevent a Serious Public Health Problem* (Atlanta: Center for Disease Control and Prevention, 2003).

Olver, J.H., Ponsford, J.L. and Curran, C.A., "Outcome following traumatic brain injury: a comparison between 2 and 5 years after injury" (1996) *Brain Injury* 10 (11), 841–848.

REFERENCES

Onsworth, T. and Clare, L., "The association between awareness deficits and rehabilitation outcome following acquired brain injury" (2006) *Clinical Psychology Review* 26, 783–795.

Ownsworth, T. and Fleming, J., "Community Adjustment and Re-Engagement" in Levin, H.S., Shum, D.H.K. and Chan, R.C.K. (eds), *Understanding Traumatic Brain Injury: the Current Research and Future Directions* (New York: Oxford University Press, 2014).

Pagulayan, K.F., Temkin, N.R., Machamer, J.E. and Diman, S.S., "The measurement and magnitude of awareness difficulties after traumatic brain injury: a longitudinal study" (2007) *Journal of the International Neuropsychological Society* 13, 561–570.

Ponsford, J., "Short and Long-Term Outcomes in Survivors of Traumatic Brain Injury" in Levin, H.S., Shum, D.H. and Chan, R.C.K. (eds), *Understanding Traumatic Brain Injury: the Current Research and Future Directions* (Oxford: Oxford University Press, 2014).

Roberts, C.M., Spitz, G. and Ponsford, J.L., "Comparing prospectively recorded post traumatic amnesia duration with retrospective accounts" (2016) *Journal of Head Trauma Rehabilitation* 31 (2), 71–77.

Rohling, M.L., Green, P., Allen, L.M. and Iverson, G.L., "Depressive symptoms and neurocognitive test scores in patients passing symptom validity tests" (2002) *Archives of Clinical Neuropsychology* 17, 205–222.

Russell, W.R. and Smith A., "Post traumatic amnesia after closed head injury" (1961) *Archives of Neurology* 5, 16–29.

Sanders, C., Ziegler E.A. and Schmitter-Edgecombe, M., "Traumatic brain and the impact of secondary influences" in Arnett, P.A. (ed.), *Secondary Influences on Neuropsychological Test Performance: Research Findings and Practical Applications* (New York: Oxford University Press, 2013).

Schweiger, A. and Parducci, A., "Nocebo: the psychologic induction of pain" (1981) *Pavlovian Journal of Biological Science* 16, 140–143.

Sherer, M., Bergloff, P., Levin, E., High, W.M., Oden K.E. and Nick, T.D. "Impaired awareness and employment outcome after traumatic brain" (1998) *Journal of Head Trauma Rehabilitation* 13 (5), 52–61.

Sherer, M., Boake, C., Levin, E., Silver, B.V., Ringholz, G. and High, W.M., "Characteristics of impaired awareness after traumatic brain injury" (1998) *Journal of the International Neuropsychological Society* 4, 380–387.

Sherer, M., Sander, A.M., Maestas, K.L., Pastorek, N.J., Nick, T.G. and Li, J., "Accuracy of Self-Reported Length of Coma and Post Traumatic Amnesia In Persons with Medically Verified Traumatic Brain Injury" (2015) *Archives of Physical Medicine and Rehabilitation* 96, 652–658.

Silver, J.M., Kramer, R., Greenwald S. and Weissman, M., "The association between head injuries and psychiatric disorders: findings from the New Haven NIMH Epidemiologic Catchment Area study" (2001) *Brain Injury* 15 (11), 935–945.

Strober, L. and Deluca, J., "Fatigue: its influence on cognition and assessment" in Arnett, P. (ed.), *Secondary influences on neuropsychological test performance. Research findings and practical applications* (New York: Oxford University Press, 2013).

Suchy, Y., *Executive Functioning: a Comprehensive Guide for Clinical Practice* (American Academy of Clinical Neuropsychology: Oxford Workshop Series, 2016).

Suhr J.A. and Gunstad, J., "'Diagnostic Threat': the effect of negative expectations on cognitive performance in head injury" (2002) *Journal of Clinical and Experimental Neuropsychology* 24 (4), 448–457.

Suhr J.A. and Gunstad, J., "Further exploration of the effect of 'diagnostic threat' on cognitive performance in individuals with mild head injury" (2005) *Journal of the International Neuropsychological Society* 11 (1), 23–29.

Suhr J.A. and Wei C., "Response expectancies and their potential influence in neuropsychological evaluation" in Arnett, P.A. (ed.), *Secondary Influences on Neuropsychological Test Performance: Research Findings and Practical Applications* (New York: Oxford University Press, 2013).

Sweet, J.J., Goldman, D.J. and Guidotti Breting, L.M., "Traumatic Brain Injury: Guidance in a Frantic Context from Outcome, Dose-Response, and Response Bias Research" (2013) *Behavioural Sciences and the Law* 31, 756–778.

Trontel, H.G., Hall, S., Ashendorf L. and O'Connor, M.K., "Impact of diagnostic threat on academic self-efficacy in mild traumatic brain injury" (2013) *Journal of Clinical and Experimental Neuropsychology* 35 (9), 960–970.

Uomoto, J.M. and Esselman, P.C., "Traumatic brain and chronic pain: differential types and rates by head injury severity" (1993) *Archives of Physical Medicine and Rehabilitation* 74 (1), 61–64.

Van Veldhoven, L.M., Sander, A.M., Struchen, M.A., Sherer, M, Clark, A.M., Hudnall G.E. and Hannay, H.J., "Predictive ability of preinjury stressful life events and post-dramatic stress symptoms for outcomes following mild traumatic brain: analysis in a prospective emergency room sample" (2011) *Journal of Neurology, Neurosurgery, and Psychiatry* 82, 782–787.

Veeramuthu, V., Narayanan, V., Ramli, N., Hernowo, A., Waran, V., Bondi, M.W., Delano-Wood, L. and Ganesan, D., "Neuropsychological outcomes in patients with complicated versus uncomplicated mild traumatic brain: 6-month follow-up" (2017) *World Neurosurgery* 97, 416–423.

Walker, W.C., Ketchum, J.M., Marwitz, J.H., Chen, T., Hammond, F.S., Sherer, M. and Meythaler, J., "A multicentre study on the clinical utility of post-traumatic amnesia duration in predicting global outcome after moderate-severe traumatic brain" (2010) *Journal of Neurology, Neurosurgery and Psychiatry*, 81, 87–89.

Wang, Y., Chan, R.C.K. and Deng, Y., "Examination of postconcussion-like symptoms in healthy university students: Relationships to subjective and objective neuropsychological function performance" (2006) *Archives of Clinical Neuropsychology* 21, 339–347.

Whelan-Goodinson, R., Ponsford, J., Johnston, L. and Grant, F., "Psychiatric Disorders Following Traumatic Brain: Their Nature and Frequency" (2009) *Journal of Head Trauma Rehabilitation* 24 (5), 324–332.

Wood, R.L., "Understanding the 'miserable minority': a diathesis-stress paradigms for post-concussion syndrome" (2004) *Brain Injury* 18 (11), 1135–1153.

Wood R.L. and Rutterford, N.A., "Psychosocial adjustment 17 years after severe brain injury" (2006) *Journal of Neurology, Neurosurgery and Psychiatry* 77, 71–73.

Wood, R., "Traumatic Brain Injury" in Young, S., Kopelman, M. and Gudjonsson, G. (eds), *Forensic Neuropsychology in Practice: a Guide to Assessment and Legal Processes* (Oxford: Oxford University Press, 2009).

Youngjohn, J.R., Davis, D., and Wolf, I., "Head injury and the MMPI-2: paradoxical severity effects and the influence of litigation" (1997) *Psychological Assessment* 9(3), 177–184.

Youngjohn, J.R., Wershba, R., Stevenson, M., Sturgeon, J. and Thomas, M.L., "Independent validation of the MMPI-2-RF somatic/cognitive and validity scales in TBI litigants tested for effort" (2011) *Clinical Neuropsychologist* 25 (3), 463–476.

REFERENCES

Zakzanis, K.K. and Yeung, E., "Base rates of post-concussive symptoms in a non-concussed multicultural sample" (2011) *Archives of Clinical Neuropsychology* 26, 461–465.

Zuercher, M., Ummenhofer, W., Baltussen A. and Walder, B., "The use of Glasgow Coma Scale in injury assessment: a critical review" (2009) *Brain Injury* 23 (5), 371–384.

CHAPTER 6

Neuropsychiatric Aspects of Brain Injury

Niruj Agrawal

INTRODUCTION

It is thought that humans knew about head injury and its consequences as early as a few millennia ago. Ancient Egyptian and Greek texts refer to various neurological and neurocognitive consequences of head injury, including seizures, paralysis and loss of sight, hearing or speech (Levin et al., 1982). Trepanation to reduce intracranial pressure to treat brain injury was practised widely in the world from prehistoric times. Despite that, until very recently, survival after a brain injury was the main challenge and a strong focus remained on the initial surgical treatment. If the initial neurosurgical intervention turned out to be successful, those who survived were offered very little in form of further treatment.

6–001

It wasn't until the nineteenth century that we began to see a number of neuropsychiatric problems following brain injury being described. Perhaps one of the first descriptions of psychological and neuropsychiatric problems was in the case of Phineas Gage, who suffered personality change after a railway track accident in which a large iron rod was driven through his frontal lobe (Mattson and Levin, 1990). Further descriptions gradually emerged of neuropsychiatric conditions such as psychosis and post-concussion syndrome developing following a brain injury.

The twentieth century witnessed exponential advances in medical science, with improvements in neuroimaging, neurosurgical techniques and early post-trauma management. This led to significant improvement in mortality rates following brain injury and brought with it an increasing focus on the challenges associated with the long term consequences of brain injury. Consequences that included the neuropsychiatric conditions such as emotional and behavioural problems.

There are a number of terms used, often interchangeably, to describe brain injury. This can lead to confusion, especially for those who are not experts in this field. Figure 1 provides a simple scheme to understand the terminology and types of brain injury. Acquired brain injury (ABI) is an umbrella term, referring to both Traumatic Brain Injury (TBI) and other non-traumatic brain injuries. Examples of non-traumatic brain injuries are anoxic brain injury (hypoxic-ischemic injury), stroke, intracranial infections such as encephalitis, brain tumours or metabolic injury etc. All of these ABIs can be associated with a range of neuropsychiatric consequences that could be similar but may differ depending upon the nature of ABI. For the sake of clarity this chapter will focus on the neuropsychiatric consequences of TBI only.

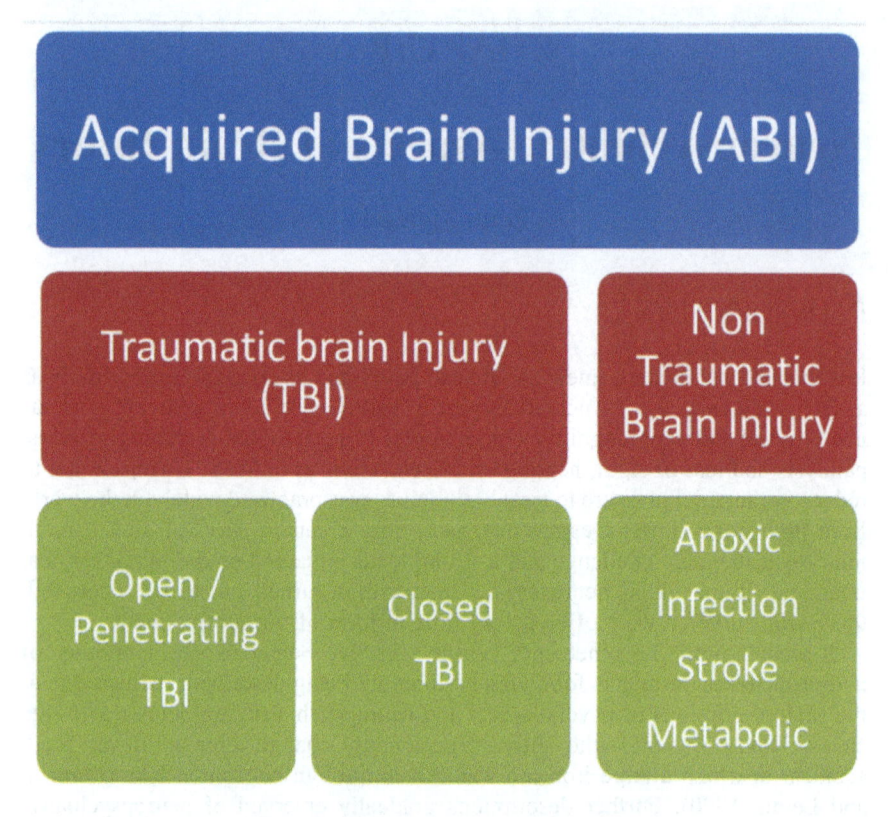

Figure 1: Terminology and types of brain injury

1. EXTENT OF PROBLEM

6–002   According to the World Health Organisation TBI will surpass many common diseases as a major cause of death and disability in world. Generally it is well recognised that the rate of admission to hospital after a TBI is 250–300/100 000 population. However, this is a significant under-estimation of the actual prevalence of TBI in the general population. Incidence of TBI in Europe and North America is noted to be between 47–618/100,000 population and in a New Zealand study incidence was 790/100,000 population (Feigin et al., 2013).

The most common causes of TBI are falls (28%), road traffic accidents (20%), struck by or against events (19%), assaults (11%) and blast injuries in war zones (Langlois et al., 2006). Sports and recreation are also a major cause of TBI and are increasingly being recognised. Falls are the leading cause of TBI in young children and the elderly, whereas in young adults the commonest causes are road traffic accidents followed by sports-related injuries, assaults and occupational injuries (Bruns and Hauser, 2003). In terms of emergency department visits, hospitalisations, and deaths combined, children aged 0 to 4 years and older

EXTENT OF PROBLEM

adolescents aged 15 to 19 years are more likely to sustain a TBI compared to persons in other age groups (Langlois et al., 2006). For hospitalisations only, adults aged 75 years or older have the highest incidence of TBI. TBI is twice as common in men as women. Mild injuries constitute a vast majority of injuries, (approximately 3/4th of injuries), whereas severe injuries constitute approximately 10% of cases. Moderate and severe TBIs are seen more frequently in adolescent and older adults than in other age groups (Andelic, 2013).

Traumatic Brain injuries are commonly associated with a range of emotional, behavioural and other neuropsychiatric problems in addition to various neurological and neurocognitive difficulties (Figure 2). The rate of neuropsychiatric problems after a TBI are significantly high with a wide range of clinical presentations.

Neurological
- Sensory
- Headache
- Dizziness
- Headache
- Epilepsy

Neurocognitive
- Memory
- Executive functions
- Language
- Visuo-spatial

Emotional
- Emotional lability
- Depression
- Anxiety
- Irritability / Anger
- Apathy

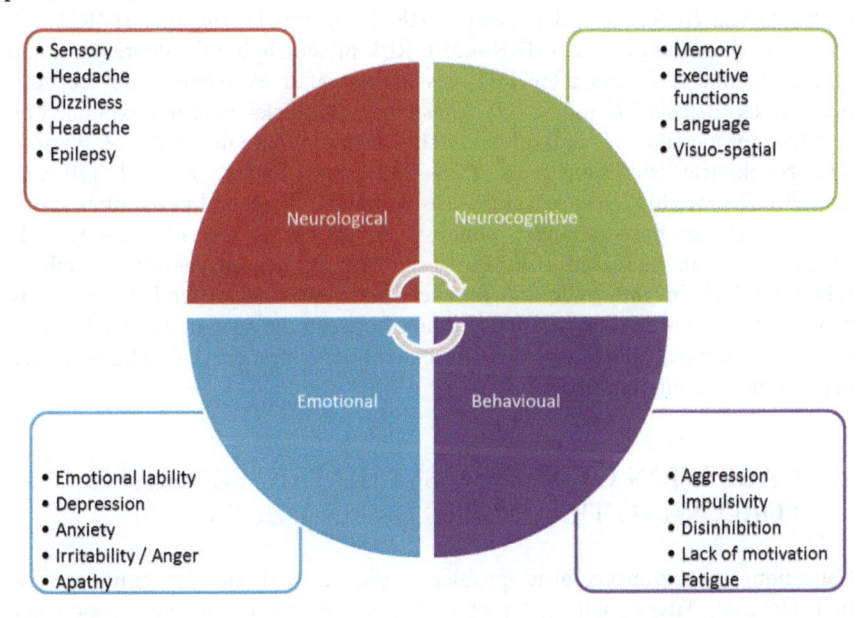

Behavioual
- Aggression
- Impulsivity
- Disinhibition
- Lack of motivation
- Fatigue

Figure 2: Long term consequences of TBI

In a 30-year-follow up study in Finland, Koponen et al. (2002) noted a life-time prevalence of neuropsychiatric problems following TBI as 61.7%, which was twice as high when compared to the general population rate of 32.7%. In their study they noted a cross sectional current prevalence of neuropsychiatric problems post TBI as 40% as compared to a general population rate of 15.7%. They noted that not all neuropsychiatric problems following TBI start immediately after the TBI and some can start years after the TBI. Koponen et al. (2002) described a vulnerability for neuropsychiatric conditions post TBI lasting decades.

In a prospective observational study one year after TBI, using very robust clinical structured interviews including Schedules for Clinical Assessment in Neuropsychiatry (SCAN) and the Structured Clinical Interview for DSM-IV Personality Disorders (SCID-II); Koponen et al. (2011) noted high rates of neuropsychiatric problems including Axis I disorders in 47.4% of subjects and

6–003

Axis II disorders in 29% of patients after TBI. Taking all the neuropsychiatric disorders into account nearly half of patients (47.4%) following TBI had a neuropsychiatric problem in the first year after TBI. They also noted 12 months before the TBI, the occurrence of major psychiatric disorders was relatively high at 39.5% and alcohol dependence was also commonly noted in 18.4% of patients. Onset of a new neuropsychiatric condition de-novo after TBI was noted in 15.8% of patients in the first year.

A Danish nationwide population-based register study (Orlovska et al., 2014) investigated the incidence of common neuropsychiatric problems such as schizophrenia spectrum disorders, depression, bipolar disorder, and organic mental disorders in 113,906 persons who had suffered head injuries. It noted head injury was associated with a higher risk (Incident risk ratio (IRR)) of schizophrenia (IRR 1.65), depression (IRR 1.59), bipolar disorder (IRR 1.28), and organic mental disorders (IRR 4.39). Risk of schizophrenia, depression, and organic mental disorders after TBI was highest after exposure to severe head injury (IRR: 2.16, 1.77, and 36.22). These increased risks were not explained by accident proneness of individuals. This means that the risk of various neuropsychiatric conditions was 1.28–4.39 times higher in mild TBI and 2.16–36.22 times higher in severe TBI as compared to general population. Other factors such as post-traumatic epilepsy or infections did not significantly contribute to an increased risk. Increased risk of neuropsychiatric problems following TBI, in both male and female gender, was not dependent on family history of psychiatric illnesses. Head injury between the ages of 11 and 15 years was the strongest predictor for subsequent development of schizophrenia, depression, and bipolar disorder.

2. CAUSATION OF NEUROPSYCHIATRIC PROBLEMS FOLLOWING TRAUMATIC BRAIN INJURY

6-004 Causation of neuropsychiatric problems after a TBI can be complex and multifactorial. Traditionally a lot of emphasis was placed on the location and extent of brain damage as evident on the brain scans. However, only a minority of patients show structural lesions visible on scans, whereas rates of neuropsychiatric problems are significantly higher. Some injuries, particularly those affecting the frontal lobes with associated behavioural problems are very easy to understand as a direct consequence of a brain lesion. Often people perceive emotional or behavioural problems after a TBI as an understandable psychological reaction to the injury, implying it is not really a direct effect of the injury and hence may have a different prognostic trajectory. Whilst psychological reaction to an injury may be a causative factor, quite often there are other brain injury related factors (Figure 3) that are equally if not more important.

Prior vulnerability, including genetic factors in the form of family history, past psychiatric problems or premorbid personality (including person's mental constitution) can be an important determinant of post-TBI neuropsychiatric presentation. People with pre-existing or past problems may be more likely to present with neuropsychiatric problems. However, more recent and emerging evidence suggests that this may have a smaller effect than previously believed.

Orlovska et al. (2014) showed that family history of psychiatric illnesses was not a significant predictor of post-TBI neuropsychiatric problems.

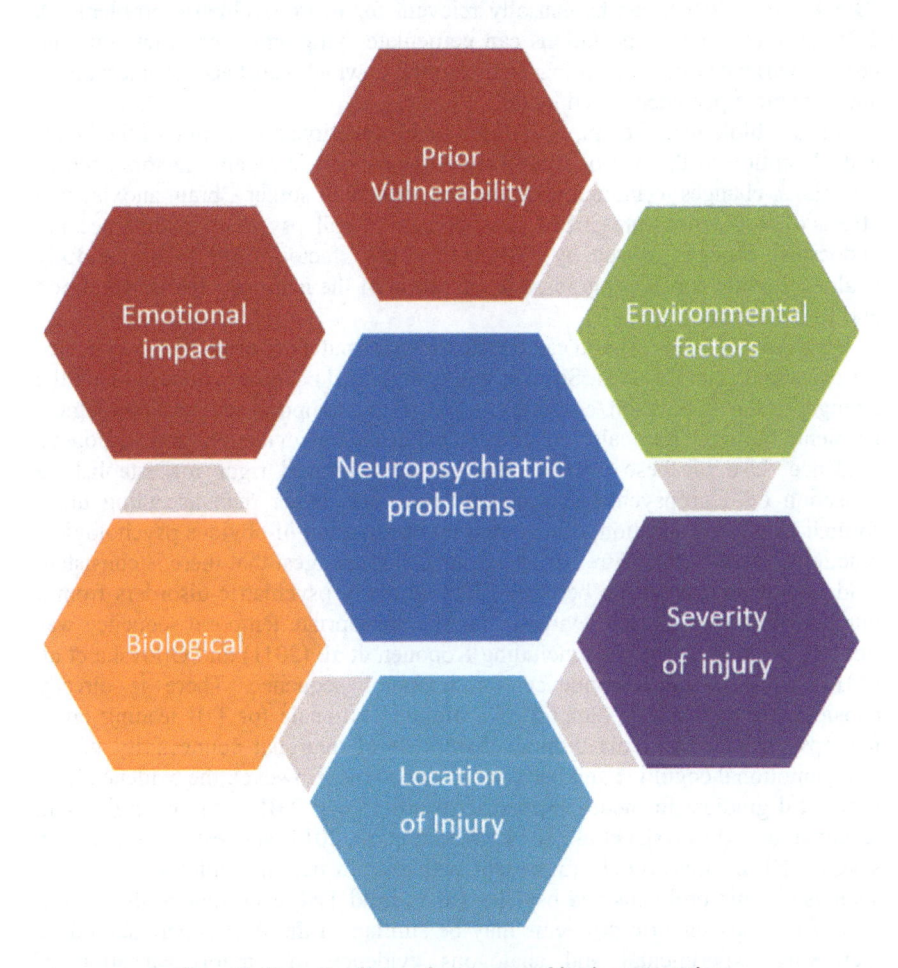

Figure 3: Causative factors for neuropsychiatric presentation

Environmental factors including level of social support available, response of family, friends and employers to the impact of the injury and a patient's own personal expectations can affect how they emotionally and behaviourally respond to their problems. Both ends of the spectrum in terms of support and concern, from lack of support to an overprotective family, can be equally problematic. Emotional factors, such as the circumstances and setting of the injury, particularly how psychologically frightening or traumatic the injury was, can determine the severity of psychological problems suffered. Repercussions of the injury on a patient's personal and social life, including the impact on finances and work could influence neuropsychiatric presentation. Personal expectations regarding the injury and its outcome and a person's illness belief system about the nature and severity of the injury can determine neuropsychiatric symptomatology. Misattributions and misconceptions including attribution biases, survivors' expectations of the aetiology of their symptoms and attributional biases, such as when behaviours are attributed to internal rather than environmental factors (Block et al., 2016), can be causally relevant for neuropsychiatric problems. A TBI survivor's own expectations can perpetuate symptoms when they attribute normal variances in functioning to their injury, which can become internalised and become a persistent fixed belief.

6–005 Various biological factors, in addition to the severity and location of the injury and disruption to the neuronal networks, can include iatrogenic factors such as infections, changes to intracranial pressure, effects of surgery, brain anoxia, side effects of medications prescribed, development of epilepsy, sleep disturbance and endocrinal changes caused by TBI itself. These factors need to be carefully evaluated while considering possible causation of the neuropsychiatric condition and its treatment.

Sir Bradford Hill's criteria can be used to systematically evaluate the evidence for causation (van Reekum, Streiner and Conn, 2001). These criteria include the strength of the association, consistency, specificity, temporal sequence, biological gradient, biologic rationale, coherence, experimental evidence, and analogous evidence. Use of these criteria can provide increased rigor for establishing causation of neuropsychiatric problems post TBI rather than accepting uninformed views on causation, often based on observation of obvious psychological reactions. van Reekum, Streiner and Conn (2001) suggest that there is consistent evidence of an association between TBI and many psychiatric disorders from a number of studies, but the evidence for the appropriate temporal sequence was limited. More recent studies including Koponen et al. (2011) and Orlovska et al. (2014) provide added evidence for temporal sequence. There is already considerable evidence in support of a biologic rationale for TBI leading on to neuropsychiatric problems through disruption of neuronal connectivity underlying emotional cognitive and behavioural functions. However, the evidence for a biological gradient for neuropsychiatric disorders post TBI is still emerging and recent studies (Orlovska et al., 2014; Osborn et al., 2014) suggest that those with severe TBI are more likely to present with certain neuropsychiatric conditions such as organic problems and psychosis than mild TBI, even though the overall rate of neuropsychiatric problems may be similar. In the future there should be increasing experimental and analogous evidence to support causation of neuropsychiatric conditions especially with improvements in neuroimaging techniques.

3. MILD TRAUMATIC BRAIN INJURY AND POST-CONCUSSION SYNDROME

6–006 A vast majority of TBI are mild closed head injury that commonly present with a combination of somatic, cognitive and psychiatric symptoms, which are commonly described as post-concussional syndrome (PCS). Despite being known about for many decades, PCS remains a poorly understood and controversial disorder with some clinicians arguing it doesn't exist, and others arguing at least some of the cases may be due to compensation seeking or malingering (Carr, 2007). However, organic factors such as changes to cerebral blood flow, glucose utilisation on SPECT or PET scans (Umile et al., 2002), and blood and cerebrospinal fluid (CSF) biomarkers (including elevated total tau and neurofilament light polypeptide in the CSF and raised total tau levels in plasma), have been described in mTBI and PCS (Zetterberg et al., 2013). While none of these are so far clinically useful investigations, they suggest biological mechanisms that may underlie the development of PCS. Routine clinical imaging with CT or MRI brain scan is mostly not useful as they do not show any abnormality. However, some of the specific MRI sequences such as diffusion tensor imaging (DTI), gradient echo and susceptibility weighted imaging (SWI) can show white matter damage and micro bleeds. In a prospective study of persistent PCS (Wäljas et al., 2015) using DTI, intracranial abnormalities were present in 12.1% and multifocal areas of unusual white matter were present in 50.7% compared with 12.4% of controls. Structural MRI abnormalities and microstructural white matter findings were not significantly associated with greater post-concussion symptom reporting.

Commonly reported symptoms of PCS include somatic symptoms of noise or light intolerance, blurred vision, double vision, headache, dizziness, fatigue, neurocognitive symptoms including difficulties with attention and concentration, memory and psychiatric symptoms of irritability, sleep disturbance, emotional lability, anxiety and depression. International classification of diseases: ICD-10 (WHO 1993) provides diagnostic criteria for PCS. The American diagnostic classification system, DSM-IV included the diagnostic criteria for PCS, but in the latest edition (DSM-5), it has removed the criteria for PCS, subsuming it under the category of Mild Neurocognitive Disorder, which is a rather unsatisfactory classification. Sharpe and Jenkins (2015) have argued that use of the term concussion is confusing and should be avoided. They advocate the use of severity of TBI diagnosis and aetiologically-based additional diagnosis. However, in the absence of a clear aetiological understanding of most of the PCS symptoms as yet, such an approach can be unhelpful for recognition of a patient's problems and provision of treatment.

There are considerable differences in the reported prevalence of PCS after mild TBI, due to differences in methods of assessment, diagnostic criteria and patient population studied, with some estimating PCS prevalence ranging from 29–90% after mild TBI (Carr, 2007). In a one-year prospective study (Sigurdardottir et al., 2009) in Norway, based on self-report questionnaires, in adults with TBI of all severity, PCS was noted to have developed in 27.8% of cases at three months, and 23.6% at 12 months post injury. The mild and moderate TBI groups showed a decline of PCS symptoms over time, in contrast to the severe TBI group. Greater levels of somatic, cognitive and anxiety symptoms at three months, as well as shorter PTA duration, were found to be important predictors for the severity of PCS symptoms at 12 months. Intracranial pathology and Glasgow Coma Scale (GCS) score were not related to the severity of PCS symptoms. Another prospective study (Roe et al., 2009) just focused on mild TBI. They followed up at three, six and 12 months using the Rivermead Post-Concussion Symptoms Questionnaire, 29/52 patients met the post-concussion syndrome criteria at three months, and 22/52 patients at six and 12 months. This indicates a significant persistence of PCS symptoms a year after the mild TBI. They also noted a considerable individual variability in the symptom pattern.

6-007　　Traditionally, it is widely believed that most patients with PCS show recovery within the first three months following TBI, and only 10–15% of patients present with a persistent PCS one year after mild TBI. This is based on very old estimates and new systematic studies based on specific questionnaires now give a much higher figure. A high proportion of people are left with disability after so called "minor TBI", a term often used for mild TBI and PCS. In a cross-sectional cohort study of 148 adults with minor TBI (Deb et al., 1998), using Glasgow outcome scale, at one year follow up 2.9% patients had a severe disability, 25.5% had a moderate disability, and 69.3% had no disability. This suggests nearly a third of patients with PCS are left with significant disability at one year. This figure is much higher than the commonly accepted rate of 10–15% of persistent PCS and is consistent with recent studies using specific questionnaires that show persistent symptoms in a quarter to a third of patients. Deb et al. (1998) noted that the most common neurobehavioral problems one year after minor TBI were irritability (30%), sleep disturbance (29%), and impatience (27%). King (2014) has highlighted inconsistent use of terminology and the proposed term permanent PCS could reasonably be applied to symptoms lasting 18 months and beyond and prolonged PCS for symptoms persisting for 12–18 months. A uniform acceptance and use of terminology will not only help with communication but also with future research.

Causation of PCS remains controversial. Lishman (1988) described compelling evidence for both physiogenic and psychogenic causes for the development of PCS and suggested a complex interaction between the two. He described a time-dependent interplay of factors in the genesis of the PCS, with an intertwining of organic and non-organic contributions. This suggests that over many weeks and months there is a shifting balance, as the patient's innate proclivities and his individual problems and conflicts affect the initial symptoms of cerebral dysfunction. However, Lishman (1988) noted that development of PCS differs from one individual to another, some patients responding to cerebral dysfunction and others to psychological influences. Nevertheless, most patients will have both factors responsible for the causation of PCS.

Alexander (1992) examined the neuropsychiatric correlates of persistent PCS and noted that it may be a manifestation of an interaction between chronic pain and depression in most cases. They noted a complex interaction of premorbid factors of age, past TBI and previous psychological problems along with post-injury factors. They described that elderly patients with apparently mild TBI have a much-reduced ability to recover and therefore present with persistent symptoms. This observation may not just apply to people in old age, generally with increasing age outcomes from PCS may be poorer. King (2014) in a systematic review noted that those with poor prolonged outcome from PCS had a significantly higher mean age (35.9) compared to mild head injury patients in general (29.9). The proportion of men in these samples (48.6%) was significantly lower than mild head injury patients in general (66.7%). King (2014) hence proposed that older age and female gender are vulnerability factors in the development of prolonged PCS.

A number of psychological factors can be associated with persistent and prolonged PCS. In a review of PCS and psychological factors associated with concussion, Broshek et al. (2015) describe pre-morbid and concurrent anxiety increases the risk for prolonged concussion recovery. They suggest cognitive biases, including good-old-days' bias and misattribution of symptoms contribute to a lengthy recovery from concussion. In addition, they highlight that medically prescribed excessive cognitive and physical rest may contribute to a protracted concussion recovery. Hou et al. (2012) analysed data from 107 patients with mild TBI and found that negative mTBI perceptions, stress, anxiety, depression and all-or-nothing behaviour were associated with the risk of developing PCS. A further multivariate analysis revealed that all-or-nothing behaviour was the key predictor for the onset of PCS at three months, while negative mTBI perceptions predicted PCS at six months. They propose a cognitive behavioural model of PCS to guide early intervention.

A prospective study (Wäljas et al., 2015) of persistent post-concussion symptoms following mTBI examined the impact of multiple biopsychosocial factors, including structural imaging (CT and MRI) and microstructural neuroimaging (diffusion tensor imaging (DTI)), on persistence of symptoms. Significant predictors of persistent PCS at one month were pre-injury mental health problems and the presence of extra-cranial bodily injuries. They noted that being symptomatic at one month was a significant predictor of being symptomatic at one year, and depression was significantly related to persistent PCS at one month and one year. Structural intracranial abnormalities visible on MRI were present in 12.1% and multifocal white matter abnormalities as measured by DTI were present in 50.7% (compared with 12.4% of controls). Structural MRI and DTI microstructural white matter abnormalities were not significantly associated with greater post-concussion symptom reporting. They concluded that reporting of persistent post-concussion symptoms is likely to represent the cumulative effect of genetics, mental health history, current life stress, medical problems, chronic pain, depression, personality factors, and other psychosocial and environmental factors. This highlights that the extent to which damage to the structure of the brain contributes to the persistence of post-concussion symptoms remains unclear.

Maruta et al. (2016) sought to characterise cognitive deficits of adult patients who had persistent symptoms after a concussion, to determine whether the original injury retained associations with the cognitive deficits, after accounting for the symptoms that overlap with PTSD and depression. They noted that patients generally produced accurate responses on reaction time-based tests, but with reduced efficiency. On visual tracking, patients displayed increased gaze position error variability following an attention-demanding task, an effect that may reflect greater fatigability. When neurocognitive performance was examined in the context of demographic factors (e.g. gender and ethnicity) and symptom-related variables (e.g. depression and PTSD), the original injury was still associated with reduced performance at a statistically significant level. They concluded that for some patients, reduced cognitive efficiency and fatigability may represent key elements of interference when interacting with the environment, leading to varied paths of recovery after a concussion. Their results are consistent with the notion that a reduction in cognitive performance may not be due to greater symptom report itself, but can be associated with the initial concussive injury (Dean and Sterr, 2013).

6–009   Pre-existing neurocognitive difficulties and reduced cognitive reserve is associated with increased risk of PCS presentation. A Swedish prospective inception mTBI cohort study (Oldenburg et al., 2016) recruited 122 adult patients and 35 healthy controls from emergency departments within 24 hours of an mTBI. Three months post-injury, participants completed the Rivermead Post Concussion Symptoms Questionnaire and a neuropsychological assessment. They estimated cognitive reserve based upon a sub-test from Wechsler Adult Intelligence Scale and international classifications of educational level and occupational skill level. They found that mTBI patients showed reduced memory performance and subtle executive memory deficits. Patients with lower cognitive reserve were 4.14 times more likely to suffer from PCS, indicating lower cognitive reserve is a risk factor and a prognostic factor for PCS.

Patients with mTBI can often have one or more previous mTBI with or without PCS. These past injuries can increase the chances of developing persistent PCS. A large prospective longitudinal study in US army soldiers looked at prognostic indicators of persistent PCS after mTBI (Stein et al., 2016), using a conservative measure of PCS (excluding symptoms that are also defining features of anxiety and mood disorders), and noted that past mTBI increases risk for persistent PCS. In addition, pre-deployment psychological distress, severe deployment stress, and loss of consciousness, or lapse of memory resulting from mTBI were prognostic indicators of persistent PCS after a mTBI.

Silverberg et al. (2015) carried out a systematic review of multivariable prognostic models for mTBI. They found no multivariable prognostic model that adequately predicts individual patient outcomes from mTBI. The most robust prognostic factors in the context of multivariable models were pre-injury mental health and early post-injury neuropsychological functioning. Women and adults with early post-injury anxiety also have worse prognoses. Relative to these factors, the severity of mTBI had little long-term prognostic value. This suggests that while we understand relative factors contributing to the outcome from mTBI and PCS, no specific model can be applied rigidly and vulnerability factors should be considered in an individual in order to produce a person specific model.

6–010   Updated Canadian clinical practice guidelines (Marshall et al., 2015) for concussion/mild traumatic brain injury and persistent symptoms used a modified Delphi process and produced 96 recommendations, addressing the diagnosis and management of mTBI and persistent concussion symptoms, including post-traumatic headache, sleep disturbances, mental health disorders, cognitive difficulties, vestibular and vision dysfunction, fatigue and return to activity/work/ school. They suggest that clinicians should assess, interpret, and subsequently manage symptoms, taking into consideration other potential pre-injury, injury and post-injury biopsychosocial factors and conditions that may have contributed to the symptoms. Suggested acute assessment includes standardised assessment of post-traumatic amnesia and immediate complications of TBI, such as haemorrhage and potential neurologic deterioration. Subsequently, management should include assessment of symptoms combined with education and reassurance that the symptoms generally resolve within days to weeks. Further guidance should be provided to patients on stress reduction and gradual return to activities and life roles.

Zurich Consensus statement (McCrory et al., 2013) on sport-related concussion suggests that patients should rest for 24 to 48 hours after a concussion as symptoms can increase with mental and physical exertion in the immediate aftermath of concussion. This suggestion also applies to non-sports related concussion patients. Functional MRI (fMRI) studies, in those performing cognitive tasks, have reported that excessive (compensatory) brain activation (as measured by fMRI blood flow) is a feature of concussion. This suggests that the brain should be rested after concussion because the threshold for physical exertion may also be lowered (Leddy, Baker and Willer, 2016). There are emerging data that excessive cognitive activity soon after concussion exacerbates symptoms and may delay recovery (Brown et al., 2014).

Psychological treatment such as cognitive behavioural therapy (CBT) has been recommended for treatment of persistent PCS symptoms. Potter, Brown and Fleminger (2016) carried out an RCT of CBT in 46 adults with persistent PCS after predominantly mild-to-moderate TBI (52% with post-traumatic amnesia ≤24 hours), but including some with severe TBIs (20% with PTA>7 days). They noted improvements associated with CBT relating to quality of life, on measures of anxiety and fatigue, but no improvements on measures of depression or post-traumatic stress disorder. Improvements were more apparent for those completing CBT sessions over a shorter period of time, but were unrelated to medicolegal status, injury severity or length of time since injury. An explicit, concomitant cognitive rehabilitation component did not appear necessary for these improvements.

Other potentially useful treatments for PCS include hyperbaric oxygen therapy which has moderately strong evidence for improvement in physical cognitive and neuropsychiatric symptoms (Boussi-Gross, 2013), mindfulness-based stress reduction, pharmacotherapy with antimigraine drugs, selective serotonin reuptake inhibitors (SSRIs), cognitive rehabilitation programme and aerobic exercise after initial rest. Repetitive transcranial magnetic stimulation (rTMS) could be a potential future treatment but it remains in experimental phase.

4. ACUTE POST-TRAUMATIC AMNESIA/POST-TRAUMATIC AGITATION

After a significant TBI, depending upon the severity, there is commonly a transient state of a pronounced inability to encode new memories, difficulty sustaining attention associated with confusion and disorientation along with lack of insight and awareness. This state is called post-traumatic amnesia (PTA). It is commonly associated with agitation, attempting to leave the acute brain injury unit, impulsivity and aggression. PTA could last for minutes to months. Duration of PTA is commonly used as a reliable measure of severity of TBI along with other indices such as GCS score and duration of loss of consciousness. It is now widely recognised that PTA is an important predictor of functional outcome after a TBI.

6–011

In addition to cognitive and behavioural difficulties including agitation, PTA is commonly associated with disordered language and cognitive communication. Various reported communication difficulties include impairment of naming, word-finding, auditory comprehension, verbal fluency, syntax and discourse production. Confusion may also manifest in communication impairments such as confabulation, perseveration and disorganised discourse (Steel et al., 2015). It is suggested that these useful and clinically relevant observations during the time of PTA may be useful for prognostic, predictive and planning purposes, in addition to the focus on cognitive difficulties and behavioural problems.

The pathophysiology of PTA is not yet fully understood. Various brain structures linked with memory functions, including limbic structures such as the hippocampus, parahippocampus gyrus, cingulate cortex and wider brain networks such as the default mode network, have been implicated. De Simoni et al. (2016), in a functional MRI study, showed evidence of abnormal functional connectivity between the default mode network and medial temporal lobes in post-traumatic amnesia. They noted that the strength of this functional disconnection correlated with features of cognitive difficulties associated with PTA, such as associative memory and information processing speed, and normalised when these functions improved. It is hence postulated that PTA occurs secondary to the effects of diffuse axonal injury on white matter tracts connecting limbic structures that are involved in memory processing.

6–012   PTA duration is widely used as a measure to help with clinical decision making in acute trauma centres, including decisions about level of support and supervision required, timing of discharge, prognostic assessment including functional outcomes, and decisions about patient's mental capacity to leave the ward and making decisions for them. Various standardised tools are now commonly used in well-functioning brain injury units to assess the PTA and its duration. These include, Westmead PTA Scale (WPTAS) (Shores et al., 1986) and Galveston Orientation and Amnesia Test (GOAT) (Levin, O'Donnell and Grossman, 1979).

Agitation in PTA is associated with psychomotor restlessness, emotional lability, disturbed diurnal rhythm, impaired insight, impulsiveness, automatisms, and verbal and physical aggression. Other features commonly seen in PTA may include perseveration, confabulation, and restlessness associated with pacing. It is noted that agitation can be floridly present even when memory for recent events is intact (Marshman et al., 2013). Agitation and behavioural problems are not included in the commonly used PTA assessment scales that generally focus on cognitive impairments. Hence, the assessment of agitation is more clinically based, involving a neuropsychiatrist to exclude other causes of agitation such as psychosis or substance misuse. Agitation is generally a negative prognostic factor for long term psychological and psychiatric outcomes, including development of later personality and behavioural change.

Management of PTA related symptoms requires a multidisciplinary approach focused on predominant symptoms. Cognitive difficulties require reorientation strategies along with involvement of occupational therapists for assessment of functioning, speech and language therapists for communication disorders. PTA associated agitation is frequently managed with the use of pharmacological agents, but currently there is a lack of good evidence and there is no consensus on the most efficacious and safest strategy to treat these complications (Williamson et al., 2016). A Cochrane systematic review published in 2006 noted lack of good evidence except for beta blockers. In this study propranolol was used in rather large doses (Fleminger et al., 2006) and most clinicians now recognise that beta blockers are not useful in all people with agitation, and perhaps only in a minority. Other agents commonly used include atypical antipsychotic agents, mood stabilisers such as carbamazepine or valproate, clonidine, and sometimes benzodiazepines.

A prospective study of consecutive TBI admissions over 30 months to a regional neurorehabilitation unit in Sheffield looked at predictors of outcome of agitation after TBI (Singh et al., 2014). Agitation was measured using the agitation behaviour scale. They found that over a third of TBI admissions developed agitation. Rates of agitation in other studies were noted to be between 10–96%, but studies using standardised measures of agitation find similar rates to Singh et al. (2014). Poor functional outcome of agitation was associated with CT scan findings, and severity and duration of agitation. Those with contusions had a better outcome than those with intracranial haemorrhage, and a markedly better outcome than those with diffuse axonal injury. This suggests again that more severe and more widespread brain lesions are associated with more agitation and poor outcome. Pre-existing alcohol and substance misuse was not a significant prognostic factor on multivariate analysis.

5. MOOD DISORDERS

Depression

Psychological difficulties are a common consequence of TBI. The commonest of these is depression. Depression is associated with distress, delayed recovery, increased dysfunction, and has the potential to affect quality of life significantly. Another commonly associated psychological problem is dysthymia, chronic low grade subclinical depressive symptoms, which are associated with impairment of functioning.

6–013

Depression is caused by a complex interaction between a range of biological, psychological and social factors (Osborn, Mathias and Fairweather-Schmidt, 2014). Biological factors include, neuroanatomical changes such as diffuse axonal injury, or focal lesions in the frontal and temporal lobes disrupting the neural circuitry between the prefrontal cortex, amygdala, hippocampus, basal ganglia, and thalamus. Neurochemical changes, such as serotonergic deficits, neuroendocrine abnormalities such as compromised hypothalamic–pituitary–adrenal axis function, occurring after TBI can cause depression (Jorge and Starkstein, 2005). Psychological variables commonly include reaction to psychological trauma, loss of function and role, diminished tolerance to frustration, low self-esteem, and maladaptive coping strategies, which could contribute to development of depression after a TBI. Social factors in addition can contribute to development of depression. These include lack of adequate social support, difficulties with relationships, unrealistic expectations and involvement in litigation. These biological, psychological and social factors commonly co-exist and interact with each other leading on to depression, and hence clinical assessment should be focused on all of these and not just on superficially apparent psychological or social factors.

Osborn, Mathias and Fairweather-Schmidt (2014) carried out a meta-analysis of point prevalence depression following adult, non-penetrating traumatic brain injury. They noted that based on self-report measures the prevalence of clinically significant depression was 38%, but differed according to scales used (Hospital Anxiety and Depression Scale (HADS): 32%; Centre for Epidemiological Studies Depression Scale (CES-D): 48%) method of administration (phone: 26%; mail 46%), post-injury interval (range: 33–42%), and injury severity (mild: 64%; severe: 39%). However, the rate of clinically diagnosable major depression was a bit lower at 27%. Estimates of major depression varied according to diagnostic criteria (ICD-10: 14%; DSM-IV: 25%; DSM-III: 47%) and injury severity (mild: 16%; severe: 30%).

6–014 Using a large prospective cohort design at a level one trauma centre in the US, Bombardier et al. (2010) noted 53.1% met criteria for major depression at least once in the first year after injury. Point prevalence ranged between 31% at 1 month and 21% at 6 months. In a multivariate model, risk of major depression after TBI was associated with major depression at the time of injury (risk ratio [RR], 1.62), history of major depression prior to injury (but not at the time of injury) (RR, 1.54), age (RR, 0.61 for >60 years vs 18–29 years), and lifetime alcohol dependence (RR, 1.34). Those with major depression were more likely to report comorbid anxiety disorders after TBI than those without major depression (60% vs 7%; RR, 8.77). This shows that people with TBI are 1.34–1.62 times more likely to develop depression after TBI than the general population. After adjusting for predictors of Major Depressive Disorder (MDD), persons with MDD reported lower quality of life at one year compared with the non-depressed group.

Depression following TBI can often go undetected, and sometimes patients and carers themselves may be reluctant to recognise depression. This could be due to stigma of mental illness or may be a consequence of symptoms of depression being seen as expected normal reaction to TBI. Bombardier et al. (2010) noted in their prospective study that only 44% of those with major depression received antidepressants or counselling. Evidence suggests that antidepressants are effective in treating depression in neurological settings (Agrawal and Rickards, 2011). Hence, clinicians should have a low threshold for diagnosing and treating depression, given the costs for not doing so in terms of outcomes and quality of life. A systematic review (Fann, Hart and Schomer, 2009) of treatment for depression after TBI documented that there is a paucity of randomised controlled trials for depression following TBI. They found that serotonergic antidepressants and cognitive behavioural interventions appeared to have the best preliminary evidence for treating depression following TBI.

Suicide

6–015 Suicide is common after TBI, more common than non-cranial trauma. In a large Danish population study (Teasdale and Engberg, 2001) register of admissions to hospital covering the years 1979–93, patients were selected who had either had a concussion (n=126 114), a cranial fracture (n=7560), or a cerebral contusion or traumatic intracranial haemorrhage (n=11 766). In the three diagnostic groups there had been 750 (0.59%), 46 (0.61%), and 99 (0.84%) cases of suicide respectively. Standardised mortality ratios, stratified by sex and age, showed that the incidence of suicide among the three diagnostic groups increased relative to the general population (3.0, 2.7, and 4.1 respectively). In all diagnostic groups the ratios were higher for females than for males, and lower for patients injured before the age of 21 or after the age of 60. The presence of co-morbid substance misuse was associated with increased suicide rates in all diagnostic groups. There was a tendency, among patients with cerebral contusions or traumatic intracranial haemorrhages, for suicide risk to increase with duration of stay in hospital. There was a significantly greater risk of suicide among patients with cerebral contusions or traumatic intracranial haemorrhages than among patients with concussion or cranial fractures (hazard ratios 1.42 and 1.50 respectively). This suggests that at that specific point risk of suicide was 1.42–1.50 times higher in people with cerebral contusion or haemorrhage than in people with concussion. There was, however, no evidence of a specific risk period for suicide after injury. Increased risk of suicide, associated with more serious injury, longer hospital stay, female gender and young adulthood at the time of injury, has implication for early and accurate identification and treatment of psychiatric conditions (such as depression), and ongoing risk assessment during brain injury rehabilitation.

In a retrospective study, relations between suicide and TBI, psychiatric diagnoses, and relationship problems, was studied in the US armed forces between 2001–2009 (Scopp et al., 2012). Multivariate analyses showed increased odds of suicide were associated with mood disorders, partner relationship problems and family circumstance problems, but not with mild TBI, alcohol dependence, or PTSD. A separate analysis revealed that psychiatric comorbidities increased odds of suicide: odds ratio was 1.5 with one psychiatric co-morbidity, increasing to 6.4 with three co-morbidities. This suggests a clear relationship with psychiatric conditions and suicide after TBI, which makes it important to identify and treat psychiatric conditions.

Affective dysregulation

Mood problems after TBI can take a lot of unusual forms. Many patients with mood problems in the aftermath of TBI may not present with sustained depressed mood representative of depression. There can be reports of sudden outbursts of crying or laughter, without any obvious reason, that even surprise the patient. This is often called pathological laughter/crying or called pseudobulbar affect. This is different from the emotional lability associated with frontal lobe dysfunction, where there are constant changes in emotions. These cases can be misdiagnosed as depression if the crying spells are frequent, but this should be avoided for diagnostic clarity and prognosis, even though the pharmacological treatment is similar to depression. These cases benefit from use of SSRI medication with evidence being best for citalopram. Psychological approaches such as CBT are not helpful for this condition.

6–016

Anxiety disorders

6–017   TBI can result in a wide spectrum of anxiety disorders that may include acute stress reaction, generalised anxiety disorder (GAD), specific phobic anxiety, social phobia, panic disorders, obsessive compulsive disorder (OCD) or post-traumatic stress disorder (PTSD). Some of these anxiety disorders, such as acute stress reaction, are transient and settle with time. Others such as phobic anxiety can be quite distressing and may affect an individual's functioning quite significantly. While travel-related anxiety is fairly common after road traffic accidents, other specific phobias could relate to stairs after a fall, or going out to public places in cases of assaults. These can be highly disabling with a huge impact on functioning and in some cases on finances.

Koponen et al. (2011), in a prospective observational study using Schedules for Clinical Assessment in Neuropsychiatry (SCAN), reported specific phobia in 5.3%, social phobia in 5.3%, and PTSD in 2.6% of patients one year after TBI. The same group, using similar methodology, but in a 30 year follow up study noted specific phobia in 8.3%, panic disorder in 8.3% and generalised anxiety disorder in 1.7% patients (Koponen, 2002).

Generalised anxiety disorder is reported in 1.7% to 44% of patients (Rogers and Read, 2007), depending upon method of assessment and different ways in which distress and anxiety can be reported. A recent meta-analysis of anxiety disorders after TBI noted prevalence estimates varied for different diagnostic criteria (range: 2%–19%), interview schedules (range: 2%–28%), and self-report measures (range: 36%–50%). GAD and anxiety were most prevalent two to five years post injury (Osborn and Mathias, 2016). The rates of clinically significant GAD increased with injury severity (mild: 11%, severe 15%), but frequency of reported anxiety decreased (mild: 53%, severe: 38%). There is no evidence for a biological gradient, or relationship with the severity of the injury, though the GAD can be persistent after injury for years. Panic disorder similarly has no specific biological basis or biological gradient with severity of injury. In a majority of patients it can occur years after TBI, suggesting psychological and coping mechanisms being responsible for the panic disorder (Rogers and Read, 2007).

6–018   Obsessive compulsive disorder (OCD) is characterised by recurrent intrusive thoughts that are recognised by the patient as their own, but are ego dystonic and anxiety-provoking, particularly if an attempt is made to stop them from coming to mind. Obsessional thoughts are commonly associated with compulsive behaviours such as checking, cleaning and counting etc. In order to deal with their cognitive impairments, patients with TBI may get involved in a restrictive and repetitive routine that is comfortable for them. This can be confused with OCD as these behaviours are commonly termed obsessional by patients and carers. Truly speaking these behaviours are not obsessional and are rather an attempt to cope with the difficulties caused by their injury and have greater control over their life.

A wide range of prevalence figures is quoted in published literature, which is due to methodological issues such as small sample size, different duration from the TBI, and different severity of TBI. Some studies quote rates similar to the general population, while others quote much higher rates with a range of prevalence from 1.6% (Deb et al., 1999) to 11%, with a higher prevalence of up to 28% in one study in mild TBI (van Reekum et al., 1996). In a comprehensive prospective study Koponen et al., (2011) noted OCD in 4% of sample. OCD can occur in focal injuries or more global injuries with diffuse axonal injury. OCD can be an early or late presentation after a TBI. Aetiology for OCD following TBI can be a mix of organic effect of TBI on brain pathways, or a psychological reaction to injury and coping mechanisms. Currently imaging evidence is weak and inconclusive.

PTSD rates after a TBI are reported to be significantly higher than the general population with relative risk being approximately five times higher (Rogers and Reed, 2007). Estimated prevalence of PTSD ranges from 1–50% after TBI (Tanev et al., 2014). Rates of PTSD are higher in mTBI than severe TBI, with disruption to memory and cognitive function considered to be a protective factor. While a lack of memory for the traumatic event appears to be a protective factor, consciousness at the time of trauma and subsequent memories might not be necessary for the development of PTSD. There have been reports that PTSD can occur after TBI even when there is a significant disturbance of consciousness or disrupted memory for the trauma (Rogers and Read, 2007).

PTSD presents with symptoms of intrusive memories such as flashbacks and nightmares, avoidance of reminders of the trauma, and hyperarousal. PTSD is commonly associated with co-morbid psychiatric conditions. Most common of these are depression, substance misuse and other anxiety disorders. People suffering from co-morbid PTSD and TBI complain of more severe neurocognitive symptoms and disability. Sleep disturbance is common in PTSD after TBI and may hinder recovery if not treated. PTSD commonly affects behaviour and may exacerbate TBI-associated irritability, agitation and aggression. 6–019

Diagnosis of PTSD relies on a good clinical assessment, and while some screening instruments may help with recognition, they are not diagnostic of the condition. Treatment is often a combination of psychological therapy, either cognitive behavioural therapy (CBT) or eye movement desensitisation reprocessing (EMDR), along with pharmacological measures such as use of SSRI medications. CBT in PTSD after TBI may not optimally work for a variety of reasons, including impaired cognitive functions, co-morbid psychiatric conditions, substance misuse, and high drop-out rates. In such circumstances, predominantly pharmacological treatment may be necessary, at least in the beginning.

6. APATHY—AMOTIVATION

Apathy following TBI is commonly associated with reduced goal-directed behaviour, lack of motivation, impaired initiative, diminished activity, and lack of concern (Marin, 1991). These symptoms of apathy are commonly divided into three dimensions: behavioural, cognitive and emotional. Apathy can be associated with poor outcomes due to lack of engagement in neurorehabilitation, and may impact on family, social and occupational functioning, as well as contributing to increased caregiver distress. People with apathy demonstrate significant differences in quality of life, particularly in regard to mental health, compared to those without apathy. In addition, people with apathy show 6–020 significantly more difficulties with functioning, including social integration and problem solving. Hence, apathy can pose significant challenges during rehabilitation if it remains unrecognised and untreated.

Various terms have been used to describe apathy in clinical settings. These include amotivation, and abulia, and it is generally described by lay people as "reduced get up and go". Individuals with apathy may also exhibit greater levels of depression, although apathy commonly gets mistaken for depression and treated as such. Hence, accurate diagnosis is important as treatment is different for depression and apathy. Apathy is more likely to occur in moderate to severe TBI than in mTBI. A common differential for apathy, apart from depression, would be pituitary dysfunction, agoraphobic anxiety, and impact of severe cognitive impairment on functioning.

Apathy is thought to result from the disruption of connections between the anterior cingulate cortex (ACC) and other cortical and subcortical regions. The ACC and orbitofrontal cortex (OFC) receive input from the limbic system (basolateral amygdala and nucleus accumbens), which are areas involved in reward mechanisms (Knutson et al., 2014). These limbic areas feed into an ascending pathway to the dorsolateral prefrontal cortex, which selects and executes behavioural responses. Apathy is caused by damage to ACC or OFC, or if any parts of this circuit is disrupted. Using a voxel-based lesion-symptom mapping imaging study, Knutson et al. (2014) noted apathy symptoms were associated with brain damage in limbic and cortical areas of the left hemisphere including the anterior cingulate, inferior, middle, and superior frontal regions, insula, and supplementary motor area. This is consistent with other studies implicating these areas. They also noted that apathy was negatively correlated with post-injury intelligence, and positively correlated with Beck Depression Inventory scores and fatigability. They suggest that the neural correlates of fatigability and apathy overlapped to some degree in that both included ACC and the frontal cortex. Increased apathy was also associated with damage to the supplementary motor area and insula, and to white matter in the left corona radiata and corpus callosum.

6–021 Clinical assessment consists of obtaining a good history and account of symptoms from carers and the wider multidisciplinary team. Distinction should be made between apathy as a symptom of mood disorder, altered level of consciousness, or cognitive impairment, and apathy as a syndrome of acquired changes in mood, behaviour, and cognition not due to mood disorder, altered level of consciousness or cognitive impairment (van Reekum et al., 2005). Use of measures such as the Apathy Evaluation Scale (Marin, 1991) or Apathy inventory (Robert et al., 2002) can help with diagnosis, but other causes such as depression and pituitary dysfunction should be excluded through clinical assessment with a neuropsychiatrist.

Treatment in the initial instance can be only non-pharmacological, particularly in milder cases. This involves behavioural approaches and structure to daily routine. In more severe cases, a combination of pharmacological and non-pharmacological approaches is recommended. Cognitive interventions are the most commonly used strategy, but other interventions such as music therapy and cognitive rehabilitation have been used (Lane-Brown and Tate, 2009). Practical behavioural approaches such as activity scheduling are also commonly used clinically. Various pharmacological treatments, including dopaminergic drugs such as Selegiline, stimulants such as Methylphenidate, and cholinesterase inhibitors such as Donepezil, and others such as SSRIs and Modafinil have been tried with variable efficacy.

7. PSYCHOSIS

Psychosis with frank delusions or hallucinations is not uncommon after moderate to severe TBI. Prevalence rates quoted in the literature range from 1.35% to 9.4% (Batty et al., 2013). In Finland, Koponen et al. (2002), in a 30-year follow-up study noted rates of psychosis of 7.6 % which is seven times the risk in the general population. However, there are still some clinicians who do not believe that TBI can cause psychosis, even though the rates of psychosis are much higher after TBI than in the general population. It is argued that this increase may partly be related to a cohort of young males with substance misuse who are more likely to have psychosis as well as TBI. Conversely it is also argued that people who are going to have psychosis may be somehow more vulnerable to have brain injury. As a result, it is suggested that the combined effect of these two factors may explain why psychosis is more common after TBI. Psychosis, however, can occur not only in first year after injury, but can first present any time after the injury—even 10 or more years after TBI. It is suggested that TBI leads to decades-lasting vulnerability to psychosis with over 42% of psychosis after TBI emerging over 10 years after TBI (Koponen et al., 2002). This may suggest a role of TBI as a causative factor, and given that rates are much higher than general population, it is unlikely that the entirety of the increased risk could be explained by the non TBI factors.

6–022

Factors that increase the risk of developing psychosis after TBI include male gender, substance misuse including cannabis and alcohol misuse, and comorbid mood and anxiety disorders. Continuing cognitive and behavioural impairments following TBI may also mediate the development of psychotic symptoms. Reduced behavioural control, with irritability, aggression, impulsivity disinhibition and/or lack of initiative is also common after a TBI, as is a lack of awareness of these changes. Similar cognitive and behavioural dysfunction including amotivation, disinhibition and social isolation is documented in psychotic disorders. It is suggested that these cognitive and behavioural changes post TBI may constitute chronic stress that may predispose for psychosis (Batty et al., 2013). Increased vulnerability for psychosis has been reported, in people with TBI with frontal, temporal or hippocampal lesions, though the evidence is still emerging. Common neuropsychological correlates of psychosis in TBI are impairment of memory and executive functions.

Psychosis following TBI most commonly presents as a delusional disorder, or schizophrenia-like psychoses. Delusional disorder may present with Capgras syndrome, reduplicative paramnesia, delusional jealousy regarding spouses resulting in marital conflict, Cotard syndrome or somatic delusions related to parts of the body. Schizophrenia-like psychosis commonly presents with auditory hallucinations and persecutory delusions whereas negative symptoms of schizophrenia are not common. Delusional disorders tend to develop earlier, generally in the first year after TBI in contrast to schizophrenia like psychosis which commonly starts late after the injury.

Assessment is mainly clinical with the involvement of a neuropsychiatrist. Assessment should focus on establishing the phenomenology of psychotic symptoms, and ruling out other causes of psychosis including substance-induced psychosis, psychosis related to epilepsy, and a primary psychotic disorder. Initial post-TBI presentation with agitation and behavioural problems associated with PTA can be commonly confused with psychosis and should be excluded. Diagnosis of psychosis when a patient is still in PTA should be avoided, unless the psychosis is very prominent and obvious. Treatment of psychosis after TBI is similar to treatment of psychosis in general, with use of atypical antipsychotic agents such as risperidone or olanzapine. Consideration should be given to interactions with other medication, sensitivity to side effects and their impact on neurocognitive functions.

8. ORGANIC PERSONALITY AND BEHAVIOURAL CHANGE

6–023   Persistent changes in behaviour, how people control their emotions and impulses and react to various external stimuli is commonly referred to as personality change or more specifically organic personality change/disorder. This has to be a significant change from pre-injury personality, and is generally pervasive, prolonged, and causes distress and/or dysfunction to reach the clinical threshold of diagnosis. Manifestations of personality change commonly overlap with changes in mood, sleep, fatigue and cognitive functions. People who have these emotional and neurocognitive problems after a TBI will inevitably show some changes in their behaviour, which would not necessarily be classified as a personality and behavioural change unless there are specific features that fulfil such a diagnosis.

Personality and behavioural changes after TBI present with significant barriers to engagement in neurorehabilitative treatment, and can have a negative impact on recovery and ability to return back to work. It is noted that patients with organic personality disorder (OPD) after TBI develop more psychosocial adjustment and emotional problems than patients with TBI without OPD diagnosis. This difference is independent of severity of cognitive impairments or severity of injury based on GCS score (Franulic et al., 2000). A Brazilian study using logistic regression analysis found that the diagnosis of personality changes after severe TBI remained an independent predictor of non-return to work with an adjusted odds ratio of 10.92 (Diaz et al., 2014). This means that people who had severe TBI and organic personality disorder had nearly 11 times higher odds of not returning to work than people with people with severe TBI without organic personality change.

In a long-term Finnish study (Koponen et al., 2002), using a structured clinical interview for DSM-IV standard personality disorders, definite personality disorders were found in 23.3%, and subthreshold personality disorders were found in an additional 18.3%. The most prevalent disorders were avoidant (15.0%), paranoid (8.3%), and schizoid (6.7%). They found 15.0%, had a definite organic personality syndrome. Overall, personality disorder or organic personality syndrome was observed in 30.0%. In another study, a quarter of people with TBI had pre-TBI personality disorder, and two thirds had an Axis II personality disorder after TBI (Hibbard et al., 2000). The most frequent Axis II diagnoses post-TBI in this study were borderline, obsessive compulsive, avoidant, paranoid, antisocial, and narcissistic. This study's findings argue against a specific TBI personality syndrome, but rather a diversity of personality disorders, reflective of the persistent challenges and compensatory coping strategies developed by people post-TBI. Rates of personality disorders post TBI can depend on severity of injury with reported rates as low as 3.5% in individuals with mild TBI and 84% in individuals with severe TBI (Obonsawin et al., 2007).

Typical personality and behavioural change symptoms in moderate to severe TBI include irritability, anger, impulsivity, disinhibition, apathy, labile mood, and self-centred and thoughtless behaviour. It is often associated with a lack of full insight into behaviour. People may show lack of goal-directed behaviour, lack of judgment, superficial jocularity, reduced social awareness, and tactlessness. People may regress into a childlike-behaviour requiring extra help and supervision. These behavioural problems often cause a high level of distress to a patient's family and people involved in caring for them. Obonsawin et al. (2007) attempted to develop a model of personality change after TBI based on information provided by the TBI survivor and a significant other, and suggested three factors that encompass personality change: affective regulation, behavioural regulation and engagement.

6–024

TBI can lead on to either focal injury such as a contusion or haemorrhages in various parts of brain or more widespread damage such as a diffuse axonal injury. Commonly lesions in orbito-frontal cortex and temporal lobes may lead to disruption of pathways involved in integrated affective processing and modulation of emotional, motivational, and behavioural states that result in personality and behavioural changes. Personality and behavioural change symptoms are commonly associated with neurocognitive impairments, particularly impairment of frontal lobe executive functions, although these impairments are not always seen (particularly in patients who had right frontal lesions).

Assessment may be facilitated by use of questionnaires such as The Frontal Systems Behaviour Scale (FrSBe), Neuropsychiatric Inventory (NPI), Frontal Behavioural Inventory (FBI) or Dysexecutive questionnaire (DEX). Most neuropsychiatrists would base their assessment on their clinical assessment facilitated by information from family and carers and other members of multidisciplinary team. It is important to establish pre-morbid personality and functioning, and rule out other psychiatric conditions that may explain the behavioural problems observed. Correlation with neurocognitive impairments and neuroimaging findings help, but are neither necessary nor sufficient.

Management routinely consists of a combination of neurorehabilitative treatment with behavioural approach, educational strategies, and pharmacological treatments. Generally, there is a paucity of high level evidence for various commonly used medications, which are recommended based on expert consensus and clinical experience. A number of different classes of medications are used to control symptoms of personality and behavioural change, depending upon the predominant manifestations. SSRIs are commonly prescribed for symptoms of irritability, depression, and emotional lability. Some of these symptoms, particularly if associated with prominent impulsivity and aggression, would be treated with atypical neuroleptic medications such as risperidone or olanzapine. Mood stabilisers, such as carbamazepine or valproate, have been used to achieve reduction in anger, agitation, aggression and affective lability. More recently, novel approaches include stimulants, including methylphenidate, amphetamines and other medications such as modafinil, amantidine, and bromocriptine, which are particularly used in treating symptoms like poor initiation, reduction in attention, apathy, motivational difficulties, and fatigue.

9. ALCOHOL AND DRUGS

6–025 Alcohol is a major risk factor for injury: 30% to 50% of all patients hospitalised with trauma are intoxicated at the time of injury. Alcohol and drug use are common in young men who present with TBI. It is commonly assumed that these substances are associated with emotional, behavioural and neurocognitive problems after TBI. People can present with increased emotional lability, depression, and aggression. They may also show reduced tolerance to the same substance (used pre-injury) increasing the likelihood of post-injury intoxication. People may in addition present with pathological intoxication, where even a small amount of the substances used previously leads on to very significant problems with memory, emotions and behaviour. Conversely people after TBI may use alcohol as a coping mechanism for low mood, sleep disturbance, pain, or use alcohol due to lack of judgment or impulsivity. Substance misuse after TBI is associated with poor psycho-social adjustment and outcomes.

Animal models show that alcohol exposure after TBI accentuated neuroinflammation, as indicated by enhanced astroglial activation and increased expression of the danger-signalling molecule HMGB1. The exacerbated neuroinflammatory state, marked by increased cellular reactivity in brain, was accompanied by impaired neurological recovery and increased anxiety-like behaviour in TBI animals exposed to alcohol vapour during the post-TBI period (Teng et al., 2015). Implications of this finding for humans remains to be established.

Alcohol consumption on the day of injury may increase the risk of sustaining a TBI, but does not appear to be associated with substantially poorer outcomes after a TBI (Mathias and Osborn, 2016). This is contrary to the commonly held belief amongst clinicians. Individuals with positive or high day-of-injury blood alcohol levels have slightly poorer cognitive outcomes, but largely comparable medical functional outcomes, as compared to those who have lower or zero blood alcohol readings at the time of their injury. Hence, persons with alcohol in their system when they sustain their TBI are not expected to have substantially poorer outcomes as a consequence of having consumed alcohol. Rather, any substantial cognitive problems and/or poor medical/functional outcomes are more likely to reflect other factors, such as the severity or type of injury (Mathias and Osborn, 2016).

6–026 Association between alcohol levels at the time of injury and mortality in patients with severe TBI seems to be complicated. In a large retrospective cohort study (Tien et al., 2006), low to moderate blood alcohol concentration post injury was associated with lower mortality compared to when there was no blood alcohol (27.9% vs 36.3%). High blood alcohol concentration was associated with higher mortality than was no blood alcohol (44.7% vs 36.3%), although this was not statistically significant. They conclude that low to moderate blood alcohol concentration may be beneficial in patients with severe brain injury from blunt head trauma. In contrast, high blood alcohol concentration seems to have a deleterious effect on in-hospital death. They suggest alcohol may have neuroprotective effects at low and moderate doses, however, these effects are likely overshadowed at higher doses by its hemodynamic and physiologic effects.

In a controlled prospective study of alcohol use post TBI (Ponsford et al., 2007) similar levels of drug and alcohol use were found in people with TBI compared to controls pre-injury, with 31.4% of the TBI group and 29.3% of controls drinking at hazardous levels. Alcohol and drug use declined in the first year post-injury, but increased by two years post-injury, with only 21.4% of participants with TBI reporting abstinence from alcohol and 25.4% drinking at hazardous levels. Only 9% showed a drug problem, but 24% had returned to some drug use. Those showing heavy alcohol use post-injury were young, male and heavy drinkers pre-injury. This suggests a window of opportunity in the first year after TBI to act and help people who are at high risk of starting or returning to substance misuse after TBI. Hence, there is a need for intervention at an early stage after TBI to educate people about the impact of alcohol, and using motivational interviewing, particularly in individuals who had heavy substance use prior to their TBI.

A history of alcohol drinking prior to injury is a strong predictor of heavy drinking after TBI. Patients with less education tend to have higher rates of relapse of drinking, but higher alcohol levels on admission may also predict a decrease in drinking after TBI. A more severe TBI, as defined by initial GCS, seems to also predict decreased drinking after TBI (Opreanu et al., 2010).

In the immediate aftermath of TBI, GCS is frequently used to assess the severity of TBI and inform further management. It is commonly assumed that being under influence of alcohol at the time of injury reduces GCS score, thus limiting its utility in intoxicated patients. Stuke et al. (2007) show that alcohol use does not result in a clinically significant reduction in GCS in trauma patients. They suggest that attributing low GCS to alcohol intoxication in TBI patients may delay necessary diagnostic and therapeutic interventions.

However, alcohol-use after TBI carries several risks. These include increased risk of recurrent TBI due to falls, more atrophy of the cerebral cortex, development of post-traumatic seizures and deterioration of behavioural functioning (Opreanu, 2010). In addition, people may have worsening of neurocognitive difficulties, increased emotional difficulties and aggression.

Similarly, substance abuse is a risk factor for TBI due to impact on cognitive function, behaviour and judgment. Substance misuse pre and post-TBI is commonly associated with alcohol misuse. Evidence suggests approximately 50 to 60% of persons with TBI have significant issues with alcohol and/or drugs. Substance misuse may increase after the TBI with odds of 4.5 within the first year post-injury, and 1.4 at three years post-injury (Allen, 2016). This indicates that people with TBI have 4.5 times higher odds of having substance misuse in the first year and 1.4 times higher odds after three years than without TBI. However, others suggest that there may be a decline in substance misuse for a while after TBI, similar to what is reported in relation to alcohol misuse. A history of substance abuse predicts increased disability, poorer prognosis, and delayed recovery. Difficulties in psychosocial adjustment and coping skills that a person had pre-injury combined with the subtle cognitive impairments in neurocognitive functioning caused by the mild TBI, may increase the risk for chronic substance abuse (Allen 2016). Substance misuse post-injury could lead to problems with emotions, behaviour, motivation, neurocognitive functions, and overall poor outcome from TBI.

10. FUNCTIONAL NEUROLOGICAL DISORDERS AND FACTITIOUS DISORDER

6–028 A group of conditions where patients present with neurological symptoms, but without a clear underlying neurological basis are well recognised in neurosciences settings. Various names have been given in the past including hysteria, psychogenic disorders, psychosomatic disorders, somatoform disorders, conversion disorders and dissociative disorders. More recently the term functional neurological disorder (FND) has become more popular and acceptable to patients to describe this condition (Stone et al., 2002). These conditions commonly occur after a stressful life event or psychological trauma, but can be associated with other neurological conditions. The main psychopathological process is considered to be subconscious without any primary external gain. The functional disorder spectrum comes close to conditions such as factitious disorder where the psychopathological process is conscious but there is no external gain. Patients presenting with factitious disorders have a strong desire to remain in the patient role, even when it is not leading to any external gains for them. This condition has also been called Munchausen's syndrome. With these conditions, another differential diagnosis is malingering where there is a conscious process with clear external gains. In the clinical settings, it may be rather difficult to be certain about the relative role of conscious and subconscious processes. Frequently, significant inconsistencies, accumulation of specific patterns of behaviours, or surveillance evidence helps clarify the diagnosis.

Eames (1992) found that of the 167 patients referred to a unit treating severe behaviour disorders after brain injury, 54 showed clinical features closely resembling those of gross hysteria (conversion disorder) as described by Charcot. Close correlation was found with very diffuse insults (hypoxia and hypoglycaemia), but not with severity of injury or with family or personal history of hysteria (conversion disorder) or other psychiatric disorders. Despite the predominance of men within the brain injury group, women were more likely to present with hysteria, as is the case in general population. Eames (1992) was of the view that the evidence did not support that the clinical picture represents a disorder reactive to the psychological stresses of severe brain injury and the personal and functional losses it produced. He noted hysteria was at least as pronounced in subjects who did not display psychological stress, and he argued for some kind of organic process. He highlighted that neither family history nor past psychiatric history was associated, suggesting no specific vulnerability. Eames noted that there were a few patients in the hysteria (conversion disorder) group in whom the clinical features clearly did derive from pre-existing personality disorder, but they were a very small minority.

Eames' paper is one of the rare papers where people have tried to look into post-brain injury presentation with functional disorders. His sample being from a highly specialised inpatient unit represented a subgroup of patients with more severe brain injury who do not represent the whole TBI spectrum. Generally, neuropsychiatrists who deal with the aftermath of TBI know a number of patients where a range of functional neurological disorders have been produced after TBI. Systematic studies are however rare. Clinical experience suggests that mild injuries may be more likely to present with functional disorders than severe injuries. Psychological stress is considered to be the main factor leading on to development of FND.

Westbrook, Devinsky and Geocadin (1998) explored the role of head injury as a risk factor in the development of non-epileptic seizures, a form of FND that presents with fits that resemble epileptic fits. They carried out a retrospective record review of patients referred and noted that out of 102 patients with non-epileptic seizures referred, nearly one-third (32%) had an antecedent head injury. They found multiple psychiatric disorders were common (79%), and a history of abuse was found in 35% of sample. They concluded that head trauma may be a frequent precipitant to psychogenic non-epileptic seizures. This study identified several characteristics of patients with non-epileptic seizures after head injury that does not appear typical of those with post-traumatic epilepsy or of the general non-epileptic seizures population. The injury severity levels were predominantly mild or minimal (85%), which is in contrast to the relative risk of epilepsy after mild or minimal head injury, and is widely accepted to be no greater than the risk for the general population. They concluded that mild head injury plays a substantially larger role as a risk factor in the epidemiology of non-epileptic seizures than it does in epilepsy. These non-epileptic seizures after TBI are equally likely to occur in men as in women, contrary to female preponderance in general population. Factitious disorders and malingering may be more common co-morbid diagnoses among patients with non-epileptic seizures after head injury than reported in the general non-epileptic seizures population.

6–029

In another study looking at non epileptic attacks after TBI (Barry et al., 1998), using a similar methodology, found that of the 157 patients with video-EEG confirmed non-epileptic seizures, 37 (24%) had the onset of their seizures attributed to a head injury. In this study there was female preponderance (68%), and non-epileptic seizures usually developed within the first year after head injury (89%). The majority (78%) of patients with non-epileptic seizures sustained only mild head injury, consistent with the Westbrook, Devinsky and Geocadin (1998) study. In this study, Barry et al. (1998) noted that patients with non-epileptic seizures after head injury resemble patients with persistent post-concussional syndrome with symptoms closely associated, including poor concentration and memory, headache, and other episodic neurologic symptoms. These patients often reported surprisingly severe symptoms and major disability after only a mild head injury. This often raises concerns that such patients may embellish or exaggerate these symptoms bringing in a differential diagnosis of malingering.

More recently a systematic and narrative review (Stone et al., 2009) of the role of physical injury in motor and sensory conversion symptoms (FND) noted that physical injury prior to symptom onset was reported in 324 patients (37%). They noted that in 131 out of the 324 cases in which injury was reported, road traffic accident was by far the most common type of injury, followed by 'falls' and minor injuries. Concussion, sporting injuries, ankle sprain, exercise, war injuries, and assault were all mentioned more than once. Although some of these injuries were potentially life-threatening, a substantial minority (and because of a lack of detail possibly more) were minor in nature (Parees et al., 2014).

Hence, functional spectrum disorders after the TBI are common and are generally seen after mild TBI. A range of presentation can be seen including non-epileptic seizures, paralysis, abnormal movements, sensory problems, speech problems, gait disturbance, visual problems, or problems with memory. People may present with failure on a test of effort within neurocognitive testing in addition to FND. But this is not necessary or invariable. Effort tests will be covered in more details elsewhere in this book. Functional disorders can be difficult to treat but if they are diagnosed early, and people are able to understand and accept their condition then prognosis for full recovery can be good with appropriate and intensive multidisciplinary treatment.

11. RISK FOR DEMENTIA

6–030 Over the last few decades of the twentieth century, there was a growing recognition that repetitive brain injuries could lead on to neurological damage sufficient enough to cause a dementia like syndrome later in life. However, it remained controversial and was not generally accepted that a single brain injury could predispose a person to cognitive decline later in life and result in dementia. More recently however, there have been a number of pieces of emerging evidence that suggest there is an increased risk of dementia after a single TBI.

Lye and Shores (2000) carried out a review and they suggest that accumulating epidemiological evidence implicates traumatic brain injury as a pathogenic agent in the development of Alzheimer's disease (AD). They noted that Satz's threshold theory of acquired brain injury (Satz, 1993), including the concept of brain reserve, appear to have made a valuable contribution toward establishing a plausible theoretical foundation to explain the association between these two neuropsychiatric conditions. They suggested that trauma-induced neuronal damage may interact with age-related neuronal attrition to exhaust brain reserve capacity, thereby lowering the neuropathological threshold for dementia onset. Additionally, neuropathological and biochemical findings provide powerful evidence that brain trauma could trigger the central neurodegenerative processes of AD (Lye and Shores, 2000).

Support for the reduced cognitive reserve hypothesis comes from neuro-radiological source too. Cole, Leach and Sharpe (2015) using a neuroimaging model attempted to find out whether long term effects of TBI may resemble normal aging, and whether TBI may accelerate aging process. They found that TBI brains were 5–6 years older than expected, and this effect increased with time since injury—indicating brain tissue loss increases throughout the post-injury phase. The discrepancy between chronological and predicted age was related to severity of injury. Moderate to severe injuries had an effect, whereas the effect of mild injury was not dissimilar to controls. They noted that it was yet unclear whether their observation suggests ongoing neurodegeneration triggered by TBI or an interaction with normal aging.

There is now accumulating epidemiological data to support the view that TBI increases the risk for dementia. Long term epidemiological studies such as Koponen et al. (2002) found dementia in 5% of their patients after TBI, and an additional 5% had subclinical dementia. A large nationwide cohort study in Sweden (Nordstrom et al., 2014), comprising of 811,622 Swedish men, investigated the association between TBI and the risk of young onset dementia. During a median follow-up period of 33 years, there were 45,249 men with at least 1 TBI in the cohort. They found strong associations between dementia and TBI, and after adjustment for unrelated risk factors. The hazard ratio for dementia after one mild TBI was 1.7, two mild TBI was 1.7 and one severe TBI was 2.6, confirming the association. This indicates that at any point in time risk of dementia is 1.7–2.6 times higher in one or more mild TBI than without any mild TBI.

6–031

Nordstrom and Nordstrom (2018) subsequently looked at another Swedish cohort of people over 50 years of age (n = 3,329,360) with mean follow-up period of 15 years. Diagnoses of dementia and TBI were tracked through nationwide databases. They found people with TBI had strong association with dementia (adjusted odds ratio (OR), 1.81; 95% confidence interval (CI), 1.75±1.86). The association was strongest in the first year after TBI (OR, 3.52; 95% CI, 3.23±3.84), but the risk remained significant >30 years (OR, 1.25; 95% CI, 1.11±1.41). Single mild TBI showed a weaker association with dementia (OR, 1.63; 95% CI, 1.57±1.70) than did more severe TBI (OR, 2.06; 95% CI, 1.95±2.19) and multiple TBIs (OR, 2.81; 95% CI, 2.51±3.15).

Risk of dementia after TBI is influenced not just by the severity of the initial injury, but also by the patient's age at the time of injury (Johnson and Stewart, 2015). It appears that while mild TBI may not increase the risk in younger adults, it increases dementia risk in those aged ≥65 years. This suggests increasing age may make people more vulnerable to the effects of TBI, where reducing severity may pose risks similar to moderate to severe injury. Li et al. (2017) noted age at the time of injury is associated with the long-term cognitive outcome of TBI. They carried out a retrospective study investigating the association between age at injury and the long-term cognitive outcome in elderly participants with a TBI history. They noted that people with TBI occurring before age 22 years had better cognitive performance in language and episodic memory/recognition than those with TBI in adulthood after 22 years age, suggesting that older age at the time of TBI is associated with poorer long term cognitive outcome. The other risk factor identified was multiple injuries.

In the US, in a retrospective cohort study of 188,764 US veterans (Barnes et al., 2014) aged 55 years or older who did not have a dementia diagnosis at baseline, during the nine-year follow-up period, 16% of those with TBI

6–032

developed dementia compared with 10% of those without TBI (adjusted hazard ratio, 1.57). They concluded that TBI in older veterans was associated with a 60% increase in the risk of developing dementia over nine years after accounting for competing risks and potential confounders.

A recent Danish nationwide population-based observational cohort study (Fann et al., 2018) used data from a cohort of 2,794,852 people for a total of 27,632,020 person-years (mean 9·89 years per patient) at risk of dementia. They found that after fully adjusting risk of all-cause dementia in people with a history of TBI was higher (hazard ratio 1·24, 95% CI 1·21–1·27) than in those without a history of TBI, as was the specific risk of Alzheimer's disease (1·16, 1·12–1·22). The risk of dementia was highest in the first six months after TBI (HR 4·06, 3·79–4·34) and also increased with increasing number of events (1·22, 1·19–1·25 with one TBI to 2·83, 2·14–3·75 with five or more TBIs). They noted that younger a person was when sustaining a TBI, the higher the HRs for dementia when stratified by time since TBI.

It is now generally accepted that moderate to severe TBI increases risk of dementia, however, association of mTBI with dementia remains controversial. The relationship between mild TBI and dementia was investigated in a nationwide cohort study in Taiwan (Lee et al., 2013) that identified 28,551 patients with mTBI and 692,382 without. They controlled for various independent risk factors for dementia including age, gender, urbanisation level, socioeconomic status, diabetes, hypertension, coronary artery disease, hyperlipidaemia, history of alcohol intoxication, history of ischemic stroke, history of intracranial haemorrhage and Charlson Comorbidity Index Score. They found that mTBI was associated with increased risk of dementia with the adjusted hazard ratio of 3.26. This indicates that people with mTBI have 3.26 times higher risk of dementia those without TBI. They concluded that TBI is an independent significant risk factor of developing dementia, even in the mild TBI. This finding will require replication before it can be widely accepted. There are of course inherent difficulties in doing such a study with mTBI as it is often difficult to define mTBI and these patients may not present to hospitals.

Generally, the data provide good support for the suggestion that TBI is associated with increased risk of dementia later in life. The hazard ratio is approximately 2–3 times for severe TBI and 1.2–2.6 times for mild TBI, particularly higher for multiple mild TBI. It is suggested that TBI is perhaps the best established environmental risk factor for dementia (Shively et al., 2012). Severity of TBI, age at the time of TBI, time since TBI and number of TBI are all relevant factors in determining the risk of dementia after TBI. The debate has now moved on from whether or not there is association and whether this indicates causation to try and understand the mechanism and pathophysiology of such increased risk. Proposed mechanisms for dementia risk after TBI includes neurodegeneration, interaction with aging, chronic traumatic encephalopathy, neuroinflammation, vascular changes, immune mechanisms and the simple model of reduced cognitive reserve.

12. MANAGEMENT

Patients with TBI are generally managed within the multidisciplinary TBI pathways with initial admission and treatment at a regional trauma centre, and subsequent inpatient and or community neuro-rehabilitation. This involves various therapists including neuropsychologists, physiotherapists, occupational therapists, speech and language therapists. A neuropsychiatrist should be an integral part of such teams but at many centres this is still not the case. Treatments are individualised following a detailed assessment of a patient's problems, and their strengths and weaknesses, using a goal-planning approach. Neuropsychiatric conditions following TBI are treated within such neurorehabilitative teams, or later on as an outpatient in the community with a combination of pharmacological, psychological, behavioural and social approaches.

Pharmacological approaches require attention to issues specific to TBI, including sensitivity to side effects, impact on energy levels and cognitive functions, interactions with other medications, and risk for post-traumatic epilepsy. These are specifically targeted at the main symptoms such as agitation, sleep disturbance or specific neuropsychiatric conditions such as depression or organic personality change. A general rule is to start low and go slow, and remove medications that are not helpful, with regular planned reviews. Many patients will however require full therapeutic doses as in non-TBI populations.

There is a dearth of evidence-based pharmacological treatments post TBI supported by strong randomised controlled trial evidence. Almost any psychotropic medication that is used for any psychiatric disorder has been used in patients following TBI. This is a growing field with gradual accumulation of evidence. Currently, no medications are specifically approved to be used post TBI by FDA, European or UK regulators. Hence, currently, the treatment is based on available evidence from open label studies and clinical experience. Various expert consensus guidelines (Warden et al., 2006; Plantier et al., 2016) and pragmatic reviews (Deb and Crownshaw, 2009; Chew and Zafonte, 2009; Bhatnagar et al., 2016) are available, which can guide management of neuropsychiatric problems post TBI.

REFERENCES

Agrawal, N. and Rickards, H., "Detection and treatment of depression in neurological disorders" (2011) *Journal of Neurology, Neurosurgery & Psychiatry* 82, 828–829.

Alexander, M.P., "Neuropsychiatric correlates of persistent postconcussive syndrome" (1992) *The Journal of Head Trauma Rehabilitation*, 7(2), 60–69.

Allen, S., Stewart, S.H., Cusimano, M. and Asbridge, M., "Examining the relationship between traumatic brain injury and substance use outcomes in the Canadian population" (2016) *Substance Use & Misuse*, 51(12), 1577–1586.

Andelic, N., "The epidemiology of traumatic brain injury" (2013) *The Lancet Neurology*, 12(1), p.28.

Barnes, D.E., Kaup, A., Kirby, K.A., Byers, A.L., Diaz-Arrastia, R. and Yaffe, K., "Traumatic brain injury and risk of dementia in older veterans" (2014) *Neurology*, 83(4), 312–319.

Barry, E., Krumholz, A., Bergey, G.K., Chatha, H., Alemayehu, S. and Grattan, L., "Nonepileptic posttraumatic seizures" (1998) *Epilepsia*, 39(4), 427–431.

Batty, R.A., Rossell, S.L., Francis, A.J. and Ponsford, J., "Psychosis following traumatic brain injury" (2013) *Brain Impairment*, 14(01), 21–41.

Bhatnagar, S., Iaccarino, M.A. and Zafonte, R., "Pharmacotherapy in rehabilitation of post-acute traumatic brain injury" (2016) *Brain Research*, 1640, 164–179.

Block, C.K., West, S.E. and Goldin, Y., "Misconceptions and misattributions about traumatic brain injury: An integrated conceptual framework" (2016) *P.M.&R.*, 8(1), 58–68.

Bombardier, C.H., Fann, J.R., Temkin, N.R., Esselman, P.C., Barber, J. and Dikmen, S.S., "Rates of major depressive disorder and clinical outcomes following traumatic brain injury" (2010) *Jama*, 303(19), 1938–1945.

Boussi-Gross R., Golan H., Fishlev G., et al., "Hyperbaric oxygen therapy can improve post concussion syndrome years after mild traumatic brain injury—randomized prospective trial" (2013) *PLoS One* 8(11):e79995.

Broshek, D.K., De Marco, A.P. and Freeman, J.R., "A review of post-concussion syndrome and psychological factors associated with concussion" (2015) *Brain Injury*, 29(2), 228–237.

Brown N.J., Mannix R.C., O'Brien M.J., et al., "Effect of cognitive activity level on duration

of post-concussion symptoms" (2014) *Pediatrics* 133(2):e299–304.

Bruns, J. and Hauser, W.A., "The epidemiology of traumatic brain injury: a review" (2003) *Epilepsia*, 44(s10), 2–10.

Carr, J., "Postconcussion syndrome: a review" (2007) *Trauma*, 9(1), 21–27.

Chew, E. and Zafonte, R.D., "Pharmacological management of neurobehavioral disorders following traumatic brain injury-a state-of-the-art review" (2009) *Journal of Rehabilitation Research and Development*, 46(6), p.851.

Cole, J.H., Leech, R. and Sharp, D.J., "Prediction of brain age suggests accelerated atrophy after traumatic brain injury" (2015) *Annals of Neurology*, 77(4), 571–581.

Dean P. J., Sterr A., "Long-term effects of mild traumatic brain injury on cognitive performance" (2013) *Front. Hum. Neurosci.* 7:30.

Deb, S., Lyons, I. and Koutzoukis, C., "Neuropsychiatric sequelae one year after a minor head injury" (1998) *Journal of Neurology, Neurosurgery & Psychiatry*, 65(6), 899–902.

Deb S., Lyons I., Koutzoukis C., Ali I., McCarthy G., "Rate of psychiatric illness 1 year after traumatic brain injury" (1999) *American Journal of Psychiatry* 44: 374–378.

Deb, S. and Crownshaw, T., "Review of subject: The role of pharmacotherapy in the management of behaviour disorders in traumatic brain injury patients" (2004) *Brain Injury*, 18(1), 1–31.

De Simoni, S., Grover, P.J., Jenkins, P.O., Honeyfield, L., Quest, R.A., Ross, E., Scott, G., Wilson, M.H., Majewska, P., Waldman, A.D. and Patel, M.C., "Disconnection between the default mode network and medial temporal lobes in post-traumatic amnesia" (2016) *Brain*, 139 (12): 3137–3150.

Diaz, A.P., Schwarzbold, M.L., Thais, M.E., Cavallazzi, G.G., Schmoeller, R., Nunes, J.C., Hohl, A., Guarnieri, R., Linhares, M.N. and Walz, R., "Personality changes and return to work after severe traumatic brain injury: a prospective study" (2014) Revista Brasileira de Psiquiatria, 36(3), 213–219.

Eames, P., "Hysteria following brain injury" (1992) *Journal of Neurology, Neurosurgery & Psychiatry*, 55(11), 1046–1053.

REFERENCES

Fann J.R., Hart T., and Schomer K.G., "Treatment for depression after traumatic brain injury: a systematic review" (2009) *J. Neurotrauma* 26, 2383–2402

Fann, J.R., Ribe, A.R., Pedersen, H.S., Fenger-Grøn, M., Christensen, J., Benros, M.E. and Vestergaard, M., "Long-term risk of dementia among people with traumatic brain injury in Denmark: a population-based observational cohort study" (2018) *The Lancet Psychiatry*, 5(5), 424–431.

Feigin, V.L., Theadom, A., Barker-Collo, S., Starkey, N.J., McPherson, K., Kahan, M., Dowell, A., Brown, P., Parag, V., Kydd, R. and Jones, K., "Incidence of traumatic brain injury in New Zealand: a population-based study" (2013) *The Lancet Neurology*, 12(1), 53–64.

Fleminger S., Greenwood R.J., Oliver D.L., "Pharmacological management for agitation and aggression in people with acquired brain injury" (2006) *Cochrane Database Syst Rev.* 4:CD003299.

Franulic, A., Horta, E., Maturana, R., Scherpenisse, J. and Carbonell, C., "Organic personality disorder after traumatic brain injury: Cognitive, anatomic and psychosocial factors. A 6 month follow-up" (2000) *Brain Injury*, 14(5), 431–439.

Hibbard, M.R., Bogdany, J., Uysal, S., Kepler, K., Silver, J.M., Gordon, W.A. and Haddad, L., "Axis II psychopathology in individuals with traumatic brain injury" (2000) *Brain Injury*, 14(1), 45–61.

Hou, R., Moss-Morris, R., Peveler, R., Mogg, K., Bradley, B.P. and Belli, A., "When a minor head injury results in enduring symptoms: a prospective investigation of risk factors for postconcussional syndrome after mild traumatic brain injury" (2012) *Journal of Neurology, Neurosurgery & Psychiatry*, 83(2), 217–223.

Johnson, V.E. and Stewart, W., "Traumatic brain injury: age at injury influences dementia risk after TBI" (2015) *Nature Reviews Neurology*, 11(3), 128–130.

Jorge, R.E., Starkstein, S.E., "Pathophysiologic aspects of major depression following traumatic brain injury" (2005) *J. Head Trauma Rehabil.* 6, 475–487.

King, N.S., "A systematic review of age and gender factors in prolonged post-concussion symptoms after mild head injury" (2014) *Brain Injury*, 28(13–14), 1639–1645.

Knutson, K.M., Monte, O.D., Raymont, V., Wassermann, E.M., Krueger, F. and Grafman, J., "Neural correlates of apathy revealed by lesion mapping in participants with traumatic brain injuries" (2014) *Human Brain Mapping*, 35(3), 943–953.

Koponen, S., Taiminen, T., Portin, R., Himanen, L., Isoniemi, H., Heinonen, H., Hinkka, S. and Tenovuo, O., "Axis I and II psychiatric disorders after traumatic brain injury: a 30-year follow-up study" (2002) *American Journal of Psychiatry*, 159(8), 1315–1321.

Koponen, S., Taiminen, T., Hiekkanen, H. and Tenovuo, O., "Axis I and II psychiatric disorders in patients with traumatic brain injury: a 12-month follow-up study" (2011) *Brain Injury*, 25(11), 1029–1034.

Lane-Brown, A.T. and Tate, R.L., "Apathy after acquired brain impairment: a systematic review of non-pharmacological interventions" (2009) *Neuropsychological Rehabilitation*, 19(4), 481–516.

Langlois, J.A., Rutland-Brown, W. and Wald, M.M., "The epidemiology and impact of traumatic brain injury: a brief overview" (2006) *The Journal of Head Trauma Rehabilitation*, 21(5), 375–378.

Leddy, J.J., Baker, J.G. and Willer, B., "Active rehabilitation of concussion and post-concussion syndrome" (2016) *Physical Medicine and Rehabilitation Clinics of North America*, 27(2), 437–454.

Lee, Y.K., Hou, S.W., Lee, C.C., Hsu, C.Y., Huang, Y.S. and Su, Y.C., "Increased risk of dementia in patients with mild traumatic brain injury: a nationwide cohort study" (2013) *PLoS One*, 8(5), p.e62422.

Levin H.S., O'Donnell V.M., Grossman R.G., "The Galveston Orientation and Amnesia Test: a practical scale to assess cognition after head injury" (1979) *J Nerv Ment Dis* 167:675–84.

Levin H.S., Benton A.L., Grossman R., "Historical review of head injury" in *Neurobehavioral Consequences of Closed Head Injury* (Oxford: Oxford University Press, 1982) pp.3–5. ISBN 0-19-503008-7.

Li, W., Risacher, S.L., McAllister, T.W., Saykin, A.J., "Alzheimer's Disease Neuroimaging Initiative, 2017. Age at injury is associated with the long-term cognitive outcome of traumatic brain injuries". *Alzheimer's & Dementia: Diagnosis, Assessment & Disease Monitoring*, 6, 196–200.

Lishman, W.A., "Physiogenesis and psychogenesis in the 'post-concussional syndrome'" (1988) *The British Journal of Psychiatry*, 153(4), 460–469.

Lye, T.C. and Shores, E.A., "Traumatic brain injury as a risk factor for Alzheimer's disease: a review" (2000) *Neuropsychology Review*, 10(2), 115–129.

Marshall, S., Bayley, M., McCullagh, S., Velikonja, D., Berrigan, L., Ouchterlony, D. and Weegar, K., "Updated clinical practice guidelines for concussion/mild traumatic brain injury and persistent symptoms" (2015) *Brain Injury*, 29(6), 688–700.

Marin R.S., Biedrzycki R.C., Firinciogullar S., "Reliability and validity of the Apathy Evaluation Scale" (1991) *Psychiatry Res* 38:143–162.

Marshman, L.A., Jakabek, D., Hennessy, M., Quirk, F. and Guazzo, E.P., "Post-traumatic amnesia" (2013) *Journal of Clinical Neuroscience*, 20(11), 1475–1481.

Maruta, J., Spielman, L.A., Yarusi, B.B., Wang, Y., Silver, J.M. and Ghajar, J., "Chronic post-concussion neurocognitive deficits. II. Relationship with persistent symptoms" (2016) *Frontiers in Human Neuroscience*, 10.

Mathias, J.L. and Osborn, A.J., "Impact of day-of-injury alcohol consumption on outcomes after traumatic brain injury: A meta-analysis" (2016) *Neuropsychological Rehabilitation*, 1: 1-22.

Mattson, A. J.; Levin, H.S., "Frontal lobe dysfunction following closed head injury. A review of the literature" (1990) *Journal of Nervous & Mental Disorders* 178 (5): 282–291.

McCrory P., Meeuwisse W., Aubry M., et al., "Consensus statement on concussion in sport–the 4th International Conference on Concussion in Sport held in Zurich, November 2012" (2013) *Clin J Sport Med* 23(2):89–117.

Nordström, P., Michaëlsson, K., Gustafson, Y. and Nordström, A., "Traumatic brain injury and young onset dementia: a nationwide cohort study" (2014) *Annals of Neurology*, 75(3), 374–381.

Nordström, A. and Nordström, P., "Traumatic brain injury and the risk of dementia diagnosis: A nationwide cohort study" (2018) *PLoS Medicine*, 15(1), p.e1002496.

Obonsawin, M.C., Jefferis, S., Lowe, R., Crawford, J.R., Fernandes, J., Holland, L., Woldt, K., Worthington, E. and Bowie, G., "A model of personality change after traumatic brain injury and the development of the Brain Injury Personality Scales" (2007) *Journal of Neurology, Neurosurgery & Psychiatry*, 78(11), 1239–1247.

Orlovska, S., Pedersen, M.S., Benros, M.E., Mortensen, P.B., Agerbo, E. and Nordentoft, M., "Head injury as risk factor for psychiatric disorders: a nationwide register-based follow-up study of 113,906 persons with head injury" (2014) *American Journal of Psychiatry*, 171(4), 463–469.

REFERENCES

Oldenburg, C., Lundin, A., Edman, G., Nygren-de Boussard, C. and Bartfai, A., "Cognitive reserve and persistent post-concussion symptoms—A prospective mild traumatic brain injury (mTBI) cohort study" (2016) *Brain Injury*, 30(2), 146–155.

Opreanu, R.C., Kuhn, D. and Basson, M.D., "The Influence of Alcohol on Mortality in Traumatic Brain Injury" (2010) *Journal of the American College of Surgeons*, 210(6).

Osborn, A.J., Mathias, J.L. and Fairweather-Schmidt, A.K., "Depression following adult, non-penetrating traumatic brain injury: a meta-analysis examining methodological variables and sample characteristics" (2014) *Neuroscience & Biobehavioral Reviews*, 47, 1–15.

Osborn, A.J., Mathias, J.L. and Fairweather-Schmidt, A.K., "Prevalence of anxiety following adult traumatic brain injury: A meta-analysis comparing measures, samples and postinjury intervals" (2016) *Neuropsychology*, 30(2), p.247.

Pareés, I., Kojovic, M., Pires, C., Rubio-Agusti, I., Saifee, T.A., Sadnicka, A., Kassavetis, P., Macerollo, A., Bhatia, K.P., Carson, A. and Stone, J., "Physical precipitating factors in functional movement disorders" (2014) *Journal of the Neurological Sciences*, 338(1), 174–177.

Plantier, D. and Luauté, J., "Drugs for behavior disorders after traumatic brain injury: Systematic review and expert consensus leading to French recommendations for good practice" (2016) *Annals of Physical and Rehabilitation Medicine*, 59(1), 42–57.

Ponsford, J., Whelan-Goodinson, R. and Bahar-Fuchs, A., "Alcohol and drug use following traumatic brain injury: a prospective study" (2007) *Brain Injury*, 21(13–14), 1385–1392.

Potter, S.D., Brown, R.G. and Fleminger, S., "Randomised, waiting list controlled trial of cognitive–behavioural therapy for persistent postconcussional symptoms after predominantly mild–moderate traumatic brain injury" (2016) *Journal of Neurology, Neurosurgery & Psychiatry*, 87:1075–1083.

Robert P.H., Clairet S., Benoit M., Koutaich J., Bertogliati C., Tible O., Caci H., Borg M., Brocker P., Bedoucha P., "The apathy inventory: Assessment of apathy and awareness in Alzheimer's disease, Parkinson's disease and mild cognitive impairment" (2002) *International Journal of Geriatric Psychiatr* 17:1099–1105.

Røe, C., Sveen, U., Alvsåker, K. and Bautz-Holter, E., "Post-concussion symptoms after mild traumatic brain injury: influence of demographic factors and injury severity in a 1-year cohort study" (2009) *Disability and Rehabilitation*, 31(15), 1235–1243.

Rogers, J.M. and Read, C.A., "Psychiatric comorbidity following traumatic brain injury" (2007) *Brain Injury*, 21(13–14), 1321–1333.

Satz, P., "Brain reserve capacity on symptom onset after brain injury: A formulation and review of evidence for threshold theory" (1993) *Neuropsychology* 7: 273–295.

Skopp, N.A., Trofimovich, L., Grimes, J., Oetjen-Gerdes, L. and Gahm, G.A., "Relations between suicide and traumatic brain injury, psychiatric diagnoses, and relationship problems, active component, US Armed Forces", 2001-2009. Air Force Medical Support Agency Fort Detrick Md Air Force Medical Evaluation Support Activity. Vol. 19 No. 2 MSMR.

Sharp, D.J. and Jenkins, P.O., "Concussion is confusing us all" (2015) *Practical Neurology*, 15(3), 172–186.

Shively, S., Scher, A.I., Perl, D.P. and Diaz-Arrastia, R., "Dementia resulting from traumatic brain injury: what is the pathology?" (2012) *Archives of Neurology*, 69(10), 1245–1251.

Shores E.A., Marosszeky J.E., Sandanam J., Batchelor J., "Preliminary validation of a clinical scale for measuring the duration of post-traumatic amnesia" (1986) *Med J Aust Internet*. 144 (11): 569–72.

Sigurdardottir, S., Andelic, N., Roe, C., Jerstad, T. and Schanke, A.K., "Post-concussion symptoms after traumatic brain injury at 3 and 12 months post-injury: a prospective study" (2009) *Brain Injury*, 23(6), 489–497.

Silverberg, N.D., Gardner, A.J., Brubacher, J.R., Panenka, W.J., Li, J.J. and Iverson, G.L., "Systematic review of multivariable prognostic models for mild traumatic brain injury" (2015) *Journal of Neurotrauma*, 32(8), 517–526.

Singh, R., Venkateshwara, G., Nair, K.P., Khan, M. and Saad, R., "Agitation after traumatic brain injury and predictors of outcome" (2014) *Brain Injury*, 28(3), 336–340.

Steel, J., Ferguson, A., Spencer, E. and Togher, L., "Language and cognitive communication during post-traumatic amnesia: A critical synthesis" (2015) *NeuroRehabilitation*, 37(2), 221–234.

Stein, M.B., Ursano, R.J., Campbell-Sills, L., Colpe, L.J., Fullerton, C.S., Heeringa, S.G., Nock, M.K., Sampson, N.A., Schoenbaum, M., Sun, X. and Jain, S., "Prognostic indicators of persistent post-concussive symptoms after deployment-related mild traumatic brain injury: a prospective longitudinal study in US Army soldiers" (2016) *Journal of Neurotrauma*, 33(23), 2125–2132.

Stone, J., Wojcik, W., Durrance, D., Carson, A., Lewis, S., MacKenzie, L., Warlow, C.P. and Sharpe, M., "What should we say to patients with symptoms unexplained by disease? The 'number needed to offend'". (2002) *B.M.J.*, 325(7378), p.1449.

Stone, J., Carson, A., Aditya, H., Prescott, R., Zaubi, M., Warlow, C. and Sharpe, M., "The role of physical injury in motor and sensory conversion symptoms: a systematic and narrative review" (2009) *Journal of Psychosomatic Research*, 66(5), 383–390.

Stuke, L., Diaz-Arrastia, R., Gentilello, L.M. and Shafi, S., "Effect of alcohol on Glasgow Coma Scale in head-injured patients" (2007) *Annals of Surgery*, 245(4), 651–655.

Teasdale, T.W. and Engberg, A.W., "Suicide after traumatic brain injury: a population study" (2001) *Journal of Neurology, Neurosurgery & Psychiatry*, 71(4), 436–440.

Tanev, K.S., Pentel, K.Z., Kredlow, M.A. and Charney, M.E., "PTSD and TBI co-morbidity: scope, clinical presentation and treatment options" (2014) *Brain Injury*, 28(3), 261–270.

Teng, S.X., Katz, P.S., Maxi, J.K., Mayeux, J.P., Gilpin, N.W. and Molina, P.E., "Alcohol exposure after mild focal traumatic brain injury impairs neurological recovery and exacerbates localized neuroinflammation" (2015) *Brain, Behavior, and Immunity*, 45, 145–156.

Tien, H.C., Tremblay, L.N., Rizoli, S.B., Gelberg, J., Chughtai, T., Tikuisis, P., Shek, P. and Brenneman, F.D., "Association between alcohol and mortality in patients with severe traumatic head injury" (2006) *Archives of Surgery*, 141(12), 1185–1191.

Umile E.M., Sandel M.E., Alavi A., Terry C.M., Plotkin R.C., "Dynamic imaging in mild traumatic brain injury: support for the theory of medial temporal vulnerability" (2002) *Arch Phys Med Rehab* 83:1506–13.

van Reekum R., Bolago I., Finlayson S., Garner S., Links P.S., "Psychiatric disorders after traumatic brain injury" (1996) *Brain Injury* 10: 319–327.

van Reekum, R., Streiner, D.L. and Conn, D.K., "Applying Bradford Hill's criteria for causation to neuropsychiatry: challenges and opportunities" (2001) *The Journal of Neuropsychiatry and Clinical Neurosciences*, 13(3), 318–325.

van Reekum, R., Stuss, D.T. and Ostrander, L., "Apathy: why care?" (2005) *The Journal of Neuropsychiatry and Clinical Neurosciences*, 17(1), 7–19.

REFERENCES

Wäljas, M., Iverson, G.L., Lange, R.T., Hakulinen, U., Dastidar, P., Huhtala, H., Liimatainen, S., Hartikainen, K. and Öhman, J., "A prospective biopsychosocial study of the persistent post-concussion symptoms following mild traumatic brain injury" (2015) *Journal of Neurotrauma*, 32(8), 534–547.

Warden, D.L., Gordon, B., McAllister, T.W., Silver, J.M., Barth, J.T., Bruns, J., Drake, A., Gentry, T., Jagoda, A., Katz, D.I. and Kraus, J., "Guidelines for the pharmacologic treatment of neurobehavioral sequelae of traumatic brain injury" (2006) *Journal of Neurotrauma*, 23(10), 1468–1501.

Westbrook, L.E., Devinsky, O. and Geocadin, R., "Nonepileptic seizures after head injury" (1998) *Epilepsia*, 39(9), 978–982.

Williamson, D.R., Frenette, A.J., Burry, L., Perreault, M.M., Charbonney, E., Lamontagne, F., Potvin, M.J., Giguère, J.F., Mehta, S. and Bernard, F., "Pharmacological interventions for agitation in patients with traumatic brain injury: protocol for a systematic review and meta-analysis" (2016) *Systematic Reviews*, 5(1), p.193.

World Health Organization (1993). The ICD-10 classification of mental and behavioral disorders: Diagnostic criteria for research. World Health Organization: Geneva.

Zetterberg H, Smith DH, Blennow K., "Biomarkers of mild traumatic brain injury in cerebrospinal fluid and blood" (2013) *Nat Rev Neurol* 9:201–10.

CHAPTER 7

Malingering and Exaggeration

Martin van den Broek and Sundeep Sembi

1. VALIDITY ISSUES IN LITIGATION

In recent years an international consensus has emerged that the assessment of response validity should be a feature of neuropsychological and psychological evaluations, particularly of individuals involved in personal injury claims. In 2009 the Professional Practice Board of the British Psychological Society (British Psychological Society, 2009) recommended that effort tests be given routinely as part of an assessment and in 2005 the National Academy of Neuropsychology Policy and Planning Committee concluded that neuropsychological assessments were a medically necessary investigation to understand an individual's functioning and the assessment of response validity was also medically necessary (Bush et al., 2005). In 2009 the American Academy of Clinical Neuropsychology recommended that stand-alone effort measures and embedded validity indicators should be employed (Heilbronner et al., 2009) and the Association for Scientific Advancement in Psychological Injury and Law (Bush et al., 2014) stated that the assessment of validity in forensic psychological valuations was essential. Similar recommendations have been made not only for forensic examinations, but also for Social Security claimants (Chafetz et al., 2015). These Position Papers have followed an explosion of research into the topics of malingering and exaggeration. Berry and Nelson (2010) noted that in the early 1980s only two or three papers a year were published on malingering, but in 2009 alone there were more than 90 papers and between 1989 and 2009 there were over 1,200 (see Figure 1). Sweet (2011) reported that the majority of malingering research was published in neuropsychology or psychology journals and 90% of the first authors were psychologists.

7–001

The driver for this interest has been the increasing involvement of neuropsychologists in personal injury litigation, particularly in North America, and more recently in European countries (Merten et al., 2013). Kaufmann (2009) reported that a Lexis search revealed 4,358 legal cases involving neuropsychological evidence during the previous 70 years, 71% of which were in the preceding decade, and he projected accelerating involvement in the future (see Figure 2).

Neuropsychological evidence can play an important, and sometimes central role in a claim, because people with brain injuries often have little in the way of physical disability and the primary limiting factors that curtail their independence and ability to manage their lives, resume social relationships and work, are the

MALINGERING AND EXAGGERATION

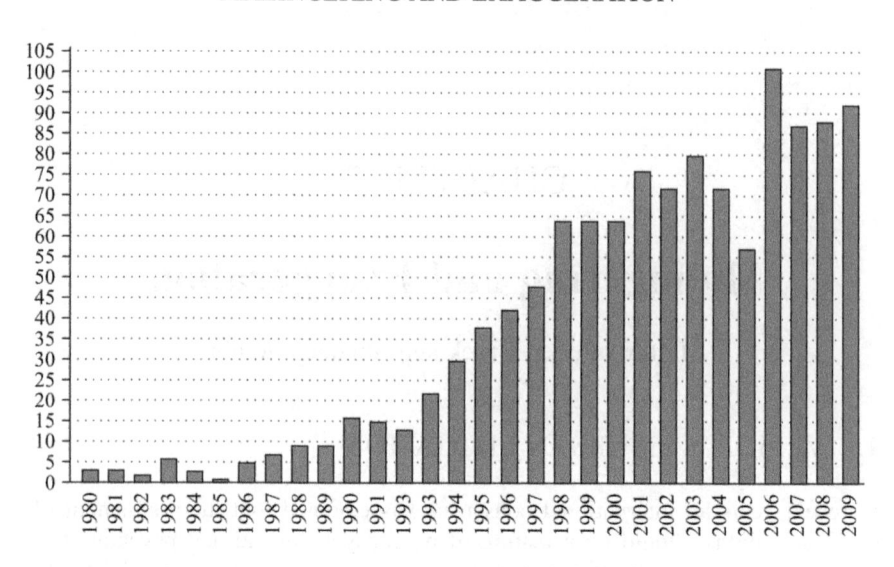

Figure 1: Number of publications annually with the keyword "malingering" from 1980 to 2009 (Berry and Nelson, 2010)

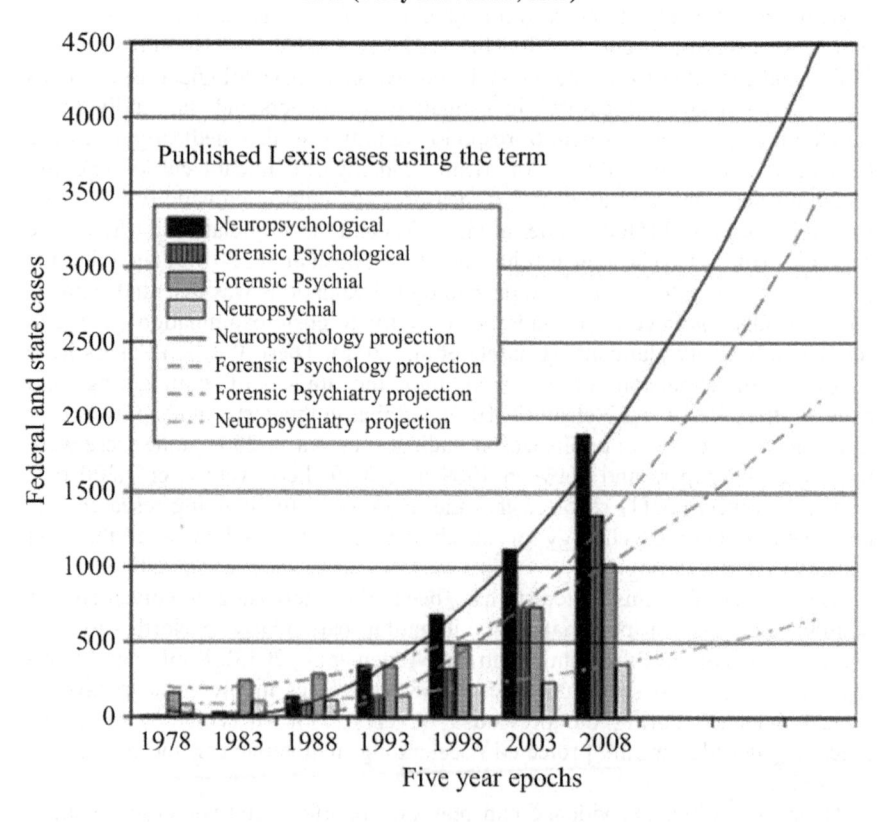

Figure 2: Number of US federal and state cases in five-year epochs between 1978 and 2008 used as a basis for polynomial regression for the subsequent 15 years (Kaufmann, 2009)

cognitive, emotional and personality changes they have undergone (Ponsford, 2014; Onsworth and Fleming, 2014). However, neuropsychological and psychological examinations rely on claimants accurately reporting their complaints and, in the case of cognitive testing, engaging appropriately and applying satisfactory effort, which in civil litigation with its obvious incentives, cannot be taken for granted. Brain injuries are notable for the fact that the claimant is the victim of the head trauma, the primary witness of their difficulties and the primary beneficiary of the claim and, apart from the most disabled, they are able to turn their condition to their advantage should they choose to do so. In the event that the assessment is distorted, the clinician's diagnosis, prognosis and treatment recommendations will necessarily be affected, leading to erroneous opinions being provided to the court. Traditionally clinicians have assumed that malingering and exaggeration are rare and not significant issues, and in the event that patients feigned complaints, they would find it difficult to evade detection by an experienced clinician. Both views have been found wanting, although many clinicians still subscribe to them and some continue to rule out malingering on the basis of clinical judgment alone. However, as Faust (1991) has pointed out, in the event a clinician was fooled by a claimant they will necessarily know nothing about it and so, a priori, such assurances are meaningless. Moreover, the more believable, honest and credible a claimant appears to be the more, rather than less, likely it is that they are a successful malingerer as successful malingerers present in that manner and it is only the unsuccessful, non-credible malingerers that are detected. In short, the clinician and lawyer are never more vulnerable to deception than when they confidently believe that they are dealing with a credible claimant. It is perhaps not surprising that having invested time, effort and resources in a claim they then respond with anger, and sometimes incredulity, when it is suggested that the claimant is not genuine and they question the motives of those who suggest otherwise.

It has been known for some time that clinicians' ability to detect feigning is poor. Ekman and O'Sullivan (1991) took videotaped interviews of people either lying or telling the truth when describing their feelings and showed them to judges, psychiatrists, college students and working adults, as well as those involved in law enforcement. They found that law enforcement personnel were the only group to perform better than chance when judging honesty or deception. Vrij and Mann (2003) reported that in studies of students' ability to detect true statements and lies, the accuracy rate was as low as 56.6%, bearing in mind that 50% accuracy was chance. There was also a bias towards correctly judging when someone was telling the truth and worse accuracy when detecting lies, with assessors being more likely to consider statements as being truthful than not. In the case of professionals, such as police and custom officers, accuracy rates were similar to those found with students, although some were more accurate than others and the truth bias was less of an issue. In a classic study Faust et al. (1988a) instructed three children aged between nine and 12 years to complete a number of cognitive tests in a way that was worse than usual, but without the examiner knowing that they were faking. The results were then given to a group of neuropsychologists, 93% of whom judged them to be abnormal, 87% of whom thought they had some kind of brain disorder and none concluded malingering. In a further study Faust et al. (1988b) asked normal adolescents to fake on testing

7–002

and on this occasion the clinicians were told the results would be drawn from a group of half malingerers and half genuine cases. In these circumstances some practitioners concluded malingering, but the identification of malingering fell below chance, despite being forewarned. Comparable limitations have been found with psychiatrists when identifying feigned mental illness (Rosenhan, 1973). Guilmette (2013) outlined a number of obstacles to clinicians concluding malingering that included their expectations when approaching an assessment. For example, a clinician who expects that cognitive difficulties and permanent disability will follow a mild head injury and who believes there is a low incidence of malingering when that is not necessarily the case, may have a low likelihood of detecting malingering. Guilmette (2013) pointed out that clinicians, and it might be added lawyers, may be susceptible to confirmatory bias, that is, have a tendency to seek information that confirms their views, rather than refutes them. A clinician who believes that a patient is genuine and their difficulties are due to brain trauma, may ignore conflicting evidence, such as other potential causes of their difficulties, like chronic pain. Guilmette (2013) pointed out that the errors inherent in relying on clinical judgment alone are typically reinforced and amplified by a lack of corrective feedback. A clinician who has come to believe that a malingerer's complaints are genuine will usually never learn that their conclusions were erroneous and so learn from their mistakes. Moreover, without feedback, they potentially become more confident about their decision-making over time with an increasing likelihood of repeating the same erroneous opinions.

It is perhaps unsurprising that clinicians have been poor at detecting feigning as their training typically emphasises the importance of developing trusting, empathic relationships with their patients characterised by qualities such as unconditional positive regard. These characteristics are highly desirable in a therapeutic relationship, but may leave an examiner insufficiently questioning and ill-prepared for work in a forensic setting. The limitations of clinical judgment have now long been accepted by neuropsychologists and, in turn, stimulated research into malingering and actuarial methods for detecting invalid presentations. However, it remains the case that many, if not most, medical and non-medical professionals still rely on clinical judgment alone when providing medico-legal opinions and they cite their judgment and experience when seeking to refute contrary views or the results of symptom validity tests. Guilmette's (2013) observations relate particularly to neuropsychological experts but, of course, they apply equally to other clinical disciplines and lawyers. In the event that a clinician relies on their clinical judgment or experience alone, it is reasonable for lawyers to enquire whether their ability to detect malingering has been subjected to empirical evaluation, safe in the knowledge that the answer will inevitably be negative.

2. BASE-RATE OF NON-CREDIBLE PRESENTATIONS

7–003 LoCascio (2003) drew attention to the emergence of a disability paradox, namely, that despite an increasingly healthy society and less physically demanding and safer workplaces, there is increasing disability. He pointed out that figures on fraud and financial abuse are difficult to obtain, not least because by their nature malingerers tend to go undetected, but he estimated that about 10% of expenditure in US Health and Disability payments is appropriated by fraud and that malingering represented a substantial proportion of that loss. Kitchen (2003) estimated that £2 billion was lost annually to fraud on welfare benefits in the UK and noted that just under 15% of the Department of Work and Pensions investigatory resources were deployed against health-related benefit fraud at that time. Chafetz and Underhill (2013) estimated that the financial costs of malingered mental disorders in US Social Security Disability payments was in the order of $20.02 billion in 2011 for adult claimants, but suggested that this was a significant underestimate and the true costs were likely to be higher. These conditions included people with intellectual disabilities, mood disorders, organic mental disorders, psychotic disorders, and "other" conditions including mild brain injuries, as well as eating disorders, autistic and developmental disorders and various childhood-adolescent disorders. In the UK the National Fraud Authority (2012) estimated that in 2006 all fraud amounted to £13 billion, rising to £30 billion in 2010, £38 billion in 2011, and £73 billion in 2012. Insurance fraud was estimated at £2.1 billion and benefit fraud was appraised by the Department of Work and Pensions to be around £1.2 billion. The costs of malingering are not confined to financial considerations alone and potentially have important health, social and legal implications. Rohling et al. (2003) suggested that differentiating between malingerers and those with real neurological impairment is essential because inaccurate diagnosis potentially results in compensation that may worsen a person's condition. They argued that the provision of unnecessary or inappropriate healthcare risks causing iatrogenic conditions such as depression and somatisation, and insurance costs may rise due to the unfair distribution of healthcare with less funding being available for legitimate cases. In addition, inappropriate claims may result in lawyers and healthcare professionals, losing credibility by initiating unmerited claims, so bringing the field into disrepute.

A key issue in brain injury litigation is the base rate of invalid presentations and the likelihood of the claimant's credibility being an issue. When considering this issue, however, a difficulty that arises is defining what constitutes an invalid presentation. Greiffenstein et al. (2002) examined the consistency between self-reported and actual educational performance in litigating head injury claimants. Their patient group was divided into a late post-concussion sample that had sustained neck or mild concussive trauma and a moderate-severe closed head injury sample. They found that the post-concussion litigants tended to be biased historians and inflated their previous grades compared with their actual educational records and a similar, but lesser, bias was found in the moderate-severe group. On the other hand, non-litigating, non-compensation seeking patients showed lower rates of bias, although there was no correlation between biased reporting and performance on various indices of malingering. Greiffenstein et al. (2002) concluded that reporting was distorted by the prospect of compensation and the litigants' self-report may be unreliable due to bias shaped by the adversarial context of litigation, rather than by malingering per se. Lees-Haley et al. (1996) examined response bias in litigants (predominantly, but not exclusively brain injuries) and non-litigants who were asked to report the severity of cognitive, emotional and somatic symptoms, both in the past and the present. They found that the litigants rated themselves as having fewer problems in the past than non-litigants and they also viewed their current situation more negatively. Lees-Haley et al. (1996) concluded there was no empirical reason to believe the litigants were healthier and functioned better pre-injury and their hindsight bias was attributed to the legal context. However, they pointed out that this might not necessarily be intentional or purposeful, but rather litigation may guide claimants' recollection of previous functioning and their current status in a way that is consistent with their injury. Lees-Haley et al. (1997) compared a group of claimants undergoing neuropsychological evaluations with non-litigating adults on a symptom questionnaire in which the groups were asked to rate their past and current cognitive (e.g. concentration and memory) and emotional (e.g. depression, anxiety, irritability, self-esteem, fatigue) functioning and other aspects of their life (e.g. life in general, alcohol, drug use, work-school issues, and self-esteem) both currently and in the past. The litigating sample tended to perceive their current functioning as more problematical than the non-litigants and their earlier functioning as having been more satisfactory. Lees-Haley et al. (1997) concluded that response bias should be taken into account by forensic examiners when considering a litigant's report of themselves as the results suggested that they viewed themselves as "hypernormal" pre-accident compared with other individuals. As there is no reason to believe that people who are injured tend to be cognitively and emotionally higher functioning, they concluded that the results indicated that they inflated their self-report. While such biases are potentially self-serving Lees-Haley et al. (1997) suggested that it was unclear that this was intentional and there might be a tendency to recall the past in the context of the present and being dissatisfied with an aspect of their life, such as with their memory, results in seeing the past as having been particularly satisfactory. Inaccurate reporting has been found to extend to issues that are sometimes central in brain injury claims. Mayou et al. (2000) examined a head injury group involved in motor accidents, all of whom had said they had been unconscious following their injuries, but only 15% were found to have been definitely unconscious as indicated by evidence from bystanders and rescuers and 23% had probably been unconscious. For the remainder there was clear evidence that they had not lost consciousness, although some had been confused. On the other hand, only two patients out of 874 who said they had not been unconscious had been observed by others to be unconscious. It was concluded that the patients' report of their unconsciousness was unreliable. Similarly, Sherer et al. (2015) examined the accuracy of self-reported length of coma and post-traumatic amnesia (PTA) in a group with verified traumatic brain injuries and compared their report with the length of coma and PTA duration documented in their medical records. The average discrepancy between the reported and actual durations was substantial, amounting to over a week for the length of coma and 64 days for PTA, with the over-estimations being sufficiently large to change injury severity classification and result in misdiagnosis. Clearly a patient's self-report either about the past, present or their injuries can be significantly and sometimes profoundly inaccurate and clinicians would be unwise to rely primarily on their accounts when formulating an opinion, even though such biases may not necessarily reflect a deliberate intention to mislead.

In a classic and much cited study Mittenberg et al. (2002) surveyed the membership of the American Board of Clinical Neuropsychology to determine the base rate of malingering and symptom exaggeration. They found that probable malingering or symptom exaggeration in litigating cases varied according to diagnosis and was thought to range from 41% in mild head injuries to 34% in pain or somatoform disorders and 9% in moderate or severe head injuries (see Table 1). Sullivan et al. (2005) in Australia estimated the base rate of probable malingering or symptom exaggeration to be 13% in personal injury cases, 13% in disability or workers compensation cases, 17% in criminal cases, and 3% in medical or psychiatric cases. They found that mild head injuries were most likely to be viewed as malingering with a base rate of 23%, followed by pain and somatoform disorders (15%), moderate or severe head injury (15%), fibromyalgia and chronic fatigue (15%), and depressive disorders, neurotoxic disorders, and anxiety disorders each at 11%. In a British study Moss et al. (2003) studied 78 brain injured claimants involved in compensation claims and found that 31% had non-credible presentations. They also found a negative correlation between head injury severity and intellectual and memory functioning in those who passed effort testing, in other words the greater the injury severity, the greater the degree of cognitive impairment. However, this was not found in those who failed effort testing.

Table 1: Base rate of probable malingering or symptom exaggeration in litigating/compensation seeking cases by diagnosis (Mittenberg, Patton, Canyock and Condit, 2002)

Diagnosis	Mean base rate
Mild head injury	41%
Fibromyalgia or chronic fatigue	39%
Pain or somatoform disorders	34%
Neurotoxic disorders	30%
Electrical injury	26%
Depressive disorders	16%
Anxiety disorders	14%
Dissociative disorders	11%
Seizure disorders	9%
Moderate or severe head injury	9%
Vascular dementia	2%

Traumatic brain injuries have been viewed as a "signature injury" in recent US military conflicts following which soldiers and military personnel may potentially be entitled to significant financial benefits. Denning (2015) reviewed

43 studies involving a total of 7,959 military personnel over half of whom had traumatic brain injuries and found the overall failure rate was 29% across all samples. Larrabee (2003) reviewed 11 studies accounting for 1,363 subjects and found that symptom exaggeration in personal injury litigants ranged from 15%–64% and the overall base rate was 40%. Subsequently Larrabee (2012) noted there was a high level of invalid presentations in individuals with external incentives including 54.3% in those undergoing pre-trial pre-sentencing neuropsychological assessments (Ardolf et al., 2007), 57.2% in those claiming toxic injury (Van Hout et al., 2006) and 40% in those claiming exposure to occupational and environmental substances (Greve et al., 2006). Larrabee et al. (2009) proposed a "magic number" of 40% plus or minus 10% as representing the base rate of invalid findings when there are external incentives, a figure that has now been widely accepted as the expected rate of invalid presentations in brain injured claimants. Rogers (2008) pointed out that it is unlikely that malingering has stable base rates and variations may occur depending on the referral question and individual circumstances. Green and Merten (2013) said that although it is widely assumed that exaggeration of existing complaints is more common than deliberate malingering, there is no way of calculating the proportion of pure malingering. Likewise Bass and Halligan (2014) commented that malingering, and factitious disorders, are not clinical entities, but rather fluctuating behaviours and responses shaped by cost-benefit influences. These factors doubtless account for the variable estimates of invalidity in personal injury samples, but given that 30–50% of claimants may have invalid presentations, the likelihood of concerns about the genuineness of a claimant's presentation arising is significant.

3. DEFINITIONS OF MALINGERING

7–005 The various versions of the Diagnostic and Statistical Manual of Mental Disorders (DSM) have maintained essentially the same definition of malingering throughout with the most recent edition, DSM-5 (American Psychiatric Association, 2013), again defining malingering as involving the intentional production of false or grossly exaggerated physical or psychological symptoms that are motivated by an external incentive such as avoiding military duty or work and obtaining financial compensation or some other gain. As malingering is not considered to be a mental illness, and in some circumstances may be adaptive, such as when individuals feign illness in wartime captivity, DSM-5 does not provide diagnostic criteria as such, but it is recommended that it should be strongly suspected when there is any combination of the following:

(1) Medico-legal context: where the individual is referred by a lawyer for examination or they are involved in litigation or criminal charges are pending.
(2) There is a marked discrepancy between the individual's claimed stress or disability and objective findings and observations.
(3) There is a lack of cooperation during the diagnostic evaluation and compliance with prescribed treatment.

DEFINITIONS OF MALINGERING

(4) The patient presents with an antisocial personality disorder.

Young (2014) pointed out, however, that the guidelines inappropriately label all claimants as potential malingerers and discrepancies or a lack of cooperation may simply reflect the confrontational nature of examinations. In addition, malingering is not necessarily associated with having antisocial characteristics and Niesten et al. (2015) found that individuals with an antisocial personality disorder do not necessarily fake bad on cognitive testing and many accurately present their symptoms. In the earlier criteria outlined in DSM-IV-TR (American Psychiatric Association, 2000) the clinician was required to determine whether symptoms were intentionally produced or not with disorders such as somatisation disorder, undifferentiated somatoform disorder, conversion disorder and pain disorder all being considered to be unintentional, in contrast to malingering which was viewed as intentional. In the case of factitious disorder, the individual was viewed as intentionally producing symptoms, but for an internal goal such as assuming a sick role, rather than for external goals, such as economic gain or avoiding legal responsibilities. However, this approach has been criticised as there are no criteria for satisfactorily distinguishing between intentional and unintentional symptom production or ascertaining whether it is for an internal or external gain (Hamilton et al., 2008; Scott, 2015). In addition, individuals may have both conscious and unconscious motives that shape their behaviour and, for example, they may simultaneously seek attention and support through illness behaviour while also being motivated to obtain monetary compensation and such motives are not mutually exclusive. In DSM-5 (American Psychiatric Association, 2013) somatoform disorders have been replaced by a new category of "Somatic Symptom and Related Disorders" in which clinicians are not required to determine whether the individual's motivation is conscious or unconscious. The category includes somatic symptom disorder, illness anxiety disorder, conversion disorder (functional neurological symptom disorder) and psychological factors affecting other medical conditions, as well as factitious disorder. Malingering is still thought to involve the intentional production of symptoms for external gain, whereas factitious disorder requires deceptive behaviour in the absence of external rewards. The DSM-5 guidelines suggest that the assessment of conscious intention is unreliable, although factitious disorder is nevertheless thought to be indicated when there is definite evidence of feigning and the individual's apparent aim is to assume a sick role, whereas malingering is inferred if the aim is to obtain an incentive such as money.

Resnick et al., (2008) proposed that malingering can be categorised into three types, pure malingering, partial malingering and false imputation. Pure malingering is when an individual feigns a disorder that they do not have, whereas partial malingering is when the individual has symptoms, but consciously exaggerates them. False imputation is when a claimant deliberately attributes their symptoms from an unrelated cause to the index injury. Resnick et al. (2008) noted that false imputation is particularly difficult to identify because the individual can accurately describe complaints and some individuals also have difficulty recognising causal relationships and so their misattribution may not be deliberate. They suggested that pure malingering is probably the least common and partial malingering is the most frequent. Hall et al., (2007) described a

7–006

number of faking bad response styles that claimants may adopt ranging from claiming difficulties that do not exist, exaggerating real difficulties arising from the injury or denying that they have retained abilities or attributing problems from one cause (such as long-standing learning difficulties) to the index event. These strategies and examples are listed in Table 2. Any one may be observed at some time in a legal assessment, although their significance will depend on the extent to which they distort the assessment. They may also adopt strategies to invalidate the assessment, for example, by arriving late, failing to attend appointments or shortening the assessment by claiming fatigue. Iverson (2006) made a distinction between poor effort, exaggeration and malingering. He proposed that poor effort is used to describe when claimants under-perform on neuropsychological testing whereas exaggeration is used when they over-report complaints on questionnaires with malingering referring to deliberate exaggeration or under-performance to influence the outcome of the litigation. He pointed out that the distinction between exaggeration and poor effort is often blurred and they are not synonymous, although there is a conceptual overlap as illustrated in Figure 3. He suggested that exaggeration and poor effort, either on their own or in combination, may occur without malingering, for example, in an individual with a factitious disorder who exaggerates and under-performs on testing not for external gain, but to assume a sick role. Similarly, poor effort may occur in the absence of malingering and exaggeration when a person is uncooperative because they do not want to undergo an assessment and so do not engage.

Table 2: Faking bad response styles (adapted from Hall, Thompson and Poirier, 2007).

Style	Behavioural Strategy
1. Verbal fabrication	Claiming a non-existent problem ("I have ringing in my ear")
2. Verbal exaggeration	Amplifying real problem ("I'm more forgetful than usual")
3. Verbal denial	Disclaiming an ability ("I can't smell anything")
4. Verbal minimising	Downplaying an ability ("I can walk only one block")
5. Misattribution	Stating deficit due to false cause rather than the true aetiology
6. Behavioural fractionalising	Shows crudely estimated fraction of ability
7. Behavioural approximating	Gets a close, but not exact answer
8. Behavioural infrequency	Sprinkles errors throughout performance on graduated scale
9. Behavioural disengagement	Shows confusion and frustration, may give up
10. Impulsivity	Answers quickly, presents first thing on mind
11. Perseveration	Persists with one response mode, regardless of feedback
12. Randomising	No consistent pattern of errors

DEFINITIONS OF MALINGERING

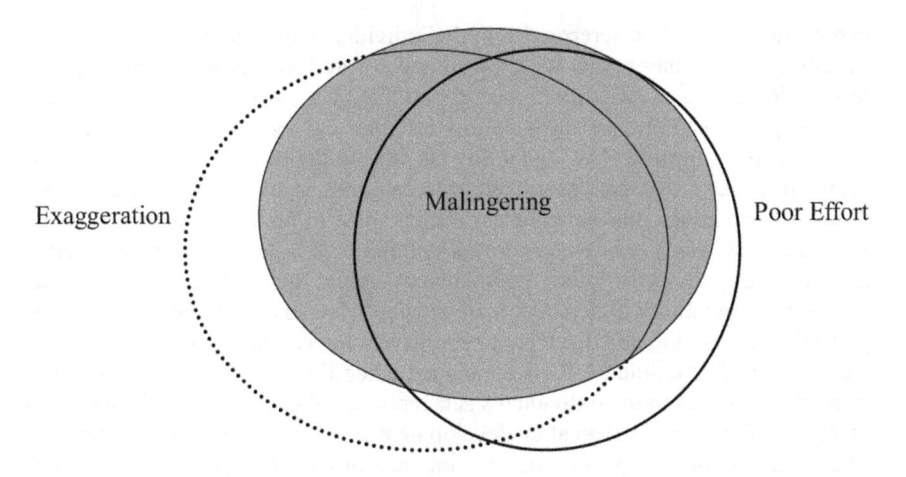

Figure 3: Iverson's (2006) schematic model outlining the overlap between exaggeration, poor effort, and malingering (shaded are represents malingering, the dotted circle exaggeration, and the solid circle poor effort)

Slick et al., (1999) proposed formal criteria for what they termed malingering of neurocognitive dysfunction (MND) which they defined as "the volitional exaggeration or fabrication of cognitive dysfunction for the purpose of obtaining substantial material gain, or avoiding or escaping formal duty or responsibility". Substantial material gain is considered to include money, goods or services, such as financial compensation following a personal injury. They pointed out that no diagnosis can be made with absolute confidence and so they outlined a diagnostic system incorporating different levels of probability, ranging from *definite* malingering to *probable* and *possible* malingering, with criteria for each level of probability (see Panel). Definite malingering is present when there is "clear and compelling evidence of volitional exaggeration or fabrication" and no alternative explanation can satisfactorily account for the findings. An essential requirement for all levels of probability is that there is a significant incentive, such as the individual being involved in a claim or pursuing some other external gain, such as avoiding criminal responsibility. In addition, the criteria require that the person shows definite evidence of response bias, which might be shown by the claimant's performance on a memory test falling significantly below chance. Such a finding is so severe that it is inconsistent with a real amnesic disorder and has been called "the smoking gun of intent" (Pankratz and Erickson, 1990). In addition, the criteria require that the claimant's behaviour cannot be fully explained or accounted for by a concomitant psychiatric or neurological condition or some developmental disorder. This is significant in stipulating that these other conditions should *fully* account for the individual's behaviour and implicitly acknowledges that an individual may also have a genuine condition but nevertheless show malingering. For example, a person who has had a mild brain injury confirmed by the medical records and who also shows definite response bias and who is depressed due to family issues and being unemployed, may nevertheless meet the criteria for Definite MND if the coexisting depression does not completely account for their behaviour which, in many, or even most, instances will not be the case. Probable malingering is indicated when there are

7–007

two or more types of discrepancies in the individual's presentation; for example, cognitive testing may reveal widespread and severe limitations, but the medical records indicate that only a whiplash-type injury was sustained or the claimant showed poor performance on an effort test that can be passed by those with severe brain injuries. The reliability in the individual's account of their complaints may also be considered; for example, a claimant who describes disabling limitations, but nevertheless spends most of their time unaccompanied and copes satisfactorily or who endorses symptoms on a questionnaire to a degree far exceeding those of other complainants might be viewed as unreliable. However, unreliability of self-report alone is not viewed as sufficient to conclude probable malingering and discrepant neuropsychological data is also required. On the other hand, Possible MND is concluded when the evidence comes primarily from discrepancies in the individual's self-report or, alternatively, the influence of other psychiatric, neurological or developmental conditions cannot be excluded. This reflects the emphasis placed on neuropsychological test data with discrepancies in self-report being assigned as having the weakest level of probability.

4. PANEL: DIAGNOSTIC CATEGORIES AND CRITERIA FOR MALINGERING OF NEUROCOGNITIVE DYSFUNCTION (MND; SLICK ET AL., 1999)

7–008

Definite MND
Definite MND is indicated by clear and compelling evidence of volitional exaggeration or fabrication of cognitive dysfunction and the absence of plausible alternative explanations. The specific diagnostic criteria are:
1. Presence of a substantial external incentive [Criterion A]
2. Definite negative response bias [Criterion B1]
3. Behaviours meeting necessary criteria from group B are not fully accounted for by psychiatric, neurological or developmental factors [Criterion D]

Probable MND
Probable MND is indicated by evidence strongly suggesting volitional exaggeration or fabrication of cognitive dysfunction and the absence of plausible alternative explanations. The specific diagnostic criteria necessary for Probable MND are:
1. Presence of a substantial external incentive [Criterion A]
2. Two or more types of evidence from neuropsychological testing, excluding definite negative response bias (two or more of criteria B2–B6), or, one type of evidence from neuropsychological testing, excluding definite negative response bias, and one or more types of evidence from self-report (one of criteria B2–B6 and one or more of criteria C1–C5)
3. Behaviours meeting necessary criteria for groups B and C are not fully accounted for by psychiatric, neurological, or developmental factors [Criterion D]

Possible MND
This is indicated by the presence of evidence suggesting volitional exaggeration or fabrication of cognitive dysfunction and the absence of plausible alternative explanations. Alternatively, Possible MND is indicated by the presence of criteria

necessary for Definite or Probable MND except that other primary aetiologies cannot be ruled out. The specific diagnostic criteria are:
1. Presence of a substantial external incentive [Criterion A]
2. Evidence from self-report [one or more of criteria C1–C5]
3. Behaviours meeting necessary criteria from group C are not fully accounted for by psychiatric, neurological, or developmental factors [Criterion D], or, criteria for Definite or Probable MND are met except for Criterion D (i.e. primary psychiatric, neurological, or developmental aetiologies cannot be ruled out)

Explanation of Criteria
Criteria A: Presence of a substantial external incentive: At least one clearly identifiable and substantial external incentive for exaggeration or fabrication of symptoms is present at the time of the examination (such as a personal injury settlement, disability pension, evasion from criminal prosecution, or release from military service).

Criteria B: Evidence from neuropsychological testing: As demonstrated by at least one of the following:
1. Definite negative response bias (e.g. when performance on cognitive testing falls significantly below chance).
2. Probable response bias. Performance on one or more well-validated psychometric tests or indices designed to measure exaggeration or fabrication of cognitive deficits which is consistent with feigning.
3. Discrepancy between test data and known patterns of brain functioning.
4. Discrepancy between test data and observed behaviour.
5. Discrepancy between test data and reliable collateral reports.
6. Discrepancy between test data and documented background history.

Criteria C: Evidence from self-report: These criteria involve significant inconsistencies or discrepancies in the patient's self-reported symptoms that suggest a deliberate attempt to exaggerate or fabricate cognitive deficits:
1. Self-reported history is discrepant with documented history.
2. Self-reported symptoms are discrepant with known patterns of brain functioning.
3. Self-reported symptoms are discrepant with behavioural observations.
4. Self-reported symptoms are discrepant with information obtained from collateral informants.
5. Evidence of exaggerated or fabricated psychological dysfunction (e.g. on well validated validity scales such as the MMPI-2-RF).

Criteria D: Behaviours meeting necessary criteria from groups B or C are not fully accounted for by psychiatric, neurological or developmental factors: Behaviours meeting the criteria from groups B and C are the product of an informed, rational, and volitional effort aimed at least in part towards acquiring or achieving external incentives as defined in Criteria A. As such, behaviours meeting criteria from groups B or C cannot be fully accounted for by psychiatric, developmental or neurological disorders that result in significantly diminished capacity to appreciate laws or mores against malingering."

The Slick criteria, as they have become known, have been widely adopted in research settings as a key standard for defining malingering and they have also been modified for use in other areas such as the assessment of malingered pain disability (Bianchini et al., 2005a). More recently Slick and Sherman (2012; 2013) suggested that they be adjusted to place greater weight on compelling inconsistencies in the way individuals report their symptoms and when their complaints are incompatible with or directly contradicted by their behaviour or performance on testing. For example, a litigating patient who says that they can no longer read since a brain injury, but who is later observed reading would, in the absence of a satisfactory explanation, be considered to show definite malingering because of the direct contradiction between their report and their observed abilities. In addition, Slick and Sherman (2013) proposed that failure on multiple validity measures should be considered to be diagnostically equivalent to performance falling below chance and therefore viewed as indicating feigning. They suggested there may also be occasions when a person exaggerates symptoms of a brain injury to receive a substantial financial award, but do so because of impaired judgment or reasoning from a severe brain injury. In these circumstances they proposed a diagnosis of "secondary malingering", that is, malingering secondary to the brain injury. They pointed out that symptom exaggeration and fabrication may coexist with genuine neuropsychological problems, and established brain trauma and malingering are not mutually exclusive. Therefore, when there is compelling evidence of malingering they recommended that the clinician still consider and, where possible, estimate the extent of the patient's real deficits.

5. LITIGATION AND ITS EFFECTS

7–009 A key issue is the impact of litigation on claimants' presentations. Binder and Rohling (1996) conducted an analysis of research examining the influence of financial incentives on maintaining disability after brain injury. Their investigation covered data from 2,353 brain injured subjects and they found that litigation had a significant influence on patients' complaints, particularly in the case of mild head injuries. They reported that if compensation was removed as a factor, there would be a 23% reduction in abnormal findings and complaints. Carroll et al. (2004) reviewed the factors determining the maintenance of complaints after mild brain injury and found only compensation claims were a factor and there was little support for other factors. The factors implicated in non-genuine presentation, however, can be multifaceted. In some, conscious processes may be the starting point which over time gradually metamorphoses into less conscious processes and move subtly from other-deception to self-deception. Merckelbach and Merten (2012) proposed that some may initially consciously feign complaints, but the discrepancy between their behaviour and their beliefs and views of themselves as honest and trustworthy, may set up an uncomfortable state of cognitive dissonance which is resolved by changing their beliefs and believing that they do suffer from the claimed symptoms. Repeat examinations and diagnostic tests with professionals have the potential to reinforce and consolidate the self-deception, so entrenching complaints that the individual then believes are real. Merckelbach et al. (2011) suggested that the distinction between consciously and non-consciously creating complaints may not be clearly demarcated. They asked normal participants to exaggerate in an experiment in which they were asked to credibly feign symptoms on a symptom scale as though they were a defendant in a criminal case. Subsequently they were given the symptom list again, and instructed to respond honestly and they found that those who were asked to malinger continued to report more cognitive and psychiatric symptoms than a non-malingering group. Merckelbach et al. (2011) suggested that intentional faking may develop into a less conscious form of exaggeration and some forget the feigned origins of their complaints and so the distinction between conscious and non-consciously created symptoms may lie on a continuum, rather than being strictly demarcated. Boone (2017) has proposed that malingering and somatoform conditions, rather than being discrete conditions, may lie on a dimension ranging from "other deception" at one end, involving malingering, to "self-deception" at the other, indicated by somatoform conditions, and where an individual lies may not be fixed.

Claimants may be motivated by perceived injustice, anger, or a desire for retribution or because of pre-existing life dissatisfactions or stresses that are resolved through illness and a claim. Misdiagnosis and labelling an individual as brain injured may also establish a disability and sickness role and a wish for compensation and so involve a complex interaction between iatrogenic and conscious processes. The legal claim itself may reinforce invalidism and illness behaviour through the provision of care, support and rehabilitation which, in some cases, continues for unduly long periods during which professionals inadvertently reinforce disability and even treat a condition that does not exist and stressful litigation can cause critogenic, that is, lawyer-induced, harm. Rehabilitation in brain injury claims can be driven as much, and sometimes more, by the wishes of the lawyers than by the clinicians, with lawyers commissioning services, requesting records, updates, reports and witness statements from the rehabilitation professionals, and even attending clinical team meetings, so blurring the boundaries between the legal and clinical domains. Gutheil et al. (2000) proposed that litigation can have both critogenic benefits and harms. The benefits include feeling empowered and being heard, acting as a witness and making those responsible aware of the harm that they have done and prevailing over a denial of injury. Some may be motivated and feel vindicated by righting a perceived wrong. However, they suggested there may also be significant harm due to the stress of becoming involved in a drawn-out process with the denials, counter-assertions and frustrations that are inevitably associated with adversarial proceedings. Repeat examinations and responding to legal enquiries and requests can cause re-traumatisation and hold back recovery and the disclosure of personal information and violation of privacy through document review and examinations or a public trial may further aggravate matters. Gutheil et al. (2000) suggested that while many, if not most, life situations involve complex, ambiguous emotions, litigation potentially drives the claimant to perceive their situation in artificially dichotomous terms with the other party viewed as being entirely bad. Such a situation potentially encourages victimhood and a failure to cope appropriately and maturely with their circumstances.

Grant et al. (2014) studied 1,010 patients (excluding moderate and severe brain injuries) who had been admitted to trauma centres and become involved in litigation. They found 34% reported high levels of stress about understanding what they were required to do for the claim, and 27% were stressed with the number of medical assessments, and 30% with delays in the claim, and 26% with the amount of compensation they were awarded. Gabbe et al. (2015) examined the issue of fault (i.e. blame) on the outcomes of 2,605 orthopaedic trauma patients from motor accidents and found those who were not at fault (according to the police and patient) were at greater risk of having a worse return to work and health status outcome, than those for whom the fault was ascribed to the patient or their vehicle. Those who considered the other party at fault, even when that was contradicted by the police, also had worse outcomes. Strasburger (1999) argued that ironically the process by which claimants seek redress may itself cause injury and claimants may be referred for treatment by lawyers with a litigation agenda aimed at enhancing the case, rather than helping the claimant to improve, and therapists may be pressured to support the case and therapy time used by the claimant to promote their cause. However, litigation is not always associated with harmful influences. Wood and Rutterford (2006) noted that while the majority of studies suggest that litigants have more and longer lasting symptoms, greater distress and take longer to return to work, they found no differences between severe head injury litigants and non-litigants either on cognitive tests or self-ratings of their mood. On the other hand, Matsuzawa and Dijkers (2014) suggested that litigation can have a stagnating effect on brain injured claimants, holding them back from progressing due to the time-consuming nature of the claim and becoming consumed by developments in the proceedings. They suggested recovery may be prolonged as litigants aim to prove they were affected, particularly when it is thought they were feigning or not injured or as severely injured as claimed, and they then feel they have to demonstrate that something is wrong. Weissman (1990) suggested there may be an interaction between the effects of the original injury and the stress of the adversarial proceedings, which may interact with certain personality styles. The result may be amplified complaints or the inaccurate attribution and false imputation of symptoms and a need for justice, revenge or vindication, which may intensify anger and resentment, so making false or exaggerated complaints of symptoms more likely. Rogers and Payne (2006) pointed out that sustained investigation of an individual's complaints may inevitably be construed as questioning their credibility and the client may then respond with anger and aim to prove their impairments by emphasising or exaggerating their difficulties.

6. ASSESSMENT OF NON-CREDIBLE PRESENTATIONS

7–010   That clinical judgment alone is insufficient to determine the veracity of claimants' complaints has long been accepted by neuropsychologists and led to the development of specialised measures of response credibility and there is now a wide range of such measures available. In broad terms, they are one of two types, those that assess effort or under-performance on cognitive testing, and those that assess exaggeration or over-reporting of complaints on questionnaires. Effort tests, or as they have more recently been termed performance validity tests (PVTs), are perhaps the best known, and can be further divided into stand-alone and embedded measures of effort. Stand-alone PVT measures have been specifically designed to assess effort during neuropsychological examinations and some of the more widely known are the Test of Memory Malingering (TOMM, Tombaugh, 1996) and the Word Memory Test (Green, 2005). On the other hand, embedded measures are built into the conventional tests that neuropsychologists use and have a dual role, both to assess a particular cognitive function, but also to assess effort during the examination. Embedded measures are therefore potentially more time-efficient, although many examiners use both kinds of PVT. Effort tests assess under-performance, that is, whether there is a lack of appropriate engagement which may result in poor results that do not accurately reflect the claimant's abilities, whereas the quantitative assessment of exaggeration relies primarily on questionnaires. There is a plethora of questionnaires available that assess a wide range of difficulties relating to a claimant's mood, psychopathology, pain, and somatic complaints, although the majority are not suitable for medico-legal evaluations as they do not include checks on response validity. However, measures are available that have well developed validity scales such as the Minnesota Multiphasic Personality Inventory-2 (MMPI-2) (Butcher et al., 2001), Minnesota Multiphasic Personality Inventory-2-Restructured Form (MMPI-2-RF) (Ben-Porath and Tellegen, 2008), and the Personality Assessment Inventory (PAI) (Morey, 1991). These instruments are now termed symptom validity tests (SVTs) and include scales to detect claimants' tendencies to endorse, or over-report (i.e. exaggerate), complaints and difficulties to a greater degree than other individuals. Under-performance and over-reporting are potentially two aspects of invalid responding that may, although not necessarily, occur together and arguably both require careful assessment. However, it is fair to say that while PVTs are increasingly employed by UK neuropsychologists, although not universally (McCarter et al., 2009), the use of SVTs has tended to lag behind, which in turn necessarily has significant implications for the weight that can be attached to the resulting opinions.

7. PERFORMANCE VALIDITY ASSESSMENT

There are numerous effort tests or PVTs available to the clinician, although despite the variety, they are similar inasmuch as they typically involve tasks that appear to be taxing and often feel difficult to the examinee, but in practice they are cognitively undemanding, such that even those with severe injuries have little difficulty completing them and the performance of people with severe brain injuries do not differ, or differ non-significantly, from those who are neurologically intact. Poor effort is then indicated when the individual's performance falls below expectations set from normative data. Carone et al., (2013) assessed two patients who had undergone surgical resections in the left anterior temporal region of their brains to treat chronic epilepsy and they had also had suffered post-operative strokes. Although they underwent removal of the left anterior hippocampus and the parahippocampal gyrus and had substantial memory difficulties, they were nevertheless capable of passing PVT testing. Similarly, Goodrich-Hunsaker and Hopkins (2009) found patients with bilateral hippocampal atrophy were able to pass effort measures. Carone (2013) reported the case of a nine-year-old girl, CJ, who had severe congenital bilateral brain damage, chronic epilepsy, cognitive impairments with an IQ exceeded by over 99% of her peers, as well as developmental and adaptive difficulties, and she was also treated with high-dose benzodiazepines. CJ's MRI scan at the age of one

7–011

year is shown on the right in Figure 4 and illustrates the severe bilateral volume loss affecting her brain. On the left is a normal comparison scan. Despite her multiple difficulties CJ was nevertheless able to pass two effort tests (Word Memory Test and Medical Symptom Validity Test). Green and Flaro (2015) found no significant differences on the same tests between adults with intellectual deficits (i.e. IQ <70) and those with higher intellectual abilities (i.e. IQ ≥70). On the other hand, they found that parents seeking custody of their children (a group motivated to do well to have custody of their children) and who had to undergo a neuropsychological assessment, performed significantly better on the same measures than adults claiming disability benefits, financial support or compensation and who potentially had an incentive to appear impaired. Green and Flaro (2016) reported similar findings in the case of children with intellectual disabilities. Green and Flaro (2015) proposed that in the event those with less significant disabilities (such as those with a mild brain injury) fail such tests, this is evidently contrary to expectation and denotes poor effort. With the exception of dementia, validity tests such as the TOMM have been found to be largely unaffected by a range of conditions including learning disability (Simon, 2007), depression (Ashendorf et al., 2004; Rees et al., 2001), pain and chronic depression (Etherton et al., 2005; Iverson et al., 2007), schizophrenia and psychotic disorders (Duncan, 2005). In short, if a measure is sufficiently undemanding that even children with a learning disability or those with other disabling conditions can complete it and produce results comparable to normal individuals, then failure cannot be attributed to these factors and indicates suboptimal engagement.

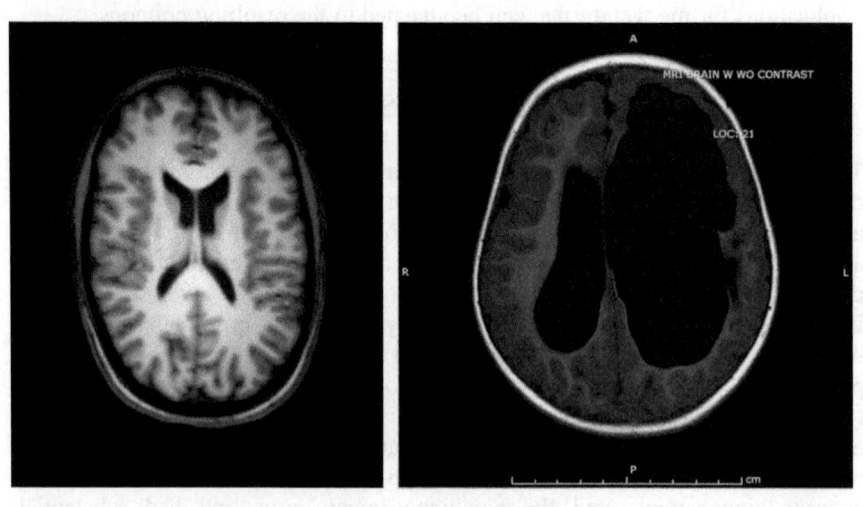

Figure 4: CJ's brain MRI (on right) at one year of age showing bilateral volume loss (from Carone, 2013). This image shows marked expansion of the ventricles, particularly in the left frontal lobe, and generalised loss of white matter around the ventricles. As a comparison, the figure on left is from a normal scan in a child of the same age and shows normal white matter thickness and ventricular size.

An important issue is the degree to which a PVT is sensitive to suboptimal effort (test sensitivity) while also avoiding misclassifying individuals as having poor effort when that is not the case (test specificity). As a rule, the more sensitive a measure is to a condition, the greater the likelihood of making a false-positive error, that is, concluding a person has the condition when they do not. On the other hand, the more conservative a measure becomes, then the risk is that it also becomes less sensitive to detecting the condition (false negative error). This is an important consideration because clinicians may differ in the PVT's they use in forensic assessments, with some measures being less sensitive to suboptimal effort and therefore erring towards suggesting effort was optimal, whereas other tests may be more sensitive, but also risk erroneously suggesting effort was suboptimal. These differences sometimes explain the differing conclusions of opposing experts. For example, one widely used PVT is the Rey 15 item test (FIT) (Rey, 1964), which has been found to be used by 24% of UK clinicians in forensic assessments (McCarter et al., 2009). In common with other effort tests the claimant completes a simple task and suboptimal effort is inferred when low scores are obtained. However, despite its popularity the FIT has long been found to lack satisfactory validity due to its insensitivity to malingered cognitive deficits and it has been argued that it is not suitable for forensic practice (Vallabhajosula and van Gorp, 2001; Guilmette et al., 2007; Flaherty et al., 2015). In the event that one clinician uses the FIT and another uses a more appropriate and sensitive measure, then quite different conclusions are likely to be drawn. Gervais et al. (2004) compared the sensitivity of three PVTs in a sample of disability and personal injury claimants and found 32% failed a verbal PVT (Word Memory Test), 17% failed a digit PVT (Computerised Assessment of Response Bias), and 11% failed a visual task (TOMM), with the differences indicating that quite different conclusions would likely be drawn depending on the measure employed. Iverson (2006) highlighted that the use of different tests depending on the side that retains the clinician raises ethical issues and, for example, employing the FIT in claimant cases and so reducing the likelihood of detecting poor effort, and using more sensitive measures in defence cases, would have the opposite bias. In short, not all PVTs are equally good at detecting suboptimal effort, with differences in their sensitivity and specificity leading to different conclusions.

Even when satisfactory PVTs are employed, it is not unusual for clinicians to differ, sometimes quite dramatically, in the way they interpret their findings and the conclusions they draw. On some occasions clinicians may inadvertently advance erroneous views and some of the more common pitfalls and problems are outlined below.

State full effort was applied

When an examinee passes a PVT clinicians may conclude they showed "full effort" during the examination and that the claimant's cognitive profile is therefore valid. However, as PVTs are typically easy to pass even by those who have had severe injuries or other disabling conditions, it is not appropriate to conclude full effort was deployed and indeed only a modicum of effort may have been engaged to produce a satisfactory result. Unfortunately, when a claimant passes effort testing, some clinicians are lulled into a false state of reassurance and may conclude effort was maximal and ignore or overlook other implausible findings and observations that clearly indicate that effort was not optimal.

7–012

Over-state good effort

7–013   An allied problem occurs when an examinee passes a well-regarded and validated PVT. In these circumstances the clinician may again be tempted to conclude effort was good and therefore the claimant's results are valid. This is commonly observed when a clinician uses a satisfactory PVT, but does not continue to sample effort. Slick and Sherman (2013) noted that complete compliance and credibility across an entire assessment cannot be inferred from effort testing alone as claimants may produce normal PVT scores, while suppressing their performance on other tests administered during the same assessment. In short, effort is not necessarily constant throughout an examination, but a dynamic process that can potentially fluctuate from time to time. Consequently a PVT pass only indicates that effort was satisfactory at the time in the examination that the PVT was administered. Relatively few clinicians assess effort throughout their examinations, although they often last several hours during which an individual's engagement may fluctuate for benign or intentional reasons. Reliance on one PVT, no matter how well validated, exposes the clinician to erroneous conclusions and so effort should be regularly assessed throughout using a combination of stand-alone and embedded indices.

Ignore the performance validity test

7–014   Some experts when faced with PVT data indicating suboptimal engagement may acknowledge the finding, but nevertheless skate over it and go on to interpret the neuropsychological data as though the results were still valid. Experts may engage in all manner of intellectual gymnastics to justify such an approach, for example, stating that other sources of information, such as witness statements or other experts or therapists, have not suggested effort is an issue, despite such sources invariably not being amenable to the kind of verification provided by a PVT. Some slip into emphasising their personal judgment despite the known limitations of such an approach, or they emphasise correct, but irrelevant observations, such as the patient having known brain damage on neuroimaging. The range of justifications is limited only by the inventiveness of the clinician, but regrettably the only sensible response to PVT failure is to conclude that the claimant did not engage appropriately, which in turn calls into question the validity of any abnormal findings.

Ignore other performance validity test results

7–015   A not uncommon observation is to find that a claimant passes PVT testing on one occasion when assessed by one expert, but fails when seen by another. In these circumstances, clinicians may resist information contradictory to their conclusions and be only willing to consider their own results, rather than utilise all the available data. A claimant expert may assert that they found no evidence of motivational factors and sidestep later contradictory additional information and so fail to form a more nuanced and comprehensive opinion. Similarly, a defence expert may conclude that motivational factors coloured the case and not properly consider other data that may be valid.

Performance validity test failure coexisting with genuine deficits

Some clinicians, and lawyers, are reluctant to agree poor effort has been found due to their anxiety that genuine deficits are then discredited and the claim is under-valued. However, PVT failure does not mean that the individual does not have genuine deficits and suboptimal effort can potentially coexist with genuine disability. People with established brain injuries are capable of having aspirations and developing motivations and in some cases they may include attempts to maximise financial compensation for perceived wrongs. Alternatively, poor effort may reflect a long-standing disinterest in assessments, a failure to appreciate the relevance of the examination or motivational characteristics unrelated to or predating the injury. Malingering may also be secondary to poor judgment arising from the brain injury (Slick and Sherman, 2013). PVT failure does not negate the fact that the individual has impairments, but nevertheless makes it difficult and sometimes impossible for the assessor to delineate their extent and severity.

7–016

Performance validity test and malingering

Clinicians and lawyers may resist evidence of poor effort as they view it as synonymous with a claim of malingering. However, PVT data indicate whether or not the individual engaged appropriately during the examination, but do not identify the *intention* of the examinee. PVT results represent one source of information to be included with other data including neuropsychological results, self-report, documentary evidence, and other information such as video evidence, that allow the clinician to determine the likelihood of malingering, rather than the determination being based on PVT results alone.

7–017

Schroeder et al. (2016) surveyed a group of neuropsychologists who were experts in the field of symptom validity assessment (as defined by their research activity and publications) and asked them to rate the most likely causes of invalidity in both forensic (e.g. medico-legal) and routine clinical settings. In forensic settings the most commonly-cited reason was malingering and in clinical settings, somatoform or conversion disorders were thought to be the most likely. In both, malingering, somatoform/conversion disorders, and attitude towards testing, were viewed as the top three causes of invalidity. They found that 90% of the experts often, or always, used both embedded and stand-alone validity measures, although they placed greater weight on stand-alone instruments, with the majority often or always concluding that an assessment was invalid when stand-alone measures were failed and embedded measures were passed, whereas only a minority thought the opposite. This preference likely reflects that stand-alone measures tend to be more sensitive to suboptimal engagement and embedded measures are more conservative. In addition, the experts reported that they relied primarily on validity testing in preference to their own clinical impressions and they disregarded their own impressions in favour of validity tests when the two were discrepant, an approach that Schroeder et al. (2016) noted was consistent with the known limitations of clinical judgment.

8. SYMPTOM VALIDITY ASSESSMENT

7–018 As well as cognitive issues, brain injured claimants typically report a range of psychopathology and personality complaints such as problems with fatigue, irritability, low mood or loss of confidence, as well as somatic and behavioural issues (Ponsford, 2014; Onsworth and Fleming, 2014; Scott and Schoenberg, 2011). These problems are usually documented during the course of an interview and not uncommonly the claimant is also asked to fill out a questionnaire or read a checklist of symptoms and indicate which complaints they have. Questionnaires have many advantages as they potentially allow the clinician to gather information across a range of areas quickly and efficiently and at relatively little cost, both financial and in time. In addition, they are uncomplicated to score and normally there are (or should be) normative data against which to assess whether the claimant's responses are within a normal range for people of the same age or gender, or some other relevant factor, and elevated scores may indicate areas of difficulty. As the format and questions do not change, they can also be used to check progress over time to ascertain whether the issues assessed are improving, static or deteriorating and in routine clinical practice one of their primary uses is to indicate whether a person is benefiting from treatment or rehabilitation, and they are widely used in clinical trials to assess treatment efficacy. There are a wide range of measures available such as the Hospital Anxiety and Depression Scale (HADS) (Zigmond and Snaith, 1983), Beck Depression Inventory (BDI) (Beck, 1987), Beck Anxiety Inventory (BAI) (Beck and Steer, 1993) and Rivermead Post-Concussion Symptoms Questionnaire (King et al., 1995) to name but a few. Typically they consist of a list of statements or questions that the claimant reads and then indicates the degree to which they agree or have the problem. A numerical score is attached to the rating and the results may be interpreted as supporting or corroborating their complaints with apparent consistency suggested as verifying their self-report. This approach implicitly acknowledges that interview data are inherently dependent on the veracity of the claimant and seeks to minimise the appearance of potential unreliability by using a quantitative measure. However, the limitation of this approach is that although a plethora of measures are available the majority are unsuitable for legal use as their purpose is invariably transparent to the claimant and therefore the results can be easily manipulated. For example, it is unsurprising if a claimant who reports at interview that they are prone to irritability and low mood after an accident, then endorses items relating to irritation and depression when presented with a questionnaire. Nevertheless, some experts will cite the results as being "consistent with" or corroborating the claimant's account and some even prefer such data to more objective sources of evidence. For example, when a cognitive assessment indicates normal performance on tests of executive function, the results may be dismissed as not indicating the true extent or nature of an individual's difficulties in preference to the claimant's self-assessment of their executive skills on a questionnaire and the expert may claim the self-ratings are more valid and accurate and corroborate the claimant's account.

Self-report measures necessarily assume that the claimant is able to comment on the area or characteristics assessed by the questionnaire and that they can do so accurately, whereas that may not be the case. Some people are inclined to give a favourable account of themselves either because they lack insight into aspects of their personality and their limitations or because of a long-standing predisposition towards self-deception and self-enhancement. Others may provide acquiescent responses and agree with whatever complaint or symptom is put to them, or alternatively, have the opposite bias (yea-sayers and nay-sayers). Those with brain injuries may have difficulty understanding questions and statements or fail to sustain their attention sufficiently to complete the measure appropriately or provide ill-considered or contradictory responses. Unless a measure has some way of detecting these issues, it will necessarily be unclear whether elevated or low scores reflect these factors, rather than providing an accurate account of the individual's situation. Unfortunately, the majority of questionnaires or scales used in legal settings do not include validity scales to assess whether the claimant has completed the measure in a consistent manner and whether they have over- or under-reported their complaints and difficulties.

Although questionnaires with well-designed validity scales are available, in the UK they have been curiously underused, with only a minority of practitioners employing them in legal settings in contrast to North America where their use is widespread (McCarter et al., 2009). Measures that have satisfactory, or even excellent, validity measures include the MMPI-2 (Butcher et al., 2001) and the PAI (Morey, 1991), as well as instruments specifically designed to assess response validity, such as the Structured Inventory of Malingered Symptoms (SIMS) (Smith and Burger, 1997). Failure to use an appropriate instrument represents a significant shortcoming in an examination as exaggerated reporting or a tendency to under-report issues may result in an inaccurate assessment and diagnosis and misleading conclusions. Schroeder et al. (2016) reported that the most common instruments used by their expert neuropsychologists were the PAI and the various versions of the Minnesota Multiphasic Personality Inventory (MMPI). The PAI was used by 29% of experts and the most frequently used measure was the MMPI-2-RF, employed by 71%. Although the MMPI-2-RF is the most recently developed member of the MMPI family of tests, it has been quickly adopted by experts in the field, probably because it has a range of validity indices. The measure consists of 338 statements relating to emotional, somatic and cognitive difficulties. A range of scales are derived which allow the clinician to identify problem areas such as tendencies to anger, irritability, anxiety and somatic and cognitive complaints. Prior to interpreting the profile, however, the clinician determines whether the statements have been responded to consistently and, in the event there are a high proportion of inconsistent or contradictory responses, which may be due to a number of factors such as inadequate understanding, confusion or non-compliance, the results are disregarded and no further interpretation is made. The measure also has scales to assess over-reporting and under-reporting of difficulties. Over-reporting refers to the tendency to endorse an excessive number of complaints, greater than that of healthy individuals and those with the same condition, whereas under-reporting refers to the tendency to present oneself as particularly well-adjusted or morally virtuous. The MMPI-2-RF over-reporting scales assess excessive reporting of psychological distress (F-r scale), psychiatric symptoms (F-p scale), somatic symptoms (Fs scale), exaggerated cognitive and somatic complaints (Symptom Validity Scale, FBS-r) and complaints associated with failure on performance validity tests (Response Bias Scale, RBS). Under-reporting is assessed by examining the claimant's tendency to present themselves as unduly virtuous (L-r scale) or well-adjusted (K-r scale). Elevated scores on the over-reporting scales call into question the claimant's self-report and indicates exaggerated complaining and, if the tendency is sufficiently pronounced, the clinician may then view the claimant's report as invalid. Alternatively, under-reporting potentially calls into question low scores on those scales that identify difficulties, as the claimant may lack insight or be responding in a naïve or socially desirable manner. Ben-Porath (2012) reviewed the evidence base for the MMPI-2-RF and argued that it met standards for use in US legal settings and others have endorsed its use in forensic settings (Schroeder et al., 2016; Greene, 2011; Boone, 2013; Young, 2014). Carone and Ben-Porath (2014) found that a patient with dementia resulting in significant memory and executive dysfunction could nevertheless complete the MMPI-2-RF in a consistent manner and with no sign of over- or under-reporting of complaints. McBride et al. (2013) examined the relationship between brain lesions in subjects involved in litigation and their results on PVTs and response bias on the MMPI-2-RF. They found no association between a tendency to over-report complaints and individuals' brain lesions, indicating that a brain injury did not lead to over-reporting. They also found no association between the presence of lesions and the results on PVT testing, indicating that PVT tests reflect response bias, rather than the effects of a brain injury. In other words, brain damage does not negate the possibility of the claimant both under-performing on tests of effort and over-reporting their difficulties on a questionnaire.

7–019   An issue of interest is the relationship between PVTs and SVTs and how they relate to each other. Over-reporting on a questionnaire and under-performing on an effort test might be expected to be associated and this has proved to be the case, although the relationship is not invariant. Gervais et al. (2007) developed the RBS to differentiate between those who passed and failed effort testing with elevated scores being associated with PVT failure. Whitney et al. (2008) confirmed that over-reporting and PVT failure were related and Youngjohn et al. (2011) found the FBS-r scale was related to passing and failing effort testing. Nguyen et al. (2015) studied a group of claimants and found that those who claimed to have neurological injuries were more likely to be considered to be malingering using the Slick criteria than those who claimed to have medical or psychiatric conditions. In particular, 16% of psychiatric complainants were suspected feigners, 38% of the medical group were suspected, and 41% of the neurological group. Those who met Slick criteria for feigning were also more likely to show over-reporting. Gervais et al. (2011) compared those who failed no PVTs with those who failed three PVTs and found elevated reporting of complaints in those who failed the effort tests. They concluded that those who showed poor effort on PVTs also took the opportunity to demonstrate emotional and somatic distress and they used the measures in combination to communicate their claimed cognitive limitations, as well as physical and emotional problems.

As might be expected, however, PVT and over-reporting measures do not always converge because the results necessarily depend on the strategy adopted by the individual taking the measures. Some aim to present as cognitively impaired and under-perform on cognitive tests, but do not over-endorse emotional or somatic complaints, whereas others take the opportunity of demonstrating their difficulties on an SVT measure, but not during cognitive testing. SVT measures are potentially valuable in confirming suspicions that the claimant is exaggerating or, alternatively, disabusing suspicions about the validity of a claimant's presentation. The latter is particularly useful in those cases where the claimant may have unlikable or unattractive characteristics that have the potential to inadvertently prejudice their assessment; in these circumstances satisfactory SVT and PVT results can highlight to the assessor their own inclinations and prejudices and lead to a more balanced opinion. On the other hand, over-reporting on an SVT measure is potentially highly significant in providing what is likely to be the only quantitative evidence of exaggeration.

9. FAKING GOOD AND FAKING BAD

On occasions there are circumstances when individuals fake good to fake bad. This may occur when claimants provide information about their lives before their injury or alternatively when they describe their post-accident complaints. For example, some describe their pre-accident functioning in idealised terms and portray their lives as having been trouble-free and uncomplicated and without significant, or any, psychological, physical or social problems (Lees-Haley et al., 1996; Lees-Haley et al., 1997). This has been termed the "good old days" bias whereby the claimant describes an ideal past life, which is contrasted with the debilitating impact of the brain trauma. Faking good about the past may be intended to communicate to the examiner how badly they have been affected and emphasise the impact of the injury, the changes they have undergone and the distress they have experienced. Lees-Haley et al. (1996) suggested this may not necessarily be deceitful, but rather represent a bias that is shaped by the legal proceedings and influenced by litigation guiding the individual to unintentionally recall details, and their current situation, in a way that is consistent with the injury. Idealisation may be accompanied by the omission of information that is perceived as being likely to adversely affect the claim. For example, past psychological or physical complaints may not be reported or minimised, as may previous accidents and injuries and convictions or a history of drug or alcohol misuse. Idealisation and omission may be difficult for the clinician to determine confidently on the basis of an interview, although their suspicions may be aroused in the event that the claimant describes their previous life in unduly positive terms. However, whatever misgivings the clinician may have, there may be concern that the claimant's account is nevertheless essentially accurate and so it is usually by documentary review of the records, such as the general practitioner notes, that the historical account is confirmed or not.

7–020

Just as claimants may edit the past, they may edit the present and omit details relevant to understanding their post-accident difficulties. Current stressors, such as other injuries or illness, housing, financial and relationship problems, recent bereavement, and family illnesses, may not be reported so as to maintain the assessor's focus on the injury and its effects. As a rule the more comprehensive the assessment, taking into account all the factors that shape a claimant's presentation, the greater the risk of weakening a simple or straightforward causal link between injury and complaints. Some individuals are aware of this and fear that their difficulties will not receive appropriate recognition and so modify their reporting. Some may become challenging and contest the relevance of enquiries about such issues during the assessment or later register complaints about the clinician's manner and conduct. It is possible to observe both over- and under-reporting in an individual's profile in the same assessment. Schroeder et al. (2011) found that individuals who were identified as malingering according to the Slick criteria had elevated scores on the over-reporting scales of the MMPI-2-RF. This is consistent with what would be expected, namely, that malingering is associated with exaggerated reporting of complaints and difficulties. However, they also found that 14% of the malingerers also obtained elevated scores on the L-r scale, a measure of under-reporting. They suggested that exaggeration among malingerers may also be accompanied by a tendency to present themselves as well-adjusted and morally virtuous while nevertheless experiencing cognitive and somatic problems due to their injuries.

An intriguing variation of malingering from outside the field of litigation has been the finding that some athletes fake bad to look good. Repeat cognitive testing has increasingly been used to track students' functioning following sports-concussions and some have been found to intentionally under-perform during baseline assessments to accelerate their return to play after a head injury. They may be highly motivated to maintain their position in the team, for reasons of personal recognition or to preserve their team's standing, and therefore seek to minimise the effects of a mild brain injury by under-performing during baseline assessments to later look good and avoid deficits being apparent in the event that they have a head injury (Bailey et al., 2006; Siedlik et al., 2015).

10. MALINGERING, EXAGGERATION AND THE COURTS

7–021 Although the base-rate of malingering and exaggeration among claimants is high, in the order of 30–50% (Larrabee, 2003; Larrabee et al., 2009), clinicians are often extremely reluctant to conclude malingering and rarely do so. In contrast, they are often happy to rule the issue out and say there was no evidence the claimant was simulating limitations, even when they have not used validity measures to confirm their opinion or stated the criteria used to discount it. Given the limitations of clinical judgment, an assessor who takes such an approach is at considerable risk of providing the court with an unverifiable and unfalsifiable opinion that is of limited value and potentially misleading. A reluctance to comment on malingering is justified by some experts on the grounds that the issue involves commenting on intention and therefore the honesty of the claimant, that being a matter for the court alone. However, such an approach is difficult to justify as the courts do not object when clinicians conclude that claimants are not exaggerating or malingering which is as much a judgment on intention and honesty, as when the clinician concludes otherwise. Similarly, clinicians routinely decide that a claimant warrants a psychological or psychiatric diagnosis, such as a major depression, anxiety, or some other condition, and in doing so they inevitably pass a judgment on the claimant's mental state and motivation and honesty, namely, that they have a genuine condition. Without necessarily intending to, and sometimes while actively seeking to avoid commenting on malingering, clinicians who diagnose are already addressing the issue and it is therefore unsound not to do so directly. Clinicians may be reluctant to conclude malingering or exaggeration because of the potential impact on the claimant, particularly in the event their opinion is wrong. Pella et al. (2012) pointed out that labelling an individual as malingering may cause them to lose benefits, certain types of insurance cover, and lead to the denial of services and their role as a patient, and potentially result in untreated complications. They concluded, with masterly understatement, that the term provides patients with few advantages, although it may help other agencies, such as the court, make decisions and assist with formulating appropriate legal judgments. As well as being potentially detrimental to the claimant, there may also be considerable detriment to the expert. The clinician may have to feedback that the claimant did not engage appropriately which, as Lippa et al. (2014) suggested, may be why some clinicians are reticent about using validity measures. As many clinicians are reluctant to conclude malingering in a claim, an expert who does is likely to find themselves in the invidious position of being in a minority, and sometimes a minority of one. In these circumstances, relatives may be called upon to confirm the claimant's complaints and refute suggestions that they are not valid, along with other involved individuals, such as those paid to provide rehabilitation for the injured party.

As Boone (2013) pointed out, while it is possible to use PVTs and SVTs to determine whether the claimant is reliable in the information they provide, no measures are available for verifying information from collateral informants, such as family or friends, some of whom may also become beneficiaries from the proceedings or at least be sympathetic to the claimant. A similar view might be taken of the information provided by treating clinicians who, like their colleagues, may be inherently reluctant to diagnose malingering and who may take on the role of advocate for their patient, as well as having an additional remunerative interest in discounting misgivings. Boone (2013) reported that she does not gather collateral information as its accuracy is necessarily unknown and while her approach is arguably radical, most experts would nowadays accept the need to include validity measures when assessing a claimant, but still uncritically accept unverified opinions from collateral informants. Nevertheless, clinicians may find it difficult to sustain a minority position and faced with a "show of hands" against them and mindful of the complexities involved in assessing behaviour, they may select another diagnosis. Green and Merten (2013) suggested that when presented with complaints that do not make sense an alternative diagnosis may reflect the political and economic choices of the clinician, rather than clinical reality. They suggested that clinicians run the risk of facing complaints and threats or legal action when they thwart a claimant's pursuit of compensation and therefore an unobjectionable diagnosis, such as post-concussion syndrome or somatoform disorder, may be preferable.

An important difficulty is that malingering or exaggerated illness behaviour are invariably complex in their presentations and do not necessarily take one form that can be easily identified. Although guidelines, such as the Slick criteria are available, nevertheless, this does not detract from the fact that there can be considerable variability and subtlety in how individuals may potentially misrepresent complaints, with some emphasising cognitive problems, such as memory difficulties, but not perceptual or linguistic limitations, and others amplifying somatic and emotional complaints, but not cognitive difficulties, or some other combination. Pella et al. (2012) noted that an individual's presentation may be multifaceted and it can be difficult to rule out the contribution of other conditions they may have to what appears to be malingering, so making the determination more difficult. Green and Merten (2013) suggested there may also be substantial vested interests that seek to avoid concluding malingering. They described the case of a claimant who had a vehicle accident resulting in a head injury and who also reported the implausible loss of the use of both of his hands. The claimed limitations were such that he maintained he could not work, drive, or look after himself, and lacking the use of his hands, he had to be cared for by his wife. Although PVT testing showed that his memory complaints were non-credible and video evidence also showed that he had normal hand use, none of the many experts who examined him concluded malingering and various opinions were advanced, including that he had a somatoform disorder. Green and Merten (2013) suggested that avoiding concluding malingering may suit all the parties, inasmuch as medical practitioners and psychologists avoid unpleasant confrontations, complaints and professional isolation, and lawyers may be satisfied by other diagnoses as they can then compromise a settlement.

11. PRACTICAL SIGNIFICANCE OF VALIDITY MEASURES

7–022   Invalid presentations on PVT and SVT measures have been found to have significant implications in a range of areas. PVT measures were initially designed to assess engagement during forensic neuropsychological examinations and, as might be expected, when effort is suboptimal lower scores are obtained on conventional cognitive tests. Green et al. (2001) studied a group of 904 patients that included 470 head injuries and 80 neurological patients, and found that effort reduced test scores 4.5 times more than moderate-severe brain injury. Green (2007) examined 1,307 patients with various diagnoses, 668 of whom had head injuries, and the majority had financial incentives, such as compensation claims. He found that 31% of the total sample failed PVT assessment and decreasing effort was associated with decreasing performance on a range of measures including tests of intelligence, memory and executive functioning. Even when effort was relatively good, nevertheless, those scoring towards the lower range performed less well than those at the upper range. This is consistent with the view that effort is a dimensional rather than a categorical construct (with "pass" and "fail" categories) and that it has a ubiquitous influence. Similarly, Grills and Armistead-Jehle (2016) examined US Army service members and found that PVT failure was associated with suppressed cognitive performance.

Non-credible presentations have been found in a range of clinical groups including children. Chafetz (2015) reported that 10% of children being evaluated for disability scored below chance on PVT assessment, 16% obtained chance-level results, and 28–34% failed one or two validity tests. He suggested that the children's malingering was mostly due to their parents and might be seen as "malingering by proxy". Chafetz and Prentowski (2011) reported the case of a nine-year-old referred for assessment whose mother was seeking benefits on his behalf and who failed validity measures. Baker and Kirkwood (2015) commented that apart from psychiatric conditions, such as conversion disorder, non-credible presentations in children may relate to issues such as school and sport avoidance, bullying, parental disharmony and iatrogenic influences. Chafetz (2015) thought that parental coaching was implicated in children's presentations and by becoming part of the parents' economies, with the need to continue playing a disabled role, this might be viewed as a form of child abuse.

Invalid presentations have been found in other diagnostic groups. Bianchini et al. (2005b) found that over half of a group of claimants following electrical injury met criteria for probable malingering. Johnson-Green et al. (2013) found 37% of a group with fibromyalgia failed one or more validity measures; the results did not always relate to whether the patients were claiming benefits and they suggested a simple explanation was that once established in a sick role, patients maintained their impairments irrespective of whether there was a financial incentive. Schwand et al. (1998) found an elevated rate of invalid responding in whiplash claimants compared with non-claimants. Flaro et al. (2007) examined 118 parents who were seeking child custody and therefore presumed to be highly motivated. As expected, 98% passed PVT testing, in contrast to 60% of a group of mild brain injuries. The PVT failure rate was 23 times higher in the mild brain injury group than the parents. Those with the least significant head injuries failed PVT testing more than those with more severe injuries (40% vs 21%). The parents who failed effort testing were subsequently interviewed and it transpired that they had changed their minds and they did not want their children after all. Chafetz et al. (2011) examined three groups of low functioning individuals each with an IQ of less than 80. None of those who were seeking to regain custody of their children failed effort testing, whereas 46% of disability claimants failed, as did 7% of those assessed for vocational rehabilitation. Although it might be expected that the vocational group would be motivated to do well, Chafetz et al. (2011) suggested that their failure rate may have been due to them seeking to retain or obtain benefits and they were complying with requirements to participate in a programme.

An interesting development in recent years has been examining the relationship between validity measures and the use of healthcare resources and community functioning. Horner et al. (2014) examined the records of 355 individuals seen for routine neuropsychological assessments and found that 80% showed adequate effort on PVT measures and 20% showed inadequate effort. The majority had been referred from mental health services, but also neurological and primary care sources, and brain injury and infectious diseases clinics. They followed their progress for a year after the examinations and found that the adequate effort group made fewer Emergency Department visits, required fewer hospitalisations, and spent fewer days in hospital, although they nevertheless had more comorbidities, that is, additional health conditions. Compared with the adequate effort group, the suboptimal effort group therefore tended to use more health resources without benefit, not only at the time of the assessment, but later when they used more resources than those making adequate effort. Horner et al. (2014) suggested that having had an inconclusive and inaccurate neuropsychological examination, their conditions may have remained unclear leading to

7–023

additional resources being spent on them or alternatively PVT failure was a marker for a general tendency to be uncooperative with services or they continued to embellish symptoms. Anestis et al. (2015) examined the issue of premature termination from treatment in a group of 511 patients attending a psychology clinic. Early termination from treatment is a common problem, resulting in incomplete progress and wasted resources. The patients completed the MMPI-2-RF during an initial assessment and subsequently it was found that 299 terminated therapy early with the remainder finishing treatment as planned. Anestis et al. (2015) found that over-reporting of complaints and difficulties on the MMPI-2-RF validity measures was associated with a lack of engagement in treatment and premature termination. Lippa et al. (2014) examined the relationship between validity measures and how patients functioned in the community. They administered both PVT and SVT measures to 131 individuals with traumatic brain injuries and had them rate their community participation. They found that those who failed effort testing were more likely to exaggerate complaints and report having greater participation restrictions. As they pointed out, this may indicate that exaggerated disability was associated with a volitional reduction in community activities or simply that they exaggerated their lack of involvement.

PVT measures have been found to have implications for disciplines other than neuropsychology. Amistead-Jehle et al. (2017) examined the relationship between effort testing and the validity of balance testing undertaken by an otolaryngologist. They assessed 78 individuals undergoing disability examinations, the majority of whom had mild head injuries, and found that 35% failed PVT testing and there was a significant level of agreement between poor effort and invalid presentations on balance testing using computerised dynamic posturagraphy. They concluded that symptom exaggeration potentially crosses the areas of cognition and balance. Fleming and Rucas (2015) examined the incidence of suboptimal engagement during occupational therapy assessments of claimants seen for compensation claims. Their group consisted of individuals with head injuries, musculoskeletal injuries and depression, and each completed one of two PVTs and 48% showed non-credible responding. Richman et al. (2006) found 42% of disability claimants with predominantly soft tissue injuries and fibromyalgia failed PVT assessment. Gill et al. (2007) included PVT testing when assessing 119 psychiatric claimants and found that 62% showed non-credible responding. This is perhaps not surprising as a significant proportion of psychiatric patients undergoing treatment and not involved in litigation have nevertheless been found to pursue advantages by attending for treatment. Van Egmond and Kummeling (2002) examined a group of 166 patients attending a psychiatric outpatient department and using questionnaires asked the patients and their treating clinicians whether they expected to receive "benefits" from being in treatment. They found that 42% of the patients expected some form of secondary gain such as getting assistance with work, social security and legal issues, help with accommodation or help with relatives. However, only 6% told their psychiatrist about their expectations and it was concluded that secondary gain was a veiled motive for having therapy. In addition, those patients who had expectations of secondary gain were significantly more likely to have a worse therapeutic outcome. Van Egmond et al. (2005) examined another group of psychiatric patients and found that 41% had expectations of some kind of secondary gain from being in therapy and again only a minority (9.5%) told their psychiatrist about their expectations and in most cases the treating psychiatrist had no knowledge of them. Sullivan et al. (2007) concluded that 25–48% of a group assessed for attention deficit hyperactivity disorder showed suboptimal effort on assessment. Their group were not involved in litigation, but they pointed out that they had other potential gains including being eligible for allowances as a disabled person and psychostimulant medication. These findings are noteworthy in illustrating that even outside litigation a significant proportion of patients can have undisclosed motives for attending for treatment which in turn potentially contaminates their progress in therapy. These investigations sound a cautionary note for those who view reports and assessments undertaken outside of litigation as in some way providing a more objective account of a claimant's presentation. In addition, given the high base-rate of non-valid presentations in neuropsychological studies, it is perhaps unsurprising that a high incidence of invalid presentations have been found by other professionals. While unsurprising, it is a concern that the assessment of response validity and the development of measures to address the issue, remains almost exclusively the province of neuropsychologists and other clinicians continue to rely primarily on clinical judgment alone.

12. CONCLUSIONS

The development of PVT and SVT measures has led to what has been called a paradigm shift in neuropsychological assessment and had a significant and arguably beneficial influence on brain injury litigation and led to more accurate and informative opinions being offered to the courts (Green, 2003). Previous assumptions that claimants rarely feign or exaggerate disability and were they to do so they would be readily identified have been found to be wanting and, on the contrary, the base rate of invalid presentations among brain injured claimants is in the order of 30–50%. The likelihood of claimant credibility becoming an issue in proceedings is therefore high, particularly when complaints are predominantly cognitive, emotional or behavioural, which is the case in the majority of cases. While financial compensation is an important potential driver for invalid presentations, this is not the only relevant factor, however, and other motivations include a wish to correct an injustice, anger, resentment or a desire for acknowledgement. Invalid presentations are sufficiently common that Bush et al. (2005) proposed that neuropsychologists should be required to justify why they have not used measures of response validity in their examinations. However, while increasingly they have been adopted, other professions have lagged well behind despite studies showing that issues of credibility occur across a range of disciplines. Such a situation is unlikely to be tenable in the long term and a demand for these professions to address validity concerns and develop specialised measures relevant to their disciplines can be expected.

7–024

REFERENCES

7–025 American Psychiatric Association, *Diagnostic and Statistical Manual of Mental Disorders, 4th Edition, Text Revision: DSM-IV-TR* (Washington DC: American Psychiatric Association, 2000).

American Psychiatric Association, *Diagnostic and Statistical Manual of Mental Disorders, 5th Edition: DSM-5* (Arlington, VA: American Psychiatric Association, 2013).

Anestis, J.C., Finn, J.A., Gottfried, E., Arbisi, P.A. and Joiner, T.E., "Reading the Road Signs: The Utility of the MMPI-2-RF Restructured Form Validity Scales in the Prediction of Premature Termination" (2015) *Assessment* 22(3):279–88.

Ardolf, B.R., Denney, R.L. and Houston, C.M., "Base rates of negative response bias and malingered neurocognitive dysfunction among criminal defendants referred for neuropsychological evaluation" (2007) *Clinical Neuropsychologist* 20, 145–159.

Armistead-Jehle, P., Lange, B.J. and Green, P., "A comparison of neuropsychological and balance performance validity testing" (2017) *Applied Neuropsychology: Adult* 24 (2), 190–197.

Ashendorf, L., Constantinou, M. and McCaffrey, R.J., "The effect of depression and anxiety on the TOMM in community-dwelling older adults" (2004) *Archives of Clinical Neuropsychology* 19, 125–130.

Baker, D. and Kirkwood, M.W., "Motivations behind and non-credible presentations: why children feign and how to make this determination" in Kirkwood, M.W. (ed.), *Validity Testing in Child and Adolescent Assessment: Evaluating Exaggeration, Feigning and Noncredible Effort* (New York: Guilford Press, 2015).

Bailey, C.M., Echemendia, R.J. and Arnett, P.A., "The impact of motivation on neuropsychological performance in sports-related mild traumatic brain injury" (2006) *Journal of the International Neuropsychological Society* 12, 475–484.

Bass, C. and Halligan, P., "Factitious disorders and malingering: challenges for clinical assessment and management" (2014) *The Lancet* 383, 1422–1432.

Beck, A.T., *Beck Depression Inventory* (San Antonio: Psychological Corporation, 1987).

Beck, A.T. and Steer, R.A., *Beck Anxiety Inventory Manual* (San Antonio: TX: PsychCorp/Pearson, 1993).

Ben-Porath, Y.S. and Tellegen, A., *MMPI-2-RF: Manual for administration, scoring an interpretation* (Minneapolis: University of Minnesota Press, 2008).

Berry, D.T.R. and Nelson, N.W., "DSM-5 and Malingering: a modest proposal" (2010) *Psychological Injury and Law* 3 (4), 295–303.

Ben-Porath, Y.S., "Addressing Challenges to MMPI-2-RF-Based Testimony: Questions and Answers" (2012) *Archives of Clinical Neuropsychology* 27, 1–15.

Bianchini, K.J., Greve, K.W. and Glynn, G., "On the diagnosis of malingered pain-related disability: lessons from cognitive malingering research" (2005a) *The Spine Journal* 5, 404–417.

Bianchini, K.J., Love, J.M., Greve, K.W. and Adams, D., "Detection and diagnosis of malingering in electrical injury" (2005b) *Archives of Clinical Neuropsychology* 20, 365–373.

Binder, L.M. and Rohling, M.L., "Money Matters: A meta-analytic review of the effects of financial incentives on recovery after closed-head injury" (1996) *American Journal of Psychiatry* 153 (1), 7–10.

Boone, K.B., *Clinical Practice of Forensic Neuropsychology: an Evidence-based Approach* (New York: Guilford Press, 2013).

REFERENCES

Boone, K.B., "Self-deception in somatoform conditions: differentiating between conscious and unconscious symptom feigning" in Boone, K.B. (ed.), *Neuropsychological evaluation of somatoform and other functional somatic conditions: Assessment Primer* (New York: American Academy of Clinical Neuropsychology, Routledge, 2017).

British Psychological Society, *Assessment of effort in clinical testing of cognitive functioning for adults* (Professional Practice Board, 2009).

Bush, S.S., Heilbronner, R.L. and Ruff, R.M., "Psychological Assessment of Symptom and Performance Validity, Response Bias, and Malingering: Official Position of the Association for Scientific Advancement in Psychological Injury and Law" (2014) *Psychological Injury and Law* 7, 197–205.

Bush, S.S., Ruff, R.M., Troster, A.I., Barth, J.T., Koffler S.P., Pliskin, N.H., Reynolds, C.R. and Silver, C.H., "Symptom Validity Assessment: Practice issues and medical necessity. NAN Policy & Planning Committee" (2005) *Archives of Clinical Neuropsychology* 20, 419–425.

Butcher, J.N., Graham, J.R., Ben-Porath, Y.S., Tellegen, A., Dahlstrom W.G. and Kaemmer, B., *MMPI-2: Manual for administration and scoring* (Minneapolis: University of Minnesota Press, 2001).

Carone, D.A. and Ben-Porath, Y.S., "Dementia does not preclude very reliable responding on the MMPI-2-RF: a case report" (2014) *Clinical Neuropsychologist* 28 (6), 1019–1029.

Carone, D.A., Green, P. and Drane, D.L., "Word Memory Test profiles into cases with surgical removal of the left anterior hippocampus and parahippocampal gyrus" (2013) *Applied Neuropsychology: Adult* 21 (2), 155–160.

Carone, D.A., "Young Child with Severe Brain Volume Loss Easily Passes the Word Memory Test and Medical Symptom Validity Test: Implications for Mild TBI" (2013) *Clinical Neuropsychologist* 28 (1), 146–162.

Carroll, L.J., Cassidy, D., Peloso, P.M., Borg, J., von Holst, H., Holm, L., Paniak, C. and Pepin, M., "Prognosis for mild traumatic brain injury: rests of the WHO Collaborating Centre Task Force on Mild Traumatic Brain Injury" (2004) *Journal of Rehabilitation Medicine* 43, 84–105.

Chafetz, M.D., "Disability: Social Security Supplemental Security Income Exams for Children" in Kirkwood, M.W. (ed.), *Validity Testing in Child and Adolescent Assessment: Evaluating Exaggeration, Training and Non-Credible Effort* (New York: Guilford Press, 2015).

Chafetz, M.D. and Prentowski, E., "A case of malingering by proxy in a Social Security disability psychological consultative examination" (2011) *Applied Neuropsychology* 18, 143–149.

Chafetz, M.D., Prentkowski, E. and Rao, A., "To Work or Not to Work: Motivation (Not a Low IQ) Determines Symptom Validity Test Findings" (2011) *Archives of Clinical Neuropsychologist* 26, 306–313.

Chafetz, M. and Underhill, J., "Estimated Costs of Malingered Disability" (2013) *Archives of Clinical Neuropsychology* 28, 633–639.

Chafetz, M.D., Williams, M.A., Ben-Porath, Y.S., Bianchini, K.J., Boone, K.B., Kirkwood, M.W., Larrabee, G.J. and Ord, J.S., "Official Position of the American Academy of Clinical Neuropsychology Social Security Administration Policy on Validity Testing: Guidance and Recommendations for Change" (2015) *Clinical Neuropsychologist* 29 (6), 723–740.

Denning, J.H., "Performance Validity Test Failure Rates in Military and Veteran Populations: The Impact on Clinical, Research, and Disability Findings" (American Academy of Clinical Neuropsychology, 2015).

Duncan, A., "The impact of cognitive and psychiatric impairment of psychotic disorders on the test of memory malingering (TOMM)" (2005) *Assessment* 12 (2), 123–129.

Ekman, P. and O'Sullivan, M., "Who Can Catch a Liar?" (1991) *American Psychologist* 46 (9), 913–920.

Etherton, J.L., Bianchini, K.J., Greve, K.W. and Ciota, M.A., "Test of Memory malingering performances unaffected by laboratory-induced pain: implications for clinical use" (2005) *Archives of Clinical Neuropsychology* 20, 375–384.

Faust, D., Hart, K., and Guilmette, T.J., "Paediatric malingering: the capacity of children to fake believable deficits on neuropsychological testing" (1988a) *Journal of Consulting and Clinical Psychology* 56 (4), 578–582.

Faust, D., Hart, K., Guilmette, T.J. and Arkes, H.R., "Neuropsychologist's capacity to detect adolescent malingerers" (1988b) *Professional Psychology: Research and Practice* 19 (5), 508–515.

Faust, D., *Brain Damage Claims: Coping with Neuropsychological Evidence* (California: Law and Psychology Press, 1991).

Flaro, L., Green, P., and Robertson, E., "Word Memory Test failure 23 times higher in mild brain injury than in parents seeking custody: The power of external incentives" (2007) *Brain Injury* 21 (4), 373–383.

Fleming, A., and Rucas, K., "Welcoming a paradigm shift in Occupational Therapy: Symptom Validity Measures and Cognitive Assessment" (2015) *Applied Neuropsychology: Adult* 22, 23–31.

Flaherty, J.M., Spencer, R.J., Drag, L.L., Pangilinan, P.H. and Bieliauskas, L.A., "Limited usefulness of the Rey Fifteen-Item Test in detection of invalid performance in veterans suspected of mild traumatic brain injury" (2015) *Brain Injury* 29 (13–14), 1630–1634.

Gabbe, B.J., Simpson, P.M., Cameron, P.A., Ekegren, C.L., Edwards, E.R., Page, R., Liew, S., Bucknill, A. and de Steiger, R., "Association between perception of fault for the crash and function, return to work and health status 1 year after road traffic injury: a registry-based cohort study" (2015) *BMJ Open* 5(11), 1–7.

Gervais, R.O., Ben-Porath, Y.S., Wygant, D.B. and Green, P., "Development and validation of a Response Bias Scale (RBS) for the MMPI-2" (2007) *Assessment* 14; 196–208.

Gervais, R.O., Rohling, M.L., Green, P. and Ford, W., "A comparison of WMT, CARB, and TOMM failure rates in non-head injury disability claimants" (2004) *Archives of Clinical Neuropsychology* 19, 475–487.

Gervais, R.O., Wygant, D., Sellbom, M. and Ben-Porath, Y.S., "Associations between Symptom Validity Test failure and scores on the MMPI-2-RF validity and substantive scales" (2011) *Journal of Personality Assessment* 93 (5), 508–517.

Gill, D., Green, P.W., and Flaro, L. and Pucci, T., "The role of effort testing in Independent Medical Examinations" (2007) *Medico-Legal Journal* 75 (2), 64–71.

Goodrich-Hunsaker, N.J. and Hopkins, R.O., "Word Memory Test performance in amnesic patients with hippocampal damage" (2009) *Neuropsychology* 23 (4), 529–534.

Grant, G.M., O'Donnell, M.L., Spittal, M.J., Creamer, M. and Studdert, D.M., "Relationship between Stressfulness of Claiming for Injury Compensation and Long-Term Recovery: A Prospective Cohort Study" (2014) *JAMA Psychiatry* 1:71(4), 446–453.

Green, P., "Welcoming a paradigm shift in neuropsychology" (2003) *Archives of Clinical Neuropsychology* 18, 625–627.

Green, P., *Green's Word Memory Test* (Kelowna, BC: Green's Publishing Inc, 2005).

Green, P., "The pervasive influence of effort on neuropsychological tests" (2007) *Physical Medicine and Rehabilitation Clinics of North America* 18, 43–68.

REFERENCES

Green, P. and Flaro, L., "Results from three Performance Validity Tests (PVTs) in adults with intellectual deficits" (2015) *Applied Neuropsychology: Adult* 22(4), 293–303.

Green, P. and Flaro, L., "Results from three Performance Validity Tests in children with intellectual disability" (2016) *Applied Neuropsychology: Child* 5 (1), 25–34.

Green, P., Rohling, M.L., Lees-Haley, P.R. and Allen, L.M., "Effort has a greater effect on test scores than severe brain injury in compensation claimants" (2001) *Brain Injury*, 12, 1045–1060.

Green, P. and Merten, T., "Non-Credible Explanations of Non-Credible Performance on Symptom Validity Tests" in Carone, D.A. and Bush, S. (eds), *Mild Traumatic Brain Injury: Symptom Validity Assessment and Malingering* (New York: Springer, 2013).

Greene, R.L., *The MMPI-2 and MMPI-2-RF: an interpretive manual*, 3rd edn (Boston, MA: Allyn & Bacon, 2011).

Greiffenstein, M.F., Baker, W.J. and Johnson-Greene, D., "Actual versus self-reported scholastic achievement of litigating postconcussion and severe closed head injury claimants" (2002) *Psychological Assessment* 14 (2), 202–208.

Greve, K.W., Bianchini, K.J., Love, J.M., Brennan, A. and Heinly, M.T.D., "Sensitivity and specificity of MMPI-2 validity scales and indicators to malingered neurocognitive dysfunction in traumatic brain injury" (2006) *Clinical Neuropsychologist* 20, 491–512.

Grills, C.E. and Armistead-Jehle, P.J., "Performance Validity Test and Neuropsychological Assessment Battery Screening Module Performances in Active-Duty Sample with a History of Concussion" (2016) *Applied Neuropsychology: Adult* 23 (4), 1–7.

Guilmette, T.J., Hart, K.J., Giuliano, A.J. and Leininger, B.E., "Detecting simulated memory impairment: comparison of the Rey fifteen-item test and the Hiscock forced-choice procedure" (2007) *Clinical Neuropsychologist* 8 (3), 283–294.

Guilmette, T.J., "The Role of Clinical Judgement in Symptom Validity Assessment" in Carone, D.A. and Bush, S. (eds), *Mild traumatic brain injury: symptom validity assessment and malingering* (New York: Springer, 2013).

Gutheil, T.G., Bursztajn, H., Brodksy, A. and Strasburger, L.H., "Preventing "Critogenic" Harms: Minimizing Emotional Injury from Civil Litigation" (2000) *Journal of Psychiatry and Law* 28(1), 1 5–18.

Hall, H.V, Thompson, J.S. and Poirier, J.S., "Detecting deception in neuropsychological cases: towards an applied model" (2007) *The Forensic Examiner*, Fall, 7–15.

Hamilton, J.C., Feldman M.D. and Cunnien, A.J., "Factitious Disorder in Medical and Psychiatric Practices" in Rogers, R. (ed.), *Clinical Assessment of Malingering and Deception*, 3rd edition (New York: Guildford Press, 2008).

Heilbronner, R.L., Sweet, J.J., Morgan, J.E., Larrabee, G.J., Millis, S.R. and Conference Participants, "American Academy of Clinical Neuropsychology Consensus Conference Statement on the neuropsychological assessment of effort, response bias, and malingering" (2009) *Clinical Neuropsychologist* 23, 1093–1129.

Horner, M.D., VanKirk, K.K., Dismuke, C.E., Turner, T.H. and Muzzy, W., "Inadequate Effort on Neuropsychological Evaluation Is Associated with Increased Healthcare Utilisation" (2014) *Clinical Neuropsychologist* 28(5), 703–13.

Iverson, G.L., "Ethical Issues Associated with the Assessment of Exaggeration, Poor Effort, and Malingering" (2006) *Applied Neuropsychology* 13 (2), 77–90.

Iverson, G.L., Page, J.L., Koehler, B.E., Shojania, K. and Badii, M., "Test of memory malingering (TOMM) scores are not affected by chronic pain or depression in patients with fibromyalgia" (2007) *Clinical Neuropsychologist* 21, 532–546.

Johnson-Greene, D., Brooks, L. and Ference, T., "Relationship between performance validity testing, disability status, and somatic complaints in patients with fibromyalgia" (2013) *Clinical Neuropsychologist* 27 (1), 148–158.

Kaufmann, P.M., "Protecting raw data and psychological tests from wrongful disclosure: a primer on the law and other persuasive strategies" (2009) *Clinical Neuropsychologist* 23, 1130–1159.

King, N.S., Crawford, S., Wende, F.J., Moss N.E., and Wade, D.T., "The Rivermead Post Concussion Symptoms Questionnaire: a measure of symptoms commonly experienced after head injury and its reliability" (1995) *Journal of Neurology* 242 (9), 587–592.

Kitchen, R., "Investigating benefit fraud and illness deception in the United Kingdom" in Halligan, P.W., Bass, C. and Oakley, D.A. (eds), *Malingering and Illness Deception* (Oxford: Oxford University Press, 2003).

Larrabee, G.J., "Detection of Malingering Using Atypical Performance Patterns on Standard Neuropsychological Tests" (2003) *Clinical Neuropsychologist* 17 (3), 410–425.

Larrabee, G.J., "Assessment of malingering" in Larrabee, G.J. (ed.), *Forensic Neuropsychology: a Scientific Approach* (New York: Oxford University Press, 2012).

Larrabee, G.J., Millis, S.R., and Meyers, J.E., "40 Plus or Minus 10, a New Magical Number: Reply to Russell" (2009) *Clinical Neuropsychologist* 23 (5), 841–849.

Lees-Haley, P.R., Williams, C.W. and English, L.T., "Response bias in self-reported history of plaintiffs compared with non-litigating patients" (1996) *Psychological Reports* 79, 811–818.

Lees-Haley, P.R., Williams, C.W., Zasler, M.D., Marguilies, S., English, L.T. and Stevens, K.B., "Response bias in plaintiffs' histories" (1997) *Brain Injury*, 11 (11), 791–799.

Lippa, S.M., Pastorek, M.J., Romesser, J., Linck, J., Sim, A.H., Wisdom N.M. and Miller, B.I., "Ecological Validity of Performance Validity Testing" (2014) *Archives of Clinical Neuropsychologist* 29(3): 236–244.

LoCascio, J., "Malingering, insurance medicine, and the medicalisation of fraud" in Halligan, P.W., Bass, C., and Oakley, D.A. (eds), *Malingering and Illness Deception* (Oxford: Oxford University Press, 2003).

Matsuzawa, Y.K. and Dijkers, M.P., "The experience of litigation after TBI I: Barriers to Recovery" (2014) *Psychological Injury and Law* 7, 388–396.

Mayou, R.A., Black, J. and Bryant, B., "Unconsciousness, amnesia and psychiatric symptoms following road traffic accident injury" (2000) *British Journal of Psychiatry* 177, 540–545.

Merckelbach, H., Jelicic, M. and Pieters, M., "The residual effect of feigning: how intentional faking may evolve into a less conscious form of symptom reporting" (2011) *Journal of Clinical and Experimental Neuropsychology* 33 (1), 131–139.

Merckelbach, H., and Merten, T., "A Note on Cognitive Dissonance and Malingering" (2012) *Clinical Neuropsychologist* 26 (7), 1217–1229.

Merten T., Dandachi-FitzGerald, B., Hall, V., Schmand, B.A., Santamaría, P. and González-Ordi, H., "Symptom validity assessment in European countries: development and state-of-the-art" (2013) *Clinica Salud* 24, 129–138.

McBride, W.F., Crighton, A.H., Wygant, D.B. and Granacher, R.P., "It's not all in your head (or at least your brain): associations of traumatic brain lesion presence and location with performance on measures of response bias in forensic evaluation" (2013) *Behavioural Sciences and the Law* 31, 779–788.

McCarter R.J., Walton N.H., Brooks D.N. and Powell G.E., "Effort testing in contemporary UK Neuropsychological Practice" (2009) *Clinical Neuropsychologist*, 23, 1050–1066.

REFERENCES

Mittenberg, W., Patton, C., Canyock, T.M. and Condit, D.C., "Base Rates of Malingering and Symptom Exaggeration" (2002) *Journal of Clinical and Experimental Neuropsychology* 24 (8), 1094–1102.

Morey, L.C., *Personality Assessment Inventory (PAI) technical manual* (Odessa, FL: Psychological Assessment Resources, 1991).

Moss, A., Jones, C., Fokias, D. and Quinn, D., "The mediating effects of effort upon the relationship between head injury severity and cognitive functioning" (2003) *Brain Injury* 17 (5), 377–387.

National Fraud Authority, *Annual Fraud Indicator, March 2012* (UK Government, 2012).

Nguyen, C.T., Green, D. and Barr, W.B., "Evaluation of the MMPI-2-RF for detecting over-reported symptoms in a civil forensic and disability setting" (2015) *Clinical Neuropsychologist* 29 (2), 255–271.

Niesten, I.J.M., Nentjes, L., Merckelbach, H. and Bernstein, D.P., "Antisocial features and 'faking bad': a critical note" (2015) *International Journal of Law and Psychiatry* 41, 34–42.

Onsworth, T. and Fleming, J., "Community adjustment and re-engagement" in Levin, H.S., Shum, D.H. and Chan, R.C.K. (eds), *Understanding traumatic brain injury: current research and future directions* (New York: Oxford University Press, 2014).

Pankratz, L. and Erickson, R.D., "Two views of malingering" (1990) *Clinical Neuropsychologist* 4, 379–389.

Pella, R.D., Hill, B.D., Singh, A.N., Hayes, J.S. and Gouvier, W.D., "Non-Credible Performance in Mild Traumatic Brain Injury" in Reynolds, C.R. and Horton, A.M. (eds), *Detection of Malingering during Head Injury Litigation*, 2nd edn (New York: Springer, 2012).

Ponsford, J., "Short and Long-Term Outcomes in Survivors of Traumatic Brain Injury" in Levin, H.S., Shum, D.H. and Chan, R.C.K. (eds), *Understanding Traumatic Brain Injury: Current Research and Future Directions* (New York: Oxford University Press, 2014).

Rees, L.M., Tombaugh, T.N. and Boulay, L., "Depression and the Test of Memory Malingering" (2001) *Archives of Clinical Neuropsychology* 16, 501–506.

Resnick, P.J., West, S. and Payne, J.W., "Malingering of Post-Traumatic Disorders" in Rogers, R. (ed.), *Clinical Assessment of Malingering and Deception*. 3rd edn (New York: Guildford Press, 2008).

Rey, A., *L'examen clinique en psychologie* (Paris: Presses Universitaires de France, 1964).

Richman, J., Green, P., Gervais, R., Flaro, L., Merten, T., Brockhaus, R. and Ranks, D., "Objective tests of symptom exaggeration in independent medical examinations" (2006) *Journal of Occupational and Environmental Medicine* 48 (3), 303–311.

Rogers, R., "An Introduction to Response Styles" in Rogers, R. (ed.), *Clinical Assessment of Malingering and Deception*, 3rd edn (New York: Guildford Press, 2008).

Rogers, R. and Payne, J.W., "Damages and Rewards: assessment of malinger disorders in compensation cases" (2006) *Behavioural Sciences and the Law* 24, 645–658.

Rohling, M.L, Langhinrichsen-Rohling, J., and Miller, L., "Actuarial Assessment of Malingering: Rohling's interpretive method" in Franklin, R.D. (ed.), *Prediction in Forensic and Neuropsychology: Sound Statistical Practices* (New Jersey: Lawrence Erlbaum Associates, 2003).

Rosenhan, D.L., "On being sane in insane places" (1973) *Science* 179, 250–258.

Schmand, B., Lindeboom, J., Schagen, S., Heijt, R., Koene, T. and Hamburger, H.L., "Cognitive complaints in patients after whiplash injury: the impact of malingering" (1998) *Journal of Neurology, Neurosurgery and Psychiatry* 64, 339–343.

Schroeder, R.W., Baade, L.E., Peck, C.P., VonDran, E.J., Brockman, C.J., Webster, B.K. and Heinrichs, R.J., "Validity of MMPI-2-RF validity scales in criterion group neuropsychological samples" (2011) *Clinical Neuropsychologist* 1–18.

Schroeder, R.W., Martin, P.K. and Odland, A.P., "Expert beliefs and practices regarding neuropsychological validity testing" (2016) *Clinical Neuropsychologist* 30(4), 515–535.

Scott, C., *DSM-5 and the Law* (New York: Oxford University Press, 2015).

Scott, J.G. and Schoenberg, M.R., "Affect, Emotions and Mood" in Schoenberg, M.R., and Scott, J.G. (eds), *The Little Black Book of Neuropsychology: a syndrome-based approach* (New York: Springer, 2011).

Sherer, M., Sander, A.M., Maestas, K.L., Pastorek, N.J., Nick, T.G. and Li, J., "Accuracy of Self-Reported Length of Coma and Post Traumatic Amnesia In Persons with Medically Verified Traumatic Brain Injury" (2015) *Archives of Physical Medicine and Rehabilitation* 96, 652–658.

Siedlik, J.A., Siscos, S.M., Evans, K., Rolf, A., Gallagher, M., Seeley, J. and Verdiman, J.P., "Computerized neurocognitive assessments and detection of the malingering athlete" (2015) *Journal of Sports Medicine and Physical Fitness* 56 (9), 1086–1091.

Simon, M.J., "Performance of mentally retarded forensic patients on the Test of Memory malingering" (2007) *Journal of Clinical Psychology* 63 (4), 339–344.

Slick, D.J., Sherman, E.M.S. and Iverson, G.L., "Diagnostic Criteria for Malingered Neurocognitive Dysfunction: Proposed Standards for Clinical Practice and Research" (1999) *Clinical Neuropsychologist* 13 (4), 545–561.

Slick, D.J. and Sherman, E.M.S., "Differential diagnosis of malingering and related clinical presentations" in Sherman, E.M.S. and Brooks, B.L. (eds), *Paediatric Forensic Neuropsychology* (New York: Oxford University Press, 2012).

Slick, D.J. and Sherman, E.M.S., "Differential Diagnosis of Malingering" in Carone, D.A. and Bush, S.S. (eds), *Mild Traumatic Brain Injury: Symptom Validity Assessment and Malingering* (New York: Springer, 2013).

Smith, G.P. and Burger, G.K., "Detection of malingering: Validation of the Structured Inventory of Malingered Symptomatology (SIMS)" (1997) *Journal of the American Academy on Psychiatry and Law* 25, 180–183.

Strasburger, L.H., "The Litigant-Patient: mental health consequences of civil litigation" (1999) *Journal of the American Academy of Psychiatry and the Law* 27 (2), 203–211.

Sullivan, B.K., May, K. and Galbally, L., "Symptom exaggeration by College adults in attention-deficit hyperactivity disorder and learning disorder assessments" (2007) *Applied Neuropsychology* 14 (3), 189–207.

Sullivan, K., Lange, R.T., and Dawes, S., "Methods of Detecting Malingering and Estimated Symptom Exaggeration Base Rates in Australia" (2005) *Journal of Forensic Neuropsychology* 4 (4), 49–70.

Sweet, J., "Professional practice guidelines for the use and interpretation of SVTs: The Time Has Come" (European Symposium on Symptom Validity, London, 2011).

Tombaugh, T.N., *Test of Memory Malingering* (Toronto: Multi-Health Systems, 1996).

Vallabhajosula, B. and van Gorp, W.G., "Post-Daubert admissibility of scientific evidence on malingering of cognitive deficits" (2001) *Journal of the American Academy of Psychiatric and the Law* 29 (2), 207–215.

Van Egmond, J. and Kummeling, I., "A blind spot for secondary gain affecting therapy outcomes" (2002) *European Psychiatry* 17 (1), 46–54.

Van Egmond, J., Kummeling, I. and Balkom, T.A., "Secondary gain has hidden motive for getting psychiatric treatment" (2005) *European Psychiatry* 20 (5–6), 416–421.

REFERENCES

Vrij, A. and Mann, S., "Deceptive responses and detecting deceit" in Halligan, P.W., Bass, C. and Oakley, D.A. (eds), *Malingering and Illness Deception* (New York: Oxford University Press, 2003).

van Hout, M.S.E., Schmand, B., Wekking, E.M. and Deelman, B.G., "Cognitive functioning in patients with suspected chronic toxic encephalopathy: evidence for neuropsychological disturbances after controlling for insufficient effort" (2006) *Journal of Neurology, Neurosurgery and Psychiatry* 77, 296–303.

Weissman, H.N., "Distortions and Deceptions in self presentation: effects of protracted litigation in personal injury cases" (1990) *Behavioural Sciences and the Law* 8, 67–74.

Whitney, K.A., Davis, J.J., Shepard, P.H. and Herman, S.M., "Utility of the Response Bias Scale (RBS) and other MMPI-2 validity scales in predicting TOMM performance" (2008) *Archives of Clinical Neuropsychology* 23, 777–786.

Wood, R.L. and Rutterford, N.A., "The effect of litigation on long-term cognitive and psychosocial outcome after severe brain injury" (2006) *Archives of Clinical Neuropsychology* 21, 239–246.

Young, G., *Malingering, Feigning and Response Bias in Psychiatric/Psychological Injury: Implications for Practice and Court* (New York: Springer, 2014).

Youngjohn, J.R., Wershba, R., Stevenson, M., Sturgeon, J. and Thomas, M.L., "Independent validation of the MMPI-2-RF Somatic/Cognitive and validity scales in TBI litigants tested for effort" (2011) *Clinical Neuropsychologist* 25 (3), 463–476.

Zigmond, A.S. and Snaith, R.P., "The Hospital Anxiety and Depression Scale" (1983) *Acta Psychiatrica Scandinavica* 67, 361–370.

CHAPTER 8

Neurorehabilitation After Acquired Brain Injury

Andrew Worthington

INTRODUCTION

Rehabilitation is essential to achieving an optimal outcome after brain injury and typically constitutes a key component of brain injury claims. How this is achieved in order to capitalise on potential for recovery and utilise resources effectively is the subject of the present chapter. The value of rehabilitation to many brain injury claims is recognised in the Rehabilitation Code, with which lawyers, case managers and most clinicians working in this area are familiar. The Code also acknowledges the importance of early intervention and attempts to provide a framework for maximising recovery. It is axiomatic that rehabilitation is a good thing, worthwhile and makes a difference, but there are many myths and misunderstandings about rehabilitation that can be challenged if not dispelled altogether, and equally good reason to question the wisdom of certain practices and always to ask "could we not do better?". Certain assumptions about rehabilitation are embedded in mainstream thinking and implicitly accepted in litigation. If the aim of rehabilitation is to help people to better fit into society, for example, this risks maintaining a particular world view where the "problem", if there is one, rests within the individual who needs "rehabilitating". This is contrary to many current views which identify disability as residing outside the individual, within the environment and attitudes of others. Likewise ability is of little value without opportunity yet therapy often treats rehabilitation as an end in itself rather than a means to an end.

8–001

Disability is not to be equated with ill-health. It follows that rehabilitation is a multidisciplinary enterprise which is not simply a subspecialty of medicine and any attempt to encompass the diverse aspects of rehabilitation under the rubric of rehabilitation medicine is to suggest the primacy of one perspective and professional discipline over all others. Whilst undoubtedly medical knowledge and expertise can contribute significantly to the care of children and adults with neurological conditions, the majority of recipients are medically stable and where this is not the case, for example, before stability is achieved or in the event of serious medical events, such as autonomic dysreflexia, status epilepticus or chest infection then a range of clinicians are likely to be involved in providing care. Rehabilitation is fundamentally about learning—learning new skills, re-relearning old ones, learning to adapt, learning how to compensate for deficits, and learning to hope and believe in the future. If rehabilitation is about trying to restore people as far as possible to the position they would have occupied had the brain injury not occurred, then in addition to promoting optimal physical health, rehabilitation must focus on the psychological, behavioural, social, vocational and environmental factors that otherwise limit the individual's participation in society, and where possible address those barriers that exist outside the individual and within their community and wider society.

This chapter will address the principal methods and means of delivery of rehabilitation from hospital to home, reviewing evidence on best practice and outcomes, whilst addressing some of the challenges and poor practice of which legal and clinical practitioners should be mindful. We start with a brief discussion of the main problems typically to be addressed after brain injury, followed by a summary of rehabilitation and service provision. The impact of brain injury in terms of physical, neuropsychological and neurobehavioural sequelae is reviewed before discussion of how these problems are addressed in terms of service organisation, teamwork, goal setting and outcome evaluation. The difficulties inherent in obtaining evidence of efficacy and of setting down appropriate quality standards are discussed, and the chapter ends with a look at future trends, notably the likely impact of technology on rehabilitation and initiatives to enhance cost-effectiveness.

1. BRAIN INJURY AND BRAIN RECOVERY

Acute treatment: preventing nerve cell death

8–002 What happens to nerves when they are damaged, do brain cells regenerate or grow back, and how many can you afford to lose before you start to get into difficulties? Lawyers and families often raise questions of this kind—straightforward queries without simple answers. Therefore this chapter begins with a brief incursion into what is known about the brain's ability to repair itself.

The modern concept of brain cells is little more than 100 years old (Finger, 2000) as reflected in the birth of terms such as dendrite (1890), neuron (1891), axon (1896) and synapse (1897). The traditional and rather gloomy view of brain injury is encapsulated by the Nobel prize-winning anatomist Cajal who stated, "In adult centres the nerve paths are something fixed, ended, immutable. Everything may die, nothing may regenerate" (see Finger, 2000) though presciently he added, "It is for the science of the future to change, if possible, this harsh decree".

Human neurons are amongst the most long-lived of cells but brain trauma subjects them to a range a range of mechanical and physiological mechanisms of damage. Cell death is linked to loss of membrane permeability, polarisation and rupture with consequent loss of intracellular contents. Shearing forces acting on surviving neurons damage the intricate axonal pathways by which nerve cells communicate (diffuse axonal injury). The precise relationship between neuron damage and functional consequences is unclear and depends on the nature of injury and the location and extent of damage, but diffuse axonal injury may be the primary mechanism responsible for the neuropsychological sequelae of brain injury (Smith et al., 2003). Recent evidence also suggests that axonal injury may be insidiously progressive and continue long after the initial injury (Johnson et al., 2013), which may explain some instances of late deterioration in function.

Unlike peripheral nerves, neurons of the central nervous system do not have the capability for spontaneous axonal regrowth (which is promoted by Schwann cells that envelope peripheral but not central nervous system axons). No new neurons can be born, which means that recovery is based upon surviving neurons sprouting new axons (see Barker and Dunnett, 1999). Thus, around an area of cell death, there will be a region of surviving damaged neurons that may provide a basis in time for taking over the functions of their neighbours. Some brain regions have more specialised functions than others so there may be less spare capacity to take on the functions of defunct cells. The conditions under which surviving neurons may extend new axons is unclear but experimental studies where this has been stimulated show that fibres grow around rather than through the area of damage. As Stichel and Muller (1998) comment, "this implicates misrouting of axons with a high risk of inappropriate pathway choices and failure to innervate the normal target as well as possible troublesome interference with surrounding projections" (p.126). At a behavioural level one can easily understand how this might translate into problems such as cognitive inefficiency, slow information processing and mental fatigue.

8–003

The notion that cell damage is irreversible has precipitated a focus within medical science on minimising the brain injury from the outset as far as possible. This has led to a range of interventions all designed to reduce the so-called second brain injury, (i.e. the consequence of rapid metabolic disturbance that follows the initial damage, and especially the control of inflammation and intracranial pressure). Decompressive craniectomies are standard practice and can be life-saving; early intervention, especially for extradural bleeds, may lead to good recovery (Rivas et al., 1988; Kuday et al., 1994).

By contrast progress in other respects has been disappointing and clinical guidelines are in short supply (Bayr et al., 2003). In a significant review paper Roberts et al. (1998) argued that there was no evidence to support the use of any of five specific intensive care interventions routinely employed in the management of severe head injury, none of which had been shown to reduce death or disability. Readers should bear this in mind because rehabilitation is often unfairly criticised as lacking evidence, as if acute treatments were backed by strong empirical support.

Moreover, the picture has barely changed in the 20 years since Roberts et al. published their paper. A recent systematic review of sedation for acutely ill, severely brain injured adults found no evidence for one form of sedative over another, whilst high doses of opioids should be avoided (Roberts et al., 2011). At best reducing intracranial pressure with hypertonic or isotonic saline may be superior to Mannitol (Wakai et al., 2007). Therapeutic cooling or targeted temperature management has theoretical benefits but is not without risk (Choi et al., 2012) and there is little support for induced hyperthermia after TBI (Clifton et al., 2001; 2011). Evidence is also against the routine use of corticosteroids (Alderson and Roberts, 1997; CRASH Trial Collaborators, 2005), but randomised studies suggest that progesterone has neuroprotective benefits (Wright et al., 2007; Ma et al., 2012). In one small study patients with severe brain injury given progesterone within eight hours of injury had significantly lower mortality than the placebo group and survivors showed higher scores on a measure of functional independence at six months (Xiao et al., 2008). Overall, however, the evidence is insufficient to warrant a clinical treatment guideline.

Does (lesion) size matter?

8-004 Many years ago it was believed that the severity of impairment after brain injury reflected the overall amount of brain cells lost, as if the brain were a kind of porridge within the skull and an injury was akin to losing a certain overall volume. Thus Lashley (1930) stated

> "After injuries to the brain, the rate of formation of some habits is directly proportional to the extent of injury and independent of the position within any part of the cortex. This shows that the rate of learning is not dependent upon the properties of individual cells, but is somehow a function of the total mass of tissue" (p.6).

The idea behind this notion was that all of the brain was involved in all (mental) activities and came to be known as "mass action".

This view of mass participation by the brain meant that the location of damage was largely irrelevant as there was no specialisation within the brain. This was a challenge to late nineteenth century received wisdom that different areas of the brain performed different functions (localisationism). An alternative notion posited that brain regions may have different specialisms but a portion of any given area was able to produce the behaviour normally controlled by the entire area (equipotentiality) which meant that partial damage to a region was compensated for by the remainder. For a time in the nineteenth and early twentieth century there was considerable debate between proponents of this view and localisationists who thought otherwise (Finger, 2000). We now recognise that there is merit in both views and that the brain is organised in networks of circuits of connected neurons distributed throughout the brain, with some circuits involved in several activities, whilst others are more specialised. This means that injury in a particular region may disrupt multiple brain functions, and any given function may be affected by various areas of brain damage. Depending on the extent of brain injury, the affected function may recover spontaneously, may be lost irretrievably or may be amenable to a degree of recovery subject to the right environmental stimulation (Robertson and Murre, 1999).

Neuroplasticity and rehabilitation

8-005 Whilst damaged nerve cells have very limited properties of recovery, the idea that the brain changes in response to experience (neuroplasticity) has been attributed to the so-called father of psychology, William James, in the late nineteenth century (Berlucchi and Buchtel, 2009). The brain is constantly learning, regardless of rehabilitation. Even something as routine as using touch screen technology changes the way the brain represents the fingertips in the somatosensory cortex. Remarkably the more recently someone has been using a touch screen the greater the activity in their somatosensory region (Gindrat et al.,

2015). It is assumed that this dynamic organisation, continually being updated by experience, which characterises the healthy brain, also provides a means to exploit surviving neurons in damaged networks. It means that the brain has a propensity to develop compensatory behavioural strategies to perform activities in response to lost function (Worthington, 2001).

This has been demonstrated in brain scans measuring cerebral activity after therapy. For example, hemiparesis causes a person to rely solely on their intact limbs on the non-affected side and this is associated with a reorganisation of brain activity (Weiller et al., 1993; Schaechter et al., 2002). Conversely, restricting the use of the "good" limb to ensure use of the affected limb is shown to lead to improved activation in the damaged region of the brain (Liepert et. al., 2000; Levy et al., 2001), although it has been difficult to translate this into a safe effective therapy (Page et al., 2002; Charles et al., 2005).

There is an exciting range of technologies for exploiting neuroplasticity ranging from neural tissue grafts and stem cell implants, transcranial magnetic stimulation and deep brain stimulation, to cognitive enhancing medication and virtual reality training, but their potential remains largely unfulfilled (Kleim et al., 2011; Cramer et al., 2011). Still, there are some established features of neuroplasticity that should guide the provision of good quality rehabilitation and it is worth reviewing these before considering how effectively they are applied in practice. Kleim and Jones (2008) distilled the evidence into 10 core principles which are succinctly summarised in Table 1 and which the author has developed as follows.

Use it or lose it

Research into sensory deprivation indicates that brain circuits not engaged in task performance for an extended period of time begin to degrade and the corresponding region may be taken over by another modality. For example, it has been suggested that extended PEG feeding may disengage neurons involved in swallowing, which then makes recovery of this function more difficult (Robbins et al., 2007). It follows that consideration needs to be given from an early stage to maintaining stimulation for preservation of functions, whether they are likely to be recruited behaviourally later in recovery or purely for quality of life.

8–006

Use it and improve it

The adage "practice makes perfect" finds support in research showing that the more a skill is rehearsed performance becomes less effortful and more technically adept. Much effort was invested in trying to identify a law that explained this phenomenon, Newell and Rosenbloom (1981) claiming task speed conformed to a mathematical power law "plotting the logarithm of the time to perform a task against the logarithm of the trial number always yields a straight line, more or less" (p.1). In reality rehabilitation is often about identifying an appropriate trade-off between speed and accuracy, so by task improvement we often wish to focus on efficiency although speed, accuracy, fluency, error reduction, and overall ability to sustain focus may all be appropriate measures of improvement.

8–007

The key point is that the brain has a natural response to reorganise itself and is driven to develop compensatory strategies which rehabilitation can capitalise upon. Professionally guided rehabilitation can enhance this propensity and ensure such behavioural alternatives or the well-meaning efforts of others do not become maladaptive.

Specificity

8–008   Research shows that repetition of existing or unskilled movements does not excite neurons to the extent of the performance of a newly acquired skill. In other words, the brain responds optimally to new learning rather than old knowledge (which is presumably using existing networks rather than establishing new ones). However, the brain changes are often highly specific to particular regions, so training one aspect of a task is likely to activate a subset of neurons involved in the complete task, which may be important, but may not lead to improvement in other aspects depending on the extent of damage. For therapists this means that careful attention needs to be paid to whether improvement reflects practice on what was trained or has generalised to encompass a broader set of related skills.

Repetition matters

8–009   In order to develop a skill it must be practised consistently. Like a flow of water gouging a path out of the landscape, new neural pathways are believed to be formed by repetitive activation. Both behaviour management and re-training of daily living skills rely on this principle. Once acquired however, it is important to continue to rehearse a skill lest the newly formed neural circuitry should degrade or be superseded by other behaviours. The reader must remember that (i) *skill acquisition* is rarely sufficient for sustainable change and must be followed by (ii) *skill consolidation*, which itself is no guarantee of (iii) skill application, and often further training is required to address the spontaneous deployment of skills or strategies taught in therapy. Thus a certain level of repetitive practice is considered necessary for a person to be able to use a skill outside therapy sessions in their daily life.

Intensity matters

8–010   As a general rule more intense training reaps rewards and is associated with increased neural sensitivity and synaptic efficiency (long term potentiation). However, there are caveats. First, evidence indicates this is unlikely to work where damage is so severe that the core knowledge is lost. Ellis and Young (1988) spent a full school year with a child with prosopagnosia (inability to identify faces) receiving daily treatment in over 1,000 sessions with little impact on face identification. Second, diffuse brain injury may also render ineffective any neighbouring neurons that might otherwise take over the responsibilities of dead cells meaning that any residual learning potential is excruciatingly slow. Francis et al. (2001) used mnemonics to help a man with agnosia (loss of knowledge about objects) re-learn letters with pain-staking commitment to therapy (the letter X alone took 10 weeks to recognise), but there was no generalisation to normal reading. Third, over-intense stimulation reduces function, causes fatigue and loss of motivation. The latter reduces commitment to future practice, while the fatigue may lead to deterioration in performance, inefficient learning and reinforcement of inappropriate neural activity, as well as potentially exacerbating other symptoms.

Time matters

Therapy that promotes neural restructuring should work at any stage but there are good reasons why early intervention is generally more effective than the same input at a later stage of recovery. Animal studies in motor learning, for example, have shown that environmental stimulation is associated with greater dendritic growth if commenced five days after ischaemic injury than after 30 days, which has potential implications for stroke rehabilitation in adults (Biernaskie et al., 2004). As discussed further in para.8–020, studies have shown that rehabilitative interventions can be commenced even whilst patients are receiving life support, which will enhance recovery and reduce the prospects of complications associated with prolonged intensive care such as muscle weakness, respiratory problems and infection (Parker et al., 2013).

8–011

Salience matters

Leaning can only take place if one event is consistently identified as being of greater importance to the learning experience than surrounding events. This simple fact has major implications for how rehabilitation is practised. It means that salient events need to be very clearly indicated by the therapist and delivered in an environment that facilitates this process. It also means that clinicians need to take into account impairments in motivation, attention and working memory that undermine learning after brain injury. Pharmacological agents that purport to increase neurotransmitters involved in arousal (such as dopamine), attention (like noradrenaline), learning (acetylcholine) or sensitivity to reward (dopamine) may be able to increase potential for rehabilitation, although reports of cognitive enhancement are largely anecdotal.

8–012

Age matters

In the healthy brain, ageing is characterised by neuronal and synaptic atrophy for which plastic brain changes do not altogether compensate, although what we think of as cognitive decline may be less evident for those involved in greater physical and mental activity. The idea that the younger brain recovers better than the aged brain is often associated with the work of Margaret Kennard whose work in the mid-twentieth century demonstrated that lesions at an earlier age in animals (and from observing recovery in children) were more recoverable. This has become known as the "Kennard principle" but, in fact, she acknowledged the limits of this observation which was largely concerned with motor impairments, and also recognised that symptoms could worsen or manifest afresh with the passage of time or in the course of maturation (Finger and Almli, 1988).

8–013

Much current thinking suggests that juvenile brain injury is linked to poorer outcomes, although this is influenced by many factors. It may also depend on how one measures outcome; Anderson et al. (2009), for example, reported that cognitive outcomes were poorest amongst children injured before two years of age, whereas behavioural outcomes were worse amongst children injured between seven and nine years of age than those who received their injuries aged three to six years, but similar to those of children injured before two years of age.

Transference

8–014   Pascual-Leone et al. (1995) showed that training on a finger movement task increased neuron excitability and enlarged the area of motor cortex which represented the hand. This suggests that repeated stimulation of neural circuits involved in one task promotes plasticity in neighbouring circuits that can be recruited in related tasks. Regular players of video games, for instance, are usually better at tasks utilising similar cognitive skills than novice players (Boot et al., 2008). It is also believed that unrelated activity in the form of physical exercise has a generalised beneficial effect by stimulating nerve growth chemicals, improving cognitive performance and increasing resistance to brain insult (Cotman and Berchtold, 2002; Vaynman and Gomez-Pinilla, 2005).

Interference

8–015   Studies with electrical and magnetic stimulation have shown that new learning is vulnerable to disruption from simultaneous or subsequent events. It is therefore important that due consideration is given in treatment to how people learn so that factors facilitating learning are optimised and interference is minimised. This is discussed below with reference to types of rehabilitation. Given the plasticity of neural circuitry any interference may lead to alternative pathways being established rather than the pattern of activation associated with a desired behaviour. It is not only people with brain injury who may adopt a path of least resistance, but family and carers can often unwittingly reinforce habits that make it more difficult to establish alternative ways of behaving once rehabilitation is underway. This is one reason why it is important that people receive early rehabilitation and that families are provided with information and guidance on what to expect during the course of recovery and how to respond.

Table 1: Principles of experience-dependent neural plasticity applied to rehabilitation

Principle	Description
1. Use It or Lose It	Failure to drive specific brain functions can lead to functional degradation.
2. Use It and Improve It	Training that drives a specific brain function can lead to an enhancement of that function.
3. Specificity	The nature of the training experience dictates the nature of the plasticity.
4. Repetition Matters	Induction of plasticity requires sufficient repetition.
5. Intensity Matters	Induction of plasticity requires sufficient training intensity.
6. Time Matters	Different forms of plasticity occur at different times during training.
7. Salience Matters	The training experience must be sufficiently salient to induce plasticity.
8. Age Matters	Training-induced plasticity occurs more readily in younger brains.
9. Transference	Plasticity in response to one training experience can enhance the acquisition of similar behaviours.
10. Interference	Plasticity in response to one experience can interfere with the acquisition of other behaviours.

2. UNDERSTANDING DISABILITY

The World Health Organization (WHO) (1980) International Classification of Impairment, Disability and Handicap (ICIDH) set out a simplified framework that attempted to explain the difference between these terms and their inter-relationships (see Figure 1).

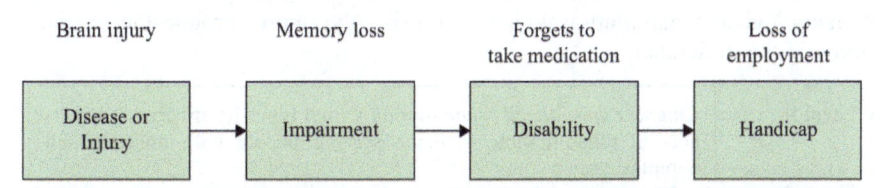

Brain injury → Memory loss → Forgets to take medication → Loss of employment

Disease or Injury → Impairment → Disability → Handicap

Figure 1: World Health Organization (1980), International Classification of Impairment, Disability and Handicap Classification Framework

This was interpreted by some as suggesting a narrow linear process of causation with the emphasis very much on the impact of the underlying impairment, although research showed that impairment does not predict disability or handicap (Johnston and Pollard, 2001). It was criticised particularly by people with disability for ignoring the influence of personal attributes (e.g. resilience), social influences (e.g. social support) and environmental factors (e.g. accessibility of public services). A revised scheme (see Figure 2) was introduced in 2001—the International Classification of Functioning, Disability and Health (ICF) (WHO, 2001), acknowledging these missing factors and also focusing on ability (rather than disability) and participation (as opposed to handicap).

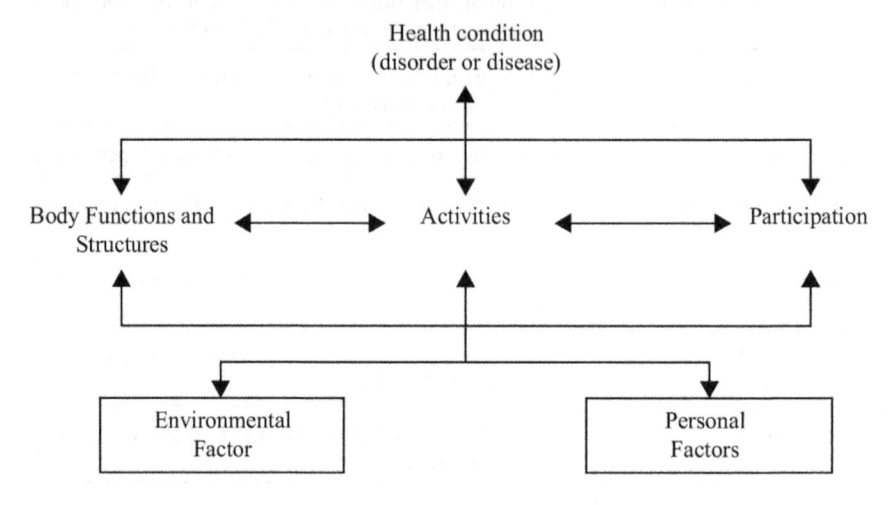

Figure 2: World Health Organization (2001), International Classification of Functioning, Disability and Health

This in turn has been criticised for merely relabelling rather than fundamentally changing the way disability is construed and for lacking precision. There are alternatives such as the Disability Creation model (Leplege et al., 2015) but the ICF is still the most widely referenced in rehabilitation.

3. MODELS OF REHABILITATION AND SERVICE PROVISION

8–017   The British Society of Rehabilitation Medicine (BSRM) recognises three aspects of neurological rehabilitation which unsurprisingly centres around the medical needs of the individual.

Level I:	*Complex specialised rehabilitation* which typically involves consultants in rehabilitation medicine serving people with multiple and complex needs.
Level II:	*Local specialist rehabilitation* which entails a multi-disciplinary team is usually medically-led or supported by a rehabilitation consultant catering for specific diagnostic groups.

Level III	*General rehabilitation* which applies to a wide range of conditions, not necessarily neurological, with access to medical advice but often led by non-medical staff. These are considered non-specialist and provide a range of services in hospital or the community

The BSRM has strongly advocated for an explicit commissioning system based upon level of specialism, with all services expected to produce data for the UK using specific outcome measures that potentially can be used to benchmark services (Turner-Stokes et al., 2012a). Whilst there is a need for quality performance metrics, the imposition of a set of clinical measures, given the diverse nature of rehabilitation, risks misrepresenting certain services and constraining innovation. For instance, one such measure, the Rehabilitation Complexity Scale, is supposed to reflect clinical needs (Turner-Stokes et al., 2012b). Leaving aside the question as to whether an individual's rehabilitation can be reduced to a set of clinical needs, this measure conflates the need for treatment with actual therapy, in other words, needs tend to be defined in terms of what inputs are being provided. This assumes that intervention would not be provided unnecessarily but does not address unmet needs and risks, under-estimating both complexity and severity.

The BSRM inevitably tends to focus on the medical aspects of rehabilitation and the role of rehabilitation physicians but it has an important role to play in this respect. Consultants in rehabilitation medicine tend to be based in specialist inpatient neurological centres but may also be attached to community teams. According to the BSRM, rehabilitation medicine consultants lead and coordinate neurological rehabilitation for people with complex needs. This may be the case in hospital, where most doctors are based, but as people continue a potentially life-long process of recovery and adjustment it is increasingly likely that environmental, social and psychological factors rather than medical issues will dictate long term outcomes. Research confirms how difficult it is to predict life satisfaction (Corrigan et al., 2001) and quality of life after brain injury (Steadman-Pare et al., 2001). Most studies show that medical indices like severity of injury do not predict later quality of life (Dikmen et al., 2003; Dijkers, 2004). In contrast, Teasdale and Engberg (2005) found there was a correlation between the two but subjective well-being was unrelated to injury severity, supporting other research suggesting that long term outcome is more a matter of psychological perspective than objective medical condition (Brown et al., 2000; Cicerone and Azulay, 2007).

This is not to diminish the influence on prognosis of long-term medical complications from conditions such as epilepsy, diabetes, respiratory and urinary infections, which need medical care from nurses and GPs, as well as medical specialists. Rather it is to query whether an expensive and scarce resource is necessary to be leading the care of medically stable patients in the community. In fact, more as a matter of expediency than anything else, many community neurorehabilitation teams are led by other healthcare professionals, although often such services may lack back-up from key medical disciplines such as rehabilitation medicine and neuropsychiatry.

8–018

There are good reasons, both practical and theoretical, why rehabilitation in the post-acute period should take place away from hospitals. These are summarised in Table 2 below and discussed later in the chapter, but perhaps the main difference is succinctly captured in the words of the late Sheldon Berrol, an eminent American rehabilitation physician, who commented that whilst hospitals are for people who are ill, rehabilitation is an educative process requiring active engagement, and yet from an early age the one thing we all learn is "when we are sick we don't have to go to school". Consequently Eames, a neuropsychiatrist, proposed that "rehabilitation units for the head-injured should be developed separately from patients with other sorts of disorders and should be located, as far as possible, away from hospitals" (Eames, 1989, p.51).

Table 2: Key differences between hospital care and non-hospital provision

Hospital	**Non-hospital settings**
Treats people who are ill/unstable	Manages people who are well/medically stable
Led by medical consultant	Often has a non-medical lead
Populated by nurses and doctors	Populated by therapists and support workers
Focus on medical interventions	Focus on educational and activity
Medication commonly used	Medication kept to a minimum
Patients as passive recipients of care	Clients as active participants in therapy
Multidisciplinary teams	Inter or transdisciplinary team working
Focus on impairments/ability	Focus on ability/participation
Therapists tend to set goals	More emphasis on client-led goals
Comprises therapy sessions	Focus on real life activities
Often risk averse	Generally more embracing of risk

Rehabilitation pathways

8–019 The majority of rehabilitation takes place outside hospital and this is entirely appropriate except for those cases where premature discharge or inadequate resources have failed to ensure a person had obtained maximum benefit from hospital admission. In many cases, however, to use current terminology, patients embark on a "journey" through a "pathway" where they should receive appropriate assistance from the right professionals in the light of their needs at that time. We have already seen that various factors determine whether this occurs and different geographical regions will have different brain injury pathways but, in principle at least, one can distinguish between acute hospital services, specialist neurological rehabilitation and neurobehavioural services, outpatient rehabilitation in hospital or a day centre, and community rehabilitation provided in the home.

Figure 3 below provides a schematic representation of these components, with darker shaded arrows reflecting the path more typically taken after brain injury.

MODELS OF REHABILITATION AND SERVICE PROVISION

No attempt is made to distinguish between services provided by the NHS, charities, private companies and independent practitioners. This is partly to avoid over-complication but also because the landscape is constantly changing and what is most important is that the rehabilitation is appropriate rather than who provides it.

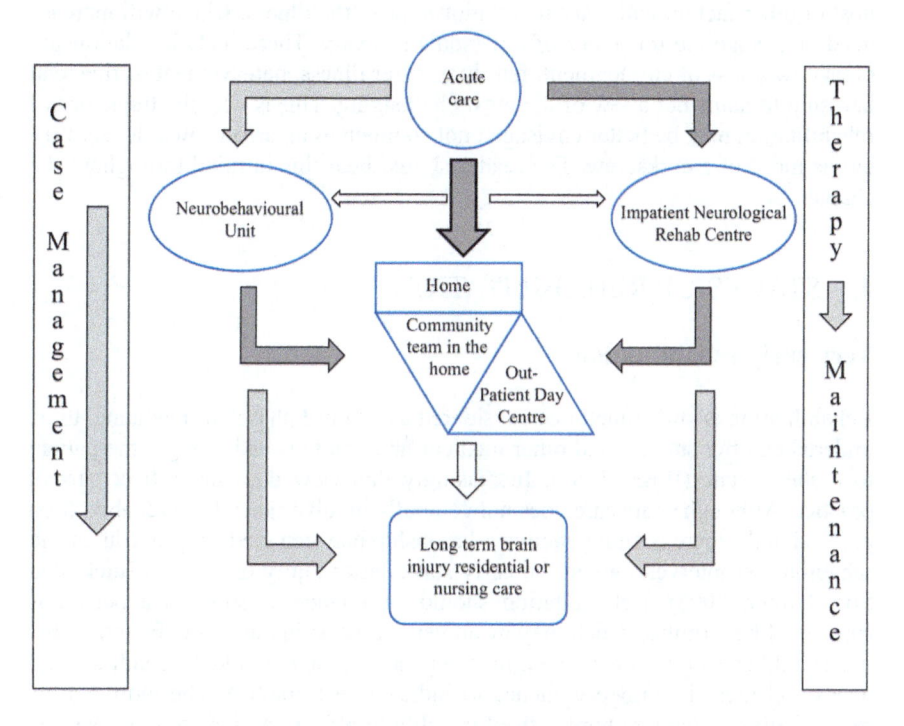

Figure 3: Schematic Brain Injury Pathway

As illustrated above, the process of rehabilitation has multiple components. In the next section the types of intervention at various stages of recovery are discussed, emphasising both the importance of early intervention and also the increasing role of non-statutory services. Although recovery may be considered in terms of acute, subacute and post-acute care, the division is somewhat arbitrary at the margins and it is often misunderstood to apply to specific types of treatment when, in fact, rehabilitation can begin at different times depending on the nature and severity of injury and the resources available. While there is a certain appeal to the idea that there are defined stages of rehabilitation as it makes a complex process more easily understood, it must be remembered that this is a simplification and does not reflect what may happen on the ground. For example, rehabilitation does not always proceed in straightforward linear progression from intensive care to hospital to home.

Another common misconception is that following a brain injury a person presents with all sequelae at the outset, to be gradually whittled away by therapists until there is a rump of residual problems which provide the basis of the future care component to a claim. In reality a multitude of later onset problems can emerge to scupper best laid plans and initiate a re-think on priorities. Some of these may be directly attributable to the injury and index events. These include organic and reactive mood disorders, post-traumatic conditions like epilepsy, complications from the original injury like heterotopic ossification (bone growth intruding into soft tissue), and procedures such as surgical revision of scars and cranioplasty. In addition, there are likely to be a host of other factors with varying relationships to the illness, which will increase need or change the trajectory of a person's recovery. These include relationship breakdown, loss of employment, family or carer illness, bereavement or financial hardship to name but a few of the most challenging. This is why the trajectory of rehabilitation may be better envisaged not so much as an arrow towards recovery but as more of a corkscrew. The reader should bear this in mind throughout the chapter.

4. STAGES OF REHABILITATION

Very early rehabilitation

8–020   Rehabilitation is still sometimes considered as a "third phase" of medicine, to be undertaken after surgery and other medical interventions had brought the patient to a stable state (Rusk, 1960). Increasingly this view does not reflect current practice. Although acute care does not generally involve specialised rehabilitation professionals, there is an interactive relationship between medical procedures and rehabilitation interventions in the early stages after injury or illness (Stucki and Stier-Jarmer, 2005). Rehabilitation should commence as soon as a person is capable of benefitting, which may mean very early on in their care. Exactly what this should constitute at any given time depends on the individual's condition and needs and there is limited evidence to indicate best practice. The term "early" rehabilitation in the literature is used variably to refer to periods of days, weeks, months and (at least in the case of traumatic brain injury (TBI)) the first year or two after injury (e.g. Wood et al., 1999).

In general, very early rehabilitation tends to focus on preventing additional complications that will be more difficult and costly to treat at a later stage, such as contractures, but is also possible to reduce impairments from an early stage. Much of the research on very early intervention has been conducted after stroke where the recovery window begins and ends earlier than TBI. For example, Musicco et al. (2003) reported that stroke patients who commenced rehabilitation within seven days had better outcomes than those who started rehabilitation after 30 days, whilst Matsui et al. (2010) reported that rehabilitation starting within three days of stroke leads to improved outcomes. Early physical mobility is associated with reduced complications of immobility (Sorbello et al., 2009) and shorter lengths of stay. Speech and language problems may also benefit, with some studies suggesting therapy can meaningfully start within a few days of stroke (Godecke et al., 2014).

After severe traumatic brain injury many patients require intensive care including mechanical ventilation for which, until recently, patients were routinely immobilised for long periods. In contrast, research now shows that early mobilisation and physical therapy is a safe and effective intervention that can have a significant impact on functional outcomes (Adler and Malone, 2012). Prolonged intensive care is itself a risk factor for the development of subsequent complications which has led to the notion of a critical illness syndrome (Bolton et al., 1984; Zochodne et al., 1987) associated with damage to function of the muscles (myopathy) and nerves (neuropathy). Although sensory fibres and cranial nerves were generally thought to be spared, cognitive impairments are now recognised amongst the possible short and long term sequelae, possibly related to hypoxia (Hopkins and Brett, 2005). In one study, Hopkins et al. (1999) reported that 30% showed a reduction on intellectual tests and 78% showed reduction in concentration and/or memory. It is important to note that none of these cases had any primary neurological injury, such as stroke or TBI, that could have accounted for these results. More recently in a study of older adults (average age: 76 years), Iwashyna et al. (2010) reported significant reductions in cognitive function and increased disability following sepsis lasting up to eight years. For this reason, early cognitive intervention has been advocated as having benefit as part of a multidisciplinary rehabilitation programme for ICU survivors (Jackson et al., 2012)

Psychological symptoms may also have their origins in intensive care. One study reported that 100 of 150 patients treated in intensive care units (ICUs) had some memory of the experience (Rotondi et al., 2002). Amongst the most commonly reported adverse recollections were difficulty speaking (65%), being thirsty (62%), feeling tense (46%), not being in control (46%) and difficulty swallowing. Patients who recalled having an endotracheal tube in situ (a breathing tube inserted down the windpipe) were bothered moderately to extremely by being unable to speak (68%), pain (56%) and anxiety (59%). Some sedated patients may have partial, incomplete recollections which are particularly disturbing. Weinert and Sprenkle (2008), for example, reported that only 18% of ventilated patients had no recollection whatsoever of ICU and those with memories in the context of delirium reported more post-traumatic symptoms, with post-traumatic stress disorder (PTSD) present in 15% of the sample at six months (see also Jones et al., 2001). However, amongst enduring psychological symptoms following ICU admission, the diagnosis of PTSD appears to be less common than depression (Jackson et al., 2014). It is now recognised that there are unmet psychological needs linked to the experience of critical care but the most effective means of meeting these is unclear. Randomised studies have shown no benefit of nurse follow-up clinics (Cuthbertson et al., 2009) or self-help manuals (Jones et al., 2003) but intervention whilst still on ICU may be more beneficial (Peris et al., 2011).

8–021

Families also suffer, especially children, with a relative in ICU. Their memories and anxieties continue long after discharge and may be unacknowledged by the brain injured person if they have no recollection of this period. To date their needs have not been widely recognised, but the term post-intensive care syndrome has also been proposed to encompass diverse and enduring patient and/or family experiences (Needham et al., 2012). In recent years more hospitals have adopted the practice of introducing critical care diaries completed by staff and visitors which have been shown to be effective in filling in gaps and reducing trauma (Bäckman and Walther, 2001; Jones et al., 2010).

Rehabilitation in hospital

8–022 Once patients are out of danger and have been medically stabilised, rehabilitation can begin in earnest. How much of this occurs in hospital depends on the condition of the patient, the resources of the hospital and the availability of alternative services. A large regional teaching hospital may have a dedicated neurological rehabilitation ward; a smaller hospital may have notional rehabilitation beds. Some hospitals have rehabilitation wards that are largely populated by older people who have suffered falls and need to get back on their feet again before they can be discharged home safely. Some rehabilitation units within hospitals focus on stroke care, and for that reason tend to be populated with older patients and may have little understanding or tolerance of agitated and confused TBI patients. Many hospital rehabilitation services focus on physical recovery and have limited, if any, access to specialist neurological rehabilitation consultants and neuropsychologists.

Thus, in many cases, what passes for rehabilitation is based upon assessment of nursing and mobility needs, risk assessment and efficient discharge planning. This is no criticism of the hard-pressed clinicians who are often given very difficult people to care for with limited resources and expertise. The focus is upon maintaining a throughput of patients to avoid the dreaded "bed-blocking" scenario. Some NHS rehabilitation services now set a limit to how many days a person should stay on the ward. This means that the care, rather than being focused on maximising recovery, shifts to determining whether a person will have sufficient support to return home, needs long term institutional care, or requires more time and input elsewhere to determine their true prognosis.

Fortunately, very early intervention can assist the timely transition through the acute care pathway. In the US, Sirois et al. (2004) reported that shorter administrative delays in transferring patients from trauma care to rehabilitation wards is associated with improved cognitive function and reduced length of stay in hospital. The problem is that many hospital rehabilitation services are ill-equipped to deal with the range of problems that arise from TBI and other acute neurological events that cause behaviour disturbance. Access to neuropsychiatry advice is extremely limited and typically ward staff have to rely on liaison psychiatrists, mental health nurses or clinical psychologists for assistance in dealing with a range of typical behavioural disturbances, ranging from post-traumatic agitation, delirium, impulsivity and violence, to smoking, consumption of alcohol and attempts to leave the hospital. Often the shock and anxiety of the family at their loved one's behaviour and perceived impotence of hospital staff to prevent this adds to the general climate of tension and frustration. In such an atmosphere there can be an understandable need to use sedating medications to prevent the brain injured person harming themselves and others, as well as a keen desire to discharge or transfer them elsewhere as soon as possible.

8–023 Evidence suggests that this problem is compounded by the demographics of head injury which show a general trend towards higher incidence in areas of higher deprivation (Bruns and Hauser, 2003; see Tennant (2005) for why London, with its public transport network is an exception). This has also been shown for children in the UK (Parslow et al., 2005). My own (unpublished) research in

Birmingham showed that over half the people presenting to their local hospital with a mild TBI resided in the most deprived 10% of postcode districts. In Scotland, Dunn et al. (2003) reported that head injured victims from more socially-economically deprived areas were more likely to be male, to have been assaulted and to have a history of alcohol and substance misuse. Significantly these patients spent less time in intensive care and had shorter hospital admissions than comparably injured patients.

This data should give cause for concern. It would be naïve to believe that referral onto specialist rehabilitation centres is based solely on clinical need. Rather, evidence suggests it has to be viewed in the broader context of care and depends on characteristics of the brain injured person and the referring professional (Foster and Tilse, 2003). Research has been conducted largely outside the UK so one has to be cautious about drawing parallels, but one early study suggests onward referral for rehabilitation was less likely if a patient was not reviewed by a rehabilitation specialist and that, when there was uncertainty about potential, social and demographics factors tended to influence decisions (Wrigley et al., 1994). Based on observations of team meetings, Foster and Tilse (2004) found that referral decisions were influenced by practitioners' selection and their interpretation of clinical and non-clinical patient factors, along with organisational pressures and resource constraints. Lest the reader be tempted to consider matters in the UK to be based more on clinical need, McCarthy (1999) provided a frank if somewhat depressing admission that without a dedicated rehabilitation budget "most neurorehabilitation purchasing is pragmatically based on individual costs, and uninformed by scientific methods or concerns for outcomes" (p.298). Yet delays in accessing rehabilitation are costly. In the UK one study of neurosurgical patients revealed that only 38% of bed occupancy days were taken up with essential acute neurosurgical ward management. Overall, 21% of bed days would have been more appropriately spent in "rapid access"/acute rehabilitation beds, 13% in "active participation" rehabilitation beds and 5% in cognitive/behavioural rehabilitation units (Bradley et al., 2006).

In an effort to improve efficiency and standardise best practice, guidelines for transfer to rehabilitation have been proposed, although there remains wide variation between and within hospitals. These were outlined by Turner-Stokes and Wade (2004):

(1) Patients in hospital more than 48 hours with impaired consciousness or mobility should be reviewed as soon as possible after injury by a rehabilitation team to advise on appropriate referral and interim management techniques to prevent secondary complications such as contractures (shortening of muscles or joints), pressure sores, malnutrition and aspiration.
(2) Severely brain injured patients still in coma should be referred to a specialist acute brain injury unit where their acute care may be supplemented by an interdisciplinary team of therapists trained in the prevention of potentially disabling complications

(3) Patients who are unable to go home directly and require a period of post-acute inpatient rehabilitation should be transferred to a specialist post-acute rehabilitation unit as soon as they are medically stable and fit to engage in rehabilitation.
(4) Patients transferring to rehabilitation services should be accompanied by their medical records or a full discharge summary.

8–024   The reality, however, is that a shortfall of experienced staff remains a major obstacle to quality rehabilitation. One survey of rehabilitation physicians identified the most common constraints to service delivery as being financial, and the lack of specialists in medicine, clinical psychology and speech and language therapy (Andrews and Turner-Stokes, 2005). The number of medical doctors specialising in rehabilitation per capita is far lower in the UK than comparable European countries such as France, Germany, Sweden and Italy (BSRM, 2007). In clinical neuropsychology, as senior clinicians leave, their posts are frozen or downgraded such that incumbents have to do more with less and often lack experience. Service leads, for example, may not have reached consultant level, which has an impact on ability to handle complex cases and on the status of the service and how it is viewed by colleagues. In the past rehabilitation has been seen as a Cinderella service and a luxury to be indulged only once the real work of surgery and critical care which keeps people alive has been completed. In case the reader considers this battle has been long won, the author has read one (defendant) medico-legal report recently in which the expert surgeon claimed that there was no evidence that rehabilitation has any benefit, and implied that rehabilitation doctors effectively conspired with surgical colleagues in order to get patients off the acute wards!

As part of the development of major trauma pathways in 2010, the Clinical Advisory Group recommended that every patient with major trauma should receive high quality rehabilitation. This led to the development of a "rehabilitation prescription" whereby each patient admitted to a Major Trauma Centre should have their rehabilitation needs assessed and documented. In the author's opinion, whilst well-intentioned, the medical terminology could hardly be more inappropriate. The notion of a prescription embodies the power imbalance in medical settings that arises when one person decides what is best for another and reinforces the outdated view that individuals are somehow passive recipients of rehabilitation. As one patient described it,

> "I wanted to be a whole person again and here my whole life was being reduced to medical reports, graphs and charts... like seeing myself examined under a microscope and having a scientist clinically describe every broken piece or part."

Residential rehabilitation

8–025   Over the past 30 years there has been a significant growth in non-NHS residential rehabilitation services. This has been fuelled by several factors but in large part it is in response to the limitations of hospital settings, particularly for managing traumatic brain injury and other conditions where the predominant sequelae are mental as opposed to physical. This includes the difficulties of providing non-medical leadership in such settings, and the need for a longer term perspective in order to bring about meaningful social and psychological changes that typically extend well beyond the timescales most busy hospitals can afford.

The NHS and Community Care Act (1990) placed the onus onto Local Authorities to provide suitable services, shifting the emphasis away from large institutional settings into smaller homes. At the same time provision by Local Authorities has steadily declined which created fertile ground for the growth of third sector and private enterprise to establish alternatives for care and rehabilitation (see Worthington and Merriman, 2008). Throughout the UK there is now a plethora of supported living homes, housing schemes and medium-sized residential facilities for adults with brain injury alongside large private hospitals. In addition, some residential schools, often run along charitable lines, provide neurorehabilitation alongside specialist education for children and adolescents. The priority for children is usually their education rather than therapy if it comes to a choice between the two, but rehabilitation teams can provide effective liaison with school staff in mainstream and special education settings. Only the most severe cases are admitted to the very few residential children's neurorehabilitation facilities. In the author's experience of working in two such services, it is very difficult to combine the cultures of education, rehabilitation and (in the case of residential establishments) hospital or children's homes, into a cohesive shared vision.

Adults and sometimes adolescents may be admitted to private hospital rehabilitation units. These tend to manage the more challenging, severely disturbed population (those with mental health, forensic or additional comorbidities for example) or the more profoundly disabled with complex physical, medical and nursing needs, including people in low awareness states and progressive degenerative conditions. Many private rehabilitation centres also have long term nursing beds, whilst some nursing homes purport to provide a degree of rehabilitation. Again, there is the problem of a clash of professional cultures. The author's experience is that it is no easy task to integrate the medically-driven care ethos of nursing with the social and psychological enabling approach characterising rehabilitation.

Slow stream rehabilitation

A psychiatrist of the author's acquaintance once described rehabilitation as a euphemism for long term care. Undoubtedly there are care homes which have latched on to the term as a means of aggrandising their care provision (and perhaps increasing their fees). Yet it would be unscientific to dismiss the evidence of plasticity in effecting late changes in behaviour. The potential for significant gains to be made over the long term underpins what is sometimes called continuing or slow stream rehabilitation. These services tend to be populated by adults too young for a nursing home who are unlikely to respond to intensive or short term rehabilitation. Consequently, such facilities are usually longer term but, unlike a traditional care facility, they include access to therapists for maintenance or slow learning of functional skills. The emphasis remains goal-oriented (see para.8–052) but there is a recognition that learning proceeds slowly and may not substantially change the long term prognosis or care needs, but optimises quality of life. On occasion, however, the steady accumulation of

8–026

small gains within a structured environment is sufficient to warrant a change of placement, such as a move from a 20-bed residential facility to a shared house locally. This may occur 10 years or more after the original brain injury; the potential of neuroplasticity even within a damaged brain should not be underestimated. In the author's experience such late transitions are not always welcomed by the family (who may have wished to approach their old age feeling their son or daughter's future was safely established rather than taking on new risks) or the funder (as the move from a larger home to a shared house or individual living arrangement may well be more costly).

Residential brain injury rehabilitation centres also have a key role to play in facilitating the timely discharge from acute hospitals or inpatient neurological rehabilitation centres. There is no specific registration for rehabilitation facilities, so unless they cater for people with heavy nursing needs, they tend to be designated as residential care homes for registration purposes. Nursing and medical input tends to be provided by GP and district nursing services, which at times means the opening of a new centre is viewed warily by already stretched primary care teams. They are also often the battle ground for funding disputes between health and social care services as to eligibility criteria for continuing healthcare funding. Sometimes considered to be an expensive resource by Local Authorities who have a duty to provide only an appropriate (but not the most appropriate) placement, there is now good evidence that such services can be very cost-effective over the longer term.

Neurobehavioural rehabilitation

8–027 Neurobehavioural units are specialist centres, often independent hospitals, that manage the minority of brain injured adults (there are no similar facilities for children) who manifest very challenging behaviour and may present significant risk to themselves and others. Alderman (2007) for example recorded 5,548 separate incidents of aggression by 108 participants over a 14-day period, including 729 physical assaults. They may require treatment under the Mental Health Act. The UK has been a pioneer in the development of such services (Eames and Wood, 1985), largely outside the NHS, which draw particularly upon neuropsychological and neuropsychiatric expertise rather than the traditional rehabilitation medicine consultant, reflecting perhaps the origin of such services in learning disability rather than other neurological conditions, such as stroke, which have tended to focus more on physical rehabilitation (Worthington et al., 2016).

These services address the disorders of cognition, behaviour, motivation and emotional regulation that undermine relationships, productive activity and participation in other forms of rehabilitation (Wood, 1987; Alderman and Wood, 2013; Worthington and Alderman, 2016). The term neurobehavioural disability refers to the wide-ranging impact of this constellation of deficits. The pattern of disability exhibited by individuals can vary considerably depending upon the nature, location, and severity of their brain injury, pre-injury behaviour and personality, and post-injury circumstances. In many cases the disability can be subtle, but still have a pervasive psychosocial impact because of problems with interpersonal relationships, an inability to adapt behaviour to changing situations, and poor temper control.

Where neurobehavioural problems are particularly severe, referral to a dedicated neurobehavioural unit may be warranted. As illustrated in Figure 1, this can be brought about by several means, such as transfer from an acute ward when a patient is disturbed whilst in PTA, from an inpatient neurological rehabilitation facility due to behaviour interfering with progress or from a community placement breaking down due to antisocial behaviour.

More than most services, there is a strong emphasis on working across traditional professional boundaries and there may be little, if any, rehabilitation medicine input. Structure is sustained through the physical environment, a daily routine and interventions derived from learning theory. Medication which may have been used to control behaviour previously (but which interferes with learning) is minimised. The result is creation of a prosthetic environment that increases awareness and motivation, whilst shaping behavioural responses into acceptable forms and optimising capacity for learning adaptive and social skills (Wood and Worthington, 2001; Worthington and Wood, 2008).

Rehabilitation in the community

The majority of rehabilitation for survivors of brain injury takes place in the community. This does not mean that the greatest progress takes place in this setting as the pace of change slows over time but, in general, rehabilitation will occur for a longer period in the community than in hospital and the gains made in the community tend to have a greater bearing on the long-term outcomes. Despite this there is a dearth of evidence as to what works. For example, Carlson et al. (2006) reviewed interventions for improving social participation, finding only 30 articles on this topic amongst 974 on rehabilitation, none of which identified best practice. As a result many practitioners fall back on the "whatever it takes" approach (Willer and Corrigan, 1994). This also means recognising the importance of a relational or systemic approach to rehabilitation in which the aim of therapy is to re-stabilise a dysfunctioning network, often within the family (Gan et al., 2006). In this endeavour the crucial role of family therapists should be recognised (Johnson and McCown, 1997). Some are dual trained in neuropsychology, but it is more important when working at this level that they have systemic therapy skills than neuropsychology training, although a clinical neuropsychologist may also be required to work alongside them and deliver one-to-one rehabilitation for other issues. This is not duplication of effort but two specialist complimentary aspects of rehabilitation.

8–028

Unfortunately, community rehabilitation has always been chronically underfunded and has never received the levels of attention, resources and prestige that practitioners working in hospitals are accorded. This probably reflects the association of rehabilitation with health and the attitude that poor health is something to be "fixed" by going to hospital. As Franz Kafka wrote in his short story A Country Doctor, "Writing prescriptions is easy but coming to an understanding of people is hard" (reprinted in Helman, 2003).

Outside the UK, Pickelsimer et al. (2007) reported that the most frequently cited barriers to services in a study of community-dwelling persons with TBI was a "lack of awareness, advocacy and case management" and help to obtain information about services. This is where advocates, charities and case managers have a key role to play in ensuring timely and appropriate rehabilitation and support. Yet statutory provision remains limited: Andrews and Tuner-Stokes (2005), for example, reported that one-third of inpatient rehabilitation facilities had no community team to refer to after discharge. McMillan and Ledder (2001) reviewed 35 community rehabilitation teams in 25 health authorities. There were fewer than 1.5 professionals per 4,000–5,000 neurologically disabled adults. Most teams focused on physical disability and 60% did not have a clinical psychologist. Neuropsychology continues to be a scarce resource with referral systems and waiting lists problematic and nearly two-thirds of PCTs describing the service as "difficult" or "very difficult" to access (Bernard et al., 2010). Unsurprisingly perhaps, research suggests that significant needs remain unaddressed within the first year following hospital discharge, particularly in regard to rehabilitation, social work support and provision of specialist equipment (Siegert et al., 2014).

8–029　The evidence base for community rehabilitation in the UK is mostly limited to individual case studies rather than overall services but research suggests that when properly resourced multidisciplinary intervention in the community is more effective than written information alone in addressing cognitive and psychological legacies of brain injury, even many years after injury (Powell et al., 2002). Evaluation of the North Wales community brain injury service showed that 71% of their clients rated themselves as improved, although this was not replicated to the same degree by carers (Coetzer et al., 2003). Outside the UK comprehensive day programmes are more widely established and have shown significant improvements in daily living skills and well-being (Malec, 2001; Cicerone et al., 2004).

While some evidence suggests more intensive therapy in the early stages of brain injury recovery pays dividends (Cifu et al., 2003) this is not necessarily desirable in the community. There is a crucial difference between providing intensive rehabilitation, which is often mistakenly considered the only way to achieve recovery potential, and extensive rehabilitation which entails a comprehensive regime that addresses all aspects required to optimise recovery, one step at a time, and at a pace which is practicable and sustainable. The "intense is best" approach by this stage is usually unhelpful and more is achieved by the therapy team prioritising various inputs at different times and adopting a "little and often" approach so as not to overwhelm the client and their family or exhaust resources prematurely. In this respect the brain injury case manager can have an important gate-keeping role.

Case management

8–030　This chapter is not directly concerned with clinical case management, but it would be remiss not to recognise that in the context of brain injury claims, the role of the case manager is frequently central. As case management is not statutorily regulated, practitioners are usually regulated by their professional body such as the Health and Care Professions Council (HCPC), for those with a therapy background, or the Nursing and Midwifery Council (NMC) for nurses. Lawyers recognise the importance of this role, enshrined in the Rehabilitation Code. The establishment of competencies for case managers is to be broadly welcomed, although some excellent case managers, who do not happen to be registered professionals such as nurses, social workers or therapists, are excluded from advanced status within the British Association of Brain Injury Case Managers (BABICM). Having set up and run a postgraduate degree in brain injury case management, with first-hand experiences of a variety of different approaches, the author's experience is that personality and professionalism are more important for competency to practise than formal qualifications in another discipline.

Research shows that case management without funding behind it has limited impact (Greenwood et al., 1994), but properly funded case management can both supplement professional therapy and enhance the overall therapeutic input. In such circumstances case managers can be vital to the success of rehabilitation, especially in complex cases. This capitalises on research elsewhere that shows that the experience of continuity of care is enhanced by access to a single trusted clinician who sees the client as a partner and assists them to navigate between clinicians and services (Haggerty et al., 2013).

Yet there are times when one might question whether funds for case management might be better spent on additional therapy, or whether therapists could not undertake some of the case management role within their therapeutic relationships. There is also a potential conflict of interest if case managers exert too much influence on spending that is not informed by the views of other team members. Instances include a deputy agreeing with a case manager that there was no need to pay for therapy whilst continuing to pay for a support worker (employed via the case management company). In such a case one might argue that further therapy would eliminate the need for both therapist and support worker in due course. Other examples in the author's experience include being removed from the role of treating clinician after refusing to endorse a computer brain training programme in one instance, and in another case, being replaced by a therapist offering to provide more frequent input for which there was little justification. Whilst differences of opinion about levels of input are to be expected at times, they should be addressed openly and with knowledge of the family and deputy to ensure that additional funds are not being spent unnecessarily. It takes a confident (and busy) clinician to state that more input with a client is not required.

Some case mangers regard their role as leading the team but most experts making recommendations will recognise the case management role as one of coordination; where clinical leadership is specified then a neuropsychologist is often identified as the most appropriate lead given the typical problems associated with traumatic brain injury. Within the broader rehabilitation team, case managers have an obligation to ensure that the therapists they engage are working effectively and appropriately, and if not, they should sensitively address the issues as best they can. Ultimately, with the client's and their family's agreement, they may wish to change therapists. By the same token therapists have a duty to raise any concerns about the conduct of the case manager.

8–031

NEUROREHABILITATION AFTER ACQUIRED BRAIN INJURY

Case managers should provide coordination and operational management of the case but should not try to manage the individual therapists; they alone are responsible for their actions and are accountable to their professional bodies, to their own line managers if employed by another company, and to the client. Having engaged a therapist the case manager should trust them to get on with the job as they see fit, not get overly involved in day-to-day issues that affect the therapeutic relationship with their client. Heavy-handed case management and micro-management is costly and unhelpful to good team working.

Neurorehabilitation in practice

8–032　This section deals with important neuropsychological and neurobehavioural factors that virtually all forms of neurorehabilitation to some degree have to contend with, appreciation of which is important to lawyers as to clinicians and families.

Identifying impairments and constraints on learning

8–033　Other chapters in this volume have detailed the neurological, psychiatric and neuropsychological sequelae of brain injury. Rehabilitation treats such impairments as either a focus for intervention or as a constraint upon treatment to be circumvented in order to optimise recovery. Bearing in mind that all types of rehabilitation involve some form of learning, there are four categories of potential impairment which should be identified and addressed in any rehabilitation programme (Table 3).

Table 3: Classification of impairments for rehabilitation programming

Sensory impairments limiting the ability to process, integrate and interpret information about the outside world and relate this to an internal bodily state.
For example, the inability to link different sources of sensory information consistently overloads the brain and undermines learning and behaviour. This arises from damage to sensory nerves, to arousal centres, primary cortical areas that receive sensory information or to association areas where multiple sensory inputs are combined.
Physical constraints on the ability to carry out learning activities.
Musculoskeletal and neurological impairments affecting motor control can either prevent or make painful and effortful key activities which means alternative approaches are required. This can arise from peripheral physical injury or as a result of damage to motor areas of the brain which send and receive signals from muscles.
Deficits in core cognitive abilities required for learning
Disorders of attention and deficits in the perception, comprehension, encoding and recall of information are all likely to affect how and what a person can understand and retain in order to relearn old skills or acquire new strategies.

STAGES OF REHABILITATION

> Impairment high-level executive processes responsible for integrating and appraising environmental events in terms of cognitive, emotional and social significance
>
> Disruption to these functions results in a range of dysexecutive and neurobehavioural disorders in initiating, regulating and adapting actions to achieve meaningful goals and social acceptability.

Neuropsychological constraints on rehabilitation

As summarised above practitioners need to take account of a wide range of physical, sensory and higher neurological deficits when planning and delivering therapies. In particular, all forms of rehabilitation need to take into account some key neuropsychological factors that constrain learning and engagement.

8–034

Attention, processing speed and learning

Processing speed relies on the integrity of multiple brain pathways whilst attention relies upon several brain regions, in the parietal cortex, the prefrontal cortex, and connected subcortical structures. Generalised brain damage such as diffuse axonal injury or those caused by brain swelling, ischaemia or hypoxia often cause slowed processing and inability to maintain focus of attention or attend selectively, resulting in distractibility. The result is impaired or inefficient learning. Although memory complaints are common after brain injury in many cases the problem is a failure to encode information due to impaired attention and processing speed. Greater mental effort is therefore required which in turn leads to problems such as fatigue and irritability. These limitations have to be recognised when designing rehabilitation programmes.

8–035

Executive functions

Executive dysfunction includes:

8–036

(1) lack of attention control and flexibility;
(2) poor working memory;
(3) impaired concept formation;
(4) problems with planning, organising and prioritising; and
(5) inability to monitor and adapt behaviour consistent with changing social circumstances.

These processes underpin rational thinking and for this reason are often referred to as "cold" executive functions, involving logic and reasoning. They are associated with the dorsolateral pre-frontal cortical regions (Chan et al., 2008). These are the skills which psychometric tests of executive function try to measure. They are distinguished from "hot" executive functions which process emotionally salient information and underpin empathy, theory of mind, social judgment and emotion regulation. Because the "cold" executive capabilities are (relatively) easy to assess their importance can easily be over-stated, for example in assessments of mental capacity or employability, without taking into account the crucial (but not so easily measured) "hot" executive abilities. The latter are mediated by the ventromedial and orbito-frontal cortices (McDonald, 2013; Baez and Ibanez, 2014) which are particularly sensitive to damage in traumatic brain injury. Brain activity in either hot or cold neural circuits is associated with reciprocal inhibition (Goel and Dolan, 2003) such that when one is operational the other is suppressed, which may explain why it is so difficult after TBI to exert self-control over emotional impulses. For rehabilitation purposes therefore, formal testing of executive functions is helpful, but more important is behavioural evidence of how hot and cold functions interact in daily life. This distinction provides a useful means of characterising the diverse nature of executive deficits that underlie neurobehavioural disorders and explains why traditional tests of executive abilities are often inadequate to encapsulate the range of real life problems often experienced after brain injury (see Wood and Worthington, 2017).

Fatigue

8–037 For many people fatigue is the most debilitating aspect of their brain injury. It can manifest in various ways but frequently results in inability to function at one's optimum level for long periods, with a follow-on impact on mood and ability to undertake other tasks. This may appear to look like inconsistency, hence the importance of activity/sleep diaries and monitoring behaviour in context. It is also a non-specific symptom, difficult to measure objectively, and for this reason is sometimes regarded suspiciously. Potentially remediable causes should be investigated such as anaemia, pituitary hormone levels and low arousal. Clinicians should take into account the cumulative impact of fatigue when structuring time and planning activities; a fuller schedule may indicate reducing levels of fatigue, but people commonly believe that keeping busy is the best way to recover whereas it can be counter-productive, especially in the first year after injury.

Constraints on psychological therapy

8–038 The author was once pestered by another neuropsychologist in the course of preparing a joint statement to omit reference to any form of psychological intervention except cognitive behaviour therapy (CBT) on the basis that "it's the only thing the lawyers understand". Without complicating matters it is at least worth recognising the limitations of CBT, particularly as many people struggling with emotional difficulties after brain injury seem to be sent to Improving Access to Psychological Therapies (IAPT) services for low intensity treatment by generic therapists who do not understand brain injury.

There is a case for using CBT in treating specific mental health problems that occur in the context of brain injury such as travel anxiety, social phobia, depression and as part of therapy for PTSD. However, to work well, CBT demands the ability to comprehend novel and abstract ideas, which requires introspection and a certain level of intellectual and emotional detachment, not to mention the ability to reflect on and articulate thoughts and feelings. It is most effective with motivated clients who can complete homework assignments and report back diligently at the next session. In contrast, neurocognitive impairment, which includes characteristics such as concrete thinking, diminished levels of self-awareness, impaired reasoning and judgment, concentration and memory problems, all mitigate against successful engagement in CBT. Cumulative effects of these and other aspects of neurobehavioural disability, including emotional volatility, awareness disorders, and presence of challenging behaviour itself, conspire to reduce ability to engage in CBT, leading to numerous modifications for us in this population, recently reviewed by Gallagher et al., (2019).

Motivation for change

Recent focus has been upon whether preparing people for change (borrowed from addiction treatment) helps to address one of the common barriers to engagement (reviewed by Medley and Powell, 2010). The evidence to date is limited, but this is likely to be increasingly important in future with specific brain injury populations such as offenders, drug addicts, adolescents and the homeless. The causes and problems linked to apathy following brain injury have been reviewed by Worthington and Wood (2018). Apathy is a common barrier to progress, and is linked to poor recovery and treatment outcome (Gray et al., 1994; Mazaux et al., 1997). It may be misinterpreted by family members and professionals as laziness or depression, while efforts made to energise individuals who are apathetic can elicit aggressive reactions. Yet disruption to what are termed conative processes (including motivation, goal-orientation, volition, will and self-direction) may explain the dissociation between having goals and being capable of working to attain them, which characterises some manifestations of apathy. People with an apathetic disposition may fail to believe they have the ability to attain a goal, or determine that there is insufficient incentive to engage meaningfully with rehabilitation. The perceived effort-to-reward ratio will be of significance, as will the goal's congruence with over-arching aims and the individual's values and beliefs (Arnould et al., 2013). It has been suggested that apathy should not be assumed to reflect depression and that diagnosis of depression should focus on symptoms of sadness, and feelings of hopelessness, helplessness and worthlessness (Levy et al., 1998; Marin and Wolkosz, 2005). Apathy may also occur secondary to intrapersonal and environmental factors that cause low self-worth. Higher levels of self-efficacy are associated with greater social participation after TBI (Dumont et al., 2004), whilst low-self-esteem is linked to an avoidant coping style (Riley et al., 2010).

8–039

Inertia and avoidance

One of the least recognised but important brain injury sequela is the inability or reluctance to act in accordance with stated intentions. This is why so much emphasis is placed on structure and implicit cueing and feedback and on the use of support workers as aids to therapy in order that behaviours will be triggered or activated at the required time by the prosthetic rehabilitative environment. This idea of behavioural activation is a crucial component in CBT, one that has been shown to be better or equivalent to more cognitively elaborate therapies (Coffman et al., 2007). Indeed, in their review, Longmore and Worrell (2007,

8–040

p.173) concluded that "there is little empirical support for the role of cognitive change as causal in the symptomatic improvements achieved in CBT". It is essential in brain injury rehabilitation where lack of initiative and planning can be a major barrier to therapeutic engagement. It works from the "outside in", utilising scheduling activities and graded exercises that promote the acquisition of skills and self-efficacy, by maximising the opportunity to positively reinforce constructive activities. It is a transdisciplinary technique which can readily be taught to non-specialists (Ekers et al., 2011).

Cognitive and behavioural rehabilitation

8–041 It is helpful to think of therapeutic intervention as comprising five overlapping stages:

(1) assessment of strengths and weaknesses;
(2) intervention to acquire knowledge and skills;
(3) consolidation and generalisation of skills;
(4) relapse prevention; and
(5) crisis intervention.

There is now good evidence for the effectiveness of a range of cognitive interventions (Cappa et al., 2005; Cicerone et al., 2005; 2011). Rehabilitative strategies for enhancing cognitive function generally fall into the following categories, each purporting to exploit the brain's plasticity (see Worthington, 2005 for a more detailed review):

Environmental modification

8–042 Challenging behaviour has historically been managed in the form of manipulation of consequences to encourage or discourage behaviour (contingency management). There is good evidence for a wide range of interventions, including differential reinforcement, token economies, extinction procedures (such as situational time-out) and response cost (see Alderman and Wood, 2013). These methods have evolved and assimilated cognitive constructs that enhance the effectiveness of the behavioural approach (Worthington and Alderman, 2017). More recently techniques that address antecedent events that trigger behaviour have been advocated, including "positive behaviour support" (PBS), which has been used successfully in educational and other learning contexts to increase the likelihood individuals engage in behaviours that enable them to succeed (Ylvisaker et al., 2003; Johnston et al., 2006).

This may entail modifying the physical environment in order to minimise irrelevant, distracting stimuli or to enhance the salience of relevant information. The objective is to simplify the information processing demands in the environment in order to facilitate task performance. Similarly, the social environment can be manipulated to facilitate social skills learning and avoid triggering inappropriate behaviour by minimising or eliminating certain trigger events. These methods have been used extensively for disturbances of perseveration (Matthey, 1996), disinhibition (Lewis et al., 1988; Turner et al., 1990), impulsiveness (Rosenstein and Price, 1994) and aggression (Manchester et al., 1997).

Compensatory strategies

Compensatory strategies may work in different ways including increased effort, changing an approach to a task, adjusting expectation or learning a new skill (Dixon and Backman, 1999), but all essentially substitute a new technique for a lost ability. Common examples include checklists and reminders which are becoming increasingly hi-tech and therefore able to compensate for an increasing array of memory and organisational difficulties. Most types of cognitive rehabilitation involve some form of compensatory strategy because lost or degraded functions are virtually impossible to restore.   8–043

Task specific training

The value of focusing on task specific training has been subject to much debate and is one of the chief criticisms of computerised training packages. This is because this form of training develops practice effects but is notoriously difficult to generalise from one task or training setting to another without further intervention specifically targeted towards improving carry-over. This method works well when a specific task needs to be achieved without worrying about generalisation (such as getting dressed or a repetitive routine in the workplace), but not so effectively when a degree of flexibility has to be applied to how a problem is tackled. A variety of techniques such as errorless learning, shaping and chaining can be recruited to assist on-task learning.   8–044

Metacognitive training

This term encompasses procedures which aim to improve self-awareness and the ability to apply strategic thinking across a range of analogous situations to regulate behaviour or solve problems. Ownsworth et al. (2010) proposed that this is more effective than repetitive practice in reducing task errors. Methods include self-instruction training (Meichenbaum, 1977), goal management training (Levine et al., 2000), problem solving therapy (von Cramon et al., 1991) and self-management training (Adlerman et al., 1995; Dayus and van den Broek, 2000). These methods are generally the procedures of choice if a person has the requisite abilities of attention, motivation, insight and initiative as they can be very effective for higher level executive difficulties and behavioural problems.   8–045

Therapy versus scaffolding

The argument is often made that therapy should be time-limited and should result in a reduction in support needs. The former point is addressed in the next subsection. The latter seems reasonable enough; after all one might well ask: why invest time and money in something that will make no difference? Yet this is to confuse making an impact with reducing support. Whilst it might be appropriate   8–046 to aim for support to gradually reduce over time this cannot be considered a necessary condition to funding intervention. The purpose of rehabilitation is to ensure that a person is able to exercise as much independence as possible, for this there may be a requirement for the same or possibly more support in future. In other words, the purpose of rehabilitation is not simply to improve functioning, but to ensure that it is maintained at an optimum. As the involvement of professional therapists reduces over time a higher level of assistance from support workers and others may be required to take up the slack and ensure gains made under the auspices of experienced clinicians are maintained or even improved upon. This may involve ensuring that activities or exercises are maintained, which is more likely to occur if they are embodied in real life tasks than basic exercise drills. It may also involve a regular system of prompting, feedback and reflection. The support regime therefore acts as a form of scaffolding which enables a person to exercise their residual capabilities.

Relapse prevention

8-047 Progress does not proceed in a linear fashion and set-backs in treatment are part and parcel of therapy. Furthermore, once therapy has ended or the claim is settled (too often these coincide as a successful claimant decides to dispense with their therapists), there are always likely adverse events threatening to derail progress. Regardless of discipline, therefore, practitioners need to include work on preventing relapse. This includes building resilience, recognising triggers to deterioration, strategies to avoid catastrophising and maintain motivation in the face of set-backs. This work can only begin once a person has acquired and consolidated skills.

Crisis intervention

8-048 The notion of a crisis is subjective and has to be seen in the context of the individual's mental state and their life situation. The departure of a support worker for example may hardly be noticed by one person yet constitute a major stressor for another. Family bereavements can trigger grief, depression and self-harm or may pass largely unregistered. The frequency of major life events varies widely (Goldberg and Comstock, 1980) but the author's rule of thumb (based on clinical judgment rather than experience) is to expect one adverse life event every five years, which seems to be acceptable to most lawyers although this may need to be amended according to circumstances.

Managing these events often requires a contingency to be set aside for management of life crises in future. In order to be reasonable this should be based as far as possible on the individual's likely future support—if support is anticipated to reduce over time then there may be an argument for a higher level of intervention at times of crisis. Unfortunately, there is no evidence as to how often these contingencies are utilised, but any such data would probably reflect willingness to seek help as originally intended, rather than the need for such contingency.

Although conventionally this is only set aside for adverse events, looking to the future, significant positive life events such as starting a new job, getting married, becoming a parent, and moving into a new home, may also require additional support as these are still stressful and additional support may determine how successfully such transitions are made. Case managers and deputies have a key role, but experience suggests they do not always exercise this to the full.

5. SERVICE ORGANISATION

Teamwork

Teamwork is essential in rehabilitation and can be considered in terms of the make-up of the professionals involved (therapy or clinical team) or all those who have a bearing on the rehabilitation process which includes the patient or client at the centre, the family, and other professionals who may be important, such as a deputy. As already noted elsewhere in the chapter hospital teams tend to work in multi-disciplinary fashion. They are usually hierarchical and the level of communication and influence each team member has on the others varies. Staff tend to be very protective of their own areas of expertise, wearing different uniforms, loyal to their departmental identity, and sometimes communicating with one another through a formal referral process from one department to another. This can create difficulties when practising rehabilitation in a hospital setting as the team needs to form a holistic view of the person's needs and within this system it can be very difficult to engage and challenge one another, which is essential to good team-working.

8–049

The development of post-acute rehabilitation services has been associated with a more fluid, less medical, more broadly clinical and, ultimately, a social form of rehabilitation, which is also reflected in the constitution of the rehabilitation team. It was recognised that learning was more effective if therapy was not limited to formal *sessions* and only with qualified *therapists* throughout the working day, but was being continually reinforced at every interaction with every member of the team. Rehabilitation was not limited to professional therapists and instead a much broader team was empowered to regard their role as that of agent for behaviour change. This meant that therapists often conducted assessments and prescribed ways of doing things, but the majority of rehabilitation was actually implemented by a range of enablers, personal care assistants and rehabilitation support workers who worked under the guidance of clinicians. This is very different from the traditional division of labour in a hospital between doctors, nurses, therapists, and auxiliaries or healthcare assistants with more domestic responsibilities. Some services, especially in hospitals, still maintain an unhelpful distinction between staff who carry out therapy and those who provide care, creating divisions within the workplace that can hinder communication and the continuity of treatment. Yet professionals can find this alternative way of working quite challenging, feeling threatened by sharing the knowledge that defines their role with others, undermining the crucial feature that is "role release" (Hall, 2005). Furthermore, in the current climate of health and social care it is not easy to follow Eames' advice that staff should embrace "a general atmosphere of positivity" and adopt "a slightly over-effusive social demeanour" in order that contingencies of positive reinforcement are more salient (Eames, 1988).

The ideal approach is the transdisciplinary model which has been recognised as best practice in a range of service delivery contexts (Guralnick, 2001). Within a transdiscipilinary team (TDT) roles are shared (the psychologist may assist someone to eat, the physiotherapist to manage their anxiety). This does not reduce skilled professionals to generic therapists but recognises that working across traditional disciplinary boundaries improves communication, interaction, and cooperation. The result is a collaborative shared vision or "shared meaning" among the team (Davies, 2007). It may also involve joint sessions with two (sometimes three) therapists on the basis that complex diverse needs are best met through input from multiple disciplines working together, rather than separately. Unfortunately, this is often misunderstood by lawyers and case managers concerned about costs and more used to a rigid "one therapist—one hour—one session" model of delivery. Of course, costs need to be controlled, and some therapists are unused to having to justify their costs; meetings can get out of hand and expenses can spiral. It is therefore important that there can be regular open discussion about the organisation of sessions, frequency of meetings, and who should attend.

8–050 Impediments to transdisciplinary working in the community include the time that is required for teams to plan, practice, and critique their work, and the travel distances involved for a team comprising therapists many miles apart from one another, which may be prohibitively costly. In practice inter-disciplinary teams are more commonly encountered, in which each discipline retains a core identify but there is some overlap between responsibilities and working. For example, a speech therapist and clinical psychologist may work together to assess mental capacity; a psychologist may join a physiotherapist to support a very anxious client to mobilise. This way of working also assists in the assessment of risk which should, as far as possible, not be left to one person to evaluate (Worthington and Archer, 2009). The team structure also has implications for goal setting and reports (see next section).

The leadership of teams may be contentious, often focused on who has the highest level of expertise or authority, but in a truly transdisciplinary team, members are on an equal footing, often delivering interventions from other disciplines under the supervision and support of team members whose disciplines are accountable for those practices. This entails being able to share expertise and value the perspectives, knowledge and skills of other team members whilst developing trust in letting go of one's specific role.

Having medical responsibility for the patient does not have to equate to responsibility for the rehabilitation team. The terms of medical responsibility are ill-defined but the author suggests they may be limited to those aspects of the person which related to ill-health. Wood (2003) argued that the different role of the medical consultant in rehabilitation makes it more difficult for them to lead a team of therapists. There should be no prescription that a specific profession has to assume the leadership role, it may not even need to be a clinician and, in certain circumstances, it could be a teacher or a rehabilitation engineer. It is not necessary nor is it appropriate, as one defendant lawyer advocated, to ensure there is a rehabilitation medicine consultant overseeing all private rehabilitation programmes in the community.

This chapter has emphasised how therapists' interventions in every discipline need to take into account neurocognitive and neurobehavioural problems that undermine many aspects of everyday behaviour. Use of psychologically-based methods can improve traditional occupational therapy activities like training washing and dressing (Worthington and Waller, 2009) and physiotherapy skills like gait re-education (Worthington et al., 1997). Thus in hospital settings leadership by a consultant in rehabilitation medicine or neurological rehabilitation is usually warranted; in specialist neurobehavioural units a neuropsychology or neuropsychiatry lead is more relevant; and in the community a clinical neuropsychologist is often the most appropriate person to lead the team.

8–051

Since the Adults with Incapacity (Scotland) Act (2000) and the Mental Capacity Act (2005) for England and Wales, capacity to make decisions for oneself is placed within a legal framework outside mental health law for the first time. The BSRM has provided guidance for the use of DOLS which has arisen out of the resulting focus on restriction of individual autonomy and personal choice, including the right to make unwise decisions. This is to be welcomed, as clinicians and others can become embroiled in disputes on contentious issues and have to accept a person's right to refuse a treatment at times from which they would probably benefit.

The case manager's role is to oversee the case and they should attend meetings of the therapy team, but not necessarily lead those meetings or consider that they have an automatic veto over clinical decisions. Decisions on what is clinically appropriate rest with the individual clinician; decisions as to whether to proceed with a recommended course of action will usually involve the case manager, (a deputy if there is one) and the family, but ultimately will rest with the client if they have capacity, otherwise a best interests meeting may be required.

Goal setting

Although difficult to trace its origin, there is an expectation that rehabilitation involves working towards explicit aims or goals. Therapy was not always thus; Freud recognised the importance of letting his patients set the agenda for the session as a means of starting from whatever surface presentation the unconscious was presenting itself. In neurorehabilitation it is always advisable to spend some time getting to know a person before being too prescriptive with objectives, yet frequently case managers and lawyers want a list of goals and measurable outcomes after an initial appointment. Sometimes this is possible because people have clear objectives (though they may not accord with what others feel is in their best interests) but more often the therapist should tease out some key themes and gradually work these into clearer concrete aims over two or three meetings. Almost inevitably they will need to be amended as therapy proceeds because circumstances change, some goals lose their relevance and others remain valid but need to be deferred to allow time to address new issues.

8–052

The acronym SMART is often cited as a useful reminder that therapeutic objectives should be as Specific as possible, easily Measurable, Achievable,

Realistic (or Relevant) and Timed. All therapy objectives should confirm to this minimum standard, yet many are ambiguous and vague (e.g. "to improve memory"; "to develop cooking skills"). It takes time to develop the habit of writing SMART goals and involves more effort initially, but it makes for clarity and easier measurement of progress. For example, a goal such as "to increase self-confidence" could be replaced with something more specific such as "to develop self-confidence over the next month by being able to talk to a stranger in a shop and make a telephone call to a customer service department with the expectation of a corresponding increase in ratings on a self-esteem scale". A bit wordy perhaps but this is clear to all what is expected within what time frame and how it will be measured, (i.e. objectively in terms of the key tasks being completed and subjectively in the form of a self-rating scale). This second, subjective, measurement is often omitted but is crucial; there is nothing to be gained by a therapist ticking off a list of achievements that have no relationship to the client attaining their goal, yet the link between the two is all too often assumed but not put to the test.

There may also be tension between the therapist's view of what is appropriate and the client's goals. Ultimately the goals need to be owned by the client and should not be determined solely by professionals but this can be difficult as brain injury often compromises insight and judgment. Some people have difficulty articulating goals, in which case the temptation to impose them should be resisted. Instead it is often helpful to work from core values—enquiring about how the person sees themselves and wants to be seen—as a measure of eliciting some tangible objectives.

8–053 Longer term goals should also reflect socially meaningful outcomes of relevance to the client, like being able to pursue a hobby and develop a relationship, rather than focus on impairments. In hospital this may mean the person's goal is to be discharged, and this can be divided into subgoals for therapists to work on. In the community a common goal is to return to work and this can be considered in terms of various steps towards this, such as regulating sleep pattern, improving personal hygiene and managing anxiety. The author had a client whose sole aim "to get laid" could be broken down into a multitude of realistic objectives addressing motivation, personal hygiene and social skills.

Transdisciplinary working in rehabilitation has been endorsed in enhancing goal setting in both residential and community rehabilitation environments (Todd, 2014). Too often multidisciplinary teams (as opposed to inter- or transdisciplinary working) leads to discipline-specific goals which does not facilitate joint-working or provide the most efficient means of addressing client goals holistically.

Measurement of outcomes is discussed in the next section, but one important way to do this is in terms of achievement of goals. The gold standard for this (though not one favoured by the author) is Goal Attainment Scaling (known as GAS goals). Essentially this is a means of benchmarking current levels of ability, setting a realistic marker for improvement and indicating whether this target has been met (designated as 0), exceeded (rated 1 or 2), remained static or performance has declined (rated -1 or -2). Several variations on this approach are possible (Turner-Stokes, 2009; 2010) and Bovend'Eerdt et al. (2009) have proposed a means of integrating GAS with SMART goal setting.

However, like all goal setting it relies on what goals are set; too easy and goal attainment is 100% and often exceeded; too difficult and they are not met. The latter can reflect adversely on either client or therapist—there is no way of knowing which. In one study barely 1% of papers on rehabilitation published in 2012 was concerned with aspects of practitioner behaviour likely to influence outcome (Kayes et al., 2015) as if to even investigate the question would undermine the scientific basis of rehabilitation, even though this kind of enquiry is commonplace in psychotherapy. Hence goal attainment ratings tend to be made by professionals, but in a mental health context Willer and Miller (1976) reported low levels of validity if rated by therapists as opposed to clients. Notwithstanding these caveats the system has many merits and is often cited by rehabilitation medicine doctors as the best way to deliver rehabilitation (though the author has yet to come across a doctor who uses it in relation to their own intervention).

Outcome evaluation

It is incumbent on therapists to evaluate the impact of their interventions but how they do this is a matter of choice as much as relevance. For example, if the physiotherapist measures mobility but not pain, or the psychologist measures memory but not the effort involved in recollection, they may well fail to appreciate the true impact of their treatment. This can be avoided by considering a range of outcome measures and through close working with colleagues. A wide range of outcomes measures for use in brain injury is reviewed by Worthington (2012).

8–054

As previously noted, it is important to measure how well patients achieve specific goals. This is because goal achievement is independent of more objective measures of disability (Liu et al., 2004). Standardised assessment tools may well be inappropriate for measuring functional outcomes underpinned by neurobehavioural sequelae of brain injury (Wood and Worthington, 1999; Wood et al., 2008). Many off-the-shelf measures have not been validated for brain injury and can easily be misconstrued. For instance, many symptoms of brain injury are also found in mental health conditions, post-concussion symptoms overlap considerably with those of PTSD, and unusually high somatic complaints can occur amongst people who have suffered major abdominal and other physical injuries in addition to brain injury. Failure to appreciate these difficulties leads to misdiagnosis.

Performance-based metrics such as walking speed or task completion are usually better than specific impairment measures (such as range of movement or test scores) because reductions in impairment do not necessarily translate into real life benefits. Individual therapies are amenable to a number of single-case methodological designs, such as withdrawal designs (where an intervention is temporarily discontinued to evaluate its impact) and multiple baseline designs (where several behaviours are assessed at the outset and treatment is applied to each one in turn, the non-treated domains acting as a control for non-treatment effects). Few clinicians utilise these but they can be powerful tools in demonstrating therapeutic efficacy.

6. QUALITY AND EVIDENCE IN BRAIN INJURY REHABILITATION

Quality standards

8-055 The UK does not have a universally recognised mark of rehabilitation quality, and there is considerable debate as to how healthcare facilities should be accredited (Jaafaripooyan et al., 2011) notwithstanding that rehabilitation cannot be reduced to healthcare. Having participated in the North American equivalent, CARF, (Commission on Accreditation of Rehabilitation Facilities) one can understand why this exhaustive process has not been widely replicated in the UK, despite some undoubted benefits to the accreditation process and the organisations which have been through this. This means the Care Quality Commission (CQC) regulatory framework remains the most universal means of identifying quality, even though it is in many ways manifestly unsuited to brain injury rehabilitation and the non-medical clinical leadership that characterises many such services.

Prospective referrers and families should look beyond glossy brochures and grand buildings. Services should demonstrate that they have a responsive rehabilitative ethos which can be undertaken in various ways, for instance, by positive decision making supports, detailed SMART rehabilitation plans, building services around the needs of clients and families, and measured outcomes. Many services claim to offer value for money without having any evidence to support their claims.

Participation in an accreditation process can be empowering and facilitate service improvement (Greenfield et al., 2010) but concern over target-driven quality initiatives has led to interest in measuring softer aspects of the healthcare which have relevance for rehabilitation, such as clinical governance climate (Freeman, 2003) and social climate (Alderman and Groucott, 2012). It remains to be demonstrated that these components of service organisation will be more predictive of benefits to both clients and staff than some of the current key performance indicators.

Inspired and disappointed in equal measure by the ill-fated National Service Framework for Long Term Conditions (2005), various regional groups and national organisations such as Headway, UKABIF (United Kingdom Acquired Brain Injury Forum) and the BSRM have proposed ideal service delivery and quality standards. The BSRM (2009) standards are the most comprehensive but none have quite the influence their contributors would have wished and one should be wary of attempts to constrain how rehabilitation should be delivered as if there was only one road to Rome. The BSRM standards for district specialist rehabilitation services, for example, equate clinical psychology with counselling (risking the likelihood that hospital managers would fund the latter, cheaper, provision) and do not explicitly recognise clinical neuropsychology in minimum recommended staffing levels (BSRM, 2009). Minimum standards are to be encouraged, raising the bar for all, but a diversity of ideologies, theories and practices ensures innovation will continue and all voices can be heard.

Efficacy and cost-effectiveness of neurorehabilitation

Long gone are the days when the doctor could claim their job was to spend money rather than save it (Jennett, 1976), yet for many years in the UK the costs of rehabilitation received little attention (McGregor and Pentland, 1997). Two decades ago, Mazaux and Richer (1998) noted, "We know we have to control rehabilitation costs… Forthcoming programmes should become cheaper, and probably shorter" (p.442). The chapter ends with a brief review of evidence to date. More detail is provided in Worthington et al. (2017).

8–056

Mild traumatic brain injury

A significant minority of people with mild brain trauma report persisting and debilitating complaints, although the aetiology remains unclear and probably has multiple causes. Post-concussion symptoms are found in non-brain injured patients, healthy controls and are correlated with mood state (Iverson et al., 2003). They may be related to other symptoms such as chronic pain (Smith-Seemiller et al., 2003). Donnell et al. (2012) reported a study of veterans in which 32% of people with mild TBI (mTBI) met diagnostic criteria for post-concussion syndrome (PCS) compared with 40% of people with PTSD, 50% generalised anxiety disorder, 57% major depression, and 91% with somatisation disorder. Therapy may therefore target a range of symptoms such as beliefs, pain and activity, but not necessarily focus on brain injury.

8–057

In a randomised trial Paniak et al. (2000) reported that improvement typically occurred within three months and people symptomatic beyond this stage tended to be symptomatic at 12 months. They argued that brief information provided at an early stage is as helpful as more intensive later treatment (and presumably more cost-effective). This is consistent with Comper et al. (2005) who reviewed 1,055 studies and found limited evidence to support patient educational interventions. Willer and Leddy (2006) reported there was limited evidence for cognitive rehabilitation, education and graded activity. Silverberg et al. (2013a) recommended that complete rest beyond three days was unproductive and activities should be gradually resumed as soon as possible thereafter. Data on the most cost-effective approaches is in short supply but one randomised trial suggested that treatment as a matter of routine offered little benefit and intervention should be targeted towards vulnerable groups such as people with pre-existing mental health difficulties (Ghaffar et al., 2006).

The key is early intervention: a pilot web-based intervention for adolescents that focused on restricting activity and symptom self-management showed benefits during the first two weeks after injury. Other evidence indicates that early CBT for at risk groups is effective after mTBI especially for people at risk of chronic pain (Silverberg et al., 2013b). In a recent randomised study Potter et al. (2016) reported that a 12-session CBT intervention was more effective if completed over a shorter period of time.

Severe brain injury

8–058 Early admission to inpatient neurorehabilitation is linked to shorter stays and improved clinical outcomes and therefore is more cost-effective (e.g. Kunik et al., 2006). If inpatient therapy is also provided at weekends this appears to be more efficient, with improved gains and reduced length of stay (Peiris et al., 2013). For older adults home-based support has been shown to be effective in reducing hospital readmission for those with cognitive and mobility problems (e.g. Melin et al., 1993) and is more cost-effective than day hospital treatment (Crotty et al., 2008).

Eames and Wood (1985) reported one of the earliest attempts to treat severe behaviour disorder following brain injury with results they described as "surprisingly good" given that their cohort were on average four years post injury. Given the high cost of placements for people with severe brain injury, more recent studies have also investigated cost-effectiveness, although for practical reasons it is difficult to identify suitable control groups. The standard procedure is therefore to compare costs of treatment with savings in care costs after rehabilitation.

Turner-Stokes et al. (2016) reported data from a five year analysis of over 5,700 patients from NHS level I and II rehabilitation facilities, reflecting a wide range of conditions (73% acquired brain injury). Average length of stay was 90 days and all groups showed significant reductions in dependency, and savings in weekly care cost ranging from a mean of £130 a week for low-dependency patients to £760 a week for the highly dependent. Even for patients with unusually long hospital admissions (average of 184 days), costs were offset by reductions in care within 14 months (Turner-Stokes, 2007). A subsequent review across 75 inpatient centres in England between 2010 and 2018 examined outcomes for over 6,000 adults with severe brain trauma (Turner-Stokes et al., 2019). Admissions for rehabilitation were between 73 and 109 days post injury in 95% of cases; duration of admission was a relatively brief 80 days on average. Excluding patients who remained in a persistent vegetative state (who show little change in care costs over time) the net average cost savings were over £32,000 (estimated lifetime savings of £740,929). A note of caution however: the authors' cost calculations assume there would be no reduction in care costs without rehabilitation but many, if not most, of these people would make some spontaneous improvement. This may well lead to reduced support costs even in the absence of rehabilitation, although there would likely be increases in costs for others whose condition deteriorated without specialist assistance.

8–059 Patients referred to facilities outside the NHS are often relatively late in recovery and tend to have severe and entrenched problems which require longer periods of rehabilitation. Wood et al. (1999) reported a cohort of 76 adults across two centres, an average of six years post injury, who underwent at least six months rehabilitation (mean: 14 months) and were followed up 1–5 years after discharge. Whereas only 4% were in some form of education of work placement prior to rehabilitation, this was 61% after rehabilitation. Care costs were significantly reduced per capita between £0.5 million and £1.1 million, especially for people admitted within two years of injury.

Worthington (2003) described a similar residential rehabilitation service, in which the majority of admissions took place within one year of injury, resulting in 56% being discharged home with support whilst one-quarter were transferred to longer-term care facilities previously inaccessible to them due to their behaviour disorder. Even when the costs of rehabilitation are factored in, this has a negligible impact on overall lifetime cost savings. Worthington et al. (2006) conducted sensitivity analysis on outcomes from 133 adults across four rehabilitation sites demonstrating projected savings of £0.8–1.1 million for adults admitted within a year of injury and £0.4–0.5 million for those admitted more than two years after injury (based on discount rates of 3–5%). Oddy and da Silva Ramos (2013) included a more conservative discount rate of 1.5% and calculated estimated cost savings between £0.19 and £1.13 million. These studies show that while earlier rehabilitation is associated with improved outcomes and lower long-term costs, this reflects a combination of natural recovery as well as rehabilitation, the latter capitalising on the former; but these data also show significant gains can be made long after the conventional two year window of optimal recovery. Moreover, follow-up confirmed that in the majority of cases improvements can continue after formal rehabilitation with the right support in place, at least up to 10 years post injury (Parish and Oddy, 2007).

Key to success is timely discharge from residential rehabilitation into the community, research showing that one of the principal reasons for delays is the point at which eligibility criteria for statutory healthcare funding are no longer met and payment responsibility passes to adult social services (Worthington and Oldham, 2006). This is why other funding sources can be vital in securing timely discharge and maintaining recovery momentum with a properly resourced support programme. For instance, one study showed how a support worker trained by a neuropsychologist to deliver cognitive intervention was able to sustain a community placement which was more cost-effective than the costs of a local care home (Pierini and Hoerold, 2014). It is difficult to compare hospital and home-based rehabilitation directly as they may both be relevant at different times. Interestingly, one review of randomised studies (not specific to brain injury) concluded that home-based treatment was notably cheaper, without necessarily compromising clinical outcomes (Brusco et al., 2014).

7. CONCLUSIONS AND FUTURE TRENDS

This chapter has provided a comprehensive though not exhaustive review of key aspects of neurorehabilitation, service organisation, delivery and outcomes in the context of neuroplasticity. It is intended to go beyond the usual brief summary provided to lawyers and clinicians who are not rehabilitation specialists as there is much to be gained in developing close working relationships and mutual understanding of roles.

In the future, technological developments are likely to have much greater bearing on how rehabilitation is practised, as mainstream technologies become more widely accessible. From individualised devices to smart homes, the role of engineers, developers and programmers is likely to be crucial in shaping the future for society and no less for those with brain injury (Worthington, 2017).

8–060

Technologies are likely to have significant impact on how community support programmes are organised. In particular, the advent of microprompting systems for memory and organisation problems is likely to prove very cost-effective over the longer term, compared to conventional support, which is both labour-intensive and in short supply (Oddy and da Silva Ramos, 2013b; Worthington, 2016).

It is important to appreciate that rehabilitation is not an entity, and it makes no more sense to ask if rehabilitation works than if medicine or "the law" works. Just as medicine encompasses many specialisms other than rehabilitation, so rehabilitation is much more than medicine. There is an overlap (or common ground) between the two because rehabilitation has medical aspects but we are still negotiating the conceptual transition of rehabilitation from a medical through a biopsychosocial to a more transformative systemic view that recognises there are no hard dividing lines between which professionals can "own" rehabilitation. The medico-legal world has been instrumental in opening up rehabilitation to the expertise of many different disciplines. This should be to the benefit of the people most affected by brain injury, though there is no reason to assume that this is always the injured party—again the more systemic view recognises that the impact of an injury, like a violent tsunami, devastates families and friends, leaving no-one, layperson or professional, untouched by its presence.

In response people want a life after brain injury, rather than a collection of services, and that means recognising what they can do, not focusing solely on what they cannot do; it means recognising the therapeutic values of spaces as much as people; music and play as much as formal treatment. Finally, it means recognising that societies are characterised by interdependence and that, ultimately, challenging though it is within the current worldview, rehabilitation is not something done to individuals, but is a way of working with families and communities. There can be no better way to reflect this than to reaffirm John Donne's celebrated words:

> "No man is an island entire of itself; every man is a piece of the continent, a part of the main. If a clod be washed away by the sea, Europe is the less, as well as if a promontory were, as well as if a manor of thy friend's or of thine own were. Any man's death diminishes me, because I am involved in Mankind".

REFERENCES

Adler, J. and Malone, D., "Early mobilization in the intensive care unit: a systematic review" (2012) *Cardiopulmonary Physical Therapy Journal* 23 (1), 5.

Alderman, N., "Prevalence, characteristics and causes of aggressive behaviour observed within a neurobehavioural rehabilitation service: predictors and implications for management" (2007) *Brain Injury* 21, 891–911.

Alderman N. and Groucott L., "Measurement of social climate within neurobehavioural rehabilitation services using the EssenCES" (2012) *Neuropsychological Rehabilitation* 22 (5): 768–793.

Alderman N. and Wood R. Ll., "Neurobehavioural approaches to the rehabilitation of challenging behaviour" (2013) *NeuroRehabilitation* 32: 761–770.

REFERENCES

Alderman N., Fry R.K. and Youngson H.A., "Improvement of self-monitoring skills, reduction of behaviour disturbance and the dysexecutive syndrome: comparison of response cost and a new programme of self-monitoring training" (1995) *Neuropsychological Rehabilitation* 5:193–221.

Alderson, P. and Roberts, I., "Corticosteroids in acute traumatic brain injury: systematic review of randomised controlled trials" (1997) *British Medical Journal* 314 (7098): 1855–1859.

Anderson, V., Spencer-Smith, M., Leventer, R., Coleman, L., Anderson, P., Williams, J., Greenham, M. and Jacobs, R., "Childhood brain insult: can age at insult help us predict outcome?" (2009) *Brain* 132 (1): 45–56.

Andrews, K. and Turner-Stokes, L., *Rehabilitation in the 21st Century: Report of three surveys* (London: Institute of Complex Neuro-disability, 2005).

Arnould, A., Rochat, L., Azouvi, P. and van der Linden, M., "A multidimensional approach to apathy after traumatic brain injury" (2013) *Neuropsychology Review* 23(3): 210–233.

Bäckman, C.G. and Walther, S.M., "Use of a personal diary written on the ICU during critical illness" *Intensive Care Medicine* 27(2): 426–429.

Baez S. and Ibanez A., "The effects of context processing on social cognition impairments in adults with Asperger's syndrome" (2014) Frontiers in Neuroscience 8: 270.

Barker R.A. and Dunnett S.B., "Neural Repair, transplantation and rehabilitation" (Hove: Psychology Press, 1999).

Bayr, H., Clark, R.S. and Kochanek, P.M., "Promising strategies to minimize secondary brain injury after head trauma" (2003) *Critical Care Medicine* 31(1), S112–S117.

Berlucchi, G. and Buchtel, H.A., "Neuronal plasticity: historical roots and evolution of meaning" (2009) *Experimental Brain Research* 192(3), 307–319.

Bernard, S., Aspinal, F., Gridley, K. and Parker, G., "Integrated services for people with long-term neurological conditions: evaluation of the impact of the national service framework" (York: Social Policy Research Unit, University of York, 2010).

Biernaskie, J., Chernenko, G. and Corbett, D., "Efficacy of rehabilitative experience declines with time after focal ischemic brain injury" (2004) *Journal of Neuroscience* 24 (5): 1245–1254.

Bolton, C.F., Gilbert, J.J., Hahn, A.F. and Sibbald, W.J., "Polyneuropathy in critically ill patients" (1984) *Journal of Neurology, Neurosurgery & Psychiatry* 47 (11): 1223–1231.

Boot, W.R., Kramer, A.F., Simons, D.J., Fabiani, M. and Gratton, G., "The effects of video game playing on attention, memory, and executive control" (2008) *Acta Psychologica* 129 (3), 387–398.

Bovend'Eerdt, T.J.H., Botell, R.E., Wade, D.T., "Writing SMART rehabilitation goals and achieving goal attainment scaling: a practical guide" (2009) *Clinical Rehabilitation* 23: 352–361.

Bradley, L.J., Kirker, S.G.B., Corteen, E., Seeley, H.M., Pickard, J.D. and Hutchinson, P.J., "Inappropriate acute neurosurgical bed occupancy and short falls in rehabilitation: implications for the National Service Framework" (2006) *British Journal of Neurosurgery* 20 (1): 36–39.

British Society of Rehabilitation Medicine, "Rehabilitation Medicine: the National Position" (London: BSRM/Royal College of Physicians, 2007).

British Society of Rehabilitation Medicine, "BSRM Standards for Rehabilitation Services Mapped onto the National Service Framework for Long-Term Conditions" (London: BSRM/Royal College of Physicians, 2009).

Brown, M., Gordon, W.A. and Haddad, L., "Models for predicting subjective quality of life in individuals with traumatic brain injury" (2000) *Brain Injury* 14 (1): 5–19.

Bruns, J. and Hauser, W.A., "The epidemiology of traumatic brain injury: a review" (2003) *Epilepsia* 44 (S10), 2–10.

Brusco, N.K., Taylor N.F., Watts J.J., Shields N., "Economic evaluation of adult rehabilitation: a systematic review and meta-analysis of randomized controlled trials in a variety of settings" (2014) *Archives of Physical and Medical Rehabilitation* 95 (1): 94–116.

Cappa, S.F., Benke, T., Clarke, S., Rossi, B., Stemmer, B., van Heugten, C.M., "EFNS guidelines on cognitive rehabilitation: Report of an EFNS Task Force" (2005) *European Journal of Neurology* 12: 665–680.

Carlson, P.M., Boudreau, M.L., Davis, J., Johnston, J., Lemsky, C., McColl, M.A. and Smith, C., "'Participate to learn': A promising practice for community ABI rehabilitation" (2006) *Brain injury* 20 (11): 1111–1117.

Charles, J. and Gordon, A.M., "A critical review of constraint-induced movement therapy and forced use in children with hemiplegia" (2005) *Neural plasticity* 12 (2–3): 245–261.

Choi, H.A., Badjatia, N. and Mayer, S.A., "Hypothermia for acute brain injury—mechanisms and practical aspects" (2012) *Nature Reviews Neurology* 8 (4): 214–222.

Cicerone, K.D. and Azulay, J., "Perceived self-efficacy and life satisfaction after traumatic brain injury" (2007) *Journal of Head Trauma Rehabilitation* 22 (5): 257–266.

Cicerone, K.D., Mott, T., Azulay, J. and Friel, J.C., "Community integration and satisfaction with functioning after intensive cognitive rehabilitation for traumatic brain injury" (2004) *Archives of Physical Medicine and Rehabilitation* 85 (6): 943–950.

Cicerone, K.D., Dahlberg, C., Malec, J.F., Langenbahn, D.M., Felicetti, T., Kneipp, S., Ellmo, W., Kalmar, K., Giacino, J.T., Harley, J.P., Laatsch, L., Morse, P.A. and Cantanese, J., "Evidence based cognitive rehabilitation: updated review of the literature from 1998 through 2002" (2005) Archives of Physical Medicine and Rehabilitation 86: 1681–1692.

Cicerone, K.D., Langenbahn, D.M., Braden, C., Malec, J.F., Kalmar, K., Fraas, M. and Ashman, T., "Evidence-Based Cognitive Rehabilitation: Updated Review of the Literature From 2003 Through 2008" (2011) *Archives of Physical Medicine and Rehabilitation* 92 (4): 519–530.

Cifu, D.X., Kreutzer, J.S., Kolakowsky-Hayner, S.A., Marwitz, J.H., and Englander, J., "The relationship between therapy intensity and rehabilitative outcomes after traumatic brain injury: a multicenter analysis" (2003) *Archives of Physical Medicine and Rehabilitation* 84 (10): 1441–1448.

Clifton, G.L., Miller, E.R., Choi, S.C., Levin, H.S., McCauley, S., Smith Jr, K.R. and Chesnut, R.M., "Lack of effect of induction of hypothermia after acute brain injury" (2001) *New England Journal of Medicine* 344 (8): 556–563.

Clifton, G.L., Valadka, A., Zygun, D., Coffey, C.S., Drever, P., Fourwinds, S. and Conley, A. "Very early hypothermia induction in patients with severe brain injury (the National Acute Brain Injury Study: Hypothermia II): a randomised trial" (2011) *The Lancet Neurology* 10 (2): 131–139.

Coetzer, B.R., Vaughan, F.L., Roberts, C.B. and Rafal, R., "The development of a holistic, community based neurorehabilitation service in a rural area" (2003) *Journal of Cognitive Rehabilitation* 21 (1): 4–15.

Coffman, S.J., Martell, C.R., Dimidjian, S., Gallop, R., Hollon, S.D., "Extreme nonresponse in cognitive therapy: Can behavioral activation succeed where cognitive therapy fails?" (2007) *Journal of Consulting and Clinical Psychology* 75 (4): 531–541.

Comper, P., Bisschop, S.M., Carnide, N. and Tricco, A., "A systematic review of treatments for mild traumatic brain injury" (2005) *Brain Injury* 19 (11): 863–880.

REFERENCES

Corrigan, J.D., Bogner, J.A., Mysiw, W.J., Clinchot, D. and Fugate, L., "Life satisfaction after traumatic brain injury" (2001) *Journal of Head Trauma Rehabilitation* 16 (6): 543–555.

Cotman, C.W. and Berchtold, N.C., "Exercise: A behavioral intervention to enhance brain health and plasticity" (2002) *Trends in Neurosciences* 25: 295–301.

Cramer, S.C., Sur, M., Dobkin, B.H., O'Brien, C., Sanger, T.D., Trojanowski, J.Q. and Chen, W.G., "Harnessing neuroplasticity for clinical applications" (2011) *Brain* 134 (6): 1591–1609.

CRASH Trial Collaborators, "Final results of MRC CRASH, a randomised placebo-controlled trial of intravenous corticosteroid in adults with head injury—outcomes at 6 months" (2005) *The Lancet* 365 (9475): 1957–1959.

Crotty M., Giles L., Halbert J., Harding J. and Miller M., "Home versus day rehabilitation: a randomised controlled trial" (2008) *Age and Ageing* 37: 628–633.

Cuthbertson, B.H., Rattray, J., Campbell, M.K., Gager, M., Roughton, S., Smith, A. and Hernandez, R., "The PRaCTICaL study of nurse led, intensive care follow-up programmes for improving long term outcomes from critical illness: a pragmatic randomised controlled trial" (2009) *British Medical Journal* 339: b3723.

Davies, S. (ed.), *Team around the child: working together in early childhood education* (Australia: Kurrajong Early Intervention Service, 2007).

Dayus, B. and Van den Broek, M.D., "Treatment of stable delusional confabulations using self-monitoring training" (2000) *Neuropsychological Rehabilitation* 10 (4): 415–427.

Dijkers, M.P., "Quality of life after traumatic brain injury: a review of research approaches and findings" (2004) *Archives of Physical Medicine and Rehabilitation* 85: 21–35.

Dikmen, S.S., Machamer, J.E., Powell, J.M. and Temkin, N.R., "Outcome 3 to 5 years after moderate to severe traumatic brain injury" (2003) *Archives of Physical Medicine and Rehabilitation* 84 (10): 1449–1457.

Dixon, R.A. and Backman, L., "Principles of compensation in cognitive neurorehabilitation" in Stuss, D.T., Winocur, G. and Robertson, I.H. (eds), *Cognitive Neurorehabilitation* (Cambridge: Cambridge University Press, 1999), 59–72.

Donnell, A.J., Kim, M.S., Silva, M.A. and Vanderploeg, R.D., "Incidence of postconcussion symptoms in psychiatric diagnostic groups, mild traumatic brain injury, and comorbid conditions" (2012) *Clinical Neuropsychologist* 26 (7): 1092–1101.

Dumont C., Gervais M., Fougeyrollas P. and Bertrand R., "Toward an explanatory model of social participation for adults with traumatic brain injury" (2004) *Journal of Head Trauma Rehabilitation* 19: 431–44.

Dunn, L., Henry, J. and Beard, D., "Social deprivation and adult head injury: a national study" (2003) *Journal of Neurology, Neurosurgery & Psychiatry* 74 (8): 1060–1064.

Eames, P., "Some aspects of the management of difficult behavior" in Hall P. and Stonier P.D. (eds), *Perspectives in Psychiatry: The Worcester lectures* (London: J Wiley & Sons, 1988), 41–58.

Eames, P., "Head injury rehabilitation: towards a 'model' service" in Wood R. Ll. and Eames P. (eds), *Models of brain injury rehabilitation* (Chapman Hall, 1989), 48–58.

Eames, P. and Wood, R.Ll., "Rehabilitation after severe brain injury: A special unit approach to behaviour disorders" (1985) *Disability and Rehabilitation* 7 (3): 130–133.

Ekers, D., Richards, D., McMillan, D., Bland, J.M., Gilbody, S., "Behavioural activation delivered by the non-specialist: phase II randomised controlled trial" (2011) *British Journal of Psychiatry* 198 (1): 66–72.

Ellis, A. and Young, A., "Training in face-processing skills for a child with acquired prosopagnosia" (1988) *Developmental Neuropsychology* 4: 283–294.

Finger, S., Minds behind the brain. A history of the pioneers and their discoveries (New York: Oxford University Press, 2000).

Finger, S. and Almli, C.R., "Margaret Kennard and her 'Principle' in historical perspective" in Finger, S., Levere, T.E., Almli C.R. and Stein D.G. (eds), *Brain Injury and Recovery. Theoretical and Controversial Issues* (New York: Plenum Press, 1988), 117–132.

Foster, M. and Tilse, C., "Referral to rehabilitation following traumatic brain injury: a model for understanding inequities in access" (2003) *Social Science & Medicine* 56 (10): 2201–2210.

Foster, M., Tilse, C. and Fleming, J., "Referral to rehabilitation following traumatic brain injury: practitioners and the process of decision-making" (2004) *Social Science & Medicine* 59 (9): 1867–1878.

Francis, D.R., Riddoch, M.J., Humphreys, G.W., "Treating agnosic alexia complicated by additional impairments" (2001) *Neuropsychological Rehabilitation* 11 (2): 113–192.

Freeman, T., "Measuring progress in clinical governance: assessing the reliability and validity of the Clinical Governance Climate Questionnaire" (2003) *Health Services Management Research* 16 (4): 234–250.

Gallagher, M., McLeod, H.J. and McMillan, T.M. "A systematic review of recommended modifications of CBT for people with cognitive impairments following brain injury" (2019) *Neuropsychological Rehabilitation* 29 (1): 1–21.

Gan, C., Campbell, K.A., Gemeinhardt, M. and McFadden, G.T., "Predictors of family system functioning after brain injury" (2006) *Brain Injury* 20 (6): 587–600.

Ghaffar, O., McCullagh, S., Ouchterlony, D. and Feinstein, A., "Randomized treatment trial in mild traumatic brain injury" (2006) *Journal of Psychosomatic Research* 61 (2): 153–160.

Gindrat, A.D., Chytiris, M., Balerna, M., Rouiller, E.M. and Ghosh, A., "Use-dependent cortical processing from fingertips in touchscreen phone users" (2015) *Current Biology* 25 (1): 109–116.

Godecke, E., Ciccone, N.A., Granger, A.S., Rai, T., West, D., Cream, A. and Hankey, G.J., "A comparison of aphasia therapy outcomes before and after a Very Early Rehabilitation programme following stroke" (2014) *International Journal of Language & Communication Disorders* 49 (2): 149–161.

Goel, V. and Dolan, R.J., "Reciprocal neural response within lateral and ventral medial prefrontal cortex during hot and cold reasoning" (2003) *Neuroimage* 20 (4): 2314–2321.

Goldberg, E.L. and Comstock, G.W., "Epidemiology of life events: Frequency in general populations" (1980) *American Journal of Epidemiology* 111 (6): 736–752.

Gray, J.M., Shepherd, M. and McKinlay, W.W., "Negative symptoms in the traumatically brain-injured during the first year post discharge, and their effect on rehabilitation status, work status and family burden" (1994) *Clinical Rehabilitation* 8 (3): 188–197.

Greenfield, D., Pawsey, M. and Braithwaite, J., "What motivates professionals to engage in the accreditation of healthcare organizations?" (2010) *International Journal for Quality in Health Care* 23 (1): 8–14.

Greenwood, R.J., McMillan, T.M., Brooks, D.N., Dunn, G., Brock, D., Dinsdale, S., and Price, J.R., "Effects of case management after severe head injury" (1994) *British Medical Journal* 308: (6938), 1199–1205.

Guralnick M.J., "A developmental systems model for early intervention" (2001) *Infants and Young Children* 14 (2): 1–18.

REFERENCES

Haggerty, J.L., Roberge, D., Freeman, G.K. and Beaulieu, C., "Experienced continuity of care when patients see multiple clinicians: a qualitative metasummary" (2013) *Annals of Family Medicine* 11 (3): 262–271.

Hall P., "Interprofessional teamwork: professional cultures as barriers" (2005) *Journal of Interprofessional Care Supp* 1: 188–196.

Helman C., *Doctors and Patients: An Anthology* (Abingdon: Oxford Medical Press, 2003).

Hopkins, R.O. and Brett, S., "Chronic neurocognitive effects of critical illness" (2005) *Current Opinion in Critical Care* 11 (4): 369–375.

Hopkins, R.O., Weaver, L.K., Pope, D., Orme Jr, J.F., Bigler, E.D. and Larson-Lohr, V., "Neuropsychological sequelae and impaired health status in survivors of severe acute respiratory distress syndrome" (1999) American Journal of Respiratory and Critical Care Medicine 160 (1): 50–56.

Iverson, G.L. and Lange, R.T., "Examination of "postconcussion-like" symptoms in a healthy sample" (2003) *Applied Neuropsychology* 10 (3): 137–144.

Iwashyna, T.J., Ely, E.W., Smith, D.M. and Langa, K.M., "Long-term cognitive impairment and functional disability among survivors of severe sepsis" (2010) *Journal of the American Medical Association* 304 (16): 1787–1794.

Jaafaripooyan, E., Agrizzi, D., Akbarai-Haghighi, F., "Healthcare accreditation systems; further perspectives on performance measures" (2011) *International Journal for Quality in Health Care* 23 (6): 645–656.

Jackson, J., Ely, E.W., Morey, M.C., Anderson, V.M., Siebert, C.S., Denne, L.B. and Schiro, E., "Cognitive and physical rehabilitation of ICU survivors: results of the RETURN randomized, controlled pilot investigation" (2012) *Critical Care Medicine* 40 (4): 1088–1097.

Jackson, J.C., Pandharipande, P.P., Girard, T.D., Brummel, N.E., Thompson, J.L., Hughes, C.G. and Hopkins, R.O., "Depression, post-traumatic stress disorder, and functional disability in survivors of critical illness in the BRAIN-ICU study: a longitudinal cohort study" (2014) *The Lancet Respiratory Medicine* 2 (5): 369–379.

Jennett, B., "Resource allocation for the severely brain damaged" (1976) *Archives of Neurology* 33 (9): 595–597.

Johnson, V.E., Stewart, W., Smith, D.H., "Axonal pathology in traumatic brain injury" (2013) *Experimental Neurology* 246: 35–43.

Johnston, M. and Pollard, B., "Consequences of disease: testing the WHO International Classification of Impairments, Disabilities and Handicaps (ICIDH) model" (2001) *Social Science and Medicine* 53 (10): 1261–1273.

Johnston, J.M., Fox R.M., Jacobson J.W., Green, G. and Mulick, J.A., "Positive behavior support and applied behavior analysis" (2006) *Behavior Analyst* 29: 51–74.

Jones, C., Griffiths, R.D., Humphris, G. and Skirrow, P.M., "Memory, delusions, and the development of acute posttraumatic stress disorder-related symptoms after intensive care" (2001) *Critical Care Medicine* 29 (3): 573–580.

Jones, C., Skirrow, P., Griffiths, R.D., Humphris, G.H., Ingleby, S., Eddleston, J. and Gager, M., "Rehabilitation after critical illness: a randomized, controlled trial" (2003) *Critical Care Medicine* 31 (10): 2456–2461.

Jones, C., Bäckman, C., Capuzzo, M., Egerod, I., Flaatten, H., Granja, C. and Griffiths, R.D., "Intensive care diaries reduce new onset post traumatic stress disorder following critical illness: a randomised, controlled trial" (2010) *Critical Care* 14 (5): R168.

Kayes, N.M., Mudge, S., Bright, F.A.S. and McPherson, K., "Whose behaviour matters? Rethinking practitioner behaviour and its influence on rehabilitation outcomes" in McPherson K., Gibson B.E. and Leplege A. (eds), *Rethinking Rehabilitation; Theory and Practice* (Boca Raton: CRC Press, 2015), 249–271.

Kleim, J.A., "Neural plasticity and neurorehabilitation: teaching the new brain old tricks" (2011) *Journal of Communication Disorders* 44 (5): 521–528.

Kleim, J.A. and Jones, T.A., "Principles of experience-dependent neural plasticity: implications for rehabilitation after brain damage" (2008) *Journal of Speech, Language and Hearing Research* 51 (1): S225–S239.

Kuday, C., Uzan, M. and Hanci, M., "Statistical analysis of the factors affecting the outcome of extradural haematomas: 115 cases" (1994) *Acta Neurochirurgica* 131 (3): 203–206.

Kunik, C.L., Flowers, L. and Kazanjian T., "Time to rehabilitation admission and associated outcomes for patients with traumatic brain injury" (2006) *Archives of Physical Medicine and Rehabilitation* 87: 1590–1596.

Lashley, K.S., "Basic neural mechanisms in behaviour" (1930) *Psychological Review* 37 (1): 1–24.

Leplege, A. Barral, C. and McPherson, K., "Conceptualizing disability to inform rehabilitation: historical and epistemological perspectives" in McPherson K., Gibson B.E. and Leplege A. (eds), *Rethinking Rehabilitation. Theory and Practice* (Boca Raton, CRC Press, 2015), 21–43.

Lewis, F.D., Nelson, J., Nelson, C. and Reusnik, P., "Effects of three feedback contingencies on the socially inappropriate talk of a brain-injured adult" (1988) *Behavior Therapy* 19: 203–211.

Levine, B., Robertson, I.H., Clare, L., Garter, G., Hong, J., Wilson B.A., Duncan J. and Stuss, D.T., "Rehabilitation of executive functioning: an experimental-clinical validation of Goal Management Training" (2000) *Journal of the International Neuropsychological Society* 6: 299–312.

Levy, M.L., Cummings, J.L., Fairbanks, L.A., Masterman, D., Miller, B.L., Craig, A.H., Paulsen, J.S. and Litvan, I., "Apathy is not depression" (1998) *Journal of Neuropsychiatry and Clinical Neurosciences* 10: 314–319.

Levy, C.E., Nichols, D.S., Schmalbrock, P.M., Keller, P. and Chakeres, D.W., "Functional MRI evidence of cortical reorganization in upper-limb stroke hemiplegia treated with constraint-induced movement therapy" (2001) *American Journal of Physical Medicine and Rehabilitation* 80 (1): 4–12.

Liepert, J., Bauder, H., Miltner, W.H., Taub, E. and Weiller, C., "Treatment-induced cortical reorganization after stroke in humans" (2000) Stroke 31 (6): 1210–1216.

Liu, C., McNeil, J. and Greenwood, R., "Rehabilitation outcomes after brain injury: disability measures of goal achievement?" (2004) *Clinical Rehabilitation* 18: 398–404.

Longmore, R.J. and Worrell, M., "Do we need to challenge thoughts in cognitive behaviour therapy?" (2007) *Clinical Psychology Review* 27: 173–187.

Ma, J., Huang, S., Qin, S. and You, C., "Progesterone for acute traumatic brain injury" (2012) *Cochrane Database Syst Rev.* 10 (10).

Malec, J.F., "Impact of comprehensive day treatment on societal participation for persons with acquired brain injury" (2001) *Archives of Physical Medicine and Rehabilitation* 82 (7): 885–895.

Manchester, D., Hodgkinson, A. and Casey, T., "Prolonged severe behavioural disturbance following traumatic brain injury: what can be done?" (1997) *Brain Injury* 11:605–617.

REFERENCES

Marin R.S. and Wilkosz, P.A., "Disorders of Diminished Motivation. Journal of Head Trauma Rehabilitation" (2005) *Journal of Head Trauma Rehabilitation* 20: 377–388.

Matsui, H., Hashimoto, H., Horiguchi, H., Yasunaga, H. and Matsuda, S., "An exploration of the association between very early rehabilitation and outcome for the patients with acute ischaemic stroke in Japan: a nationwide retrospective cohort survey" (2010) *BMC Health Services Research* 10 (1): 213.

Matthey, S., "Modification of perseverative behaviour in an adult with anoxic brain damage" (1996) *Brain Injury* 10: 219–227.

Mazaux, J.M. and Richer E., "Rehabilitation after traumatic brain injury in adults" (1998) *Disability and Rehabilitation* 20 (12): 435–447.

Mazaux, J.M., Masson, F., Levin, H.S., Alaoui, P., Maurette, P. and Barat, M., "Long-term neuropsychological outcome and loss of social autonomy after traumatic brain injury" (1997) *Archives of Physical Medicine and Rehabilitation* 78 (12): 1316–1320.

McCarthy, M., "Purchasing Neurorehabilitation in the UK National Health Service" (1999) *Neuropsychological Rehabilitation* 9 (3–4): 295–303.

McDonald, S., "Impairments in Social Cognition Following Severe Traumatic Brain Injury" (2013) *Journal International Neuropsychological Society* 19 (3): 231–246.

McGregor, K. and Pentland, B., "Head injury rehabilitation in the UK: An economic perspective" (1997) *Social Science and Medicine* 45 (2): 295–303.

McMillan, T.M. and Ledder, H., "A survey of services provided by community neurorehabilitation teams in South East England" (2001) *Clinical Rehabilitation* 15 (6): 582–588.

Medley, A.R. and Powell, T., "Motivational interviewing to promote self-awareness and engagement in rehabilitation following acquired brain injury: A conceptual review" (2010) *Neuropsychological Rehabilitation* 20 (4): 481–508.

Meichenbaum, D., "Cognitive-Behavior Modification" (New York: Plenum Press, 1977).

Melin, A., Hakansson, S. and Bygren, L.O., "The cost-effectiveness of rehabilitation in the home: a study of Swedish elderly" (1993) *American Journal of Public Health* 83 (3): 356–362.

Musicco, M., Emberti, L., Nappi, G., Caltagirone, C. and Italian Multicenter Study on Outcomes of Rehabilitation of Neurological Patients, "Early and long-term outcome of rehabilitation in stroke patients: the role of patient characteristics, time of initiation, and duration of interventions" (2003) *Archives of Physical Medicine and Rehabilitation* 84(4), 551–558.

Needham, D.M., Davidson, J., Cohen, H., Hopkins, R.O., Weinert, C., Wunsch, H. and Brady, S.L., "Improving long-term outcomes after discharge from intensive care unit: report from a stakeholders' conference" (2012) *Critical Care Medicine* 40 (2): 502–509.

Newell, A. and Rosenbloom, P.S., "Mechanisms of skill acquisition and the law of practice" in Anderson J.R. (ed.), *Cognitive skills and their acquisition* (New Jersey: Lawrence Elbaum, 1981), 1–55.

Oddy, M. and da Silva Ramos, S., "The clinical and cost-benefits of investing in neurobehavioural rehabilitation: a multi-centre study" (2013) *Brain injury* 27 (13–14): 1500–1507.

Oddy, M. and da Silva Ramos, S., "Cost effective ways of facilitating home based rehabilitation and support" (2013) *NeuroRehabilitation* 32 (4): 781–790.

Ownsworth, T., Quinn, H., Fleming, J., Kendall, M. and Shum, D., "Error self-regulation following traumatic brain injury: a single case study evaluation of metacognitive skills training and behavioural practice interventions" (2010) *Neuropsychological Rehabilitation* 20 (1): 59–80.

Page, S.J., Levine, P., Sisto, S., Bond, Q. and Johnston, M.V., "Stroke patients' and therapists' opinions of constraint-induced movement therapy" (2002) *Clinical Rehabilitation* 16 (1): 55–60.

Paniak, C., Toller-Lobe, G., Reynolds, S., Melnyk, A. and Nagy, J., "A randomized trial of two treatments for mild traumatic brain injury: 1 year follow-up" (2000) *Brain Injury* 14 (3): 219–226.

Parish, L. and Oddy, M., "Efficacy of rehabilitation for functional skills more than 10 years after extremely severe brain injury" (2007) *Neuropsychological Rehabilitation* 17 (2): 230–243.

Parker, A.M., Sricharoenchai, T. and Needham, D.M., "Early rehabilitation in the intensive care unit: Preventing impairment of physical and mental health" (2013) *Current Physical Medicine and Rehabilitation Reports* 1 (4): 307–314.

Parslow, R.C., Morris, K.P., Tasker, R.C., Forsyth, R.J. and Hawley, C., "Epidemiology of traumatic brain injury in children receiving intensive care in the UK" (2005) *Archives of Disease in Childhood* 90 (11): 1182–1187.

Pascual-Leone, A., Nguyet, D., Cohen, L.G., Brasil-Neto, J.P., Cammarota, A. and Hallett, M., "Modulation of muscle responses evoked by transcranial magnetic stimulation during the acquisition of new fine motor skills" (1995) *Journal of Neurophysiology* 74: 1037–1045.

Pierini, D. and Hoerold, D., "Back home after and acquired brain injury: building a 'low-cost' team to provide theory-driven cognitive rehabilitation after routine interventions" (2014) *NeuroRehabilitation* 34 (1): 65–80.

Peris, A., Bonizzoli, M., Iozzelli, D., Migliaccio, M.L., Zagli, G., Bacchereti, A. and Bendoni, E., "Early intra-intensive care unit psychological intervention promotes recovery from post traumatic stress disorders, anxiety and depression symptoms in critically ill patients" (2011) *Critical Care* 15 (1): R41.

Peris, C.L., Shields, N., Brusco, N.K., Watts, J.J. and Taylor N.F., "Additional Saturday rehabilitation improves functional independence and quality of life and reduces length of stay: a randomized controlled trial" (2013) *BMC Medicine* 11: 198.

Pickelsimer, E., Selassie, A., Sample, P., et al., "Unmet service needs of persons with traumatic brain injury" (2007) *Journal of Head Trauma Rehabilitation* 22: 1–13.

Potter, S.D., Brown, R.G. and Fleminger, S., "Randomised, waiting list controlled trial of cognitive–behavioural therapy for persistent post concussional symptoms after predominantly mild–moderate traumatic brain injury" (2016) *Journal of Neurology, Neurosurgery and Psychiatry* Oct; 87(10): 1075–1083.

Powell, J., Heslin, J. and Greenwood, R., "Community based rehabilitation after severe traumatic brain injury: a randomised controlled trial" (2002) *Journal of Neurology Neurosurgery and Psychiatry* 72 (2): 193–202.

Riley, G.A., Dennis, R.K. and Powell, T., "Evaluation of coping resources and self-esteem as moderators of the relationship between threat appraisals and avoidance of activities after traumatic brain injury" (2010) *Neuropsychological Rehabilitation* 20 (6): 869–882.

Rivas, J.J., Lobato, R.D., Sarabia, R., Cordobés, F., Cabrera, A. and Gomez, P., "Extradural hematoma: analysis of factors influencing the courses of 161 patients" (1988) *Neurosurgery:* 23 (1), 44–51.

Robbins, J., Butler, S.G., Daniels, S., Gross, R.D., Langmore, S., Lazarus, C., et al., "Neural plasticity, swallowing and dysphagia rehabilitation: Translating principles of neural plasticity into clinically oriented evidence" (2007) *Journal of Speech, Language, and Hearing Research* 50: S276–S300.

REFERENCES

Roberts, I., Schierhout, G. and Alderson, P., "Absence of evidence for the effectiveness of five interventions routinely used in the intensive care management of severe head injury: a systematic review" (1998) *Journal of Neurology, Neurosurgery and Psychiatry* 65 (5): 729–733.

Roberts, D.J., Hall, R.I., Kramer, A.H., Robertson, H.L., Gallagher, C.N. and Zygun, D.A., "Sedation for critically ill adults with severe traumatic brain injury: a systematic review of randomized controlled trials" (2011) *Critical Care Medicine* 39 (12): 2743–2751.

Robertson, I.H. and Murre, J.M., "Rehabilitation of brain damage: brain plasticity and principles of guided recovery" (1999) *Psychological Bulletin* 125 (5): 544.

Rosenstein, L.D. and Price, R.F., "Shaping a normal eating rate using audiotaped pacing in conjunction with a taken economy" (1994) *Neuropsychological Rehabilitation* 4: 387–398.

Rotondi, A.J., Chelluri, L., Sirio, C., Mendelsohn, A., Schulz, R., Belle, S. and Pinsky, M.R., "Patients' recollections of stressful experiences while receiving prolonged mechanical ventilation in an intensive care unit" (2002) *Critical Care Medicine* 30 (4): 746–752.

Rusk, H.A., "Rehabilitation: the third phase of medicine" (1960) *Rhode Island Medical Journal* 43: 385–387.

Schaechter, J.D., Kraft, E., Hilliard, T.S., Dijkhuizen, R.M., Benner, T., Finklestein, S.P. and Cramer, S.C., "Motor recovery and cortical reorganization after constraint-induced movement therapy in stroke patients: a preliminary study" (2002) Neurorehabilitation and Neural Repair 16 (4): 326–338.

Siegert, R.J., Jackson, D.M., Playford, E.D., Fleminger, S. and Turner-Stokes, L., "A longitudinal, multicentre, cohort study of community rehabilitation service delivery in long-term neurological conditions" (2014) *BMJ Open* 4 (2): e004231.

Silverberg, N.D. and Iverson, G.L., "Is rest after concussion 'the best medicine'?: recommendations for activity resumption following concussion in athletes, civilians, and military service members" (2013a) *Journal of Head Trauma Rehabilitation* 28 (4): 250–259.

Silverberg, N.D., Hallam, B.J., Rose, A., Underwood, H., Whitfield, K., Thornton, A.E. and Whittal, M.L., "Cognitive-behavioral prevention of postconcussion syndrome in at-risk patients: a pilot randomized controlled trial" (2013b) *Journal of Head Trauma Rehabilitation* 28 (4): 313–322.

Smith, D.H., Meaney, D.F. and Shull, W.H., "Diffuse axonal injury in head trauma" (2003) *Journal of Head Trauma Rehabilitation* 18 (4): 307–316.

Smith-Seemiller, L., Fow, N.R., Kant, R. and Franzen, M.D., "Presence of post-concussion syndrome symptoms in patients with chronic pain vs mild traumatic brain injury" (2003) *Brain Injury* 17 (3): 199–206.

Sirois, M.J., Lavoie, A. and Dionne, C.E., "Impact of transfer delays to rehabilitation in patients with severe trauma" (2004) *Archives of Physical Medicine and Rehabilitation* 85 (2): 184–191.

Sorbello, D., Dewey, H.M., Churilov, L., Thrift, A.G., Collier, J.M., Donnan, G. and Bernhardt, J., "Very early mobilisation and complications in the first 3 months after stroke: further results from phase II of A Very Early Rehabilitation Trial (AVERT)" (2009) *Cerebrovascular Diseases* 28 (4): 378–383.

Steadman-Pare, D., Colantonio, A., Ratcliff, G., Chase, S. and Vernich, L., "Factors associated with perceived quality of life many years after traumatic brain injury" (2001) *Journal of Head Trauma Rehabilitation* 16 (4): 330–342.

Stichel, C.C. and Müller, H.W., "Experimental strategies to promote axonal regeneration after traumatic central nervous system injury" (1998) *Progress in Neurobiology* 56 (2): 119–148.

Stucki, G., Stier-Jarmer, M., Grill, E. and Melvin, J., "Rationale and principles of early rehabilitation care after an acute injury or illness" (2005) *Disability and Rehabilitation* 27 (7–8): 353–359.

Teasdale, T.W. and Engberg, A.W., "Subjective well-being and quality of life following traumatic brain injury in adults: A long-term population-based follow-up" (2005) *Brain Injury* 19 (12): 1041–1048.

Tennant, A., "Admission to hospital following head injury in England: Incidence and socio-economic associations" (2005) *BMC Public Health* 5 (1): 21.

Todd, D., "Narrative approaches to goal setting" in Weatherhead, S. and Todd, D. (eds), *Narrative approaches to brain injury* (London: Karnac Books Ltd, 2014).

Turner, J.M., Green, G., and Braunling-McMorrrow, D., "Differential reinforcement of low rates of responding to reduce dysfunctional social behaviours of a head injured man" (1990) *Behaviour Residential Treatment* 5: 15–27.

Turner-Stokes, L., "Cost-efficiency of longer-stay rehabilitation programmes: can they provide value for money?" (2007) *Brain injury* 21 (10): 1015–1021.

Turner-Stokes, L., "Goal attainment scaling (GAS) in rehabilitation: a practical guide" (2009) *Clinical Rehabilitation* 23: 362–370.

Turner-Stokes, L., "Goal attainment scaling: a direct comparison of alternative rating methods" (2010) *Clinical Rehabilitation* 24: 66–73.

Turner-Stokes, L, and Wade, D., "Rehabilitation following acquired brain injury: concise guidance" (2004) *Clinical Medicine* 4 (1): 61–65.

Turner-Stokes, L., Sutch, S. and Dredge, R., "Healthcare tariffs for specialist inpatient neurorehabilitation services: rationale and development of a UK casemix and costing methodology" (2012) *Clinical rehabilitation* 26 (3): 264–279.

Turner-Stokes, L., Scott, H., Williams, H. and Siegert, R., "The Rehabilitation Complexity Scale–extended version: detection of patients with highly complex needs" (2012) *Disability and Rehabilitation* 34 (9): 715–720.

Turner-Stokes, L., Williams, H., Bill, A., Bassett, P. and Sephton, K., "Cost-efficiency of specialist inpatient rehabilitation for working-aged adults with complex neurological disabilities: a multicentre cohort analysis of a national clinical data set" (2016) BMJ Open 6 (2): e010238.

Turner-Stokes, L., Dzingina, M., Shavelle, R., Bill, A., Williams, H and Sephton, K. "Estimated life-time savings In the cost of ongoing care following specialist rehabilitation for severe traumatic brain Injury in the United Kingdom." (2019) *Journal of Head Trauma Rehabilitation* 34 (4): 205–214

Vaynman, S. and Gomez-Pinilla, F., "License to run: Exercise impacts functional plasticity in the intact and injured central nervous system by using neurotrophins" (2005) *Neurorehabilitation and Neural Repair* 19: 283–295.

von Cramon, D.Y., Cramon, G.M.V. and Mai, N., "Problem-solving deficits in brain-injured patients: A therapeutic approach" (1991) *Neuropsychological Rehabilitation*, 1 (1): 45–64.

Wakai, A., Roberts, I. and Schierhout, G., "Mannitol for acute traumatic brain injury" (2007) *Cochrane Database Syst Rev.* 1.

Weiller, C., Ramsay, S.C., Wise, R.J., Friston, K.J. and Frackowiak, R.S., "Individual patterns of functional reorganization in the human cerebral cortex after capsular infarction" (1993) *Annals of Neurology* 33 (2): 181–189.

Weinert, C.R. and Sprenkle, M., "Post-ICU consequences of patient wakefulness and sedative exposure during mechanical ventilation" (2008) *Intensive Care Medicine* 34 (1): 82–90.

REFERENCES

Willer, B. and Miller, G., "On the validity of Goal Attainment Scaling as an outcome measure in mental health" (1976) *American Journal of Public Health* 66 (12): 1197–1198.

Willer, B. and Corrigan, J.D., "Whatever it Takes: A model for community-based services" (1994) *Brain Injury* 8 (7): 647–659.

Willer, B. and Leddy, J.J., "Management of concussion and post-concussion syndrome" (2006) *Current Treatment Options in Neurology* 8 (5): 415–426.

Wood, R.Ll., Brain Injury Rehabilitation: A neurobehavioural approach (London: Croom Helm, London, 1987).

Wood, R.Ll., "The rehabilitation team" in Greenwood, R.J., Barnes, M.P., McMillan, T.M. and Ward, C.D. (eds), *Handbook of Neurological Rehabilitation*, 2nd edn (Hove: Psychology Press, 2003) 41–50.

Wood, R.Ll. and Worthington A.D., "Outcome in community rehabilitation: measuring the social impact of disability" (1999) *Neuropsychological Rehabilitation* 9: 505–516.

Wood, R.Ll. and Worthington, A.D., "Neurobehavioural rehabilitation in practice" in Wood, R.Ll. and McMillan, T.M. (eds), *Neurobehavioural Disability and Social Handicap Following Traumatic Brain Injury* (Hove: Psychology Press, 2017) 133–155.

Wood, R., LL. and Worthington, A. "Neurobehavioural abnormalities associated with executive dysfunction after traumatic brain Injury." (2017) *Frontiers in Behavioral Neuroscience* 11: 195

Wood, R.Ll., Alderman, N. and Williams, C., "Assessment of neurobehavioural disability: a review of existing measures and recommendations for a comprehensive assessment tool" (2008) *Brain Injury* 22 (12): 905–918.

Wood, R.Ll., McCrea, J.D., Wood, L.M. and Merriment, R.N., "Clinical and cost-effectiveness of post-acute neurobehavioural rehabilitation" (1999) *Brain Injury* 13 (2): 69–88.

World Health Organization, International Classification of Impairments: Disabilities and Handicaps (Geneva: WHO, 1980).

World Health Organization, International Classification of Functioning Disability and Health (Geneva: WHO, 2001).

Worthington, A., "Neural plasticity and rehabilitation" in Lamar, M. and Price, C. (eds), *Instructors' Manual for Principles of Neuropsychology* (Wadsworth: Belmont, CA, 2001), 237–238.

Worthington, A., "Out on a limb? Developing an integrated rehabilitation service for adults with acquired brain injury" (2003) *Clinical Psychology* 23: 14–18.

Worthington, A., "Rehabilitation of executive deficits: Effective treatment of related disabilities" in Halligan, P.W. and Wade, D.T. (eds), *Effectiveness of Rehabilitation for Cognitive Deficits* (New York: Oxford University Press, 2005), 357–267.

Worthington, A., "Research design and outcome evaluation" in Goldstein, L.H. and McNeil, J.E. (eds), *Clinical Neuropsychology: A Practical Guide to Assessment and Management for Clinicians*, 2nd edn (Oxford: Wiley-Blackwell, 2012), 505–525.

Worthington, A., "Treatments and technologies in the rehabilitation of apraxia and action disorganisation syndrome: A review" (2016) *NeuroRehabilitation* 39 (1): 163–174.

Worthington, A., "Emerging Technologies for the Rehabilitation of Executive Dysfunction and Action Disorganisation" (2017) *Austin Journal of Clinical Neurology* 4 (4): 1116.

Worthington, A. and Oldham, J.B., "Delayed discharge from rehabilitation after brain injury" (2006) *Clinical Rehabilitation* 20: 79–82.

Worthington, A.D. and Merriman, R.N., "Residential Services" in Tyerman, A. and King, N.S. (eds), *Psychological Approaches to rehabilitation after traumatic brain injury* (Oxford: BPS Blackwell, 2008), 91–110.

Worthington, A. and Wood, R.Ll., "Behaviour problems" in Tyerman, A. and King, N.S. (eds), *Psychological approaches to rehabilitation after traumatic brain injury* (Oxford: BPS Blackwell, 2008), 227–259.

Worthington, A. and Archer, N., "Assessment and management of risk" in Oddy, M. and Worthington, A. (eds), *Rehabilitation of executive disorders following brain injury* (Oxford: Oxford University Press, 2009) 299–326.

Worthington, A. and Waller, J., "Rehabilitation of everyday living skills in the context of executive disorders" in Oddy, M. and Worthington, A. (eds), *Rehabilitation of executive disorders* (New York: Oxford University Press, 2009) 195–210.

Worthington, A. and Alderman, N., "Neurobehavioural Rehabilitation: an evolving paradigm" in McMillan, T. and Wood, R.L. (eds), *Neurobehavioural Disability and Social handicap Following Traumatic Brain Injury*, 2nd edn (Hove: Psychology Press, 2016).

Worthington, A. and Wood R.Ll. "Apathy following traumatic brain injury: A review" (2018) *Neuropsychologia* 118: 40–47.

Worthington, A., Wood, R.Ll. and McMillan, TM, "Neurobehavioural disability over the past four decades" in McMillan, T. and Wood, R.Ll. (eds), *Neurobehavioural Disability and Social handicap Following Traumatic Brain Injury*, 2nd edn (Hove: Psychology Press, 2016).

Worthington, A., Ramos, D.S. and Oddy, M., "The Cost Effectiveness of Neuropsychological Rehabilitation" in Wilson, B.A., et al. (eds), *Neuropsychological Rehabilitation: The International Handbook* (Abingdon: Routledge, 2017).

Worthington, A., Williams, C., Young, K. and Pownall, J., "Retraining gait components for walking in the context of abulia" (1997) *Physiotherapy Theory and Practice* 13: 247–256.

Worthington, A.D., Matthews, S., Melia, Y. and Oddy, M., "Cost-benefits associated with social outcome from neurobehavioural rehabilitation" (2006) *Brain Injury* 20 (9): 947–957.

Wright, D.W., Kellermann, A.L., Hertzberg, V.S., Clark, P.L., Frankel, M., Goldstein, F.C. and Lowery, D.W., "ProTECT: a randomized clinical trial of progesterone for acute traumatic brain injury" (2007) *Annals of Emergency Medicine* 49 (4): 391–402.

Wrigley, J.M., Yoels, W.C., Webb, C.R. and Fine, P.R., "Social and physical factors in the referral of people with traumatic brain injuries to rehabilitation" (1994) *Archives of Physical Medicine and Rehabilitation* 75 (2): 149–155.

Xiao, G., Wei, J., Yan, W., Wang, W. and Lu, Z., "Improved outcomes from the administration of progesterone for patients with acute severe traumatic brain injury: a randomized controlled trial" (2008) *Critical Care* 12 (2): R61.

Ylvisaker, M., Jacobs, H. and Feeney, T., "Positive supports for people who experience behavioural and cognitive disability after brain injury. A review" (2003) *Journal of Head Trauma Rehabilitation* 18:7–32.

Zochodne, D.W., Bolton, C.F., Wells, G.A., Gilbert, J.J., Hahn, A.F., Brown, J.D. and Sibbald, W.A., "Critical illness polyneuropathy: a complication of sepsis and multiple organ failure" (1987) *Brain* 110 (4): 819–841.

CHAPTER 9

Paediatric Acquired Brain Injury

Ingram Wright

CHAPTER LAYOUT

This chapter is split into three parts. Part 1 addresses general themes related to childhood brain injury at a conceptual level. Part 2 addresses thematic issues relevant to brain injury litigation. Part 3 then addresses specific exemplar challenges relevant to litigation in paediatric acquired brain injury.

9–001

1. NEURODEVELOPMENTAL ASPECTS OF CHILDHOOD BRAIN INJURY

Why a developmental perspective matters

Understanding the impact of childhood brain injury, as opposed to injury in adulthood, requires acknowledgement of several key constructs which influence the interaction between age at the time of injury and outcome in childhood and later adult life (Anderson et al., 2016).
   These constructs include:

9–002

- understanding of central nervous system (CNS) development;
- post-injury CNS and cognitive development:
    - plasticity (biological and behavioural levels);
    - vulnerability (biological, behavioural and cognitive levels);
- critical periods in development.

Taking each of these in turn there follows a brief review of the influence of the above constructs on our understanding of the impact of childhood brain injury.

Healthy central nervous system maturation

The maturational status of the central nervous system (CNS) is a crucial determinant of the influence of brain injury during childhood. A general overview of the variety of parameters commonly used to judge CNS maturation in the pre- and post-natal periods of development is provided by Lin (2003) and also by Stiles et al. (2005). There are numerous markers of developmental maturity

9–003

including: cell migration, myelination of nerve fibres within the CNS, cellular changes influencing synaptic density and dendritic development within both the cortex and subcortical structures. Synaptic density has long been regarded as a sensitive marker of early foetal and infant brain development with density reaching a peak at around two years of age and declining thereafter (Peter, 1979). The subsequent reduction in synaptic density, far from being a pathological feature, is characteristic of normal maturation and developmental pruning.

Alongside synaptic pruning, related corresponding specialisation of brain systems is indexed by other markers of CNS maturation. The first two years of life are characterised by rapid changes in neuronal and synaptic density and the corresponding further development of gross neuroanatomic form (Knickmeyer et al., 2008). The majority of hemispheric growth results from an increase in grey matter volume of over 149% in the first year of life.

Myelination of nerve fibres is a much more protracted developmental process and elegantly described by Lebel et al. (2008), who utilised diffusion tensor imaging to study developmental changes in maturation of white matter tracts in individuals from 5 to 30 years of age. Diffusion tensor magnetic resonance imaging (DTI) is particularly sensitive to the myelination process and the development of white matter connections. Age-related development in major white matter tracts, deep grey matter, and subcortical white matter, shows considerable regional variation. It is clear that fronto-temporal connections are amongst the latest to mature with protracted developmental changes into late adolescence and early adulthood. It is clear that specific aspects of functional connectivity illustrated by such imaging studies have clear and very specific correlations in corresponding aspects of cognitive and educational development (Qiu et al., 2008).

Further developmental changes in infancy are also strongly evident in metabolic changes as reported by Chugani (1999). Regional metabolic development in the first year of life is broadly consistent with the rapid behavioural, neurophysiological, and anatomical changes known to occur during infant development. However, measurement of glucose utilisation with positron emission tomography reveals further protracted developmental change with glucose utilisation rates not reaching adult levels of maturity until age 16 to 18 years. Furthermore, the same regional variation as with myelination is present across cortical areas and specifically highlights selective late development of frontal lobe systems.

Post-injury central nervous system and cognitive development

9–004 Age is known to be a powerful influence on recovery from injury. Children generally enjoy greater capacity for recovery of function than adults in studies of outcome following traumatic brain injury (TBI) (Anderson et al., 2004; Anderson et al., 2001; Dennis et al., 2013; Ewing-Cobbs et al., 2003). In general, the maturational status of the brain at the time of injury has a profound effect on subsequent developmental course. Following injury, the course of subsequent maturation of the CNS and further development of cognitive function is perturbed and follows a distinct path.

NEURODEVELOPMENTAL ASPECTS OF CHILDHOOD BRAIN INJURY

Plasticity (biological)

The plasticity of the developing brain at a biological level permits a variety of favourable compensatory responses to focal brain injury in order to restore function (Giza and Prins, 2006). The development of new neurons and glial cells, axonal sprouting of surviving neurons, and new synapse formation serve to re-establish lost functions more rapidly than is the case for adults (Wieloch and Nikolich, 2006). The plasticity of the developing brain is superior to that of the adult brain and therefore, there exists greater capacity for full restitution of function via such mechanisms.

9–005

Similarly, whereas an adult brain tends to have committed to specialist functional architecture and localisation of specialist functions within the cortex, a child's brain shows less obvious specialisation. The relative lack of anatomical specialisation results in less predictable consequences of cortical injuries and flexibility in atypical post-injury specialisation via plasticity around damage tissue. The most powerful example of this phenomenon is the recovery of language following early injury to the left hemisphere (via stroke or surgical hemispherectomy). Language deficits following such injuries are common in adults, but almost full recovery of language function is frequently observed in young children following similar injury or surgery (Liégeois et al., 2008).

Plasticity (cognitive/behavioural)

Plasticity as a construct has a broader application to understanding childhood brain injury than its original narrow biological meaning (Chapman and McKinnon, 2000). Children typical display greater behavioural flexibility in compensating for and adjusting to life after injury. While adults may dwell or ruminate on the loss of their prior well-established function, young children will often adapt to changes surprisingly readily. Childhood naïveté, and some lack of insight, may contribute to this form of plasticity and constitute protective features.

9–006

Plasticity in development is also evident at the cognitive level. Such plasticity, or cognitive flexibility, allows children to circumvent inborn cognitive deficits or cognitive consequences of later acquired injury. For example, infants typically break down speech that they hear in their environment to develop their understanding of spoken language and drive their own vocabulary development. Infants with hearing impairment, lack the input required to drive this typical process. Nonetheless such infants develop a remarkable sensitivity to sequential gestures used in sign language and when producing language will "babble" with approximations to sequential gestures in the same way that a hearing infant does with spoken language. It is via such mechanisms of cognitive flexibility that infants are able to circumvent conventional cognitive foundations to exert positive influences on development despite fundamental cognitive deficits.

Vulnerability (biological/behavioural/cognitive)

Alongside the positive influences of plasticity on a child's recovery from early brain injury, we must also recognise the particular vulnerability of the developing

9–007

brain and corresponding cognitive and behavioural systems. At the biological level, immaturity of brain systems renders them more vulnerable to toxins and injury caused by metabolic challenges such as anoxia. A similar "dose" of injury can therefore cause a more widespread pattern damage to a young, immature brain.

The phenomenon of Wallerian degeneration is a process which involves local damage causing effects further away but linked via neuronal networks in the brain. This has the effect of producing cascading degeneration far away from the boundaries of injury due to damage to the cell bodies (Jones et al., 2013). While not exclusively a feature of childhood brain injury, similar processes in the developing brain results in rapid developmental atrophy of brain structures distant from the focus of the injury (Verger et al., 2001).

At the cognitive level, an injury resulting in a specific cognitive deficit to a foundation skill can subsequently exert a cascading influence on wider cognitive, educational and developmental outcomes. An example of such a deficit might include an impairment in working memory which forms the foundation for understanding complex spoken language. In adulthood, such a deficit would not be trivial and would have implications for language comprehension and indeed fluency of speech output. However, in children such deficits are likely to profoundly influence the fundamental course of language acquisition as the development of normal language and growth of vocabulary is crucially dependent on working memory systems.

Similarly, loss of vision in adulthood, while having an impact on social functioning and participation, would not lead directly to an impairment of social cognition. In contrast, a congenital or early acquired visual impairment is strongly associated with a high prevalence of social deficits due to the consequent impoverished ability to incorporate and make judgments regarding nonverbal cues in social situations (Dale and Salt, 2008).

Critical periods in development

9–008 As a consequence of all of the above features of childhood brain maturation, behavioural and cognitive development, there exist a number of recognised "critical periods" in childhood. These periods have a profound influence on adult functioning if a particular function is not able to mature normally within a specific early developmental time window.

A critical period for language development is powerfully illustrated by Genie, a 13-year-old girl who had been deprived and confined to a small room, devoid of stimulation for her developing language. Genie failed subsequently to develop the ability to understand or produce syntax beyond a very basic level. This was despite her notable advances in other domains such as vocabulary and non-verbal cognition. It is now understood that a critical period for language and phonological developmental exists during early childhood although opinions vary on the precise end point (Friedmann and Rusou, 2015).

The increasing growth of research into early childhood experience documents long term change in emotional functioning and behavioural regulation resulting from early adversity such as neglect and abuse and corresponding lifelong impact on brain development (Garner et al., 2015; Grimshaw et al., 1998; Szilagyi and

Halfon, 2015). Studies of Romanian orphans highlight structural changes in limbic system volumes and connectivity related to the extent of emotional adversity experienced in early years (Eluvathingal et al., 2006).

Impact of age at injury on outcome following brain injury

There are a number of factors that influence the relative contribution of early plasticity and vulnerability on the developing brain. The size of the lesion is a particularly notable factor, with small lesions causing limited perturbation to brain development. Effective reorganisation of function is, however, promoted by large lesions resulting in improved outcomes. It appears that the influence of lesion size is bimodal, with moderately sized insults sufficient to cause extensive damage, but insufficient to promote wholesale reorganisation of function. Clearly the nature of a lesion is also influential, with diffuse, generalised pathology caused by trauma or infection being more likely to expose the vulnerability of the developing brain, whereas focal lesions caused by stroke or circumscribed tumours tend to benefit from subsequent plasticity in development (Anderson et al., 2016).

9–009

The impact of a brain injury is crucially determined on CNS maturational status and particularly with regard to prenatal injuries. For example, injuries between 15 to 22 weeks' gestation result in neuronal migration defects. After about 22 weeks' gestation, oligodendrocytes are particularly vulnerable to injury. White matter wasting and periventricular leukomalacia is observed in injuries occurring towards 40 weeks' gestation and both cortical and subcortical injuries become more common alongside damage to the basal ganglia (Anderson et al., 2004; Ewing-Cobbs et al., 2003; Lin, 2003).

Forsythe (2010) notes the influence of early unilateral brain injury on subsequent recovery from hemiplegia. In an adult, coordinated control of a limb is controlled by the opposite hemisphere of the brain (i.e. the right arm is controlled by the left motor cortex). However, in the pre-natal brain, control is served by both sides of the brain for each limb. Subsequent pruning leads to progression towards the adult pattern of cortical control. Pre-natal and early post-natal injuries to the left motor cortex hemisphere result in preservation of right sided control of the limb, minimising the damaging outcome for right hand function. In contrast, late post-natal injures that occur after pruning of the control pathways result in a dense and permanent hemiplegia, as is the case with adults facing a similar pattern of injury.

2. ISSUES IN CHILDHOOD BRAIN INJURY LITIGATION

Age at which reliable prognosis can be determined

Ascertaining levels of functional independence and the individual's corresponding support/care needs, employment prospects and capability to manage finances and everyday affairs is a crucial task in the management of childhood brain injury cases. In younger children, reliably identifying the presence of specific cognitive, behavioural or emotional issues will lead to recommendations regarding

9–010

appropriate and timely intervention. However, understanding the trajectory of the development of intellectual and cognitive abilities allows experts to make claims not only about contemporaneous needs, but also to determine likely future needs based on the likely evolution of deficits over time.

It is clearly recognised and reflected in the literature on trajectories of childhood cognitive development, that predictions based on assessments conducted at a young age are fraught with far greater uncertainty than assessments carried out close to adulthood. The reason for this uncertainty includes the restricted behavioural repertoire of the young child. For example, it is clearly not possible to directly assess detailed financial knowledge in a child of two years. Future capacity in this regard is therefore often inferred from judgment based on the child's level of numeracy, assuming that this will be predictive of function with regard to financial management. Test instruments designed to assess cognitive functioning are also limited in younger children and lead to greater levels of uncertainty with regard to contemporaneous memory, attention and language abilities. Such uncertainty results in corresponding unreliability about the prognosis and future functioning.

In older children, there is notable enhancement of the cognitive repertoire and maturation of brain systems and the child benefits from increasing experience and opportunities for everyday challenges. Such challenges provide a direct means of identifying cognitive limitations. In addition, typically developing or uninjured children begin to exhibit a stronger association with genetic factors including, but not exclusively, intellectual and cognitive abilities inherited from their parents. Improved assessment qualities also render prognostic judgments with test instruments more reliable and stable with regard to predictions of adult functioning (Blaga et al., 2009).

9–011 There are specific cases where a prognosis can be determined with greater confidence. Those children at the extremes of the distribution of functioning (i.e. those with severe impairment), are likely to demonstrate greater continuity and therefore it is possible to determine the likelihood of corresponding high support needs at an early stage in life. Conversely, there is great uncertainty with regard to subtle deficits; fluctuations in performance over time are greatest for those children scoring closer to the mean range of ability.

Assessments in young children are constrained with regard to both reliability and validity and, except in cases where cognitive function is severely impaired, there is significant residual uncertainty about the long-term outcome. The prognostic value of any assessment is constrained by the limited stability of cognitive tests in children for which empirical studies suggest increasing stabilisation of cognitive trajectory in IQ by mid-childhood (Bornstein et al., 2006; DeFries et al., 1987).

Assessments of infants are particularly lacking in validity and obtaining clarity with regard to their long-term prognosis is particularly challenging. However, extreme performance on cognitive tests tends to show greater continuity. Therefore, assessments of infants showing significant developmental delay leads to reasonable confidence of a poor outcome and the likelihood of learning disability in adulthood.

9–012 The prognostic value of cognitive tests is more complex when one considers cognitive and behavioural characteristics which are immaturely represented in young children or have yet to emerge. This applies to the assessment of executive function, which is considered to be a particular challenge. The challenge is essentially that, due to late maturation of frontal sub-cortical circuitry within the child's brain, deficits in executive function may emerge gradually over time, becoming more prominent when maturation exposes a previously hidden deficit as a result of early brain injury.

Continuity and discontinuity of other behavioural and emotional sequalae of brain injury are also a key consideration in paediatric cases. Early emotional or behavioural problems may signal a risk of later amplification or lifelong problems that will have profound implications for the value of a claim when care costs are considered. A child who presents with persistent challenging behaviour may be regarded as likely to present with ongoing challenging behaviour into adulthood and therefore require an enhanced care regime with the provision of 2:1 support, rather than from a single carer.

However, despite understandable concerns about the emergence of behavioural difficulties following a brain injury in childhood, literature from the development of non-injured children provides a guide as to the likely discontinuity of such behaviour. Children with ADHD commonly recover and are a large proportion of those meeting diagnostic criteria in early childhood, but no longer do so on reaching adolescence (Hill and Schoener, 1996). There is acknowledged to be greater continuity at the symptom level (as opposed to diagnostic entities) and symptoms such as inattention are more likely to persist than the full spectrum of difficulties leading to the diagnosis of the behavioural disorder itself. Conversely, individual symptoms, such as hyperactivity or impulse control problems, although changing in form and impact, show reasonable continuity throughout life (Faraone et al., 2002; Willoughby, 2003).

9–013

Emotional disturbance in early childhood may herald an adulthood characterised by significant mental health risk with attendant implications for unemployment, low income and support needs. Again, however, emotional disturbance in uninjured young children does not necessarily predict adult mental health with sufficient certainty to be useful to the legal expert. It must be borne in mind that continuity of symptoms is crucially dependent on aetiology and the cause of such symptoms. Symptoms originating due to brain injury are likely to prove less amenable to fluctuation or respond to natural maturation of regulatory systems within the brain. Essentially, it is more challenging for a damaged brain system to correct dysfunctional regulatory mechanisms.

Later adult adaptive functioning or independence is often of significance in cases of childhood brain injury. We are keen to predict whether a particular level of learning disability or cognitive impairment is likely to preclude remunerative employment or necessitate a high level of care and supervision. However, it is clear that intellectual ability, other than in cases where this is very low, is a relatively poor predictor of support needs. Those with low IQ will often function with relative independence and many individuals with high IQ, particularly those limited by other impairments or motor disability, may require a higher level of assistance with daily tasks.

Estimating pre-injury functioning in childhood

9–014   Questions about the impact of injury or clinical negligence resulting in brain injury often raise how a child would have developed without the injury or negligence. In adulthood, there are well established methods of estimating pre-morbid functioning to quantify the impact of injury on cognition. Formal educational attainment, employment status and functioning alongside standardised tests can be used to determine prior cognitive abilities and thus assist in quantifying losses resulting from an injury (Vanderploeg, 1994).

In children, particularly those injured at a young age, there may be limited evidence of any trajectory sufficiently reliable to indicate prior functional abilities. In the case of neonatal injuries, claims often rely on assertions based on parental functioning, functioning of siblings and the quality of the home environment and aspirations of parents for the child. The utility of such mechanisms is, however, significantly constrained, and correlations with sibling or parental IQ typically explain less than 40% of the variance in childhood ability. Thus, even knowing parental IQ (if such measures are available) would result in significant uncertainty as to the likely outcome for a child absent an injury.

Peri-natal brain injury presents particular challenges in litigation, and those with global or diffuse patterns of damage have the poorest outcome (Ewing-Cobbs et al., 2003). However, in such cases there is no period of normal development in order to delineate separable pre- and post-injury courses to more precisely determine the specific influence of the injury on development. Such claims are often necessarily based on approximations, in turn based on parental intellectual abilities, their educational attainment and family socioeconomic status.

In cases of later-acquired injury, the increasing availability of cognitive tests undertaken in schools allows a direct prediction of premorbid intellectual ability (Wright et al., 2005). Such a methodology circumvents the problems associated with predicting IQ on the basis of academic attainment. Again, it is clear that while correlated, the relationship between academic attainment and intellectual ability is modest, systematically absent in underprivileged groups and shows marked variance over developmental time.

Impact of intervention and rehabilitation in childhood

9–015   Recommendations for early intervention are often requested to mitigate the risk of adverse outcomes in adulthood. Intervention in the psychological domain might involve support to mitigate the risks of attentional problems on classroom-based learning or intervention to address early behavioural or emotional difficulties. There are reasonable descriptive accounts of interventions claiming efficacy for a wide range of cognitive, emotional and behavioural sequelae (Anderson and Catroa, 2006). However, systematic research demonstrating the efficacy of childhood neurorehabilitation is sadly lacking and often methodologically compromised.

The delivery of interventions in childhood requires particular sensitivity to the developmental context (Wright and Limond, 2004). Intervention with young children and those in mid-childhood is limited by developmental restrictions on insight. The priorities for the rehabilitation team with regard to longer term outcomes are unlikely to be shared by a child at an early developmental stage. Children are unlikely to recognise the problematic nature of some restrictions and therefore struggle to engage. Intervention may therefore be indirect and imposed on the wider system rather than relying on engagement with the individual child. Support in the classroom and in promoting social functioning must be deployed sensitively to avoid causing unintended harm to a child's developing sense of self-efficacy and confidence. There is some evidence that classroom-based support may have a detrimental impact on some aspects of pupil functioning, particularly in the social domain (Alborz et al., 2009; van de Pol et al., 2015).

There is limited evidence to support early intervention to address childhood emotional and behavioural problems (Bellini et al., 2007; Farrell and Barrett, 2007) and the presence of difficulties in childhood heralds a risk of emotional and behavioural problems in adulthood. Adverse childhood experiences, impaired social functioning, social isolation and limited emotional resilience are strongly linked to poor mental health in adulthood and compromised independence.

Educational interventions include appropriate school provision, securing classroom-based support for learning and advising regarding the management of specific cognitive problems. Additional support and advice may be required with the management of emotional disturbance or challenging behaviour.

9–016

Realistic expectations with regard to educational attainment may need to be set for young people with acquired brain injury and in some circumstances they may benefit from reduced academic loading and focussing on a smaller number of subjects in which success is achievable. Such reductions may allow children to rehearse material with tutors to circumvent memory problems or mitigate the impact of severe attentional problems with opportunities to take breaks and learn in smaller chunks of time. At a more extreme end of the injury severity, children may benefit significantly from opportunities to engage in functionally-oriented education designed to support skill development with everyday finances, domestic independence, and aspects of social and emotional functioning.

Clinical neuropsychologists have a clear role in the multidisciplinary team. However, intervention to address neuropsychological and neurocognitive issues, in addition to emotional and behavioural problems, requires clear and effective coordination with other treating therapies. In some cases, the emotional and behavioural issues may prevent or significantly constrain the effectiveness of other interventions. In more challenging circumstances, the intervention from other clinicians may serve to inadvertently reinforce or exacerbate challenging behaviour and emotional difficulties. In such circumstances, it may be sensible for the treating neuropsychologist to take the lead role and influence neuropsychological intervention indirectly through individual therapists or the team as a whole and the wider family and educational system.

3. SPECIFIC CHALLENGES IN PAEDIATRIC ACQUIRED BRAIN INJURY

Mild traumatic brain injury and normal brain imaging

9–017 It is relatively common for children with marked cognitive problems to have no significant abnormalities on imaging. In the case of uncomplicated mild TBI (mTBI), we would not expect to see abnormalities on initial CT imaging otherwise the injury would be a complicated mild or moderate injury, even if there is no loss of consciousness. However, microstructural imaging abnormalities in mTBI may be revealed by particular imaging sequences showing up microstructural injury not amenable to conventional imaging (Aoki et al., 2012; Mechtler et al., 2014).

It is clear that in children, there is a possibility of an injury precipitating psychological and emotional symptoms such as fatigue and concentration problems recognised as a post-concussion syndrome. Evidence suggests variable severity within the mTBI population with some individuals having subtle injuries not evident on conventional MRI. However, it is not clear that such subtle injuries are causally associated with evident neurocognitive deficits in the population (van der Horn et al., 2018). Regardless of the extent of objective signs of brain injury, there are some children for whom the experience of an injury destabilises psychological and emotional function, establishes negative patterns of illness, or exposes previous vulnerabilities (Micklewright et al., 2012).

Special case of frontal lobe functioning and emergence of dysexecutive symptoms

9–018 The impact of early brain injury on the development of executive functions presents a particular challenge with regard to the timing of a confident prognosis. Myelination of the dorsolateral pre-frontal cortex is amongst the most protracted of cortical regions (Qiu et al., 2008). Given that the frontal lobe systems are relative late maturing, and the emergence of executive competence to the standard of healthy adults is also late to emerge, many view the prognosis with regard to executive function as particularly fraught with uncertainty.

Children are not expected to have established competence with regard to planning, multitasking, goal directed behaviour or inhibition of inappropriate of irrelevant behaviour. Furthermore, the underlying cognitive systems which support competent functioning are not well established until mid- to late-adolescence to support functioning comparable to adults. Environmental challenges and expectations with regard to executive competence are also deferred to late childhood for similar reasons. Therefore, children who may be showing early signs of immaturity or deficits in frontal lobe functioning are not particularly conspicuous in exhibiting failure.

It is possible for children with frontal lobe damage to show relatively modest signs of difficulty in early childhood but, as the frontal lobe systems mature, latent behavioural and anatomical pathology becomes more evident. Even in those children not showing obvious signs of specific focal frontal injury, subtle damage to brain regions related to the healthy development of frontal systems may show patterns of gradual amplification of initially subtle signs of executive dysfunction. There are numerous case examples of early frontal lobe injury showing emergence of frank pathology and dysfunction in later life (Anderson et al., 1999).

From a legal perspective, these features of frontal lobe injury mean that it is difficult to confidently rule out the later emergence of behavioural difficulties and functional compromise that might link an early brain injury to later executive dysfunction. In these circumstances, monitoring for the emergence of executive dysfunction into at least mid-adolescence supports a more confident opinion on functional prognosis and the corresponding implications for adult care and support requirements.

9–019

There are, however, reasonable counter arguments to this view. Young children do show a capability with regard to inhibition, aspects of multitasking, attentional control and aspects of goal-directed behaviour. It is simply the case that such behaviours are present in immature forms and require the development of other areas to fully mature in an adult form (Wright et al., 2003). Furthermore, it is clear that pathology related to frontal dysfunction does show reasonable continuity from childhood into adolescence. Thus, it is possible to predict adult functioning to some extent from the functioning of a child. Sensitive assessment of young children using appropriately valid measures may be employed to demonstrate the absence of even subtle signs of difficulty and the risk of the likely emergence of frontal pathology.

In any case, a child who is showing few signs of executive dysfunction by 12 years old is significantly less likely to show severe problems in late adolescence or early adulthood. In other cases, a severe general cognitive or intellectual disability is an evident feature of early development. In such cases it is unlikely that specific executive dysfunction is likely to present any further additional challenges to future care or support needs.

Capacity to litigate and manage finances and broader issues on reaching majority

Experts are often asked to comment on the likelihood that a child will have capacity to manage finances or to litigate on reaching majority. The Mental Capacity Act applies to children under 16 years in that the Court of Protection can make decisions about the property and affairs of a child and may continue if the child lacks capacity to make those decisions when they reach 16 years old.

9–020

Some children, having suffered early brain injury, may suffer such significant impairment that the capacity to manage finances, as with other aspects of cognition and functional independence, can be ruled out at an early stage. However, in cases where injury has a more subtle impact on cognition, assessment in relation to capacity is more challenging. The appropriate test of capacity refers to the ability to understand, communicate, retain and weigh information. These areas, to an extent, translate into comprehension, memory and executive functions at a cognitive level. Thus, a child with significant comprehension problems will, by definition, struggle to understand information presented to them. A child with memory problems will be unable to retain a volume of information. Finally, those with executive difficulties would struggle to hold two scenarios in mind while judging which to execute in order to make an effective decision. Thus, compromise within any of these broad cognitive domains can be used to predict future corresponding restrictions on capacity. Capacity is, of course, related to specific decisions such as the ability to manage financial investments of the order of several thousand pounds, or to instruct a solicitor with regard to pursuing a case to settlement given the risks if a case goes to trial. Such decisions not only rely on the underlying cognitive processes supporting the understanding, retention and comparison of information, but also an ability to manage the conceptual content. In the case of finances, a child's emerging numerical ability is likely to be significant and of prognostic value. In the case of litigation, the ability to learn and acquire knowledge of legal processes at a conceptual level will be important.

It is possible to support quite complex decision making in individuals through a diligent effort to bolster their conceptual knowledge. Thus, detailed knowledge of investment practices and options, and awareness of the terminology can support effective decision making despite subtle compromises to comprehension, memory and executive function. In this way, development of the content domain (i.e. knowledge of specific terminology and processes) can bolster performance. This is commonly witnessed in individuals able to make calculations about shopping and dietary intake using knowledge of context to bolster numerical performance (Greiffenhagen and Sharrock, 2008).

9–021   Children who have had acquired brain injuries may not only suffer cognitive deficits, but also struggle educationally. Slow educational development or fragmented education (due to hospitalisation for example) may lead to the poor development of conceptual knowledge to support decision making. Children may also have limited experience of practical aspects of decision making due to restricted independence, for example because of restricted mobility or medical complications such as epilepsy. In the absence of experience and poor educational progress, children may be destined to lack capacity because of the poor development of content knowledge and expertise, rather than fundamental cognitive problems with comprehension, memory and executive function. Such restrictions on capacity may be short-lived with support and education to promote development.

Once again, confidence with regard to prognosis is often dependent on the severity of the injury and the corresponding cognitive impairment. Adolescents with age equivalent levels of comprehension below six years and levels of numeracy at similarly restrictive levels would likely struggle to manage even basic finances on reaching adulthood. However, those children with levels of functioning at the eight–nine-year level may reasonably manage weekly budgets within a restricted area, such as grocery shopping. Full independence with regard to finances clearly involves a level of complex understanding of issues such as contactless card payments, internet purchasing and risks of fraud and/or financial exploitation.

SPECIFIC CHALLENGES IN PAEDIATRIC ACQUIRED BRAIN INJURY

Intellectual ability and adaptive function/care needs, employment

Age equivalent functioning is commonly used as a communicative tool to illustrate the level of impairment characteristic of the equivalent level of a younger child (e.g. an adult of 25 years of age may be described as having the mental age of a five year old). Corresponding claims about level of care and support can be made on the basis of common sense understanding of the level of care appropriate to the developmental age equivalent.

9–022

Age equivalent scores, while superficially potent in illustrating the extent of a deficit, neglect a number of important limitations of developmental age as a construct. Referring to a mental or developmental age uses the average (mean) level of performance across the childhood age range as a reference point (Wright et al., 2005).

Thus, referring to a child of eight years as having a reading age of six years, highlights the fact that the performance is equivalent to the average six year old. What such a metric does not tell us is how unusual such a "deficit" is in the population of children at eight years of age. In this particular case, around 20% of individuals at eight years of age will have reading ages at or below six years. This is a reflection of the fact that reading develops relatively slowly at this age and there is significant variance in capabilities. A counter example is in the development of a child's head circumference. Here, development is relatively rapid in young infants and the variance at any given age is relatively small. Describing a child's head circumference as equivalent to that of a younger child, in this case, highlights a significant and notable anomaly (Baxter et al., 2009).

There is, of course, a relationship between general intellectual ability and adaptive functioning and levels of independence. However, this relationship is neither straightforward nor linear. Those individuals with an IQ below 70 (or 1st percentile) may be characterised as having a learning disability (Department of Health, 2001). However, currently employed criteria are based on impairment of everyday skills rather than merely a threshold of intellectual ability. There are several definitions of learning disability used in the UK. A commonly used definition is from "Valuing People: a new strategy for learning disability for the 21st century", the Government White Paper for England about health and social care support for people with a learning disability (Department of Health, 2001). It explains that a learning disability includes the presence of:

9–023

- a significantly reduced ability to understand new or complex information or to learn new skills;
- a reduced ability to cope independently; and
- an impairment that started before adulthood, with a lasting effect on development.

It is clear that there is a threshold level of intellectual impairment below which the prospects of successful independent living are remote indeed. However, IQ alone is not a straightforward determinant of functional independence and support needs. Ability below the 5th percentile is not necessarily a barrier to largely normal levels of independence and remunerative employment. Furthermore, there are many individuals with impaired ability below the 1st percentile who are nonetheless able to care for themselves and live independently with relatively limited support. Discrete additional features common in acquired brain injury in childhood such as motor disability, medical needs and discrete domains of cognitive dysfunction (memory or executive difficulties), will also exert marked additional restrictions on later independence. The extent of motor disability, for example, explains around 70% of the variance in functional competence of adults with cerebral palsy (Donkervoort et al., 2007).

Employment prospects are clearly a function not only of intellectual ability and academic attainment, but aspects of physical, social, behavioural and emotional functioning. Deficits in any of these domains may severely restrict employment despite adequate functioning in all other areas. Social communication, memory and language difficulties are noted to have a particularly pronounced effect on employment in those with otherwise preserved intellectual ability (Liss et al., 2001; Taylor et al., 2015).

SUMMARY

9–024 In general, an understanding of the impact of childhood acquired brain injury is based on detailed knowledge of maturational pathways of brain systems coupled with an understanding of the developmental timing of a brain injury from a biological, cognitive, behavioural and emotional perspective. Experts are regularly challenged with regard to the need to provide contemporaneous and evidence-based recommendations regarding rehabilitation. In addition, judgments around pre-injury functioning are particularly challenging in paediatric personal injury or neonatal negligence cases. Experts face significant uncertainty with regard to prognostic judgments.

REFERENCES

9–025 Alborz, A., Pearson, D., Farrell, P., and Howes, A. (2009). *The impact of adult support staff on pupils and mainstream schools: A systematic review of evidence*. London: EI-Centre Social Science Research Unit UCL Institute of Education, University College London, 2009.

Anderson, S.W., Bechara, A., Damasio, H., Tranel, D., and Damasio, A.R., "Impairment of social and moral behavior related to early damage in human prefrontal cortex" (1999) *Nature Neuroscience*, 2(11), 1032–1037.

Anderson, V.A., Morse, S.A., Catroa, C., Haritou, F., and Rosenfeld, J.V., "Thirty month outcome from early childhood head injury: A prospective analysis of neurobehavioural recovery" (2004) *Brain*, 127(12), 2608–2620.

Anderson, V., Anderson, P., Northam, E., Jacobs, R., and Catroa, C., "Development of executive functions through late childhood and adolescence in an Australian sample" (2001) *Developmental Neuropsychology*, 20(1), 385–406.

Anderson, V., and Catropa, C., "Advances in postacute rehabilitation after childhood-acquired brain injury: A focus on cognitive, behavioral, and social domains" (2006) *American Journal of Physical Medicine and Rehabilitation*, 85, 767–778.

Anderson, V., Northam, E., and Wrennall, J., *Developmental Neuropsychology: A Clinical Approach*. (London: Routledge, 2016)

REFERENCES

Aoki, Y., Inokuchi, R., Gunshin, M., Yahagi, N., and Suwa, H., "Diffusion tensor imaging studies of mild traumatic brain injury: A meta-analysis" (2012) *Journal of Neurology, Neurosurgery and Psychiatry*, 83(9), 870–876.

Baxter, P.S., Rigby, A.S., Rotsaert, M.H.E.P.D., and Wright, I. "Acquired microcephaly: causes, patterns, motor and IQ effects, and associated growth changes" (2009) *Pediatrics*, 124(2), 590–595.

Bellini, S., Peters, J. K., Benner, L., and Hopf, A., "A Meta-Analysis of School-Based Social Skills Interventions for Children With Autism Spectrum Disorders" (2007) *Remedial and Special Education*, 28(3), 153–162.

Blaga, O.M., Shaddy, D.J., Anderson, C.J., Kannass, K.N., Little, T.D., and Colombo, J., "Structure and continuity of intellectual development in early childhood" (2009) *Intelligence*, 37(1), 106–113.

Bornstein, M.H., Hahn, C.S., Bell, C., Haynes, O.M., Slater, A., Golding, J., and Wolke, D., "Stability in cognition across early childhood a developmental cascade" (2006) *Psychological Science*, 17(2), 151–158.

Chapman, S.B., and McKinnon, L. "Discussion of developmental plasticity: Factors affecting cognitive outcome after pediatric traumatic brain injury" (2000) *Journal of Communication Disorders*, 33, 333–344. Elsevier Inc.

Chugani, H.T. "Metabolic imaging: A window on brain development and plasticity" (1999) *Neuroscientist*, 5, 29–40.

Dale, N., and Salt, A., "Social identity, autism and visual impairment (VI) in the early years" (2008) *British Journal of Visual Impairment*, 26(2), 135–146.

DeFries, J.C., Plomin, R., and LaBuda, M.C., "Genetic Stability of Cognitive Development From Childhood to Adulthood" (1987) *Developmental Psychology*, 23(1), 4–12.

Dennis, M., Yeates, K., Taylor, G., and Fletcher, J. "Brain reserve capacity, cognitive reserve capacity, and age-based functional plasticity after congenital and acquired brain injury in children". In Y. Stern (ed.), *Cognitive Reserve: Theory and Applications* (New York: Psychology Press, 2013).

Department of Health, "Valuing people – a new strategy for learning disability for the 21st century: a White Paper", Department of Health Publications, 2001.

Donkervoort, M., Roebroeck, M., Wiegerink, D., van der Heijden-Maessen, H., and Stam, H., "Determinants of functioning of adolescents and young adults with cerebral palsy" (2007) *Disability and Rehabilitation*, 29(6), 453–463.

Eluvathingal, T. J., Chugani, H. T., Behen, M. E., Juhász, C., Muzik, O., Maqbool, M., Makki, M., "Abnormal brain connectivity in children after early severe socioemotional deprivation: A diffusion tensor imaging study" (2006) *Pediatrics*, 117(6), 2093–2100.

Ewing-Cobbs, L., Barnes, M.A., and Fletcher, J.M., "Early Brain Injury in Children: Development and Reorganization of Cognitive Function" (2003) *Developmental Neuropsychology*, 24(2–3), 669–704.

Faraone, S., Biederman, J., and Monuteaux, M.C., "Further evidence for the diagnostic continuity between child and adolescent ADHD" (2002) *Journal of Attention Disorders*, 6(1), 5–13.

Farrell, L.J., and Barrett, P.M., "Prevention of Childhood Emotional Disorders: Reducing the Burden of Suffering Associated with Anxiety and Depression" (2007) *Child and Adolescent Mental Health*, 12(2), 58–65.

Forsyth, R.J., "Back to the future: Rehabilitation of children after brain injury" (2010, July) *Archives of Disease in Childhood*, 95, 554–559.

Friedmann, N., and Rusou, D. "Critical period for first language: The crucial role of language input during the first year of life" (2015) *Current Opinion in Neurobiology*, 35, 27–34. Elsevier Ltd.

Garner, A.S., Forkey, H., and Szilagyi, M., "Translating Developmental Science to Address Childhood Adversity" (2015) *Academic Pediatrics*, 15, 493–502. Elsevier Inc.

Giza, C.C., and Prins, M.L., "Is being plastic fantastic? Mechanisms of altered plasticity after developmental traumatic brain injury" (2006) *Developmental Neuroscience*, 28, 364–379.

Greiffenhagen, C., and Sharrock, W., "School mathematics and its everyday other? Revisiting Lave's 'Cognition in Practice.'" (2008) *Educational Studies in Mathematics*, 69(1), 1–21.

Grimshaw, G.M., Adelstein, A., Bryden, M.P., and MacKinnon, G.E., "First-language acquisition in adolescence: Evidence for a critical period for verbal language development" (1998) *Brain and Language*, 63(2), 237–255.

Hill, J.C., and Schoener, E.P., "Age-dependent decline of attention deficit hyperactivity disorder" (1996) *American Journal of Psychiatry*, 153(2), 1143–1146.

Jones, K.C., Hawkins, C., Armstrong, D., Deveber, G., Macgregor, D., Moharir, M., and Askalan, R., "Association between radiographic Wallerian degeneration and neuropathological changes post childhood stroke" (2013) *Developmental Medicine and Child Neurology*, 55(2), 173–177.

Knickmeyer, R.C., Gouttard, S., Kang, C., Evans, D., Wilber, K., Smith, J.K., Gilmore, J.H., "A structural MRI study of human brain development from birth to 2 years" (2008) *Journal of Neuroscience*, 28(47), 12176–12182.

Lebel, C., Walker, L., Leemans, A., Phillips, L., and Beaulieu, C., "Microstructural maturation of the human brain from childhood to adulthood" (2008) *NeuroImage*, 40(3), 1044–1055.

Liégeois, F., Cross, J.H., Polkey, C., Harkness, W., and Vargha-Khadem, F., "Language after hemispherectomy in childhood: Contributions from memory and intelligence" (2008) *Neuropsychologia*, 46(13), 3101–3107.

Lin, J.P., "The cerebral palsies: A physiological approach" (2003, March) *Neurology in Practice*, 74, i23–i29.

Liss, M., Harel, B., Fein, D., Allen, D., Dunn, M., Feinstein, C., Rapin, I., "Predictors and Correlates of Adaptive Functioning in Children with Developmental Disorders" (2001) *Journal of Autism and Developmental Disorders*, 31(2), 219–230.

Mechtler, L.L., Shastri, K.K., and Crutchfield, K.E., "Advanced Neuroimaging of Mild Traumatic Brain Injury" (2014) *Neurologic Clinics*, 32(1), 31–58.

Micklewright, J.L., King, T.Z., O'Toole, K., Henrich, C., and Floyd, F.J., "Parental distress, parenting practices, and child adaptive outcomes following traumatic brain injury" (2012) *Journal of the International Neuropsychological Society*, 18(2), 343–350.

Peter R.H., "Synaptic density in human frontal cortex—Developmental changes and effects of aging" (1979) *Brain Research*, 163(2), 195–205.

Qiu, D., Tan, L.H., Zhou, K., and Khong, P.L., "Diffusion tensor imaging of normal white matter maturation from late childhood to young adulthood: Voxel-wise evaluation of mean diffusivity, fractional anisotropy, radial and axial diffusivities, and correlation with reading development." (2008) *NeuroImage*, 41(2), 223–232.

Stiles, J., Reilly, J., Paul, B., and Moses, P., "Cognitive development following early brain injury: Evidence for neural adaptation" (2005) *Trends in Cognitive Sciences*, 9(3 SPEC. ISS.), 136–143. Elsevier Ltd.

REFERENCES

Szilagyi, M., and Halfon, N., "Pediatric Adverse Childhood Experiences: Implications for Life Course Health Trajectories" (2015) *Academic Pediatrics*, 15, 467–468. Elsevier Inc.

Taylor, J.L., Henninger, N.A., and Mailick, M.R., "Longitudinal patterns of employment and postsecondary education for adults with autism and average-range IQ" (2015) *Autism*, 19(7), 785–793.

van de Pol, J., Volman, M., Oort, F., and Beishuizen, J., "The effects of scaffolding in the classroom: support contingency and student independent working time in relation to student achievement, task effort and appreciation of support" (2015) *Instructional Science*, 43(5), 615–641.

van der Horn, H.J., de Haan, S., Spikman, J. M., de Groot, J.C., and van der Naalt, J., "Clinical relevance of microhemorrhagic lesions in subacute mild traumatic brain injury" (2018) *Brain Imaging and Behavior*, 12(3), 912–916.

Vanderploeg, R.D., *Clinicians Guide to Neuropsychological Assessment* (Hilsdale, NJ: Lawrence Erlbaum Associates, 1994).

Verger, K., Junqué, C., Levin, H. S., Jurado, M.A., Pérez-Gómez, M., Bartrés-Faz, D., Mercader, J.M., "Correlation of atrophy measures on MRI with neuropsychological sequelae in children and adolescents with traumatic brain injury" (2001) *Brain Injury*, 15(3), 211–221.

Wieloch, T., and Nikolich, K., "Mechanisms of neural plasticity following brain injury" (2006) *Current Opinion in Neurobiology*, 16, 258–264.

Willoughby, M.T., "Developmental course of ADHD symptomatology during the transition from childhood to adolescence: A review with recommendations" (2003) *Journal of Child Psychology and Psychiatry and Allied Disciplines*, 44, 88–106.

Wright, I., and Limond, J., "A developmental framework for memory rehabilitation in children" (2004) *Pediatric Rehabilitation*, 7, 85–96.

Wright, I., Strand, S., and Wonders, S., "Estimation of premorbid general cognitive abilities in children" (2005) *Educational and Child Psychology*, 22, 100–107.

Wright, I., Waterman, M., Prescott, H., and Murdoch-Eaton, D., "A new Stroop-like measure of inhibitory function development: Typical developmental trends" (2003) *Journal of Child Psychology and Psychiatry and Allied Disciplines*, 44(4), 561–575.

CHAPTER 10

Subtle Brain Injury Claims

Jonathan Watt-Pringle QC and Martin van den Broek

INTRODUCTION

In recent years a new and controversial type of claim has emerged in brain injury litigation relating to what has become known as subtle brain injury claims. Although now well known within the legal arena, the term "subtle brain injury" has no clear medical meaning; nor is it a recognised diagnosis, and it does not appear in any of the conventional diagnostic manuals. If told that an individual has a subtle brain injury, many clinicians would be likely to assume that the individual had some subtle, unspecified effects from an injury, but they would not necessarily link the term to a particular aetiology or diagnosis. On the other hand, clinicians working in the medico-legal field will be very familiar with the expression and aware that it has become an active and controversial area of litigation and, as such, subtle brain injury exists in a world parallel to routine clinical practice. The absence of a clear definition and diagnostic criteria means that the term is often used in somewhat vague or different ways depending on the particular case, and sometimes it is not defined at all. Madan (2016) provided a legal monograph on subtle brain injuries but, despite advising lawyers on how to assess and manage such claims, no definition of the condition was provided. The appellation has been used in a number of ways and may refer to a moderate or severe brain injury that has long-term, but subtle effects, such as diminishing an individual's concentration and memory, and so downgrading their performance at work. In these instances, where there is clear evidence of brain trauma, such as on CT or MRI imaging, and incontrovertible evidence of cognitive changes, such as from ward observations, there may be little disagreement that the individual has been affected. However, a motif of subtle brain injury claims is that clear-cut evidence of brain trauma is usually absent; indeed, a brain injury may not have been suspected for some years post-injury and the claim may have been advanced on some other basis, such as the claimant having suffered whiplash. Only later in the course of litigation is a brain injury diagnosed, so elevating the claim into a different league of gravity and inevitably meeting with resistance from defendants sceptical about this turn of events.

10–001

There are no universally agreed diagnostic criteria for traumatic brain injuries, but among the most widely used are the Mayo system (Malec et al., 2007; see Chapter 4) and DSM-5 (American Psychiatric Association, 2013; see Chapter 5). Typically, brain trauma is inferred by reference to a number of indicators, including whether there has been a loss of consciousness, Glasgow Coma Scale

(GCS) scores, the duration of post-traumatic amnesia (PTA), and neuroimaging. The Mayo criteria define a moderate-severe brain injury as involving a loss of consciousness for 30 minutes or more, PTA of 24 hours or more, and an initial GCS of less than 13, or evidence of brain trauma on neuroimaging. On the other hand, DSM-5 does not include neuroimaging in its criteria and instead the diagnosis and injury severity rest on the length of any loss of consciousness, the duration of PTA, and GCS readings. Although the criteria differ, they share a common feature in that the injury is diagnosed on the basis of the individual's clinical characteristics in the aftermath of the injurious event. In contrast, subtle brain injuries have tended to take a different approach and, instead of relying on contemporaneous acute, peri-trauma observations, the diagnosis is inferred on the basis of a combination of symptoms and complaints reported some time, perhaps years, later and the patient's retrospectively reported PTA, that is, the period of disorientation and discontinuous recall following the index accident.

The duration of PTA has been viewed as particularly important, if not pivotal, when inferring that a brain injury has taken place.[1] In addition, complaints of poor memory, slowness and reduced empathy may be interpreted as "neurogenic" and therefore indicative that a diffuse axonal injury (DAI) has occurred, thereby reinforcing the diagnosis. Beyond acute care, such as attending A&E, there may have been a relative absence of engagement with NHS services or other clinicians. In the event that the claimant later undergoes treatment, the persistence of complaints following improvement in their mood may then be interpreted as ruling out a psychological or psychiatric explanation for their symptoms and indicating an organic brain injury. However, while the PTA may be described as having been lengthy and indicating a severe initial injury, the long-term effects are often described as being relatively mild or subtle, but nevertheless disabling. A further characteristic of such claims is that the claimant may have been particularly able or intelligent and so high-functioning and, although the long-term effects of the injury may be modest, in the context of their previous occupational attainments, they are thought to be significantly disadvantaged.[2] Finally, although the claimant is said to have had an injury of some severity, there may nevertheless be an absence of physical evidence that objectively confirms the presence of brain trauma, and normal neuroimaging may be viewed as consistent with a DAI. Similarly, while neuropsychological assessment may be said to confirm the patient's complaints, the absence of demonstrable impairments on cognitive testing may also be argued as not contradicting the existence of cerebral trauma.[3]

1. POST-TRAUMATIC AMNESIA

10–002 The term post-traumatic amnesia (PTA) was used by Symonds (1940) to refer to a condition in which the individual shows a defect in cerebral function after consciousness has been restored, and it is considered to end when they can

---

[1] e.g. *Siegel v Pummel* [2014] EWHC 4309 (QB), and *Mann v Bahri* unreported 12 March 2012, Central London County Court.
[2] See, e.g. *Clark v Maltby* [2010] EWHC 1201 (QB); *Van Wees v Karkour* [2007] EWHC 165 (QB); and *Siegel v Pummell* [2014] EWHC 4309 (QB).
[3] See, e.g. *Mann v Bahri* unreported 12 March 2012.

provide a clear and sequential account of events. PTA is associated with clinical outcomes and neuropsychological limitations (Walker et al., 2010), although Ashla et al. (2009) found that retrospective PTA (as assessed by the Rivermead Post-Traumatic Amnesia Protocol, see below) was correlated with cognitive deficits for only up to five years post-injury, and not thereafter. The post-traumatic phase is characterised by disorientation when the individual is confused in time and place and their situation, as well as amnesia during which events are not stored in memory. Later questioning may reveal that they cannot remember an interval of time after the accident or they have patchy memories ("islands" of memories), before again becoming oriented and having a sequential recollection. The post-traumatic duration is therefore the interval from the original head injury, including any loss of consciousness (i.e. coma), until the person has continuous recall. The interval to the first memory has sometimes been used to define its end, but as there may still be some impaired recall due to the brain insult, the first memory does not necessarily mark the restitution of sequential awareness. In some cases, PTA ends abruptly and, for instance, there may be a clearly delineated period, such as a weekend, that the person cannot remember, whereas for others the end is less clear cut and more ragged. In addition, there may be amnesia for events preceding the injury (i.e. retrograde amnesia), which is also associated with injury severity, and a long interval may denote a severe injury. However, the relationship is imperfect and severe injuries can nevertheless be accompanied by only short retrograde amnesia. It may also be difficult for the person to define, as it relies on their recollection of events and their pre-accident activities may have been unremarkable and without distinctive features. Retrograde amnesia is also not always fixed and can shrink over time before settling to an unchanging interval.

In subtle brain injury claims some experts spend a significant amount of time interviewing claimants to determine the length of their PTA, whereas others spend only minutes on the task. In practice an adequate assessment can be undertaken within minutes and, indeed, longer is not necessary or even possible in the routine clinic or research studies, and may indicate inexperience. In *Van Wees v Karkour*[4] at [35], Langstaff J made the following pertinent observation:

> "Although the length of post traumatic amnesia was described by Dr Lewis, consultant neurologist, called on behalf of the defendants, as 'the gold standard', it is one of a number of means by which an estimation (no more than that) can be made as to whether an individual has suffered a head injury and if so, of what likely severity it is. I can understand the importance of it for the purposes of treatment. What is a good servant for those purposes becomes in my view a bad master in a compensation claim. I do not think there is any inherent magic, such as Mr Grant [claimant's counsel] appeared to claim, to the process of assessing the length of post traumatic amnesia. Dr Lewis said it would take about 10 minutes. Criticisms of this by Mr Grant as being unreasonably short are in my view misplaced. The task is a relatively simple one: identifying what memories an individual actually has following an accident, until the time of return of 'normal' memory (which inevitably will not play with the smooth continuity of a cinema film). I see no reason why this cannot and should not be done entirely adequately within such a period as Dr Lewis suggested, and I accept his evidence on this."

---

[4] [2007] EWHC 165 (QB).

PTA may be especially significant when there is no contemporaneous medical assessment of the claimant's condition after the injury. If they are seen, there may be pointers to injury severity, such as a record of a loss of consciousness and GCS scores; but some claimants do not go to hospital or they are seen and not thought to be significantly injured or to have a head injury at all. However, subsequently they report amnesia post-accident, which in hindsight is interpreted as indicating that a brain injury occurred. A key problem is that in many cases PTA is assessed retrospectively, months and sometimes years afterwards. Inevitably, that raises concern about the accuracy and reliability of such assessments although, as Friedland and Swash (2016) pointed out, retrospective assessments have tended to go unchallenged in the courts. King et al. (1997) described a procedure for retrospectively assessing PTA and evaluated its reliability. Their approach, which they termed the Rivermead Post-Traumatic Amnesia Protocol, is in line with that taken by most clinicians and therefore repays examination. It involves a loosely-structured interview and they provided the following guidelines:

> "Patients are asked to record their memories after the injury in chronological order. It is emphasised that they should relate what they can actually recall rather than what they have been told. After each event, the patient is asked "what is the next thing you remember?" and thus it is clarified whether each memory is an isolated one or part of a longer memory sequence. This process is continued until the assessor is satisfied that normal continuous memory is being described. The patient is then asked if this is the point at which he or she thinks that normal continuous memory for events returned. The patient might need to compare memory for that point with memory for a time a few days or weeks before the injury (when it was normal). If the assessor and patient disagree after discussion, the assessor's measure is used."

10–003 King et al. (1997) studied four groups of brain injured patients ranging from a mean of 11 days to 38 weeks post-injury and concluded that retrospective assessment was reasonably reliable, and McMillan et al. (1996) came to similar conclusions. However, the limitations of retrospective assessment are readily apparent, inasmuch as the individual's ability to provide sequential recollections is unknown. An individual may provide a consistent, but nevertheless wholly erroneous, account of their memories and the clinician will be none the wiser. King et al. (1997) recommended that the clinician continue with the assessment until they are satisfied that normal continuous memory is being described; but inevitably this is a subjective judgment, as is the patient's judgment as to when they think continuous memory returned. Neither the clinician's nor the patient's judgments can be verified although, if they concur, the clinician may nevertheless develop a potentially false sense of certainty that the end of PTA has been defined. Finally, King et al. (1997) recommended that, in the event that there is a disagreement between the assessor and the patient, the assessor's opinion is to be preferred; but again the clinician has no way of knowing whether their opinion is correct and any more accurate than the patient's. The difficulty is that in the absence of a truly objective assessment of PTA the clinician is in the dark, and in the absence of feedback about the accuracy of their opinion, they may become unduly confident, both in a particular case and more generally. Even when different clinicians come to similar conclusions, that does not necessarily provide reassurance about their accuracy: it may simply reflect the patient's consistent but erroneous account of their memories, or similarities in the mindset and approach of the clinicians, or both.

An important consideration is that memories are not laid down in a continuous, uninterrupted stream as with a tape or video recorder, but instead they are discontinuous and fragmentary and, importantly, they degrade over time (McNally, 2005). Accordingly, it might be expected that any individual, even someone healthy and without a brain injury, will have a discontinuous, patchy and imperfect recollection of events months or years later due to normal forgetfulness alone. Friedland and Swash (2016) pointed out a further problem, which is when the claimant inadvertently provides the assessor with learnt material rather than genuine memories. Both in clinical and in legal settings the patient may begin to present learnt responses, which neither assessor nor patient recognises. This may be a particular problem for later examiners.

An additional issue is that where a claimant has reported cognitive impairments such as an impaired memory, it is counter-intuitive to assume that they are nevertheless able to recall accurately events from months or years earlier with sufficient accuracy to define a period of PTA that then accounts for their current impaired abilities. The individual's mental state at the time of the assessment or at the time of the injury may also influence the reliability of their account. Many claimants have emotional and physical symptoms, such as anxiety, low mood and irritability, as well as headaches and pain, which may interfere with their recall at the time they are being assessed. On the other hand, the claimant's emotional state at the time of the accident may affect their recollection and produce a PTA-type experience. Kemp et al. (2010) found that over a third of patients who had orthopaedic injuries, but no brain trauma, appeared to have PTA that was related to anxiety after their injury and anaesthetic drugs, and that nearly a third were amnesic for 24 hours or more, suggesting that they had a substantial brain injury. Other researchers have also found that analgesia can induce a PTA-type presentation (McCarter et al., 2007). Similarly, emotional trauma associated with the index event can result in amnesia for it. Post-traumatic stress disorder has as one of its diagnostic criteria the inability to remember important aspects of the traumatic event or events, as well as problems with concentration (American Psychiatric Association, 2013). In these circumstances the clinician has no way of differentiating between amnesia that may be due to a head injury and that attributable to emotional trauma. Lees-Hayley (2001) found that approximately one in five of non-brain injured claimants described having a PTA experience, despite having no head injury.

King et al. (1997) suggested that the retrospective assessment of PTA is reliable, but nevertheless found that when PTA was assessed and later reassessed 21% of their patient group changed their injury classification; and among those who had been classed as having severe injuries 32% changed classification. Sherer et al. (2015) found that patients retrospectively overestimated both the length of time that they were unconscious and their PTA duration and the overestimation was sufficient to change their injury classification. Statistical modelling suggested that those who had never been unconscious might report lengthy intervals of coma amounting to days. Similarly, retrospective PTA was erroneous and potentially resulted in significant diagnostic error and, as might be

10-004

expected, the longer the interval between the injury and the PTA assessment, the less reliable were patients' accounts. Roberts et al. (2016) also found that retrospective PTA was invariably inconsistent with the documented duration and that more than half of patients over-estimated their PTA, while approximately a third underestimated the duration.

On occasions, clinicians do not attempt to define the PTA duration in its entirety and instead discontinue the assessment when they conclude it was over 24 hours, suggesting that the injury was severe (see Lezak et al., 2012). This approach of "getting across the line" illustrates an additional problem in PTA assessment, which is the difficulty in defining its end (assuming it is present) and distinguishing that from patchy, discontinuous recollections characteristic of normal memory. In these circumstances it is difficult for the clinician to define the PTA duration and requiring a clear endpoint may illustrate the limitations of the assessment.

In research studies these issues also come into play, but they are less of a problem when researchers aggregate data across groups of patients and, for instance, examine the relationship between PTA and clinical outcomes, but when assessing an individual in a legal context they are a significant concern.

10–005 Given the concerns about retrospective assessment, if PTA is the only or primary clinical indicator, there is a risk that it is given undue significance. Arguably in view of the concerns about patients' reliability, clinicians' judgment, the influence of mood and the vagaries of human memory, as well as the paradoxical nature of presuming accuracy when a claimant is also viewed as cognitively impaired, and the non-specific nature of PTA, few diagnosing clinicians rely upon retrospective PTA alone. A report of PTA raises the possibility that the patient had a brain injury, but most will seek corroboration from other sources, such as contemporaneous medical records and neuroimaging. In the absence of corroboration, reliance upon retrospective PTA is fraught with risk. A useful and cautionary reminder against placing reliance upon an individual's memory was provided by Leggatt J in *Gestmin SGPS SA v Credit Suisse (UK) Ltd*.[5] While commenting on a case quite unrelated to brain injury litigation and PTA, the judge made a number of perceptive observations that are highly relevant to the weight which can properly be placed upon retrospective PTA assessments:

> "An obvious difficulty which affects allegations and oral evidence based on recollection of events which occurred several years ago is the unreliability of human memory.
>
> While everyone knows that memory is fallible, I do not believe that the legal system has sufficiently absorbed the lessons of a century of psychological research into the nature of memory and the unreliability of eyewitness testimony. One of the most important lessons of such research is that in everyday life we are not aware of the extent to which our own and other people's memories are unreliable and believe our memories to be more faithful than they are. Two common (and related) errors are to suppose: (1) that the stronger and more vivid is our feeling or experience of recollection, the more likely the recollection is to be accurate; and (2) that the more confident another person is in their recollection, the more likely their recollection is to be accurate.

---

[5] [2013] EWHC 3560 (Comm) at [15]–[22].

Underlying both these errors is a faulty model of memory as a mental record which is fixed at the time of experience of an event and then fades (more or less slowly) over time. In fact, psychological research has demonstrated that memories are fluid and malleable, being constantly rewritten whenever they are retrieved. This is true even of so-called 'flashbulb' memories, that is memories of experiencing or learning of a particularly shocking or traumatic event. (The very description 'flashbulb' memory is in fact misleading, reflecting as it does the misconception that memory operates like a camera or other device that makes a fixed record of an experience.) External information can intrude into a witness's memory, as can his or her own thoughts and beliefs, and both can cause dramatic changes in recollection. Events can come to be recalled as memories which did not happen at all or which happened to someone else (referred to in the literature as a failure of source memory).

Memory is especially unreliable when it comes to recalling past beliefs. Our memories of past beliefs are revised to make them more consistent with our present beliefs. Studies have also shown that memory is particularly vulnerable to interference and alteration when a person is presented with new information or suggestions about an event in circumstances where his or her memory of it is already weak due to the passage of time.

The process of civil litigation itself subjects the memories of witnesses to powerful biases. The nature of litigation is such that witnesses often have a stake in a particular version of events. This is obvious where the witness is a party or has a tie of loyalty (such as an employment relationship) to a party to the proceedings. Other, more subtle influences include allegiances created by the process of preparing a witness statement and of coming to court to give evidence for one side in the dispute. A desire to assist, or at least not to prejudice, the party who has called the witness or that party's lawyers, as well as a natural desire to give a good impression in a public forum, can be significant.

Considerable interference with memory is also introduced in civil litigation by the procedure of preparing for trial. A witness is asked to make a statement, often (as in the present case) when a long time has already elapsed since the relevant events. The statement is usually drafted for the witness by a lawyer who is inevitably conscious of the significance for the issues in the case of what the witness does nor does not say. The statement is made after the witness's memory has been 'refreshed' by reading documents. The documents considered often include statements of case and other argumentative material as well as documents which the witness did not see at the time or which came into existence after the events which he or she is being asked to recall. The statement may go through several iterations before it is finalised. Then, usually months later, the witness will be asked to re-read his or her statement and review documents again before giving evidence in court. The effect of this process is to establish in the mind of the witness the matters recorded in his or her own statement and other written material, whether they be true or false, and to cause the witness's memory of events to be based increasingly on this material and later interpretations of it rather than on the original experience of the events.

It is not uncommon (and the present case was no exception) for witnesses to be asked in cross-examination if they understand the difference between recollection and reconstruction or whether their evidence is a genuine recollection or a reconstruction of events. Such questions are misguided in at least two ways. First, they erroneously presuppose that there is a clear distinction between recollection and reconstruction, when all remembering of distant events involves reconstructive processes. Second, such questions disregard the fact that such processes are largely unconscious and that the strength, vividness and apparent authenticity of memories is not a reliable measure of their truth.

In the light of these considerations, the best approach for a judge to adopt in the trial of a commercial case is, in my view, to place little if any reliance at all on witnesses' recollections of what was said in meetings and conversations, and to base factual findings on inferences drawn from the documentary evidence and known or probable facts. This does not mean that oral testimony serves no useful purpose – though its utility is often disproportionate to its length. But its value lies largely, as I see it, in the opportunity which cross-examination affords to subject the documentary record to critical scrutiny and to gauge the personality, motivations and working practices of a witness, rather than in testimony of what the witness recalls of particular conversations and events. Above all, it is important to avoid the fallacy of supposing that, because a witness has confidence in his or her recollection and is honest, evidence based on that recollection provides any reliable guide to the truth."

2. POST-INJURY COMPLAINTS

10–006 "… [T]he cluster of symptoms of which the Claimant now complains is consistent with his having suffered a brain injury."[6]

It has long been established that brain trauma can precipitate cognitive, behavioural and emotional changes, whereas physical changes are less common. Ponsford et al. (1995) found that two years post-injury memory and planning difficulties were reported by 74% and 48% of patients respectively, as well as issues with thinking speed (64%) and concentration (62%). Fatigue was also reported (72%), as well as word finding difficulties (68%), anxiety (58%) and depression (59%). On the other hand, few were non-ambulant or wheelchair-bound (3%) and the majority were able to walk, run and jump (60%). Van Zomeren and van den Burg (1985) followed up patients two years post injury and found that the most common complaints were forgetfulness (54%), irritability (39%), and slowness (33%). Brooks et al. (1986) obtained relatives' perspectives at five years post injury and the predominant complaints concerned psychological and behavioural problems, with the most common being personality changes (74%), slowness (67%) and poor memory (67%). The majority were fully independently mobile (93%), although minor problems with vision (41%) and balance (48%) were reported. Acute and post-acute cognitive, behavioural and physical symptoms are therefore expected, particularly after mild brain injuries, but also following moderate or severe trauma.

When such complaints are reported after an injurious event, clinicians may conclude that they are consistent with, or indicative of, a neurological event which, together with a report of PTA, leads to a diagnosis of subtle brain injury. Such a view appears to make sense given the known relationships between brain trauma and symptomatology and symptoms reported in the immediate aftermath can be particularly persuasive and reinforce this view. However, Lees-Haley et al. (2001) drew attention to the difficulty in differentiating between the effects of brain trauma and other possible injuries. They observed that many life events can cause a person to feel dazed or confused and orthopaedic injuries or chronic pain can also alter cognitive and psychosocial functioning. They looked at the incidence of complaints in a mild brain injury group and a group of personal injury claimants who had no history of head injury or toxic exposure, and both were asked to record their symptoms immediately after their injuries. The brain

---

[6] *Siegel v Pummel* [2014] EWHC 4309 (QB) at [569].

injured group reported a partial loss of consciousness and having more problems with reading. The personal injury group endorsed trembling, depression and anxiety more often, but loss of memory was endorsed at similar rates, as were headaches. Concentration difficulties were reported by both the personal injury (65%) and brain injury (63%) groups. The personal injury participants also reported having a partial loss of consciousness (24%) and PTA (21%), and there was no significant difference in the total number of complaints reported by the two samples. Lees-Haley et al. (2001) concluded that caution is needed before drawing causal inferences from upsetting events when there is no objective evidence of cerebral injury.

Dunn et al. (1995) administered a symptom checklist to a personal injury group pursuing litigation for psychological injuries, none of whom had a brain injury. The claimants had undergone a range of stressful experiences including overwork, wrongful termination, verbal harassment and discrimination, physical injuries, pain, vehicle accidents, physical and sexual assaults, other types of accidents, as well as orthopaedic conditions and muscle pain. The personal injury litigants endorsed having neuropsychological and neurotoxic symptoms significantly more often than non-litigating subjects who had suffered brain trauma or toxic exposure. Dunn et al. (1995) suggested that the high rate of symptom reporting when none of the group had a brain injury indicated that claims of cognitive impairment in litigation should not be based solely on self-report. Iverson and Lange (2003) pointed out that post-concussional complaints can follow a brain injury of any severity, not only mild injuries, and suggested that it is a mistake to accept uncritically self-reported symptoms as being due to a past injury, because uncomplicated mild brain injuries recover quickly and such symptoms are non-specific.

Iverson (2006) cautioned that those experiencing low mood and depression may be at particular risk of being diagnosed as having a post-concussion syndrome. He pointed out that the diagnostic criteria for depression includes a diminished ability to think and concentrate, indecisiveness, fatigue or loss of energy, and problems with sleep. Depressed patients may also suffer from irritability, excessive health worry and headaches, and have social problems such as strained relationships. Iverson (2006) administered a post-concussion symptom checklist to a group diagnosed with major depression, dysthymic disorder or depressive disorder and found that between 31.2% and 85.6% of symptoms were endorsed to a mild or greater degree. Those who endorsed symptoms as being moderate-to-severe ranged from 10.9% to 57.8%. Iverson (2006) pointed out that the overlapping symptoms between depression and brain injury represent a significant challenge to the diagnostician, and that those with depression or chronic pain or a combination of the two are likely to report the same symptoms as those with a mild brain injury.

10–007

Gasquoine (2000) administered a checklist of brain injury-related complaints to patients with traumatic back pain, none of whom had a history of injury to the head, concussion or neurological events, and compared their responses with a head injury group. The back-pain participants endorsed symptoms at a similar rate to the concussion group, suggesting that the self-reported symptoms were not specific to head injury. On the other hand, correlations were found between self-reported brain injury symptoms and measures of emotional distress, with the highest correlation being with depression. Iverson and McCracken (1997) found that 39% of a chronic pain sample met the DSM-IV criteria for post-concussive disorder, although none had a brain injury. McCracken and Iverson (2001) studied patients attending a pain management service, none of whom had brain trauma, and found that self-reported cognitive problems were common, with over half of the sample having at least one cognitive complaint. Forgetfulness was reported (23.4%), not finishing things (20.5%), and difficulty reasoning and problem-solving (12.8%) and reacting slowly (9.2%). Emotional distress was associated with an enhanced perception of cognitive dysfunction. Fear et al. (2009) examined a large group of UK military personnel who had been deployed in Iraq and who completed a checklist of seven symptoms (headache, dizziness, irritability or outburst of anger, double vision, ringing in the ears, loss of concentration and forgetfulness). Symptom endorsement was associated with self-reported exposure to a blast injury while in a combat zone (which might precipitate a mild brain injury), but the same symptoms were also linked with other in-theatre exposures that were not associated with brain injury.

Iverson and Lange (2003) examined the incidence of brain injury-related complaints in healthy individuals living in the community. They administered a symptom checklist and found that post concussion-like symptoms were reported by between 35.9% and 75.7% of the group. The most frequently reported mild symptoms included fatigue (75.7%), irritability (71.8%), and feeling sad or down in the dumps (61.2%). Poor concentration was endorsed by a significant proportion (61.2%), as were memory problems (50.5%). Similarly, having extra sensitivity to noise (39.8%) and nausea/feeling sick (37.9%) were frequently reported. When the participants were asked to rate whether their complaints were present to a moderate-severe degree, lower endorsement rates were found, although fatigue was still endorsed by a significant proportion (13.6%), as was poor concentration (15.5%) and memory problems (13.6%). Garden and Sullivan (2010) conducted a similar study and noted that concentration difficulties, fatigue and sleep problems have been associated with both depression and post-concussion complaints. They examined the rate of brain injury symptoms endorsed by healthy individuals and the most common complaints were headaches (81.3%), dizziness (52.1%) and nausea (53.2%). Cognitive issues were also common, with poor concentration (73.4%) and memory problems (56.3%) being endorsed. A significant number also reported having symptoms to a moderate to severe degree and they were more frequent in a subgroup who reported depression, although none had a history of brain injury or neurological disease. Similar results have been found by other clinicians (Zakzanis and Yeung, 2011; see Chapter 5, Table 6).

10–008 An important consideration is whether self-reported complaints, such as forgetfulness or executive difficulties, are associated with objective limitations. It might be expected that a report of cognitive difficulties, such as forgetfulness or poor concentration, will reflect impairments that can be objectively demonstrated in an assessment. Green (2019) reported on the relationship between self-reported verbal memory difficulties and performance on a verbal memory test (California Verbal Learning Test) and, after excluding those who failed effort tests, found no correlation between subjective complaints and objective difficulties on testing. Schiehser et al. (2011) examined patients with mild to moderate head injuries and explored the relationship between performance on objective cognitive tests (assessing executive functioning, attention/processing speed and memory) and self-reported cognitive changes on a questionnaire. Patients' reports of executive difficulties did not predict objective performance on executive and memory measures, while they did predict poor performance on measures of attention/processing speed. The authors found that self-reported depression predicted worse performance on executive and memory measures.

Jamora et al. (2012) observed that while subjective complaints are an integral part of any assessment, self-report has tended to be viewed as unreliable and potentially inconsistent and prone to bias. Some investigations have shown that following TBI subjective complaints and neuropsychological performance are correlated, and others have not. Investigations have tended to find that those with mild brain injuries over-report (or exaggerate) their symptoms, whereas those with severe injuries under-report, potentially due to poor self-awareness and insight. Jamora et al. (2012) examined the relationship between injury severity and cognitive outcome and found that moderate-to-severe TBI patients' self-report predicted their results on measures of memory and learning, but that that was not true of a mild TBI group. On the other hand, self-reported attention problems were not correlated with objective performance in the moderate-to-severe group. Among mild TBI subjects, self-reported attention problems predicted their objective performance. The authors also found that the mild group rated themselves as being equally or more impaired than the moderate-to-severe group.

Spencer et al. (2010) studied Iraq military veterans with mild brain injuries and examined the relationship between self-reported cognitive functioning and their objective performance on testing. Objective and subjective assessments were not significantly correlated, and they proposed that objective testing should be used when cognitive weaknesses are suspected. They found that subjective self-reported deficits were associated with mood issues, including depression, anxiety and post-traumatic stress disorder. French et al. (2014) studied US military service personnel who had mild or moderate-severe traumatic brain injuries and found that subjective cognitive complaints were largely unrelated to cognitive measures, but they were related to measures of psychological distress. Wang et al. (2006) administered a symptom checklist to a group of healthy individuals who endorsed having high levels of symptoms, such as fatigue (76.9%), needing longer time to think (60.3%) and poor concentration (58.7%). They found that having more symptoms was associated with greater self-reported depression, which was consistent with previous studies. However, those who rated themselves as having a high number of symptoms mostly did not differ on cognitive tests from those who reported fewer symptoms.

The non-specific nature of many complaints associated with brain injuries and their imperfect association with objective functioning indicates that circumspection should be the rule when considering an individual's self-report. Some accurately appraise their difficulties, others overestimate, some underestimate, and some show variable self-awareness, and so subjective reporting can have an uncertain relationship to a person's actual abilities. Madan (2016) suggested that, when preparing a case, lawyers should look for a number of indicators of a subtle brain injury, such as mood swings, apathy, and tiredness, as well as headaches,

10–009

poor concentration and memory. In clinical lore these complaints have been particularly associated with brain trauma, but this association is not unique and they are common in other conditions such as pain, low mood, psychiatric conditions and other injuries giving rise to litigation. Indeed, such complaints are also made by healthy people. In addition, some problems that are thought to be particularly associated with neurological trauma may not be. Madan (2016) suggested that the development of alcohol intolerance is especially significant and commented that it was difficult to see how it could be a psychological symptom. However, Iverson (2006) found that 39% of depressed patients endorsed being more affected by alcohol to some degree compared with the past, and 5% endorsed being very much affected. Iverson and Lange (2003) found that even among healthy normal individuals, 18.6% endorsed being more affected by alcohol than in the past. Similarly, fatigue is often viewed as being particularly associated with neurological trauma, but it is common in those with depression, pain, and in the normal population (Lees-Haley and Brown, 1993; Garden and Sullivan, 2010; Iverson and McCracken, 1997; Wang et al., 2006). As with other symptoms, altered alcohol sensitivity and fatigue do not have a unique association with neurological injury. Hartlage (1995) pointed out that people can be "aggressive, belligerent, contumacious, or depressed" when they have not had a neurological event, and that failure to take into account the base rate of such complaints potentially leads to erroneous conclusions about changes that are attributed to a brain injury. In short, it is unwise to infer a specific cause (i.e. brain trauma) from symptoms and complaints that are non-specific and may reflect the presence of a range of conditions or none. Similarly, the absence of a consistent association between complaints and objectively-assessed impairments is problematic. It has been suggested that failure to demonstrate impairments on cognitive testing or even the failure of friends and family to notice impairments is not inconsistent with the individual having a subtle brain injury resulting in cognitive impairments. This has been termed the frontal lobe paradox, which refers to the situation when a brain injured person presents well during a conventional neurological or neuropsychological examination, but nevertheless has problems in their daily life. While there is no doubt that some individuals, particularly those who have had severe brain trauma, may present in this manner, there are nevertheless problems when citing the frontal lobe paradox as an explanatory concept in litigation. Such an explanation is invariably advanced post hoc and can be misused so that positive findings of impairment are accepted, but failure to corroborate the claimant's complaints are not. Some lawyers have misinterpreted the paradox as suggesting that deficits can only be demonstrated on assessment, but not their absence. Such an assumption could cause the assessor to slip into error by concluding that the claimant is impaired irrespective of the objective evidence. As HHJ Saggerson observed in *Hibberd-Little v Carlton*[7]:

> "There were several points during the trial when it seemed that the claimant was in an unassailable position; if she did poorly (in tests or evidence) it was indicative of a brain injury and if she did well (in any context) it was due to the frontal lobe paradox or 'buffering'."

---

[7] [2018] EWHC 1787 (QB) at [144].

Roth and Spencer (2013) pointed out that an erroneous diagnosis of brain trauma can arise when the practitioner relies more on persistent post-injury sequelae (i.e., the individual's complaints) rather than the acute, peri-trauma symptoms. The presence of apparent head injury symptoms may lead the clinician to infer that the cause is a brain injury and refer the individual to neurological services. They pointed out that as many clinicians are aware that a wide range of symptoms are associated with moderate and severe brain injuries, and that such symptoms can be permanent, there is the potential for confusing non-specific complaints with the permanent neurodisability associated with moderate and severe brain trauma, particularly when the individual has other serious physical injuries, such as orthopaedic trauma. When the individual's account of their injury, such as PTA, and their subsequent difficulties are the only or the primary source of information, there is a significant risk of misdiagnosis.

3. EXPLANATIONS FOR SUBTLE BRAIN INJURY COMPLAINTS

"How often have I said to you that, when you have eliminated the impossible, whatever remains, however improbable, must be the truth?" [Sherlock Holmes in *The Sign of Four*]

10–010

Where there is an absence of objective corroboration of a brain injury by reference to contemporaneous medical records and neuro-imaging, it is common for a claimant to argue that they should succeed on the basis of the retrospective PTA assessment and a cluster of symptoms consistent with a DAI, particularly where the defendant has failed (i) to allege or establish fraud, or (ii) to establish an alternative explanation for the claimant's presentation. Indeed, by means of Part 18 requests for further information and Part 35 requests for clarification under the CPR, claimants' lawyers sometimes seek to drive defendants' lawyers and medical experts to allege fraud or exaggeration. Unless there is cogent evidence to support such a defence, the temptation should be resisted. Indeed, even where there is a strong suspicion that the claim is dishonest or exaggerated, defendants are often better advised to avoid assuming the onus of proving a positive case of dishonesty.

There are sound legal grounds, recognised by the House of Lords and lower courts, for simply requiring claimants to prove their case of organic brain damage. In *Rhesa Shipping Co SA v Edmunds (The Popi M)*[8] the Popi M had sunk in calm weather in the Mediterranean Sea and the court was concerned with a claim for an indemnity under the marine insurance policy. The trial judge concluded that the claimant's hypothesis as to the cause of the ship's loss was "extremely improbable". Nevertheless, he found for the claimant because he considered the defendant's theory of the cause of the shipwreck to be doubtful. The House of Lords overturned the decision on the following emphatic basis, at 951B–D and 955H–956A:

---

[8] [1985] 1 W.L.R. 948.

"In approaching this question it is important that two matters should be borne constantly in mind. The first matter is that the burden of proving, on a balance of probabilities, that the ship was lost by perils of the sea, is and remains throughout on the shipowners. Although it is open to underwriters to suggest and seek to prove some other cause of loss, against which the ship was not insured, there is no obligation on them to do so. Moreover, if they chose to do so, there is no obligation on them to prove, even on a balance of probabilities, the truth of their alternative case.

The second matter is that it is always open to a court, even after the kind of prolonged inquiry with a mass of expert evidence which took place in this case, to conclude, at the end of the day, that the proximate cause of the ship's loss, even on a balance of probabilities, remains in doubt, with the consequence that the shipowners have failed to discharge the burden of proof which lay upon them.

... [T]he judge is not bound always to make a finding one way or the other with regard to the facts averred by the parties. He has open to him the third alternative of saying that the party on whom the burden of proof lies in relation to any averment made by him has failed to discharge that burden. No judge likes to decide cases on burden of proof if he can legitimately avoid having to do so. There are cases, however, in which, owing to the unsatisfactory state of the evidence or otherwise, deciding on the burden of proof is the only just course for him to take."

10–011 The same orthodox approach was adopted by the House of Lords in *Pickford v Imperial Chemical Industries Plc*,[9] which concerned a claim for damages in respect of repetitive strain injury sustained by a typist. She alleged that her disorder was an organic one, whereas the defendant countered that it was psychogenic. The judge dismissed the claim because he was not satisfied on the balance of probabilities that the claimant's disorder was organic. The Court of Appeal overturned the judgment and found for the claimant. In a further appeal the House of Lords reinstated the original decision, despite the fact that the trial judge had concluded that the claimant was not a malingerer and that her problem was not psychogenic in nature:

"There is no doubt that in most cases the question of onus ceases to be of any importance once all the evidence is out and before the court. But in this case it was not so simple. As Lord Thankerton observed in *Watt v. Thomas* [1947] A.C. 484, 487 the question of burden of proof as a determining factor does not arise at the end of the case except in so far as the court is ultimately unable to come to a definite conclusion on the evidence, or some part of it, and the question arises as to which party has to suffer from this. From time to time cases arise which are of that exceptional character. *They include cases which depend on the assessment of complex and disputed medical evidence, where the court finds itself in difficulty in reaching a decision as to which side of the argument is the more acceptable.* I think that this was such a case, and that the judge was justified in reminding himself where the onus lay as he examined the evidence. [1200 A–C. Italics supplied]

...

In the first place what [the Court of Appeal was] doing was to invert the onus of proof. The [claimant's] whole case was that her cramp had an organic cause. It was essential to her success that it was proved to have been caused by repetitive movements while typing. So, according to the ordinary rule, the onus was on her to prove that the cause which she had alleged was the right one. It was open to the appellants to lead evidence in rebuttal to the effect that its cause was a psychogenic one. But they did not have to prove that it was due to a conversion hysteria. Failure

---

[9] [1998] 1 W.L.R. 1189.

to prove this alternative explanation was a factor to be taken into account in the decision as to whether the respondent had established an organic cause, but it was no more than that. It still left open the question, in the light of the wider dispute revealed by the medical evidence, whether an organic cause had been established for the cramp so that it could be said to have been due to the respondent's typing work. It was precisely because he was unable to answer this question in her favour on the medical evidence that the judge turned for such assistance as it might offer to the other evidence." [1201 A–E]

Newman v Laver[10] concerned a claim in respect of neurological injuries, including bilateral monocular diplopia (BMD), which were alleged to have been caused by a rear-end shunt. The Court of Appeal upheld a judgment dismissing the claim in respect of the unusual eye condition. Giving the judgment of the court, Rix LJ set out the correct legal approach at [81]:

"In my judgment, there was no need of any blanket allegation of fraud, fakery or fabrication in the pleaded defence ... The defence and its counter schedule of damages, together with the expert reports served pursuant to the defence, and the video provided for trial, sufficiently put in issue the defendant's lack of acceptance that Mr Newman had suffered the injuries and sequelae of which he complained, including in particular BMD ... In truth there was no wholesale attack of fabrication, no general attack on Mr Newman's honesty, at trial, as the defendant's written closing submissions demonstrate. Instead, there was, as must occur at the close of many a trial, a detailed submission by reference to specific points which had arisen in the evidence as to why the judge should regard Mr Newman's credibility as being both at the heart of his claim and as being suspect. The submission divided its fire between specific allegations of falsehood, exaggeration, and inconsistency, to be balanced, it was said, against the lack of objective verification of the symptoms relied on."

The above approach to adjudication was followed in *Hibberd-Little v Carlton* at [6]–[16].[11] The trial judge correctly observed at [16] that "... if the medical opinion about the claimant is substantially based on her accuracy, and her accuracy is questionable, then the medical conclusion may also be questionable regardless of whether a plausible alternative cause or diagnosis is forthcoming."

10–012

When a brain injury is mild and therefore not expected to lead to enduring disability, or it is disputed that there was a brain injury, persisting accounts of poor concentration, forgetfulness, headaches, and dizziness may suggest that a neurological event has occurred. In these circumstances a defendant will not be required to provide an alternative explanation for the claimant's symptoms, although it is germane to consider factors that might be implicated, if not brain trauma. Often there will not be a single factor, but rather several or even numerous influences, with a complex interaction between the individual's pre-existing personality characteristics (such as long-standing dependency needs, catastrophising, insecurity, or somatic focusing/somatisation), as well as interpersonal and social influences. These may arise from family dynamics and other relationships, or the individual may seek to take advantage of their injury in order, for instance, to give up an unrewarding job. When there has been a mild neurological event, acute symptomatology may be present and then resolve and

---

[10] [2006] EWCA Civ 1135.
[11] [2018] EWHC 1787 (QB).

be overtaken by the attribution of non-specific normal symptoms to the injury. Other influences may also come into play, such as substance or alcohol misuse, which themselves may bring about symptoms. In short, myriad influences potentially become relevant and require careful review.

Emotional and mood disorders

10–013   Depression, anxiety, and other dysfunctional mood states, tend to be associated with subjective neuropsychological and post-concussional difficulties and represent potentially important drivers for symptom reporting. Feelings of pessimism, hopelessness and failure may colour an individual's perception of their abilities and cause them to be unduly negative in their self-appraisal and report difficulties that may not be corroborated by objective assessment. Low mood may also interfere with a willingness to engage with effortful tasks, particularly as depression progresses, so causing deterioration in their performance, which may be reversible. Gervais et al. (2009) examined the relationship between subjective cognitive complaints reported on a questionnaire (MMPI-2-RF) and mood and psychological symptoms on another self-report measure (Multifactor Health Inventory). The group comprised disability claimants predominantly presenting with chronic pain, traumatic stress, depression and other emotional complaints due to workplace, road traffic and other accidents. Subjective cognitive complaints were strongly correlated with the claimants' assessment of their emotional distress. On the other hand, after controlling for suboptimal effort on performance validity tests, the reported cognitive complaints were unrelated to their objective performance on cognitive tests. In other words, the patients' account of their difficulties most closely reflected emotional factors and their mood, rather than real and demonstrable limitations.

Fox et al. (1995) studied a group of psychiatric patients referred for treatment for a range of conditions, including anxiety, depression, and marital and family problems. Before being interviewed they were asked to complete a checklist of post-concussional symptoms. The authors found that the rate of reported symptoms was so high that they provided little information about the presence of a neuropsychological condition and they pointed out that many with post-concussional conditions experienced emotional distress. Farrin et al. (2003) examined the relationship between subjective and objective cognitive difficulties in a group suffering from depression and a non-depressed group and found that subjective cognitive complaints were more strongly related to mood issues and only weakly linked to demonstrable performance.

A feature of subtle brain injury claims has been that following treatment for mood issues or other psychopathology, residual cognitive and behavioural complaints have been attributed to the effects of brain trauma. However, while having intuitive appeal, such an interpretation may not be justified. Garden and Sullivan (2010) found that those who endorsed having mild to severe depression on a questionnaire showed higher frequencies and severities of complaints, again indicating that depression drives complaining even in the absence of brain trauma. However, among non-depressed healthy individuals without a history of head injury or other neurological problems a high incidence of such complaints has consistently been found, indicating that it would be unwise to assume that complaints are indicative of brain trauma and, on the contrary, they may be quite normal (Zakzanis and Yeung, 2011; Iverson and Lange, 2003; Gouvier et al., 1988; Machulda et al., 1998; Sawchyn et al., 1999; Trahan et al., 2001; see Chapter 5).

Acute and chronic pain

Many injuries, whether involving the brain or other parts of the body, are associated with acute pain and if the pain persists for six months or more, it is then characterised as chronic. Nampiaparampil (2008) reviewed the prevalence of pain after head injury and found that chronic headache had a prevalence of 57.8%. Chronic pain was more common in civilians with mild head injuries (75.3%), as opposed to moderate or severe brain injuries (32.1%). Martelli et al. (1999) noted that the incidence of post-traumatic headache following head, brain and neck trauma was 90% and that chronic headache (i.e., headache lasting more than six months) was 44%, and after four years the incidence was 20%. A particular difficulty for the assessor is that those who have not had a brain injury, but suffer from pain also report a high incidence of complaints characteristic of brain trauma. Munoz and Esteve (2005) examined a group with various types of pain, including neuropathic pain, bone, joint, and visceral pain, headaches, vascular pain and fibromyalgia. Memory complaints were common, involving difficulty remembering films and books (61%), forgetfulness (44%), handling of everyday things (38%) and remembering conversations (38%), and depression, anxiety and ruminations were associated with having subjective complaints. McCracken and Iverson (2001) examined a group with chronic pain and found that 54% reported having at least one cognitive problem. They suggested that their results were consistent with the literature, indicating that perceived cognitive impairment is non-specific, and found in many groups and associated with depression and pain-related anxiety. Pain has been associated not only with subjective complaints, but also objective limitations affecting memory, attention, processing speed, and executive functioning in the absence of a brain injury. Martelli et al. (1999) concluded that headache generally exerts a negative effect on cognitive functioning in those with persistent subjective complaints, with decrements in information processing speed and complex attention being the most common.

10–014

Objective limitations in the context of chronic pain can have a complex aetiology and may stem from myriad influences. Some investigations have pointed to the importance of comorbid mood states, particularly depression, as well as sleep disturbance and the use of multiple pharmacological agents, including opioid and psychotropic medications and over-the-counter drugs, all of which can affect functioning (Mazza et al., 2018; Nicholson et al., 2001; Schultz et al., 2018; Uomoto et al., 1993; Hart et al., 2000). Other concomitant psychiatric conditions, such as anxiety, post-traumatic stress disorder, personality disorders, and substance misuse, may also influence the experience of pain and the individual's presentation. Schultz et al. (2018) pointed out the importance of disentangling the influence of pain from brain injury factors and noted that this can be particularly difficult. Failure to take pain into account, including its severity, duration and course, together with the cumulative influence of comorbidities and their interactions, can lead to misdiagnosis and inferring from subjective complaints and even objective limitations, that neurological trauma is present when it is not.

Iatrogenesis

10–015 Iatrogenesis refers to outcomes, positive or negative, arising from a healthcare provider, although usually it refers to negative outcomes that are unintended (Carone, 2018). Harmful outcomes can occur either in the course of diagnosis or as a result of treatment or both. Medical iatrogenesis is well known and refers to the harmful effects of diagnostic procedures, medications and their side effects, drug interactions, and harmful reactions from stopping medications, surgery and hospitalisation (Krishnan and Kasthuri, 2005). Less attention has been paid to psychological iatrogenesis, that is, when the individual develops new or worsening health problems as a result of interactions with a healthcare provider in the course of their diagnostic endeavours or treatment. Carone (2018) distinguished between three types of diagnostic error that can cause iatrogenic harm. First, when the clinician diagnoses the wrong condition when an actual condition exists; secondly, when the clinician diagnoses a condition where none exists; and thirdly, when the clinician does not provide a diagnosis when a condition is present. In addition, some clinicians may avoid communicating a diagnosis, such as a mental health diagnosis, as it may be perceived as unacceptable to the individual. Carone (2018) suggested that these errors are particularly common when the clinician's opinion is based on subjective symptom reporting, rather than objective information, such as test scores, and when they see themselves as a patient advocate, rather than an objective scientist practitioner. The patient's retrospective report of PTA is potentially significantly error-prone and unreliable, and a diagnosis of brain trauma that rests on that may carry a substantial iatrogenic risk.

Bender and Matusewicz (2013) pointed out that providing a diagnosis is not a neutral act and that labelling has consequences: an individual may feel that their symptoms have been legitimised and no longer viewed as due to their imagination, but it also provides entry to a sick role. Communicating a diagnosis of brain injury can be particularly potent and cause the individual to focus on symptoms that are incorrectly attributed to neurological trauma, when they are due to other causes or even normal. It may also exacerbate complaints or precipitate the emergence of new symptoms that then become real to the individual. Roth and Spencer (2013) described the case of a serviceman who was erroneously diagnosed as having brain injury and who then identified with the diagnosis such that he referred repeatedly to "my TBI" and expressed dissatisfaction with those he felt did not understand his condition and he travelled widely giving talks about living with his injury. Carone (2018) observed that patients' beliefs about a condition may be shaped by a range of influences, such as film, TV programmes and social media, and so influence their response to head trauma and initial symptoms following a mild blow to the head: while symptoms might resolve naturally within weeks, patients may misinterpret unremarkable everyday lapses and physical symptoms as concussion symptoms indicative of a serious neurological condition. In this situation the individual's expectations and beliefs, potentially shaped by social influences, perpetuate their symptoms.

Some assessment practices can lead to greater symptom endorsement than others: for instance, more complaints tend to be endorsed when subjects are provided with a checklist than they spontaneously report in the course of an interview. Iverson et al. (2010) examined the symptom reports of patients temporarily off work due to a mild brain injury, who were receiving compensation. They were initially asked to report their symptoms and difficulties in an interview and they then completed a checklist of symptoms. During the interview they reported an average of 3.3 symptoms, but on the questionnaire they endorsed having 9.1 symptoms. They found that 44.4% reported four or more symptoms during the interview, and 91.8% endorsed having four or more symptoms on the questionnaire. Villemure et al. (2011) asked mild brain injury patients to report their symptoms spontaneously and then using a standardised checklist, and more symptoms were reported with the checklist. Roth and Spencer (2013) suggested that checklists provide the opportunity for the individual to express, and be influenced by, the perception of significant impairments thought to be due to a brain injury. Vanderploeg and Belanger (2013) cautioned against the use of checklist screening in the US military because of the risks of reinforcing negative expectations and beliefs about brain trauma, potentially derived from sources such as the media or individual expectations resulting in the misattribution of symptoms, such as headaches, fatigue and normal memory lapses, to a perceived brain injury. Similarly, symptoms that might be due to psychological problems, such as post-traumatic stress disorder and depression, and which are treatable, may be attributed to brain trauma. Suhr and Gunstad (2002, 2005) also highlighted that the process of assessment may affect the individual's presentation. They found that when an individual's attention is drawn to having a history of concussion, this may adversely affect their performance on cognitive testing.

Page and Wesseley (2003) suggested that extensive assessments may be harmful to those with unexplained symptoms and patients may be unwilling to accept, or be reassured by, the results of investigations which are normal, particularly when they have issues with their mood. Merckelbach et al. (2018) drew attention to the influence of misinformation in engendering symptoms. Misinformation refers to the provision of erroneous or false information which influences the individual's perception of events and symptom reporting. In these circumstances erroneous memories have been found to be readily established in a wide range of situations. For instance, Murphy et al. (2019) presented true and fabricated stories about the Irish abortion referendum to participants and almost half of the sample reported having a false memory for at least one fabricated event with "yes" voters (i.e. those favouring legalising abortion) being more likely than "no" voters to "remember" a fabricated scandal about the "no" campaign, and vice versa. These effects also occur in health settings; Baumann et al. (1989) found that suggesting that individuals have high blood pressure can lead them to report symptoms associated with that condition and Urban et al. (2019) found misinformation affected people's memory for pain. Merckelbach et al. (2018) asked participants to complete a symptom checklist and afterwards altered these self-ratings, either to indicate that they had more or fewer

10–016

difficulties than they had reported. Approximately 82% of participants accepted the upward symptom misinformation and 67% accepted the downward change. Furthermore, 27% then gave reasons for the increased symptom ratings and 8% provided explanations for the lowered ratings. Merckelbach et al. (2011) also misinformed students about their symptom ratings and found that many failed to detect that they had been misinformed; they tended to accept and adopt the misinformation. Merckelbach et al. (2012) suggested that misinformation influences are particularly potent under certain conditions. When erroneous information is communicated by a trusted person, such as a doctor, it is more likely to be accepted. It is also likely to have a significant impact when it is repeated and associated with some real details in the individual's life, which are inherently plausible, and so internalised by the recipient. In the course of litigation, many of these conditions exist.

Bender and Matusewicz (2013) commented that repeat examinations potentially contribute to iatrogenic symptoms. Litigation is invariably characterised by numerous examinations over the course of several years involving various specialists. In contrast to other neurological conditions, such as stroke, claimants are required repeatedly to prove their symptoms to doctors, lawyers and ultimately the court. Instead of improving over time, the symptoms may become entrenched and distorted as a result of the protracted legal proceedings. The authors noted that the concept of compensation neurosis has fallen out of favour, but the factors implicated in such a presentation include unjustified implications of long-term injury (for instance, from lawyers and/or family), prolonged litigation, and personality characteristics such as dependency, avoidance or exaggeration, rationalisation and retaliation.

Iatrogenic effects are not limited to assessment and diagnostic issues, but can also occur in treatment. Litigation is commonly associated with recommendations for rehabilitation involving a range of disciplines, both medical and non-medical, as well as support worker involvement and case management. Treatment may continue for long periods, sometimes years, and not conclude during the course of the legal proceedings. It may also be initiated with a litigation, rather than a therapeutic, agenda, with lengthy treatment viewed as indicating the severity of the claimant's injuries. It may also lead to cascading iatrogenesis, where multiple complications develop after an initial innocuous intervention with one problem following after another, so exacerbating the individual's condition. For example, side-effects from medication may cause a patient to fall, resulting in orthopaedic injury, leading to admission, which in turn leads to a hospital-acquired infection and further illness. Similar cascades can occur when an individual has multidisciplinary rehabilitation and support, which reduces coping and self-reliance, so having a disempowering effect with resulting dependency and increased care and support. Brain injury rehabilitation often includes efforts to raise the individual's insight through education and endeavouring to help them recognise that they have difficulties and link them causally to the index injury. When a brain injury is in doubt, this may have significant iatrogenic effects. While the adverse effects of pharmacological treatments have been extensively examined, the same is not true of psychological interventions, even though, as Parry et al. (2016) pointed out, such treatments cannot be both psychoactive and harmless. Psychological interventions are often thought to be either neutral or positive in their impact. However, Crawford et al. (2016) conducted a survey of people receiving a range of different therapies for depression and anxiety in services in England and Wales and asked whether they had suffered lasting bad effects from treatment and of 14,587 respondents, 5.2% reported having such effects. People who were from sexual and ethnic minorities, or unsure of the type of treatment they had received, were more likely to report negative effects, whereas those over the age of 65 were less likely. Parry et al. (2016) commented that harmful effects may come from damaging interactions between the therapist and patient, inappropriate therapeutic methods or lack of skill, a poor fit between therapist and patient, or attachment issues. Therapists may also have excessive caseloads and some interventions, such as group treatments, may be inappropriate. Moritz et al. (2018) studied patients with depression and found that 95.6% reported positive benefits from treatment, but nevertheless around half of the sample (52.6%) reported at least one adverse effect including side effects (38.5%), issues with the therapist's malpractice (26.7%) and unethical conduct (8.1%). Unfortunately, the incidence of harmful effects from private rehabilitation services, particularly among the ad hoc groups of therapists who treat most brain injury claimants, is unknown and rarely documented.

Validity issues

The validity of claimants' cognitive difficulties is usually assessed using either stand alone or embedded performance validity tests (PVT), better known as effort tests. They involve asking the individual to take a task that appears to be difficult, but in practice is easy and can be completed satisfactorily even by those with severe brain injuries or other conditions, such as depression and learning disabilities. Suboptimal effort is inferred when they perform unduly poorly. The base rate of invalid responding among brain injured litigants has been found to be relatively high and in the order of 30–50% (see Chapter 7). In addition, subjective brain injury symptoms have not consistently been found to be associated with objective performance; they have tended to be associated more with distress, such as depression and anxiety (Dunn et al., 1995; Fox et al., 1995; Iversen, 2006). An important issue is the extent to which subjective complaints are also associated with over-reporting. Gervais et al. (2008) examined a group with chronic pain and anxiety and depressive disorders, the majority of whom were applying for benefits or involved in litigation. They completed cognitive tests and were also assessed using the MMPI-2-RF questionnaire, which includes a number of validity scales designed to assess over-reporting of difficulties. One of these, the Response Bias Scale (RBS), has been found to predict those who fail PVTs. Participants were also asked to complete a questionnaire that assessed their self-reported memory difficulties and they found that increasing memory complaints was associated with elevated RBS scores. In other words, more frequent complaints about their memory was associated with over-reporting. They also examined the relationship between self-reported memory complaints and performance on a memory test and found little in the way of association, this being consistent with other investigations.

Tsanadis et al. (2008) examined the rate of symptom endorsement by a mild head trauma litigant group who also showed poor effort on PVT tests and by a

10–017

group of moderate to severe brain injured litigant group, and found that the former endorsed having more symptoms. However, the moderate-to-severe litigants reported having more symptoms than non-litigating moderate-to-severe participants. The association between cognitive complaints and underperformance on PVTs was investigated by Armistead-Jehle et al. (2016). They studied a group with a history of concussion, who completed a self-report questionnaire enquiring about memory complaints and they also took two PVTs (Medical Symptom Validity Test, Non-Verbal Medical Symptom Validity Test). Failure on the effort tests was associated with higher scores on all of the self-reported memory complaints scales. In other words, increasing reports of memory difficulties was associated with less valid objective performance. Jones et al. (2012) examined a group of patients with predominantly mild traumatic brain injuries and those who failed PVTs obtained higher scores on the MMPI-2-RF validity scales compared with a group who passed PVTs: underperformance on effort testing was associated with over-reporting of subjective complaints. They also found that the more PVTs that were failed, the greater the degree of reporting.

Critogenic influences

10–018   "Litigation as violence" (Cardi, 2014).

Gutheil et al. (2000) defined the term critogenic harm as referring to harm or injury caused by the litigation process itself, not due to bad laws or poor legal practice or inept lawyers, but rather the harm caused by litigation when the process is working exactly as it should. Critogenic harm, that is, lawyer-induced harm, parallels the more widely recognised problem of iatrogenic harm and has also been termed "litigation response syndrome" (Lees-Haley, 1988). It refers to the psychological damage and symptoms arising from involvement in litigation, irrespective of the effects of the initial injury. Cardi (2014) likened the potential effects of litigation to those following a violent physical assault causing stress, anxiety, low mood and irritability, difficulty concentrating, loss of motivation and social involvement, diminished enjoyment and pleasure in life, somatic symptoms (e.g. aches and pains), diminished self-esteem, startle responses and ruminations about the litigation. These effects may be experienced by claimants, although not all are affected, and also by others such as spouses and relatives who are drawn into the proceedings. Critogenic harms may also apply to defendants and much attention has been paid to the harmful effects of litigation on medical practitioners accused of malpractice (medical malpractice stress syndrome). This comprises similar symptoms, such as restlessness, fatigue, irritability and difficulty concentrating, insomnia and anxiety, and may also include complications such as alcohol misuse and self-medication. Charles (2001) commented that the impact on medical practitioners can be significant depending on the individual's personality, with depression being common (27%–39%), as well as adjustment disorders (20%–53%), and the onset or exacerbation of a physical illness (2%–15%). The issue has been of sufficient concern that a "survival guide" has been provided for practitioners (James and Davies, 2006). Aurbach

(2013) pointed out that both claimant and defence lawyers potentially contribute to critogenesis, although this may be done unwittingly and without insight or awareness.

The involvement of lawyers has been found to be associated with poor outcomes in a range of clinical conditions, including health after major trauma, whiplash, orthopaedic injury, amputation, and mild brain injuries (Harris et al., 2008; Bhandari et al., 2006; Cassidy et al., 2000; McKenzie et al., 2005; Osti et al., 2005; Carroll et al., 2004; Binder and Rohling, 1996; Paniak et al., 2002). Matsuzawa and Dijkers (2014) commented that litigation can be stressful and challenging and precipitate sleeplessness, anger, frustration and humiliation, as well as a heightened sense of vulnerability and anger. They conducted a qualitative study of current and past litigants and suggested that a number of factors accounted for their complaints, including stagnation, confusion, and being misunderstood. Stagnation arose from the time-consuming nature of litigation which prevented recovery because of the hours spent on the case; this in turn detracted from daily living, including time with family, work and other activities. Claimants reported spending excessive time attempting to understand their case, feeling overwhelmed by its complexity and being unable to move on until it had settled. Stagnation also arose from anxiety about working and considerations about whether to return to work and feeling paranoid and stuck. Feelings of confusion occurred when attending court and being unable to understand proceedings and feeling misunderstood and disbelieved. Others reported stress due to being viewed as a liar. Matsuzawa and Dijkers (2014) suggested that the process of confirming an injury and determining fault risks the claimant coming to perceive themselves as a victim or feeling victimised and having to demonstrate that there is something wrong.

Gutteil et al. (2000) also drew attention to the ubiquitous nature of delay, with claims lasting years so that stresses are prolonged. They suggested that even when litigation is successful, the passage of years may make it feel like a hollow victory and so lacking in resolution. Strasburger (1987) commented on the devastating effect of hearing psychiatric testimony at trial: a defendant commented that it felt as though he was on an operating table and being dissected with a knife for everyone to see and wanting to be dead. Strasburger (1999) observed that when litigation concludes both claimant and defendant then have to deal with the residue of having gone through the process. Aurbach (2013) observed that at that juncture there may be further disruption with the abrupt abandonment of the client by the lawyer. Charles and Kennedy (1985) commented that on completion there may be no sense of victory, but rather sadness and disruption on both sides of the case. Aurbach (2013) observed that during delay individuals may obsess about their condition and feel ill treated; treatment may be withheld or interrupted, and the claimant may ruminate on the injustice of compensation being withheld, with economic hardship being a particular stressor.

The adversarial nature of proceedings is an additional critogenic influence. Aurbach (2013) differentiated between harms caused by claimant and defendant lawyers. Claimant lawyers may reinforce a focus on the potential size of an award, rather than the individual recovering and returning to their previous life and work and so overlook their best interests, which may be quite unrelated to the

10–019

outcome of the proceedings. There may be an interaction between iatrogenesis and critogenesis when lawyers instruct experts who opine on a prognosis that is beneficial to the claim, but when internalised by the claimant becomes harmful. Repeat examinations, sometimes to find favourable opinions, can maintain their focus on symptoms and reinforce a sense of loss of control. Defendant lawyers may cause harm by questioning the claimant's honesty, initiating surveillance and introducing delay while pursuing a defence, so contributing to the development of disability. Aurbach (2013) observed that claimants may feel the need to demonstrate their disability by maintaining the role of a disabled person to negate those impugning their veracity. Keet et al. (2017) noted that adversarial proceedings can create a noxious environment and an "aura of combat"; meetings with lawyers can become distressing and intimidating; and having to disclose information which claimants know may affect their case can cause distress, as may repeat examinations, so having an exhausting and disempowering influence. Gutheil et al. (2000) commented that there may be repeat traumatisation and boundary violations when claimants are required to disclose health records, including those relating to sensitive health issues and psychological or psychiatric difficulties, so violating their privacy and potentially setting back recovery. Boundary violations may occur when lawyers attend meetings held by those treating their client, thereby introducing legal considerations into the process of recovery. Arrested recovery, particularly failure to return expeditiously to employment, can be particularly harmful as prolonged unemployment is associated with eventual failure to work. However, critogenesis is not inevitable and can be avoided by considering the best interests of the claimant in much the same way that medical practitioners advise their patients about the pros and cons of a course of treatment or surgery.

A new development is that critogenic effects have been reported in respect of medico-legal experts subject to covert recording by claimants. The stated intention behind covert recordings is to protect the claimant's rights and to ensure that clinicians accurately report their examination and findings. They have been a particular feature of subtle brain injury cases and especially focused on defendant rather than claimant experts, although there is no reason to think that claimant experts are any more competent or accurate in their assessments than defendant experts. In some cases recordings have been undertaken overtly with the assessor's knowledge and agreement, but in others they have been surreptitious and clinicians who have later learnt that they were recorded have reported feeling sullied, violated, distressed, angry and disillusioned.[12] Goldstein (1989) suggested that covert recording raises concerns about both the morality of such practices and the validity of the recorded examination. He noted that deceit is equated with violence and most psychiatrists who have been spied upon claim to have felt assaulted in their relationship with the examinee. Gross et al. (2018) suggested that clandestine recordings are inherently wrong, that rights should be bilateral and equivalent rather than unilateral, and that recordings should be undertaken openly and by mutual consent. Bush et al. (2009) addressed the ethics of recording in a neuropsychological context and suggested that it should be avoided, even when the claimant or their representative, give consent. They advised that recording patients without their consent involves deception which

---

[12] See *Mustard v Flower* [2019] EWHC 2623 (QB) at [11].

conflicts with professional ethical standards; similarly, the examiner also has a right to be protected from deception during the examination and intentional deception by covertly recording the assessor is inconsistent with ethical practice. The authors concluded that neuropsychologists should not encourage, condone or engage in secret recording and, arguably, lawyers should have at least the same ethical standards as experts. Elwyn and Buckman (2015) observed that recording clandestinely, instead of opting to record openly and by mutual consent, inevitably suggests that the intention is to deliberately entrap or trip up the doctor.

Aside from the issue of morality, recording also raises questions about the validity of the resulting examination and, paradoxically, may have additional critogenic effects on the claimant. Bush et al. (2009) noted that claimant's behaviour may be affected by being recorded. Gross et al. (2018) suggested that the claimant may seek to influence the assessment in ways that are unknown to the assessor, potentially by emphasising or minimising issues, and so affecting interpretation and the outcome. When recordings are undertaken secretively and on legal advice, the perceived need to record may result in the claimant approaching the assessment with a lack of trust and viewing the assessor as hostile; that may cause them to adopt a critical, fault-finding manner, so affecting the consultation and rapport. On the other hand, claimants may "play to the audience" or conversely become inhibited, knowing that a range of people will later listen to their most personal disclosures, even in an open court, and so not discuss issues of relevance which cause embarrassment. The individual may experience apprehension and anxiety about being found out or have ethical quandaries and feelings of guilt and shame about the deception. There may be a complex amalgam of feelings and reactions, some contradictory, particularly when most people are unfamiliar with deceptive practices, which may affect their mental state both during the assessment and subsequently, so causing further critogenesis.

4. CONCLUSIONS

Although subtle brain injury claims have commonly relied on the assessment of PTA and the claimant's self-reported complaints, such an approach is potentially fraught with difficulty. Retrospective PTA assessment is potentially unreliable, and complaints assumed to be associated with brain trauma are often non-specific and found in a range of conditions including depression, pain, stress and other injuries, and they are also common in the normal, healthy population. Many factors may account for claimants being symptomatic, such as issues with their mood, including depression, stress, anxiety and somatic symptoms; iatrogenic influences when claimants interact with assessors or enter into treatment; and involvement with the legal process itself. The diagnosis of brain injury should therefore rely on acute, peri-trauma observations following an injurious event, in particular, on the contemporaneous ambulance and medical assessments, including any documented loss of consciousness and GCS readings. In addition, neuro-imaging provides objective evidence that may establish that brain trauma has occurred. In the event that a neurological injury is confirmed, patients may experience subtle impairments which, in the case of high functioning individuals,

10–020

may be significant, and neuropsychological assessment may provide objective evidence of such limitations. However, they should be interpreted with caution as the results may be influenced by patients' motivation, with suboptimal effort leading to under-performance and lowered scores on tests; alternatively, patients may over-report complaints and so present as more symptomatic than they are, or they may do both (see Chapter 7). Importantly, low performance even in high functioning individuals may not be unusual: Iverson et al. (2012) pointed out that among those of high average intellectual ability it is common to have up to 10% of their scores on intelligence testing at or below the 10th percentile, that is, in the low average range or lower, and up to 5% of their results at or below the 5th percentile. Similarly, low performance may be observed in other domains, including memory, concentration, processing speed and executive functioning, while nevertheless being quite normal (see Chapter 5). Failure to take into account these factors may lead to misdiagnosis and misconstruing normal variation for acquired limitations, and so have iatrogenic effects. A combination of contemporaneous medical observations, neuro-imaging, and neuropsychological investigations may establish that the claimant has verifiable impairments but, in their absence, a diagnosis of brain trauma may be unwarranted. However, even when it can be confidently asserted that a neurological injury has occurred, this does not necessarily rule out other factors playing a role, which may be substantial, and critogenic and iatrogenic influences and factors relating to the claimant's mood may influence and shape their presentation.

Case Study 1

Van Wees v Karkour [2007] EWHC 165 (QB)

10–021 **Judge:** Langstaff J

This was the first major trial in which the High Court dealt with a multi-million pound claim arising out of a subtle brain injury. The claimant (V), aged 33, was a pillion passenger on a scooter travelling at about 25 to 30 mph when it was involved in a collision with a car travelling at about 5 to 10 mph. She was knocked off the scooter and her helmet was damaged. She lost consciousness, appeared to be fitting and to turn blue. She was noted by the ambulance crew to be "concussed" and had a GCS score of 14. She vomited at the scene and again in the ambulance. On arrival at hospital she was recorded as fully alert and orientated, but was unable to recall events and complained of a headache. The admitting doctor recorded that she had been unconscious for two minutes, that she remembered "ambulance only" (indicating a degree of PTA) and that she had suffered a significant concussion. She was detained overnight for observation. On the basis of this evidence, Langstaff J held that (a) V was unconscious for at least 5 minutes, and (b) she suffered a brain injury, which was epileptic, and the loss of some control of breathing (hence her turning blue). The subsequent history was one of dislocation of the claimant's life for about three months. V's case was that the duration of her post traumatic amnesia was so long that her brain injury should be classified as at least severe. Her neurosurgical expert estimated that it had lasted more than nine days, whereas her clinical psychologist concluded that it had lasted over 24 hours. The judge noted, at [32],

CONCLUSIONS

that PTA is not necessarily a complete absence of memory. By definition, it begins at the time of the accident and lasts until the return of *continuous* memory: thus the existence of "islands of memory ... in a sea of non-recollection" is characteristic of PTA. The judge had difficulty in determining when V's continuous memory had recommenced, because she had been on her own at home after discharge from hospital; but he concluded that it was "just a little over the 24 hours" suggested by the psychologist: see [40].

Given the importance that retrospective assessments of PTA have played in subtle brain injury claims, Langstaff J's approach is interesting:

> "[35] The claimant herself referred more than once in her evidence to various experts having performed a 'proper' PTA assessment, and others (those instructed by the defendant) not having done so. This view, however, seems to me to be largely a forensic construct. Although the length of post traumatic amnesia was described by Dr Lewis, consultant neurologist, called on behalf of the defendants, as 'the gold standard', it is one of a number of means by which an estimation (no more than that) can be made as to whether an individual has suffered a head injury and if so, of what likely severity it is. I can understand the importance of it for the purposes of treatment. What is a good servant for those purposes becomes in my view a bad master in a compensation claim. I do not think there is any inherent magic, such as Mr Grant [V's counsel] appeared to claim, to the process of assessing the length of post traumatic amnesia. Dr Lewis said it would take about 10 minutes. Criticisms of this by Mr Grant as being unreasonably short are in my view misplaced. The task is a relatively simple one: identifying what memories an individual actually has following an accident, until the time of return of 'normal' memory (which inevitably will not play with the smooth continuity of a cinema film). I see no reason why this cannot and should not be done entirely adequately within such a period as Dr Lewis suggested, and I accept his evidence on this. [36] The defendant's case as to post traumatic amnesia was that much of it was contrived. Taking as his starting point that those matters which stand out as islands of memory in a sea which is otherwise misty will remain stark and constant, Mr Featherby [defendants' counsel] invites comparison of the reports given by six different doctors (one of them Mr Price on two occasions) and by the claimant's witness statement, with a view to demonstrating that these do not show consistent memories. This overlooks the fact that it should not be thought surprising that slightly different reflections of such clear individual memories as the claimant has should be given to different listeners (who then separately report what they see of importance). Far from demonstrating an inconsistency in report, I regard there as having been a consistency of those reports over time, from February 2002 to June 2006, in the specific memories which the claimant says she has." The Judge accepted the PTA assessment of the Psychologist, Ms Levett, as lasting more than 24 hours but cautioned against "the elevation of the process of identifying when continuous memory returned into an art form, and attempting to pigeon hole the claimant into a pre-existing box [determined by the length of PTA] rather than present her as she was": see [59].

As is often the case in subtle brain injury cases, the claimant was highly intelligent and well educated. She had a full-scale IQ of 128 measured post-accident. She had a degree in Mechanical Engineering from Delft University in the Netherlands, though her degree "was not at the very top level". Six years later she obtained an MBA at INSEAD.

V did not suggest that her organic brain injury had rendered her unemployable. On the contrary, a year after the accident she had obtained a high-level corporate

10–022

job with an annual package well into six figures. Yet she contended that, "if uninjured she would have had a yet higher IQ, and without the subtle diminutions in her abilities to perform at a high corporate level would command a yet greater salary": see [4]. The abiding symptoms complained of included "a subtle degree of short term memory loss, low grade headaches which occasionally become severe, a diminished ability to concentrate, and mental (not physical) fatigue particularly noticeable as the day wears on": see [15] and [17].

The defendants' main line of defence was that V was consciously exaggerating; alternatively, there was sub-conscious exaggeration; or non-organic, psychological factors, such as a post-concussional syndrome, were present and she had a prospect of recovery: see [19].

Although there were aspects of V's evidence which gave the judge "cause for concern" (see, for instance, [20], [21] and [44]–[46]), on balance he did not consider that she was consciously exaggerating her case.

> "[48] ... I had a considerable opportunity to observe her. In the main, I accept her account as being that which she believes. (However, in the light of my view that she had too high expectations of herself, and tended to exaggerate her difficulties caused by the accident as self-justification for her failures to achieve them, this is not to conclude that I accept her case). [49]. She was in my view, plainly not incapable. She displayed no marked fatigue. She was not depressed. She was not slow in processing information. She did not display a poor memory. She showed no lack of concentration (though on occasions she appeared to think that she needed to concentrate harder than perhaps she did). She showed very little dis-inhibition (thought there were a couple of flashes of this, which could have been a Dutch unfamiliarity with English legal process). She can plainly multi-task. ... [50] I am quite sure she genuinely feels that she is not the person that she once was. Much of the lay evidence supported this from a number of different perspectives. Broadly, I accept that evidence. Although as Mr Featherby points out, a number of her friends saw only snapshots of her, and on occasions when (as I conclude) her presentation was affected by depression superimposed on top of any deficiencies she may have suffered in the accident, I accept that she does not have the 'edge' she once did. However, this is a fine judgment: the deficit is not a gross one. I have to be careful to disentangle the symptoms of depression, and the effects of natural ageing (an active, sporty 33 year old, absent any brain injury, may appear brighter, fresher and more active than the same individual at 40, absent any brain injury at all). [51] I incline to think that the accident in 2000 has been a handy explanation, to herself, as to the reason for the inability of her career to progress as she had expected it would."

10–023   The judge accepted the evidence of the claimant's neuropsychologist, at [52]:

> "The deficits are technically mild, but sufficient to have a substantial effect on her otherwise superior range abilities, hence the way she describes her impairments. In other words, mild deficits in the context of a high functioning individual are likely to have a substantial impact on perceived functioning, particularly where their occupation requires a superior range of abilities".

V was awarded general damages of £42,500 for subtle brain injury which had been overlaid with psychological reactions. Langstaff J rejected the notion that V's psychological symptoms could be given the controversial label "Post Concussion Syndrome": see [61]. The basis of his award was set out as follows:

CONCLUSIONS

"[160] ... There was, here, a head injury of moderate severity. It resulted in a post traumatic amnesia, described above. It dislocated the claimant's life, social, domestic, personal, and at work for the best part of 4 months to a significant extent, but also to some extent thereafter. It contributed to depressions. It has left her with permanent cognitive deficits, which are mild (relatively viewed) but which have a significant impact upon this particular claimant. She has always placed a great store upon success particularly in employment, and with some (but not total) justification sees the deficits as responsible for her never achieving the success she had placed such store by. It has caused her headaches of a nagging intensity throughout much of the time since the accident. It contributed to the loss of her job at Vodafone, which in turn caused significant depression with symptoms which, if explored, were not far removed from those of post traumatic stress disorder. All this happened to someone who was relatively young: 33. Balancing this are the fact that the deficits are not in themselves severe. She remains able to function at a level well above that of the average uninjured employee. A large component of her depression has been caused by a failure to achieve success, for which her injuries were not primarily responsible. [161] In my view, an appropriate award falls within the range identified by the eighth edition of the JSB Guidelines at 2(A)(c)(iii), up-rated by inflation since the date to which the awards were calculated (some eight months ago). It is £42,500. I include in this sum particular recognition of the career consequences for the claimant: this is not a suitable case for a separate award by way of damages for loss of congenial employment."

In assessing the loss of earnings, Langstaff J had considerable reservations about the two employment experts who had provided reports and given evidence: see [113]–[128]. Whereas the claimant's expert "wrote his report with an excess of hyperbole, as though he were advertising the claimant rather than reporting realistically upon her prospects," the defendant's expert appeared to regard a balanced report as one which highlighted matters which were adverse to the claimant. In the event, the judge accepted the defendant's submission that the loss of earnings should be assessed as in *Blamire v Cumbria Health Authority*,[13] rather than in the conventional multiplier/multiplicand manner. Langstaff J awarded £100,000 in respect of 6.75 years of past loss of earnings, £850,000 in respect of future loss of earnings and £100,000 in respect of loss of pension.

In addition, the claimant was awarded £9,216 for past and future CBT from Ms Levett, who acted as both a treating psychologist and an expert in the case. On a claim which was advanced at £9,976,319, the claimant was awarded £1,105,012.50 inclusive of interest.

Case Study 2

Clarke v Maltby [2010] EWHC 1201 (QB); [2010] EWHC 1856 (QB)

Judge: Owen J

10–024

The claimant (C) was a solicitor in private practice who suffered serious injuries as a passenger in a car, including undisplaced fractures of C2 and C3 vertebrae; fractures of the collar bone, ribs, wrist and ankle; pneumothorax; abdominal scarring; and lacerations to the chin and facial bruising. The collision impact was estimated to be between 80 and 110 miles per hour. In addition to her multiple injuries, C sustained a head injury which rendered her unconscious. She

---

[13] [1993] PIQR Q1.

was an inpatient for 12 days, initially in the Intensive Care Unit for three days, followed by a period in the High Dependency Unit. She made a good, but incomplete, recovery from her physical and psychological injuries. She made a full recovery from a major depressive disorder and, after a 9-month period of CBT, her PTSD had improved to a sub-clinical level.

The trial took place some five and a half years after the accident. C continued to complain of symptoms which were indicative of organic brain damage. These symptoms included dizziness and vertigo, intermittent throbbing headaches, mild sensorineural hearing loss and a cluster of cognitive dysfunctions: mental fatigue, disinhibited temper, impaired short-term and medium-term memory, impaired concentration, impaired processing function and speed, inability to multi-task, compromised language and speech, disinhibited speech, impulsive spending habits, impaired organisational and planning capability, obsessional behavioural traits and alcohol intolerance.

C's neurologist, neuropsychologist and psychiatrist all recognised that many of these symptoms were compatible with TBI, particularly to the frontal lobes, but could equally be indicative of depression, anxiety and PTSD. The judge accepted the evidence of the claimant's psychiatric expert and treating psychologist that she had recovered from her psychiatric problems; and adopted the conclusions of C's neurological and neuropsychological experts that her symptoms must therefore have been caused by a substantial brain injury.

10–025 Although the issue of PTA was not discussed in any detail in the judgment, the judge described it "as an important indicator of the severity of head injury" and criticised the defendant's neuropsychologist for failing to take a history to ascertain whether or not there had been PTA: [63].

The major head of claim was for loss of past and future earnings. Accordingly, there was a detailed examination of C's pre- and post-accident career as a solicitor, and evidence from a jointly instructed expert in legal recruitment was also heard. She had a high IQ falling within the top 3%, but her memory function was only in the top 50%. The judge accepted the evidence of C's experts that the problem for people with high functional intellectual responsibilities was that even a slight decrease in ability can produce seemingly catastrophic results; whereas the same apparent disability in someone with a lower IQ to start with may leave that person relatively unscathed. Whilst not accepting that C would only work part-time in the future, the judge assessed the loss of earnings award on the basis of the concession made by the defendant, that it would be reasonable for C to withdraw from private practice and take a less onerous job as an employed lawyer.

Owen J ordered the defendant to pay the claimant's costs on an indemnity basis, for three reasons. First, although there was no allegation of fraud, the Counter-Schedule had questioned the genuineness of C's symptoms; and the prolonged cross-examination of the claimant and other witnesses was on the basis that she was deliberately exaggerating her symptoms. There was no support for such exaggeration in any of the medical evidence. Secondly, the allegation was plainly distressing for C and would have had the most serious consequences for a practising solicitor. Thirdly, the Counter-Schedule implied serious professional impropriety on the part of C's solicitors, viz that they had influenced her to

CONCLUSIONS

reduce her working hours in order to inflate the value of her claim, and had been unreservedly withdrawn only at the start of the trial.

Case Study 3

Siegel v Pummell [2014] EWHC 4309 (QB); [2015] EWHC 195 (QB)

Judge: Wilkie J

10–026

Mr Siegel (S) was a highly intelligent man with an IQ of 136. He was described by the judge as a high-achieving, driven person who operated at a high intellectual level throughout his working life and had good physical and mental stamina; he had a non-conformist streak and had experienced periods of psychological illness, but these had not interfered with his ability to operate at a high level. On 16 November 2009 when his car was stationary in traffic, it was struck in the rear at a speed of between 20 and 35 miles per hour. S was aged 38 at the time and brought a claim for £2,172,235 on the basis that he had suffered a "severe, subtle, permanent closed brain injury secondary to diffuse axonal injury ('DAI')". His case was that, immediately after the accident, he had a severe headache, problems with his vision and cervical spine pain. He had a persistent headache the following day and his recollection of the period of some two weeks after the accident was patchy. He was certified unfit for two months, during which time he became aware of a range of physical and cognitive problems involving his short-term memory, concentration, and difficulty with organising and planning. He lost his libido, became indecisive, lost the ability to multi-task, lacked social judgment, would suddenly blurt out inappropriate comments, and suffered pervasive mental fatigue. He also lost his previous tolerance for alcohol and became susceptible to uncontrollable outbursts of temper for no reason. He showed less empathy to others. Almost a year after the accident his barrister told him that he had sustained brain damage in the accident. According to S, his wife and a host of friends who gave evidence at trial, those symptoms still troubled him five years later when the case was eventually tried. Some three and half years after the accident, S had undergone three sessions of CBT for symptoms of mild PTSD, and he said that these resolved his problems with anxiety and agoraphobia. However, the psychotherapy had not alleviated his cognitive symptoms.

The defendant viewed the accident and its consequences in a rather different light, contending that S had not suffered a brain injury. It was not suggested that he was a malingerer or putting forward a false claim. But, assuming that his reported symptoms were genuine, it was said that he had suffered, at most, a minor whiplash injury. His symptoms were psychologically based in two respects: first, his psychological condition had always been vulnerable to the upsets in his life; and secondly, the persistence of his symptoms were "iatrogenic" in nature—i.e. they arose from S's unconsciously reflecting the expectations of his medical and legal advisers, who have erroneously informed him that he sustained a brain injury in the accident. Accordingly, the claim was worth only £5,000, which was sufficient to compensate S for a minor whiplash neck injury.

Having heard evidence from neurologists and neuropsychologists for each party, a clinical psychologist for the claimant and a neuropsychiatrist for the defendant, the judge concluded that he was satisfied that S had made out his case on DAI.

10–027 On balance, he preferred the expert neurological evidence of Dr Allder to that of Prof Swash. In particular, at [519] to [528]:

- Dr Allder explained the mechanism of injury by reference to the paper by Smith and Meaney. The extremely rapid acceleration/deceleration attributable to a significant rear-end shunt provided a mechanism of injury consistent with the development of DAI at the microscopic level. The chance of DAI was exacerbated if there was an element of rotation, as there was in this case; for S specifically recalled that his head was turned to the left whilst he tuned his car radio.
- Dr Allder cited literature in support of his contention that surprisingly extensive DAI could occur even without a marked loss of consciousness.
- He also contended that S's responses during various assessments by the experts were consistent with PTA, which was a phenomenon associated with brain injury, but not with psychogenic injury. "Functional" or psychogenic amnesia tended to produce a blanket memory loss without interspersed snapshots of vivid recall. S did not present with that pattern of memory, but rather with durable snapshots of recollection. Furthermore, a greater number of snapshots in the early post-traumatic period was not inconsistent with DAI: the literature indicated that axonal pathology could develop over the course of hours and days following the injury.
- Each of the cluster of enduring physical, cognitive and behavioural symptoms of DAI was linked to tracts within the white matter. Whilst an overlap with co-existing psychopathology was possible, S's psychological symptoms had been successfully treated with CBT.
- Dr Allder explained that S's compromised sense of smell indicated that DAI was the explanation for the cognitive and behavioural symptoms, because the same shearing forces capable of causing DAI were sufficient to cause partial shearing to the delicate fibres of the olfactory bulb, passing behind the frontal lobe.
- The judge considered that Professor Swash, by comparison, had been overly prescriptive and had failed to engage with the concept of microscopic DAI arising where scanning equipment did not reveal any damage to the white matter. Instead, the nub of his evidence was to the effect that there was such a mismatch between the symptoms complained of on the one hand and, on the other hand, the nature and severity of the accident, the absence of immediate head injury or loss of consciousness or scans showing damage that he concluded that S's symptoms were not genuine.

The judge also preferred the claimant's expert neuropsychological evidence to the defendant's. In particular, at [529]–[543]:

CONCLUSIONS

- Professor Morris found that there was a discrepancy between the claimant's very superior IQ and his average delayed memory function. Whilst he acknowledged that the two do not necessarily have to correlate, he considered that where, as here, S had required a sustained high level of intellectual performance to undertake his work, the presence post-accident of an "average" delayed memory function was evidence of a significant deficit.
- Professor Morris considered that S's residual psychological symptoms were not potent enough to explain the cluster and severity of his cognitive symptoms.
- He also considered that the extra effort required to compensate at work for the deficit resulting from the brain injury would give rise to fatigue. The brain would have to work harder. The patient would become fatigued, which would impact on his cognitive functions, setting up a vicious circle.
- Dr Connolly, the defendant's expert, undertook a PTA assessment, though she was aware that S had done this exercise on previous occasions. Without suggesting that it was deliberate, she had the impression that his responses were rehearsed. She did conclude that there was a brief period of PTA, less than 24 hours.
- She emphasised that there was a body of medical opinion that a persistent cluster of symptoms was observed after a number of different events—some involving trauma, some not, some based on anxiety, some on depression—so that such symptoms were not unusual amongst people who did not fit into any medical category. The state of current research was not conclusive on why such symptoms persist and she was unable to identify what the mechanism of the persistence might be.
- Dr Connolly drew attention to the fact that there was no diminution of S's processing speed. She observed that the most prominent neuropsychological signs of DAI were related to processing speed and memory, particularly processing speed. Whilst she did not assert that a high level of processing speed excluded DAI, she emphasised that changes to processing speed and memory were the cardinal signs of DAI.
- Dr Connolly's evidence was that up to 25% of the population might be expected to have a very superior level of IQ but have an average delayed memory score, so that the presence of those outcomes in Professor Morris's assessment did not, of itself, denote a deficit which had to be explained by an extraneous cause.
- Her conclusion was that S's history of anxiety and depression made him more prone to suffering from symptoms. She considered his symptoms had persisted because of information given to the claimant (the iatrogenic effect).
- Although the judge considered that the neuropsychologists were genuinely seeking to engage with the issues raised by each other, on balance he concluded that Prof Morris' formulation was more likely to be correct than Dr Connolly's. The judge did not reject her contention that there was a body of professional opinion which acknowledges the persistence of such symptoms where there was no evident cause other than a psychological one. Nevertheless, where there was a specific history which gave rise to an

alternative explanation that more readily fitted S's circumstances, the judge preferred Professor Morris's formulation.

10–028 S relied upon the evidence of Ms Levett as his expert in psychology. The judge felt that he had to approach her evidence with particular care, since her name had been struck off the register of practitioner psychologists by the Health and Care Professions Council and her appeal to the Administrative Court had been dismissed in trenchant terms. However, at the trial Ms Levett had a further appeal against that decision pending in the Court of Appeal.

In this and other cases, she had occupied the dual role of treating psychotherapist and expert witness, giving evidence about the detailed retrospective PTA assessment she had undertaken. Although the defendant accepted that she was a talented psychotherapist who had helped alleviate some of S's symptoms, he contended that she was a consistent advocate of DAI or subtle brain damage in circumstances where she could find no other explanation for a claimant's symptoms. Further, it was said that in her formulations of DAI she went beyond the reach of her professional expertise; and that her objectivity was compromised by the fact that she had acted both as treating psychologist to S and as an expert witness with obligations to the court. This was said to be particularly important where it was contended that S's symptoms were caused by his belief in the diagnosis of DAI that he had been given by others, including Ms Levett.

The judge decided that there was no evidence that Ms Levett had failed to conduct herself in an objective and professionally appropriate way. Further, the history taken by her was similar to that obtained by other experts—no retrograde amnesia, but snapshots of recall from the time of the accident lasting several days.

10–029 Following the above analysis of the evidence, the judge decided that S had proved on the balance of probabilities that his cluster of symptoms was caused by DAI, sustained in the rear-end shunt. In summary, at [562]–[573]:

- He rejected the defendant's contention that DAI should be ruled out because there was no loss of consciousness, a normal Glasgow Coma Scale and an absence of evidence of brain lesions on the CT and MRI scans.
- There were a number of factors pointing towards there having been DAI on a microscopic level, as described by Dr Allder and by the literature upon which he relied.
- First, the collision was not as minor as the defendant suggested.
- Secondly, within 10 days of the accident the A&E department had found evidence of loss of consciousness (the consistent reports by S that he had no recollection of having heard the bang when the accident occurred), albeit for seconds, and of PTA.
- Thirdly, S had given consistent accounts to each of the experts of his snapshots of memory, and a PTA in excess of 24 hours was therefore appropriate. His account was supported by evidence of his confusion for some days after the accident and the description of "islands of memory" during the period covered by the PTA.

CONCLUSIONS

- Fourthly, the mechanism of the accident—a rapid acceleration/deceleration of the head, even without a concurrent blow—was consistent with DAI. In any event there was evidence that S struck his head against his head rest.
- Fifthly, the cluster of symptoms which the claimant reported was consistent with a brain injury.
- The judge made a point of stating, at [570], that he did not reject out of hand the alternative explanations put forward by the defendant's experts, Professor Trimble and Dr Connolly. He accepted that there were elements of S's personality and past medical history which might be thought to provide a basis for an explanation of continuing symptoms caused by psychological rather than physical factors. However, the judge accepted Professor Morris's opinion that the cluster of persisting symptoms was caused by a diffuse axonal injury rather than by psychological causes.
- Whilst the judge accepted the concept of an iatrogenic cause for continuing symptoms, it did not apply in this case.
- Although previous cases on DAI were decided on their own facts and did not set a binding precedent, the Judge was reassured that the conclusion to which he had come was similar to conclusions reached in *Williams v Jervis*[14]; *Clarke v Maltby*,[15] and *Mann v Bahri* in the Central London County Court.

Having decided that S had established his case of DAI, the judge awarded him general damages of £65,000 and special damages of £1,446,431. These included past loss of earnings, treatment costs and, most significantly, future loss of earning capacity by a factor of two thirds of his pre-accident earnings.

The judge declined to award indemnity costs on the grounds that there had been personal attacks on Ms Levett and that there had been an improper allegation of dishonesty against S. The judge held that the defendant was entitled to object to Ms Levett's dual role as treating psychologist and expert witness; and that defence counsel was entitled to cross-examine on the basis that the claimant's symptoms were of iatrogenic origin and that he was prone to exaggerate.

Case Summary 4

Hibberd-Little v Carlton [2018] EWHC 1787 (QB)

Judge: HHJ Saggerson (sitting as a Judge of the High Court)

Like many of the DAI claims, this case started with a rear-end shunt. On 29 March 2013 Mrs Hibberd-Little (HS), a primary school teacher aged 29, was stuck by the defendant's car in stop-start traffic. There was no accident reconstruction evidence and the judge held that the impact speed would have been appreciably less than 30 mph, that HS did not strike her head or lose consciousness, and that, despite her evidence, it was not possible to say whether or not HL's head had been affected by any significant rotational forces. HL was able to drive herself home. When seen at the local A&E later that day she

---

[14] [2008] EWHC 2346 (QB).
[15] [2010] EWHC 1201 (QB).

complained of cervical spine tenderness and neck pain, a severe headache and tingling sensation in her arms; she scored 15 on the Glasgow Coma Scale, and it was noted that there had been no loss of consciousness and no history of a head injury. HL was discharged home with analgesics.

There were a number of unusual features of the claim. Mr and Mrs Hibberd-Little were friends of Peter Siegel and a few weeks before her accident they had both provided witness statements in support of Mr Siegel's claim against Mr Pummell. Their statements corroborated the various changes that he had undergone since his accident, many of which HL complained of in due course. On the 14 November 2014 they gave evidence at Mr Siegel's trial and on 18 December 2014 he was awarded substantial damages. In late 2014 his solicitors replaced HL's former solicitors and arranged for her to be seen by the same core medical experts in neurology, neuropsychology and psychology, who had given evidence in Mr Siegel's case. Having started as a modest claim in the Portal, HL's claim transmogrified into a £4.4 million brain damage claim in the High Court. In addition to her whiplash injuries, she claimed to have suffered a diffuse axonal injury, concussion of the auditory and vestibular systems resulting in vestibular migraine and hyperacusis, PTSD and associated agoraphobic consequences with panic attacks and OCD-type symptoms. Her case was that she had been left with a cluster of life-changing cognitive, behavioural and physical problems, had lost a very promising career as a primary school teacher, and was at a heightened risk of dementia.

In a detailed judgment the judge emphasised that DAI was not on trial in this claim. Indeed, previous cases in the last decade demonstrated that it was an established diagnosis in appropriate cases. The real issue was whether HL could prove that she had suffered DAI in the accident. In order to do so it was important that she was a consistent and accurate historian, that the evidence established a clear temporal link between the accident and the onset of her symptoms, and that those symptoms were consistent with DAI: [93] and [98]. The neurological experts had agreed that, "without specific high-risk factors such as side impact, significant rotational forces, or significant contact injuries, when a healthy individual is considered, low speed impacts are very unlikely to cause diffuse axonal injury." The judge found that none of these high-risk factors was present and, therefore, that this made HL's reliability and the reliability of the information she presented during the PTA assessments all the more critical.

10–031 The absence of an alternative diagnosis was an important consideration, but not conclusive. Given that the Smith and Meaney papers recognise that DAI is a "diagnosis of exclusion", the judge remarked that it would have been helpful to have imaging results in this exclusionary process, particularly since scanning had become more sophisticated since the papers were published. Indeed, there was even a possibility that imaging would have revealed other potential causes for the claimant's enduring symptoms.

Dr Allder, the claimant's neurological expert, considered that HL had suffered a DAI in this collision. Dr Heaney, the defendant's expert, whilst recognising that such a conclusion was theoretically plausible, concluded that HL's case lacked the necessary temporal coherence. The judge preferred Dr Heaney's opinion, which was

CONCLUSIONS

"... anchored more securely and realistically in clinical experience and practise and is less theoretical and academic than that of Dr Allder. Dr Allder approaches his opinion from the perspective of exclusion without, in my judgment, sufficient regard to the whole picture. In recognising, as he did, that the claimant's case might fall within a small cohort of a small cohort (microscopic DAI with progressive amnesia whilst functioning apparently normally) and accepting that whilst this was not the norm, '*it can happen*', I came to the conclusion that Dr Allder focused too much on theoretical plausibility and not enough on the kind of coherence in the overall presentation of a particular patient (the claimant) he agrees is essential": [101]–[102].

The judge found HL's evidence

"... to be unsettling (due largely to its internal inconsistencies and inconsistency with documents, together with the mismatch between her reporting of enduring symptoms and her actual presentation in court) and ultimately profoundly unsatisfactory": [72].

She was not a reliable or accurate witness: inter alia, she was "prepared to say whatever she thinks is necessary to get what she wants" and had a capacity for wishful thinking, an over-inflated idea of her pre-accident capabilities and a tendency to exaggerate and jump to unwarranted conclusions. The evidence of HL and her husband about their contact with their friend, Mr Siegel, lacked transparency and candour and was evasive. There was a lack of consistency or coherence between her reporting of symptoms in the early stages and the information later provided during the retrospective PTA assessments; the onset and trajectory of her symptoms "was not right"; and her case was "full of oddness": [102] and [122].

The medical case was put in the same way as the claimant's lawyers had put it in previous subtle brain injury cases. Since many of the symptoms complained of were not specific to DAI, great reliance was placed on the PTA assessment as an exclusionary diagnostic tool. The judge emphasised, at [98(8)], that

"DAI should never be diagnosed on the strength of a PTA assessment alone but it is a necessary tool. It is better if a prospective PTA assessment can be undertaken, but if it has not been done, the closer to the time of an accident a retrospective assessment can be made, the better (due to the passage of time and confusion caused by received information). Retrospective assessment of PTA is nonetheless viable and helpful when undertaken carefully with a recognised diagnostic tool and in such circumstances, can be just as useful as a prospective assessment—assuming the history given is accurate and consistent. The first retrospective PTA assessment is likely to be the most informative, if carried out appropriately and this can be the best single indicator of the severity of a closed head injury."

Some 28 months after the accident Ms Levett, a psychologist, began to carry out retrospective PTA (rPTA) assessments. Initially, she was instructed as an expert, but later continued to see HL as a treating therapist. Her evidence was that HL had suffered PTA for between two and three weeks after the accident. The judge rejected this evidence for a number of reasons. First, he was highly critical of the "positively Byzantine" evidence she gave concerning her professional status and the disciplinary proceedings against her. He considered that her evidence should be treated with suspicion, that she lacked the transparency that the courts expect

10–032

of expert witnesses, was evasive and also lacked insight into why her professional standing was relevant. He was not satisfied that Ms Levett was sufficiently independent and objective as an expert witness and found that there was a real possibility that she had allowed her specialist interest in this type of case to stray into advocacy "for the identification of DAI in cases where previously none would have been found": [117]. Secondly, there was a troublesome overlap between Ms Levett's dual function as an expert and a treating specialist, which gave rise to concerns that she had too readily accepted at face value information provided by an unreliable historian. In the absence of a recording of the rPTA assessment, it was impossible to know how much of the assessment was the product of leading or suggestive questions. Her evidence about her knowledge of the part HL played in the Siegel case verged on the evasive and lacked candour. Thirdly, there were inconsistencies in the histories taken by the various experts, but these did not give Ms Levett any pause for thought before or during the trial. She had closed her mind to the potential importance of inconsistencies in HL's history and reporting of symptoms and the need for a reflective re-evaluation of the history as recounted to Ms Levett. Fourthly, there was HL's evidence. Although he did not find that she was dishonest or malingering, the judge concluded that she was unreliable, inaccurate and very confused as an historian.

The judge accepted the evidence of Dr Grace, the consultant neuropsychiatrist called by the defendant, which he described as impressive and less dogmatic than that of Ms Levett, who "... thought that her rPTA was more or less all that was needed to close the case in the claimant's favour." Dr Grace regarded the cluster of symptoms of which HL complained as non-specific to DAI; and, like Dr Heaney, she had never encountered a patient with between two and four weeks' PTA, who did not display signs of disorientation as to time and place and who was not discernibly disorganised and incomprehensible to others. The judge noted Dr Allder's evidence that 1% of patients with brain injury and PTA for two to three weeks can present normally to the outside world, but felt that this very small possibility could be discounted in this case.

10–033 Prof Morris, the claimant's neuropsychological expert, gave evidence that HL had weaknesses in memory and executive functioning and that her high intelligence provided her with some cognitive reserve that enabled her to maintain a degree of function. Dr McCulloch, the defendant's expert, disagreed and found no evidence of brain damage based on the neuropsychological test results; in her opinion, the results showed strong performances across a range of functions. Both experts accepted that it was normal for any patient to get a range of scores across different tests and that someone scoring well or very well on many tests might still get a low score in other tests. Prof Morris also recognised that a low score within a battery of tests (such as memory) was only consistent with brain injury, not diagnostic of it. The main focus of dispute between Prof Morris and Dr McCulloch concerned the Delayed Memory Index (DMI). The judge was satisfied that the testing of both Prof Morris and Dr McCulloch revealed a significant difference (described as a "mismatch") between her Full Scale IQ and her score on the DMI. Only a small percentage of the population (1.53%) would have such a distinctive discrepancy between these two measurements. Dr McCulloch agreed that, on the basis of a discrepancy of the order identified by both neuropsychologists, the explanation was (subject always to a rogue test result) either constitutional or due to damage caused to neural networks and connections associated with memory. However, she noted that the test results, as a whole, did not show any demonstrable impairment of the claimant's intellectual or cognitive functioning. With this in mind, the judge accepted the thrust of Dr McCulloch's evidence as a matter of common sense, to the effect that there might be a host of reasons (tiredness, anxiety, boredom) why a patient might do worse than their actual potential on a test. Both Prof Morris and Dr McCulloch agreed that the test results cannot tell the whole story and much depends on the patient's description of function and symptoms. Had HL been a consistent, coherent, accurate and reliable witness about her social, domestic and professional background and the onset and trajectory of the enduring symptoms, the discrepancy between her FSIQ and the comparatively low score on the DMI would have given the hypothesis advanced on behalf of the claimant added plausibility. However, the judge concluded that this single aspect of the test results was insufficient to outweigh all the other shortcomings or "oddness" in the claimant's case. He preferred Dr McCulloch's evidence as being more sharply focused on the presentation of the particular patient in particular circumstances and in the context of the evidence, as opposed to being attached to an academic hypothesis.

The judge rejected the claim based on DAI. He found that HL had sustained a whiplash injury of some severity and suffered symptoms consistent with some of the criteria of PTSD in addition to OCD and a period of anxiety. He awarded her general damages of £25,000, past losses of £15,594 (covering Ms Levett's treatment costs, gratuitous care, travel costs etc.) and interest of £655.94. HL was awarded only 25% of her costs up until the expiry of the 21-day period under Part 36, and was ordered to pay the defendant's costs thereafter, plus interest of 2.5%; and the defendant was granted permission to set off the costs against the costs awarded to the claimant.

The claimant's application for permission to appeal against the judgment was dismissed by Coulson LJ. Permission was granted to appeal against the costs order, but the appeal was subsequently dismissed by consent.

REFERENCES

American Psychiatric Association, *Diagnostic and Statistical Manual of Mental Disorders, 5th Edition: DSM-5* (Arlington, VA: American Psychiatric Association, 2013). **10–034**

Armistead-Jehle, P., Grills, C.E., Bieu, R.K., and Kulas, J.F., "Clinical utility of the memory complaints inventory to detect invalid test performance" (2016) *The Clinical Neuropsychologist*, 30, 610–628.

Ashla, P.M., McMurtray, A.M., Licht, E. and Mendez, M.F., "Retrospective posttraumatic amnesia in traumatic brain injury" (2009) *Journal of Neuropsychiatry and Clinical Neurosciences*, 21 (4), 468.

Aurbach, R., "Suppose Hippocrates had been a lawyer: a conceptual model of harm to litigants; Part 2" (2013) *Psychological Injury and Law*, 6 (3), 228–237.

Baumann, L.J., Cameron, L.D., Zimmerman, R.S., and Leventhal, H., "Illness representations and matching labels with symptoms" (1989) *Health Psychology*, 8, 449–469.

Bender, S.D., and Matusewicz, M., "PCS, Iatrogenic symptoms, and Malingering following concussion" (2013) *Psychological Injury and Law,* 6 (2), 113, 121.

Binder, L.M., and Rohling, M.L., "Money matters: a meta-analytic review of the effects of financial incentives on recovery after closed-head injury" (1996) *The American Journal of Psychiatry*, 153(1), 7–10.

Bhandari, M., Busse, J.W., Hanson, B.P., Leece, P., Ayeni, O.R., and Schemitsch, E.H., "Psychological distress and quality-of-life after orthopedic trauma: an observational study" (2008) *Canadian Journal of Surgery*, 51 (1), 15–22.

Brooks, N., Campsie, L., Symington, C., Beattie, A., and McKinlay, W., "The 5 year outcome of severe blunt head injury: a relative's view." (1986) *Journal of Neurology, Neurosurgery, and Psychiatry*, 49, 764–770.

Bush, S.S., Pimenthal, P.A., Ruff, R.M., Iverson, G.L., Barth, J.T., and Broshek, D.K., "Position paper. Secretive recording of Neuropsychological Testing and Interviewing: official position of the National Academy of Neuropsychology" (2009) *Archives of Clinical Neuropsychology*, 24, 1–2.

Cardi, V., "Litigation as violence" (2014) *Wake Forest Law Review*, 49 (3), 677–686.

Carone, D.A., "Medical and Psychological Iatrogenesis in Neuropsychological Assessment". In, Morgan, J.E. and Ricker, J.H. (eds), *Textbook of Clinical Neuropsychology* (New York: Routledge, 2018)

Carroll, L.J., Cassidy, J.D., Peloso, P.M., Borg, J., von Holst, H., Holm, L., Paniak, C., and Pepin, M., "Prognosis for mild traumatic brain injury: Results of the WHO collaborating centre task force on mild traumatic brain injury" (2004) *Journal of Rehabilitation Medicine*, 84–105.

Cassidy, J.T., Caroll, L.J., Cote, P., Lemstra, M., Berglund, A., and Nygren, A., "Effect of eliminating compensation for pain and suffering on the outcome of insurance claims for whiplash injury" (2000) *The New England Journal of Medicine*, 342 (16),1179–1186.

Charles, S.E., and Kennedy, E., *Defendant* (New York: The Free Press, 1985).

Charles, S.E., "Coping with a medical malpractice suit" (2001) *Western Journal of Medicine*, 174 (1), 55–58.

Crawford, M.J., Thana, L., Farquharson, L., Palmer, L., Hancock, E., Bassett, P., Clarke, J., and Parry, G.D., "Patient experience of negative effects of psychological treatment: results of a national survey" (2016) *The British Journal of Psychiatry*, 208, 260–265.

Dunn, J.T., Lees-Haley, P.R., Brown, R.S., Williams, C.W., and English, L.T., "Neurotoxic complaint base rates of personal injury claimants: implications for Neuropsychological assessment" (1995) *Journal of Clinical Psychology*, 51 (4), 577–584.

Elwyn, G., and Buckman, L., "Should doctors encourage patients to record consultations?" (2015) *British Medical Journal*, 1–3.

Farrin, L., Hull, L., Unwin, C., Wykes, T., and David, A., "Effects of Depressed Mood on Objective and Subjective Measures of Attention" (2003) *The Journal of Neuropsychiatry and Clinical Neurosciences*, 1, 98–104.

Fear, N.T., Jones, E., Groom, M., Greenberg, N., Hull, L., Hodgetts, T.J., and Wessely, S., "Symptoms of post-concussional syndrome are non-specifically related to mild traumatic brain injury in UK Armed Forces personnel on return from deployment in Iraq: an analysis of self-reported data" (2009) *Psychological Medicine*, 39, 1379–1387.

Fox, D.D., Lees-Haley, P.R., Earnest, K., and Dolezal-Wood, S., "Post-concussive symptoms: base rates and etiology in psychiatric patients" (1995) *The Clinical Neuropsychologist*, 9 (1), 89–92.

REFERENCES

French, L.M., Lange, R.T., and Brickell, T.A., "Subjective cognitive complaints and Neuropsychological test performance following military-related traumatic brain injury" (2014) *Journal of Rehabilitation Research & Development,* 51 (6), 933–950.

Friedland, D., and Swash, M., "Post-traumatic amnesia and confusional state: hazards of retrospective assessment" (2016) *Journal of Neurology, Neurosurgery and Psychiatry,* 87 (10), 1–7.

Garden, N., and Sullivan, K.A., "An examination of the base rates of post-concussion symptoms: the influence of demographics and depression" (2010) *Applied Neuropsychology,* 17, 1–7.

Gasquoine, P.G., "Postconcussional symptoms in chronic back pain" (2000) *Applied Neuropsychology,* 7 (2), 83–89.

Gervais, R.O., Ben-Porath, Y.S., Wygant, D.B., and Green, P., "Differential sensitivity of the Response bias Scale (RBS) and MMPI-2 validity scales to memory complaints" (2008) *The Clinical Neuropsychologist,* 22, 1061–1079.

Gervais, R.O., Ben-Porath, Y.S., and Wygant, D.B., "Empirical Correlates and Interpretation of the MMPI-2-RF Cognitive Complaints (COG) Scale" (2009) *The Clinical Neuropsychologist,* 1–20.

Goldstein, R.L., "Spying on psychiatrists: surreptitious surveillance of the forensic psychiatric examination by the patient himself" (1989) *The Journal of the American Academy of Psychiatry and the Law,* 17(4), 367–372.

Green, P., *Memory Complaints Inventory* (Kelowna, BC: Green's Publishing Inc, 2019).

Gross, M.J., Doyal, L., and Swash, M., "The covert recording of medico-legal consultations" (2018) *Medico-Legal Journal,* 86 (4), 202–207.

Gutheil, T.G., Bursztajn, H., Brodsky, A., and Strasburger, L.H., (2000) "Preventing "critogenic" harms: minimising emotional injury from civil litigation". *The Journal of Psychiatry and Law,* 28 (1), 5–18.

Harris, I.A., Young, J.M., Rae, H., Jalaludin, B.B., and Solomon, M.J., "Predictors of general health after major trauma" (2008) *Journal of Trauma: Injury, Infection, and Critical Care,* 64 (4), 969–974.

Hart, R.P., Martelli, M.F., and Zasler, N.D., "Chronic pain and Neuropsychological functioning" (2000) *Neuropsychological Review,* 10 (3), 131–149.

Hartlage, L.C., "Neuropsychological complaint base rates in personal injury, revisited" (1995) *Archives of Clinical Neuropsychology,* 10 (3), 279–280.

Iverson, G.L., "Misdiagnosis of the persistent postconcussion syndrome in patients with depression" (2006) *Archives of Clinical Neuropsychology,* 21, 303–310.

Iverson, G.L., Brooks, B.L., Ashton, V.L., and Lange, R.T., "Interview versus questionnaire symptom reporting in people with post-concussion syndrome" (2010) *Journal of Head Trauma Rehabilitation,* 25 (1), 23–30.

Iverson, G.L., Brooks, B.L., and Holdnack, J.A., "Evidence-based Neuropsychological assessment following work-related injury". In, Bush, S.S., and Iverson, G.L. (eds), *Neuropsychological Assessment of Work-Related Injuries* (London: Guilford press, 2012).

Iverson, G.L., and Lange, R.T., "Examination of "post-concussion -like" symptoms in a healthy sample" (2003) *Applied Neuropsychology,* 10 (3), 137–144.

Iverson, G.L., and McCracken, L.M., "'Postconcussive' symptoms in persons with chronic pain" (1997) *Brain Injury,* 11, 783–790.

James, J.M., and Davis, W.E., Physicians Survival Guide to Litigation Stress: Understanding, Managing, and Transcending a Malpractice Crisis (Physician Health Publications, 2006).

Jamora, C.W., Young, A., and Ruff, R.M., "Comparison of subjective cognitive complaints with US tests in individuals with mild vs Severe Traumatic Brain Injuries" (2012) *Brain Injury*, 26 (1), 36–47.

Jones, A., Ingram, M.V., and Ben-Porath, Y.S., "Scores on the MMPI-2-RF Scales as a Function of Increasing Levels of Failure on Cognitive Symptom Validity Tests in a Military Sample" (2012) *The Clinical Neuropsychologist*, 26, 790–815.

Keet, M., Heavin, H., and Sparrow, S., "Anticipating and managing the psychological cost of civil litigation" (2017) *Windsor Yearbook of Access to Justice*, Vol.34(1), 73–98.

Kemp, S., Agostinis, A., House, A., and Coughlan, A.K., "Analgesia and other causes of amnesia that mimic post-traumatic amnesia (PTA): a cohort study" (2010) *Journal of Neuropsychology*, 4, 231–236.

King, N.S., Crawford, S., Wenden, F.J., Moss, N.E.G., Wade, D.T., and Cadwell, F.T., "Measurement of post-traumatic amnesia: how reliable is it?" (1997) *Journal of Neurology, Neurosurgery and Psychiatry*, 62 (1), 38–42.

Krishnan, N.R., and Kasthuri, A.S., "Iatrogenic Disorders" (2005) *Medical Journal Armed Forces India*, 61 (1), 2–6.

Lees-Haley, P.R., "Litigation Response Syndrome" (1988) *American Journal of Forensic Psychology*, 6 (1), 3–12.

Lees-Haley, P.R., and Brown, R.S., "Neuropsychological complaint base rates of 170 personal injury claimants" (1993) *Archives of Clinical Neuropsychology*, 8, 203–209.

Lees-Haley, P.R., Fox, D.D., and Courtney, J.C., "A comparison of complaints by mild brain injury claimants and other claimants describing subjective experiences immediately following their injury" (2001) *Archives of Clinical Neuropsychology*, 16, 689–695.

Lezak, M.D., Howieson, D.B., Bigler, E.D., and Tranel, D., *Neuropsychological Assessment*. 5th Edition, (Oxford University Press, 2012).

Machulda, M.M., Bergquist, T.F., Ito, V., and Chew, S., "Relationship between stress, coping, and post-concussion symptoms in a healthy adult population" (1998) *Archives of Clinical Neuropsychology*, 13 (5), 415–44.

MacKenzie, E.J., Bosse, M.J., Pollak, A.N., Webb, L.X., Swiontkowski, M.F., Kellam, J.F., Sanders, R.W., Jones, A.L., Starr, A.J., McAndrew, M.P., Patterson, B.M., Burgess, A.R., and Castillo, R.C., "Long-term persistence of disability following severe lower-limb trauma. Results of a 7-year follow-up" (2005) *Journal of Bone and Joint Surgery*, 87 (8), 1801–1809.

Madan, P., A Practical Guide to Subtle Brain Injury Claims (Law Brief Publishing, 2016).

Malec, J.F., Brown, A.W., Leibson, C.L., Flaada, J.T., Mandrekar, J.N., Diehl, N.N., and Perkins, P.K., "The Mayo Classification System for Traumatic Brain Injury Severity" (2007) *Journal of Neurotrauma*, 24, 1417–1424.

Martelli, M.F., Revonda, G., and Zasler, N.D., "Post-traumatic headache: Neuropsychological and psychological effects and treatment implications" (1999) *Journal of Head Trauma Rehabilitation*, 14 (1), 49–69.

Matsuzawa, Y.K., and Dijkers, M.P., "The experience of litigation after TBI I: barriers to recovery" (2014) *Psychological Injury and Law*, 7, 388–396.

Mazza, S., Frot, M., and Rey, E., "A comprehensive literature review of chronic pain and memory" (2018) *Progress in Neuropsychopharmacology and Biological Psychiatry*, 20, 183–192.

McCarter, R.J., Walton, N.H., Moore, C., Ward, A., and Nelson, I., "PTA testing, the Westmead post-traumatic amnesia scale and opiate analgesia: a cautionary note" (2007) *Brain Injury*, 21, 1393–1397.

REFERENCES

McMillan, T.M., Jongen, E.L.M.M., and Greenwood, R.J., "Assessment of post-traumatic amnesia after severe closed head injury: retrospective or prospective?" (1996) *Journal of Neurology, Neurosurgery, and Psychiatry*, 60 (4), 422–427.

Merckelbach, H., Jelicic, M., and Jonker, C., "Planting a misdiagnosis of Alzheimer's disease in a person's mind" (2012) *Acta Neuropsychiatrica*, 24, 60–62.

Merckelbach, H., Jelicic, M., and Pieters, M., "Misinformation increases symptom reporting: a test-retest study" (2011) *Journal of the Royal Society of Medicine*, 2 (10), 1–6.

Merckelbach, H., Dalsklev, M., van Helvoot, D., Boskovic, I., and Otgaar, H. "Symptom self-reports are susceptible to misinformation" (2018) *Psychology of Consciousness: Theory, Research and Practice*, 5 (4), 384–397.

McNally, R.J., "Debunking myths about trauma and memory" (2005) *Canadian Journal of Psychiatry*, 50, 13, 817–822.

Moritz, S., Nestoriuc, Y., Rief, W., Klein, J.P., Jelinek, L., Peth, J., "It can't hurt, right? Adverse effects of psychotherapy in patients with depression" (2018) *European Archives of Psychiatry and Clinical Neuroscience,* 269 (5), 577–586.

Munoz, M., and Esteve, R., "Reports of memory functioning by patients with Chronic Pain" (2005) *Clinical Journal of Pain*, 21 (4), 287–291.

Murphy, G., Loftus, E.F., Grady, R.H., Levine, L.J., and Greene, C.M., "False memories for fake news during Ireland's abortion referendum" (2019) *Psychological Science*, 30 (10), 1449–1459.

McCracken, L.M., and Iverson, G.L., "Predicting Complaints of Impaired Cognitive Functioning in Patients with Chronic Pain" (2001) *Journal of Pain and Symptom Management*, 21 (5), 392–396.

Nampiaparampil, D.E., "Prevalence of chronic pain after traumatic brain injury: a systematic review" (2008) *Journal of the American Medical Association* 13, 300 (6): 711–719.

Nicholson, K., Martelli, M.F., and Zasler, N.D., "Does pain confound interpretation of Neuropsychological test results?" (2001) *Neurorehabilitation*, 16, 225–230.

Osti, O.L., Gun, R.T., Abraham, G., Pratt, N.L., Eckerwall, G., and Nakamura, H., "Potential risk factors for prolonged recovery following whiplash injury" (2005) *European Spine Journal*, 14, 90–94.

Page, L.A., and Wesseley, S., "Medically unexplained symptoms: exacerbating factors in the doctor-patient encounter" (2003) *Journal of the Royal Society of Medicine*, 96, 223–227.

Paniak, C., Reynolds, S., Toller-Lobe, G., Melnyk, A., Nagy, J., and Schmidt, D., "A longitudinal study of the relationship between financial compensation and symptoms after treated mild traumatic brain injury" (2002) *Journal of Clinical and Experimental Neuropsychology*, 24(2), 187–193.

Parry, G.D., Crawford, M.J., and Duggan, C., "Iatrogenic harm from psychological therapies—time to move on" (2016) *The British Journal of Psychiatry*, 208, 210–212.

Ponsford, J.L., Olver, J.H., and Curran, C., "A profile of outcome: 2 years after traumatic brain injury" (1995) *Brain Injury*, 9 (1), 1–10.

Roberts, C.M., Spitz, G., and Ponsford, J.L., "Comparing prospectively recorded posttraumatic amnesia duration with retrospective accounts" (2016) *Journal of Head Trauma Rehabilitation*, 31 (2), 71–77.

Roth, R.S., and Spencer, R.J., "Iatrogenic risk in the management of mild traumatic brain injury among combat veterans: a case illustration and commentary" (2013) *International Journal of Physical Medicine and Rehabilitation*, 1(1), 105.

Sawchyn, J.N., Brulot, M.M., and Strauss, E., "Note on the use of the post-concussion syndrome checklist" (1999) *Archives of Clinical Neuropsychology*, 15 (1), 1–8.

Schiehser, D.M., Delis, D.C., Filoteo, J.V., Delano-Wood, L., Han, D., Jak, a J., Drake, A.I., and Bondi, M.W., "Are self-reported symptoms of executive dysfunction associated with objective executive function performance following mild to moderate traumatic brain injury?" (2011) *Journal of Clinical and Experimental Neuropsychology*, 33 (6), 704–714.

Sherer, M., Sander, A.M., Maestas, K.L., Pastorek, N.J., Nick, T.G., and Li, J., "Accuracy of self-reported length of Coma and posttraumatic amnesia in persons with medically verified traumatic brain injury" (2015) *Archives of Physical Medicine and Rehabilitation*, 96, 652–658.

Schultz, I.Z., Sepehry, A.A., and Greer, S.C., "Impact of Pain on Cognitive Function in Forensic Neuropsychology context" (2018) *Psychological Injury and Law*, 11, 129–138.

Spencer, R.J., Drag, L.L., Walker, S.J., and Bieliauskas, L.A., "Self-reported cognitive symptoms following mild traumatic brain injury are poorly associated with Neuropsychological performance in OIF/OEF veterans" (2010) *Journal of Rehabilitation Research & Development*, 47 (6), 521–530.

Strasburger, L.H., "'Crudely, without any finesse': the defendant hears his psychiatric evaluation" (1987) *The Journal of the American Academy of Psychiatry and the Law*, 15 (3), 229–233.

Strasburger, L.H., "The litigant-patient: mental health consequences of civil litigation" (1999) *Journal of the American Academy of Psychiatry and the Law*, 29 (2), 203–211.

Suhr, J.A., and Gunstad, J., "'Diagnostic Threat': the effect of negative expectations on cognitive performance in head injury" (2002) *Journal of Clinical and Experimental Neuropsychology*, 24 (4), 448–457.

Suhr, J.A., and Gunstad, J., "Further exploration of the effect of 'diagnostic threat' on cognitive performance in individuals with mild head injury" (2005) *Journal of the International Neuropsychological Society*, 11 (1), 23–29.

Symonds, C.P., "Concussion and contusion of the brain and their sequelae". In Brock, S., (ed). *Injuries of the skull, brain and spinal-cord: Neuro- psychiatric, and surgical and medico-legal aspects* (London: Bailliere, Tindall & Cox, 1940).

Trahan, D.E., Ross, C.E., and Trahan, S.L., "Relationships among post-concussional-type symptoms, depression, and anxiety in neurologically normal young adults and victims of mild brain injury" (2001) *Archives of Clinical Neuropsychology*, 16, 435–445.

Tsanadis, J., Montoya, E., Hanks, R.A., Millis, S.R., Fichtenberg, N.L., and Axelrod, B.N., "Brain injury severity, litigation status, and self-report of postconcussive symptoms" (2008) *The Clinical Neuropsychologist*, 22 (6), 1080–92.

Uomoto, J.M., and Esselman, P.C., "Traumatic brain injury and Chronic Pain: Differential types and rates by head injury severity" (1993) *Archives of Physical Medicine and Rehabilitation*, 74(1)), 61–64.

Urban, E.J., Cochran, K.J., Acevedo, A.M., Cross, M.P., Pressman, S.D., and Loftus, E.F., "Misremembering Pain: a memory blindness approach to adding a better end" (2019) *Memory and Cognition*, 47, 954–967.

Vanderploeg, R.D., and Belanger, H.G., "Screening for a remote history of mild traumatic brain injury: when a good idea is bad" (2013) *Journal of Head Trauma Rehabilitation*, 28 (3), 211–218.

van Zomeren, A.H., and van den Burg, W., "Residual complaints of patients 2 years after severe head injury" (1985) *Journal of Neurology, Neurosurgery, and Psychiatry*, 48, 21–28.

REFERENCES

Villemure, R., Nolin, P., and Le Sage, N., "Self-reported symptoms during post-mild traumatic brain injury in acute phase: influence of interview method" (2011) *Brain Injury*, 25, 53–64.

Walker, W.C., Ketchum, J.M., Marwitz J.H., Chen, T., Hammond, F.S., Sherer, M., and Meythaler, J., "A multicentre study on the clinical utility of post-traumatic amnesia duration in predicting global outcome after moderate-severe traumatic brain injury" (2010) *Journal of Neurology, Neurosurgery and Psychiatry*, 21, 339–347.

Wang, Y., Chan, R.C.K., and Deng, Y., "Examination of post-concussion-like symptoms in healthy University students: relationships to subjective and objective neuropsychological function performance" (2006) *Archives of Clinical Neuropsychology*, 21, 339–347.

Zakzanis, K.K., and Yeung, E., "Base rates of post-concussive symptoms in a non-concussed multicultural sample" (2011) *Archives of Clinical Neuropsychology*, 26, 461–465.

CHAPTER 11

Return to Work and Vocational Rehabilitation

Andy Tyerman, Nigel King and Martin Hillier

INTRODUCTION

"The right to work is a fundamental human right. The Universal Declaration on Human Rights recognizes that everyone has the right to work, to free choice of employment, to just and favourable conditions of work and to protection against unemployment (art. 23, para. 1). The right to work is essential for realizing other human rights and forms an inseparable and inherent part of human dignity. Work usually provides livelihood to the person and her or his family, and insofar as work is freely chosen or accepted, it contributes to the person's development and recognition within the community." (Office of the United Nations High Commissioner for Human Rights, 2012).

11–001

Employment prospects for people with disability remain relatively low. In the UK, 50.7% of people with disability aged 16–64 were in work in early 2018 compared with 81.1% of those without disabilities with the resultant disability employment gap of 30.4% noted to be "large and persistent" (Equality and Human Rights Commission (EHRC), 2018). It is generally accepted that work provides personal and social benefits including a sense of personal worth, connection to a social community and structure to the day (Jahoda, 1982). Absence or loss of work has negative consequences (Vinokur and Price, 2015) and unemployment is associated with a decline in both psychological and physical health and increased risk of suicide (see Wanberg, 2012). Of the mental health effects, depressive symptoms are widely documented but they also commonly include stress reactions, anxiety and lowered self-esteem (see Price et al., 2002). For those with common health conditions there is a strong association between worklessness and ill-health, manifested in higher mortality, poorer general health and poorer mental health, with parallel evidence of the restorative effect of re-employment (Waddell and Burton, 2006).

Returning to or remaining in work is a key element in quality of life and life satisfaction for people with a traumatic brain injury (TBI) (Webb et al., 1995; O'Neill et al., 1998; Corrigan et al., 2001; Steadman-Pare et al., 2001; Jacobsson et al., 2010). However, only a minority of people with TBI return to employment (Sander et al., 1996; Kreutzer et al., 2003; van Velzen et al., 2009a). The prospects of a return to work (RtW) after TBI reflect "a complex interaction between pre-morbid characteristics, injury factors, post-injury impairments, personal and environmental factors" (Shames et al., 2007). Unemployment after TBI has major economic implications (McMordie and Barker, 1988; Johnstone et al., 2003; Gamboa et al., 2006; Brown et al., 2008), as well as marked personal and family effects.

11–002 Vocational rehabilitation (VR) is defined by the British Society of Rehabilitation Medicine (BSRM) as the overall process of "enabling individuals with either temporary or permanent disability to access, return to, or to remain in employment" (BSRM, 2000, p.11). (This process is also sometimes referred to as occupational rehabilitation or work rehabilitation.) The World Health Organization (2011) states that VR services "develop or restore the capabilities of people with disabilities so that they can participate in the competitive labour market". However, in this chapter the term VR is used broadly to refer to the process of assisting people to enter, return to and/or remain in employment, education/ training or alternative occupation (e.g. voluntary work or family carer). In discussing return to work (RtW) after TBI it is important to recognise the distinctions between a return to previous work and a return to alternative employment or other occupation.

The chapter will review RtW after TBI and some of the factors reported to be associated with RtW and VR needs after TBI. The legal context provided by the United Nations Convention on the Rights of Persons with Disabilities and the UK Equality Act 2010 will be reviewed. The process of vocational assessment and VR will then be outlined, along with a summary of effectiveness and of VR provision in the UK. This chapter builds on previous reviews of VR after ABI (Tyerman, 2008; Tyerman, Tyerman and Viney, 2008; Tyerman, 2012; Tyerman, Meehan and Tyerman, 2017).

1. VOCATIONAL OUTCOMES/NEEDS

Return to work after traumatic brain injury

11–003 The extent of difficulties in RtW after TBI in the UK were highlighted 30 years ago in a neurosurgical follow-up study in Glasgow, with 86% employed pre-injury but just 29% at two to seven-year follow-up (Brooks et al., 1987). Whilst few of this group received rehabilitation, RtW outcomes from neurorehabilitation centres in the UK were also disappointing at around 35–40%. For example, only 36% were in full-time employment at two year follow-up from the then Wolfson Medical Rehabilitation Centre, Wimbledon, with most working in a reduced capacity rather than in former jobs (Weddell et al., 1980). When seen again at seven years, some had progressed to jobs comparable to those pre-injury but no-one unemployed at two years had since found employment (Oddy et al., 1985). Subsequent RtW outcomes at two years post-injury from two UK demonstration centres in rehabilitation highlighted extensive unmet VR needs with just 20% in paid employment (5% former work/study, 11% working in a reduced capacity and 4% in sheltered work) and over half (54%) of this young adult group at home with no occupation (Tyerman, 1987).

Even with specific advice in RtW, a successful return was accomplished by just 38% of people with very severe TBI at Addenbrooke's Hospital, Cambridge, with a further 28% attempting but failing to RtW (Johnson, 1987). In a 10-year follow-up 34% were employed full-time and 10% part-time with 6% in sheltered work, but 50% remained unemployed (Johnson, 1998). It was noted that those successful in RtW did so without employment rehabilitation services, which were found to be of limited value, not geared to the needs of TBI, of too short a duration and too late to be effective (Johnson, 1989). The particular challenge of RtW in an economically disadvantaged rural area in North Wales was highlighted by Coetzer et al. (2002) with employment falling from 80% pre-injury to just 25% overall and from 58% to 15% for those with severe TBI.

Similar RtW rates have been reported in the USA and Australia. In a multi-centre study of the Model Systems TBI programs in the USA (which include access to VR) competitive employment rates were 23% at one year, 17% at two years and 25% at three years and under 40% even for those previously employed (Sander et al., 1996). "Job instability" among those who RtW has also been highlighted (Kreutzer et al., 2003; Machamer et al., 2005). Similarly, in an Australian rehabilitation follow-up, 33% of those employed prior to injury were employed full-time and 9% part-time at two-year follow-up (Ponsford et al., 1995). However, by five years, 32% of those employed at two years were no longer in work and, of those at school at time of injury, only 29% were employed (Olver et al., 1996).

RtW rates after TBI are noted to vary from 15–90% in systematic reviews (Kendal et al., 2006; Nightingale et al., 2007). This "enormous variability" is thought to reflect the heterogeneous nature of rehabilitation, prevalence of methodological problems, lack of a standardised definition of outcome and measurement insensitivity to RtW outcomes (Kendall et al., 2006). Definitive RtW rates after both TBI and acquired brain injury (ABI) more generally have been compounded by variable diagnostic groups across TBI and other forms of ABI (e.g. stroke, encephalitis, cerebral hypoxia and cerebral tumour), unclear work status (pre-injury and pre-rehabilitation), lack of detail of the rehabilitation provided, differential time post-injury and variable definition of RtW (Tyerman, 2012). The latter varies from full-time competitive employment to more inclusive definitions incorporating paid, supported/sheltered, voluntary work, vocational training, further education and homemaking. For those in paid employment it is often unclear if this is previous or alterative work, with or without modifications, full- or part-time, at an equivalent or reduced level, with or without extra training and at a competitive level or not (Shames et al., 2007).

In an attempt to address the above concerns, a systematic review of studies reporting RtW after non-progressive forms of ABI for those in paid employment or voluntary work prior to injury was reported by van Velzen et al. (2009a). Of 49 studies meeting the inclusion criteria, 35 studies were of people with ABI from traumatic causes. After excluding outliers with very high or very low percentages of RtW, results were pooled. This resulted in a RtW rate of 40.7% for 4709 participants at one year and 40.8% for 276 participants at two years. In a parallel review for stroke RtW rates ranged from 3–60% across 12 studies with a mean of 39% at two years (van Velzen et al., 2009a), which was slightly below the 44% (70 studies, n=8,810) reported by Daniel et al. (2009). A RtW rate of 40% would seem the best current estimate after TBI for those previously in paid or voluntary

11–004

work with lower rates expected for those who were not previously in employment. Most people with a moderate or severe TBI of working age are therefore not in paid work.

Whilst RtW is quite reasonably a key goal for rehabilitation services we need to be alert to the risks of a premature RtW without adequate support, which can have negative effects both vocationally and psychologically (Tyerman, 2012). It is noted that RtW sometimes leads to "catastrophic" consequences in terms of stress, psychological well-being and quality of life (Levack et al., 2004). As such, the need to consider how the job contributes to "feelings of meaningful productivity" and to a positive sense of identity and self-worth is stressed. It is important to consider what constitutes the optimal vocational option for each individual. For some this will involve an alternative to paid employment (e.g. voluntary work, being a home-maker or carer and/or further or adult education).

Factors influencing return to work

11–005   There is an extensive literature exploring the factors that can influence RtW after brain injury. In a meta analysis of 41 studies Crepeau and Scherzer (1993) found a wide range of predictors and indicators to be related to RtW after TBI but only weakly or moderately, with the highest and most reliable correlations with unemployment being with executive dysfunction, emotional disturbances, deficits in activities of daily living and less VR services. In a subsequent review of 50 studies Ownsworth and McKenna (2004) found that the factors most consistently associated with RtW after TBI included pre-injury occupational status, functional status at discharge, global cognitive functioning, perceptual ability, executive functioning, involvement in VR services and emotional status.

Neuropsychological impairment has long been linked with poor vocational outcome, as noted previously (Tyerman, 2008). In the early long-term UK neurosurgical follow-up Brooks et al. (1987) found that those in work had fewer cognitive difficulties and also fewer problems emotionally/behaviourally. Cognitive impairment (including executive difficulties such as cognitive inflexibility and problem-solving) at one-month post-injury was reported to differentiate between those in and out of work at one year (Fraser et al., 1988). The role of self-awareness has attracted particular attention with improvements in self-awareness reported to be one of the principal factors in successful RtW, along with increased effectiveness in information processing and improvements in acceptance by patients of their existential situation (Ben-Yishay et al., 1987). In a further study Ezrachi et al. (1991) reported that capacity for acceptance is the single most potent variable in determining capacity to benefit from rehabilitation and RtW. Scherer et al. (1998; 2003) report a positive relationship between self-awareness and positive employment outcomes and advocate interventions to improve self-awareness. Wise et al. (2005) reported a similar relationship and advocated the routine use of standardised measures of self-awareness to identify those that may benefit from additional intervention.

Numerous other studies have reported a link between neuropsychological function and RtW (e.g. Ryan et al., 1992; Girard et al., 1996; Sander et al., 1997; Teasdale et al., 1997; Cattelani et al., 2002; Simpson and Schmitter-Edgecombe, 2002; Machamer et al., 2005). However, as noted (Tyerman, 2012), a link between neuropsychological test results and RtW has not always been found (e.g. Johnstone et al., 1999, 2003; Tyerman and Young, 1999; McCrimmon and Oddy, 2006). Other studies have highlighted difficulties in work behaviour—in "work conformance" (mainly relating to social judgment, inappropriate behaviour and communication); in "task orientation" (work persistence and need for close supervision, in part due to poor error recognition); and poor "work tolerance" (Price and Baumann, 1990). "Job separation" (i.e. loss of job) for people with ABI in supported employment has been attributed to poor work skills (25.0%), insufficient motivation to work (20.3%) and aberrant/inappropriate behaviour (23.5%) as well as to external factors (20.3%) and economic layoffs (10.9%) (Kregel et al., 1994). People with ABI were also noted to be more likely than people with other disabilities (i.e. learning disabilities, mental illness or cerebral palsy) to be separated from work due to aberrant/inappropriate behaviour.

Whilst many factors have been associated with RtW after TBI, a systematic review of 55 studies concluded that there was insufficient evidence to reliably and validly identify variables with prognostic significance for RtW (Nightingale et al., 2007). A systematic review of a wide range of potential prognostic factors (e.g. injury severity, length of hospital stay, time since injury, physical variables, behaviour, external factors (e.g. family) and personal factors (e.g. age, gender, race, income, etc)) was reported by van Velzen et al. (2009b). Most of the variables were found to have little or no prognostic value in terms of RtW.

11–006

A subsequent review of 80 studies similarly concluded that the evidence for predicting vocational outcome after TBI from a range of pre/post-injury variables (including age, educational level, pre/post-injury occupational status, severity of TBI, functional status, level of depression and anxiety, gender and race) is weak (Saltychev et al., 2013). However strong evidence has been reported of a negative association of comorbid psychiatric disorders with RtW after ABI (Garrelfs et al., 2015). A recent review of 27 studies found "strong evidence" that high educational level is positively associated with RtW after TBI and low educational level, being unemployed pre-injury and length of stay in rehabilitation negatively associated with RtW after TBI (Donker-Cools et al., 2016b).

Over the last decade a parallel qualitative research literature has evolved. Investigating the factors supporting a RtW from the perspective of professionals, as well individuals with ABI, two significant themes (personal and social) were identified with six major categories: self-continuity, coping, social factors, rehabilitation interventions, professionalism and health insurance (Lundqvist and Samuelsson, 2012). Of the social factors, having employment and a positive employer was seen as important. Having a job was seen as important personally and socially (over and above its economic benefits), for example, for identity, self-image and quality of life. A difficult and painful experience with a "distinct grief reaction" in exploring re-engagement in occupation after TBI was identified by Hooson et al. (2013).

A qualitative analysis of views of people with a TBI of what was important in the process of RtW identified four key themes (Stergiou-Kita et al., 2012):

- *Meaning of work*—RtW was seen as an important goal, denoting success and a return to "normality", including a sense of social re-integration, purpose and structure to the day, financial independence and respect from others.
- *Process of RtW and reconciling a new identity*—RtW was seen not as a single event, but rather as a process that individuals engage in striving for normality, learning about post-injury capabilities and reconciling abilities and disabilities.
- *Opportunities to try versus risks of failure*—Participants viewed opportunities to try out work skills as a vital element in the RtW process, providing new insights into abilities and limitations. However, some participants saw a need for such opportunities to be weighed against the risks of unsuccessful work trials.
- *Significance of support*—This theme is related to available support including structured opportunities to try out abilities with guidance and feedback and/or both instrumental and emotional support (e.g. help with travel, aids and adaptations and encouragement from peers or professionals, supervisors and colleagues). Educating family, colleagues and supervisors concerning both expectations and their role was also seen as important.

11–007   In a grounded theory qualitative analysis two years after TBI, Johannson et al. (2016) described participants' experiences of mastering daily activities with the ultimate aim of RtW. A core theme, "desire for control: focusing on high priority issues", was identified. Participants were unsure to what extent they had the ability to RtW. Whilst seen as desirable, RtW was also regarded as a challenge with a need for work adjustments and support with strategies to enable them to prioritise tasks and sustain effort at work. All participants saw RtW as providing structure, routine and order. As such, it was concluded that support with work-related issues (e.g. strategies, routines, structure, and feedback about performance) would help people in mastering life in general with the workplace potentially an ideal context in which to deliver such support (Johannson et al., 2016).

In a specific study of self-efficacy and quality of life after TBI, both employment related self-efficacy and general self-efficacy were reported to be important (Tsauosides et al., 2009). As such, when considering VR interventions after TBI, it was recommended to consider including measures of self-efficacy, both general and specific (e.g. job search self-efficacy), and designing interventions to enhance work-related skills and abilities and underlying beliefs in the ability to perform successfully in the workplace. Other studies have highlighted factors that both impede and facilitate RtW. Identified barriers include the following: personal factors, psychosocial adaptation, injury-related consequences and factors in the working environment—workplace demands, attitudes of employers and colleagues, complicated information, excessive bureaucracy, too little practice before RtW and physical barriers (Ellingsen and Aas, 2009); fatigue (Van Velzen et al., 2011); and sensory overload, fatigue, poor guidance and support (Donker-Cools et al., 2018).

Identified facilitative factors have included: optimism and determination but also resources—social support, time-related flexibility, relevant tasks and accommodations (Ellingsen and Aas, 2009); the will to RtW, ongoing recovery and the knowledge and support of the employer, colleagues, occupational physician and VR specialist (Van Velzen et al., 2011); individually-tailored rehabilitation, at least moderate motivation for RtW and awareness of the person's cognitive and social abilities (Materne et al., 2017); rehabilitation, personal factors and work support (Moller et al., 2017) and work-related solutions (backed up by professional supervision), understanding and acceptance of limitations of ABI (Donker-Cools et al., 2018). In a study of participants experiencing different RtW pathways (pre-injury employment, job seeking for new employment and not yet worked post-injury) both universal and pathway-specific themes were identified (McRae et al., 2016). The three universal themes were the importance of working, the impact of injury and determination. The five pathway-specific themes (i.e. understanding, adjustment, access, support and disclosure) reflect distinct characteristics across the different pathways. A final theme of intervention also varied across pathways such that it was concluded that approaches to VR need to be tailored to individual circumstances, opportunities and support needs.

In a meta-synthesis of 16 qualitative studies four key concepts were identified in RtW after ABI (i.e. empowerment, self-awareness, motivation and facilitation) (Liaset and Loras, 2016). It was concluded that personal development was experienced as essential (including awareness of strengths and weaknesses) and that these personal factors intersect with the employer providing facilitation in the workplace. This qualitative research is adding depth to our understanding and identifying additional factors to be considered in the relationship between TBI, VR interventions and work.

11–008

In the meantime, we are unable to predict RtW for individuals with TBI based on current research. Whilst this may be compounded by methodological inconsistencies, even with consensus on data collection, definitive prediction of RtW is likely to prove elusive due to the complex interaction of differentially relevant factors relating to the individual, their work situation at time of injury, the nature of the TBI, the rehabilitation received and the specific demands of the job. People with a similar TBI who receive comparable rehabilitation will be differentially restricted in their prospects of RtW depending on their profession and job specific role, whilst those with a similar job role will be differentially restricted depending on the nature and severity of TBI and the rehabilitation received. The prospects for those required to seek alternative employment will also vary according to access to suitable VR and the employment market across occupational sectors, both geographically and over time. Whilst it is clearly sensible to be mindful of the factors most commonly reported to be associated with RtW, reaching a view of an individual's prospects of RtW after TBI remains a matter of expert judgment, weighing up the positive and negative influences of all known relevant factors. As such, whilst we might reasonably expect to be able to inform the design of VR service developments, individual RtW prospects and VR needs are likely to remain a matter of individual judgment, at least for the foreseeable future.

Vocational needs after brain injury

11–009   Whilst definitive predictive factors have proved elusive, there are numerous studies documenting the challenges faced by people with TBI in RtW. These include reduced cognitive and motor skills, a wide range of subjective complaints (somatic, cognitive, behavioural, and communication), difficulties in work attitude, skills, performance, behaviour and social interaction at work, environmental/organisational obstacles and health and safety concerns. As noted, such concerns stem from a wide variety of sources including self/family reports, formal VR assessments, experiences of VR practitioners, calls to the Job Accommodation Network and feedback from supported placements (Tyerman, 2012).

In a survey of "employment concerns" of 1,052 people of whom 30% were employed and 70% unemployed at on average seven years after TBI, respondents were not satisfied with the availability and quality of VR (Roessler et al., 1992). Whilst 40% reported receiving vocational counselling, less than 20% had received either job training or job placement assistance. Vocational potential was reported not to be recognised and work preparation needs not met with specific gaps in career counselling and job training. Problems with job training included failure to develop programmes that meet the needs of people with TBI and lack of access to training related to local job opportunities. The most important employment problem was inadequate access to placement support by a professional knowledgeable about TBI. Lack of long-term follow-up enhanced the problem of job retention (Roessler et al., 1992). In a study of unemployed people over five years post-TBI, relatives reported a high incidence of cognitive, motor and emotional problems (most commonly boredom, frustration, slowness, loss of train of thought, difficulties in decision-making, fatigue and impatience) (Witol et al., 1996). The top five perceived obstacles to RtW were noted to be diverse: memory, "trouble using hands, arms or legs", "thinking problems", transportation and "poor vision".

For those seen by VR providers numerous difficulties have been highlighted. Of people seen on a supported employment program after moderate-to-severe TBI at an average of five years post-injury (range 13 days to 28 years) a "diverse and global pattern of cognitive impairment" was evident on neuropsychological testing (Devany et al., 1991). The most common difficulties were with attention and information processing (affecting more than 90%), slowed motor ability/ impaired dexterity (more than 70%) and in free recall verbal learning and memory for geometric figures (more than 70%). On self-report a wide range of items were endorsed: somatic problems (40–72%); cognitive problems (64–70%); behavioural problems (56–83%); and communication and social problems (44–72%). All 10 cognitive and 10 behaviour items, six of 10 communication and social items and five of 10 somatic were endorsed by over 50% of the group (Devany et al., 1991). Job coaches working with people with TBI considered six of 31 survey items to be major problems affecting job coaching success: slow acquisition of job skills, verbal memory, judgment, visual memory, inflexibility of thinking and anxiety (Stapleton et al., 1989). Another 12 items were considered to be a moderate problems: completion of work in a timely fashion, obsessive/compulsive behaviour, inability to detect/correct errors, inability to work independently, attention/concentration deficits, poor social interaction skills, intellectual limitations, inability to prioritise/organise talks, distractibility or difficulty staying on task, physical limitations, inability to work without structure and inability to make plans independently (Stapleton et al., 1989). In a further study, staff members involved in vocational assessment, training and job placement noted the following client difficulties: restrictions arising from the need for structure, inability to complete a task and tendency to make errors. Slowness, attention deficit, inability to act independently, limited ability to prioritise, poor judgment and limited intellectual skills were all consistently found to be in the top 10 problems (Parente and Stapleton, 1996).

Another perspective of VR needs is provided by the TBI-related difficulties that prompted contact with the Job Accommodation Network in the US (Hirsh et al., 1996). Contact was made by a service provider (e.g. rehabilitation counsellor, job coach) (45%), the individual with TBI or family member (32%), or the employer or their representative (23%). Three-quarters of callers were seeking information related to cognitive difficulties (e.g. remembering, organising, staying on task, prioritising and learning new tasks) at work in order to meet performance standards. The five most common job functions requiring accommodation were as follows: remember task or sequence (37%), concentrate on work details (33%), prioritise, sequence task (18%), learning new task or information (15%), draw conclusions, evaluate information (10%). Whilst over half the issues were in the "perform efficiently" category for all respondents, safety issues were primarily a concern for employers (38%) rather than individual/families (10%) or service providers (13%), and a higher proportion of employers reported concerns about behaviour (19%) than did individual/families (12%) or service providers (9%). 11–010

In spite of the above challenges, Shames et al. (2007) expressed the view that "a significant proportion" of people with TBI (including those with severe injuries) are able to RtW "if sufficient and appropriate rehabilitation effort is invested". However, it was noted that the model of VR employed varies greatly depending on the location and the type of health care system. Before considering VR interventions to assess and address vocational needs, we will explore the legal context in the UK.

2. DISABILITY DISCRIMINATION

Article 27 of the United Nations Convention on the Rights of Persons with Disabilities sets out the right to work of persons with disabilities. This obligates States to recognise the right of persons with disabilities to work on an equal basis with others including "the opportunity to gain a living by work freely chosen or accepted in a labour market and work environment that is open, inclusive and accessible to persons with disabilities" (Office of the United Nations High Commissioner for Human Rights, 2012). As such, States are to take steps, including through legislation, to safeguard and promote the realisation of the right to work in order to create an enabling and conducive environment for employment that welcomes persons with disabilities as employees. 11–011

Guidance on implementation includes standards relating to the following:

(1) non-discrimination: the right to work on an equal basis with others;
(2) accessibility: the opportunity to gain a living in a work environment that is accessible, identifying and removing barriers that hinder persons with disabilities from working on an equal basis with others;
(3) reasonable accommodation: ensuring that reasonable accommodation is provided to persons with disabilities who request it, taking effective steps to ensure that the denial of reasonable accommodation constitutes discrimination; and
(4) positive measures: adopting positive measures to promote employment opportunities for persons with disabilities (Office of the United Nations High Commissioner for Human Rights, 2012).

In the UK these obligations are incorporated within the Equality Act 2010.

The Equality Act 2010

11-012   The Equality Act 2010 protects anyone who has, or has had, a "protected characteristic" (i.e. age, disability, gender reassignment, marriage and civil partnership, pregnancy and maternity, race, religion or belief, sex, sexual orientation) against discrimination in a wide range of situations including education, employment and as a service user (EHRC, 2011). While it is recognised that small employers may have more informal practices, fewer written policies and greater financial constraints, no employer is exempt because of size (EHRC, 2011, para.1.20). The summary of the Equality Act below is taken from the Equality Act 2010 Employment Statutory Code of Practice (EHRC, 2011), which covers both employment and other work-related activity.

Disability is defined broadly as "a physical or mental impairment which has a long-term and substantial adverse effect on the ability to carry out normal day-to-day activities" (para.2.12). "Long-term" means that the impairment has lasted or is likely to last for at least 12 months or for the rest of the affected person's life (para.2.14). "Substantial" means more than minor or trivial (para.2.15). Even when no longer adversely affected in their daily activities, people with disability (including TBI) are still protected if the effects lasted for over 12 months (para.2.9). Discrimination arises when someone is treated differently because of a protected characteristic in a situation covered by the Act, which includes employment and education. There are six types of disability discrimination:

Direct discrimination

11-013   Direct discrimination occurs when a person treats another less favourably than they treat (or would treat others) because of a protected characteristic (para.3.2) or based on a stereotype relating to a protected characteristic (para.3.15) (e.g. not offering a job to a person with TBI because it is assumed that they will not be able to do the job). Direct discrimination is unlawful, regardless of motive, intent, whether done consciously or unconsciously or whether the employer is aware of treating the worker differently because of a protected characteristic (para.3.14). It is also direct discrimination if an employer treats a worker less favourably

DISABILITY DISCRIMINATION

because of their association with a person with a protected characteristic, because they campaigned to help someone with such a characteristic or refused to act in a way that would disadvantage such a person (paras 3.18–3.21).

Indirect discrimination

Indirect discrimination may occur when an employer applies an apparently neutral provision, criterion or practice which puts workers sharing a protected characteristic at a particular disadvantage (para.4.3). An example would be an employer requiring all job applicants to use an online application process which is not accessible for a person with TBI as a result of cognitive impairment with no alternative means of application. For indirect discrimination to take place, four requirements must be met (para.4.4):

11–014

- the employer applies (or would apply) the provision, criterion or practice equally to everyone within the relevant group including a particular worker;
- the provision, criterion or practice puts, or would put, people who share the worker's protected characteristic at a particular disadvantage when compared with people who do not have that characteristic;
- the provision, criterion or practice puts, or would put, the worker at that disadvantage; and
- the employer cannot show that the provision, criterion or practice is a proportionate means of achieving a legitimate aim.

A "provision, criterion or practice" includes any policies, rules, practices, arrangements, criteria, conditions, prerequisites, qualifications or provisions (para.4.5). "Disadvantage" includes denial of an opportunity or choice, deterrence, rejection or exclusion and does not have to be quantifiable or involve actual loss (para.4.9) or to be intentional (para.4.24).

Discrimination arising from disability

Discrimination arising from disability occurs when a person is treated unfavourably because of something arising in consequence of their disability (para.5.1) (e.g. disciplining a person with TBI for multiple memory lapses). However, if the employer can show that the detrimental treatment is a "proportionate means of achieving a legitimate aim" (para.5.11) or that they did not know, and could not reasonably have been expected to know, about the disability, then it is not discriminatory. If an employer's agent or employee (e.g. occupational health (OH) adviser or HR officer) is aware of the disability, the employer will not usually be able to claim a lack of knowledge (para.5.17).

11–015

Failure to make reasonable adjustments

The duty to make reasonable adjustments requires employers to take positive steps to ensure that people with disability can access and progress in employment. This requires not only avoiding treating job applicants and workers with a disability unfavourably, but also taking additional steps to ensure that they

11–016

RETURN TO WORK AND VOCATIONAL REHABILITATION

can access jobs, education and services as easily as people without disability (para.6.4), for example, allowing an employee (e.g. with TBI) to take several short breaks instead of one longer break in order to manage fatigue. The duty requires employers to take reasonable steps to (para.6.5):

- Avoid the substantial disadvantage where a provision, criterion or practice applied by or on behalf of the employer puts a disabled person at a substantial disadvantage compared to others (i.e. those who are not disabled).
- Remove or alter a physical feature or provide a reasonable means of avoiding such a feature where it puts a disabled person at a substantial disadvantage compared to others.
- Provide an auxiliary aid (including an auxiliary service) where a disabled person would, but for the provision of that auxiliary aid, be put at a substantial disadvantage to others.

An employer only has a duty to make an adjustment if they know, or could reasonably be expected to know, that a worker has a disability and is, or is likely to be, placed at a substantial disadvantage. Employers must do all they can reasonably be expected to do to find out whether this is the case. However, if a person keeps a disability confidential it is likely that the employer will not be under a duty to make an adjustment, unless they could reasonably be expected to know about the disability anyway (para.6.20). There is no onus on an employee to suggest what adjustments should be made (para.6.24).

It is noted that effective adjustments often involve little or no cost or disruption and are therefore very likely to be reasonable for an employer to make. Even if there is significant cost, adjustments may still be cost-effective (e.g. relative to recruiting and training a new staff member) and may still be a reasonable adjustment (para.6.25).

11–017 When the duty to make a reasonable adjustment applies, the question of "reasonableness" alone determines whether it has to be made. Whilst "reasonableness" will depend on individual circumstances (paras 6.29–6.30), factors which might be taken into account when deciding what is a reasonable step include the following (para.6.28):

- whether taking any particular steps would be effective in preventing the disadvantage;
- the practicability of the step;
- financial and other costs of making the adjustment and extent of any disruption caused;
- the extent of the employer's financial or other resources;
- availability of financial or other assistance to help the employer make an adjustment; and
- the type and size of the employer.

If an adjustment poses an increased health and safety risk to anyone, risk assessments should be undertaken to help determine whether the risk is likely to arise (para.6.27).

Harassment

Harassment occurs when unwanted conduct related to a protected characteristic has the purpose or effect of violating the dignity of a person or of making them feel humiliated, offended or degraded (para.7.6). "Unwanted conduct" covers spoken or written words or abuse, imagery, graffiti, physical gestures, facial expressions, mimicry, jokes, pranks, acts affecting a person's surroundings or other physical behaviour (para.7.7). An example could include mimicking the slurred speech of someone with a TBI. Deciding whether conduct had such an effect requires consideration of the personal circumstances of the person with disability, the environment in which the conduct takes place and whether it is reasonable for the conduct to have that effect (para.7.18).

11–018

Victimisation

Victimisation occurs when a person with a disability is subjected to a "detriment" because of making (or supporting someone in making) a complaint about discrimination (para.9.2). This includes having done a "protected act", defined as any of the following: bringing proceedings under the Act; giving evidence or information in connection with proceedings under the Act; doing anything related to the provisions of the Act; making an allegation that another person has done something in breach of the Act; or making or seeking a "relevant pay disclosure" to or from a current or former colleague (para.9.5). The resultant "detriment" is defined broadly including being rejected for promotion, denied an opportunity, excluded from training opportunities, overlooked in allocation of discretionary bonuses or performance-related awards (para.9.8) or a threat which a complainant takes (and it is reasonable for them to take) seriously (para.9.9).

11–019

It is also unlawful to instruct someone to discriminate or to help, cause or induce (or to attempt to cause or induce) another person to discriminate against or harass a third person because of a protected characteristic or to victimise a third person because they have done a protected act (paras 9.16–9.17). It is unlawful knowingly to help someone to discriminate against, harass or victimise another person (para.9.5). Employers and employees in the public sector in the UK also have additional responsibilities under the Public Sector Equality Duty.

Public Sector Equality Duty and positive action

The Public Sector Equality Duty requires public bodies to consider the needs of all individuals in their day-to-day work—in shaping policy, delivering services and in relation to their own employees, so that policies and services are appropriate and accessible to all and meet different people's needs (Government Equality Office, 2011). The Equality Duty has three aims, requiring public bodies to have due regard to the need to:

11–020

- eliminate unlawful discrimination, harassment, victimisation and any other conduct prohibited by the Act;
- advance equality of opportunity between people who share a protected characteristic and people who do not share it; and

- foster good relations between people who share a protected characteristic and people who do not share it.

"Advancing equality of opportunity" involves consideration of the need to: remove or minimise disadvantages suffered by people due to a protected characteristic; meet the needs of people with a protected characteristic; and encourage people with a protected characteristic to participate in public life or in other activities where participation is low (Government Equality Office, 2011). All public bodies are expected to recognise that the needs of people with a disability differ from those of non-disabled people and to take this into account in policies or services. This includes making reasonable adjustments or treating disabled people better than non-disabled people in order to meet their needs.

The Act also permits employers to take voluntary positive action to help to alleviate disadvantage in the labour market by groups who share a protected characteristic (para.12.9). Such action may be taken when an employer reasonably thinks that people who share a protected characteristic: experience a disadvantage connected to that characteristic; have needs that are different from the needs of persons without that characteristic; or have disproportionately low participation in an activity compared to others without that characteristic (para.12.11). Examples of positive action include exclusive training, support and mentoring, creation of a work-based support group, providing bursaries to train for a profession where participation is disproportionately low and reserving training course places for people with a protected characteristic (para.12.19).

As it is not unlawful to treat a person with disability more favourably than a "non-disabled" person, an employer can, if they wish, lawfully restrict recruitment, training and promotion to people with disability (para.12.32). In order to achieve equality of opportunity between people with different disabilities, an employer can take positive action to overcome disadvantage, meet different needs or increase participation of people with a specific type of disability but not others (para.12.33). However, any actions which do not meet the stated requirements for positive action could be unlawful (see para.12.35).

Obligations of employers

11–021 An employer has obligations not to discriminate against, victimise or harass job applicants and employees (para.10.6). The summary of employers' obligations below is again taken from the Equality Act 2010 Employment Statutory Code of Practice (EHRC, 2011).

Selection

11–022 In selection the Act seeks to ensure that applicants with a disability are assessed objectively for their ability to do the job in question and not rejected because of their disability. Employers must not discriminate against or victimise job applicants (para.10.7) in:

- the arrangements they make for deciding who should be offered employment;

- in the terms on which they offer employment; or
- by not offering employment to the applicant.

Selection "arrangements" refer to all policies, criteria and practices used in the recruitment process including job advertisements, the application process and interview stage, and not just the decision-making process (para.10.8). Employers have a duty to make reasonable adjustments in recruitment and selection. This might mean providing and accepting information in accessible formats and amending policies and procedures to ensure that applicants with a disability are not at a substantial disadvantage (para.10.18). With the exception of enquiries to determine reasonable adjustments necessary to assess a person's suitability for the job, employers should not make enquiries about disability or health before the offer of a job is made (para.10.10). Information on disability obtained for the purpose of making adjustments in selection should, as far as possible, be held separately and not form any part of decision-making about a job offer (para.10.29).

It is unlawful for an employer (or their agent or employee) to ask a job applicant about their disability or health until the applicant has been offered a job—this includes questions about previous sickness absence that relate to disability (para.10.25). An employer cannot refer an applicant to an OH practitioner or ask an applicant to fill in an OH questionnaire before a job offer is made (para.10.26) except in six specific circumstances: in making reasonable adjustment in recruitment (paras 10.29–10.31), to monitor diversity (para.10.32), to implement positive action (para.10.33), to demonstrate an occupational requirement if having a specific disability is a job requirement (para.10.34), for purposes of national security (para.10.35) or to determine a person's ability (with adjustments, as required), to carry out a function intrinsic to the job (para.10.36).

When an applicant voluntarily discloses information about a disability, the employer must ensure that they only ask further questions about reasonable adjustments required to enable the person to carry out an intrinsic function of the job (para.10.37). Although job offers can be made conditional on satisfactory responses to pre-employment disability or health enquiries or satisfactory health checks, employers must ensure they do not discriminate against an applicant with a disability on the basis of any such response. For example, it will amount to direct discrimination to reject an applicant purely on the grounds that a health check reveals that they have a disability. Employers should also consider whether there are reasonable adjustments that should be made in relation to any disability disclosed by these enquiries or checks (para.10.39).

Ongoing employment and adjustments

Once selected, employers must not discriminate against an employee with a disability: in the terms of employment; in access to opportunities (e.g. promotion, transfer, training or any other benefit); through dismissal (including expiry of a fixed-term contract); or any other detriment (paras 10.11–10.13). Policies and procedures may need to be amended to ensure that employees with a disability are not put at a substantial disadvantage. The duty to make reasonable adjustments applies to all stages of employment and such adjustments should be

11–023

implemented in a timely fashion (para.6.32). In some cases a reasonable adjustment will not succeed without the cooperation of co-workers. Subject to confidentiality, employers must ensure that this happens. If other staff are obstructive or unhelpful, an employer is expected to deal with this appropriately (para.6.35).

Examples of steps it might be reasonable for employers to take include (para.6.33):

- Making adjustments to premises.
- Providing information in accessible formats.
- Allocating some of the disabled person's duties to another worker.
- Altering the disabled worker's hours of work or training.
- Transferring the disabled worker to fill an existing vacancy.
- Assignment to a different place of work or training or arranging home-working.
- Allowing absence to attend for rehabilitation, assessment or treatment.
- Giving, or arranging for, training or mentoring (for a person with disability or others).
- Acquiring or modifying equipment.
- Modifying procedures for testing or assessment.
- Providing a reader or interpreter.
- Providing supervision or other support.
- Allowing a disabled worker to take a period of disability leave.
- Participating in supported employment schemes.
- Employing a support worker to assist a disabled worker.
- Modifying disciplinary or grievance procedures for a disabled worker.
- Adjusting redundancy selection criteria for a disabled worker.
- Modifying performance-related pay arrangements for a disabled worker.

An employee with concerns about discrimination is advised, as far as possible, to raise this first with the employer, who should investigate whether there is any substance to the complaint and, if so, whether it can be resolved (para.15.5). Employees need to be aware that there may be time-limits within which a claim has to be made (paras 15.20–15.31).

Obligations in higher and further education

11–024 The Equality Act applies to further or higher education based on the principle that students with a protected characteristic should not be discriminated against and that education may need to be provided in a different way (including on more favourable terms), so that they can receive the same standard of education, as far as this is possible (EHRC, 2014). The legal requirements and discrimination relating to students applying to or in further and higher education parallel those for employment. The summary below is taken from the Equality Act 2010 Technical Guidance on Further and Higher Education (EHRC, 2014).

As in employment, disability discrimination in education can be direct (EHRC, 2014 paras 4.1–4.48), indirect (paras 5.1–5.40) or as result of something arising in consequence of disability (paras 6.1–6.21). With respect to the latter some such consequences are obvious (e.g. unable to walk unaided), others less so (e.g. unable to concentrate for long periods, need for regular breaks or for instructions to be repeated) (para.6.9), as is often the case with hidden disabilities arising from TBI.

The duty to make reasonable adjustments requires education providers to take positive steps to ensure that students with a disability can participate fully in education and enjoy related benefits, facilities and services as close as is reasonably possible to that offered to other students (para.7.3). This applies to potential and actual applicants and at all stages of education (para.7.18). In education this duty is "anticipatory", requiring consideration of, and action in relation to, barriers that impede people with a disability prior to an individual seeking access (para.7.19). Failure to anticipate such needs may render it too late to comply with the duty to make adjustments (para.7.20). The duty is ongoing; when an initial step is no longer sufficient further adjustments might be required (paras 7.26–7.27). When a provision, criterion or practice places students with a disability at substantial disadvantage, providers must take such steps as it is reasonable for them to have to take, in all the circumstances, so that it no longer has such an effect. This may mean waiving a criterion, amending a practice to allow exceptions or abandoning it all together (para.7.31).

As public bodies, most further and higher education institutions will also have additional obligations under the Public Sector Equality Duty (para.10.8). This proactive duty is designed to enable institutions to identify and tackle inequalities arising from the way they act and to improve education outcomes for those with protected characteristics (para.10.45). In addition, they may wish to consider positive action to seek to ensure that all sections of the community are able to benefit from the education, facilities, benefits and services that they provide (para.10.43). If desired it can be lawful to restrict courses, benefits, facilities or services to people with a disability, or to offer them on more favourable terms, provided such action meets the stated requirements (para.10.44).

11–025

In essence, the Act says that it is unlawful for a further or higher education institution to discriminate against or victimise a person with a disability (para.10.5) in the arrangements it makes for deciding who is offered admission, the terms of admission, by not admitting a person, in the way it provides education, in the way it affords access to a benefit, facility or service, by not providing education, by not affording access to a benefit, facility or service, by excluding the student, and by subjecting the student to any other detriment (para.10.5).

As in employment, discrimination can arise both at selection and for current students.

Selection

It is unlawful to discriminate both in admission processes and in how courses are set up. The latter includes course design/requirements, marketing, open days, campus tours, summer schools, taster sessions, mentoring schemes, recruitment fairs/activities, applications, interviews and tests, and in informal admission processes (para.10.10). In all of the above reasonable adjustments should be made for applicants with a disability (para.10.14), who, if selected, should not be

11–026

offered admission on less favourable terms (para.10.16). Any requirement that is not "a proportionate means of achieving a legitimate aim" may be discriminatory (e.g. stating that a certain personal, medical or health-related characteristic is required or preferred) if this is not necessary or if reasonable adjustments could be made for an applicant with a disability to meet that requirement (para.10.19).

Applying blanket policies that do not take into account individual circumstances or that do not consider reasonable adjustments may result in discrimination (para.10.20), as can the way in which a person's ability to meet course requirements and criteria is assessed (para.10.21). This includes making reasonable adjustments to course requirements unless they are a competence standard (para.10.23). Education providers must consider its duty to make reasonable adjustments before rejecting an applicant with a disability (para.10.24).

Current students

11–027 The duties under the Equality Act cover all of the services, facilities and benefits provided or offered to students, not just the specific teaching and examination component of education (see para.10.25). It is unlawful to provide education or access to any benefit, facility or service in such a way that students with a disability cannot access them (para.10.26). The reasonable adjustment requirements are wide-ranging and include changes to provisions, criteria or practices, the provision of auxiliary aids and services and making adjustments to physical features (para.10.35). However, it is important to be aware that a provision, criterion or practice would not normally include a "competence standard" (para.7.31).

A competence standard is defined as "an academic, medical, or other standard applied for the purpose of determining whether or not a person has a particular level of competence or ability" (paras 7.33–7.34). It is important to note that a condition that a person can do something within a certain period of time will not be a competence standard if time does not determine a particular level of competence (para.7.35). Furthermore, whilst the duty to make adjustments does not include altering a competence standard (para.7.37), it does apply to the process by which competence is assessed. As such, an education provider has a duty to consider whether or not a reasonable adjustment could be made to some aspect of the process by which it assesses a competence standard (para.7.38).

Where there is an adjustment that could reasonably be put in place in order to reduce a disadvantage, it is not sufficient to take some lesser step (para.7.57). Whilst it is recognised that there may be no steps that it would be reasonable to take to make education, benefits, facilities or services accessible, this is likely to be rare (para.7.60).

Students who believe that their education provider has committed an unlawful act against them may bring civil proceedings. However, it may be appropriate first to see if concerns can be resolved directly with the provider (e.g. using complaints procedure) or through the Office of the Independent Adjudicator (OIA) (see paras 15.8–15.10). It is important to be aware that making a claim may be subject to time limits from the date of the act or when the person became aware that such an act had occurred (see paras 15.16–15.26).

Disability discrimination in vocational rehabilitation practice

As recognised by the Select Committee on the Equality Act 2010 and Disability (2016), integrating disability legislation with that of other protected characteristics "ignores a crucial distinction" between disability and other protected characteristics under the Act, for whom equality of opportunity is largely achieved by equality of treatment. In contrast, equality for people with a disability often requires different treatment. It is noted that in evidence submitted by the Trades Union Congress it is suggested that employers "struggle with the concept of treating disabled people more favourably to achieve equality in practice" and by the Disability Law Service that "many employers do not understand that they can, and should treat disabled people more favourably than others when making adjustments" under the Act. The Select Committee (2016) report provides evidence of problems in obtaining reasonable adjustments "emanating from almost every part of society" (para.196). Some employers were reported to have responded to requests for adjustments by making an employee redundant or offering a termination package as their first response (para.197). Some were noted to have poor understanding of the duty to make reasonable adjustments (paras 204–206), some still saw this as showing "favouritism" (para.207) and some believed that the need to make adjustments applied only to physical and sensory disabilities not "hidden" disabilities (para.208), of which TBI is, of course, a primary example.

In the UK the Women and Equalities Committee (2019a) note repeated reports of barriers to enforcing rights under the Equality Act 2010, which is often breached without challenge. "… what little enforcement is happening is insufficient to tackle the systemic or routine discrimination that too many people experience as a simple fact of life". Whilst preserving the right of individuals to challenge discrimination in the courts, the need for a fundamental shift in the enforcement of the Act is highlighted, so that this is only rarely needed. In a separate report the Women and Equalities Committee (2019b) raise serious concerns about allegations of unlawful discrimination and harassment in the workplace being routinely covered up by employers with legally drafted non-disclosure agreements (NDAs). It is noted that difficulties in pursuing a legal case and the imbalance of power between employers and employees means that employees feel they have little choice but to reach a settlement that prohibits them from speaking out. However, those signing a NDA may find it difficult to work in the same sector again, may suffer psychological damage (which may affect ability to work) and some suffer financially as a result of losing their job and bringing a case against an employer. Other victims may be reluctant to report their experiences for fear of losing their job. It is concluded that "NDAs should not be used to silence victims of discrimination and harassment and that employers and their legal advisers should not be complicit in using NDAs to cover up allegations of unlawful acts". Recommendations for Government action to limit the use of NDAs to cover up discrimination are proposed.

In providing VR interventions to assist people in returning to and retaining employment or another occupation, it is highly likely that disability discrimination will be encountered. For example in providing "Working Out", a brain injury vocational rehabilitation programme run by the Community Head Injury Service,

11–028

RETURN TO WORK AND VOCATIONAL REHABILITATION

Buckinghamshire Healthcare NHS Trust, we have encountered many examples of disability-related discrimination, both in relation to employment/voluntary work and in further and higher education.

In employment

11–029   Examples of apparent disability discrimination have occurred when people have applied for both paid and voluntary work. Sometimes this has been blatant, with our work placement consultant being told by one senior executive with a relative with ABI that on this basis they would not employ anyone with ABI and, on another occasion, on enquiring about voluntary work being told "we've already got one of those"! After visiting a supermarket about possible work experience with a person who has use of one arm, we received a telephone call from the health and safety department saying they cannot accommodate a person with one arm as this would be too risky, without any consideration of reasonable adjustments. On visiting a public sector employer, a manager commented that now was not the right time and suggested waiting until another vacancy arose, but no response was received to our contact or the person's application to this vacancy. On other occasions people have applied to employers who are signed up to the "two ticks" scheme, under which an interview is guaranteed if applicants meet the minimum criteria, and yet no interview was forthcoming. Follow-up enquiries with employers are often ignored or dismissed on broad or questionable grounds (e.g. there were "better candidates for the role"). In practice, suspicions of discrimination are often difficult to prove and usually go unchallenged.

Discrimination encountered by staff on the Working Out programme has included the following: people being offered a salary below the minimum wage; employers ignoring advice about voluntary work or permitted earnings rules, thereby putting benefits at risk; employers failing to explore and make work adjustments in spite of disability disclosure; pressure on people to work overtime in spite of disclosure of fatigue, thereby putting their health and job at risk; refusing requests to meet our staff to explain difficulties; refusing to allow staff to support people with a disability at work even when a job is at risk; very slow response to concerns or grievances, thereby exacerbating peoples' anxiety and distress.

Some employers can be actively hostile. A person with social communication difficulties was reported to have been taken advantage of, leading to a claim of gross misconduct. The person wanted support at the disciplinary hearing, but HR would not allow this, even when asked to consider this as a reasonable adjustment. Following a letter outlining the person's difficulties and requesting OH input, this was agreed "reluctantly", leading to a joint discussion with HR about the person's capability to carry out the role and possible adjustments. HR remained "very hostile" and the disciplinary meeting took place eventually without our input, as it was felt pushing for this could have adversely affected the outcome. Whilst the person remained in work, the six-month process was highly stressful.

11–030   Even when thwarted in our efforts to support people with ABI, contact with employers may still be beneficial as they are aware of the involvement of people with knowledge of their employees' rights. On one occasion a staff member was told "I don't care who you are, I don't want to know who you are", yet the employer's attitude changed and more positive relationships were established. Whilst we can advise and support people with a disability and intervene, as appropriate, on their behalf to explain their needs and recommend adjustments, this can still be very stressful and people with ABI without access to VR support commonly struggle to secure the reasonable adjustments that they need.

Employees have a range of options if they believe that their rights under the Equality Act are not being realised, such as raising informal concerns, taking out a formal grievance and/or making a claim to an employment tribunal. It is vital to ensure that anyone considering raising concerns is aware of appropriate sources of advice and support such as OH and independent advice, advocacy and support (e.g. Trade Union, Citizen's Advice Bureau, Equality and Human Rights Commission, legal advice), particularly as raising concerns can lead to an escalation of discriminatory practices. If the person chooses to pursue action against their employer, this is likely to lead to a great deal of stress and will require significant ongoing support. A person contacted us to report that he was facing dismissal following alleged gross misconduct relating to a reporting error. We intervened to explain that the error was likely to reflect the effects of TBI (rather than misconduct). We completed a vocational assessment and made recommendations about adjustments. However, following re-organisation, the person was redeployed in an alternative role and appeared to be the subject of "micro-management", which undermined his self-confidence. Support in adjusting to and maintaining the new role was provided as part of broader psychological therapy monthly for two years, reducing gradually to quarterly, six-monthly and annually over several years (see Example D, in Tyerman et al., 2017).

Even when a person with TBI can cope cognitively with the process and emotionally with the stress, few can afford to pay for legal advice in order to take an employer to a tribunal, particularly in the context of welfare changes that "have disproportionately and adversely affected the rights of people with disabilities" (Committee on the Rights of People with Disabilities, 2016). Access to justice for people in relation to disability discrimination has not been helped by the imposition of tribunal fees, withdrawing legal aid and cost rule changes (Select Committee, 2016), with a 49% reduction in claims to employment tribunals noted from 2012–2015. As such, supporting a person in securing alternative employment with a new employer who accepts the person's disability and is happy to make adjustments is often a safer and preferable option. However, this often leaves the discrimination unchallenged.

Further and higher education

Our experience of the support for people with a disability in further and higher education has usually been positive, but this has not always been the case. For example, a person applied for a post-graduate certificate in education course and disclosed his ABI. He was told he would not be able to do the course, with no knowledge of his difficulties and no consideration of what adjustments could be made to accommodate his needs. He is now working as a teacher!

11–031

Our experience is that most education providers are supportive with established disability support policies and services providing advice, assessments (e.g. for dyslexia) and recommendations for adjustments, including learning support equipment such as computer hardware (e.g. laptops, printers, scanners), software (e.g. reading and speech recognition), tape recorder etc. However, learning support services will require guidance on specific brain injury needs and additional adjustment recommendations are often required, for example, in non-standard teaching (e.g. practical skills training sessions) and support for deadline extensions on full-time professional training courses. As such, ongoing monitoring by the VR practitioner may be advisable, thereby allowing for timely additional recommendations, as required. Furthermore, individual departments may be reluctant or slow to implement core learning support or additional VR recommendations. Some appear unaware of their responsibilities to take all reasonable steps to implement adjustments to enable people with a disability to have equality of access (as far as this is possible). For example, some departments mistakenly insist that standard course teaching and assessment processes cannot be changed and/or that "everyone has to be treated the same". The latter is a well-recognised misunderstanding of the Equality Act with respect to disability (Government Equality Office, 2011; Select Committee, 2016).

As in employment, when people raise concerns, they can be subjected to a wide range of detrimental treatment, including further discrimination, harassment and victimisation. Even if the response to raising concerns does not involve further discrimination, complex and protracted appeals and complaints procedures and high levels of resultant stress make it very difficult for anyone with a disability to pursue formal proceedings whilst continuing with their studies. Furthermore, even when the evidence appears to be clear cut, this is no guarantee of a positive outcome in terms of course progression raising concerns about discrimination. As such, the potential benefits need to be weighed carefully against the potential risks and the student would be well advised to consult student support and/or take legal advice, particularly if the detrimental treatment involves harassment and/or victimisation. If the concerns relate to a lack of effective adjustments then working with disability support services to review, recommend and support the implementation of any additional adjustments may involve less risk and stress than taking formal action. As in employment, if a student chooses to pursue a formal complaint or legal claim, they are likely to require a great deal of support over a prolonged period.

3. VOCATIONAL ASSESSMENT

What is vocational assessment?

11-032 Vocational assessment (VA) has been defined as a "global appraisal of an individual's work/training background, general functional capacities and social/behavioural characteristics" and includes "an evaluation of medical factors, psychological makeup, educational background, social behaviours, attitudes, values, work skills and abilities" (Wesolek and McFarlane, 1992). As such, VA is a broad term encompassing a wide range of assessments relating to vocational strengths, weaknesses, needs and prospects.

As noted in recommendations for best practice in VA and VR for people with long-term neurological conditions (BSRM, 2010), VA for people with a neurological condition (including TBI) should take into account the following: the person's personal and family circumstances; an evaluation of motor, sensory, communication and cognitive function; behavioural control and emotional status; the effects of current medication and other interventions; the demands of the current or desired occupation; the current skills and employment assets of the individual; the practical obstacles to accessing and undertaking that occupation; and potential work solutions to facilitate successful job performance (BSRM, 2010). As such, VA for people with a neurological condition including TBI may draw on a combination of many components, depending on the specific condition, individual circumstances and specific vocational needs (BSRM, 2010), as detailed below:

- Interview with person (e.g. educational, vocational, medical and rehabilitation history, current difficulties, work experience, and current vocational interests/aspirations).
- Interview, as appropriate, with a close relative to assist the person in providing a full history, in describing needs and in identifying relevant personal/family circumstances.
- Review of past clinical information including previous assessment or rehabilitation reports and/or consultation with health or other practitioners with knowledge both of the person's current difficulties and of their overall health status (e.g. from the GP).
- Formal interview, testing and/or examination of work-related skills (e.g. motor, sensory, cognitive, communication, educational and social), work capacity (e.g. strength, endurance, fatigue etc) and related management/coping strategies.
- Psychological adjustment as expressed, whenever possible, either in the workplace or on work-related activities.
- Structured evaluation and/or ratings of work attitude, performance and behaviours based on direct observation and/or feedback/reports of current or recent work or placements.
- Assessment of obstacles that might prevent a person from getting to work, accessing facilities at work and/or undertaking a specific work role.
- Review of the requirements of a job (e.g. job description/person specification).
- Worksite assessment to evaluate the actual requirements of a work role, performance in the role and/or work adjustments to enable a person to undertake the work role.
- Consideration of training programmes to update current and/or develop new skills, including how training might be adapted to meet the needs of the individual.
- Careers guidance and/or job matching to identify alternative occupation/job goal.

- Assessment of the financial consequences of a reduction or withdrawal from work.

11-033 The contribution of neuropsychological evaluation to vocational planning was reviewed in detail by Uomoto (2000). Whilst neuropsychological evaluations were considered to assist decision-making about jobs and appropriate job tasks, their predictive limitations were acknowledged. As such, in-vivo community assessment (e.g. work trials) were advocated to augment neuropsychological assessments in order to "test the limits" and evaluate at what point neuropsychological difficulties interfere with job performance in the workplace (Uomoto, 2000). Given the difficulty in generalising to the workplace, the need to simulate closely the actual work situation is stressed. Specific vocational implications of executive dysfunction are identified:

(1) utilising work trials, "job stations" or "on-the-job" training (to examine new learning, help in assessing the person's ability to adjust to novel situations and perform multiple tasks simultaneously and to observe how problem-solving deficits impede job performance);
(2) utilising familiar tasks thereby minimising the need for new learning;
(3) training in a method of problem-solving that is job or task specific (due to difficulty in transferring learned skills from one group of tasks or job setting to another); and
(4) supervision by co-workers or others for people with problem-solving deficits (Uomoto, 2000).

It is suggested that job coaches or co-worker trainers provide feedback and cues to reduce errors. The need to assess the meaning of work for the individual, work-related goals, perceptions of work competency and readiness and anticipated challenges has been stressed (Stergiou et al., 2012), as has the need to assess general and work-related self-efficacy (e.g. in job search) (Tsauosides et al., 2009).

Whilst the specific assessment components will vary for different vocational needs (BSRM, 2010), an example of an ABI vocational assessment process is provided by the Working Out Programme (Tyerman et al., 2008).

Illustrative acquired brain injury vocational assessment programme

11-034 All persons referred to the Working Out Programme are seen first for an initial suitability assessment, as outlined by Tyerman et al. (2008). This comprises a Brain Injury Background Interview Schedule, a Head Injury Problem Schedule, a Head Injury Semantic Differential scale (renamed the Brain Injury Well-being Index), Hospital Anxiety and Depression Scale and a Family Screening Assessment (when appropriate). This provides a detailed social, clinical and work history and a profile of current problems and the person's work situation, from which individual VA needs are identified (Tyerman et al., 2008). The VA programme combines vocational interviews, formal assessments (typically neuropsychological and occupational therapy plus additional medical, physiotherapy, speech and language, as needed), attendance at a weekly work preparation group, self-ratings and staff observations and ratings of work attitude, performance and behaviour on practical community VR activities and, when appropriate, a vocational guidance interview.

A neuropsychological assessment is routinely undertaken unless recently completed elsewhere, in which case only selected tests are administered. Assessment has typically included tests of the following: general intellectual ability (i.e. Wechsler Adult Intelligence Scale); memory and information processing (i.e. BIRT Memory and Information Processing Battery) and attention/executive function including the Test of Everyday Attention; Trail Making Test; and Modified Six Elements or other tests from the Behavioural Assessment of the Dysexecutive Syndrome (BADS) or Delis Kaplan Executive Function System (D-KEFS), plus other language, perceptual and spatial skills, as appropriate (Tyerman et al., 2008). Additional tests of executive function (including Key search and Zoo Map from the BADS, Hayling and Brixton from the D-KEFS) and of social cognition have been added subsequently (e.g. Benton Facial Recognition Test; Test of Awareness of Social Inference (TASIT); Recognition of Faux Pas Test; Reading the Mind in the Eyes Test; Social Situations Task; Bangor Gamble Task, see Yeates et al. (2016).

The Chessington Occupational Therapy Neurological Assessment Battery (COTNAB) (Tyerman et al., 1986) was originally designed specifically for assessing RtW after TBI. The battery comprises 12 sub-tests, three in each of four functional areas: visual perception (overlapping figures, hidden figures and sequencing); constructional ability (2D construction, 3D construction and block printing); sensory motor ability (stereognosis, dexterity and coordination); and ability to follow instructions (written, visual and spoken instructions). The assessment provides separate ability and time grades and combined overall performance grades for each sub-test.

Whilst formal assessments clarify the nature of cognitive, motor and other difficulties, the assessment of work attitude, performance and behaviour, as reported and/or observed on practical work activities, is noted to be of at least equal importance (Tyerman et al., 2008). As such, people on assessment typically attend a weekly work preparation group, one or more community-based VR activities and/or an individual assessment project set up in the workplace, in the centre, in a community setting or at home. This enables staff to observe work attitude, performance and behaviour and complete a structured "functional work assessment" and two vocational rating scales: Functional Assessment Inventory (FAI) (Crew and Athelstan, 1981) and Work Personality Profile (WPP) (Bolton and Roessler, 1986).

11–035

The FAI has 30 items of vocational strengths/limitations rated on a four-point scale from 0 (no significant impairment) to 3 (severe impairment) across seven factors:

- "adaptive behaviour"—behaviour, interaction, work habits and social support;
- "motor functioning"—hand/arm function and motor speed;
- "cognition"—learning, reading/writing, memory and perception;
- "physical condition"—mobility, exertion, endurance, sickness and stability of condition;

- "communication"—hearing, speech and language;
- "vocational qualifications"—work history, acceptability, attractiveness, skills, economic disincentives, access to job opportunities and need for special working conditions; and
- "vision"—visual impairment.

Normative data is reported for 1,716 persons consulting VR counsellors in the US.

The WPP has 58 items relating to work attitudes, values, habits and behaviours, rated on a four-point scale from 4 ("a definite strength, an employment asset") to 1 ("a problem area" which "will definitely limit the chance for employment") across five factors:

- "task orientation"—cognitive skills and good work habits (e.g. learning, initiative, independence, adaptability, responsibility);
- "social skills"—interaction with co-workers (e.g. appropriately sociable, outgoing, friendly and emotionally expressive);
- "work motivation"—willingness to accept work assignments, move readily to new tasks, and work at routine jobs without complaining;
- "work conformance"—appropriate behaviour at work with respect to "good judgment" in the expression of negative behaviour and the ability to exercise an even-temper and "controlled self-presentation"; and
- "personal presentation"—interaction with supervisory personnel and attention to personal hygiene and appearance.

The WPP was standardised on 243 persons receiving vocational rehabilitation in the US.

11-036 When a person has recently been in work or on a work placement, feedback will normally be sought from past employers (including, when appropriate, completion of the above vocational rating scales). The vocational guidance interview undertaken by the work placement consultant provides an in-depth assessment of educational history, vocational qualifications, pre-injury employment (including profiling of past jobs), vocational interests/aspirations and leisure/social interests. This is balanced by the understanding of vocational restrictions arising from TBI, as highlighted by the other assessments.

The difficulties experienced by 45 people with severe TBI (median post-traumatic amnesia 42 days) seen for assessment in the pilot phase of the Working Out programme at on average 41 months post-injury were extensive (Tyerman and Young, 1999; 2000). The neuropsychological tests identified considerable cognitive impairment (notably in psychomotor speed, attention, speed of information processing, verbal memory/learning and executive function). Whilst those who were able to RtW successfully scored higher on almost all tests than those who did not, no significant differences were found on any of the neuropsychological tests. The COTNAB confirmed difficulties affecting all four sections (visual perception; constructional ability; sensory motor ability; and following instructions). The proportion scoring more than one standard deviation below the mean in overall performance on individual tests ranged from 31% to 88% (with over half scoring below average on seven of 12 tests) but with the low scores on "dexterity" and "co-ordination" the most striking. In contrast with the neuropsychological tests, those returning to work did score significantly higher (p<0.01) on two COTNAB constructional tests (Tyerman and Young, 1999; 2000).

Staff ratings on the vocational ratings scales were compared with normative data for people with all forms of disability: on the FAI staff rated the participants as having greater problems on four of the seven factors—adaptive behaviour, cognition, physical condition and vocational qualifications. Compared with self-rating, staff rated significantly greater problems on three factors—adaptive behaviour, physical condition and vocational qualifications. On the WPP staff ratings were significantly lower than the normative group on all factors (i.e. task orientation, social skills, work motivation, work conformance and personal presentation). Compared with self-ratings, staff ratings were significantly less positive on all five WPP factors. Those returning to employment on programme completion were rated significantly more positively on four factors of the FAI (motor function, cognitive function, physical condition and vocational qualifications) and on two factors of the WPP (task orientation and social skills) with two others (i.e. work motivation and personal presentation) nearing statistical significance.

Experience on the Working Out programme is that vocational rating scales such as the FAI and WPP are of value in providing a structured assessment of work attitudes, performance and behaviour. The greater difficulties recorded by staff endorses the value of direct observation in parallel with self report, both in assessing work potential and in facilitating dialogue about related interventions in VR. As illustrated in VR examples (Tyerman et al., 2008; 2017), observations of practical work performance provides valuable indications of how underlying ABI difficulties restrict work skills, but also how they influence, and are influenced by, productivity, confidence and emotional state. They also provide an opportunity to observe concentration and fatigue over an extended period in a busy social environment as opposed to a one-to-one formal assessment session.

Expert neuropsychological assessment and opinion

People with TBI attempting a RtW will often simultaneously be involved in medico-legal compensation claims. Clinical neuropsychologists acting as expert witnesses within civil medico-legal settings will often be asked to comment on a range of issues. These can include: the person's cognitive strengths and weaknesses; their emotional sequelae and how these may affect cognitive functioning; the extent to which an index event and/or other factors contribute to their cognitive and emotional functioning; the extent and duration of any suffering, impairment or disability they may have suffered; their capacity to litigate or manage their financial affairs; the impact that cognitive or emotional impairments have on their daily living skills; any tests, treatment or rehabilitation which might reduce their disabilities, impairments or suffering; the timescale and cost implications of any further tests or treatment; their prognosis.

From a vocational perspective clinical neuropsychologists will frequently be asked their opinion on: the person's capacity for work; how close they may be to their pre-injury work performance levels; the reasonableness or otherwise of the

11–037

amount of time they had off work; the extent to which any injuries are disadvantageous to them in the work environment; what type of work they are capable of currently and in the future. Potential loss of future earnings and the costs associated with the provision of treatment or rehabilitation which might militate against such will often make up a substantial part of a compensation claim. The clinical neuropsychologists' opinion on these vocational questions may therefore be of substantial medico-legal importance.

In many medico-legal contexts these types of questions will often fall within the expertise of a clinical neuropsychologist. Specialist vocational assessment and opinion is therefore only sought in a minority of cases. Also the availability of specialist ABI vocational rehabilitation services within the UK is very limited. Treatment recommendations, outside of those that would be typically made by clinical neuropsychologists, may therefore be restricted to a few areas of the country where specialist ABI VR is available. This is made even more likely in the light of VR at distance being a viable treatment option only in very rare circumstances.

11–038 Specialist vocational opinion is therefore normally only sought when cases raise work-related issues which are very complex. There are four main areas where it is likely that a clinical neuropsychologist or other expert health clinicians will have insufficient understanding of the work issues under question and therefore where a specialist vocational assessment may be required:

(1) When the person is young and has yet to establish a clear work history. Ascertaining their likely career trajectory and the impact that an index event may have had on this can be particularly difficult in such circumstances. This judgment is further complicated when the person has an atypical educational history, or one which is inconsistent in nature. In such circumstances the career they intended to work towards may appear at odds with their educational attainment but militated by significant non-scholastic strengths like high levels of energy, a strong work ethic, passion and enthusiasm for their work and highly developed interpersonal skills. Such qualities may have led to an "over-achieving" career trajectory when compared to formal academic competencies. Conversely a person with high educational attainment may not, on closer and more expert analysis, have possessed the requisite non-academic qualities required for their anticipated work aspirations.

(2) When there is an unusual discrepancy between a person's apparent work potential and their actual attainment. This may make judgments regarding how realistic future work intentions are much more complex. This might involve someone with high premorbid academic attainment with a modest vocational history in comparison, but who states they intended to pursue more lucrative employment later on in their working life. They may have deliberately chosen to take lower paid jobs in order to gain the appropriate experience required for a more lucrative career later on or as a temporary arrangement with the anticipation of pursuing more lucrative work when personal circumstances became more favourable (e.g. when they no longer had a substantial caring role within their family). Conversely the discrepancy might also include those with more modest intellectual skills

but who were "overachieving" vocationally before an index event and who anticipated even greater career advancement.

(3) When people have unusual jobs without a clear or conventional career trajectory. This might involve jobs with a very wide range of responsibilities requiring very disparate abilities. Such jobs may be more financially rewarding than similar jobs with a more restricted range of responsibilities. Similarly, jobs with very high levels of specialism may make judgments about the likelihood or type of career progression very difficult.

(4) When people have highly demanding job roles, working long hours and/or at a very high intensity and where even very subtle or mild changes to their work capacity may lead to severe disability within the work place and/or a substantial impact on their career advancement. In such circumstances any, even very small impairment, may mean that: they are no longer able to fulfil their current work responsibilities; there is insufficient flexibility or "wiggle room" in their work role to accommodate such changes; and/or judgments regarding what alternative roles may be possible in the future are highly complex and nuanced.

4. VOCATIONAL REHABILITATION

11–039 Vocational rehabilitation (VR) is a key provision in implementing the right to work for people with disability, with States required to enable persons with disabilities to have effective access to technical and vocational training and rehabilitation (Office of the United Nations High Commissioner for Human Rights, 2012). Our experience of running a specialist ABI VR programme is that different interventions are best suited to different vocational needs. A wide range of models have been developed to address vocational needs for people after ABI including neurorehabilitation services with integrated or added VR elements, VR models adapted for TBI/ABI, case coordination models, consumer-directed models and hybrid models combining different approaches (Tyerman, 2012). Key illustrative models will be discussed in the context of different vocational needs—supported return to previous work, preparation for alternative employment, alternative occupation and long-term job retention.

Supported return to previous work

11–040 Interventions to support return to previous work (RtPW) may include the following: identifying vocational goals; education about work-related difficulties; development of required skills and behaviours; restoring work-related routines (e.g. travel); building up attention, work/study tolerance, stamina and confidence; advice about aids, assistive technology and coping strategies; and working on material drawn from, or relevant to, the person's work (BSRM, 2010). This is typically followed by a gradual and supported re-orientation to the workplace (Tyerman, 2012). An early example of interventions to support people with TBI in a managed return to previous work under "special conditions" following post-acute rehabilitation was reported by Johnson (1987) at Addenbrooke's Hospital, Cambridge, UK. This might include part-time work, "easier" work (i.e.

easier job or restricted duties), a work trial (same or different job), an informal return (unpaid, reduced/flexible hours), liaison with employers, training to address specific work problems, workplace support (e.g. by a work colleague) and/or "tolerance" (e.g. about unscheduled days off). A successful RtW was achieved by 38% of people with severe TBI—a further 28% attempted but failed to RtW. In a 10-year follow-up 34% were employed full-time, 10% part-time with 6% in sheltered work (Johnson, 1998).

A "Vocational Case Coordinator" model at the Mayo Medical Centre, Minnesota, integrated medical and VR services through an ABI vocational coordinator. Key elements of the role include the integration of vocational goals into core rehabilitation, assessing vocational readiness, developing comprehensive RtW plans, providing vocational counselling/evaluation and adjustment to disability counselling, linking with local work rehabilitation centres, completing on-the-job evaluations, educating employers and providing follow-up support (Buffington and Malec, 1997). Of 80 participants with ABI (52 with TBI) 70% were placed within 12 months. In a replication study (138 participants with ABI, 61% TBI, of whom 84% were unemployed and the remainder failing at work), 80% remained in community-based employment one-year post-placement (56% with no support) (Malec and Moessner, 2006). In a related development "resource facilitators" contacted participants every two weeks and organised regular case conferences and focused, when appropriate, on pro-actively engaging former employers in a RtW plan. Employer education, "titrating" RtW schedules and functions and facilitating utilisation of job supports through both clinical and employment specialists were noted to be common strategies (Trexler et al., 2010).

A "client-centred" ABI vocational "case management" model was provided by the Australia Commonwealth Rehabilitation Service in Melbourne, Australia (O'Brien, 2007). People seen at a median of 21 weeks post-onset were allocated a "rehabilitation consultant", with whom they worked for an average of 36 hours. In an audit of 27 files, the minimum number of interventions used was 14. A "work training placement" was rated the most effective, followed by "graded RtW programmes", "teaching compensatory strategies", "coaching people regarding the hidden job market", "vocational counselling" and "coaching regarding work behaviours". Post-placement support was included by telephone (person and employer), scheduled workplace visits, ongoing support/counselling outside work hours and email support. The employment rate for people with ABI completing the programme was 50%.

11–041 A UK example of occupational therapy guided RtPW after TBI in Nottingham is reported by Radford et al. (2013). This involved:

(1) assessing impact of TBI on the participant, family and their roles (e.g. as a worker or student);
(2) educating participants and families about TBI effects and impact on work/education and related strategies;
(3) community reintegration training (e.g. using transport, increasing confidence in community activities);
(4) pre-work training (i.e. help to establish structured routines with gradually increasing activity and opportunities to practice work-related skills); and

(5) liaison with employers, tutors or employment advisors to advise about effects of TBI and to plan/monitor graded RtPW.

A higher proportion (75%) of 40 people with TBI of mixed severity returned to work after the specialist intervention than in a control group (60%) who received less specialist care.

The above programme is consistent with the process of return to previous employment, education or training in UK guidelines on VR for people with ABI (BSRM/Jobcentre Plus/RCP, 2004, paras 8.1–8.9). Central to the recommended process is assessment of readiness to RtW, incorporation of work-related goals and interventions within core ABI rehabilitation, liaison with the employer and other relevant parties (e.g. GP, occupational health) to formulate an agreed RtW plan, ongoing monitoring of progress and proactive review. The RtW plan may incorporate a wide range of potential reasonable adjustments: changes in hours and/or duties; adaptations, equipment and coping strategies; and additional training, supervision and support (see BSRM, 2010, para.5.57). Sources of advice on work adjustments include specialist websites (e.g. the Job Accommodation Network), voluntary groups and government employment services, occupational health and VR services (for example in the UK, the Equality and Human Rights Commission, Employers' Forum on Disability, Health and Safety Executive). A parallel range of support may be required for those seeking to return to education or training (see BSRM, 2010, para.5.61) with joint working with the student disability support service. Proactive review of progress in return to employment, education or training by the VR practitioner is vital to respond to any emergent concerns.

Preparation for new or alternative employment

Some models of VR after TBI are rooted in ABI rehabilitation but with specific VR elements, either integrated within the programme or added as a supplementary phase (Tyerman, 2012). One of the most influential of such models has been the New York University Head Trauma Program (Ben-Yishay et al., 1987). This involved three phases:

11–042

(1) remedial intervention (intensive individual/group work four days a week for 20 weeks, focusing on cognitive remediation, self-awareness/ acceptance and social skills);
(2) guided voluntary occupational trials under the guidance/supervision/ tutoring of a vocational counsellor (3–9 months); and
(3) assistance in finding suitable work, in job familiarisation and, as needed, in making early adjustments to a new work environment.

Of 94 people with very severe TBI entering the programme on average three years post-injury, 84% were considered to have the ability to engage in "productive endeavours" on completion of the occupational work trial phase (63% at a competitive and 21% at a sheltered/subsidised level). "The great majority" were employed over the next three years and employability ratings held up well at three years (Ben-Yishay et al., 1987).

Numerous examples of holistic out-patient ABI programmes with VR elements have been developed, as noted by Tyerman (2012), including in the UK (Wilson et al., 2000). A contrasting approach involves the adaptation of existing VR models for people with TBI or ABI. A primary such model is the supported placement model developed at Virginia Medical College characterised by on-site training, counselling and support by a job coach (Wehman et al., 1988). This has four phases:

(1) job placement (matching job needs to abilities/potential, encouraging communication, establishing travel arrangements/travel training, and analysing the job environment to verify potential obstacles);
(2) job site training and advocacy—behavioural training (e.g. skills, time-keeping, behaviour and communication) and advocacy on behalf of the person (e.g. orientation to workplace, communication between all parties, counselling about work behaviours);
(3) ongoing assessment: evaluation from both the supervisor and the person; and
(4) job retention and "follow along" through regular on-site visits, phone calls, reviews of supervisor evaluations, client progress reports and family/caretaker evaluations.

11–043 Of 53 people referred at on average seven years after severe TBI, 41 were placed in competitive employment, requiring an average of 291 hours of job coaching, with 71% remaining in work at on average 10 months follow-up (Wehman et al., 1990). In a further study of 73 people who required 245 hours of intervention over 18 weeks to achieve "job stabilization", plus 2.24 hours per week of support to enhance job retention over the first year, the total average costs were $10,198 (Wehman et al., 1994). In a long-term follow-up of 59 people with TBI (91.7% severe) the average number of months of employment was 42.58 months with over half working for less than two years but 25% worked for over seven years and 10% for over 12 years (Wehman et al., 2003). A supported placement model has been adopted by several other providers in the US where six of 16 TBI Model Systems programs were reported to use this approach (Hart et al., 2006).

An example of a hybrid model is provided by the flexible, "highly individualized", VR model of the Work Reentry Program at Sharp Memorial Rehabilitation Center, San Diego (Abrams et al., 1993). With a philosophy that there is more than one 'blueprint' for VR after TBI, the programme includes flexible access to elements of both work rehabilitation (i.e. vocational evaluation, simulated work samples, work hardening, 'work adjustment experience', vocational counselling and job seeking/keeping skills) and supported placements (including on-site job coaching and an off-site adjustment/support group). People received typically about 60 hours of input and significantly less (around 41 hours) for those returning to previous employment (Haffey and Abrams, 1991). Of 142 people with TBI (of variable severity), who had been unable to obtain or sustain RTW, 75% obtained employment within the study's 45-month observation period and 55% at the last follow-up (Abrams et al., 1993). Of those successful in RTW, half were working full-time and 75% more than half-time, with 24% returning to their previous employer.

In the UK, Momentum (formerly Rehab UK) programmes in Birmingham, London and Newcastle reported a combined model incorporating supported placements following a centre-based pre-placement VR phase in a three stage process:

- Pre-placement work preparation: focusing on compensatory strategies, work-related social skills, training in numeracy, literacy and information technology, self-awareness/ABI knowledge and identification of "realistic and appealing vocational goals".
- In-situ vocational trial phase: work placements in real settings—sourced, overseen and monitored by a job coach, who supported both the person and the employer.
- Final placement phase: support with job search, job applications/interviews and job coaching into new work role with follow-up support for up to five years.

The following vocational outcomes were reported for 232 people with ABI (62% with TBI) after an average of 50 weeks on the programme: paid competitive employment (41%), mainstream training/education (15%), voluntary work (16%), discharged to other treatment (15%) and withdrew from programme (13%) (Murphy et al., 2006).

In the NHS the Working Out programme provided by the Community Head Injury Service, Buckinghamshire Healthcare NHS Trust, was developed originally for people unable to RtPW after TBI, but broadened subsequently to include ABI and complex long-term job retention interventions. The programme blends ABI rehabilitation and VR through flexible individually-tailored access to four overall service areas: vocational assessment, work preparation, voluntary work trials and supported work placements (Tyerman et al., 2008).

Following specialist assessment (described above), the work preparation phase has integrated elements of VR (i.e. work preparation group, voluntary VR activities in the community, individual work projects and vocational counselling) and core ABI rehabilitation (e.g. educational programme, cognitive rehabilitation group, communication group, psychological support group, and individual psychological therapy). Individually selected voluntary work trials are set up with local employers with on-site job coaching (when required) and off-site support including a fortnightly work-related support group. People are then assisted in finding, applying for and establishing themselves in work with ongoing monitoring and support and on-site job coaching, as required. Once established there is usually a phased withdrawal of support but with ongoing access to the work-related support group and open re-access to further guidance, as required.

In the original research and development phase 40 people with severe TBI completed the programme: 50% returned to paid employment or vocational training with another 35% to "permitted" work or voluntary work, with outcomes maintained at one and two year follow-up (Tyerman and Young, 2000). Of a subsequent consecutive series of 100 people unable to RtPW after ABI seen at a median of 45 months post-injury, 36% returned to paid employment (23%

full-time, 25% part-time) or training/higher education (8%), plus another 30% to alternative unpaid occupations. However, it is important to note that many have required intermittent access to specialist VR support in order to maintain their positive vocational outcomes. This includes those returning to alternatives to paid employment such as voluntary work.

Return to alternative occupation

11-045　An alternative model for those considered to be unsuitable for, or who have been unsuccessful in, other VR programmes is provided by the Clubhouse in the USA. Developed originally to provide peer support for people with mental health conditions, the Clubhouse is reported to have potential in assisting people with ABI in RtW. This is a "consumer-directed, community-based, day programme", "operated by and for its members" (Jacobs, 1997). Staff act in a facilitative role—reviewing progress, establishing goals and identifying resources. Members are involved in practical centre-based tasks within work units selected by participants. Those with the requisite skills are supported in seeking paid work. Over a 3.5 years period 24% progressed to "compensated community work experience", 9% participated in transitional employment and 18% entered competitive employment, of whom half remained employed (Jacobs and De Mello, 1996).

　　Kolakowsky-Hayner and Kreutzer (2001) described a "self-guided therapeutic" RtW program and Niemeier et al. (2010) reported a controlled trial of a Vocational Transitions Program (VTP), a "consumer-driven", "manualized, employability enhancing intervention", for people with ABI attending work-centred clubhouses in Virginia. 20 group sessions include the following:

(1)　discussion of a typical challenge after ABI and how it may affect RtW;
(2)　a brief survey or questionnaire of peoples' experiences;
(3)　a "skit" depicting ways of coping or a compensatory strategy;
(4)　demonstration of strategies and ideas for addressing ABI challenges; and
(5)　"wrap-up" time to reinforce the session.

"Modestly significant" treatment effects were reported: in the VTP group the percentage working increased from 13.5% pre-treatment to 23.1% post-treatment and productivity (i.e. working and/or volunteering) from 75.7% to 80.8%. In contrast, in the control group (n=32) the percentage working fell from 26.9% to 14.3% and productivity from 65.4% to 46.4%.

11-046　The need for VR to facilitate alternatives to employment, either as an interim step towards an eventual RtW or as part of long-term alternative occupation, is critical. Even with extensive specialist VR provision, a significant number of people with ABI will not be able to RtW. Those severely injured as children or as young adults potentially face 50 years of lack of paid employment and need an alternative occupation to add structure and meaning to their lives. Back in the 1970s there was very little suitable alternative occupation provision for people with TBI in the UK. The development of Headway Houses provided by voluntary groups and branches of Headway, the brain injury association, has done much to fill this gap. There is currently a network of more than 125 groups and branches of Headway that provide physical, cognitive and social rehabilitation and support to individuals and families (*https://www.headway.org.uk*), some of whom offer specific advice about paid and voluntary work. However, not all people with ABI who are unable to RtW are content to attend Headway groups and alternative opportunities (e.g. social enterprise projects, adult education and alternative leisure pursuits) are also required. The role of the charitable and voluntary sector to VR in the UK is reviewed by Frank (2016). Recommendations on alternative occupation provision for people with long-term neurological conditions are provided in BSRM (2010, paras 5.111–5.116).

Our experience is that alternatives to employment (e.g. social enterprises, voluntary work, adult education, leisure pursuits) often require significant VR input, ongoing support and, potentially further placements in new similar opportunities as many of these activities are time-limited and not permanent. It is vital to see alternative occupation (such as voluntary work or taking on a family caring role) in a positive light, even for those who appear to have the skills for a return to paid employment as there are numerous reasons why this may not be viable. This includes marked fatigue, behavioural difficulties (e.g. aggression and disinhibition) and emotional concerns (e.g. mood swings, anxiety and depression). This was highlighted early on the Working Out programme by a person who demonstrated the skills for alternative paid employment but who could not tolerate the frustration of working in a support role, having previously worked in senior management. His wife expressed concern about the frustration that he was taking home to her and their two young children. Voluntary work, undertaking duties of his choosing, working at his own pace, proved a more viable option. A compensation claim enabled him to continue with rewarding voluntary work rather than struggle with frustrating low level paid employment.

As in all VR interventions, proactive review is vital to ensure that the person is managing the work role without undue stress, excessive fatigue or dissatisfaction and to identify as early as possible any concerns on the part of the employer or education provider. This allows the VR practitioner to consider and discuss any emergent difficulties and make further recommendations to adapt the job role or course requirements (as required) in order to secure and maintain the work role or progression in academic study or training.

Effectiveness of vocational rehabilitation after brain injury

Evaluation of models of VR after TBI report generally positive outcomes with, in most cases, over half the group returning to paid employment—the relatively low figures for the Clubhouse model is not surprising given the severity of the population involved. As previously noted, direct comparison across programmes is not possible both as they differ in target population (TBI vs ABI), severity, time post-injury and exclusion criteria, and also the nature and amount of VR interventions is often not specified (Tyerman, 2012). However, in a quantitative synthesis of 26 outcome studies involving 3,688 adults with TBI, aggregated results indicated that VR programmes produced higher and quicker RtW than that reported in non-intervention follow-up studies (Kendall et al., 2006). In order to increase the number of people with TBI in competitive employment, earlier and intensive emphasis on preparation for full-time work was recommended.

11–047

There is also evidence that ABI VR programmes are cost-effective. For example, total operational costs over five years in the early 1990s were on average $4,377 per person on the Work Reentry Programme in San Diego: taking into account taxes paid and savings in state benefits, the average payback period was just 20 months for people who would otherwise most likely face a lifetime of unemployment and financial dependency (Abrams et al., 1993). Experience in the UK also indicates the value of health economic input in evaluating costs and benefits (Radford et al., 2013). Further such analyses are required.

Fadyl and McPherson (2009) report a systematic review of the evidence for three broad models of VR after TBI: "program-based", "supported employment" and "case coordination". Disappointingly few studies met the inclusion criteria and of these, only five were judged to be of high quality and none compared different VR approaches. It was concluded that there is currently little clear evidence to suggest what constitutes best practice in VR after TBI. However, as noted, our experience on the Working Out programme is that different VR models are differentially suited to different VR needs.

11–048 This view is supported by a comparative study of vocational outcomes for 114 people with ABI (64% with TBI) (Malec and Degiorgio, 2002). Participants were accepted at a median of just over a year post-injury onto one of three VR pathways, determined clinically: specialist vocational service (SVS) only, SVS plus a three hour per week community re-integration outpatient group and SVS plus a six hour per day comprehensive day treatment programme. At one-year follow-up community-based employment outcomes did not differ across groups (77%, 85% and 84% respectively). It was concluded that different pathways can result in RtW after ABI if the intensity of the service matches the severity of the disability, time since injury and other participant characteristics (Malec and Degiorgio, 2002). A similar conclusion was reached in a review of five US TBI Model Systems programmes providing post-placement interventions (Hart et al., 2010). Support in the six months after placement varied markedly with mean hours of input ranging from four to 88 hours across centres and mean proportion of treatment delivered in the workplace ranging from less than 1% to over 50%. The programmes providing less intensive VR interventions were noted to be supporting less impaired people early post-injury, mostly in a return to previous work. It was concluded that "less intensive, clinic-based treatment" may be "sufficient" for people with milder injuries and existing jobs, whereas more intensive VR programmes may have evolved to meet the long-term needs of people with more severe injuries (Hart et al., 2010).

A recent review of 12 ABI studies found "strong evidence" that work-directed interventions in combination with education/coaching are effective in promoting RTW and "indicative findings" for the effectiveness of work-directed interventions in combination with skills training and education/coaching (Donker-Cools et al., 2016a). The most effective interventions were reported to be a tailored approach, early intervention, involvement of the patient and the employer, work or workplace accommodations, work practice and training of social and work-related skills, including coping and emotional support.

Further research is needed to evaluate the relative efficacy of VR models for different vocational needs and their cost-effectiveness to build a stronger evidence base. In the meantime, the case for VR is persuasive in terms of practice-based evidence of the benefit of specialist ABI VR programmes, over and above core ABI rehabilitation. For example on our own programme, 56% of those previously unable to RtW (seen at a median of 45 months post-injury) were supported into paid employment (or training 8%), as illustrated by examples described by Tyerman et al. (2017). Very few of this group would be expected to achieve positive work outcomes without the benefit of specialist VR. Those who have their TBI as a child or a young adult face up to half a century of unemployment. Whilst we have been fortunate to be able to promote such outcomes for people previously unable to re-establish themselves in work post-injury, currently such opportunities are rare in the UK.

5. VOCATIONAL REHABILITATION SERVICE PROVISION IN THE UK

Developing specialist VR services to address unmet vocational need after TBI in the UK has proved challenging. In a key development, specialist ABI VR providers worked with Jobcentre Plus, an executive agency of the Department for Work and Pensions (DWP), to develop a national DWP framework for contracting for brain injury work preparation, geared to the needs of people with ABI (BSRM/JobcentrePlus/RCP, 2004, Appendix 5). This was incorporated in inter-agency guidelines on VA and VR for people with ABI in the UK (BSRM/JobcentrePlus/RCP, 2004). This provided guidance on

11–049

(1) support on return to previous employment, education or training;
(2) vocational/employment assessment to determine alternative avenues of employment or training;
(3) VR to prepare for return to alternative employment, education or training;
(4) supported employment for those requiring ongoing support and/or additional training; and
(5) alternative occupation—permitted work, voluntary work or other occupational/educational provision.

In a survey of VR provision after ABI in the UK, 62% of neurorehabilitation services reported that they address vocational issues, but only 8% provided specialist VR (Deshpande and Turner-Stokes, 2004). However, 80% referred to VR services provided by a variety of agencies including the National Health Service (NHS), independent brain injury services, VR providers and Further Education providers. Of the 36 vocational services identified some were specialist ABI VR programmes (most with Jobcentre Plus brain injury work preparation contracts), some were ABI services with added VR elements and some were generic vocational, educational or training programmes open to people with ABI. Not surprisingly, specialist VR programmes in the NHS tend to use an ABI model with additional VR components, whereas those in the independent sector tend to use adapted supported employment models. A case coordination approach may be adopted by vocational case managers funded through compensation claims. Headway, the brain injury association, is likely to favour a consumer-directed approach. It was estimated that VR provision was less than 10% of that required with very few services geared to ABI.

In the UK a specific Quality Requirement on VR was included in a National Service Framework for Long-term Conditions (Department of Health, 2005). This requires access to appropriate vocational assessment, rehabilitation and ongoing support (from local rehabilitation and/or specialist VR services) to enable people with a long-term neurological condition to find, regain or remain in work and access other occupational and educational opportunities. Implementation has, however, been severely constrained by a lack of any dedicated funding. There has been increased interest within ABI services in supporting people in RtPW. As noted, a "preliminary cohort comparison study", evaluating the effectiveness of a guided/supported return to work by an occupational therapist within a specialist TBI team was completed in Nottingham (Radford et al., 2013).

11–050   In contrast, there has been limited opportunity to develop specialist VR provision for those unable to RtPW. This is of great concern, given that only 18% of people with disability and only around 14% of new Employment Support Allowance claimants secure employment through the DWP Work Programme (EHRC, 2017; Work and Pensions Committee, 2017). Current Jobcentre Plus funded disability employment provision (Work Choice) replaced the previous specialist work preparation contracts in 2010. Work Choice is a voluntary programme which aims to help disabled people who experience difficulty in finding and keeping a job. It can help with training and skills development, confidence building and coaching for job interviews. There are three levels: work entry support which provides advice on work and skills to facilitate return to work (up to six months); in-work support which provides help in taking up work and remaining in work (up to two years); and long term in work support, aimed at helping individuals to make progress and perform their job without support (long term). Whilst overall outcomes for Work Choice are more positive, there has been concern that it had been poorly targeted towards those with the most significant barriers to work (Work and Pensions Committee, 2017). This would be expected to include TBI. Other key DWP provision includes the Access to Work scheme which pays for practical support to help people who have a disability, health or mental health condition to start work, stay in work or become self-employed. For a summary of DWP disability provision see BSRM (2010, paras 3.14–3.43), Frank (2016) or go to *https://www.gov.uk/browse/working/finding-job*.

Given the move away from DWP funded specialist provision, joint working across the NHS, Jobcentre Plus, local councils and other statutory, independent and voluntary agencies is essential in addressing complex vocational needs after TBI. This was incorporated in guidance on VR for people with a neurological condition (BSRM, 2010), updating and extending the earlier ABI guidelines with additional recommendations for job retention, transition from education to employment and withdrawing from work. Recommendations for implementation include the need for: inter-agency review of local services, development of local inter-agency referral criteria and protocols, establishment of ongoing service links, review of training in VR by all relevant professional groups, an inter-agency approach to training, research to identify new and effective VR and audit of current provision against relevant standards and guidelines (BSRM, 2010). However, progress has been limited.

VOCATIONAL REHABILITATION SERVICE PROVISION IN THE UK

In a UK mapping exercise of VR provision for people with a long-term neurological condition, only 23% of services identified were dedicated VR services with the rest offering VR as part of broader rehabilitation with highly variable provision. Only 18% of services offered help with job-seeking as well as job retention, and most saw fewer than 10 people for VR per year (Playford et al., 2011). It was concluded that VR services in England are under-resourced and do not meet the needs of people with neurological conditions. This finding is inconsistent with the requirement to ensure that people with disability have effective access to VR programmes that adequately take into account their needs (Office of the United Nations High Commissioner for Human Rights, 2012).

In the absence of any funding to develop specialist VR provision, ABI services are encouraged to prioritise RtW and extend their services to assist as many people with TBI as possible to return to and maintain previous employment, albeit potentially in a reduced role (Tyerman, 2012). For those unable to return to previous work we strive to retain the existing specialist provision, but also advocate pro-active joint working across ABI services, Jobcentre Plus, Social Services and independent/voluntary providers in order to pool respective expertise and resources to support as many people with TBI as possible into alternative employment or alternatives to employment. In the current funding climate a pragmatic joint approach is key in addressing unmet vocational need after TBI (Tyerman, 2012). This includes accessing funding and services through legal claims when available.

11–051

When the legal process is able to facilitate a successful RtW it ultimately benefits both the claimant (in successfully being able to RtW) and the defendant (in reducing the loss of earnings that will need to be compensated for). Where suitable VR is not available from statutory services and appropriate non-statutory services are available, interim payments to claimants in civil cases can be a highly beneficial means of accessing timely input. Equally a case manager, appointed as part of interim service provision, can also have a significant positive impact in sourcing alternative occupational opportunities and in accessing and coordinating services with a VR focus. In some circumstances solicitors themselves end up providing a form of case management for their client, facilitating access to professionals and services to increase the likelihood of a successful RtW. Conversely, however, the litigation and rehabilitative processes can work in direct opposition to each other. For example, discussion about a claim may leave a person with TBI with a perception that, because a successful RtW will reduce their compensation for loss of earnings, they should not attempt a RtW until the completion of their case, thereby maximising their financial remuneration. However, if the opportunity to return to a previous and familiar job is lost, later attempts to return to new alternative employment may prove a greater challenge, particularly if this is unsupported. When services are provided through the legal process, close collaboration and joint decision-making with statutory and any other services involved is essential both to avoid any contradictory advice and to facilitate complementary service provision.

When identifying and evaluating vocational needs and prospects after TBI in clinical practice or in assessments for insurance or legal purposes, conclusions and recommendations need to take into consideration the availability of suitable VR services. We are fortunate on the Working Out programme to have had the opportunity to see what can be achieved with a specialist brain injury VR programme. This is not only able to prepare people for new or alternative employment, but also to provide ongoing input until the person is established at work (including short-term job coaching if required) and long-term troubleshooting as and when a person runs into difficulty at work years after a RtW or starting a new job. However, this level of VR support is very rare in the UK and only a small minority of people have access to any VR support in job-seeking (Playford et al., 2011). As such, it is important to recognise that specialist VR support is not usually available to avoid raising unrealistic expectations of RtW for people with TBI, which is likely to add significantly to their frustration and dissatisfaction.

6. CONCLUSIONS

11-052 From the review of outcome studies, it seems reasonable to conclude that overall up to around 40% of people with moderate-to-severe TBI who were in work at time of injury will RtW. Relatively high rates of RtW would be expected for those who have access to specialist ABI VR, but relatively low rates both for those without such access and for those not previously in work. Whilst many factors have been found to be associated with RtW in individual studies, systematic reviews have concluded that it is not possible to predict RtW for individuals on the basis of these factors. This probably reflects the complex interaction of multiple factors related to the person, their educational and work history, the nature and effects of brain injury, rehabilitation received (both general and VR), and the nature/demands of the job to which they seek to return.

A number of models of ABI VR have been developed (e.g. case coordination, ABI rehabilitation with added VR elements, VR models adapted to ABI, consumer-based models and hybrid models combining elements of the above). Specialist models of ABI VR generally report positive vocational outcomes. There is some evidence to support our clinical experience that models may be differentially suited to different VR needs, as well as recent research identifying some common factors underlying the effectiveness of VR. There remains a need for more controlled studies including cost-effectiveness.

Currently in the UK few people with TBI receive specialist VR interventions and it is likely that only a minority achieve their full vocational potential as a result. In the short-term, recommendations regarding the vocational potential and needs of people with TBI need to take into account the scarcity of specialist VR support. Even if there is a suitable local VR service available it cannot be assumed that funding for such support will be available to provide long-term support. The extent of unmet need requires ABI rehabilitation practitioners to prioritise RtW and to extend their services from the rehabilitation centre, community and home to address vocational needs, working in partnership with relevant agencies as appropriate. Assisting people with TBI to retain an existing job and/or to return to new or alternative employment or other occupation when they would not otherwise be able to do so, is invaluable and can help to transform lives.

REFERENCES

Abrams, D., Barker, L.T., Haffey, W. and Nelson, H., "The economics of return to work for survivors of traumatic brain injury. Vocational services are worth the investment" (1993) *Journal of Head Trauma Rehabilitation* 8, 59–76.

Ben-Yishay, T., Silver, S.M., Piasetsky, E. and Rattok, J., "Relationship between employability and vocational outcome after intensive holistic cognitive rehabilitation" (1987) *Journal of Head Trauma Rehabilitation* 2, 35–48.

Bolton, B. and Roessler, R., "The Work Personality Profile: Factor scales, reliability, validity and norms" (1986) *Vocational Evaluation and Work Adjustment Bulletin* 19, 143–149.

Brooks, N., McKinlay, W., Symington, C., Beattie, A. and Campsie, L., "Return to work within the first seven years of severe head injury" (1987) *Brain Injury* 1, 5–19.

Brown, A.W., Elovic, E.P., Kothari, S., Flanagan, S.R. and Kwasnica, C., "Congenital and acquired brain injury. 1. Epidemiology, pathophysiology, prognostication, innovative treatments and prevention" (2008) *Archives of Physical Medicine and Rehabilitation* 89, Suppl 1, S3–8.

BSRM, *Vocational rehabilitation: The way forward* (London: British Society of Rehabilitation Medicine, 2000).

BSRM, *Vocational rehabilitation for people with a neurological condition: Inter-agency guidelines*, edited by M.J. Meehan, V. Neumann and A. Tyerman (London: British Society of Rehabilitation Medicine, 2010).

BSRM, *Vocational Assessment and Rehabilitation after Acquired Brain Injury. Inter-Agency Guidelines*, edited by A. Tyerman and M.J. Meehan (London: British Society of Rehabilitation Medicine, Jobcentre Plus and Royal College of Physicians, 2004).

Buffington, A.L.H. and Malec, J.F., "The vocational rehabilitation continuum: Maximising outcomes though bridging the gap from hospital to community based services" (1997) *Journal of Head Trauma Rehabilitation* 12, 1–13.

Cattelani, R., Tanzi, F., Lombardi, F. and Mazzucchi, A., "Competitive re-employment after severe traumatic brain injury: clinical, cognitive and behavioural predictive variables" (2002) *Brain Injury* 16, 51–64.

Coetzer, B.R., Hayes, N.M. and Du Toit, P.L., "Long-term employment outcomes in a rural area following traumatic brain injury" (2002) *Australian Journal of Rural Health* 10, 229–232.

Committee on the Rights of People with Disabilities, "Inquiry concerning the United Kingdom of Great Britain and Northern Ireland carried out by the Committee under article 6 of the Operational Protocol to the United Nations Convention on the Rights of Persons with Disabilities: Report of the Committee" (2016) *http://www.ohchr.org/_layouts/15/ WopiFrame.aspx?sourcedoc=/Documents/HRBodies/CRPD/CRPD.C.15.R.2.Rev.1-ENG.doc&action=default&DefaultItemOpen=1*.

Corrigan, J.D., Bogner, J.A., Mysiw, W.J., Clinchot, D. and Fugate, L., "Life satisfaction after traumatic brain injury" (2001) *Journal of Head Trauma Rehabilitation* 16, 543–555.

Crepeau, F. and Scherzer, P., "Predictors and indicators of work status after traumatic brain injury: A meta-analysis" (1993) *Neuropsychological Rehabilitation* 3, 5–35.

Crewe, N.M. and Athelstan, G.T., "Functional assessment in vocational rehabilitation: A systematic approach to diagnosis and goal-setting" (1981) *Archives in Physical Medicine and Rehabilitation* 62, 299–305.

Daniel, K., Wolfe, C.D.A., Busch, M.A. and McKevitt, C., "What are the social consequences of stroke for working aged adults" (2009) *Stroke* 40, 431–440.

11–053

Department of Health, *The National Service Framework for Long-term Conditions* (London: Department of Health, 2005).

Deshpande, P. and Turner Stokes, L., "Survey of vocational rehabilitation services available to people with acquired brain injury in the UK" (2004) *BSRM/Jobcentre Plus/RCP*.

Devany, C.W., Kreutzer, J.S., Halberstadt, L.J. and West D.D., "Referrals for supported employment after brain injury: Neuropsychological, behavioural and emotional characteristics" (1991) *Journal of Head Trauma Rehabilitation* 6, 59–70.

Donker-Cools, B.H., Daams, J.G., Wind, H., Frings-Dresen, M.H., "Effective return-to-work interventions after acquired brain injury: a systematic review" (2016a) *Brain Injury* 30, 113–131.

Donker-Cools, B.H., Wind, H. and Frings-Dresen, M., "Prognostic factors of return to work after traumatic or non-traumatic acquired brain injury" (2016b) *Disability and Rehabilitation* 38, 733–741.

Donker-Cools, B.H., Schouten, M.J., Wind, H. & Frings-Dresen, M.H.W., "Return to work following acquired brain injury: the views of patients and employers" (2018) *Disability and Rehabilitation*, 40, 185–191.

Equality and Human Rights Commission, Equality Act 2010 Employment Statutory Code of Practice (London: The Stationary Office, 2011), https://www.equalityhumanrights.com/sites/default/files/employercode.pdf.

Equality and Human Rights Commission, Equality Act 2010 Technical Guidance on Further and Higher Education Equality and Human Rights Commission (London: The Stationary Office, 2014), https://www.equalityhumanrights.com/sites/default/files/equalityact2010-technicalguidance-feandhe-2015.pdf.

Equality and Human Rights Commission (2017). Being disabled in Britain. A journey less equal. London: Equality and Human Rights Commission. https://www.equalityhumanrights.com/sites/default/files/being-disabled-in-britain.pdf.

Equality and Human Rights Commission (2018). Is Britain Fairer? The state of equality and human rights in 2018. London: Equality and Human Rights Commission. https://www.equalityhumanrights.com/sites/default/files/is-britain-fairer-accessible.pdf.

Ellingsen K.L. and Aas R.W., "Work Participation After Acquired Brain Injury: Experiences of Inhibiting and Facilitating Factors" (2009) *International Journal of Disability Management Research*, 4, 1–11.

Ezrachi, O., Ben-Yishay, Y., Kay, T., Diller, L. and Rattok, J., "Predicting employment in traumatic brain injury following neuropsychological rehabilitation" (1991) *Journal of Head Trauma Rehabilitation* 6, 71–84.

Fadyl, J.K. and McPherson, K.M., "Approaches to vocational rehabilitation after traumatic brain injury: a review of the evidence" (2009) *Journal of Head Trauma Rehabilitation* 24, 195–212.

Frank, A., "Vocational rehabilitation: Supporting ill and disabled individuals in (to) work: A UK perspective" (2016) *Healthcare* 4(3), 46.

Fraser, R., Dikmen, S., McLean, A., Miller, B. and Temkin, N., "Employability of head injury survivors: first year post-injury" (1988) *Rehabilitation Counselling Bulletin* 31, 276–288.

Gamboa, A.M., Holland, G.H., Tierney, J.P. and Gibson, D.S., "American community survey: earnings and employment for persons with traumatic brain injury" (2006) *Neurorehabilitation* 21, 327–333.

REFERENCES

Garrelfs, S.F., Donker-Cools, B.H.P.M., Wind, H. and Frings-Dresen, M.H.W., "Return-to-work in patients with acquired brain injury and psychiatric disorders as a comorbidity: A systematic review" (2015) *Brain Injury* 29, 550–557.

Girard, D., Brown, J., Burnett-Stolnack, M., Hashimoto, N., Hier-Wellmer, S., Perlman, O.Z. and Seigerman, C., "The relationship of neuropsychological status and productive outcomes following traumatic brain injury" (1996) *Brain Injury* 10, 663–676.

Government Equality Office, Equality Act 2010: Public sector equality duty. What do I need to know? A quick start guide for public sector organisations (2011), https://www.gov.uk/government/uploads/system/uploads/attachment_data/file/85019/equality-duty.pdf.

Haffey, W.J. and Abrams, D.L., "Employment outcomes for participants in a brain injury work reentry program: Preliminary findings" (1991) *Journal of Head Trauma Rehabilitation* 6, 24–34.

Hart, T., Dijkers, M., Fraser, R., Cicerone, K., Bogner, J.A., Whyte, J., Malec, J. and Waldron, B., "Vocational services for traumatic brain injury: treatment definition and diversity within model systems of care" (2006) *Journal of Head Trauma Rehabilitation* 21, 467–482.

Hart, T., Dijkers, M., Whyte, J., Braden, C., Trott, C.T. and Fraser, R., "Vocational interventions and supports following job placement for persons with traumatic brain injury" (2010) *Journal of Vocational Rehabilitation* 32, 135–150.

Hirsh. A., Duckworth, K., Hendricks, D. and Dowler, D., "Accommodating workers with traumatic brain injury: Issues related to TBI and ADA" (1996) *Journal of Vocational Rehabilitation* 7, 217–226.

Hooson. J.M., Coetzer, R., Stew, G. and Moore, A., "Patients' experience of return to work rehabilitation following traumatic brain injury: A phenomenological study" (2013) *Neuropsychological Rehabilitation*, 23, 19–44.

Jacobs, H.E., "The Clubhouse: Addressing work-related behavioral challenges through a supportive social community" (1997) *Journal of Head Trauma Rehabilitation* 12, 14–27.

Jacobs, H.E. and De Mello, C., "The Clubhouse model and employment following brain injury" (1996) *Journal of Vocational Rehabilitation* 7, 169–179.

Jacobsson, L.J., Westerberg, M. and Lexell, J., "Health-related quality of life and life satisfaction 6–15 years after traumatic brain injuries in northern Sweden" (2010) *Brain Injury* 24, 1075–1086.

Jahoda, M., Employment and Unemployment: A social-psychological analysis (London: Cambridge University Press, 1982).

Johansson, A.E.M., Haugstad, T., Berg, M. and Johansson, U., "Participation in the workforce after a traumatic brain injury: a matter of control" (2016) *Disability and Rehabilitation* 38(5), 423–432.

Johnson, R.P., "Return to work after severe head injury" (1987) *International Disability Studies* 9, 49–54.

Johnson, R., "Employment after severe head injury: do Manpower Services Commission schemes work?" (1989) *Injury* 20, 5–9.

Johnson, R. "How do people get back to work after severe head injury? A 10 year follow-up study" (1998) *Neuropsychological Rehabilitation* 8, 61–79.

Johnstone, B., Schopp, L.H., Harper, J. and Koscuilek, J., "Neuropsychological impairments, vocational outcomes, and financial costs for individuals with traumatic brain injury receiving state vocational rehabilitation services" (1999) *Journal of Head Trauma Rehabilitation* 14, 220–232.

Johnstone, B., Mount, D. and Schopp, L.H. "Financial and vocational outcomes 1 year after traumatic brain injury" (2003) *Archives of Physical Medicine and Rehabilitation* 84, 238–241.

Kendall, E., Muenchberger, H. and Gee, T., "Vocational rehabilitation following traumatic brain injury: A quantitative synthesis of outcome studies" (2006) *Journal of Vocational Rehabilitation* 25, 149–160.

Kolakowsky-Hayner, S.A. and Kreutzer, J.S., "Return to work after brain injury: a self-directed approach" (2001) *Neurorehabilitation* 16, 41–47.

Kregel, J., Parent, W. and West, M., "The impact of behavioral deficits on employment retention: An illustration from supported employment" (1994) *Neurorehabilitation* 4, 1–14.

Kreutzer, J.S., Marwitz, J.H., Walker, W., Sander, A., Sherer, M., Bogner, J., Fraser, R. and Bushnic, B., "Moderating factors in return to work and job stability after traumatic brain injury" (2003) *Journal of Head Trauma Rehabilitation* 18, 128–138.

Levack, W.N., McPherson, K. and McNaughton, H., "Success in the workplace following traumatic brain injury: are we evaluating what is more important?" (2004) *Disability and Rehabilitation* 26, 290–298.

Liaset, I.F. & Loras, H. (2016) Perceived factors in return to work after acquired brain injury: A qualitative meta-synthesis. *Scandinavian Journal of Occupational Therapy*, 23, 446-457.

Lundqvist, A. and Samuelsson, K., "Return to work after acquired brain injury: A patient perspective" (2012) *Brain injury* 26(13–14), 1574–1585.

McCrimmon, S. and Oddy, M., "Return to worm following moderate-to-severe traumatic brain injury" (2006) *Brain Injury* 20, 1037–1046.

Machamer, J., Temkin, N., Fraser, R., Doctor, J.N. and Dikmen, S., "Stability of employment after traumatic brain injury" (2005) *Journal of the International Neuropsychological Society* 11, 807–816.

McMordie, W.R. and Barker, S.L., "The financial trauma of head injury" (1988) *Brain Injury* 2, 357–364.

McRae, P., Hallab, L. & Simpson, G. (2016). Navigating Employment Pathways and Supports Following Brain Injury in Australia: Client Perspectives. *Australian Journal of Rehabilitation Counselling*, 22, 76-92.

Malec, J.F. and Degiorgio, L., "Characteristics of successful and unsuccessful completers of 3 postacute brain injury rehabilitation pathways." (2002) *Archives of Physical Medicine and Rehabilitation* 83, 1759–1764.

Malec, J.F. and Moessner, A.M., "Replicated positive results for the VCC model of vocational intervention after ABI within the social model of disability" (2006) *Brain Injury* 20, 227–236.

Materne, M., Lundqvist, L.O. & Strandberg, T. 2017). Opportunities and barriers for successful return to work after acquired brain injury: A patient perspective. *Work*, 56,:125-134.

Moller, C., Lingah, T. & Phehlukwayo, S.M. (2017). "We all need employment". An exploration of the factors which influence the return-to-work after a severe traumatic brain injury. *South African Journal of Occupational Therapy*, 47, 17-24.

Murphy, L., Chamberlain, E., Weir, J., Berry, A., Nathaniel-James, D. and Agnew, R., "Effectiveness of vocational rehabilitation following acquired brain injury: preliminary evaluation of a UK specialist rehabilitation programme" (2006) *Brain Injury* 20, 1119–1129.

REFERENCES

Niemeier, J.P., DeGrace, S.M., Farrar, L.F., Ketchum, J.S., Berman, A.J. and Young, J.A., "Effectiveness of a comprehensive, manualized intervention for improving productivity and employability following brain injury" (2010) *Journal of Vocational Rehabilitation* 33, 167–179.

Nightingale, E.J., Soo, C.A. and Tate, R.L., "A systematic review of early prognostic factors for return to work after traumatic brain injury" (2007) *Brain Impairment* 8, 101–142.

O'Brien, L., "Achieving a successful and sustainable return to the workforce after ABI: a client-centred approach" (2007) *Brain Injury* 21, 465–478.

Oddy, M., Coughlan, A., Tyerman, A. and Jenkins, D., "Social adjustment after closed head injury: a further follow—up seven years after injury" (1985) *Journal of Neurology, Neurosurgery and Psychiatry* 48, 564–568.

Office of the United Nations High Commissioner for Human Rights, "Thematic study on the work and employment of persons with disabilities" (2012) *http://www.ohchr.org/_layouts/15/WopiFrame.aspx?sourcedoc=/Documents/Issues/Disability/A-HRC-22-25_en.doc&action=default&DefaultItemOpen=1*.

Olver, J.H., Ponsford, J.L. and Curran, C.A., "Outcome following traumatic brain injury: a comparison between 2 and 5 years after injury" (1996) *Brain Injury* 10, 841–848.

O'Neill, J., Hibbard, M.R., Brown, M., Jaffe, M., Sliwinski, M., Vandergoot, D. and Weiss, M.J., "The effect of employment on quality of life and community integration after traumatic brain injury" (1998) *Journal of Head Trauma Rehabilitation* 13, 68–79.

Ownsworth, T. and McKenna, K., "Investigation of factors related to employment outcome following traumatic brain injury: a critical review and conceptual model" (2004) *Disability and Rehabilitation* 26, 765–784.

Parente, R. and Stapleton, M., "Vocational evaluation, training, and job placement after traumatic brain injury: problems and solutions" (1996) *Journal of Vocational Rehabilitation* 7, 181–191.

Playford, E.D., Radford, K., Burton, C., Gibson, A., Jellie, B., Sweetland, J. and Waykins, C., "Mapping vocational rehabilitation services for people with long-term neurological conditions. Summary report" (2011), https://www.networks.nhs.uk/nhs-networks/vocational-rehabilitation/documents/FinalReport.pdf.

Ponsford, J.L., Olver, J.H. and Curran, C., "A profile of outcome: 2 years after traumatic brain injury" (1995) *Brain Injury* 9, 1–10.

Price, P.L. and Baumann, W.L., "Working: the key to normalisation after brain injury" in D.E. Tupper and K.D. Cicerone (eds), *The neuropsychology of everyday issues: Issues in development and rehabilitation* (Massachusetts: Kluwer Academic, 1990).

Price, R.H., Vinokur, R.D. and Friedland, D.S., "The jobseeker role as resource: achieving reemployment and enhancing mental health" in A. Maney and J. Ramos (eds), *Socioeconomic conditions, stress and mental health disorders: Towards a new synthesis of research and public policy* (Washington DC: NIMH, 2002).

Radford, K.A., Phillips, J., Drummond, A., Sach, T., Walker, M., Tyerman, A., Haboubi, N. and Jones, T., "Return to work after traumatic brain injury: Cohort comparison and economic evaluation" (2013) *Brain Injury* 27, 507–520.

Roessler, R.T., Schriner, K.F. and Price, P., "Employment concerns of people with head injuries" (1992) *Journal of Rehabilitation* January/February/March, 17–22.

Ryan, T.V., Sautter, S.W., Capps, C.F., Meneese, W. and Marth, J.T., "Utilizing neuropsychological measures to predict vocational outcome in a head trauma population" (1992) *Brain Injury* 6, 175–182.

Saltychev, M., Eskola, M., Tenovuo, O. and Laimi, K., "Return to work after traumatic brain injury: Systematic review" (2013) *Brain Injury* 27(13–14), 1516–1527.

Sander, A.M., Kreutzer, J.S. and Fernandez, C.C., "Neurobehavioral functioning, substance abuse, and employment after brain injury: implications for vocational rehabilitation" (1997) *Journal of Head Trauma Rehabilitation* 12, 28–41.

Sander, A.M., Kreutzer, J.S., Rosenthal, M., Delmonico, R. and Young, M.E., "A multi-center longitudinal investigation of return to work and community integration following traumatic brain injury" (1996) *Journal of Head Trauma Rehabilitation* 11, 70–84.

Scherer, M., Bergloff, P., Levin, E., High, W.M., Oden, K.E. and Nick, T.G., "Impaired awareness and employment outcome after traumatic brain injury" (1998) *Journal of Head Trauma Rehabilitation* 13, 52–61.

Scherer, M., Hart, T., Nick, T.G., Whyte, J., Thompson. R.N. and Yablon, S.A., "Early impaired self-awareness after traumatic brain injury" (2003) *Archives of Physical Medicine and Rehabilitation* 84, 168–176.

Select Committee, The Equality Act 2010: the impact on disabled people. Report of House of Lords Select Committee on the Equality Act 2010 and Disability (The Stationary Office, 2016), https://www.publications.parliament.uk/pa/ld201516/ldselect/ldeqact/117/117.pdf.

Shames, J., Treger, I., Ring, H. and Giaquinto, S., "Return to work following traumatic brain injury: Trends and challenges" (2007) *Disability and Rehabilitation* 29, 1387–1395.

Simpson, A. and Schmihtter-Edgecombe, M., "Prediction of employment status following traumatic brain injury using a behavioural measure of frontal lobe functioning" (2002) *Brain Injury* 16, 1075–1091.

Stapleton, M., Parente, R. and Bennett, P., "Job coaching traumatically brain injured individuals: Lessons learned" (1989) *Cognitive Rehabilitation* July/August, 18–21.

Steadman-Pare, D., Colantonio, A., Ratcliff, G., Chase, S. and Vernich, L., "Factors associated with perceived quality of life many years after traumatic brain injury" (2001) *Journal of Head Trauma Rehabilitation* 16, 330–342.

Stergiou-Kita, M., Rappolt, S. and Dawson, D., "Towards developing a guideline for vocational evaluation following traumatic brain injury: the qualitative synthesis of clients' perspectives" (2012) *Disability and Rehabilitation* 34,179–188.

Teasdale, T.W., Hansen, S., Gade, A. and Christensen, A-L., "Neuropsychological test scores before and after brain-injury rehabilitation in relation to return to employment" (1997) *Neuropsychological Rehabilitation* 7, 23–42.

Trexler, L.E., Trexler, L.C., Malec, J.F., Klyce, D. and Parrott, D., "Prospective randomized controlled trial of resource facilitation on community participation and vocational outcome following brain injury" (2010) *Journal of Head Trauma Rehabilitation* 25, 440–446.

Tsaousides, T., Warshowsky, T., Ashman, A., Cantor, B., Speilman, L. and Gordon, W.A., "The relationship between employment-related self-efficacy and quality of life following traumatic brain injury" (2009) *Rehabilitation Psychology* 54(3), 299–305

Tyerman, A., "Self-concept and psychological change in the rehabilitation of the severely head injured person" (Doctoral Thesis, University of London, 1987).

Tyerman, A., "Vocational rehabilitation and executive disorders" in M. Oddy and A. Worthington (eds), *Brain Injury and Executive Dysfunction* (Oxford: Oxford University Press, 2008), 211–231.

REFERENCES

Tyerman, A., "Vocational rehabilitation after traumatic brain injury: Models and services" (2012) *Neurorehabilitation* 31, 51–62.

Tyerman, A., Meehan, M. and Tyerman, R., "Vocational and occupational rehabilitation" in B. Wilson, C. van Heugten, J. Winegardner and T. Ownsworth (eds), *International Handbook of Neuropsychological Rehabilitation* (Psychology Press, 2017, 378-388).

Tyerman, A., Tyerman, R. and Viney, P., "Vocational rehabilitation programmes" in A. Tyerman and N.S. King (eds), *Psychological approaches to rehabilitation after traumatic brain injury* (Oxford: BPS Blackwell, 2008), 376–402.

Tyerman, A. and Young, K., "Vocational rehabilitation after severe traumatic brain injury: evaluation of a specialist assessment programme" (1999) *Journal of the Application of Occupational Psychology to Employment and Disability* 2, 31–41.

Tyerman, A. and Young, K., "Vocational rehabilitation after severe traumatic brain injury: II Specialist interventions and outcomes" (2000) *Journal of the Application of Occupational Psychology to Employment and Disability* 2, 13–20.

Tyerman, R., Tyerman, A., Howard, P. and Hadfield, C., *The Chessington O.T. Neurological Assessment Battery* (Nottingham: Nottingham Rehab, 1986).

Uomoto, J.M., "Application of the neuropsychological evaluation in vocational planning after brain injury" in R.T. Fraser and D.C. Clemmons (eds), *Traumatic brain injury: Practical vocational, neuropsychological and psychotherapy interventions* (Boca Raton: CRC Press, 2000), 1–94.

van Velzen, J.M, van Bennekom, C.A.M., Edelaar, M.J.A., Sluiter, J.K. and Frings-Dresen, M.H.W., "How many people return to work after acquired brain injury?: A systematic review" (2009a) *Brain Injury* 23, 473–488.

van Velzen, J.M., van Bennekom, C.A.M., Edelaar, M.J.A., Sluiter, J.K. and Frings-Dresen, M.H.W., "Prognostic factors of return to work after acquired brain injury: A systematic review" (2009b) *Brain Injury* 23, 385–395.

van Velzen, J.M., van Bennekom, C.A, van Dormolen, M., Sluiter, J.K. & Frings-Dresen M.H. (2011). Factors influencing return to work experienced by people with acquired brain injury: a qualitative research study. *Disability and Rehabilitation*, 33, 237-246.

Vinokur, A.D. and Price, R.H., "Promoting reemployment and mental health among the unemployed" in J. Vuori, R. Blonk and R.H. Price (eds), *Sustainable working Lives; Managing work transitions and health throughout the life course* (Springer Netherlands, 2015), 177–186.

Waddell, G. and Burton, A.K., *Is work good for your health and wellbeing?* (London: The Stationary Office, 2006).

Wanberg, C.R., "The Individual Experience of Unemployment" (2012) *Annual Review of Psychology* 63, 369–396.

Weddell, R., Oddy, M. and Jenkins, D., "Social adjustment after rehabilitation: a two year follow-up of patients with severe head injury" (1980) *Psychological Medicine* 10, 257–263.

Webb, C.R., Wrigley, M., Yoels, W. and Fine, P.R., "Explaining quality of life for persons with traumatic brain injuries: 2 years after injury" (1995) *Archives of Physical Medicine and Rehabilitation* 76, December, 1113–1119.

Wehman, P., Kregel, J., West, M. and Cifu, D., "Return to work for patients with traumatic brain injury: Analysis of costs" (1994) *American Journal of Physical Medicine and Rehabilitation* 73, 280–282.

Wehman, P., Kregel, J., Keyser-Marcus, L., Sherron-Targett, P., Campbell, L., West, M. and Cifu, D., "Supported employment for persons with traumatic brain injury: A preliminary investigation of long-term follow-up costs and program efficiency" (2003) *Archives of Physical Medicine and Rehabilitation* 84, 192–196.

Wehman, P.H., Kreutzer, J.S., West, M.D., Sherron, P.D., Zasler, N.D., Groah, C.H., Stonnington, H.H., Burns, C.T. and Sale, P.R., "Return to work for persons with traumatic brain injury: a supported employment approach" (1990) *Archives of Physical Medicine and Rehabilitation* 71, 1047–1052.

Wehman, P., Kreutzer, J., Wood, W. Morton, M.V. and Sherron, P., "Supported work model for persons with traumatic brain injury: toward job placement and retention" (1988) *Rehabilitation Counselling Bulletin* 31, 298–312.

Wesoleck, J. and McFarlane, F., "Vocational assessment and evaluation in the USA" (1992) *Rehab Network* Spring Edition, 15–19.

Wilson, B.A., Evans, J., Brentnall, S., Bremner, S., Keohane, C. and Williams, H., "The Oliver Zangwill Center for Neuropsychological Rehabilitation" in A-L. Christensen and B.P. Uzzell (eds), *International Handbook of Neuropsychological Rehabilitation* (New York: Kluwer Academic/Plenum Publishers, 2000), 231–246.

Wise, K., Ownsworth, T. and Fleming, J., "Convergent validity of self-awareness measures and their association with employment outcome in adults following acquired brain injury" (2005) *Brain Injury* 19, 765–775.

Witol, A.D., Sander, A.M., Seel, R.T. and Kreutzer, J.S., "Long term neurobehavioral characteristics after brain injury: Implications for vocational rehabilitation" (1996) *Journal of Vocational Rehabilitation* 7, 159–167.

Women and Equalities Committee (2019a). Enforcing the Equality Act: the law and the role of the Equality and Human Rights Commission. London: House of Commons. https://publications.parliament.uk/pa/cm201719/cmselect/cmwomeq/1470/1470.pdf.

Women and Equalities Committee (2019b). The use of non-disclosure agreements in discrimination cases. London: House of Commons. https://publications.parliament.uk/pa/cm201719/cmselect/cmwomeq/1720/1720.pdf.

Work and Pensions Committee (2017). Disability employment gap. Seventh Report of Session 2016-17. London: House of Commons. https://publications.parliament.uk/pa/cm201617/cmselect/cmworpen/56/56.pdf.

World Health Organization, World report on disability (Geneva: World Health Organization, 2011), http://www.who.int/disabilities/world_report/2011/en/.

Yeates, G., Rowberry, M., Dunne, S., Goshawk, M., Mahadevan, M., Tyerman, R., Salter, S., Hillier, M., Berry, A. and Tyerman, A., "Social cognition and executive functioning predictors of supervisors' appraisal of interpersonal behaviour in the workplace following acquired brain injury" (2016) *Neurorehabilitation* 38, 299–310.

CHAPTER 12

Assessing Care Needs After Acquired Brain Injury[1]

Caz Lyall

INTRODUCTION

This chapter focuses on the possible needs for care and support that an individual who has sustained a brain injury may have. The impairments are varied, sometimes very subtle, and can affect all aspects of function associated with daily living, and thus the needs for care and support are multifaceted too. It is crucial therefore to understand the components of brain injury and to assess each person thoroughly. The research demonstrating the complexities and subtleties of the changes experienced, which assist in understanding this complicated condition, are reported at the beginning of the chapter. The chapter also addresses the skill base of the care expert, the assessment process including past and future care, aids and adaptations, future recommendations in terms of rehabilitation, types of care packages, case management and longer-term recommendations.

For clarification, many titles are given to describe the role of "carer". These include carer, support worker, buddy and personal assistant. For the purposes of this chapter and to help the reader separate out the subtle nuances of the role of a "carer" in a medico-legal context, the following definitions are provided: carer = care giver; support worker = providing support and is quite a generic role; buddy = suggests more of a peer role working alongside someone needing more social or community support; and personal assistant = providing more of a supervisory or facilitative role with higher level tasks, such as paperwork.

12–001

1. INTRODUCTION TO ACQUIRED BRAIN INJURY

An acquired brain injury (ABI) is an injury caused to the brain since birth. There are many possible causes, such as a fall, a road accident, cerebral hypoxia and stroke.

12–002

The problems commonly associated with brain injury are multifaceted and may include physical and cognitive deficits, as well as psychological and behavioural problems. Due to the nature of these types of deficits it is usual for

---

[1] The author would like to acknowledge the contribution of Alison Somek and Kathleen Dean from Somek & Associates and Jan Harrison and Carolyn Bodiam from Harrison Associates in the preparation of this chapter.

people to continue to experience residual deficits affecting everyday function on an ongoing basis. Consequently, individuals with a brain injury typically have difficulties returning to their premorbid activities. They often struggle to live independently and experience breakdown or difficulties in their marital relationships (Kieffer-Kristensen and Teasdale, 2011; Gillen et al., 1998; Frosch et al., 1997; Mintz et al., 1995; Allen et al., 1994; Linn et al., 1994; Pessar et al., 1993; Brooks et al., 1986; Livingston et al., 1985; Thomsen, 1984, 1974). Forslund et al. (2014) found that significant predictors of relationship stability included having dependent children at the time of injury, higher education and being in a blue-collar occupation at the time of injury.

Physical problems associated with a brain injury may include hemiparesis, ataxia, impaired balance, visual problems and excessive fatigue. Due to these physical impairments people often experience problems with mobility. Cognitive difficulties may include a range of deficits such as impaired memory, concentration and problems with executive function. Executive function is the ability to establish and meet complex self-directed goals (Miller and Cohen, 2001; Morrison et al., 2013) and the ability to plan, organise, problem solve and to think flexibly (Mattson and Levin, 1990). Individuals with executive dysfunction experience problems in relation to vocational ability, interpersonal skills (Eslinger et al., 2011) and their ability to carry out social and leisure activities—all fundamental aspects of normal living. Gorporaptis et al. (2019) found that cognitive impairment was associated with poorer health-related quality of life.

12–003 In addition to physical and cognitive problems, it is not uncommon for individuals to have speech and language impairments. Some may have expressive dysphasia or receptive dysphasia and others may experience both. Quite often people with brain injury have dysarthria, causing them to have difficulty speaking clearly and fluently.

From the psychological and behavioural perspective, people with brain injury can present with an array of difficulties such as impulsivity, unrestrained and tactless behaviour, disinhibition, diminished concern for the future and mood changes such as anger and hostility (Mattson and Levin, 1990). Hammond et al. (2012) reported that following traumatic brain injury, irritability is a common long-term sequelae. Personality changes, the most prevalent being personality traits of neuroticism, extraversion, and conscientiousness, were reported after ABI in the study of Norup and Mortensen (2015).

Individuals may also become less spontaneous, have difficulty initiating thought or action, and have reduced motivation and a decreased level of self-awareness (Stuss and Benson, 1984). Cognitive and behavioural deficits have also been shown to influence social behaviour and an individual's ability to interact in a socially appropriate and adept way (Peters et al., 1992). Personality changes influence a person's ability to react in the same spontaneous and affectionate manner that they may have demonstrated towards their family or partners prior to their injury. A loss of sensitivity towards their partner's feelings and emotions also has an impact on a marriage (Peters et al., 1992). It is common for a family member to say, "he isn't the same person he was before the accident".

Impact of acquired brain injury on family members and spouses

Ennis et al. (2013) reported that spouses and parents experienced increased distress as indicated by raised levels of depression and anxiety following TBI. Research has demonstrated that it is usually the cognitive, emotional and behavioural changes that cause the most distress to the family as suggested by raised levels of anxiety and depression (Ponsford et al., 2003; Gillen et al., 1998; Marsh et al., 1998; Sander et al., 1997; Brooks et al., 1986, 1987). It is postulated that this is because family members perceive the subtle personality changes that are inherently connected with the emotional and behavioural disturbances. Marsh et al. (1998) also found that aggression elicited the greatest degree of anguish for family carers, despite a low frequency of reported aggression by carers in the study. The burden of caring for relatives has been strongly correlated with the magnitude of change in terms of behaviour, personality and emotions (Brooks et al., 1986). Guevara et al. (2016) report that the long-term effect on caregiver burden is due to dysexecutive syndrome (i.e. a combination of cognitive and behavioural factors). A study by Linn et al. (1994) also found that family carers who reported higher levels of social aggression in the person with the head injury also experienced higher levels of depression. Anderson et al. (2013) found that neurobehavioral impairments (cognitive, behavioural, and social) had a "direct effect on family functioning, which increased psychological distress". They also noted that male carers' distress was influenced more by the disrupted family functioning than female carers.

12–004

Willer et al. (1991) demonstrated that wives had greatest difficulties with their husband's change in personality, followed by their husband's cognitive deficits. In contrast, husbands identified the "loss of autonomy experienced by their wives" as their greatest problem, followed by their wives' mood swings (Willer et al., 1991).

Previous studies have demonstrated that adverse effects, such as depression, stress, ill health (McPherson et al., 2000) and poor quality of life (Moules and Chandler, 1999) are experienced both in the short and long term by parents and spouses (Hellawell et al., 2001). Marsh et al. (1998) found that 37% of their sample reported clinically significant levels of depression. Mintz et al. (1995) found that 52% of their sample had scores indicating the presence of depression, which ranged from mild to moderate-to-severe. Flanagan (1998) noted that 57% had increased levels of anxiety. Zinner et al. (1997) explored the concept of "mother's grief" using a grief experience inventory. They showed that there was a significant relationship between time since injury and grief, which was highest in the early phase following the injury. Mothers' perceptions of their child's difficulties were found to impact on the level of grief experienced.

ABI potentially leads to dramatic role changes where the spouse experiences increased responsibility, changes in the relationship and an inability to participate in social activities with their partner. The spouse must try and cope with all these changes and needs to "mourn the loss of their partner, which may result in a decision to leave the marriage or to remain as caretaker" (Zeigler, 1989). Hall et al. (1994) demonstrated that the relationship of parents was also at risk and that they also experience strains in their relationship following TBI. Wood and

12–005

Yurdakul (1997) also demonstrated that any cognitive and behavioural deficit increased the risk of marital relationships breaking down when one partner has a brain injury.

In their study, Hoofien et al. (2001) stated that even 10 years post-injury, people with TBI and their families may struggle to maintain a reasonable quality of life without the intervention of professionals. It is postulated that certain factors need to be considered in evaluating the need for care and assistance in the community, particularly level of insight, executive functioning and mood regulation. Unsurprisingly studies have demonstrated that more people have deficits in domestic and community skills compared to basic activities of daily living. Dikmen et al. (2003) reported that 60% of individuals with moderate or severe TBI after one year of inpatient rehabilitation stated they had cognitive problems when carrying out their daily activities. Consequently, they needed help, either partial or total. Powell et al. (2007) also found that 43% of their sample had difficulties in carrying out tasks, such as cooking, cleaning, shopping and laundry and 13% required assistance for most tasks.

Family members and spouses frequently find themselves in the position of having to provide care to their children or spouses who have a brain injury, commonly due to a lack of resources and funding through the statutory services.

In summary, assessing an individual with a brain injury is complex and a care assessment needs to address a wide array of potential difficulties. This calls for a holistic approach where all the psychosocial, emotional, cognitive and physical needs of the individual can be assessed to inform how they can be met in the future. In addition, the needs of the family and friends must be considered along with the potential impact their support or input would have on the individual with the brain injury; this may be positive or negative. Furthermore, it is necessary to consider the impact that caring for the person with the brain injury would have on the physical and psychological well-being of the family and friends and whether they would be able to continue to provide care in the longer term. This may change over time requiring periodic reassessment.

2. SKILL BASE OF THE CARE EXPERT

12–006 Acquired brain injury cases require a care expert to be skilled in assessing a wide range of impairments and disabilities. There are a variety of care experts with different skill bases, experience and knowledge. Most commonly they have a background in occupational therapy or nursing. It is important to consider the level of clinical complexity with which the claimant presents, as this may guide the type of expert that would be best suited to a case. For example, a nurse may be preferable if the claimant has a percutaneous endoscopic gastrostomy (PEG), ventilator and a high level of physical nursing needs in the future. On the other hand, an occupational therapist may be more suitable if the claimant requires an assessment of future aids and equipment. Occupational therapists are also skilled in assessing a claimant's rehabilitation potential and, if needed, able to recommend occupational therapy intervention to develop, recover or maintain the daily living and work skills of people with physical and cognitive difficulties.

When a nursing expert is instructed, it is often necessary to instruct an occupational therapist to address the claimant's need for aids and equipment and any occupational therapy intervention.

When instructing a care expert, if the outcome desired is for claimants to reach their maximum potential, instructing parties need to consider what approach needs to be taken to achieve this and the expert must be able to take a dynamic approach to the case. It is necessary for care experts to be able to consider both the current and premorbid level of independence and occupation of the claimant and recommend a rehabilitation programme that is goal-orientated and enabling. When considering care, it is easy to lose sight of what the aim might be, and care experts need to be mindful that the recommendations being put forward are not necessarily just about employing a carer "to do things" for the claimant. In addition, they need to think about the changing needs of the claimant at different phases of their life and consider the psychological well-being of not only the claimant, but also their family and partners.

A care expert must be clear about his/her own skill base and be able to recommend the need for specialist advice from other health professionals where necessary.

On the legal side, care experts need to be aware of the implications of only seeing themselves as claimant-instructed or defendant-instructed experts, as this may potentially and inadvertently affect their opinions and introduce bias. It is expected that the care expert will remain impartial and maintain objectivity, as required in respect of their duties under the Civil Procedure Rules 1998 (CPR) Part 35. They must not only consider the needs of the claimant, but understand the complexities of the case, particularly in respect of causation, taking into account pre-existing disabilities and/or comorbidities, as relevant to the case. Lord Blackburn outlined a statement of general principle on damages:

> "To assess objectively what is that sum of money which will put the party who has been injured in the same position, as he would have been in, if he had not sustained the wrong for which he is now getting his compensation" (Lord Blackburn, *Livingstone v Rawyards Coal Co* (1880) 5 App. Cas. 25).

3. ASSESSMENT OF A CLAIMANT WITH BRAIN INJURY

Within the framework of the medico-legal process, it needs to be acknowledged that the care expert, alongside other experts, usually only gets a snapshot view of the claimant's life during their assessment. This is not typical in a rehabilitation setting where all therapists work with other professionals, ideally over a period, helping to provide a complete picture of the individual's difficulties and their potential for improvement. Consequently, and because of the complexities of this condition, it is essential for the expert to have experience in working with people who have sustained a brain injury. In addition, they need to consider all the available medical and neuropsychological evidence when constructing his/her report. However, there may be times when the care expert has little or no medical evidence and future recommendations may be difficult to put forward until this evidence is received. The care expert must draw evidence and information from all sources including family and carers.

12–007

In many cases a case manager is instructed to implement a rehabilitation or care package and it is important for both claimant and defendant-instructed care experts, to be able to access the case manager and get feedback regarding the claimant's progress. It is possible that claimant-instructed experts may have easier access and more information at an earlier date compared to the defendant-instructed expert. Clearly, this should not happen as the case manager should be neutral and not influenced by the litigation process. The Guidance for the Instructions on Experts in Civil Claims (2014) also states that:

> "experts should try to ensure that they have access to all relevant information held by the parties, and that the same information has been disclosed to each expert in the same discipline. Experts should seek to confirm this soon after accepting instructions, notifying instructing solicitors of any omissions."

One important consideration for both care experts and the litigation team, is the fact that the claimants' abilities, and the expectations their family/spouses have of the claimants' recovery, are likely to change over time. So, if a care assessment is carried out 6–12 months post-injury as opposed to two years or more, the claimant and family/spouse may have different expectations of the care and assistance required in the longer term. In the early days post-injury both may be more optimistic about the longer-term recovery and abilities of the claimant, compared to two or more years after the event. This may influence their understanding about the level of care and assistance required in the future and their willingness to accept professional carers both in the short and long term. In contrast, some may underestimate the levels of recovery and consider that high levels of care are, and will continue to be, required. It is the role of the care expert to use their experience to assess the claimant's current difficulties and the care they are likely to require in the future, on a balance of probabilities, and to provide a comprehensive report with realistic future goals and expectations. To facilitate this process it may be necessary, and in most cases would be considered desirable, to carry out two or more assessments, particularly if a period of rehabilitation is being recommended.

4. ASSESSMENT PROCESS

Introduction

12–008 When assessing an individual with a brain injury, it is important for care experts to obtain information about the claimant's pre-injury abilities and lifestyle. This will provide a guideline as to what goals and objectives need to be set to help them return to their premorbid functioning, in so far as this may be possible. In view of the nature of brain injury, claimants may not always remember what their lifestyle was like preceding the index event and therefore it is always helpful to have a family member, spouse, partner or friend present when assessments are carried out. If this is not possible, then it is recommended that a telephone conference or meeting is arranged following the assessment with a relevant family member or partner.

ASSESSMENT PROCESS

Frequently the individual with the brain injury lacks or has reduced insight into the nature of their problems and the impact that they are having on their functional ability. Consequently, they may not be aware of their difficulties or underestimate the problems that they have and the help that they need. Therefore, having someone available who knows the claimant well at the time of the assessment can be extremely beneficial. It is well recognised that lack of awareness or poor insight is a sequelae following TBI (Bach et al., 2006). Clark-Wilson et al. (2016) reported that:

> "lack of insight is associated with increased occurrence of behavioural disturbance [Ergh et al., 2002], poorer functional recovery and rehabilitation outcome [Prigatano and Altman, 1990, O'Callaghan et al., 2012], worse employment outcomes [Shereer et al., 1998] and poorer spousal relationships [Burridge et al., 2007]."

Family members or partners can also help provide a more accurate picture of the difficulties the claimant has and the assistance they need to carry out daily activities. In addition, the individual with the brain injury may have psychological or behavioural problems following the index event and having someone familiar present may reassure them. Family can also provide invaluable insights into how the claimant's behaviour is impacting on them and the family and the care expert can observe the interaction between the claimant and the family or partner.

On the other hand, while it is beneficial to have someone familiar present, it is essential that claimants are encouraged to participate fully in the assessment and to verbalise their difficulties and needs as much as possible. This may serve to show a lack of insight. Others must not be allowed to overshadow the assessment process or influence it in any way, that is, the assessor must control the assessment process to achieve objective results. Others must not be allowed to intimidate the claimant who may lack confidence to articulate their views.

12–009

In the case of adolescents and younger adults, a regular lifestyle will not have been developed and the job of care experts and legal teams is more difficult in terms of establishing reasonable restitution. Care experts will need to look at other factors including family lifestyle, education and previously stated desires and aims, although ultimately determination of reasonable restitution will be a matter for the court.

At times claimants may have difficulty managing their anger or frustration and be verbally or physically aggressive. Experts need to be aware of this and safety precautions should be in place prior to the visit if there are concerns.

Assessment techniques

The role of care experts is to provide an objective view of claimants. One of the challenges is to assess the potential ongoing care needs and not only consider their ability to carry out their activities of daily living but, more crucially in the case of acquired brain injury, the claimant's level of executive function, insight, mood and behaviour. These factors all impact on future functional ability and return to employment.

12–010

During the assessment process, care experts need to consider claimants' current difficulties in relation to their premorbid abilities, their psychological status and potential ability to respond to therapeutic intervention. Everyone is different and every brain injury is unique to that individual so the way that he responds to what has happened and their ability to recover and regain their premorbid level of ability varies. The amount of functional recovery is not always dependent on the severity of the brain injury. Psychological factors, personality and environment all play a role in determining the longer-term outcome. Furthermore, it is also possible that dependency may be fostered, or encouraged, if a claimant is undergoing a medico-legal case and the care expert needs to be aware of the short- and long-term implications this may have for the claimant. This is particularly important as care experts rely heavily on family evidence.

When assessing claimants, a variety of techniques will need to be employed depending on the skill base and background of the care expert. A thorough assessment will help the expert provide an evaluation of both past and future care. If required, the identification of the claimant's problems and functional difficulties will enable the care expert to recommend a suitable rehabilitation programme and potentially vocational rehabilitation.

Consequently, it is expected that a variety of techniques, such as interview, questionnaires, task analysis and/or standardised tests will be used to assess the claimant's level of impairment and disability. In addition, diaries and witness statements may be used to provide further information, as the claimant's presentation may change from day to day. This all helps to provide a more objective and comprehensive view of their difficulties.

12–011 Care experts provide an important role specifically in relation to executive function which, as previously stated, is commonly affected following brain injury. It is well recognised that neuropsychological tests do not always capture executive difficulties which are often subtle and not easily identified in a structured test environment (Chan et al., 2008). Priestley et al. (2013) advocated that observation by people who know them well to be the best indicator of any executive deficits. Consequently, observation of the claimant in their home environment, where they can be asked to carry out certain daily tasks, such as making a hot drink or a snack, could provide valuable information. Specific questions regarding their ability to carry out community-based activities can also indicate the claimant's ability to function in a less structured environment and manage unexpected events.

In view of the important role that family members and partners play in supporting the claimant, it is necessary for care experts to assess the effects on the family/relationships and how this might impact on the claimant's recovery and the future care they might need.

In the case of relationships, experts need to be mindful that marital relationships may break down and that current or future relationships may be at a higher risk of breakdown. This potentially impacts on the level of care or support that the claimant may need in the future. In the case of younger people, it is also necessary to consider their ability to look after offspring should they have children in the future, so that any additional support can be factored into the claimant's longer-term care needs.

ASSESSMENT PROCESS

When preparing a care report, it is extremely beneficial for the expert to read any available medical and neuropsychological evidence, particularly in terms of prognosis. This can help guide and inform the expert as to what future care needs the claimant may have and their rehabilitation potential. However, it is expected that the care expert will come to his own conclusions regarding the presenting difficulties and the type of rehabilitation or care that is required. It is outside a neuropsychologist's or medical expert's expertise to provide recommendations as to the level of care or case management that a claimant requires in the future. However, equally the care expert must be able to justify the recommendations that are put forward and this can be assisted by the medical and neuropsychological evidence, which along with the care expert's own assessment provides comprehensive information upon which recommendations are based.

12–012

The assessment could potentially be influenced by external personnel, but the care expert must form his own view. In some cases, case managers are present for the assessment, which is not unreasonable for claimants who do not have family members or a partner. However, the case manager should not be present unless there is a clear identified need and this has been agreed in advance. Claimants can find the presence of the case manager inhibiting, particularly if family members are present too as they may find the number of people overwhelming. In addition, they may not feel able to discuss their problems or progress as openly. In some cases, they may not be given the opportunity to answer the questions being posed to them as case managers or others answer on their behalf. In these situations, care experts must be very clear about who is leading the assessment and request to see the claimant on their own, if necessary. It is advisable for the expert to speak to a case manager who is planning to be present to discuss this approach, in advance of the assessment.

Depending on the assistance that is being provided to the claimant at the assessment, it may be appropriate for support workers to be present. However, it is recommended that separate discussions take place with case managers and support workers. Clearly, solicitors and legal personnel should not be present.

It is recognised that claimants can feel intimidated by the assessment and therefore it is important for the care expert to develop a rapport. It is important for the experts to reassure the claimant, particularly when defendant instructed, so that they know that the expert is there in a non-biased role. It is advocated that experts (regardless of whether they are claimant or defendant instructed) set up their own assessments by telephone to enable an initial brief discussion, ideally with the claimant. This can serve as part of the assessment process but, more importantly, it is the start of developing rapport and enables the claimant to know a bit about the assessor.

Pre-existing disabilities

A challenge to care experts is when claimants have pre-existing disabilities. Here the expert needs to carefully assess the difficulties and care needs, if not for the index event. A widely reported case, *Reaney v University Hospital of North Staffordshire NHS Trust and Mid Staffordshire NHS Foundation Trust*[2] was heard in the Court of Appeal in October 2015. Mrs Reaney sustained pressure ulcers

12–013

---

[2] [2015] EWCA Civ 1119; [2016] P.I.Q.R. Q3.

due to admitted negligence by the NHS Trust and although she had pre-existing paraplegia, she sought to recover damages for all her overall needs. The defendants argued that they should only pay for the additional needs caused by the pressure sores and any pre-existing needs should be paid for by the local authority or Mrs Reaney. Initially Mr Justice Foskett held that the defendants were responsible for all of Mrs Reaney's care needs, but the Court of Appeal concluded that:

> "a disabled claimant who suffers additional injury as a result of negligence is now only entitled to compensation for the additional injury and associated loss. Only where there is no real comparison between the pre and post negligence position can the 'but for' test be disregarded" *(http://www.capsticks.com/resources/news/read/547/pre-existing-injuries-court-of-appeal-rules-defend).*

The case has helped to clarify the circumstances in which future care can be discounted to demonstrate the care that would have been needed in any event.

Experts need to consider any available quantitative and qualitative evidence as to the claimant's pre- and post-negligence positions. However, it may not be easy to separate out the pre-existing and current difficulties. The care expert may need to revert to the medical experts for their opinion in terms of future prognosis of the pre-existing condition and how this may have impacted on their functional ability in any event. This is particularly important where pre-existing disabilities are likely to have changed care needs in the future.

There may be additional challenges in identifying needs when the claimant has pre-existing cognitive, physical or psychological difficulties that are not dissimilar to the difficulties present following brain injury. Such cases may include individuals with cerebral palsy, learning difficulties or mental health problems. It is likely to be easier to tease out care needs and future care needs with pre-existing conditions that do not present as much cross-over in terms of impairment and disability.

Timing of care assessments

12–014   In some instances, it may be necessary for care experts to do more than one assessment depending on when the initial assessment was carried out, what recommendations were made, and what progress the claimant made following the assessment. It is not uncommon for reassessments to take place one or two years after the initial assessment. This is particularly relevant if a rehabilitation programme has been recommended or a trial of independent living so that the claimant's abilities can be re-evaluated and longer term needs more accurately predicted. In addition, reassessment is usually advocated when there has been significant change in the claimant's condition or social situation.

Use of standardised assessments and the potential for exaggeration

12–015   Within the litigation process, there is the possibility that the claimant or their family may consciously or unconsciously exaggerate the claimants' problems. According to Fleming and Rucas (2015) neuropsychologists are required to employ tests to establish whether claimants may be exaggerating their problems, particularly in medico-legal settings (Bush et al., 2005; Fox, 2011; Heilbronner et al., 2009). Fleming and Rucas (2015) state that:

> "the current data suggest that occupational therapists need to incorporate symptom validity measures into their assessments to objectively establish the validity of their formal cognitive and psychosocial test results. This is particularly important when reported cognitive deficits and/or subjective complaints form the basis for a monetary claim or a claim for assistance or treatment."

Fleming and Rucas (2015) are also of the view that by not using objective measures, occupational therapists may draw the wrong conclusions. Clearly, in the medico-legal setting this may have significant implications for any past and future recommendations in relation to both rehabilitation and care.

Fleming and Rucas (2015) are of the view that "occupational therapists need to incorporate symptom validity testing into their cognitive assessment protocol, which is based on neuropsychological foundations". Whilst recognising the skill of occupational therapists to assess functional impairment, it is also recommended that recommendations are based on "objective and validated assessment methods". If there is evidence of exaggeration in the neuropsychological tests, then care experts need to take this into consideration when putting forward future recommendations and carefully critique and question the validity of the information provided during the assessment.

Currently, there is no standardised way to assess the validity of information that is being collated by care experts. From this perspective alone it is crucial that experts consider all the information provided to them. The assessment undertaken must be comprehensive and practical and it will be lengthy (typically three to four hours), and thus will be more likely to show inconsistencies in presentation which may inform any judgment of exaggeration. At times DVD surveillance may be used if there is some concern that the claimant may be exaggerating, and the expert may be required to consider such evidence and comment on its impact on their opinion and recommendations.

Ultimately any exaggeration on the part of the claimant and/or their family is a matter for legal argument.

Assessment of past care

The role of the care expert is unique in that it has evolved from the medico-legal world where past, current and future care has needed to be measured and quantified in some way. At present there is no standardised way to assess the care that has been gratuitously provided by spouses, partners or family members. Care experts are reliant on the information that is usually provided at the time of the assessment or later by telephone. Witness statements can also provide invaluable information if they are available.

12–016

Most people find it challenging to remember the care and support they have provided and the time scales. A few keep a diary of events, but this is not the norm and care experts need to be skilled at helping the family or partners remember what tasks they needed to carry out over and above what they would have done in any event. This includes not only carrying out practical tasks, but can include behavioural support, such as prompting or encouraging the claimant to engage in activities, background supervision or psychological support. The latter may be given whilst supporting the claimant to engage in practical tasks and in such cases, it would not be reasonable to cost for both the practical support and psychological support.

Experts need to use their experience of brain injury and their understanding of the likely progress and assistance claimants may have needed up to the date of the care assessment to establish past care needs. This analysis can be assisted by assessing the claimant's current level of impairment and disability. Despite this, it is apparent that the estimation of past care is not an exact science and it is not unusual for claimant and defendant experts to estimate different levels of care.

Rates for valuing gratuitous care have been argued over for many years, but in recent years there has been a large degree of consensus on using the National Joint Council for Local Authorities (spinal point 8; since 2019 this has now changed to spinal point 2). The job description covers a reasonably broad range of typical care activities, including personal care, domestic support and other generic tasks. There is, however, a debate regarding whether such rates should be enhanced for care provided in unsocial hours (such as night-time and weekends) which for a paid carer attract an enhanced rate. This remains a matter for legal argument as there are judgments on both sides. However, in recent years there does appear to be a more consistent agreement that where gratuitous care levels are significant (i.e. many hours over every day of the week) then enhanced rates are acceptable. Equally where care has been minimal, perhaps a few hours of domestic support per week, basic rates are agreed. The care expert's role remains an objective one of determining the care required, the time taken and typical times of day or night, to enable the legal argument to ensue.

Conclusion

12–017 In putting a care report together, care experts have been advised not to make their reports too long. *Harman v East Kent Hospitals NHS Trust*[3] included a criticism of expert witness reports being too long. It was considered that reports should be "more focused on analysis and opinion than on history and narrative". However, whilst acknowledging that judges may not wish to wade through repetitive information that is provided in all expert reports, the care expert does need to draw on the medical and neuropsychological evidence to establish a picture of the claimant's deficits. In addition, it is important to include the claimant's background and history so that any changes in their functional abilities can be identified. It is also important for the expert to be analytical in their approach to assessment, which will then underpin future recommendations. A clear rationale for opinions, recommendations and costs are essential to assist the court. This is particularly so in high value cases, such as most acquired brain injury cases, where general damages are likely to be significant.

---

[3] [2015] EWHC 1662 (QB); [2015] P.I.Q.R. Q4.

5. FUTURE RECOMMENDATIONS IN TERMS OF REHABILITATION

Within litigation, brain injury claims are usually high value and complex. The Rehabilitation Code of Practice should be considered for all types of personal injury claims.

12–018

Introduction

The 2015 Rehabilitation Code:

12–019

> "promotes the collaborative use of rehabilitation and early intervention in the compensation process. The Code's purpose is to help the injured claimant make the best and quickest possible medical, social, vocational and psychological recovery. This means ensuring that his or her need for rehabilitation is assessed and addressed as a priority, and that the process is pursued on a collaborative basis. With this in mind, the claimant solicitor should always ensure that the compensator receives the earliest possible notification of the claim and its circumstances whenever rehabilitation may be beneficial."

Care experts can provide recommendations without the limitations imposed by finances or time constraints, as may be the case in the NHS and Social Services. Medico-legal cases give claimants the opportunity to potentially have further rehabilitation, aids or care that they might not otherwise have been able to receive through the statutory services. However, it is the care expert's role to provide reasonable and realistic recommendations so that claimants can achieve their optimal potential, as well as improve their quality of life. The aim being to try to return them to their premorbid lifestyle, as far as is possible, and to receive reasonable restitution for their injuries and losses.

Care experts need to take a holistic view of the claimant and take into consideration all the available medical and neuropsychological evidence in order to put forward the appropriate recommendations, which may need to include the claimant's rehabilitation potential. The latter may be challenging in view of the nature of the litigation process and how any one individual responds, not only to the index event, but also the litigation. For many, particularly those who have suffered a severe brain injury with catastrophic consequences, rehabilitation will be focused on trying to reach their optimal potential. However, there may be times when the claimant only makes progress once litigation has ceased.

Recommendations for rehabilitation

When care experts carry out their assessment of a claimant, some may have already received intensive rehabilitation, some may still be undergoing rehabilitation, and some may not have received any rehabilitation. The expert needs to consider what therapeutic intervention the claimant has received to date, the findings from their assessment, the available medical evidence, and then consider what intervention, if any, would potentially further develop the claimant's functional skills and independence or improve their quality of life.

12–020

If it is anticipated that the claimant may be able to regain further independence in their functional abilities, then the input of therapists, such as occupational therapists, neuropsychologists, physiotherapists and speech and language therapists, may be recommended. If this type of rehabilitation package is needed, then the care expert should emphasise that the team needs to collaborate and work together to ensure that a cohesive and structured programme is in place, particularly if community rehabilitation is recommended rather than inpatient rehabilitation. With regards to the former, this will take place at the claimant's home where it may be more challenging for goals and objectives to be monitored and a consistent approach implemented, especially where support workers have been recommended. In these cases, it is usual practice for the claimant to have a case manager and part of his role is to set up and monitor the rehabilitation programme. The length of rehabilitation will vary depending on the claimant's functional abilities and potential for improvement. In some instances, inpatient rehabilitation may be recommended, particularly if the claimant has a wide range of problems that may be difficult to resolve in a home environment.

In some cases care experts may identify that while no further improvement in the claimant's impairments and/or functional abilities is expected, a period of therapeutic intervention and support worker input will improve the claimant's quality of life.

An integral part of the assessment is to establish whether they would benefit from aids and equipment to facilitate their independence and potentially help them to maintain their dignity, such as aids that assist with personal care and toileting. Environmental and accommodation assessment is also important, as moving to more accessible accommodation or the installation of suitable adaptations to a property, may make the difference between someone needing constant support and supervision to them having more autonomy, independence and potentially less gratuitous or commercial care.

Support workers and their role in rehabilitation

12–021 Due to the complex nature of brain injury and the wide range of deficits that are usually present, particularly cognitive impairment, experts often recommend that a claimant receive assistance to implement the goals that are set by the treating therapists. As stated earlier, different terminology is used to refer to this type of support such as carers, support workers, buddies or personal assistants. It is important for care experts to be clear about the role of the person they are recommending. The term support worker is used when a rehabilitative role is discussed. If a rehabilitative approach is advocated, then it is important for the support workers to be able to engage in this process and part of their role is to help "train" the claimant to become more independent, rather than simply provide "care" or "support". Providing care and support may result in the claimant becoming more, rather than less, dependent and inadvertently facilitate learned helplessness.

Ideally individuals with a brain injury require specialist support workers who have been trained to work with people following brain injury. Specialist brain injury agencies may have the advantage over direct employment as they have a plethora of people to choose from to provide suitable support workers with the

FUTURE RECOMMENDATIONS IN TERMS OF REHABILITATION

experience and skills that claimants need. It is very difficult for claimants where there may only be a narrow window of opportunity to regain their lost independence to be matched with people who do not possess the requisite skills. Inexperienced or poorly trained support workers can make the difference between becoming more independent and gaining confidence in their abilities, to becoming more dependent on other people and not reaching their optimum level.

For a rehabilitative approach, it is therefore recommended that the case manager recruits support workers who have the skills and understanding to implement the goals and objectives set by the team. The most successful outcomes are achieved when skilled support workers are employed and notably psychological assistants/graduates lend themselves very well to this process. This is particularly apparent when higher level cognitive deficits or behavioural problems are present and cognitive strategies and behavioural strategies need to be employed. People with a psychology background have the advantage of having appropriate knowledge and training and appreciate the difference between facilitating and training claimants rather than "doing" tasks for them. Support workers without this background or who do not understand executive dysfunction and the impact on claimants' ability to carry out their daily activities will struggle to implement the rehabilitation programme effectively. For example, they may expect claimants to take the lead on what they need to do in a session, expecting them to provide ideas or solutions, an impossible task for claimants with executive dysfunction. Alternatively, support workers may be tempted to take over doing tasks to be supportive or helpful.

In summary, the skills required by a support worker should never be underestimated as it may make the difference between the rehabilitation programme being a success or a failure.

12–022

The number of hours of input from support workers and the length of time that is required varies from individual to individual and is not an exact science. Ideally, claimants need to be reassessed by the care expert or treating therapist after a period of intervention, but this is not always feasible within the litigation process.

Care experts need to be mindful that despite appropriate intervention and rehabilitation, some claimants are likely to require ongoing support. The amount will clearly be dictated by the extent of the residual cognitive deficits and physical impairments, as well as any behavioural sequelae. Developing routines and a structured lifestyle may help to reduce the level of support, but it is well recognised that claimants with executive dysfunction, following brain injury, frequently struggle to manage new or complex tasks. Therefore, while some may regain their independence, it is often the case that others require ongoing assistance. This may be on a daily, weekly or monthly basis and the input may be from a variety of sources such as therapists, support workers, family members, partners and/or a case manager. This ongoing support needs to be factored in by care experts.

Trials of independent living

12–023 One recommendation that is often put forward to establish longer-term care needs is a trial of independent living. This is usually made for younger people who have not had the opportunity to develop the skills of independent living and were either living in the parental home or returned to the parental home following the index event. This is not that dissimilar to the idea of a transitional living period in the NHS when individuals are about to be discharged from inpatient treatment on a brain injury unit. Individuals can sometimes spend time in a flat on the grounds of the rehabilitation centre to assess their ability to manage with daily activities, such as personal care, domestic tasks, meal preparation and shopping.

A trial of independent living in their own rented property is, however, unique to the litigation process. To date there is no research or clinical evidence as to the benefits of this type of intervention; however, it does seem to provide the impetus for claimants and/or their families to consider them living more independently. In some cases, this may be appropriate, but in others it may be too soon and not something that the family or claimant would have considered. For the trial to have meaning, it needs to take place for at least six months to a year. As with the rehabilitation programme, care experts need to recommend the input of a case manager to help organise and set up the trial.

If the trial is well organised by the case manager, it can help establish the extent to which claimants can live independently. However, it needs to be carefully managed with clear goals and objectives. In addition, strategies need to be in place for gradually reducing the level of input from therapists and support workers at the appropriate stages of increased skill and independence. Unfortunately, independent living trials are not always carried out this way and claimants can be provided with too much "care", no rehabilitation goals or objectives, and become dependent on the high level of support that has been provided. In this situation it is then very difficult to change the status quo.

Care packages where active rehabilitation approach is not required

12–024 Care experts assess claimants with a variety of needs following severe brain injury. In some cases, claimants have significant physical and personal care needs due to the extent of their injury. Increasingly, claimants who are in a minimally conscious state or who require 24-hour care are being discharged from hospital and care homes, into their own accommodation, often at the request of family members or partners. In these cases, care experts must ensure that claimants care needs will be met and make recommendations that enable carers to receive appropriate training, for example, to use percutaneous endoscopy gastrotomy (PEG) tubes, catheters or cough and assist machines.

If the expert is not an occupational therapist, then usually a separate report is obtained from one to assess and provide advice on suitable aids and equipment that will be needed in the home. In addition, the occupational therapist can provide recommendations on the type of accommodation that claimants need. However, the cost of any future accommodation and the feasibility and implementation of adaptations needed will be provided by an accommodation expert.

FUTURE RECOMMENDATIONS IN TERMS OF REHABILITATION

Predicting future care needs and differing view of care experts

Predicting future care needs can be a challenging process. The care expert needs to consider to what extent claimants need support both in the short term, when a rehabilitation programme may be in place, and the longer-term. Any emotional and behavioural problems also need to be considered in relation to the safety of family members and/or support workers/carers. Here medical and neuropsychological evidence can help guide care experts with regard to maintaining the health and safety of the claimant, their prognosis and life-span.

If the support workers have been providing rehabilitation, then it is expected that their role will change from a "training" role to a more "facilitative" or "practical" role. In this way it is expected that claimants will be assisted to live their life more independently and have a good quality of life. At this point, psychology graduates/assistants are no longer required.

When putting forward possible future care and therapeutic interventions, care experts need to consider different future scenarios. For example, the care needs of a claimant may vary depending on whether they have children in the future, they lose or gain the support of a partner, move to a new house, change job or experience other life changing events. In addition, care experts need to consider additional future care needs if the medical experts are of the view that the claimant is likely to experience cognitive decline with age.

Every person who sustains a brain injury is different and how they respond to what has happened to them will be unique. The severity of the brain injury will not necessarily indicate a high level of future care or support and equally someone with a mild brain injury will not always equate to little or no support. In addition, the level of support required may be dependent on the claimant's pre-existing functional abilities and expectation in attaining a similar level of ability.

The opinion provided by care experts should not be influenced by the fact that they are instructed by the defendant or the claimant. However, this is not always the case and some experts who are claimant-instructed recommend high levels of care when it is not required. When challenged in court this may not then be substantiated. It is therefore important for experts to analyse each claimant's level of impairment and disability and their potential for further recovery, and then provide recommendations accordingly. Equally, some defendant-instructed experts make inadequate recommendations, arguably having not completed a sufficiently comprehensive assessment and fully understood the impact and level of impairment and need. This emphasises the requirement to ensure that the care expert instructed, whether by claimant or defendant, has the required background and experience to undertake a thorough and appropriate assessment of need.

CPR rule 35.3 states that "it is the duty of the expert to help the court on matters within their expertise" and "this duty overrides any obligation to the person from whom the expert has received instructions or by whom they are paid". The care expert can ensure they are not being biased to either side by self-checking and asking *"what would I recommend if I was on the other side?"*

ASSESSING CARE NEEDS AFTER ACQUIRED BRAIN INJURY

What are the main areas of disagreement between care experts?

12–027 Potentially, there are many areas of disagreement between care experts. For example:

- the need for a second carer;
- the need for overnight support;
- the need for a waking night carer versus a sleep-in carer;
- the hours of support required during the day;
- holiday needs;
- transport needs;
- the level of case management;
- the need for therapeutic intervention in the long and short term; and
- the need for aids and equipment and the potential benefit of these aids.

Currently, there is no single standardised format of care that can be provided across the board and no single calculation as to the number of hours of support that an individual will need. Consequently, the hours of care and the type of care packages that are recommended by care experts on the same claimant may be quite different.

Care experts are usually required to discuss the case with their counterpart in an experts' meeting after which they produce a joint statement on issues agreed and not agreed. Here the opportunity is provided for each to explain how they came to their recommendations and establish whether an agreement can be reached in relation to past and future care. In some cases, there are similarities in the recommendations, but it is often the case that the views are disparate. The latter may, in part, reflect the disparity between the claimant's and defendant's medical and neuropsychology experts. On this basis, each expert may consider that his views and opinions are the most appropriate and, therefore, no fundamental changes in the recommendations are put forward in the joint statement.

Unless the case goes to court, care experts do not find out which view may have been accepted by the judge or the outcome of any settlement meeting. Furthermore, once the case settles care experts are generally not privy to what happens to the claimant in the longer term and whether the recommendations that have been put forward in reports have been implemented or not. It is therefore difficult to present outcomes of cases.

Management of neuropsychiatric conditions

12–028 In some cases, individuals may have neuropsychiatric conditions as part of their presenting problems. This may give rise to self-harm risk or challenging behaviours that put themselves or others at risk. The care expert will need to consider the expert opinion of the neuropsychiatrist when making recommendations. In extreme cases, if the challenging behaviours were to place a risk to the claimant and/or others (including support workers) some form of institutional care may be appropriate.

6. "CARE" PACKAGES AND WORKING TIME DIRECTIVES

When assessing a claimant, there is the expectation that the care expert will provide recommendations for a suitable care package, if needed. However, "care" packages are perhaps not the best term to use as this suggests that care is being provided, whereas claimants do not always need "care" per se. In some cases, claimants need physical and practical assistance with their activities of daily living, including basic self-care tasks, such as personal care and toileting. However, in many cases claimants require someone to prompt, remind and/or facilitate them to engage in daily activities, rather than physical assistance. An experienced care expert will be able to identify and make recommendations for the most suitable package of support.

12–029

Packages need to be individually tailored towards each claimant as what works for one person may not work for another. However, there are a few generic considerations that apply for all claimants:

(1) How the support workers are recruited (through a care agency or by direct recruitment).
(2) Live-in carer versus day and night carers.
(3) Sleep-in carer versus waking night carer.

When putting forward potential care packages, care experts need to highlight the importance of selecting the right candidates and consider what training the support workers may need. They also need to consider the level of case management input that may be required, depending on whether the support workers are directly employed or employed through an agency.

Case managers play a crucial role in setting up the appropriate care package. Part of their role is to help claimants find suitable support workers who not only have the requisite skills, but the right "personality". The extent to which case managers are directly involved in this process depends on whether the support workers are directly employed or employed through an agency.

12–030

Setting up a care package, particularly one with a high level of input, can take time to arrange. The care expert also needs to be mindful that some claimants and their families/partners may need time to come to terms with having support. It can take both claimants and their families/partners time to adjust to having support workers in their home and some may perceive the support as being intrusive or unnecessary. It may therefore be necessary for the support to be introduced gradually. In addition, when recommending a package, care experts need to be mindful that the quality of support worker input may be variable.

At present there are minimum standards that support workers are required to achieve and they are outlined in the care certificate. A useful website that outlines the basic requirements is: *http://www.skillsforcare.org.uk/Learning-development/Care-Certificate/Care-Certificate.aspx*.[4] The care certificate is meant to ensure that workers have the same induction to enable them to provide "compassionate, safe and high quality care and support". However, this is only the minimum requirement and further training may be required depending on the role they are required to undertake.

---

[4] [Accessed 6 February 2020].

12–031 Care experts should take into consideration that support workers will need specialist training to work with a claimant with an acquired brain injury. This may include the following:

- Conflict management and de-escalation.
- Management of violence and aggression and breakaway techniques.
- Personal safety.
- Privacy and dignity.
- Mental Capacity Act and deprivation of liberty safeguards.
- Acquired brain injury.
- Cognitive behavioural principles.
- Moving and handling.
- Protection of vulnerable adults and safeguarding.

Monitoring the care package

12–032 Frequently care experts are requested to analyse a care package that is in situ and review the support worker and case management records. This can be a challenging task as there is no standardised way to measure or monitor the input that is provided by support workers or how successful this has been. Case managers may use recording methods and goal setting to monitor this input, particularly when a more rehabilitative approach is being implemented. However, this is not always the case and care experts may therefore struggle to establish the effectiveness of the package. This potentially impacts on their ability to predict any future care needs.

Research needs to be carried out to identify stringent and reliable methods of analysing support and the outcome, that is, whether individuals are more independent and/or have a better quality of life compared to those who do not have this input.

Agency and direct employment

12–033 Currently care experts usually recommend that support workers are employed through an agency or via direct recruitment. Each case needs to be considered on its own merits as both regimes have their pros and cons and the expert needs to take this into account when recommending how the package should be implemented. When using an agency, it is recommended that this is through one that specialises in brain injury rather than a generic agency where support workers may not have experience or the requisite skills. Specialist brain injury agencies provide their support workers with the training needed and have the benefit of a wider range of people and resources to choose from. Workers will be specifically recruited for each service user to ensure continuity of care, cover or back-up when required.

In cases where direct recruitment is preferred, care experts need to take into consideration that case managers will be required to recruit support workers and provide or buy in training. This will be a much more time-consuming process compared to the time taken to recruit carers through an agency. However, this type of package may be suitable where claimants require a substantial amount of care and a large team of support workers. Furthermore, some claimants prefer to recruit their own carers rather than going through an agency. Recruiting the right people is crucial to the success of the package.

Live-in care and working time directives

Where the claimant only requires a relatively low level of "arms-length" supervision during the day and no care at night, other than to manage emergency situations, then it may be appropriate to employ a live-in carer (LIC). A LIC plays an important role in providing care within the home and can be cost effective. Another advantage of having a LIC is they are not bound by shift changes time, so they potentially have more time to develop a good rapport with claimants as well as more opportunities to allow for spontaneity of activity.

12–034

Regarding the Working Time Regulations 1998, LIC differs from other care models in that the work pattern is not set in stone and is therefore considered to be unmeasured work. The United Kingdom Home Care Association (UKHCA) is the national professional association for homecare agencies. In a Position Statement (UKHCA, 2007) they stated:

> "UKHCA does not accept the interpretation that live-in care should be treated in the same way as shift work, and believes that live-in care should continue to be regarded as 'unmeasured work' for the purposes of both National Minimum Wage and Working Time Regulations."

LICs can provide up to two minor interventions at night, but the "care" tasks on average should take no more than 10 hours of hands-on support per day. When considering a LIC regime it is also important to consider the intensity of support. For those claimants who need some input to organise their day, prompting to carry out daily tasks such as personal care, but also require support at night due to reduced ability to manage emergency situations, a LIC would be ideal. The advantage of a LIC is that they can provide ad hoc care when required and their role can be tailored to the claimant's needs. However, if claimants have challenging behaviour and need a high level of assistance to carry out daily activities, then the intensity of support required may be such that the LIC would burn out within days or a week. Consequently, in this type of scenario a LIC would not be appropriate.

LICs can be employed through an agency or directly. If employed through an agency, they typically work for 4–6 weeks and then have one to two weeks off while another LIC takes over. LICs are also entitled to 14 hours off a week, which can be accommodated if claimants do not require someone at all times or by employing a second carer to cover the 14 hours. There is some flexibility as to when LICs take their 14 hours per week and it should be agreed in advance between the relevant parties. Some like to take two hours a day, others a half day every other day and there may be times when LICs prefer to add the hours up and take a whole day off. When the hands-on care is not being provided the LIC is not considered to be working.

12–035

One additional factor to bear in mind, if the LIC option were to be recommended, is that they need to have their own bedroom and use of a bathroom.

Double-up care

12–036 A potential argument that may arise in some litigation cases is the need for two support workers. In most cases, claimants require assistance from one person to provide the verbal prompts or practical assistance needed. However, there may be times when it could be argued that two people are required, such as when there are physical impairments affecting the individual's ability to transfer independently or when there are behavioural difficulties.

The need for double-up care needs to be carefully assessed and each case needs to be considered on its own merits due to the number of factors that have to be taken into consideration. Experts need to assess the claimant's level of disability and behaviour. When the claimant is unable to transfer independently, they need to establish the need for aids and adaptations and the size and weight of the claimant. Any aggressive behaviour is likely to warrant the need for at least two people with moving and handling tasks, such as hoisting. In some cases, it may be possible to have one person to transfer a claimant using an overhead tracking hoist. However, this needs to be risk assessed on a case-by-case basis taking the aforementioned factors into account.

Similarly, for some claimants where there are no physical impairments, but behavioural problems, such as inappropriate sexual behaviour or disinhibited behaviour, two people may be required for some activities at home and/or in the community.

As with the above case, consideration needs to be given as to the extent the claimant requires the assistance of two people throughout the day. Where claimants have specific tasks that require two and the tasks take place at a certain time of day, such as personal care or community support, then it may be hard to justify the need for two carers throughout the day. When the claimant requires two people to carry out tasks on a more ad hoc and flexible basis, it is more likely that the expert will need to consider recommending two people to provide care. The type of assistance required at night will also need to be carefully assessed. The need for a second person has been explored in the judgment of *Farrugia v Burtenshaw*.[5] Mr Farrugia was a young man who suffered a very severe brain injury and required two people to assist him to transfer and address incontinence at night. The case went to court to establish whether he needed a second carer on a full-time basis or whether periodic attendances would suffice. Mr Justice Jay considered that two carers were required in view of the nature of his difficulties and that his routine was unpredictable.

7. RECOMMENDATIONS FOR CASE MANAGEMENT INPUT

12–037 In many medico-legal cases, a case manager has not been recommended and is not working with the claimant when the care expert carries out the first assessment. Part of the role of the expert is therefore to consider whether it is necessary to recommend a case manager both in the short and longer term. Evidently, the need for input and its extent will depend on the claimant's

---

[5] unreported 22 January 2014 Queen's Bench Division.

RECOMMENDATIONS FOR CASE MANAGEMENT INPUT

difficulties and what the recommendations are likely to be in terms of rehabilitation, facilitation or support. The time post-injury is also likely to play a role.

Case manager role and standards of practice

Case managers and care/support can be funded either through litigation claims or statutory services (i.e. through Social Services or Clinical Commissioning Groups). Regarding statutory services, individuals must fulfil certain criteria to be eligible for funding. As per Clark-Wilson et al. (2016), the criteria for eligibility may not include "full range of cognitive and behavioural deficits that may follow TBI". Furthermore, any provision of services depends on the resources available and frequently family members, partners or spouses take on the role of care provider. Within litigation claims, the funding for services, including case management, can be provided where it is needed. 12–038

The British Association of Brain Injury and Complex Case Management (BABICM) was established in 1996 to promote the development of case management in brain injury (*https://www.babicm.org/about-us/*). On their website, BABICM is described as the "representative body providing a structure for the continued professional advancement of case management and promoting best practice to address and manage the needs of people with brain injury and other complex conditions".

According to the BABICM the "practice of case management developed in the United Kingdom in recognition of gaps in services for those individuals whose needs did not fall conveniently within the boundaries of a single agency or professional group". Another association of case management is the Case Management Society UK (CMSUK) which also aims to "ensure the delivery of quality case management through standards of best practice while promoting the individual and collective development of case management throughout the United Kingdom" *(https://www.cmsuk.org)*.

Case managers have increasingly played a role in brain injury over the past 10–15 years and case manager agencies have emerged accordingly. 12–039

As stated by the Rehabilitation Code 2015, "the parties are encouraged to try to agree the selection of an appropriately qualified independent case manager best suited to the claimant's needs to undertake an Initial Needs Assessment (INA)". This is recommended in medium, severe and catastrophic cases, and required to be in compliance with NICE guidelines.

A case manager's overriding duty is to the claimant in all circumstances and to act in their best interests. It is stated that case managers need to use their professional judgment and evidence base to establish the appropriate recommendations for the claimant. Case managers are reminded in the Rehabilitation Code that when attending a meeting with the claimant's legal team they should not "allow themselves to be open to undue influence". However, this may be difficult to achieve as case managers are usually recommended by the claimant's solicitor.

The 2015 Rehabilitation Code has helped to crystallise the role of the case manager in complex cases, particularly in the early stages of the litigation process. It has become increasingly apparent that claimants need someone 12–040 proactive and knowledgeable about their condition to coordinate rehabilitation and/or care packages to achieve their maximum potential and this role is usually filled by a case manager.

The amount of case management recommended by care experts will depend on the outcome of the assessment of the claimant and the need for therapeutic intervention and/or care package. Where possible, care experts benefit from seeing medical and neuropsychological evidence to help predict future recommendations. However, this evidence may not always be available.

In addition, whether an agency model of employing care workers is used or they are recruited through the direct employment route, the expert needs to be aware that the role of the case manager will differ. In the former, as the employer, the agency will be responsible for the recruitment and retention of staff, monitoring annual leave, sickness and absence, ensuring effective training and formal supervision of staff. In the latter, the case manager will assume responsibility for these roles, although the claimant will be the employer. With respect to the costs, therefore, it is very likely that the cost of case management in a directly recruited care package will be higher.

Effectiveness of a dynamic and well managed rehabilitation programme and care package

12–041 When case managers are effective, the positive outcomes achieved for claimants can be impressive. However, not all case managers are up to the task and at times inappropriate rehabilitation packages are implemented and managed. The latter could entail insufficient monitoring of tasks being carried out by support workers, such that the claimant is not facilitated or enabled to carry out their daily activities more independently.

Consequently, a claimant may be at risk of either not progressing or becoming a "cared for person". That is, they can become so used to other people intervening or doing things for them that they lose the motivation and/or confidence to carry out activities. The situation may arise where the claimant is worse off than had rehabilitation not been implemented in the first place. This leads to the question, what training and qualifications are needed for someone to call themselves a case manager. Case management is not a profession per se. Case managers usually have a background in occupational therapy, nursing or social work and therefore they have a variety of skills and experience. This can be either positive or negative, depending on how these skills are implemented.

A further challenge for case managers is the dual role they are required to play, providing input into the legal process, as well as providing management of the case. Clearly case managers are required to provide records to the legal team, but it is important for them to provide a non-biased view.

12–042 Increasingly the input that case managers and their team provide is being scrutinised, as demonstrated by the judgment of *Loughlin v Singh*.[6] Here the case manager was criticised for not implementing a sleep regime once difficulties with sleep in the claimant were identified. In addition, the care package was criticised by two neuropsychologists when they reported that:

---

[6] [2013] EWHC 1641 (QB); [2013] Med. L.R. 513.

"... the goals of the support package are not as clearly specified or challenging as they need to be and that there is evidence that support sometimes takes the form of provision of services such as transport or carrying out domestic tasks without Mr Loughlin's participation. We agree that to the extent to which this occurs, this is not an appropriate use of support and will tend to foster dependence rather than independence."

In this type of case the care experts should critique the rehabilitation/care package as this will be an important part of estimating future care or assistance. Mr Justice Kenneth Parker noted:

"... it does seem to me that principle requires that I should take due account of the fact, that I have found, that the standard of the care and case management services did, in an important respect, fall significantly below the standard that could reasonably have been expected."

In respect of this, a reduction of 20% in the charges claimed was made.

The case of *Loughlin v Singh* reinforced the responsibilities of a case manager and the role of the care expert in critically analysing care packages and the recommendations that have been implemented. It is imperative that care experts and case managers are alert to the changing clinical and social needs and circumstances of the claimant. Failure to do so can lead not just to worse outcomes for a claimant, but also to financial penalties for the case manager or provider.

Where there are concerns that the Rehabilitation Code has not been followed, insurance companies may start to use "shadow case managers" and employ their own case manager to ensure that an efficient and cost-effective service is being implemented.

On the other hand, while there may be some negative press when case managers fail to achieve positive outcomes, it is also apparent that when an appropriate rehabilitation package is in place, the converse is true. With a dynamic and effective case manager and a rehabilitation team (usually comprising an occupational therapist, neuropsychologist, physiotherapist, sometimes a speech and language therapist and a support worker), claimants can achieve their potential and be more likely to require less support and have a better quality of life.

Effectiveness of case management after brain injury

When care experts recommend rehabilitation and care/support it is expected that case managers will play a pivotal role in setting up the recommendations outlined by the expert and ensuring a successful outcome. However, to date there is little evidence as to the effectiveness of case management for individuals after brain injury. Greenwood et al. (1994) found that case managers increased "contact with formal rehabilitation" in the first two years post-injury, but the outcome was no different in a group that did not have case management input. Outcome was measured in terms of functional ability at home and in the community, vocational ability, family, supervision and care. The authors posited that this may be because while there were increased referrals to brain injury rehabilitation services, the hours of treatment the claimants received did not, in fact, increase. The model of case management that was implemented in the study was one of providing "advice, support, advocacy, goal planning and referral but not interventional training itself". It would seem, therefore, that case managers were only able to guide and recommend rehabilitation and the lack of effectiveness was more due to the lack of rehabilitation services and the inability of case managers to influence a change.

Further research is needed to establish the effectiveness of case management following brain injury to ensure future funding, not only in the medico-legal setting, but also in statutory services.

8. LONGER-TERM RECOMMENDATIONS

12–045 Currently there is no published evidence as to the extent to which claimants continue with their recommended care package or continue to employ case managers once litigation has ceased. Clark-Wilson et al. (2016) state that "individuals with ongoing severe problems in community living are likely to continue to need case management …". However, they did not explore the extent to which claimants retain case manager input once the litigation ended.

Part of the care experts' role is to put forward long-term recommendations for care and case management. Due to the residual deficits of people with acquired brain injury, in terms of cognition, behaviour and psychological status, case management is often recommended on an ongoing basis. The role can include tasks such as arranging future therapeutic intervention or care, aiding with unexpected events or crises and acting as the claimant's advocate. Estimating the level of ongoing case management can be a particularly challenging task when claimants have not undergone or completed rehabilitation at the time of finalising reports. Care experts need to consider all the available medical and neuropsychological evidence and when the future is uncertain, put forward preliminary recommendations to reflect this uncertainty. At other times the level of need is more apparent, such as when claimants have significant physical difficulties requiring a high level of ongoing care and support.

Case management companies have indicated that it is usual for claimants who have had more severe injuries and high care needs to retain their services following settlement. However, research is warranted to explore to what extent case managers continue to provide input or whether claimants choose to rely on a family member, partners or friends, when litigation has ceased.

Further areas that are worthy of investigation include addressing the general long-term outcome, such as whether claimants continue to employ paid carers or take up recommended therapeutic interventions or whether they run out of money, and whether they maintain a higher quality of life compared to those who have not received compensation.

REFERENCES

12–046 Allen, K., Linn, R.T., Gutierrez, H., and Willer, B.S., "Family burden following traumatic brain injury" (1994) *Rehabilitation Psychology* 39 (1), 29–48.

REFERENCES

Anderson, M.I., Simpson, G.K. and Morey, P.J., "The impact of neurobehavioral impairment on family functioning and the psychological well-being of male versus female caregivers of relatives with severe traumatic brain injury: multigroup analysis" (2013) *Journal of Head Trauma Rehabilitation* Nov–Dec; 28(6):453–463.

Bach, L.J. and David, A.S., "Self-awareness after acquired and traumatic brain injury" (2006) *Neuropsychological Rehabilitation* 16:397–414.

Brooks, D.N, Campsie, L., Symington, C., Beattie, A. and McKinlay, W., "The Five Year Outcome of Severe Blunt Head Injury: A Relative's View" (1986) *Journal of Neurology, Neurosurgery and Psychiatry*, 49: 764–770.

Brooks, D.N, Campsie, L., Symington, C., Beattie, A. and McKinlay, W., "The effects of severe head injury on patient and relative within seven years of injury" (1987) *Journal of Head Trauma Rehabilitation* 2 (3): 1–13.

Burridge, A.C., Williams, W.H., Yates, P.J., Harris, A., Ward, C., "Spousal relationship satisfaction following acquired brain injury: the role of insight and socio-emotional skill" (2007) *Neuropsychological Rehabilitation* 17:95–105.

Bush, S., Ruff, R., Troster, A., Barth, J., Koffler, S., Pliskin, N., Reynolds, C. and Silver, C., "Symptom validity assessment: Practice issues and medical necessity: NAN Policy and Planning Committee" (2005) *Archives of Clinical Neuropsychology* 20, 419–426.

Chan, R.C.K., Shum, D., Toulopoulou, T., Chen, E.Y.H., "Assessment of executive functions: review of instruments and identification of critical issues" (2008) *Archives of Clinical Neuropsychology* 23:201–216.

Clark-Wilson, J., Muir Giles, G., Seymour, S., Tasker, R., Baxter, D.M. and Holloway M., "Factors influencing community case management and care hours for claimants with traumatic brain injury living in the UK" (2016) *Brain Injury* 1–11.

Dikmen, S.S., Machamer, J.E., Powell, J.M. and Temkin, N.R., "Outcome 3 to5 years after moderate to severe traumatic brain injury" (2003) *Archives of Physical Medicine and Rehabilitation* 84:1449–1457.

Ennis, N., Rosenbloom, B.N., Canzian, S. and Topolovec-Vranic, J., "Depression and anxiety in parent versus spouse caregivers of adult patients with traumatic brain injury: a systematic review" (2013) *Neuropsychological Rehabilitation* 23(1):1–18.

Ergh, T.C., Rapport, L.J., Coleman, R.D. and Hanks, R.A. "Predictors of caregiver and family functioning following traumatic brain injury: social support moderated caregiver distress" (2002) *Journal of Head Trauma Rehabilitation* 17: 155–174.

Eslinger, P.J., Moore, P., Anderson, C. and Grossman, M., "Social cognition, executive functioning, and neuroimaging correlates of empathic deficits in frontotemporal dementia" (2011) *Journal of Neuropsychiatry and Clinical Neurosciences* 23:74–82.

Flanagan, D.A.J., "A Retrospective Analysis of Expressed Emotion (EE) and Affective Distress in a Sample of Relatives Caring for Traumatically Brain-Injured (TBI) Family Members" (1998) *British Journal of Clinical Psychology* 37: 431–439.

Fleming, A. and Rucas K., "Welcoming a paradigm shift in occupational therapy: Symptom validity measures and cognitive assessment" (2015) *Applied Neuropsychology: Adult* 22: 23–31,.

Forslund, M.V., Arango-Lasprilla, J.C., Roe, C., Perrin, P.B. and Andelic, N., "Multilevel modeling of partnered relationship trajectories and relationship stability at 1, 2, and 5 years after traumatic brain injury in Norway" (2014) *Neurorehabilitation* 34(4):781–788.

Fox, D., "Symptom validity test failure indicates invalidity of neuropsychological tests" (2011) *Clinical Neuropsychologist*, 25, 488–495.

Frosch, S., Gruber, A., Jones, C., Myers, S., Noel, E., Westerlund, A. and Zavisin, T., "The long-term effects of traumatic brain injury on the roles of caregivers" (1997) *Brain Injury* 11 (12), 891–906.

Gillen, R., Tennen, H., Affleck, G. and Steinpreis, R., "Distress, depressive symptoms and depressive disorder among caregivers of patients with brain injury" (1998) *Journal of Head Trauma Rehabilitation* 13 (3), 31–43.

Gorgoraptis, N., Zaw-Linn, J., Feeney, C.Y., Tenorio-Jimenez, C., Niemi, M., Malik, A., Ham, T., Goldstone, A.P. and Sharp, D.J., (2019) *Neurorehabilitation* 44 (3), 321-331

Guevara, A.B., Demonet, J.F., Polejaeva, E., Knutson, K.M., Wassermann, E.M., Grafman, J. and Krueger, F., "Association between traumatic brain injury-related brain lesions and long-term caregiver burden" (2016) *Journal of Head Trauma Rehabilitation* 31 (2), 48–58

Greenwood, R.J., McMillan, T.M., Brooks, D.N., Dunn, G., Brock, D., Dinsdale, S., Murphy, L.D. and Price, J.R., "Effects of case management after severe head injury" (1994) *British Medical Journal,* 308:1199.

Hall, K.M, Karzmark, P., Stevens, M., Englander, J., O'Hare, P. and Wright, J., "Family Stressors in Traumatic Brain Injury: A Two-Year Follow-up" (1994) *Archives of Physical Medicine and Rehabilitation* 75: 876–884.

Hammond, F.M., Davis, C.S., Cook, J.R., Philbrick, P. and Hirsch, M.A., "Relational dimension of irritability following traumatic brain injury: a qualitative analysis" (2012) *Brain Injury* 26(11):1287–1296.

Heilbronner, R., Sweet, J., Morgan, J., Larrabee, G., Millis, S. and Conference Participants, "American Academy of Clinical Neuropsychology consensus conference statement on the neuropsychological assessment of effort, response bias, and malingering" (2009) *Clinical Neuropsychologist,* 23, 1093–1129.

Hellawell, D.J. and Pentland, B., "Relatives' reports of long-term problems following traumatic brain injury or subarachnoid haemorrhage" (2001) *Disability and Rehabilitation An International Multidisciplinary Journal,* 23(7): 300–305.

Hoofien, D., Gilboa, A., Vakil, E. and Donovick, P.J., "Traumatic brain injury (TBI) 10–20 years later: a comprehensive outcome study of psychiatric symptomatology, cognitive abilities and psychosocial functioning" (2001) *Brain Injury* 15:189–209.

Kieffer-Kristensen, R. and Teasdale, T.W., "Parental stress and marital relationships among patients with brain injury and their spouses" (2011) *Neurorehabilitation* 28(4):321–330.

Linn, R.T., Allen, K. and Willer, B.S., "Affective symptoms in the chronic stage of traumatic brain injury: A study of married couples" (1994) *Brain Injury* 8 (2), 135–147.

Livingston, M.G, Brooks, D.N. and Bond, M.R., "Patient Outcomes in the Year Following Severe Head Injury and Relatives' Psychiatric and Social Functioning" (1985) *Journal of Neurology, Neurosurgery and Psychiatry* 48: 876–881.

Marsh, N.V, Kersel, D.A., Havill, J.H. and Sleigh J.W., "Caregiver Burden at 6 Months following Severe Traumatic Brain Injury" (1998) *Brain Injury* 12 (3): 225–238.

Mattson, A.J. and Levin H.S., "Frontal Lobe Dysfunction following Closed Head Injury" (1990) *Journal of Nervous and Mental Disease* 178 (5): 282–291.

McPherson, K.M, Pentland, B. and McNaughton, H.K., "Brain injury – the perceived health of carers" (2000) Disability and Rehabilitation: An International Multidisciplinary Journal 22(15): 683–689.

Miller, E.K. and Cohen, J.D., "An integrative theory of prefrontal cortex function" (2001) *Annual Review of Neuroscience* 24:167–202.

REFERENCES

Mintz, M.C., van Horn, K.R. and Levine, M.J., "Developmental models of social cognition in assessing the role of family stress in relatives predictions following traumatic brain injury" (1995) *Brain Injury* 9 (2), 173–186.

Morrison, T.M., Giles, G.M., Ryan, J.D., Baum, C.M., Dromerick, A.W., Polatajko, H.J. and Edwards, D.F., "Multiple Errands Test-Revised (METR): a performance-based measure of executive function in people with mild cerebrovascular accident" (2013) *American Journal of Occupational Therapy* 67:460–468.

Moules, S. and Chandler, B.J., "A study of the health and social needs of carers of traumatically brain injured individuals served by one community rehabilitation team" (1999) *Brain Injury* 13(12): 983–993.

Norup, A., and Mortensen, E.L., "Prevalence and predictors of personality change after severe brain injury" (2015) *Archives Physical Medicine Rehabilitation* Jan; 96(1):56–62.

O'Callaghan, A., McCallister, L. and Wilson, L., "Insight vs readiness: factors affecting engagement in therapy from the perspectives of adults with TBI and their significant others" (2012) *Brain Injury* 26:1599–1610.

Pessar, L.F, Coad, M.L, Linn, R.T. and Willer, B.S., "The Effects of Parental Traumatic Brain Injury on the Behaviour of Parents and Children" (1993) *Brain Injury* 7 (3): 231–240.

Peters, L.C., Stambrook, M., Moore, A.D., Zubek, E., Dubo, H. and Blumenschein, S., "Differential effects of Spinal Cord Injury and Head Injury on Marital Adjustment" (1992) *Brain Injury* 6: 461–467.

Ponsford, J., Olver, J., Ponsford, M. and Nelms, R., "Long-term adjustment of families following traumatic brain injury where comprehensive rehabilitation has been provided" (2003) *Brain Injury* 17(6): 453–468.

Powell, J.M., Temkin, N.R., Machamer, J.E. and Dikmen, S.S., "Gaining insight into patients' perspectives on participation in home management activities after traumatic brain injury" (2007) *American Journal of Occupational Therapy* 61:269–279.

Priestley, N., Manchester, D. and Aram, R., "Presenting evidence of executive functions deficit in court: issues for the expert neuropsychologist" (2013) *Journal of Personal Injury Law* 4:240–247.

Prigatano, G.P. and Altman, I.M., "Impaired awareness of behavioural limitations after traumatic brain injury" (1990) *Archives of Physical Medicine and Rehabilitation* 71:1058–1064.

Sander, A.M, High, W.M. Jr, Hannay, H.J. and Sherer, M., "Predictors of Psychological Health in Caregivers of Patients with Closed Head Injury" (1997) *Brain Injury* 11 (4): 235–249.

Shereer, M., Bergloff, P., Levin, E., High W.H., Oden, K.E. and Nick T.G., "Impaired awareness and employment outcome after traumatic brain injury" (1998) *Journal of Head Trauma Rehabilitation* 13: 52–61.

Stuss, D.T. and Benson D.F., "Neuropsychological Studies of the Frontal Lobes" (1984) *Psychological Bulletin*, 95 (1): 3–28.

Guidance for the Instructions on Experts in Civil Claims August 2014: https://www.judiciary.gov.uk/wp-content/uploads/2014/08/experts-guidance-cjc-aug-2014-amended-dec-8.pdf.

The 2015 Rehabilitation Code: https://www.cmsuk.org/files/CMSUK%20General/REHAB%20CODE%20in%20full.pdf.

Thomsen, I.V., "The Patient with Severe Head Injury and His Family" (1974) *Scandinavian Journal of Rehabilitation Medicine* 6: 180–183.

Thomsen, I.V., "Late Outcome of Very Severe Blunt Head Trauma: A 10–15 year second follow-up" (1984) *Journal of Neurology, Neurosurgery and Psychiatry* (47): 260–268.

Willer, B., Allen, K., Liss, M. and Zicht, M.S., "Problems and Coping Strategies of Individuals with Traumatic Brain Injury and their Spouses" (1991) *Archives of Physical Medicine and Rehabilitation* 72, 460–464.

Wood, R.L. and Yurdakul, L.K., "Change in Relationship Status Following Traumatic Brain Injury" (1997) *Brain Injury* 11 (7): 491–502.

Zeigler, E.A., "The Importance of Mutual Support for Spouses of Head Injury Survivors" (1989) *Cognitive Rehabilitation* 7 (3): 34–37

Zinner, E.S., Ball, J.D., Stutts, M.L. and Philput, C., "Grief Reactions of Mothers of Adolescents and Young Adults with Traumatic Brain Injury" (1997) *Archives of Clinical Neuropsychology* 12 (5): 435–447.

CHAPTER 13

Whose Evidence Should We Accept? How Judges Reach Their Decisions

The Hon Mr Justice Langstaff, William Norris QC, Nathan Tavares QC and Martin van den Broek

1. THE ISSUE

This chapter addresses an issue that arises in every contested case: how will a judge decide the winner? It is relevant to a book on brain injuries not just because much of the focus of this work is on litigation but particularly because psychologists and neuropsychologists may have professional skills which may help a decision-maker to decide whether a witness is or is not telling the truth, most obviously if there are objective diagnostic criteria, such as the Slick criteria (Slick, Sherman and Iverson, 1999), which can provide a valuable basis for making such a judgment.

13–001

It is self-evident that, in some cases, the answer to our question will depend entirely on the correct application of legal principle to agreed, uncontroversial or established facts. If the trial judge gets that wrong, the appellate courts are there to correct him. If the answer is correct in law but morally or politically objectionable then it is the job of Parliament to ensure that the law is made fair for the future—or, indeed, in the instant case. A classic example of such a legislative response to a legal ruling which was generally considered to result in an unfair outcome is s.3 of the Compensation Act 2006, which was passed as a swift response to the decision of the House of Lords in *Barker v Corus UK Ltd*[1] (in which their Lordships held that a tortfeasor's liability for mesothelioma was to be apportioned in accordance with its contribution to the overall exposure).

In other cases, the answer to the question "who wins?" will depend on the judge's evaluation of the evidence. That evidence may be factual or it may be expert (or a combination of both). This chapter considers how the judge may approach this task. Is it a scientific approach, which depends on a rational evaluation of conflicting evidence on the basis of objective criteria (such as the Slick criteria) and/or psychometric tests which generate the appropriate conclusion according to a "balance of probabilities" (which is the recognised standard of proof in civil cases[2])? Or is it a more intuitive process—one in which

---

[1] *Barker v Corus UK Ltd* [2006] UKHL 20; [2006] 2 A.C. 572.
[2] It is "beyond reasonable doubt" in criminal cases. However, it is well recognised that although in a civil case, the "balance of probabilities" test is one and the same, whatever the issue, it is less likely to be satisfied the more serious the allegation is, since it is less likely that a person will commit a serious

the person or people deciding the facts reach the decision as to who is telling the truth on a more instinctive basis by reference to a wholly or partly subjective impression of the witness?

All appellate courts have consistently emphasised the primacy of the fact-finding process conducted at first instance,[3] particularly where the credibility or reliability of a witness is in issue—see, for example, the judgment of Lord Hodge in *Beacon Insurance Co Ltd v Maharaj Bookstore Ltd* and the citation from a decision of the Canadian Supreme Court in *Housen v Nikolaisen* at [14].[4]

2. EVALUATING BRAIN INJURY CLAIMS (MB)

13–002   A central difficulty for the court when assessing the merits of a brain injury claim and quantum is that much of the evidence presented to it, and on which a judgment is to be made, is invariably to a degree partisan and advanced in such a way as to present each sides' case in the most favourable and persuasive light. These biases can be either coarse or subtle. Coarse bias may be known to be present and relatively easy to detect, but nevertheless difficult to circumnavigate to get to an accurate understanding of the claimant's difficulties and therefore the merits of the case. Subtle biases by their nature are more problematical and it can be difficult to ascertain when they are present as typically they reflect sincere beliefs, usually held by professionals, particularly medico-legal experts, that influence their perception and reporting on a claimant, and lead to certain conclusions being preferred over others.

Coarse bias

13–003   The foundation for much coarse bias is arguably the adversarial nature of personal injury litigation and the conflict that inevitably arises between claimant and defendants' lawyers. A starting point for coarse bias is the preparation of evidence and the selection of experts. While experts may endeavour to provide accurate assessments of the claimant, they inevitably have their own particular preferences and ways of working, thinking and considering issues that make them more or less attractive to one side or the other. Some will be sympathetic and empathic in nature whereas others are cerebral and sceptical, and these tendencies may make them more or less attractive to instructing lawyers who invariably have a good idea of the approach the expert will take. Lawyers may seek to encourage experts to feel part of a "team", so encouraging identification with them and their case, or a team is built implicitly by selecting the same experts in different cases. Conferences with lawyers are often used overtly to arrive at a common or uniform view among the different experts which is then presented to the opposing lawyers. Additions, deletions or amendments to evidence may be requested, erasing or minimising differences of opinion, and sometimes

---

default than a minor one. Thus, in general, the more serious the fault alleged, the more proof is likely to be required to show it has happened. To allege fraud against a party will therefore place the evidential bar at a high level.

[3] By which we mean the judge (in a civil case) and the jury or magistrates in a criminal case.

[4] *Beacon Insurance Co Ltd v Maharaj Bookstore Ltd* [2014] UKPC 21; [2014] 4 All E.R. 418; *Housen v Nikolaisen* [2002] 2 S.C.R. 235 at [14].

considerable pressure is brought to bear to arrive at a common view by inviting experts to defer to other disciplines, review evidence or agree to some other face-saving way of removing obstacles. The Annual Expert Witness Survey (2016) found that 36% of medical experts and 23% of non-medical experts reported being asked or felt pressurised to change their reports by their instructing party, such that it damaged their impartiality. Ultimately, in the event that an expert's opinion is deemed unhelpful, it may not be disclosed and the court will be unaware of contrary views and the opportunity of having a different perspective.

With the development of the Rehabilitation Code brain injured claimants potentially have access to early private rehabilitation that may be of benefit to all the parties inasmuch as the claimant receives the treatment they need and, with improvement, the cost of the claim to the insurer is potentially reduced. However, the involvement of lawyers in commissioning private services can introduce another distorting influence when they ignore clinical boundaries and involve themselves in the rehabilitation process itself. Lawyers may attend or even host clinical team meetings, email members of the rehabilitation team, request updates, case management reports, witness statements, and commission support workers, so intruding into rehabilitation and reminding all involved of the importance of the proceedings to the claimant and the significance of their role in it. As with legal experts, rehabilitation therapists may be commissioned by the same lawyers in different cases and so develop a team identity, not only among themselves (which is desirable), but also with the lawyers (which is not). Lawyers may ask them to provide statements to counter expert evidence or gather evidence demonstrating a need, such as for support, and so the clinician is drawn inexorably into a dual role of providing both treatment and assisting with the case, which may not be in their patient's interests and potentially raises ethical issues for the practitioner. Claimants may be keen for a clinician to be recruited to support their case which in turn can cause problems and conflict when the clinician is aware of issues that may hinder litigation, such as exaggeration or other relevant problems like alcohol misuse. Treatment may also be sought by lawyers with a legal, rather than a therapeutic goal, with a lengthy intervention taken as reflecting the magnitude of the claimant's injuries, so leaving the claimant to stagnate in long-term rehabilitation. A tell-tale sign of legal bias affecting rehabilitation professionals is when there is a relative absence of communications between them and the claimant's general practitioner (GP), in contrast to the sometimes-voluminous documentation provided to lawyers. In these circumstances, the rehabilitation team have pivoted their attention towards the legal profession, rather than the GP who is the primary coordinator of patient care. Arguably there is no more of a role for lawyers in rehabilitation than there is for them in the operating theatre and there should be a "Chinese Wall" separating the legal and clinical domains, so leaving the rehabilitation team to do their work free from involvement with, or consideration of, the claim.

Occasionally evidence from NHS clinicians is offered to the court that is assumed as more objective and so carries greater weight than that of legal experts. Greenberg and Shuman (1997) suggested that treating therapists may be viewed as providing more efficient, candid, and neutral opinions, while nevertheless being qualified. A treating clinician will have spent time with the

13–004

claimant and, it might be assumed, knows them and their difficulties well, and to collate the same information again may be time-consuming and expensive. By being outside the legal process, the treating therapist may also provide additional information because the claimant might be more candid in therapy and the therapist may be viewed as more neutral and, in particular, not influenced by financial incentives, while nevertheless having relevant expertise. However, Greenberg and Shuman (1997) suggested that the data available to a treating clinician is rarely sufficient to allow them to provide a legal opinion and there may be conflict between their treating and legal roles. For example, treating clinicians usually work under pressure and have to formulate their opinions quickly and move expeditiously to treatment and intervention and invariably they do not have access to all the relevant sources of information, such as general practitioner and hospital records, previous psychological or psychiatric notes or details about the claimant's education and history. Not uncommonly, even hospital records relating to the index injury are unavailable and in some cases the diagnosis of brain injury relies primarily or even exclusively on the claimant's account. In recent years there has been a growing awareness of the high incidence of invalid responding among brain injured litigants with the base rate of non-credible presentations on performance validity testing being in the order of 40% (Larrabee, 2003; see Chapter 7). However, treating therapists commonly assume that their patients have sought treatment to maximise their recovery and overcome limitations and therefore that they will provide an accurate account to maximise the chances of progress, when this may not be the case. Therapists typically adopt a relatively uncritical attitude towards their patient, reflecting their training in providing a supportive and collaborative therapeutic approach and sometimes they become keen advocates on their behalf. It is therefore not surprising that few clinical evaluations include assessments of symptom validity, in contrast to forensic examinations, so inadvertently leading to erroneous conclusions. For example, McCarter et al. (2009) found that only 16% of clinicians working in clinical settings reported using symptom validity tests in more than half of their assessments, compared with 73% of those involved with medico-legal evaluations. The differences between therapeutic and forensic roles have the effect that the advantages of treating therapists may be far fewer and less compelling than might initially appear and therapeutic evidence may be compromised or erroneous. Greenberg and Shuman (1997) outlined 10 critical differences between therapeutic and forensic roles and strongly advocated that clinicians should not adopt a dual role in civil litigation (see Table 1).

Table 1: 10 Differences between Therapeutic and Forensic Relationships (adapted from Greenberg and Shuman, 1997)

	Care Provision	Forensic Evaluation
1. Whose client is patient/litigant?	The mental health practitioner	The Lawyer
2. The relational privilege that governs disclosure in each relationship	Therapist-Patient Privilege	Lawyer-Client and Lawyer work-product privilege
3. The cognitive set and evaluative attitude of each expert	Supportive, accepting, empathic	Neutral, objective, detached
4. The differing areas of competency of each expert	Therapy Techniques for treatment of the impairment	Forensic Evaluation techniques relevant to the legal claim
5. The nature of the hypotheses tested by each expert	Diagnostic criteria for the purpose of therapy	Psycholegal criteria for the purpose of legal adjudication
6. The scrutiny applied to the information utilised in the process and the role of historical truth	Mostly based on information from the person being treated with little scrutiny of that information by the therapist	Litigant information supplemented with that of collateral sources and scrutinised by the evaluator and the court
7. The amount and control of structure in each relationship	Patient structured and relatively less structured than forensic evaluation	Evaluator structured and relatively more structured than therapy
8. The nature and degree of "adversarialness" in each relationship	A helping relationship; rarely adversarial	An evaluative relationship; frequently adversarial
9. The goal of the professional in each relationship	Therapist attempts to benefit the patient by working within the therapeutic relationship	Evaluator advocates for the results and implications of the evaluation for the benefit of the court
10. The impact on each relationship critical judgment by the expert	The basis of the relationship is therapeutic alliance and critical judgment is likely to impair that alliance	The basis of the relationship is evaluative and critical judgment is unlikely to cause serious emotional harm

Brain injury claims usually feature a number of witness statements provided by the claimant and their family and friends, which detail their pre-accident functioning and the effects of the injury on their personality and cognitive and physical abilities, as well as their capacity to manage their life day-to-day. However, the limitations of witness statements provided by the claimant are readily apparent. As in the order of 40% of litigants present non-credibly on validity testing, there is no guarantee that their self-report in a witness statement will be credible or unbiased. The risks of unreliable report potentially grow given that they are essentially co-authored and drafted and amended by a lawyer who has significant incentives to present their client in a particular light. The lawyer's influence is sometimes transparent, such as when a statement lacks an authentic voice and it is written in a way that is inconsistent with the personality, education and social background of the signatory, or uses terminology recognisable to a head injury specialist, but not to a layman. Adopting the same format or making the same points across statements also betray the author. Typically, the claimant's difficulties are outlined in detail highlighting problems with their mental health and well-being, personality and cognitive abilities, and while this may reflect the situation, it may also be guided by common assumptions about the likely outcome following brain trauma. A tell-tale sign of incomplete reporting is the omission of pre- or post-accident undesirable characteristics or issues and, in some cases, the omission of positive changes following the brain injury. The impact of brain trauma is invariably negative and inevitably the focus is on the individual's diminished functioning, both interpersonal and social, and their psychological distress, cognitive difficulties and problems integrating socially. However, in recent years there has been a growing recognition that some people show post-traumatic growth after their injuries. Grace et al. (2015) proposed that post-traumatic growth involves individuals reporting that their relationship with others has been enhanced and includes a greater sense of connection or compassion towards others who have suffered, a greater appreciation of themselves and new possibilities in life, and changes in their philosophy about life and what is important. Grace et al. (2015) conducted a systematic review and meta-analysis of research and found that people with acquired brain injuries show post-traumatic growth as is also seen following other traumatic events or illnesses, such as cancer, bereavement, and surgery and, as such, they may not simply be victims of trauma. Similarly, while many caregivers experience significant burden from looking after a person with a brain injury (Knight et al., 1998; Rivera et al., 2007; Watanabe et al., 2000) this is not always the case and some report positive experiences from caring (Machamer et al., 2002).

Subtle biases

13–005 When preparing evidence for the court, professionals can be subject to particular ways of thinking about the issues that lead them to prefer some conclusions over others and subtly alter and bias their thinking and consideration of the issues and their conclusions. Typically these biases are unintentional and the individual may be quite unaware of them as they tend to arise from their training, ways of working in their professional group, or they represent common assumptions held by many people. The difficulty for the court is that they inadvertently influence the professional's opinion, particularly about aetiology, treatment and prognosis, so further complicating the judge's assessment.

Base rates

It is common that a clinician expresses the view that a claimant's presentation is consistent with, or indicative of, a brain injury. Many claimants report having problems with their thought processes and difficulty with their concentration, memory and organisational skills, as well as having emotional and behavioural issues or physical and somatic complaints. They may say they have an unreliable memory and, for instance, report mislaying items in the house or say they will go into a room and be unable to remember the reason, or complain of having difficulty concentrating on the television when there are extraneous noises. Issues with irritability or anxiety may also be said to interfere with their family or working life. When examined by an expert, the conclusion may be that these complaints are consistent with or indicate that the individual has suffered brain trauma in the index accident. In some cases, particularly in subtle brain injury claims where there may be no physical evidence of brain trauma, such as abnormalities on neuroimaging, or contemporaneous clinical evidence, such as findings recorded in an Accident and Emergency Department, these complaints can be the primary or even only evidence of a brain injury. In these circumstances, brain-related or post-concussion complaints are particularly significant and in the absence of an alternative explanation, viewed as indicating brain trauma that, if persistent, is seen as permanent. A key issue, therefore, is the extent to which these complaints are uniquely associated with, or pathognomonic of, brain trauma. In other words, it is important to know the base rate of complaints not only among those who have had a brain injury, but more particularly, in other conditions and even those who have no clinical condition. In the event that complaints are not uniquely associated with brain trauma, an expert's conclusion that they indicate a neurological injury will necessarily be erroneous and misleading.

13–006

Many symptoms presented to the court as indicating brain trauma are not particularly unusual. For example, mislaying keys or forgetting the reason for going into a room, might not be thought of as uncommon or pathological, although experts routinely rely on such incidents to diagnose a brain injury and conclude it has had adverse effects. Iverson and McCracken (1997) studied the base rate of post-concussion complaints in a group suffering from chronic pain, none of whom had a brain injury. They found that post-concussion complaints were common and, for instance, 76% complained of fatigue, 73% reported irritability and aggression following little or no provocation, 37% complained of personality changes (including being socially or sexually inappropriate) and 69% complained of apathy or lack of spontaneity, although none had a neurological injury. Iverson (2006) examined the base rate of post-concussion symptoms in patients with depression and found that nine out of 10 met liberal self-reported criteria for a post-concussion syndrome and more than half met conservative criteria for the diagnosis. He pointed out that long after the symptoms of a mild brain injury had resolved, individuals with pain, depression or both, would be likely to meet the criteria for persistent post-concussion syndrome, even though the effects of the brain injury had long resolved. Lees-Haley and Brown (1993) examined the base rate of brain injury complaints in a group of people attending a family practice with complaints such as sore throats, respiratory problems, flu and hypertension, and a claimant group involved in litigation for issues such as age, sex or race discrimination, sexual or verbal harassment, verbal threats, intimidation, and wrongful termination and emotional distress, and none had a brain injury. They found a high incidence of brain-injury symptoms reported by the claimants; 78% reported having concentration difficulties, 61% felt disorganised and 53% had memory problems. Interestingly, in the family practice group 26% had concentration complaints, 24% felt disorganised, and 20% reported having memory problems (see Chapter 5, Table 5). Lees-Haley et al. (2001) examined claimants with mild brain injuries and a group of claimants none of whom had a brain injury, but who were pursuing litigation for issues such as sexual harassment, wrongful dismissal and discrimination claims. They found that 71% of the brain injury group felt shocked immediately after their litigating injury, but so did 88% of the non-brain injury group. Among the brain injured group 71% complained of memory difficulties, 63% had difficulty paying attention and 33% felt disoriented, but in the non-brain injured group 42% complained of memory difficulties, 56% had difficulty paying attention, and 42% felt disoriented. Zakzanis and Yeung (2011) examined post-concussive symptoms in healthy normal people, that is, people who had no clinical condition. They found that fatigue, poor concentration and other complaints, such as forgetfulness and dizziness, were regularly reported, indicating that such complaints were common (see Chapter 5, Table 6). Garden and Sullivan (2010) examined a group of normal individuals and found that 92% endorsed having at least three post-concussion symptoms and 30% endorsed having at least 11 of 13 symptoms. A significant proportion who also reported having problems with their mood, endorsed having the symptoms to a moderate-to-severe degree, suggesting that mood issues were associated with complaints.

Symptoms attributed to a brain injury may not therefore necessarily reflect neurological damage and they can be found in those with other conditions and other litigating injuries and they are not uncommon in the normal population. An expert who is unaware of the base rate of "symptoms" runs the risk of over-pathologising and erroneously attributing complaints due to other conditions, such as pain or low mood, to a neurological injury or even interpreting difficulties that are common among healthy individuals as indicating pathology. This arises because of what is sometimes termed illusory correlations between conditions and complaints. For example, a neurologist who routinely hears brain injured patients complain about forgetfulness, poor concentration and diminished organisational skills, may come to associate these complaints with brain trauma and over time infer that the condition is present when complaints are reported. As most clinicians do not assess patients (or claimants) with conditions from outside their specialty, and even fewer spend any time interviewing healthy people, they may become susceptible to inferring a condition is present when complaints are reported, unaware that their conclusions are based on symptoms that are neither uncommon nor specific. Many experts are unaware of the importance of symptom base rates or, if they are, do not know the base rates of specific symptoms in any event. In these circumstances, a diagnosis of brain trauma can have iatrogenic effects and risk establishing the individual in a patient role. Lawyers can also be susceptible to illusory correlations and misinterpret complaints. A personal injury lawyer who is experienced in dealing with brain injured claimants will be familiar with the difficulties they experience and when new claimants present with similar symptoms, they may assume that they are characteristic or typical of those following brain trauma and initiate litigation accordingly. This perspective may in turn be reinforced by expert opinion and lead to services being commissioned, such as case management and a rehabilitation team, so introducing iatrogenic and critogenic influences. McCrae (2008) observed that a situation can develop where an individual with complaints, but no clear indication that they have had significant head trauma, is diagnosed as having had a brain injury and informed that they will never make a complete recovery, and the resulting harm can be long lasting and difficult to reverse.

Hindsight bias

Brain injury claims invariably generate a considerable amount of documentary evidence such as hospital, general practitioner, educational and case management records, to name but a few. These documents are forwarded to medical and care experts and occasionally also made available to those involved in rehabilitation. While this evidence can be important in understanding an individual's condition and progress, it potentially runs the risk of establishing hindsight bias whereby, with the benefit of hindsight, the clinician's perspective of the claimant is influenced, sometimes significantly. For example, knowledge that the claimant had a lengthy interval of post-traumatic amnesia or Glasgow Coma Scale readings were low at the accident scene may influence the expert to interpret current behaviour or findings as being consistent with those details. Neuroimaging arguably has a particularly powerful influence on the perceptions of both clinicians and lawyers and, for instance, knowledge that frontal lobe contusions were found on CT or MRI imaging can establish a view that neuropsychological abnormalities will also be observed in line with, or consistent with, the imaging. It is not uncommon for an expert to assert that as the patient had a severe brain injury, personality problems such as impulsiveness or disorganisation are consistent with the injury. However, such a view can be problematical as hindsight bias can lead the expert to overlook other possible causes for the claimant's difficulties, such as pre-existing personality characteristics or post-accident issues, such as dysfunctional peer group influences or substance use. Although these other factors may be important, and sometimes clearly so, the gravitational pull of hindsight bias can be substantial and cause both clinicians and lawyers to become extremely resistant to the significance of alternative factors when they are brought to their attention.

13–007

Hindsight bias can be associated with what is sometimes called the Texas sharpshooter fallacy. Iverson et al. (2008) outlined that the Texas sharpshooter was known for firing his shotgun randomly into the side of a barn after which he painted a bull's-eye around the spot where most of the shot was clustered. This is similar to the approach taken by clinicians when they argue that observations or findings must be due to the injurious event. Iverson et al. (2008) proposed that such reasoning is potentially fallacious because a cluster or pattern of findings, or low scores on cognitive tests, may simply be due to chance or some other cause. As there is a wide range of potential and unpredictable outcomes after brain trauma, clinicians are particularly susceptible to such reasoning. For example, after a severe injury some people show executive limitations, whereas others have predominant problems with their attention or memory, some show impairments on intelligence tests, whereas others do not, and some have global and severe deficits, whereas others have mild and selective limitations. Whatever the pattern, the clinician may argue their findings are consistent with the injury. In these circumstances, almost any combination of results or observations can be interpreted as consistent with the index event and the expert overlooks alternative or contributory factors. Sometimes even normal findings are interpreted as being consistent with a putative brain injury and, for instance, it may be argued that a normal cognitive profile does not rule out impairments or indicate recovery, but rather is an example of a frontal lobe paradox and that the claimant has limitations that cannot be demonstrated on conventional measures. As Iverson et al. (2008) pointed out the fallacy with this reasoning is that any inference or opinion can be selected and adjusted after the data are collected, making it impossible to test the opinion. Hindsight bias therefore establishes a mental set where the expert accepts evidence of deficit and resists a less dramatic portrayal of the claimant's difficulties, other explanations or that recovery has occurred.

Confirmatory bias

13-008 A further potential complicating issue is confirmatory bias, that is, experts' and lawyers' tendency to favour observations or clinical details that confirm or are consistent with their views and opinions while discounting, or placing less weight on alternative perspectives and contradictory views. Personal injury litigation is perhaps particularly likely to lead to entrenched positions due to its adversarial nature and high stakes for both parties. This can lead to polarised opposition, sometimes over minor matters. Confirmatory bias is evident when experts maintain their own opinions in the face of contradictory evidence that comes to light. For instance, a claimant's cognitive limitations may initially be attributed to an injury with the clinician later discounting the relevance of pre-existing dyslexia or challenging the accuracy of the diagnosis when it is subsequently found in educational records. Occasionally experts attach scientific papers to their reports to support and endorse their opinions. Invariably, however, this betrays confirmatory bias as there may be no attempt to conduct a proper literature review and sometimes even only a single paper or a small number of papers consistent with the expert's opinion are included and no contradictory research.

Faust et al. (1991) suggested that confirmatory bias can significantly influence a clinician's approach to assessment. Even basic information, such as a lawyer informing the expert in instructions that the claimant was involved in an accident and had a head injury, potentially establishes expectations that certain complaints will be found. A claimant's self-report of memory difficulties may lead to an extensive examination of memory functioning and, if a sufficient number of cognitive tests are given, some anomalous results are likely to be obtained. This occurs because there is often considerable variability in an individual's cognitive profile even in the absence of any injury, and it is common to obtain some low results on the basis of normal variation alone (see Chapter 5). Although not unusual, a clinician who expects to find an abnormality because a claimant has been injured may interpret such findings as indicating deficits attributable to the injury, so resulting in a false-positive diagnosis. Similarly, as post-concussion complaints such as dizziness, irritability and fatigue have a high base rate, even in those who have not been injured, a clinician who anticipates that a claimant will have "symptoms" is likely to have their expectations confirmed. Likewise, knowledge that a claimant has had a frontal lobe injury may lead the clinician to examine for executive limitations and potentially misinterpret normal behaviour, such as disorganisation and impulsivity in an adolescent, as indicating a pathological change. An associated issue is when the clinician selectively attends to reported problems or poor results on tests, while overlooking or placing little weight on positive observations or findings. Faust et al. (1991) pointed out that the clinician may attach particular significance to an isolated abnormal finding, while overlooking the majority of normal findings. For instance, they may emphasise the potential adverse consequences of brain damage found on MRI imaging, while overlooking relatively normal day-to-day functioning, or stress the significance of a poor cognitive test result, despite other normal results and the claimant having returned to work or being engaged in childcare. Occasionally a clinician will also use "neuro-terminology" to describe the claimant's difficulties, so forging a link or emphasising an association between injury and presentation. For example, they may describe a person as having neurobehavioural difficulties, rather than difficulties, as being impulsive, rather than impetuous, lacking insight instead of lacking acumen, or having dysexecutive impairments, rather than being feckless.

A particular form of confirmatory bias is anchoring, that is, the tendency to rely excessively on a salient piece of information and anchor an opinion on it. Iverson et al. (2008) suggested that this can result in some information having more influence than it should. For instance, being informed by a lawyer that their claimant has had catastrophic injuries with probable long-term effects may influence the clinician to seek confirmatory evidence, as opposed to an alternative opinion. Alternatively, being told at the outset that there are suspicious aspects to a claim may establish anchoring in a different direction. Aspects of the claimant's behaviour may have a similar influence and, for instance, an isolated episode of financial mismanagement may colour the clinician's views on their ability to manage their financial affairs and weigh heavily in their assessment of the claimant's financial capacity. Occasionally a dramatic incident or aspect of the claimant's behaviour may be repeated throughout the records, also influencing the perception of both lawyers and experts and have an anchoring effect, despite it having occurred some time before.

3. JUDICIAL DECISION-MAKING

There is no better starting point for an examination of judicial decision-making than a speech given by Mostyn J[5] to the University of Bristol Law School on 8 December 2014, entitled "The Craft of Judging and Legal Reasoning". It is a wise and learned discussion of the process and is at once a valuable analysis in its

13–009

---

[5] Published in Australia in *The Judicial Review* but also available to read on the website of the Judiciary of England and Wales.

own right and a very useful resource for identifying other important contributions on the subject. Mostyn J sits as a judge in the Family Division but, as he says, the facts he has to find in the course of his work are of "the utmost seriousness"[6] and the fact-finding task of a judge in civil cases cannot logically differ whether he sits in the Family, Queen's Bench or Chancery Divisions.

Mostyn J begins by recommending two works, each of which we also commend to those with any serious interest in the subject. One is *The Business of Judging* by the late Lord Bingham[7]; the other is *Reflections on Judging* by Judge Richard Posner of the US Court of Appeals for the Seventh Circuit.[8] Mostyn J continues with the following:

> "If I were to ask you what was the key factor in finding facts in a trial you might reply 'credibility'. Who does the judge believe? The primacy of the factor of credibility has an iconic, almost canonical, status. Thus Posner writes at page 123:
>
>> 'No legal catchphrase is more often repeated than that determinations by a trial judge whether to believe or disbelieve a witness can be overturned on appeal in only extraordinary circumstances. The reason is said to be the inestimable value, in assessing credibility, of seeing and hearing the witness rather than reading a transcript of his testimony, since the transcript eliminates clues to veracity that are supplied by tone of voice, hesitation, body language, and other non-verbal expressions.'
>
> Just such a line was taken in *Beacon Insurance Company Ltd v Maharaj Bookstore Ltd* [2014] UKPC 21 (9 July 2014), a recent decision of the Privy Council on an appeal from Trinidad and Tobago. Lord Hodge cited the Canadian Supreme Court in *Housen v Nikolaisen* [2002] 2 SCR 235, para 14:
>
>> 'The trial judge has sat through the entire case and his ultimate judgment reflects his total familiarity with the evidence. The insight gained by the trial judge who has lived with the case for several days, weeks or even months may be far deeper than that of the Court of Appeal whose view of the case is much more limited and narrow, often being shaped and distorted by the various orders and rulings being challenged.'
>
> He cited the famous dictum of Hoffmann J, as he then was, in *Biogen Inc v Medeva plc* [1997] RPC 1, at page 45:
>
>> 'The need for appellate caution in reversing the trial judge's evaluation of the facts is based upon much more solid grounds than professional courtesy. It is because specific findings of fact, even by the most meticulous judge, are inherently an incomplete statement of the impression which was made upon him by the primary evidence. His expressed findings are always surrounded

---

[6] There are many who consider that the facts actually determine the outcome of cases very much more often than "the law". The story generally attributed to Ognall J, when hearing a case in which counsel had devoted much attention to a lot of complicated law, is probably not apocryphal and may provide a salutary lesson for advocates. The judge listened to leading counsel's legal analysis for some 25 minutes in opening, his face growing ever redder with impatience (in both respects he had a head start on the wider population). Eventually, he could stand no more and interrupted "Thank you, Miss/Mr X, I am sure this law is all very interesting, but it may help you to know I am rather more of a merits man". He is not the only judge to harbour such sentiments.

[7] *The late Tom Bingham, The Business of Judging* (Oxford: OUP, 2000).

[8] Richard A Posner, *Reflections on Judging* (Harvard University Press, 2013).

by a penumbra of imprecision as to emphasis, relative weight, minor qualification and nuance ... of which time and language do not permit exact expression, but which may play an important part in the judge's overall evaluation.'

He cited Lord Neuberger of Abbotsbury in *Re B (A Child) (Care Proceedings: Threshold Criteria)* [2013] 1 WLR 1911 at [53]:

'This is traditionally and rightly explained by reference to good sense, namely that the trial judge has the benefit of assessing the witnesses and actually hearing and considering their evidence as it emerges. Consequently, where a trial judge has reached a conclusion on the primary facts, it is only in a rare case, such as where that conclusion was one (i) which there was no evidence to support, (ii) which was based on a misunderstanding of the evidence, or (iii) which no reasonable judge could have reached, that an appellate tribunal will interfere with it. This can also be justified on grounds of policy (parties should put forward their best case on the facts at trial and not regard the potential to appeal as a second chance), cost (appeals can be expensive), delay (appeals on fact often take a long time to get on), and practicality (in many cases, it is very hard to ascertain the facts with confidence, so a second, different, opinion is no more likely to be right than the first).'

So you can see why this feature, credibility, has gained such high importance. It has a long and heavily backed pedigree. But is it justified? Posner has his doubts. He writes at page 123:

'This is one of those commonsense propositions that may well be false. Nonverbal clues to veracity are unreliable and distract a trier of fact from the cognitive content of the witness's testimony. Yet it would occur to few judges to question the proposition that the trial judge has superior ability to judge credibility than the appellate judge, because nothing in the culture of the law encourages its insiders to be sceptical of oft-repeated propositions accepted as the old-age wisdom of the profession, and because appellate judges (indeed all judges) are happy to hand off responsibility for deciding to another adjudicator.'

And then he makes this very obvious point:

'No longer, however, are they technologically constrained to do so. Witnesses' testimony could be video-taped and the tapes of their testimony made available to an appellate judge who thought demeanour important in assessing the truthfulness of testimony.'

This convincingly undermines the argument that first instance judges somehow have some numinous exclusive power to assess credibility perfectly. But is oral testimony about an event the best source of evidence about that event? Invariably the testimony depends on the memory of the witness. In *Gestmin SGPS SA v Credit Suisse (UK) Ltd & Anor* [2013] EWHC 3560 (Comm) (15 November 2013) Leggatt J had some very potent things to say about testimony based on memory at paras 15–21:

'An obvious difficulty which affects allegations and oral evidence based on recollection of events which occurred several years ago is the unreliability of human memory

While everyone knows that memory is fallible, I do not believe that the legal system has sufficiently absorbed the lessons of a century of psychological research into the nature of memory and the unreliability of eyewitness testimony. One of the most important lessons of such research is that in everyday life we are not aware of the extent to which our own and other people's memories are unreliable and believe our memories to be more faithful than they are. Two common (and related) errors are to suppose: (1) that the stronger and more vivid is our feeling or experience of recollection, the more likely the recollection is to be accurate; and (2) that the more confident another person is in their recollection, the more likely their recollection is to be accurate.

Underlying both these errors is a faulty model of memory as a mental record which is fixed at the time of experience of an event and then fades (more or less slowly) over time. In fact, psychological research has demonstrated that memories are fluid and malleable, being constantly rewritten whenever they are retrieved. This is true even of so-called 'flashbulb' memories, that is memories of experiencing or learning of a particularly shocking or traumatic event. (The very description 'flashbulb' memory is in fact misleading, reflecting as it does the misconception that memory operates like a camera or other device that makes a fixed record of an experience.) External information can intrude into a witness's memory, as can his or her own thoughts and beliefs, and both can cause dramatic changes in recollection. Events can come to be recalled as memories which did not happen at all or which happened to someone else (referred to in the literature as a failure of source memory).

Memory is especially unreliable when it comes to recalling past beliefs. Our memories of past beliefs are revised to make them more consistent with our present beliefs. Studies have also shown that memory is particularly vulnerable to interference and alteration when a person is presented with new information or suggestions about an event in circumstances where his or her memory of it is already weak due to the passage of time.

The process of civil litigation itself subjects the memories of witnesses to powerful biases. The nature of litigation is such that witnesses often have a stake in a particular version of events. This is obvious where the witness is a party or has a tie of loyalty (such as an employment relationship) to a party to the proceedings. Other, more subtle influences include allegiances created by the process of preparing a witness statement and of coming to court to give evidence for one side in the dispute. A desire to assist, or at least not to prejudice, the party who has called the witness or that party's lawyers, as well as a natural desire to give a good impression in a public forum, can be significant motivating forces.

Considerable interference with memory is also introduced in civil litigation by the procedure of preparing for trial. A witness is asked to make a statement, often (as in the present case) when a long time has already elapsed since the relevant events. The statement is usually drafted for the witness by a lawyer who is inevitably conscious of the significance for the issues in the case of what the witness does nor does not say. The statement is made after the witness's memory has been "refreshed" by reading documents. The documents considered often include statements of case and other argumentative material as well as documents which the witness did not see at the time or which came into existence after the events which he or she is being asked to recall. The statement may go through several iterations before it is finalised. Then, usually months later, the witness will be asked to reread his or her statement and review documents again before giving evidence in court. The effect of this process is to establish in the mind of the witness the matters recorded in his or her own statement and other written material, whether they be true or false, and to cause the witness's memory of events to be based increasingly on this material and later interpretations of it rather than on the original experience of the events.

It is not uncommon (and the present case was no exception) for witnesses to be asked in cross-examination if they understand the difference between recollection and reconstruction or whether their evidence is a genuine recollection or a reconstruction of events. Such questions are misguided in at least two ways. First, they erroneously presuppose that there is a clear distinction between recollection and reconstruction, when all remembering of distant events involves reconstructive processes. Second, such questions disregard the fact that such processes are largely unconscious and that the strength, vividness and apparent authenticity of memories is not a reliable measure of their truth.'

One of Lord Bingham's essays in 'The Business of Judging' is 'The Judge as Juror: The Judicial Interpretation of Factual Issues'. There he quotes an extra-curial speech by Lord Justice Browne, who makes the same argument as Leggatt J, but more laconically:

'The human capacity for honestly believing something which bears no relation to what actually happened is unlimited.'"

[When weighing a witness's memory a trier of facts should firmly bear in mind Aleksandar Hemon's comments[9]:]

13–010

'If I try to tell you what happened to me in '91, I'll have to guess about certain things, I'll have to make up certain things, because I can't remember everything. And certain memories are not datable. You and I might remember our lunch, but some years from now we won't remember it was on a Friday. I will not connect it with what happened this morning because they are discontinuous events. To tell a story, you have to—not falsify—but you have to assemble and disassemble. Memories are creative. To treat memory as a fact is nonsense. It's inescapably fiction.'

Lord Bingham also points to a further obvious pitfall in the path of the assessment of credibility, namely the very plausible but dishonest witness:

'The ability to tell a coherent, plausible and assured story, embellished with snippets of circumstantial detail and laced with occasional shots of life-like forgetfulness, is very likely to impress any tribunal of fact. But it is also the hallmark of the confidence trickster down the ages.'

Not infrequently it is shown that lies have been told out of court. That is by no means determinative. It has been said that in the assessment of core credibility in a fact-finding inquiry it would be as well for the court to give itself the famous direction in *R. v Lucas* [1981] Q.B. 720 where it was stated by Lord Lane CJ:

'To be capable of amounting to corroboration the lie told out of court must first of all be deliberate. Secondly it must relate to a material issue. Thirdly the motive for the lie must be a realisation of guilt and a fear of the truth. The jury should in appropriate cases be reminded that people sometimes lie, for example, in an attempt to bolster up a just cause, or out of shame or out of a wish to conceal disgraceful behaviour from their family.'

---

[9] *New York Review of Books*, 4 December 2014.

Again, this is a highly important observation for a trier of facts to have in mind.

Therefore Lord Bingham argues that the better approach is, when finding facts, to look first, where possible, at contemporaneous documents and undisputed facts and to draw conclusions primarily from those sources. He cites the dissenting speech, now almost forgotten, of Lord Pearce in *Onassis v Vergottis* [1968] 2 Lloyd's Rep. 403 HL:

> '"Credibility" involves wider problems than mere "demeanour" which is mostly concerned with whether the witness appears to be telling the truth as he now believes it to be. Credibility covers the following problems. First, is the witness a truthful or untruthful person? Secondly, is he, though a truthful person, telling something less than the truth on this issue, or, though an untruthful person, telling the truth on this issue? Thirdly, though he is a truthful person telling the truth as he sees it, did he register the intentions of the conversation correctly and, if so, has his memory correctly retained them? Also, has his recollection been subsequently altered by unconscious bias or wishful thinking or by overmuch discussion of it with others? Witnesses, especially those who are emotional, who think that they are morally in the right, tend very easily and unconsciously to conjure up a legal right that did not exist. It is a truism, often used in accident cases, that with every day that passes the memory becomes fainter and the imagination becomes more active. For that reason a witness, however honest, rarely persuades a Judge that his present recollection is preferable to that which was taken down in writing immediately after the accident occurred. Therefore, contemporary documents are always of the utmost importance. And lastly, although the honest witness believes he heard or saw this or that, it is so improbable that it is on balance more likely that he was mistaken? On this point it is essential that the balance of probability is put correctly into the scales in weighing the credibility of a witness. And motive is one aspect of probability. All these problems compendiously are entailed when a Judge assesses the credibility of a witness; they are all part of one judicial process. And in the process contemporary documents and admitted or incontrovertible facts and probabilities must play their proper part.'

13–011 In a similar vein in the *Gestmin* case at para 22 Leggatt J states:

> 'In the light of these considerations, the best approach for a judge to adopt in the trial of a commercial case is, in my view, to place little if any reliance at all on witnesses' recollections of what was said in meetings and conversations, and to base factual findings on inferences drawn from the documentary evidence and known or probable facts. This does not mean that oral testimony serves no useful purpose—though its utility is often disproportionate to its length. But its value lies largely, as I see it, in the opportunity which cross-examination affords to subject the documentary record to critical scrutiny and to gauge the personality, motivations and working practices of a witness, rather than in testimony of what the witness recalls of particular conversations and events. Above all, it is important to avoid the fallacy of supposing that, because a witness has confidence in his or her recollection and is honest, evidence based on that recollection provides any reliable guide to the truth.'

If this is the more reliable approach to fact-finding then this gives rise to a paradox, or at least an irony. Lord Hodge's opinion in the *Beacon Insurance Company* [[2014] UKPC 21] case cites at para 17 Lord Bridge of Harwich in *Whitehouse v Jordan* [1981] 1 W.L.R. 246 at 269–270:

'[T]he importance of the part played by those advantages in assisting the judge to any particular conclusion of fact varies through a wide spectrum from, at one end, a straight conflict of primary fact between witnesses, where credibility is crucial and the appellate court can hardly ever interfere, to, at the other end, an inference from undisputed primary facts, where the appellate court is in just as good a position as the trial judge to make the decision.'

And Lord Hodge concluded:

'Where the honesty of a witness is a central issue in the case, one is close to the former end of the spectrum as the advantage which the trial judge has had in assessing the credibility and reliability of oral evidence is not available to the appellate court. Where a trial judge is able to make his findings of fact based entirely or almost entirely on undisputed documents, one will be close to the latter end of the spectrum.'

Thus, the more reliable the technique of fact-finding, the more it is susceptible to appellate review.

Another interesting statement of the judicial approach to assessing credibility comes from Robert Goff LJ in *The Ocean Frost* [1985] 1 Lloyd's Rep. 1 at 57:

'Speaking from my own experience, I have found it essential in cases of fraud, when considering the credibility of witnesses, always to test their veracity by reference to the objective facts proved independently of their testimony, in particular by reference to the documents in the case, and also to pay particular regard to their motives and to the overall probabilities. It is frequently very difficult to tell whether a witness is telling the truth or not; and where there is a conflict of evidence such as there was in the present case, reference to the objective facts and documents, references to the witness' motives and to the overall probabilities can be of very great assistance to a Judge in ascertaining the truth.'"

Expert evidence

This aspect of the judicial decision-making process is relatively straightforward in theory, even if it may be hard work in practice. This is not the place to discuss the merits or demerits of expert evidence generally or the extent to which experts enhance or corrode the quest for justice. As the authors explained in Chapter 1, for discussion of such issues, the reader should begin with Lord Woolf's "Access to Justice" report, consider the terms of Part 35 of the Civil Procedure Rules 1998 (CPR) and Chapter 23 of Kemp, *Personal Injury Law, Practice and Procedure*.[10] What follows is likely to be the typical approach of any judge faced with the task of evaluating and choosing between competing experts giving evidence in a given case.

It should be taken as read that the expert will have familiarised himself with what is expected when giving evidence. He must always remember that his primary duty is to the court and that trumps any obligations he may have to the party that instructs (and pays) him.[11] We shall further assume the expert will be familiar with (or, otherwise, will take the trouble to study) the judgment of

13–012

---

[10] Kemp, *Personal Injury Law, Practice and Procedure* (London: Thomson Reuters).
[11] For a reminder, see CPR r.35.3(2).

Cresswell J in *The Ikarian Reefer (No.1)*,[12] the Practice Direction to CPR Part 35 and the Protocol issued by the Civil Justice Council in June 2005 and reissued in 2012. We shall just concentrate on what distinguishes the good from the bad expert.

To be convincing and to be able to speak with authority then, as the authors have explained already, the expert needs to:

- Practise personally in and/or have recent experience of the field of which he speaks. That is as true of a doctor as it is of an engineer or an architect. The retired consultant who last operated on a patient 15 years ago and now makes a comfortable living from his medico-legal practice inevitably begins his evidence at a disadvantage.
- (Preferably) be recognised as someone who does not always give evidence for defendants against claimants or vice versa: otherwise there is a real risk of apparent (or actual) bias and of being seen as a "hired gun".
- Be familiar with the literature if there is any scope for academic or practical disagreement about the topic in question.
- Have studied all relevant written or other relevant material in the case. For example, in the case of a road traffic accident (RTA) claim and/or one involving clinical negligence, that means being familiar with all the contemporaneous documentation including accident, medical and nursing records, witness statements from lay witnesses and so forth. It may mean listening to the evidence of lay witnesses in the trial before going into the witness box himself. It usually means not having read the papers so long ago that the expert has now forgotten their contents.
- Have ensured that his knowledge or familiarity with the case is current: that may mean, for example, having examined the claimant recently or having visited the scene of the accident or having inspected the component that is said to have failed sufficiently recently so as to be able to describe it convincingly.[13]
- Be able to show that he has kept an open mind as long as possible (and that he is willing to review his conclusions), being prepared to consider alternative points of view and new or additional material and be flexible enough to give ground if that is appropriate and willing to recognise points against any such thesis as he is commending in his evidence as well as those which support it.
- Avoid being seen as an advocate for the cause that he is in fact supporting.
- Be able to express himself in writing in a way that is clear and with economy of language. That applies equally to reports and to joint statements.

If the expert in the case is able to follow those guidelines, then it is likely that he will impress the court. It is very rare that both (or all) experts are equally successful in each of those respects. The one who does best is likely to be on the "winning" (which we ought to assume is also the "right") side.

---

[12] *The Ikarian Reefer (No.1)* [1993] 2 Lloyd's Rep. 68.
[13] Better this than struggling to demonstrate how the component works in the course of oral evidence: all litigators are familiar with the well-known truth that court experiments always go wrong.

Lay witnesses: how do we decide between them?

Lord Bingham[14] reminds us that:

13–013

> "The job of the judges is to apply the law, not to indulge their personal preferences. There are areas in which they are required to exercise a discretion, but such discretions are much more closely constrained than is always acknowledged".

This is, of course, uncontroversial as a statement of principle. What it does not necessarily illuminate is how facts are decided, or the basis on which a discretion is exercised. Here, it seems, there is bound to be at least an element of subjective, intuitive, judgment.

That is most vividly apparent on issues of fact where, as a matter of logic and possibility, there is more than one choice. Just as the jury (or magistrates) in a criminal case will decide issues of fact, so the judge in a civil case will, save in a few exceptional cases such as those involving libel, have to do likewise. That may involve deciding which out of two people trying to tell the truth has the more reliable memory. It may even involve deciding whether they are lying—that is, putting forward an account which they know to be untrue. In other cases, it is by no means unusual to find that the authors of two competing accounts may each believe that theirs is correct. But they cannot both be right.

The decision-maker's role in such a case is to decide which is correct or, more strictly, which is to be preferred as rendering the decision for which he contends[15] the more probable. We do not pretend to say with any confidence whether judges or juries are any good at this, still less whether they are any better than any lay person or other professional might be in a spotting a liar, be that in court or on a television programme such as *Call My Bluff* or any of its more modern variants.

Juries, certainly, do this without any professional training: they must therefore rely on their own instincts, informed or tempered by their own personal experience and prejudices. Magistrates and judges may not have actual training in such decision-making but, by virtue of their professional lives, will inevitably have far more practical experience of the process. But, as we said at the outset, the point of this chapter is to investigate that process. Is it purely an instinctive judgment to say that A rather than B was telling the truth? Or is the process more scientific than that—or should it and can it be made so?[16]

13–014

The "golden rule", as we shall call it, of all evidential analysis when deciding questions of fact is that of the three 'C's: consistency, cogency and corroboration. But none of them is a precondition for an account being accurate, nor does the ticking of all three boxes mean that an account must in fact be true. A false account may be consistently told and its cogency may be very compelling. And it may be supported by an independent account (= corroborated) which turns out to be wholly fabricated or entirely mistaken. Hence the search for the truth has to

---

[14] Writing in *The Rule of Law*, published by Allen Lane in 2010, at p.51.
[15] This formulation is obviously careful and deliberate: the test of balance of probability loses most of its utility if it is applied to each and every dispute on the facts between witnesses, as observed by Langstaff J, in *Mugweni v NHS London* [2011] EWHC 334 (QB) at [7].
[16] There is a useful guide to analysing a witness's credibility in the speech of Lord Pearce in *Onassis v Vergottis* [1968] 2 Lloyd's Rep. 403 at 431.

take other paths if one is to decide which of two conflicting accounts is to be preferred when applying the requisite civil standard of proof of a "balance of probabilities".

At this juncture it may be as well to say a little more about the burden of proof. As the judicial system for common law civil claims is adversarial and not inquisitorial, the judge trying such claims is not in fact principally charged with eliciting the truth. Instead, his role is to decide whether or not the party advancing the claim has proven his case to the requisite degree of probability: that is, has the party discharged the burden of proof? In one of the last judgments delivered by Lord Denning, he said:

> "So I hold that when we speak of the due administration of justice this does not always mean ascertaining the truth of what happened. It often means that, as a matter of justice, a party must prove his case without any help from the other side. He must do it without discovery and without putting the other side into the witness box to answer questions."[17]

Suffice it to say, it is easier for a judge to decide whether the standard of proof has been met sufficiently to discharge the burden than to decide what, as a matter of fact, happened. However, the judge should always strive to make findings of fact where possible, and only in exceptional circumstances decide, without making findings of primary fact, that the burden has not been discharged: "a judge should only resort to the burden of proof where he is unable to resolve an issue of fact or facts after he has unsuccessfully attempted to do so by examination and evaluation of the evidence".[18]

Guthrie Featherstone and the "judicial nose"

13–015 Judges (some of them, anyway) like to think that their experience on the Bench and in practice gives them an exceptional "nose" for deciding who is telling the truth and who is not. It was just such judicial conceit that enabled Horace Rumpole to have fun at the expense of the overly self-confident Featherstone J.[19] Nevertheless, our judges often refer to the good or bad impressions they had of a witness' "demeanour" in the witness box. But that may seem a very unscientific starting point for deciding who is telling the truth. A good "demeanour" may simply indicate that the witness was personable and/or presentable or a polished or practised liar.[20] Even so, experience tells us that all those who have been in

---

[17] *Air Canada v Secretary of State for Trade* [1983] 2 A.C. 394. Whether the inquisitorial is better than the adversarial system (or vice versa) is beyond the scope of this chapter. Suffice it to say, however, that the litigation culture in England and Wales is now significantly more inquisitorial than it was, as is reflected, for example, in the CPR.
[18] Per Auld LJ in *Stephens v Cannon* [2005] EWCA Civ 222; [2005] C.P. Rep. 31 at [19].
[19] Formerly Guthrie Featherstone QC, MP.
[20] To give an example of how "demeanour" in the witness box could surely be misleading, we know of a case where the outcome depended on the circumstances of an incident in a school playground when the two boys involved (later claimant and defendant) were aged 11 and 13 at the time. It was necessary to decide not only what they had done but also their respective intentions/motivation at the time. The case came to trial eight years later and yet the judge expressly placed emphasis on the respective "demeanour" of the witnesses, who by then were adults, in the witness box when they gave evidence. It is difficult to see how an assessment of demeanour in such circumstances can really be helpful.

court to hear a particular case do generally find that they agree on who was a "good" and who was a "poor" witness. But on what are such assessments based? Is there anything scientific in the process? Or is ours simply an instinctive judgment, albeit instinct is, in the case of judges and litigators, based on very considerable experience? And is it not very easy for us to be wrong, finding ourselves over-impressed by someone who is personally appealing or simply a very skilled actor?

The task facing a trial judge in a brain injury case may be compounded by the fact that the demeanour of a claimant (if called to give evidence) may well be significantly affected by the consequences of neurotrauma. Eye contact may be abnormal or non-existent; thought processes may be slowed and/or perseverative. This may be further affected by the cultural background and expectations of the witness. The judge will have to weigh these factors on top of the ordinary difficulties of evaluating witnesses, a particular issue for the judge to determine is often the question of whether the claimant is malingering (see Chapter 7). It will be appreciated that the judicial task may be a difficult one.

Science versus art

In an unpublished lecture to the New College Law Society some years ago, Robert Jay QC (now Jay J) addressed the dichotomy between a process of assessment which is substantially scientific—that is, one based on a rational analysis of scientific probabilities—and one that is instinctive or intuitive. 13–016

He explained how he had begun his professional life with a strong sense that a rational analysis based on objective criteria was to be favoured, but, over time and with experience, came to realise that he favoured—or at least attached real value—to the subjective, intuitive assessment made through observing performance in the witness box. We sense he might have not been overly-impressed by any such tools as the Slick criteria (Slick et al., 1999), preferring to trust his own more flexible, intuitive judgment.

This, of course, brings us back to the beginning of this chapter and to the discussion by Mostyn J of the thoughts of Posner and Lord Bingham, in the context of the major importance attached by the higher judiciary to the findings of fact at first instance.

Arguably barristers look for a number of key elements when cross-examining,[21] namely; consistency, cogency and corroboration, and the search for them will inform the cross-examiner's thinking. 13–017

- Consistency: this is one of the most obvious areas for investigation and can be regarded as elementary cross-examination material as we look for

---

[21] It is worth bearing in mind that, these days, it is usually only cross-examination which offers any real opportunity to investigate and so to assess a witness's account. When some of us began our professional lives, there was no exchange of witness statements between the parties: indeed, one sometimes called witnesses who had never even given a statement (a practice which the reader may be interested to know is still the norm in civil litigation in South Africa). Later, the rules required statements to be exchanged and now a witness's statement usually stands as the entirety (or at least the vast majority) of a witness's evidence in chief. Since the statement will almost inevitably have been drafted by a lawyer (albeit it is supposed to be in the witness's own words), one loses the clarity and value of hearing the witness's own account first-hand.

inconsistencies between what the witness has said or written at different times. That may involve looking at what was said in an earlier witness statement or to the police or other investigator when they inquired into the circumstances of the accident. How does the account presented at trial compare with what was said in the aftermath of the accident or what was written in the first letters between solicitors? When the claimant asserts that, prior to the accident he never had so much as a twinge in his back or a day off with depression, do the medical notes bear that out? When he says that he had previously enjoyed an exemplary work history, do the employment records support him? Perhaps the most vivid demonstration of inconsistency will be when it is possible to show that the person's conduct and behaviour on one occasion (e.g. when observed or filmed without his knowledge or awareness that it may later be used against him) is completely at odds with his presentation in the litigation. A classic example of that is a case which went to the Supreme Court, *Summers v Fairclough Homes Ltd*,[22] where the claimant pretended to be thoroughly disabled but video and other evidence showed that he was in fact able to lead a relatively normal life.[23]

- Cogency: does the account make sense? Here, the wise decision-maker must resist the understandable temptation to jump to a conclusion until having heard all the evidence. It is very easy indeed for us to think that we can see "what must have happened" and decide that, therefore, it probably did happen that way. We may in fact be right, of course, but until we have considered all possibilities, the good decision-maker will keep an open mind: any other approach is unsound and unscientific. One should approach competing factual accounts with similar caution. Any psychiatrist or psychologist will warn of the dangers of retrospective re-attribution: "if such and such had not happened when I was a child, all these other bad things in my life would never have happened either". The same is true of retrospective reconstruction/reinterpretation: that is, the process of retrospectively coming up with a nicely ordered and detailed account of events as we look back on an event or events which may have happened in a blur over a timescale of less than 30 seconds. Our own experience tells us that this is very easily done and is probably human nature. Consider, for example, how we might seek to explain later the circumstances of the road accident in which we were involved or which we narrowly avoided. In such an example, the later account may be very much more carefully assembled than the reality of a blurred and confusing sequence of events which was one's initial impression.

---

[22] Not on the issue of whether the claimant was in fact substantially disabled but whether the fact that he had been found to have fraudulently invented more or less 90% of his claim meant that the court (a) could and (b) should strike out the whole claim in its entirety, that is, even including the "genuine" 10%. The answer was "yes" to (a) but "no" to (b) in the circumstances of that case.

[23] *Summers v Fairclough Homes Ltd* [2012] UKSC 26. One must, however, recognise that allegations of fraud by one party against another cannot be made without a sufficient evidential basis—see the judgment of Lord Woolf in *Excelsior Commercial & Industrial Holdings Ltd v Salisbury Hamer Aspden & Johnson* [2002] EWCA Civ 879; [2002] C.P. Rep. 67. An example of what can happen when, for example, a defendant unsuccessfully alleges that the claimant is a malingerer and does so on no good grounds is *Clarke v Maltby* [2010] EWHC 1201(QB) at 1856.

- Corroboration: is the witness's account supported by independent evidence—another eye witness or a contemporaneous document, for example? Clearly, two or more people can make the same mistake or gain the same false impression. Or they may be colluding dishonestly or instinctively but innocently giving an account which is supportive of a friend, colleague or family member. This sort of evidence nevertheless provides the most reliable support for the primary account which is being examined.

If those are the three main elements of any examination of the truth/accuracy or falsity/unreliability of a witness' account, there are other, more subjective, features of a witness' performance which may influence us. We like witnesses who speak clearly and with balance. We like those who do not try and argue their own case or answer back or show off. We like witnesses who are prepared to give ground or admit a mistake. We do not like witnesses who are long-winded or who will not answer the question or who seem evasive or argumentative. But none of these characteristics is necessarily decisive of whether the witness is or is not telling the truth; they are just familiar tools which we use and we must be careful lest they mislead, not least because a skilled liar can easily imitate an honest witness.

The same is true of our assessments of a witness' body-language and facial expressions or just whether we find them to be attractive or likeable characters. These must also be features which a judge or any expert assessor of the veracity of an account (which may include psychiatrists or clinical psychologists) can only use with the utmost caution, recognising the dangers of impressions which make no adequate allowance for factors such as culture and gender, personality and appearance or simply the pressure of the situation (whether it be evidence given in a witness box or the clinician's medico-legal examination). On the other hand, the value of our intuitive or instinctive judgments cannot just be ignored or treated as valueless. The fact is that any group of people who have sat in court for a day, be they lawyers or laymen, do tend to agree on who was likeable, who was believable and who was impressive, just as a group of people in a social group may have a high measure of agreement about someone they meet for the first time. It would seem, therefore, that to a greater or lesser extent we do tend to share the same capacity for intuitive judgment and very often find we have the same reaction as each other to our fellow beings. But quite how that capability can be defined or described so as to constitute any kind of identifiable measure of veracity is rather more difficult to say!

13–018

4. JUDICIAL PERSPECTIVES

One of the more intriguing observations on judicial decision-making was made in the judgment of the Privy Council in *White v Kuzych*,[24] in which the Board expressed the view that the members of a Trade Union body dispensing Union discipline could not be expected to act with the strict impartiality with which a judge should approach and decide an issue between two litigants—"that icy

13–019

---

[24] *White v Kuzych* [1951] A.C. 585.

impartiality of a Radhamanthus" which some 60 years earlier Bowen LJ, when deciding *Jackson v Barry Railway Co*,[25] had regarded as obligatory. The Bangalore principles of judicial conduct,[26] echoed in the words of the judicial oath itself, require such impartiality, even if not necessarily so "icy": absent that, there can be no justice worthy of the name, as Mummery LJ (rather more recently) observed in *AWG Group Ltd v Morrison*.[27] These eminent judges were talking, of course, about impartiality in the sense of having a predisposition to decide a case in favour of one party despite the evidence in favour of the other. But there must be a real question as to the point at which the life experience of judges, shaping their honest views, colouring their every-day perceptions—and, it may be said, influencing their judgment—shades into a "bias" which most observers would recognise as such. Judges are people, not gods, nor creatures of classical myth[28]; and like any person, they must come to pass judgment by having regard to that which life has taught them about those matters in issue before them which are likely to have happened, are unlikely, or are "possible, but ...". Since their life experiences may be widely different, then insofar as their judgment is a product of them, it too may differ to some extent from judge to judge. The Olympian detachment which principle demands is perhaps therefore better understood as the exercise of integrity—each judge being true to her or himself, without "fear or favour, affection or ill-will"[29] consciously being exercised, and making every attempt to understand the evidence rather than jumping too hastily to convenient conclusions about it.

For all that, however, the system remains essentially human, and not divine. And with that comes a preliminary point—it may not be possible to identify any particular approach to making decisions on the evidence which is applicable uniformly to all judges. It may not be any easier to identify the intrinsic approach of any particular judges, taken individually: for the approach of one and the same judge may in one case respond to the nuances of the testimony, in another to the use or abuse of language in documents, in another, positively, to the numerical superiority of the witness array on one side of an argument, yet in another seemingly negatively.

Nonetheless, it may be assumed that there is a sufficient commonality of approach to justify comment rather than defy it. How does a judge decide the facts of a case? First, a matter which is often forgotten: the judge needs to be clear what facts are needed in order to decide the issue which will determine the case—stripped to its bones, that is what any case is about. In a case where the claim is for compensation for being the victim of a road traffic accident allegedly caused by a car driver's negligence, for instance, there will be much which is undisputed—such as broadly when and where the accident occurred, who was controlling the car said to be at fault, the general nature of the injuries, and so on. It was what is in dispute that needs to be decided one way or the other: e.g. whether the pedestrian victim ran out suddenly in front of the car, giving the driver no realistic chance to stop; or the driver was travelling too fast, and the

---

[25] *Jackson v Barry Railway Co* [1893] 1 Ch. 238 at 248.
[26] Article 2.5 in particular.
[27] *AWG Group Ltd v Morrison* [2006] 1 W.L.R. 1163 (at [6]).
[28] According to legend, circa 400 BC, Radhamanthus, because of his inflexible integrity, was made one of the judges of the dead.
[29] The words of the oath.

driver simply did not see the victim until it was too late, at that speed, for him to stop so as to avoid hitting him. This may not be simple. "Suddenly", "too fast" and "too late" are matters of judgment, which depend in turn on establishing facts relating to events which took only seconds or less to materialise, set against judgments as to the way in which other motorists—being reasonably careful[30]—would behave if set in similar circumstances. If placed on the pavement immediately before the accident, looking in the same direction as the driver, an observer may instantly take a view. If on the opposite side of the street, looking the other way—or merely hearing the noises of the accident or seeing its immediate aftermath—a witness may take the opposite view. How does a judge begin? The answer—given the facts it is necessary to consider to answer these questions—is initially one of focus. Speed, visibility and distance (the relative position of the parties) are the critical factors: but all of these are indeed just that—factors in the single determinative assessment of fact (and judgment) which is whether the standard of driving has fallen below that to be expected of a reasonably competent driver on that occasion. This conclusion is that which has to be expressed on the balance of probabilities. If, for instance, the judge was not satisfied on balance whether the speed exceeded the applicable limit, nor as to the precise distance the car travelled during the time when the driver might, had he looked carefully enough, have seen his victim, he could not abdicate his function to say—well, the burden of proof hasn't been satisfied as to either. It is the combination of these factors which matters, coupled with a near instinctive view as to the way in which a reasonably careful driver would have driven on that occasion. So, the focus of the judge has to be on how such a hypothetical driver would (probably) have behaved, and whether (probably) the driver before him did not.

Secondly, before, and with a view to, deciding deceptively simple points such as these most judges will wish to be clear what may safely be established, either as obvious, or by undisputed testimony, or as agreed by the parties in the court documents, in writing before the hearing, or in front of the judge—if you like, the "objective" facts. They will provide a context, into which a judge will anticipate other evidence (documentary, photographic, direct or recorded testimony) should fit, and with which any scientific evidence should be coherent. They may even begin to enable the judge to form a view as to the likelihood of any disputed fact.

13–020

Much of the context should be set by the court documents. They should not only identify the claim to be made, but the points in dispute and—often just as important—the points upon which there is agreement. These days, a judge will have read more than the basic court documents (the "pleadings" and accompanying documents). He will almost certainly have been furnished with written cases[31] by both parties, and probably witness statements which he will read since they are likely to be the evidence in chief before him. He will, too, have a bundle of documents.[32] It is in consideration of this material that the process of decision making begins. A picture of the claims being made will (or at

---

[30] In itself a hypothetical standard.
[31] Laughingly referred to as "skeletons", though I live in hope.
[32] The preparation of this is a forgotten part of advocacy. It is rare in any case for the parties to make reference to more than a handful of the documents a bundle contains; it is common for the bundle to contain the same document not once but many times over, as where there is trail of email correspondence, which is (unhelpfully) picked up at the start, and followed by successive emails each

least should) become clear, as should the reasons and facts which go the other way. The context begins to be set—and as Lord Hoffmann is known famously to have observed, "Context is everything".

Thirdly, the judge will wish to understand the context within which critical events are placed—to look first, if you like, at "the big picture". This may be helpful in assessing whether oral testimony is likely to be reliable or not. Take an example: if a husband and wife have recently split up, somewhat acrimoniously, or an extra-marital affair has just come to light, the allegation of one that the other has physically or sexually abused their child may be seen to be less worthy of uncritical acceptance than if until the allegations were first raised by or on behalf of the child they had been (on all accounts) entirely happily married. The context is the state of the relationship between accuser and accused. Take another: if a party is emphatic, and emotional in making complaints that (say) she has been racially and sexually discriminated against, and asserts that events some five years ago which in themselves were acts of discrimination were what led to the matters of which she most recently complains, a judge will want to know in what context the alleged acts occurred. If, in the same workplace, amongst the same individuals, there had been no complaint then by someone who is vocal and determined in her complaints now, this would be surprising. It would be unlikely unless there were some good reason to explain it: the context is an absence of complaint when there was ample opportunity to make it, by someone who might be depended on to complain. These two examples are mere illustrations of a general approach, which seeks to evaluate any one piece of evidence by placing it in context, seeing against its background, "knowing where the witnesses are coming from"—not viewing it in isolation—asking whether it "fits" (all common phrases used to describe what is essentially the same process). It applies most obviously to oral testimony, but is also appropriate when considering documentation, photographic materials, and (moving on to a further area of decision making which might seem to be far removed from the witness box) even to understanding a previous decision of the courts in another case. Documents have authors. They will have roles to fulfil; they may have agendas. Photographs no longer "never lie"—leaving aside doctoring, airbrushing and the like, they are inevitably taken from a particular perspective (not merely visual, but often that of the photographer too). Scientific studies may be financed by those with pharmaceuticals to sell, religious points to make, or particular views as to the efficacy of alternative therapies. So, where is the piece of evidence coming from? The essential point is that a judge will expect one piece of evidence to be coherent with those circumstances which are more firmly established, and with other pieces of evidence before the court. Where it is not, it is unlikely to be acceptable unless there is a particularly good reason.

13–021 This approach has its limits. It depends to some extent on the decision-maker's expectation of the ways in which people behave. Unknowingly, errors may creep in—the white male Anglo-Saxon judge may for years have mistaken the lowered head and sideways glance of a man from another cultural background for indications of dishonest shiftiness, when they are truly indications of deference

---

of which has attached to it the string that went before. Good advocacy might suggest putting into the bundle only those documents which are essential, and trying to limit the number of copies of each to one.

and respect for authority. That example relates to what a judge makes of direct testimony, but it should not be thought that an understanding of the broad context set by uncontroversial evidence is free from similar instinctive biases: is it, now, considered that evidence that a woman did not cry out or fight back, or even complain contemporaneously to others, when subjected to sexual assault is evidence which puts in doubt a claim that she was actually raped? It was, not so long ago. Times change. So too do fashions for litigating particular types of claim. Take stress or "RSI"; take whiplash claims. At first, the enthusiasm of litigants for embracing such claims, and their growth in number might expose judges so often to hearing of the general circumstances in which such injuries occur that they recognise those same features in the next such case to come along, and credit the next case as all the more reliable because it has become "exactly the sort of behaviour you might expect to give rise to such injury". Then, after a while, experience that some such claims may be brought adventitiously makes the decision maker suspicious that particular features similar to those in earlier cases are claimed only in order to give a spurious authenticity to the present case before the court. In short, society changes; familiarity with certain types of facts may lead at one time to embracing them as reliable, at another time as rejecting them as all too conveniently asserted. The way society expects people to behave does not necessarily mean that they do behave in that way, for the reasons supposed. Expectations change not just with time but from one cultural group to another—and inevitably are influenced by the background of and social milieu of opinion formers within the society or those groups which are asked to recognise or reject those expectations. Accordingly, testing behaviours against expectations has its limits: but one feature of good judging is that most if not all judges are aware of this as a general problem; each when in practice earlier as an advocate is likely to have encountered cases which they thought sure-fire winners or losers because of such an approach, yet have been forced to realise by the conclusion of the hearing that the extraordinary does sometimes happen; and they will accordingly be prepared at least to be wrong, and not to rush too readily to assumptions.

All that said, although what is extraordinary may sometimes happen, it is nonetheless extraordinary. What is extraordinary is by definition less likely to happen than it is to occur. So a sense of what is exceptional, highly unusual, extraordinary (whatever phrase is used) is generally a good guide to evaluating whether in all probability it actually happened, and of anticipating that there would be evidence from a number of witnesses (or set out in a number of contemporaneous documents) remarking on it having occurred, if indeed it did, such that the absence of such witnesses or documents would be another reason to discount the event as having occurred.

Fourthly, an American jurist once remarked that it is a sound principle that the probabilities should be judged by the evidence which it is within the power to one party to adduce, and the other to refute. Take for example where it is said by A that B heard a conversation when C disputes any such conversation having

HOW JUDGES REACH THEIR DECISIONS

occurred. If it is known that B is a close relative, employee, friend or colleague of A, a judge will be more sceptical of A's case if B does not then appear.[33]

13-022 Then, fifthly, there is what a judge makes of oral testimony. It may seem useful to speak in terms of the impression a witness makes when giving evidence without first having as clear a picture of the context as the objective facts can give, and having some sense of "where the witness is coming from" which will colour the testimony. In essence, the modern approach is that a judge is not swayed overmuch by the judge's own reaction to the manner of the witness in the box—there is a great diversity of people who may give evidence, and the ways in which they do so is no less diverse. Difference does not equate to unreliability. Nonetheless, the witness who hesitates to answer difficult questions[34] and changes the subject repeatedly, or who "talks the point out" is less likely to convince than someone who seems measured, concedes points going the other way, and appears to think carefully about the answers. This is no more than human reaction, however: so fallible that without the evidence fitting the probabilities, being coherent with other material (especially contemporaneous documents)—and not being inconsistent in one part with that which is stated in another, it is likely to be insufficient on its own for definite findings that the evidence is right, or that the "impressive" witness should on that basis alone be believed—after all, it is the stock-in-trade of a confidence trickster to appear impressive and honest.

So, in summary—expect a judge to approach decision-making and evaluating evidence by:

(1) making sure what facts it is necessary to decide (the others can be ignored unless valuable as background);
(2) having regard to the context;
(3) looking for an explanation if the evidence does not fit the context and being reassured if it does;
(4) asking himself if there is available evidence which one would expect to be brought which has not been; and
(5) having regard to the way in which the witness answers the questions in substance, making as many allowances as the judge can for the fact that different people adopt different approaches, none will remember the same things in the same way if they remember them at all, and that memory is often affected by a desire to see the past differently.

A judge may ask if the witness appears broadly honest (judging this, as indicated, by very much more than "demeanour"), for if not, the evidence he gives is unlikely to be acceptable unless it chimes clearly with other unchallenged material: and then remember that he is not in a position to declare unshakeably that the evidence is true, for the judge will recognise that many will think the past was as they now wish to see it (or, maybe, wished to see it at the time) whilst being entirely honest in doing so: not at all lying, just mistaken. Finally, factoring

---

[33] A judgment of Langstaff J mentioned this principle, and drawing attention to the fact that the brother of the claimant (who could have given evidence about disputed matters) was in court but not called, was upheld by the Court of Appeal who emphasised this point far more heavily.
[34] At least where the witness is fluent in English.

in his "impression" of any witness evidence the judge will return to the facts he has identified as necessary to decide and consider the whole of the material before him to determine whether they are more likely than not[35] to have occurred.

REFERENCES

Annual Exert Witness Survey Report, *First Joint Annual Expert Witness Survey* (Bond Solon: Wilmington Legal, 2016).

Faust, D., Ziskin, J. and Hiers, J.B., *Brain Damage Claims: Coping with Neuropsychological Evidence* (Los Angeles: Law and Psychology Press, 1991).

Garden, N. and Sullivan, K.A., "An examination of the base rate of post-concussion symptoms: the influence of demographics and depression" (2010) *Applied Neuropsychology* 17(1), 1–7.

Grace, J.J., Kinsella, E.L., Muldoon, O.T. and Fortune, D.G., "Post-traumatic growth following acquired brain injury: a systematic review and meta-analysis" (2005) *Frontiers in Psychology* 6, 1–16.

Greenberg, S.A. and Shuman, D.W., "Irreconcilable conflict between therapeutic and forensic roles" (1997) *Professional Psychology: Research and Practice* 28(1), 50–57.

Iverson, G.L., "Misdiagnosis of the persistent postconcussion syndrome in patients with depression" (2006) *Archives of Clinical Neuropsychology* 21, 303–310.

Iverson, G.L., Brooks, B.L. and Holdnack, J.A., "Misdiagnosis of Cognitive Impairment in Forensic Neuropsychology" in Heilbronner, R.L. (ed.), *Neuropsychology in the Courtroom: Expert Analysis of Reports and Testimony* (Guilford Press, 2008).

Iverson, G.L. and McCracken, L.M., "Postconcussive" symptoms in persons with chronic pain" (1997) *Brain Injury* 11(11), 783–790).

Knight, R.G., Devereux, R. and Godfrey, H.P., "Caring for a family member with a traumatic brain injury" (1998) *Brain Injury* 12(6), 467–481.

Lees-Haley, P.R. and Brown, R.S., "Neuropsychological Complaint Base Rates of 170 Personal Injury Claimants" (1993) *Archives of Clinical Neuropsychology* 8, 203–209.

Lees-Haley, P.R., Fox, D.D. and Courtney, J.C., "A comparison of complaints by mild brain injury claimants and other claimants describing subjective experiences immediately following their injury" (2001) *Archives of Clinical Neuropsychology* 16, 689–695.

Machamer, J. and Dikmen, S.S. "Significant Other Burden and Factors Related to it in Traumatic Brain Injury" (2013) *Journal of Clinical and Experimental Neuropsychology* 24(4), 420–433.

McCarter, R.J., Walton, N.H., Brooks, D.N. and Powell, G.E., "Effort Testing in Contemporary UK Neuropsychological Practice" (2009) *Clinical Neuropsychologist* 23, 1050–1066.

McCrea, M.A., Mild Traumatic Brain Injury and Postconcussion Syndrome: The New Evidence Base for Diagnosis and Treatment (Oxford Workshop Series: American Academy of Clinical Neuropsychology, 2008).

Rivera, P., Elliott, T.R., Berry, J.W., Grant, J.S. and Oswald, K., "Predictors of caregiver depression among community-residing families living with traumatic brain injury" (2007) *Neurorehabilitation* 22, 3–8.

---

[35] These remarks are cast in terms of the usual civil standard—of course, the standard will be adjusted depending on the particular legal rule that operates, but the process of seeking satisfaction of that standard is much the same.

Slick, D.J., Sherman, E.M.S. and Iverson, G.L., "Diagnostic Criteria for Malingered Neurocognitive Dysfunction: Proposed Standards for Clinical Practice and Research" (1999) *Clinical Neuropsychologist* 13(4), 545–561.

Watanabe, Y., Shiel, A., Asami, T., Taki, K. and Tabouchi, K., "An evaluation of neurobehavioural problems as perceived by family members and levels of family stress 1–3 years following traumatic brain injury in Japan" (2000) *Clinical Rehabilitation* 14(2), 172–177.

Zakzanis, K.K. and Yeung, E., "Base rates of post-concussive symptoms in a non-concussed multicultural sample" (2011) *Archives of Clinical Neuropsychology* 26, 461–465.

INDEX

All references are to paragraph number

ABCDE
  initial assessment of head injuries, 3–023
Acute pain
  subtle brain injuries, 10–014
Adaptive functioning
  childhood brain injury, 9–023
Advanced Trauma Life Support
  initial management of head injuries, 3–023
Affective dysregulation
  mood disorders, 6–016
Age
  assessment of capacity, 2–054
  childhood brain injury
    effect on outcome, 9–009
    reliable prognosis, 9–010—9–013
  effect on head injuries, 3–021—3–022
Agency staff
  care packages, 12–033
Alcohol use
  neuropsychiatric problems, 6–025—6–027
  secondary influences on neuropsychological impairment, 5–018
Alzheimer's disease
  delayed consequences of traumatic brain injury, 4–022
Amnesia
  neuropsychiatric problems, 6–011—6–012
Anatomy of brain
  diagrams, 3–008
Anosmia
  see **Smell**
Anxiety
  neuropsychiatric problems, 6–017—6–019
  secondary influences on neuropsychological impairment, 5–015
Apathy
  neuropsychiatric problems, 6–020—6–021
Assessing capacity
  see **Mental capacity**
Attention
  neuropsychological assessment, 5–009—5–010
  neuropsychological constraints on rehabilitation, 8–035

Autoregulation
  effect of reduced blood flow to brain, 3–011
Avoidance
  assessing capacity, 2–122
Behavioural changes
  neuropsychiatric problems, 6–023—6–024
Behavioural rehabilitation
  compensatory strategies, 8–043
  crisis intervention, 8–048
  environmental modification, 8–042
  generally, 8–041
  metacognitive training, 8–045
  relapse prevention, 8–047
  task specific training, 8–044
  therapy versus scaffolding, 8–046
Best interests
  assessing capacity, 2–047, 2–123
Blood clots
  see **Haematomas**
Brain atrophies
  age-related patterns of head injuries, 3–022
Brain imaging
  see also **CT scans**; **MRI scans**
  childhood brain injury, 9–017
Brainstem
  anatomy of brain, 3–008
British Society of Rehabilitation Medicine
  rehabilitation, 8–017—8–018
Bulbar functions
  physical consequences of brain injuries, 4–010
Burden of proof
  capacity, 2–043, 2–094—2–095
Burr holes
  haematomas, 3–018, 3–020
Cacosmia
  see **Smell**
Capacity
  see **Mental capacity**
Care needs
  acquired brain injuries
    generally, 12–002—12–003
    impact on families and spouses, 12–004—12–005
    assessing brain-injured claimants, 12–007

INDEX

assessment process
  conclusions, 12–017
  exaggeration, 12–015
  introduction, 12–008—12–009
  past care, 12–016
  pre-existing disabilities, 12–013
  standardised assessments, 12–015
  techniques, 12–010—12–012
  timing of assessments, 12–014
care packages
  agency staff, 12–033
  care experts, 12–031
  case managers, 12–030
  direct employment, 12–033
  double-up care, 12–036
  introduction, 12–029
  live-in care, 12–034—12–035
  monitoring, 12–032
  working time directives, 12–034
case management
  effectiveness of, 12–044
  effectiveness of well managed rehabilitation programme, 12–041—12–043
  generally, 12–037
  role of care manager, 12–038—12–040
  standards of practice, 12–038—12–040
childhood brain injury, 9–023
introduction, 12–001
longer-term recommendations, 12–045
rehabilitation
  care packages where rehabilitation not required, 12–024
  code of practice, 12–018—12–019
  independent living trials, 12–023
  main areas of disagreement between care experts, 12–027
  management of neuropsychiatric conditions, 12–028
  predicting future care needs, 12–025—12–026
  recommendations, 12–020
  support workers' role, 12–021—12–022
skills base of care expert, 12–006
working time directives, 12–034

Care packages
agency staff, 12–033
care experts, 12–031
case managers, 12–030
direct employment, 12–033
double-up care, 12–036
introduction, 12–029
live-in care, 12–034—12–035
monitoring, 12–032
working time directives, 12–034

Case management
care needs
  effectiveness of, 12–044
  effectiveness of well managed rehabilitation programme, 12–041—12–043
  generally, 12–037
  role of care manager, 12–038—12–040
  standards of practice, 12–038—12–040
stages of rehabilitation, 8–030—8–031

Case studies
assessing capacity, 2–065—2–076
care needs
  assessment techniques, 12–010—12–012
  disagreements between experts, 12–027
  double-up care, 12–036
  live-in care, 12–034—12–035
  predicting future care needs, 12–025—12–026
  pre-existing disabilities, 12–013
litigation issues
  damages assessment for moderate brain injuries, 1–035—1–039
  difficulty assessing cognitive ability, 1–032—1–034
  illegality following brain injury, 1–040—1–042
  somatisation disorder, 1–043—1–045
  subtle brain injuries, 1–030—1–031

Causation
neuropsychiatric problems, 6–004—6–005

Causative nexus
assessing capacity, 2–052, 2–103—2–104

Central nervous system
childhood brain injury
  healthy maturation, 9–003
  post-injury cognitive development, 9–004

Cerebellum
anatomy of brain, 3–008

Cerebral perfusion pressure
effect of reduced blood flow to brain, 3–011—3–012

Child restraints
measures to reduce head injuries, 3–007

Childhood brain injury
adaptive functioning, 9–023
age-related patterns of head injuries, 3–021—3–022
capacity to litigate, 9–020—9–021
capacity to manage finances and broader issues on reaching majority, 9–020—9–021
care needs, 9–023
dysexecutive symptoms, 9–018—9–019
employment prospects, 9–023
frontal lobe functioning, 9–018—9–019
intellectual ability, 9–022—9–023
litigation
  age at which reliable prognosis can be determined, 9–010—9–013
  estimating pre-injury functioning in childhood, 9–014
  impact of intervention and rehabilitation in childhood, 9–015—9–016
  minor traumatic brain injury and normal brain imaging, 9–017

INDEX

neurodevelopmental aspects of childhood brain injury
  age at injury and outcome, 9–009
  critical periods in development, 9–008
  healthy central nervous system maturation, 9–003
  introduction, 9–002
  plasticity, 9–005—9–006
  post-injury central nervous system and cognitive development, 9–004
  vulnerability, 9–007
  summary, 9–024

Chronic pain
  subtle brain injuries, 10–014

Civil partnerships
  capacity to enter, 2–030

Clinical judgment
  assessing capacity, 2–101

Closed injuries
  diffuse brain injury, 3–017
  infection, 3–026
  meaning, 3–016

Codes of practice
  Mental Capacity Act 2005, 2–063

Cogency
  judicial decision-making, 13–017

Cognitive rehabilitation
  compensatory strategies, 8–043
  crisis intervention, 8–048
  environmental modification, 8–042
  generally, 8–041
  metacognitive training, 8–045
  relapse prevention, 8–047
  task specific training, 8–044
  therapy versus scaffolding, 8–046

Cognitive testing
  assessing capacity, 2–101

Community-based rehabilitation
  stages of rehabilitation, 8–028—8–029

Compound injuries
  meaning, 3–016

Computed tomography
  see **CT scans**

Confusion
  assessing capacity, 2–120—2–121

Consciousness
  assessment of, 3–015
  Glasgow Coma Score, 3–015

Consent to treatment
  capacity to consent, 2–031

Consistency
  judicial decision-making, 13–017

Contra-coup injuries
  meaning, 3–017

Contract
  capacity to enter, 2–014—2–016

Contusions
  effects of, 3–017
  intracranial haematomas and, 3–018

  meaning, 3–017

Corpus callosum
  anatomy of brain, 3–008

Corroboration
  judicial decision-making, 13–017

Craniectomy
  management of head injuries, 3–012, 3–019

Cranioplasty
  management of head injuries, 3–028

Craniotomy
  haematomas, 3–018

CRASH Study
  initial management of head injuries, 3–019

Critogenic influences
  subtle brain injuries, 10–018—10–019

CT scans
  initial management of head injuries, 3–023—3–025
  traumatic brain injuries, 4–013—4–015

Cushing reflex
  intracranial pressure and, 3–014

Delayed complications
  traumatic brain injury
    Alzheimer's disease, 4–022
    hydrocephalus, 4–019
    hypopituitarism, 4–023
    minor head injuries, 4–025—4–026
    motor neurone disease, 4–024
    movement disorders, 4–024
    multiple sclerosis, 4–024
    Parkinson's syndrome, 4–024
    persistent vegetative state, 4–027
    post-traumatic epilepsy, 4–020—4–021

Dementia risks
  neuropsychiatric problems, 6–030—6–032

Depression
  neuropsychiatric problems, 6–013—6–014
  secondary influences on neuropsychological impairment, 5–014

Diagnosis
  importance in litigation, 1–006

Diffuse axonal injury
  age and, 3–021
  meaning, 3–017

Diffuse brain injuries
  meaning, 3–017
  severe diffuse injuries, 3–019

Diplopia
  see **Vision**

Direct discrimination
  Equality Act 2010, 11–013

Direct employment
  care packages, 12–033

Disability discrimination
  employment
    generally, 11–021
    ongoing employment and adjustments, 11–023
    selection, 11–022

INDEX

vocational rehabilitation, 11–029—11–030
Equality Act 2010
   direct discrimination, 11–013
   discrimination arising from disability, 11–015
   failure to make reasonable adjustments,
      11–016—11–017
   generally, 11–012
   harassment, 11–018
   indirect discrimination, 11–014
   victimisation, 11–019
further and higher education
   current students, 11–027
   generally, 11–024—11–025
   selection, 11–026
   vocational rehabilitation, 11–031
introduction, 11–011
public sector equality duty, 11–020
vocational rehabilitation
   employment, 11–029—11–030
   further and higher education, 11–031
   generally, 11–028
Disclosure
experts
   disclosure of opinion of, 1–016
   provision of information to, 1–015
Double-up care
care packages, 12–036
Dysarthria
see **Bulbar functions**
Dysexecutive symptoms
childhood brain injury, 9–018—9–019
Dysphagia
see **Bulbar functions**
Elderly persons
age-related patterns of head injuries,
   3–021—3–022
Emotional disorders
neuropsychological assessment, 5–019—5–022
subtle brain injuries, 10–013
Employment
disability discrimination
   generally, 11–021
   ongoing employment and adjustments,
      11–023
   selection, 11–022
   vocational rehabilitation, 11–029—11–030
Employment prospects
childhood brain injury, 9–023
Epilepsy
delayed consequences of traumatic brain injury,
   4–020—4–021
Equality Act 2010
see also **Disability discrimination**
direct discrimination, 11–013
discrimination arising from disability, 11–015
failure to make reasonable adjustments,
   11–016—11–017
generally, 11–012

harassment, 11–018
indirect discrimination, 11–014
victimisation, 11–019
Exaggeration
see **Malingering**
Executive functions
neuropsychological assessment, 5–011—5–012
neuropsychological constraints on rehabilitation,
   8–036
Experts
attendance at trial, 1–017—1–018
bias, 1–014
changing, 1–011
choosing, 1–010
consultation with client, 1–013
disclosure of opinion of, 1–016
disclosure to, 1–015
funding, 1–014
importance to litigation, 1–005
independence, 1–014
judicial criticism of reports, 2–127
judicial decision-making, 13–012
preparation for trial, 1–017—1–018
role of, 1–008—1–009
treating doctors as, 1–012
Extradural haematomas
initial management, 3–018
Factitious disorders
neuropsychiatric problems, 6–028—6–029
Families
impact of brain injury on, 12–004—12–005
Fatigue
neuropsychological constraints on rehabilitation,
   8–037
secondary influences on neuropsychological
   impairment, 5–016
Financial affairs
capacity to manage, 2–009—2–013
Focal injuries
meaning, 3–016
Foraminal herniation
effects of, 3–014
Frontal lobe functioning
childhood brain injury, 9–018—9–019
Functional neurological disorders
neuropsychiatric problems, 6–028—6–029
Further and higher education
disability discrimination
   current students, 11–027
   generally, 11–024—11–025
   selection, 11–026
   vocational rehabilitation, 11–031
Gifts
capacity to make, 2–029
Haematomas
intracranial haematomas, 3–018
Harassment
Equality Act 2010, 11–018

INDEX

Head injuries
age, effect of, 3–021—3–022
anatomy of brain, 3–008
categories, 1–007
conclusions, 3–029
consciousness, assessment of, 3–015
economic impact of, 3–002
introduction, 3–001
long term surgical complications
　cranioplasty, 3–028
　hyrdrocephalus, 3–027
　infection following head injury, 3–026
management of, 3–023—3–025
pathophysiology, 3–016
physiology of brain
　blood flow to brain, 3–011–3–012
　brain herniation, 3–013—3–014
　Glasgow Coma Score, 3–015
　intracranial pressure, 3–010
　neurophysiology, 3–009
public health measures to reduce
　baby and child car seats, 3–007
　helmets, 3–005
　introduction, 3–003
　seat belts, 3–006
　speed limits, 3–004
types of injury
　chronic subdural haematomas, 3–020
　diffuse brain injuries, 3–017
　intracranial haematomas, 3–018
　introduction, 3–016
　severe diffuse injuries, 3–019

Hearing
physical consequences of brain injuries
　loss of hearing, 4–008
　tinnitus, 4–009

Herniation
intracranial pressure, 3–010, 3–013—3–014
severe diffuse injuries, 3–019

High velocity injuries
effect of, 3–016

Hospital-based rehabilitation
stages of rehabilitation, 8–022—8–024

Hypopituitarism
delayed consequences of traumatic brain injury, 4–023

Hyposmia
see **Smell**

Hyrdrocephalus
delayed consequences of traumatic brain injury, 4–019
management of head injuries, 3–027

Iatrogenesis
subtle brain injuries, 10–015—10–016

Imaging
CT scans
　initial management of head injuries, 3–014
　traumatic brain injuries, 4–013—4–015
introduction, 4–012

MRI scans, 4–016—4–017
radionuclide studies, 4–018

Inconsistency
assessing capacity, 2–120—2–121

Incontinence
physical consequences of brain injuries, 4–011

Indecision
assessing capacity
　application of all elements in full, 2–057
　code of practice, 2–063
　communicating decision, 2–062
　expert evidence, 2–064
　generally, 2–056, 2–122
　relevant information, 2–058—2–061

Independent living
trials, 12–023

Indirect discrimination
Equality Act 2010, 11–014

Infections
management of head injuries, 3–026

Intellectual ability
childhood brain injury, 9–022—9–023

Intellectual assessment
neuropsychological assessment, 5–007—5–008

Intracranial haematomas
see **Haematomas**

Intracranial pressure
head injuries, 3–010

Ischaemic core
effect of reduced blood flow to brain, 3–011

Ischaemic penumbra
effect of reduced blood flow to brain, 3–011

Judicial decision-making
cogency, 13–017
consistency, 13–017
corroboration, 13–017
evaluating brain injury claims
　base rates, 13–006
　coarse bias, 13–003—13–004
　confirmatory bias, 13–008
　hindsight bias, 13–007
　introduction, 13–002
　subtle biases, 13–005
expert evidence, 13–012
generally, 13–009—13–011
introduction, 13–001
judicial "nose", 13–015
judicial perspectives, 13–019—13–022
lay witnesses, 13–013—13–014
science versus art, 13–016—13–018

Kidney function
physical consequences of brain injuries, 4–011

Lasting powers of attorney
capacity to make, 2–017—2–024

Lay witnesses
judicial decision-making, 13–013—13–014

Learning
neuropsychological constraints on rehabilitation, 8–035

INDEX

Life expectancy
  traumatic brain injury, 4–028—4–031
Litigation
  brain injuries
    handling litigation for brain-injured individuals, 1–019—1–020
    identifying nature of, 1–004
    illegality following, 1–040—1–042
    moderate brain injuries, 1–035—1–039
    subtle brain injuries, 1–030—1–031
  capacity
    brain-injured individuals, 1–019—1–020
    incapacitated claimants, 1–025
    retained capacity with support, 1–026—1–028
    to litigate, 2–003—2–007
  case studies
    damages assessment for moderate brain injuries, 1–035—1–039
    difficulty assessing cognitive ability, 1–032—1–034
    illegality following brain injury, 1–040—1–042
    somatisation disorder, 1–043—1–045
    subtle brain injuries, 1–030—1–031
  childhood brain injury
    age at which reliable prognosis can be determined, 9–010—9–013
    estimating pre-injury functioning in childhood, 9–014
    impact of intervention and rehabilitation in childhood, 9–015—9–016
  diagnosis, 1–006
  duties owed to clients, 1–022–1–024
  head injuries
    categories, 1–007
  medical opinion
    relevance to damages, 1–003
  medico-legal experts
    attendance at trial, 1–017—1–018
    bias, 1–014
    changing, 1–011
    choosing, 1–010
    consultation with client, 1–013
    disclosure of opinion of, 1–016
    disclosure to, 1–015
    funding, 1–014
    importance to litigation, 1–005
    independence, 1–014
    preparation for trial, 1–017—1–018
    role of, 1–008—1–009
    treating doctors as, 1–012
  seriously unwell claimants, 1–021
  understanding medicine, 1–002
Live-in care
  care packages, 12–034—12–035
Long term consequences
  traumatic brain injury, 6–003

Malingering
  assessment of non-credible presentations, 7–010
  base-rate of non-credible presentations, 7–003—7–004
  care needs assessment, 12–015
  conclusions, 7–024
  diagnostic categories and criteria, 7–008
  faking good and bad, 7–020
  introduction, 7–001—7–002
  litigation and, 7–009, 7–021
  meaning, 7–005—7–007
  performance validity assessment
    generally, 7–011
    ignoring other PVT results, 7–015
    ignoring PVT, 7–014
    over-state good effort, 7–013
    PVT failure coexisting with genuine deficits, 7–016
    relationship to malingering, 7–017
    stating full effort applied, 7–012
  practical significance of validity measures, 7–022—7–023
  symptom validity assessment, 7–018—7–019
Management of patients
  neuropsychiatric problems, 6–033
Marriage
  capacity to enter, 2–030
Matter-specific impairment
  assessing capacity, 2–051
Medical opinion
  relevance to damages, 1–003
Medico-legal experts
  see **Experts**
Memory
  neuropsychological assessment, 5–009—5–010
Mental capacity
  capacity to litigate
    cases after Masterman-Lister, 2–006—2–007
    childhood brain injury, 9–020—9–021
    Masterman-Lister, 2–004—2–005
    summary, 2–003
  childhood brain injury
    capacity to litigate, 9–020—9–021
    managing finances and broader issues on reaching majority, 9–020—9–021
  common law tests
    care decisions, 2–033, 2–036
    civil partnerships, 2–030
    consent to treatment, 2–031
    contact, 2–033, 2–035
    contract, 2–014—2–016
    evidence unobtainable, 2–008
    gifts, 2–029
    internet use, 2–037
    introduction, 2–002
    knowledge of amount of award of damages, 2–038—2–040
    lasting powers of attorney, 2–017—2–024
    litigation, 2–003—2–007

INDEX

management of property and affairs, 2–009—2–013
marriage, 2–030
residence, 2–033—2–034
sexual relationships, 2–032
social media use, 2–037
testamentary capacity, 2–025—2–028
conclusions, 2–128
judicial observations on
  avoidance, 2–122
  avoiding impractical and unnecessary distinctions, 2–102
  best interests analysis, 2–123
  burden of proof, 2–094—2–095
  causative nexus, 2–103—2–104
  combination of clinical judgment and cognitive testing, 2–101
  confusion, 2–120—2–121
  court to make ultimate decision, 2–078
  criticism of expert report, 2–127
  danger of imposing too high a test, 2–100
  evaluation of all issues, 2–107
  existence of other factors, 2–106
  expertise of surgeon to assess capacity, 2–091
  forward looking focus of Court of Protection, 2–080
  impairment of brain, 2–105
  inconsistency, 2–120—2–121
  indecision, 2–122
  introduction, 2–077
  judge seeing patient in private, 2–099
  outcome approach, 2–087
  presumption of capacity, 2–081
  psychiatric tests, 2–092
  psychological tests, 2–092
  qualifications and qualities of assessor, 2–088—2–090
  reasonably foreseeable consequences, 2–111
  refined analysis, 2–119
  relevant information, 2–109—2–110
  single visit, 2–098
  standard of proof, 2–096—2–097
  stock responses, 2–093
  surveying all evidence, 2–079
  taking all practicable steps, 2–082
  understanding, 2–108
  unwise decisions, 2–083—2–086
  use or weigh, 2–112—2–118
  vacillation, 2–122
  vulnerability, 2–124
  vulnerable person's protective imperative, 2–125—2–126
litigation issues
  brain-injured individuals, 1–019—1–020
  incapacitated claimants, 1–025
  retained capacity with support, 1–026—1–028
Mental Capacity Act 2005
case studies, 2–065—2–076

inability to make decisions
  application of all elements in full, 2–057
  code of practice, 2–063
  communicating decision, 2–062
  expert evidence, 2–064
  relevant information, 2–058—2–061
  statutory provisions, 2–056
introduction, 2–041
persons lacking capacity
  age, 2–054
  assessment of, 2–050
  causative nexus, 2–052
  diagnostic threshold, 2–050
  matter specific, 2–051
  standard of proof, 2–055
  statutory provisions, 2–049
  temporary impairment, 2–053
  time specific, 2–051
principles
  all practical steps, 2–044
  best interests, 2–047
  burden of proof, 2–043
  less restrictive alternatives, 2–048
  presumption of capacity, 2–043
  statutory provision, 2–042
  supported decision-making, 2–045
  unwise decisions, 2–046
Mild traumatic brain injury
childhood brain injury, 9–017
neuropsychiatric problems, 6–006—6–010
rehabilitation
  efficacy and cost-effectiveness, 8–057
Minor head injuries
assessment of, 4–025—4–026
Mobility
physical consequences of brain injuries, 4–007
Moderate injuries
case study, 1–035—1–039
neuropsychological assessment, 5–023—5–024
Mood disorders
affective dysregulation, 6–016
anxiety disorders, 6–017—6–019
depression, 6–013—6–014
subtle brain injuries, 10–013
suicide, 6–015
Motor neurone disease
delayed consequences of traumatic brain injury, 4–024
Movement disorders
delayed consequences of traumatic brain injury, 4–024
MRI scans
imaging traumatic brain injuries, 4–016—4–017
Multiple sclerosis
delayed consequences of traumatic brain injury, 4–024
Neurobehavioural rehabilitation
stages of rehabilitation, 8–027

INDEX

Neurodevelopment
  childhood brain injury
    age at injury and outcome, 9–009
    critical periods in development, 9–008
    healthy central nervous system maturation, 9–003
    introduction, 9–002
    plasticity, 9–005—9–006
    post-injury central nervous system and cognitive development, 9–004

Neurological and neuroradiological evaluation
  traumatic brain injuries
    assessment of head injury severity, 4–002—4–003
    conclusions, 4–032
    delayed complications, 4–019—4–024
    extremes in spectrum of severity, 4–025—4–027
    imaging after traumatic brain injury, 4–012—4–018
    introduction, 4–001
    life expectancy, 4–028—4–031
    physical consequences, 4–004—4–011

Neuropsychiatry
  acute post-traumatic amnesia, 6–011—6–012
  alcohol use, 6–025—6–027
  apathy, 6–020—6–021
  behavioural changes, 6–023—6–024
  causation of neuropsychiatric problems following traumatic brain injury, 6–004—6–005
  dementia risks, 6–030—6–032
  drug use, 6–025—6–027
  extent of problem, 6–002—6–003
  factitious disorders, 6–028—6–029
  functional neurological disorders, 6–028—6–029
  introduction, 6–001
  long term consequences of traumatic brain injury, 6–003
  management of patients, 6–033
  mild traumatic brain injury, 6–006—6–010
  mood disorders
    affective dysregulation, 6–016
    anxiety disorders, 6–017—6–019
    depression, 6–013—6–014
    suicide, 6–015
  personality changes, 6–023—6–024
  post-concussion syndrome, 6–006—6–010
  post-traumatic agitation, 6–011—6–012
  psychosis, 6–022
  substance use, 6–025—6–027

Neuropsychology
  attention, 5–009—5–010
  conclusions, 5–027
  constraints on rehabilitation
    attention, 8–035
    executive functions, 8–036
    fatigue, 8–037
    generally, 8–034
    learning, 8–035
    processing speed, 8–035
  difficulties in determining injury severity, 5–003—5–004
  emotional functioning, 5–019—5–022
  executive skills, 5–011—5–012
  intellectual assessment, 5–007—5–008
  introduction, 5–001—5–002
  memory, 5–009—5–010
  moderate injuries, 5–023—5–024
  neuropsychological examination, 5–005—5–006
  psychological functioning, 5–019—5–022
  secondary influences on neuropsychological impairment
    alcohol use, 5–018
    anxiety, 5–015
    depression, 5–014
    fatigue, 5–016
    generally, 5–013
    pain, 5–017
    substance use, 5–018
  severe injuries, 5–023—5–024
  symptom endorsement percentages, 5–006
  test disclosure, 5–025
  third party observers, 5–026

Neurorehabilitation
  see **Rehabilitation**

Non-credible presentations
  see **Malingering**

Open injuries
  infection control, 3–026

Paediatric acquired brain injury
  see **Childhood brain injury**

Pain
  secondary influences on neuropsychological impairment, 5–017
  subtle brain injuries, 10–014

Parkinson's syndrome
  delayed consequences of traumatic brain injury, 4–024

Parosmia
  see **Smell**

Past care
  assessment of care needs, 12–016

Pathophysiology
  head injuries, 3–016

Performance validity assessment
  malingering
    generally, 7–011
    ignoring other PVT results, 7–015
    ignoring PVT, 7–014
    over-state good effort, 7–013
    PVT failure coexisting with genuine deficits, 7–016
    relationship to malingering, 7–017
    stating full effort applied, 7–012

INDEX

Persistent vegetative state
  assessment of, 4–027
Personality changes
  neuropsychiatric problems, 6–023—6–024
Physical consequences
  traumatic brain injuries
    bulbar function, 4–010
    double vision, 4–009
    hearing loss, 4–008
    incontinence, 4–011
    loss of smell, 4–008
    mobility impairments, 4–007
    post-traumatic syndrome, 4–004—4–006
    sphincter functions, 4–011
    tinnitus, 4–009
    visual impairment, 4–009
Plasticity
  childhood brain injury, 9–005—9–006
Post-concussion syndrome
  neuropsychiatric problems, 6–006—6–010
Post-injury complaints
  subtle brain injuries, 10–006—10–009
Post-traumatic agitation
  neuropsychiatric problems, 6–011—6–012
Post-traumatic amnesia
  neuropsychiatric problems, 6–011—6–012
  subtle brain injuries, 10–002—10–005
Post-traumatic epilepsy
  delayed consequences of traumatic brain injury, 4–020—4–021
Post-traumatic stress disorder
  physical consequences of brain injuries, 4–004—4–006
Pre-existing disabilities
  assessment of care needs, 12–013
Processing speed
  neuropsychological constraints on rehabilitation, 8–035
Property
  capacity to manage, 2–009—2–013
Protective headgear
  measures to reduce head injuries, 3–005
Psychiatric tests
  assessing capacity, 2–092
Psychological functioning
  neuropsychological assessment, 5–019—5–022
Psychological tests
  assessing capacity, 2–092
Psychological therapy
  constraints on rehabilitation
    avoidance, 8–040
    generally, 8–038
    inertia, 8–040
    motivation for change, 8–039
Psychosis
  neuropsychiatric problems, 6–022
Public health
  measures to reduce head injuries
    baby and child car seats, 3–007
    helmets, 3–005
    introduction, 3–003
    seat belts, 3–006
    speed limits, 3–004
Public sector equality duty
  disability discrimination, 11–020
Quality standards
  rehabilitation, 8–055
Radionuclide studies
  imaging traumatic brain injuries, 4–018
Reasonable adjustments
  employers' duties, 11–023
  failure to make, 11–016—11–017
Reasonable foreseeability
  assessing capacity, 2–111
Recovery factors
  acute treatment, 8–002—8–003
  age, 8–013
  intensity, 8–010
  interference, 8–015
  lesion size, 8–004
  neuroplasticity, 8–005
  preventing nerve cell death, 8–002—8–003
  repetition, 8–009
  salience, 8–012
  specificity, 8–008
  time, 8–011
  transference, 8–014
  use it and improve it, 8–007
  use it or lose it, 8–006
Refined analysis
  assessing capacity, 2–119
Rehabilitation
  care needs
    code of practice, 12–018—12–019
    independent living trials, 12–023
    main areas of disagreement between care experts, 12–027
    management of neuropsychiatric conditions, 12–028
    predicting future care needs, 12–025—12–026
    recommendations, 12–020
    support workers' role, 12–021—12–022
  cognitive and behavioural rehabilitation
    compensatory strategies, 8–043
    crisis intervention, 8–048
    environmental modification, 8–042
    generally, 8–041
    metacognitive training, 8–045
    relapse prevention, 8–047
    task specific training, 8–044
    therapy versus scaffolding, 8–046
  conclusions, 8–060
  efficacy and cost-effectiveness
    generally, 8–056
    mild traumatic brain injury, 8–057
    severe brain injury, 8–058—8–059
  introduction, 8–001

515

INDEX

models of
  British Society of Rehabilitation Medicine,
    8–017—8–018
  rehabilitation pathways, 8–019
neuropsychological constraints
  attention, 8–035
  executive functions, 8–036
  fatigue, 8–037
  generally, 8–034
  learning, 8–035
  processing speed, 8–035
practical aspects
  cognitive and behavioural rehabilitation,
    8–041—8–048
  generally, 8–032
  identifying impairments, 8–033
  learning constraints, 8–033
  neuropsychological constraints,
    8–034—8–037
  psychological therapy constraints,
    8–038—8–040
psychological therapy constraints
  avoidance, 8–040
  generally, 8–038
  inertia, 8–040
  motivation for change, 8–039
quality standards, 8–055
recovery from brain injury
  acute treatment, 8–002—8–003
  age, 8–013
  intensity, 8–010
  interference, 8–015
  lesion size, 8–004
  neuroplasticity, 8–005
  preventing nerve cell death, 8–002—8–003
  repetition, 8–009
  salience, 8–012
  specificity, 8–008
  time, 8–011
  transference, 8–014
  use it and improve it, 8–007
  use it or lose it, 8–006
service organisation
  goal setting, 8–052—8–053
  outcome evaluation, 8–054
  teamwork, 8–049—8–051
stages of
  case management, 8–030—8–031
  community-based rehabilitation,
    8–028—8–029
  hospital rehabilitation, 8–022—8–024
  neurobehavioural rehabilitation, 8–027
  residential rehabilitation, 8–025
  slow stream rehabilitation, 8–026
  very early rehabilitation, 8–020—8–021
understanding disability, 8–016
Rehabilitation pathways
  models of rehabilitation, 8–019

Residential rehabilitation
  stages of rehabilitation, 8–025
Reticular activating system
  anatomy of brain, 3–008
Return to work
  conclusions, 11–052
  disability discrimination
    employment, 11–021—11–023,
      11–029—11–030
    Equality Act 2010, 11–012—11–019
    higher and further education,
      11–024—11–027, 11–031
    introduction, 11–011
    positive action, 11–020
    public sector equality duty, 11–020
    vocational rehabilitation and,
      11–028—11–031
  introduction, 11–001—11–002
  vocational assessment
    expert neuropsychological assessment and
      opinion, 11–037—11–038
    illustrative assessment programme,
      11–034—11–036
    meaning, 11–032—11–033
  vocational needs, 11–009—11–010
  vocational outcomes
    factors influencing return to work,
      11–005—11–008
    return to work statistics, 11–003—11–004
  vocational rehabilitation
    disability discrimination, 11–028—11–031
    effectiveness, 11–047—11–048
    generally, 11–039
    preparation for new or alternative
      employment, 11–042—11–044
    return to alternative occupation,
      11–045—11–046
    service provision, 11–049—11–051
    supported return to work, 11–040—11–041
Seat belts
  measures to reduce head injuries, 3–006
Service organisation
  rehabilitation
    goal setting, 8–052—8–053
    outcome evaluation, 8–054
    teamwork, 8–049—8–051
Severe brain injury
  neuropsychological assessments, 5–023—5–024
  rehabilitation
    efficacy and cost-effectiveness,
      8–056—8–059
Sexual relationships
  capacity to consent, 2–032
Slow stream rehabilitation
  stages of rehabilitation, 8–026
Smell
  physical consequences of brain injuries, 4–008
Speed limits
  measures to reduce head injuries, 3–004

INDEX

Sphincter functions
physical consequences of brain injuries, 4–011
Spouses
impact of brain injury on, 12–004—12–005
Standard of proof
assessing capacity, 2–055, 2–096—2–097
Subdural haematomas
chronic subdural haematomas, 3–020
elderly persons, 3–022
management of, 3–018
Subfalcine herniation
effects of, 3–014
meaning, 3–014
Substance use
neuropsychiatric problems, 6–025—6–027
secondary influences on neuropsychological impairment, 5–018
Subtle brain injuries
case studies, 1–030—1–031, 10–021—10–033
conclusions, 10–020
explanations for subtle brain injury complaints
acute pain, 10–014
chronic pain, 10–014
critogenic influences, 10–018—10–019
emotional disorders, 10–013
generally, 10–010—10–012
iatrogenesis, 10–015—10–016
mood disorders, 10–013
validity issues, 10–017
introduction, 10–001
post traumatic amnesia, 10–002—10–005
post-injury complaints, 10–006—10–009
Suicide
mood disorders, 6–015
Support workers
role of, 12–021—12–022
Supported decision-making
assessing capacity, 2–045
Symptom endorsement percentages
neuropsychological assessment, 5–006
Symptom validity assessment
malingering, 7–018—7–019
Temporary impairment
assessing capacity, 2–053
Tentorial herniation
effects of, 3–014
Test disclosure
neuropsychological assessment, 5–025
Testamentary capacity
capacity to make will, 2–025—2–028
Thalamus
anatomy of brain, 3–008
Third party observers
neuropsychological assessment, 5–026
Throat
see **Bulbar functions**
Time-specific impairment
assessing capacity, 2–051

Tinnitus
see **Hearing**
Tongue
see **Bulbar functions**
Traumatic brain injuries
assessment of severity, 4–002—4–003
conclusions, 4–032
delayed complications
Alzheimer's disease, 4–022
hydrocephalus, 4–019
hypopituitarism, 4–023
motor neurone disease, 4–024
movement disorders, 4–024
multiple sclerosis, 4–024
Parkinson's syndrome, 4–024
post-traumatic epilepsy, 4–020—4–021
extremes in spectrum of severity
minor head injuries, 4–025—4–026
persistent vegetative state, 4–027
imaging
CT scans, 4–013—4–015
introduction, 4–012
MRI scans, 4–016—4–017
radionuclide studies, 4–018
introduction, 4–001
life expectancy, 4–028—4–031
neuropsychological perspectives
attention, 5–009—5–010
conclusions, 5–027
difficulties in determining injury severity, 5–003—5–004
emotional functioning, 5–019—5–022
executive skills, 5–011—5–012
intellectual assessment, 5–007—5–008
introduction, 5–001—5–002
memory, 5–009—5–010
moderate injuries, 5–023—5–024
neuropsychological examination, 5–005—5–006
psychological functioning, 5–019—5–022
secondary influences on neuropsychological impairment, 5–013—5–018
severe injuries, 5–023—5–024
symptom endorsement percentages, 5–006
test disclosure, 5–025
third party observers, 5–026
physical consequences
bulbar function, 4–010
double vision, 4–009
hearing loss, 4–008
incontinence, 4–011
loss of smell, 4–008
mobility impairments, 4–007
post-traumatic syndrome, 4–004—4–006
sphincter functions, 4–011
tinnitus, 4–009
visual impairment, 4–009

517

INDEX

Understanding
  assessing capacity, 2–108
Unwise decisions
  assessing capacity, 2–046, 2–083—2–086
Vacillation
  assessing capacity, 2–122
Very early rehabilitation
  stages of rehabilitation, 8–020—8–021
Victimisation
  Equality Act 2010, 11–019
Vision
  physical consequences of brain injuries
    double vision, 4–009
    visual impairment, 4–009
Vocational assessment
  employment, 11–029—11–030
  further and higher education, 11–031
  generally, 11–028
Vocational needs
  returning to work, 11–009—11–010
Vocational outcomes
  factors influencing return to work, 11–005—11–008
  return to work statistics, 11–003—11–004
Vocational rehabilitation
  disability discrimination, 11–028—11–031
  effectiveness, 11–047—11–048
  generally, 11–039
  preparation for new or alternative employment, 11–042—11–044
  return to alternative occupation, 11–045—11–046
  service provision, 11–049—11–051
  supported return to work, 11–040—11–041
Vulnerability
  assessing capacity, 2–124
  childhood brain injury, 9–007
Vulnerable person's protective imperative
  assessing capacity, 2–125—2–126
Working time
  care packages, 12–034

Also available:

Facts & Figures 2020/2021

General Editor: Simon Levene

ISBN: 9780414075542

Publication date: July 2020

Formats: Paperback/ProView eBook

Special Damages constitute an important part of most personal injury claims and preparing a schedule of damages is a complex process. *Facts & Figures: Tables for the Calculation of Damages* makes the entire calculation process quicker, easier and more accurate.

Facts & Figures Tables for the Calculation of Damages 2019/20 is designed to guide barristers, insurers, solicitors and all levels of the judiciary through the issues that such a calculation can involve. It is compiled with input from many sources, including lawyers, accountants and actuaries, as well as experts in nursing, housing and motoring.

Also available as a Standing order

Asbestos: Law and Litigation

General Editors: Harry Steinberg QC, Michael Rawlinson QC; James Beeton

ISBN: 9780414071698

Publication date: August 2019

Format: Hardback

Asbestos: Law & Litigation is the first comprehensive guide to claims for asbestos-related injury in the UK. It has been written by experienced practitioners involved in many of the leading cases on the subject. The scope of the book is wide-ranging; from the development of knowledge, to the law of damages, with all the legal and practical issues in between. It provides detailed and pragmatic guidance on the difficult technical issues specific to this type of case. It is an indispensable guide for practitioners, students, and anyone with an interest in the history and practice of asbestos litigation.

McGregor on Damages, 21st edition

General Editor: Hon. Justice James Edelman

Publication date: December 2020

Formats: Hardback/ProView eBook/Westlaw UK

Part of the Common Law Library, *McGregor on Damages* provides in-depth and comprehensive coverage of the law, from detailed consideration of the general principles to a full analysis of specific areas of damages.

Also available as a Standing order

Contact us on: Tel: +44 (0)345 600 9355

Order online: sweetandmaxwell.co.uk